# THE NAG HAMMADI LIBRARY
# AFTER FIFTY YEARS

# NAG HAMMADI
## AND
# MANICHAEAN STUDIES

FORMERLY

NAG HAMMADI STUDIES

EDITED BY

J.M. ROBINSON & H.J. KLIMKEIT

XLIV

# THE NAG HAMMADI LIBRARY AFTER FIFTY YEARS

## PROCEEDINGS OF THE 1995 SOCIETY OF BIBLICAL LITERATURE COMMEMORATION

EDITED BY

JOHN D. TURNER

AND

ANNE McGUIRE

BRILL

LEIDEN · NEW YORK · KÖLN

1997

This book is printed on acid-free paper.

ISSN    0929-2470
ISBN    90 04 10824 6

PRINTED IN THE NETHERLANDS

# CONTENTS

PART ONE

## PAST, PRESENT, AND FUTURE RESEARCH ON THE NAG HAMMADI CODICES

PART TWO

## THE *APOCRYPHON OF JOHN*

PART THREE

# THE *GOSPEL OF PHILIP*

PART FOUR

# THE *GOSPEL OF THOMAS*

PART FIVE

## ISSUES OF SOCIAL LOCATION, COMPOSITION, AND REWRITING

PART SIX

## BIBLIOGRAPHY

# PREFACE

At the Annual Meeting in Philadelphia, November 18-22, 1995, the Nag Hammadi and Gnosticism Section and Thomasine Christianity Group of the Society of Biblical Literature conducted a special program in recognition of the fiftieth anniversary of the discovery of the Nag Hammadi Library. The program in Philadelphia consisted of four sessions for the presentation of papers clustered around the theme: "The 50th Anniversary of the Discovery of the Nag Hammadi Library: Retrospect of Past Research and Prospect for Future Research;" two sessions were devoted specifically to the Gospel of Thomas. At a special evening session, James M. Robinson presented a plenary address on "Nag Hammadi: The First Fifty Years." These Philadelphia sessions were preceded on November 17, 1995 by a one-day meeting at Haverford College. The Haverford meeting consisted of two seminar sessions devoted to the current state of research on two highly significant texts from Nag Hammadi: a morning seminar on the *Apocryphon of John* and an afternoon seminar on the *Gospel according to Philip*.

In addition to James M. Robinson's plenary address, the Haverford and Philadelphia meetings included the presentation of twenty-eight papers and four prepared responses by scholars from Belgium, Finland, France, Germany, the Netherlands, Norway, Québec (Canada), and the United States. Among these presentations were contributions from the leaders of the three major international Nag Hammadi research teams: James M. Robinson of the Coptic Gnostic Project of the Institute for Antiquity and Christianity; Hans-Martin Schenke of the *Berliner Arbeitskreis für koptisch-gnostische Schriften*; and Paul-Hubert Poirier of the *Bibliothèque Copte de Nag Hammadi* Project at Université Laval in Québec. The papers from twenty-four of these scholars form the content of the present volume.

The Society of Biblical Literature ("SBL") has served as a vitally important venue for the presentation of scholarly research on the Nag Hammadi Library and Gnosticism since 1972, when a three-year Seminar on Nag Hammadi was established under the leadership of the late George W. MacRae, S. J. This seminar was replaced in 1975 by the Nag Hammadi and Gnosticism Section, which has convened at every SBL Annual Meeting since then. During these first two decades of the section's existence, the publication of the Facsimile edition of the Nag Hammadi Codices was completed (1972-1977), along with the single volume English translation of the entire Library (*The Nag Hammadi Library in English* was presented at the 1977 SBL Annual Meeting); the latter has appeared in three editions, with over 100,000 copies sold. It was also during this time period that the fourteen-volume critical edition, The Coptic Gnostic Library, with introductions to each tractate, followed by transcripts, translations, notes and indices, was inaugurated and completed. Begun in 1975 at E. J. Brill in Leiden with the *Gospel of the Egyptians*, the final two volumes of this critical edition, *The Apocryphon of John: Synopsis of Nag Hammadi Codices II,1; III,1; and IV,1 with BG 8502,2* and *Nag Hammadi Codex VII*, appeared precisely during the SBL commemoration of the fiftieth anniversary of the Nag Hammadi discovery represented in this volume.

Beginning in 1985, the Nag Hammadi and Gnosticism Section has regularly reserved at least one of its sessions—often held jointly with other program units of the SBL—for papers devoted to a specific theme. Among the themes treated in these thematic sessions have been "Images of the Feminine in Gnosticism" (1985), "The Social Setting of Gnosticism" (1986; jointly with the SBL Social World of Early Christianity Group), "Ritual in Gnosticism" (1987), "Gnostic Hermeneutics" (1988), "Platonism and Gnosticism" (1990-92; jointly with the Platonism and Neoplatonism Group of the American Academy of Religion [AAR]), "Gnostic Uses of Scripture" (1991), "Identifying Gnosticism(s): Rethinking Categories Used in the Study of Gnosticism" (1993), "Nag Hammadi, Gnosticism and the New Testament" (1994), and "The Place of Mani and Manichaeism within the History of Gnosticism" (1994; jointly with the SBL Manichaeism Consultation).

In addition to the Nag Hammadi and Gnosticism Section, the Society of Biblical Literature has hosted other program units devoted to the study of Gnosticism: the Female and Male in Gnosticism Group met annually from 1986 to 1992 to continue the discussion begun in the 1985 conference on Images of the Feminine in Gnosticism sponsored by the National Endowment for the Humanities and Claremont Graduate School. In 1993 the SBL Seminar on Gnosticism and Later Platonism was formed as a way of continuing the joint "Platonism and Gnosticism" project of the SBL Nag Hammadi and Gnosticism Section and the Platonism and Neoplatonism Group of the AAR.

It appears that fifty years after the discovery of the Library, the initial phase of Nag Hammadi research is coming to completion. The publication of the American critical edition (The Coptic Gnostic Library) has been completed. The French-Canadian critical edition with commentary, *La bibliothèque copte de Nag Hammadi*, directed by Paul-Hubert Poirier, began publication in 1977 and will complete its edition before the end of the decade. In 1958, the *Berliner Arbeitskreis für koptisch-gnostische Schriften*, under the leadership of Hans-Martin Schenke, began publishing German translations of the tractates in the *Theologische Literaturzeitung*, and presently intends to publish a complete German translation of the Library to appear as *Koptisch-gnostische Schriften*, volumes 2 and 3, in the series *Die griechischen christlichen Schriftsteller der ersten Jahrhunderte*.

In spite of the enormous bibliography on Nag Hammadi and Gnosticism, analysis of the Nag Hammadi texts can still be said to be in its infancy in many respects. Even the adequacy and heuristic value of the term "Gnosticism" as a designation for the religious phenomena found in these texts is being subjected to intense criticism. Nevertheless, there have emerged several areas of broad agreement. For example, the roots of Gnosticism, previously sought all over the ancient world, have become most visible in Judaism. Even more significant, the Nag Hammadi texts have revealed the unanticipated existence of a whole new sectarian movement having its origins within second temple Judaism: it was Hans-Martin Schenke who showed that eleven of the forty-eight unique Nag Hammadi texts can be ascribed to a movement now known as Gnostic Sethianism, which emerged, as did early Christianity, out of first-century C.E. Jewish baptismal sectarianism.

An entire session of the SBL's recognition of the 50th Anniversary, the morning seminar at Haverford, focused on a single such Sethian text, the *Apocryphon of John*, whose critical edition, in the form of a synopsis of its four versions edited by Michael Waldstein and Frederik Wisse, was also presented during the course of the commemoration in Philadelphia. As Michael Waldstein shows in the present volume, this work is a product of Platonizing Hellenistic Jewish intellectuals who juxtaposed the God of Israel, jealous of his identity as the only God, with the God of the Middle Platonists, who emanates his divinity without envy. These intellectuals end up splitting their God into a good and merciful upper God—identified as the Middleplatonic transcendent deity but retaining central features of the God of Israel—and an evil lower God—identified as the God of Israel but possessing features of the Platonic demiurge. This basic theologoumenon informs all four versions of this work.

Yet the existence of four separate Coptic copies of this work raises many interesting questions about its compositional history and significance. Unlike Homeric epic, the *Apocryphon of John* is a product of literary composition, and careful synoptic comparison of its four versions reveals evidence of intense editorial labor, interpolation, and revision. The modern scholar must choose whether to view the numerous manuscript variants as intentional corrections and improvements or as mere transmissional corruptions. But several papers in this volume, especially those of Karen L. King and Frederik Wisse, suggest that the attempt to resolve every issue of contradiction or difficulty by means of literary additions, omissions, redactions, etc., in pursuit of a presumed *Urtext* may give a text like the *Apocryphon of John* a coherence it never had at any stage of its literary history, and may even obscure the true significance of both the stability and fluidity of the transmissional process. Rather than attempt to reconstruct an original version that explains all the others, a recent trend in dealing with fluid texts like the *Apocryphon of John* which survive in various languages and recensions is to apply the techniques of intertextual analysis: how do the various versions with their respective literary, social-historical, or theological features converse with one other and with other texts and traditions? To what extent does actual rewriting serve as a means of receiving and appropriating a text within the circles through which it passed?

The question of literary coherence, raised by the multiple versions of a text like the Apocryphon of John, arose also in the sessions devoted to the *Gospel according to Philip* and the *Gospel according to Thomas*. As Einar Thomassen points out, the textual incoherence of the *Gospel according to Philip* is an indisputable fact, perhaps the outcome of successive stages of excerpting, collecting, independent note-composition, redaction and scribal confusion, resulting in a history of textual transmission that is probably too complex ever to be reconstructed. Martha Turner provides an extensive typology of major scholarly attempts to cope with this apparent incoherence during the last thirty-five years. But just as in the case of the *Apocryphon of John*, this textual incoherence does not preclude the presence of homogeneous clusters of material, if not throughout the entire text, at least within extended sections of it.

The question of literary coherence is again raised by the *Gospel according to Thomas*. This text clearly contains sayings that cannot be derived from the canonical Gospels, but in some cases these sayings may have the same claim to antiquity and even authenticity as the older layer of sayings in the canonical Gospels and Q. Yet *Thomas* is also a gospel that strikes many critics as a haphazard text, a series of almost isolated statements, lacking both context and sequence. As a result, scholarship on the *Gospel according to Thomas* has concentrated its efforts mostly on the individual sayings and their extra-textual history rather than on the text of the gospel as a whole. How-ever, as Philip Sellew reminds us, there is no more license to treat Thomas only as a quarry to be mined for reconstructing the Jesus tradition—without regard to literary and compositional realities of the text—than there is in the case of other Christian texts, be they canoni-cal narrative gospels or sayings gospels. Instead, the integrity of this text is perhaps better discovered by investigating its literary form and intertextual relationships with other literature, such as the *Book of Thomas* and the *Acts of Thomas*, or the Gospel of John. Thus April De Conick's article is partly directed against the recent suggestion of Gregory Riley that the doubting Thomas pericope in the Gospel of John represents a dispute between the Johannine community and the Thomasine Christians over the issue of bodily resurrection; in her view, it was rather meant to criticize the Thomasine emphasis upon visionary experience at the expense of faith. On either thesis, the *Gospel of Thomas* itself was already at some stage of completion, whether written or oral, and its contents known to the author of the Johannine gospel, probably through inter-community contact and ver-bal exchange of a polemical sort.

Such matters as textual coherence, polemical rewriting, and evi-dence of intertextuality raised by the *Apocryphon of John*, the *Gospel according to Philip*, and the *Gospel according to Thomas* obviously raise the question of the nature of the groups who used and operated upon these texts. Surely each of the Christian Nag Hammadi texts presuppose some form of church community with characteristic theo-logoumena and ritual practices, and the same seems to be true for the Sethian texts: be they predominantly Jewish, Christian or Platonic, they display a coherent mythological base which comes to expression in ritual—mostly baptismal—acts related to visionary and other types of religious experience. But almost all the texts exhibit intense interest in ancient tradition, especially deriving from the book of Genesis and Plato's *Timaeus*, suggesting that many of the authors associated themselves with various schools of interpretation devoted to exploring the similarities, differences, and even contradictions between and within those venerable accounts. As Christoph Markschies shows in the case of Valentinianism, some of these groups seem to have a structure and function much like a traditional philosophical school with lectures, commentaries, analytical methods, common meetings and meals, as well as various ritual activities. Perhaps such groups are ideal candidates for fostering the sort of intertextual activity so clearly evident in the texts singled out for discussion during this 50th anniversary of the Nag Hammadi discovery.

The editors would like to thank the administration of the Society of Biblical Literature for generously enabling a fitting commemoration of the 50th anniversary of the Nag Hammadi discovery within the context of an Annual Meeting attended by thousands of participants. We would also like to express our thanks to several members of the Haverford College community for making possible the November 17 seminar meetings on the Haverford College campus. The administration of Haverford College, particularly former President Tom Kessinger, Provost Elaine Hansen, the Office of Distinguished Visitors, and the Gest Program, deserve special thanks for generously providing financial support for meals, lodging, transportation between Philadelphia and Haverford, and a spacious meeting room for the full day of seminar discussions. In addition, we would like to thank Annette Barone, secretary of the Gest Center, for her tireless assistance in organizing and administering the seminar; and to James Gulick (reference librarian, Magill Library), Bridget Gillich (Haverford '98), and especially Kristen Rudisill (Bryn Mawr '97) for their invaluable assistance in preparing the bibliography for publication.

The day of meetings at Haverford concluded with a musical performance of "Thunder, Perfect Mind" (NHC VI,2) for Celtic harp and voice by composer Julia Haines, and a dinner at which seminar members were able informally to enjoy collegial conversation and to share perspectives on the past, present, and future of Nag Hammadi research. The editors wish to thank all of the participants and sponsors of the Haverford seminar, a splendid event that initiated the high level of discussion that continued throughout the Philadelphia SBL sessions over the following four days.

# ABBREVIATIONS TO PERIODICALS, REFERENCES WORKS, AND SERIALS

| | |
|---|---|
| AAWG.PH | Abhandlungen der Akademie der Wissenschaften in Göttingen. Philologisch-historische Klasse |
| AB | The Anchor Bible |
| ABD | D. N. Freedman et al. (eds.), Anchor Bible Dictionary. |
| AHAW.PH | Abhandlungen des Heidelberger Akademie der Wissenschaften. Philosophisch-historische Klasse. |
| ALBO | Analecta lovaniensia biblica et orientalia |
| AnBib | Analecta biblica |
| AnC | Antike und Christentum |
| ANET | J. B. Pritchard (ed.), Ancient Near Eastern Texts Relating to the Old Testament |
| ANF | A. Roberts and J. Donaldson (eds), The Ante-Nicene Fathers |
| AnOr | Analecta orientalia |
| ANRW | W. Haase et al. (eds.), Aufstieg und Niedergang der römischen Welt: Geschichte und Kultur Roms im Spiegel der neueren Forschung. |
| ARW | Archiv für Religionswissenschaft |
| ATDan | Acta theologica danica |
| BA | Biblical Archaeologist |
| BAR | Biblical Archaeologist Reader |
| BARev | Biblical Archaeology Review |
| BCNH | Bibliothèque copte de Nag Hammadi |
| BETL | Bibliotheca ephemeridum theologicarum lovaniensium |
| BEvT | Beiträge zur evangelischen Theologie |
| BHT | Beiträge zur historischen Theologie |
| Bib | Biblica |
| BiTeu | Bibliotheca Teubneriana |
| BJS | Brown Judaic Studies |
| BSac | Bibliotheca Sacra |
| BZNW | Beihefte zur ZNW |
| CAH | Cambridge Ancient History |
| CBQ | Catholic Biblical Quarterly |
| CBQMS | Catholic Biblical Quarterly--Monograph Series |
| CChr | Corpus Christianorum |
| CCSL | Corpus Christianorum, Series Latina |
| CIG | Corpus inscriptionum graecarum |
| CII | Corpus inscriptionum iudaicarum |
| CIL | Corpus inscriptionum latinarum |
| CPG | Clavis Patrum Graecorum |
| CRINT | Compendia rerum iudaicarum ad novum testamentum |
| CSCO | Corpus scriptorum christianorum orientalium |
| CSEL | Corpus scriptorum ecclesiasticorum latinorum |
| CUFr | Collection des Universités de France |
| DBSup | Dictionnaire de la Bible, Supplément |
| EPRO | Etudes préliminaires aux religions orientales dans l'empire Romain |

| ETL | Ephemerides theologicae lovanienses |
| EvT | Evangelische Theologie |
| EWNT | H. Balz and G. Schneider (eds.), Exegetisches Wörterbuch zum Neuen Testament |
| FKDG | Forschungen zur Kirchen- and Dogmengeschichte |
| FRLANT | Forschungen zur Religion und Literatur des Alten und Neuen Testaments |
| GCS | Griechischen christlichen Schriftsteller |
| GNS | Good News Studies |
| GOF.H | Göttinger Orientforschungen. Hellenistica |
| GRBS | Greek, Roman, and Byzantine Studies |
| HABES | Handbuch der Altertumswissenschaft; Byzantinisches Handbuch |
| HDR | Harvard Dissertations in Religion |
| HTKNT | Herders theologischer Kommentar zum Neuen Testament |
| HTR | Harvard Theological Review |
| ICC | International Critical Commentary |
| ILS | Inscriptiones latinae selectae |
| ISBE | G. W. Bromiley (ed.), International Standard Bible Encyclopedia, rev. |
| JAC | Jahrbuch für Antike und Christentum |
| JAC Ergb. | Jahrbuch für Antike und Christentum, Erganzungsband |
| JBL | Journal of Biblical Literature |
| JECS | Journal of Early Christian Studies |
| JEH | Journal of Ecclesiastical History |
| JSNT | Journal for the Study of the New Testament |
| JSNTSup | Journal for the Study of the New Testament—Supplement Series |
| JTS | Journal of Theological Studies |
| KlT | Kleine Texte |
| LCL | Loeb Classical Library |
| LTP | Laval théologique et philosophique |
| Mus | Le Muséon |
| NedTTs | Nederlands theologisch tijdschrift |
| Neot | Neotestamentica |
| NHLE | Nag Hammadi Library in English |
| NHMS | Nag Hammadi and Manichaean Studies |
| NHC | Nag Hammadi Codex |
| NHS | Nag Hammadi Studies |
| NorTT | Norsk Teologisk Tidsskrift |
| NovT | Novum Testamentum |
| NovTSup | Novum Testamentum, Supplements |
| NTOA | Novum Testamentum et Orbis Antiquus |
| NTS | New Testament Studies |
| NTTS | New Testament Tools and Studies |
| Numen | Numen: International Review for the History of Religions |
| NumenSup | Supplements to Numen |
| OBO | Orbis biblicus et orientalis |
| OLZ | Orientalische Literaturzeitung |
| OrChr | Oriens christianus |

| | |
|---|---|
| PhAnt | Philosophia Antiqua |
| PIOL | Publications de l'Institut orientaliste de Louvain |
| PTS | Patristische Texte und Studien |
| PW | Pauly-Wissowa, Real-Encyclopädie der classischen Altertumswissenschaft |
| RAC | Reallexikon für Antike und Christentum |
| REAug | Revue des Études Augustiniennes |
| RechBibl | Recherches Bibliques |
| REg | Revue d'égyptologie |
| RelSRev | Religious Studies Review |
| ResQ | Restoration Quarterly |
| RevScRel | Revue des sciences religieuses |
| RHPR | Revue d'histoire et de philosophie religieuses |
| RHR | Revue de l'histoire des religions |
| RTP | Revue de théologie et de philosophie |
| SAC | Sources in Antiquity and Christianity |
| SAQ | Sammlung ausgewählter kirchen- und dogmengeschichtlicher Quellenschriften |
| SBL | Society of Biblical Literature |
| SBLDS | SBL Dissertation Series |
| SBLEJL | SBL Early Judaism and Its Literature |
| SBLMS | SBL Monograph Series |
| SBLSP | SBL Seminar Papers |
| SBLTT | SBL Texts and Translations |
| SC | Sources chrétiennes |
| SCBO | Scriptorum Classicorum Bibliotheca Oxoniensis |
| SD | Studies and Documents |
| SecCent | Second Century |
| SHR | Studies in the History of Religions, Supplements to Numen |
| SJLA | Studies in Judaism in Late Antiquity |
| SP | Studia Patristica |
| SPS | Salzburger Patristische Studien |
| StTh | Studia Theologica |
| StudBib | Studia Biblica |
| SUNT | Studien zur Umwelt des Neuen Testaments |
| SUNY | State University of New York |
| TBü | Theologische Bücherei |
| TD | Theology Digest |
| TDNT | G. Kittel and G. Friedrich (eds.), Theological Dictionary of the New Testament |
| TF | Theologische Forschung |
| TLZ | Theologische Literaturzeitung |
| TRE | Theologische Realenzyklopädie |
| TRu | Theologische Rundschau |
| TU | Texte und Untersuchungen |
| TWNT | G. Kittel and G. Friedrich (eds.), Theologisches Wörterbuch zum Neuen Testament |
| TZ | Theologische Zeitschrift |

| | |
|---|---|
| UTB | Universitäts-Taschenbücher |
| UUÅ | Uppsala universitetsårsskrift |
| VC | Vigiliae christianae |
| VCSup | Supplements to Vigiliae christianae |
| VF | Verkündigung und Forschung |
| VHAAH.FF | Kungl. Vitterhets Historie och Antikvitets Akademiens Handlingar, Filologisk-filosofiska |
| WUNT | Wissenschaftliche Untersuchungen zum Neuen Testament |
| ZÄS | Zeitschrift für Ägyptische Sprache und Altertumskunde |
| ZNW | Zeitschrift für die neutestamentliche Wissenschaft |
| ZRGG | Zeitschrift für Religions- und Geistesgeschichte |
| ZTK | Zeitschrift für Theologie und Kirche |

# PART ONE

# PAST, PRESENT, AND FUTURE RESEARCH
# ON THE NAG HAMMADI CODICES

# NAG HAMMADI: THE FIRST FIFTY YEARS[*]

*James M. Robinson*
The Claremont Graduate School

## INTRODUCTION

I have been asked to speak about the significance of the discovery of the Nag Hammadi Codices 50 years ago, in terms of what the Nag Hammadi codices have meant for the discipline of New Testament scholarship. This significance is not limited to such specific issues as Gnosticism and the New Testament. My focus here is rather in terms of the sociology of knowledge: What has this important manuscript discovery, and the way it was handled over the past half-century, effected in the shaping of Biblical Studies as a discipline?

But first, to give you a taste of the discovery itself, let me begin with how we know that it took place 50 years ago, before I trace what happened during the first 50 years.

The young French graduate student and adventurer, Jean Doresse, originally the only source of information about the discovery, had dated it variously and without explanation to the beginning of 1946,[1] then more generally 1946,[2] then 1945,[3] then 1947[4] or even 1948.[5]

---

[*] A Plenary Address given at the Annual Meeting of the Society of Biblical Literature on the occasion of the Fiftieth Anniversary of the Nag Hammadi Discovery on November 19, 1995. An earlier draft of this lecture was given at the Institute for Antiquity and Christianity on September 21, 1995.

[1] Jean Doresse and Togo Mina collaborated in preparing announcements made by Henri-Charles Puech to the Académie des Inscriptions et Belles-Lettres in Paris on February 20, 1948. See H.-C. Puech and J. Doresse, "Nouveaux écrits gnostiques découverts en Egypte," Académie des Inscriptions et Belles-Lettres: *Comptes Rendus des Séances de l'Année 1948* (1948) 89. Their report was also presented by Togo Mina to the Institut d'Egypte in Cairo on March 8, 1948. See his publication, "Le papyrus gnostique du Musée Copte," *VC 2* (1948) 129, in which Togo Mina stated the date of the discovery as "about two years ago—it has not been possible to establish the exact date." The typescript composed by Doresse for the presentation to the French Academy cited the acquisition of Codex III by the Coptic Museum in October 1946 and the examination of other codices by the unnamed Jacques Schwartz "more than a year and a half ago," to conclude "as a result the find would date perhaps from the beginning of 1946." But in editing the typescript Puech deleted "more than," thus obscuring any evidence of a date prior to August 1946, though in fact Schwartz' examination took place late in March 1946, as he has informed me.

Hence I sought to find more precise information about the time, place, participants, and specifics of the discovery.

The most obvious place to begin had apparently never been consulted, the Acquisitions Registry of the Coptic Museum in Cairo. Here the name of the person who sold the first codex, Codex III, to the Coptic Museum on October 4, 1946 for LE 250 is listed by name: Rāghib Andarāwus "al-Qiss" ʿAbd al-Sayyid. I tracked him down in retirement in the town of Qinā in Upper Egypt, and he gave me information making it possible to unravel the whole story, with the help of the discoverer himself, Muḥammad ʿAlī al-Sammān in the hamlet al-Qaṣr across the Nile from Nag Hammadi.

Muḥammad ʿAlī is an illiterate field hand not capable of putting a calendar date to anything, much less the discovery. But it was associated in his mind with two things much more important to him at the time: When the local sugarcane harvest was over and the land lay fallow during the brief winter, he regularly dug soft earth at the foot

---

[2] H.-C. Puech, "Nouveaux écrits gnostiques découverts à Nag Hammadi," *RHR* 134 (1948) 244. In his essay "Les nouveaux écrits gnostiques découverts en Haute-Egypte (premier inventaire et essai d'identification)," *Coptic Studies in Honor of Walter Ewing Crum* (Boston: The Byzantine Institute of America, 1950) 93, he was even less certain: "in the course of 1946 ... at a date itself imprecise." In "Une bibliothèque gnostique copte," *La Nouvelle Clio* 2 (1949) 61, Doresse followed suit: "It was about 1946." The date of 1946 persisted even after it had been replaced: Doresse, "A Gnostic Library from Upper Egypt," *Archaeology* 3 (1950) 69; P. Labib, "Les papyrus gnostiques coptes du Musée Copte du Vieux Caire," *La Revue du Caire* 195-196 (1956) 275.

[3] "Toward 1945": Doresse, "Sur les traces des papyrus gnostiques: Recherches à Chénoboskion," Académie royale de Belgique: *Bulletin de la Classe des Lettres et des Sciences morales et politiques*, 5ème Série, 36 (1950) 433; *Les livres secrets des gnostiques d'Egypte*, I: *Introduction aux écrits gnostiques coptes découverts à Khénoboskion* (Paris: Librairie Plon, 1958) 145; II: *L'Evangile selon Thomas ou les paroles secrètes de Jésus* (Paris: Librairie Plon, 1959) 1; H.-C. Puech, "Découverte d'une bibliothèque gnostique en Haute-Egypte," *Encyclopédie Française*, Vol. 19 *Philosophie. Religion* (Paris: Societé Nouvelle de l'Encyclopédie Française, 1957) 19.42.5. "In 1945": Doresse, "Les gnostiques d'Egypte," *La Table Ronde* 107 (1956) 86.

[4] "Une importante découverte: Un papyrus gnostique copte du IVème siècle," *La Bourse Egyptienne*, January 10, 1948, reprinted in *Chronique d'Egypte* 23 (1948) 260. This dating is based on the acquisition of Codex III by the Coptic Museum, stated to have been "a few months ago." In fact this reference only fits the time when Doresse first saw it in October 1947 (the acquisition date was October 4, 1946). See Doresse, "Le roman d'une grande découverte," *Les Nouvelles Littéraires* (July 25, 1957) 1: "The discovery had begun the day when the lamented Togo Mina ... made for his collections the fortunate purchase ... . That took place in 1947. Shortly afterwards ... Togo Mina submitted this codex to me." 1947 then became the unambiguous date of the discovery itself, "Une extraordinaire découverte archéologique en Haute-Egypte: Quarante-neuf livres secrètes relèvent la religion gnostique," in "La vie littéraire" of *La Tribune de Genève*, February 1-2, 1958, 13: "the discovery made in 1947 to the north of Luxor."

[5] From an interview with Doresse by Georges Fradier, *UNESCO Features* 2 (August 1, 1949) 11: "It was a year ago, on the shore of the Nile ... ."

of the cliff that served as fertilizer for the fields. He had been digging fertilizer, he recalled, just a few weeks before the Coptic Christmas, which is January 7, when he made the discovery. This suggests the discovery was in a December.

With regard to the year, he again could speak of it only in terms more important to him at the time: The murder of his father in a blood feud.[6] He regretted he had to wait some half a year before the opportunity came to avenge his father's death, by murdering the man who did it.[7] But this new victim was from Ḥamra Dūm, the opposing village in the long-standing blood feud with al-Qaṣr. Since Ḥamra Dūm lay just at the foot of the cliff on whose talus the discovery had been made, it claimed that area as its turf. Hence Muḥammad ʿAlī's act of vengeance meant that he no longer dared return to the area of the discovery, which had taken place less than a month before he avenged his father's death. So if the date of the father's death could be established, the date of the discovery itself about half a year later could be calculated.

The Nag Hammadi Real Estate Taxation Office maintains a Registry of Deaths. A Copt I knew worked there, and was able to locate the entry, giving the cause of death as "unknown" and the date in 1945 as May 7. If the vengeance was some half a year later, about a month after the discovery, the discovery itself had to have been in November or December 1945. Voilà, our fiftieth anniversary date![8]

---

[6] Muḥammad ʿAlī's memory of that tragedy: One night his father, a night watchman for valuable irrigation machinery that had been imported from Germany, killed a marauder from the nearby village Ḥamra Dūm, a village that had an ongoing blood feud with Muḥammad ʿAlī's own village al-Qaṣr. The next day that murder was avenged, in that Muḥammad ʿAlī's father was found shot through the head, lying beside the remains of the man from Ḥamra Dūm he had killed. Muḥammad ʿAlī's mother, beside herself, told her seven sons to keep their mattocks sharp so as to be ready when an occasion for revenge presented itself.

[7] Muḥammad ʿAlī's memory of revenge: Someone ran to his house to tell the family that the murderer Aḥmad Ismā*īl was asleep in the heat of the day on a dirt road nearby, with a jug of sugarcane molasses, the local product, by his side. The sons grabbed their mattocks, fell on the hapless person before he could flee, hacked him up, cut open his heart, and, dividing it among them, ate it raw, the ultimate act of blood vengeance.

[8] The story of the blood feud came out in connection with Muḥammad ʿAlī explaining why he would not accompany me to the cliff to show me the site of the discovery. So I had to go to Ḥamra Dūm myself, find the son of Aḥmad Ismā*īl, the man Muḥammad ʿAlī had butchered, and get his assurance that, since he had long since shot up a funeral cortège of Muḥammad ʿAlī's family, wounding Muḥammad ʿAlī and killing a number of his clan, he considered the score settled. Hence he would not feel honor-bound to attack Muḥammad ʿAlī if he returned to the foot of the cliff. I took this good news back to Muḥammad ʿAlī, who opened his shirt, showed me his scar, bragged that he had been shot but not killed, yet emphasized that if he ever laid eyes on Aḥmad Ismà'īl again, he would kill him on the spot. As a result of this display of a braggadocio's fearlessness, he could

I propose now to address four dimensions of what has taken place in the half-century since the Nag Hammadi discovery.

## 1. THE FIRST HALF OF THE FIFTY YEARS: THE MONOPOLIZING OF THE BULK OF THE NAG HAMMADI CODICES FROM 1945 TO 1970

Of course, the codices had first to move from the foot of the cliff into the control of the monopolists. This happened as follows:[9]

Muḥammad ʿAlī had at first feared to open the jar (sealed with a bowl attached with bitumin to the mouth of the jar), lest it contain a jinn. But then it occurred to him it might contain gold. This gave him courage enough to break it with his mattock. Out flew, up into the air, what he thought might be an airy golden jinn, but which I suspect was only papyrus fragments. He was very let down to find only worthless old books in the jar.

He tore some up to divide them among the other camel drivers who were present, which explains some of the damage and loss that does not fit the pattern of what one would expect from the gradual deterioration of the centuries. Since the other camel drivers, no doubt out of fear of Muḥammad ʿAlī, declined his insincere offer to share, he stacked it all back up together, unrolled the turban from around his head, put the codices in it, slung it over his shoulder, unhobbled his camel, drove back home, and dumped the junk in the enclosed patio of his house where the animals and their fodder were kept. His mother confirmed to me that she had in fact burnt some along with straw as kindling in the outdoor clay oven.

The family tried to sell the books for an Egyptian Pound or so, but nobody was willing to give money. Some were bartered for cigarettes

---

be persuaded to go to the cliff, camouflaged in my clothes, in a government jeep, with me sitting on the bullets side facing the village and him on the safer cliff side, at dusk in Ramadan, when all Muslims are at home eating their fill after fasting throughout the daylight hours.

[9] For more detailed presentations see my "Introduction" in M. W. Meyer and J. M. Robinson eds., *The Nag Hammadi Library in English*, translated by members of the Coptic Gnostic Library Project of the Institute for Antiquity and Christianity (Leiden: E. J. Brill, 1977); "The Discovery of the Nag Hammadi Codices," *BA* 42 (Fall 1979) 206-24, unabridged with footnotes as "From the Cliff to Cairo: The Story of the Discoverers and the Middlemen of the Nag Hammadi Codices," in *Colloque international sur les textes de Nag Hammadi (Québec, 22-25 août 1978)*, ed. B. Barc (BCNH, Section "Etudes" 1; Québec: Les Presses de l'Université Laval, 1981 [1982]) 21-58; "The Discovering and Marketing of Coptic Manuscripts: The Nag Hammadi Codices and the Bodmer Papyri," *Sundries in honour of Torgny Säve-Söderbergh* (Acta Universitatis Uppsaliensis; Boreas: Uppsala Studies in Ancient Mediterranean and Near Eastern Civilizations 13, 1984) 97-114, reprinted in *The Roots of Egyptian Christianity*, Studies in Antiquity and Christianity, eds. B.A. Pearson and J.E. Goehring (Philadelphia: Fortress, 1986) 1-25.

or oranges. A Copt told Muḥammad ʿAlī they were books of the church, which probably meant only that the Copt could read enough to know they were not written in Arabic but in Coptic, which is more than could be said for Muḥammad ʿAlī. Since the police were repeatedly searching his home for incriminating evidence of the blood-vengeance murder, he deposited one book—Codex III—with a Coptic priest, knowing that house would not be searched. For the British had made clear to the Muslim police not to give the Copts too hard a time, for fear of inciting incidents between Copts and Muslims.

The priest gave the codex to his brother-in-law, a circuit-riding teacher of History and English in the parochial Coptic schools (the only schools in the region prior to President Nasser), who once a week stayed overnight at the priest's home the day he taught at al-Qaṣr. This parochial school teacher was named, as you already know, Rāghib Andarāwus "al-Qiss" ʿAbd al-Sayyid. At the end of the summer of 1946, he took Codex III to Cairo to sell. Instead, when he showed it to an educated Copt, Georgy "Bei" Sobhy, to learn its value, he was, much to his horror, turned in to the authorities. He felt lucky to be permitted finally to sell his book to the Coptic Museum (for ŁE 300, from which a "gift" to the Museum of ŁE 50 was deducted) and return home without being put in prison.

The Director of the Coptic Museum, Togo Mina, had been a classmate in Paris of Jean and Marianne Doresse, in fact had proposed (unsuccessfully) to Marianne before she married Jean. He welcomed them to the Coptic Museum on their first visit to Cairo in the fall of 1947, proudly showed them Codex III, and offered to co-publish with Doresse (though Mina had shown it on December 5, 1946 to François Daumas, and offered to co-publish it with him). Togo Mina also took Doresse to an antique shop in Cairo owned by Albert Eid to see some 40 leaves of a similar codex—Codex I—which was later smuggled out of Egypt and taken as far as Ann Arbor, Michigan, in an effort to sell it. Finally it was bought by the Jung Institute in Zürich for $8,000 contributed by an American expatriate, George H. (Tony) Page, and hence is known as the Jung Codex.[10]

Most of the codices were acquired ultimately by Phocion J. Tano(s), a well-known Cypriot antiquities dealer in Cairo. He was pressured into entrusting them for safe-keeping to the government, which ultimately nationalized them instead, and deposited them in the Coptic Museum. The long drawn-out but ultimately unsuccessful

---

[10] For the details, see my review article, "The Jung Codex: The Rise and Fall of a Monopoly," *RelSRev* (1977) 17-30.

legal proceedings that Tano undertook to repossess his property made
the bulk of the codices inaccessible throughout the 1950s.

When Mina, the French-educated Director of the Coptic Museum,
died prematurely in 1949, he was succeeded by the German-educated
Director Pahor Labib. Then the Egyptian revolution in 1952 led to the
expulsion of the French Director of the *Services des Antiquités*, Abbé
Etienne Drioton, under whom Mina had studied in Paris. Finally, the
Suez Crisis of 1956 resulted in a complete break in diplomatic relations between France and Egypt. All the French had left to show for
their efforts was an International Committee dominated by Doresse's
professor Henri-Charles Puech (who by now had cut Doresse himself
out of the Committee, no doubt as academically unqualified and no
longer needed). The Committee had been convened in Cairo just
before the Suez crisis, but achieved no more than to award publication rights for *The Gospel of Thomas* to itself. Official minutes of
that meeting were never made available to the Committee members,
and hence no written publication rights were actually available. The
Committee was never reconvened.

When Coptologists from former East Germany, not compromised
in the Suez Crisis, began to visit Cairo in 1958, they were welcomed
by the new Director of the Coptic Museum, Labib, who awarded
them choice publication rights. They then returned to—West Germany! Martin Krause and Pahor Labib published the three copies of
the *Apocryphon of John* in 1963,[11] while Alexander Böhlig and Labib
published *On the Origin of the World* in 1962[12] and the four *Apocalypses* of Codex V in 1963.[13] Their colleagues still in East Germany,
Hans-Martin Schenke and Peter Nagel, and of course all Coptologists
from other countries, were cut out of publication rights.

A poignant anecdote illustrates the oddity and injustice of the
situation: The greatest living Coptologist of the time, Hans Jakob
Polotsky, originally of Berlin, but by then of Jerusalem, expressed his
amazement that, after his European colleagues had consistently denied
him access to the new discovery, the texts should suddenly be offered

---

[11] *Die drei Versionen des Apokryphon des Johannes im Koptischen Museum zu Alt-
Kairo* (Abhandlungen des Deutschen Archäologischen Instituts Kairo, Koptische Reihe
1; Wiesbaden: Harrassowitz, 1962 [1963]).

[12] *Die koptisch-gnostische Schrift ohne Titel aus dem Codex II von Nag Hammadi im
Koptischen Museum zu Alt-Kairo* (Deutsche Akademie der Wissenschaften zu Berlin,
Institut für Orientforschung 58; Berlin: Akademie-Verlag, 1962).

[13] *Koptisch-gnostische Apokalypsen aus Codex V von Nag Hammadi im Koptischen
Museum zu Alt-Kairo*, *Sonderband* of the *Wissenschaftliche Zeitschrift der Martin-
Luther-Universität* (Halle-Wittenberg: Martin-Luther Universität, 1963).

to him by students from an unknown Institute for Antiquity and Christianity in California, of all places, who had come to Ann Arbor to study Coptic with him at a summer school in 1967.

Meanwhile the French had long-since counter-attacked, already in 1961, by enlisting the Paris-based UNESCO to internationalize the project. At the suggestion of its scholarly advisors, who were of course French, the UNESCO officials proposed to photograph all the material, bring it to Paris (which, after all, was where UNESCO was located), and convene in 1962 an International Committee to publish it by the end of 1964. But it soon became clear that the Coptic Museum, with Krause's help, had already assigned the unpublished plums to Krause and Böhlig. For a preliminary committee consisting of Pahor Labib, President; Martin Krause; and Michel Malinine, met in Cairo and submitted on November 4, 1961 a report, based on Krause's inventory, proposing that UNESCO assign only twenty-three of the forty-eight tractates, on the grounds the others had already been assigned, were in the press, or had already appeared.

Those listed as already published were I,3 (published 1956); II,1 III,1, IV,1 (actually published, by Krause and Labib, only in 1963); II,2 (published 1959); II,5 (actually published, by Böhlig and Labib, in 1962); and II,6-7 (actually published, by Krause and Labib, in 1972). Two items already in the public domain, by way of a very modest volume of facsimiles published by Pahor Labib in 1956,[14] were listed as assigned to the scholarly world outside of West Germany: II,3 to J.Martin Plumley of England and II,4 to the American Kendrick Grobel (who apparently was never informed of his assignment).

After consultation with Puech and Antoine Guillaumont, the relevant UNESCO official queried: "This seems to me very serious; if a large part of the treatises, and perhaps the richest, are already in the process of publication, is the creation of an International Committee of Publication really justified?" In response to UNESCO's request for an informed assessment, Guillaumont wrote on December 4, 1961:

> I admit that reading this report causes me some surprise and reveals to me a situation very different from what was presupposed in our previous correspondence relative to the Committee envisaged for the publication of the texts of Nag Hammadi. ...

---

[14] P. Labib, *Coptic Gnostic Papyri in the Coptic Museum at Old Cairo*, Vol. 1 (Cairo: Government Press, 1956). This is the only volume of this edition to appear.

I note, furthermore, that the treatises presented as already published or to be published by persons already designated are undoubtedly those that have the most interest and that give to the Nag Hammadi discovery its exceptional importance. Only those are left to be distributed by the Committee that offer the least interest and those whose publication, in view of their poor state or their fragmentary condition, will be especially thankless.

Upon the invitation addressed to me last July 4 by the Director General of UNESCO, I agreed quite gladly to become part of a Committee whose stated objective was the publication of the whole of the Nag Hammadi texts; it was, moreover, stated that this Committee would have for its task, at its first meeting, to work out the plan of the publication and to divide the work among the competent specialists. Now it seems to me evident that, in the conditions defined by the report, the Committee is from now on dispossessed of this essential antecedent task, for the major and most important part of the Nag Hammadi texts. If its role must be limited to covering with its authority a work organized without it and accomplished outside of its effective control, I for my part think that it no longer has any *raison d'être.*

UNESCO decided to limit itself to a facsimile edition, whose photography it was willing to fund. The French, now that the West Germans had gotten the remaining plums, lost interest. After all, the French had gotten control of the initial plum they had detected while France still held the monopoly, the *Gospel of Thomas* (II,2), and also had control of the Jung Codex (Codex I) in Zürich, which was all they could manage to edit for years to come.

During a sabbatical year as Annual Professor at the American School of Oriental Research in Jerusalem in 1965-66, I went in all innocence to Cairo to find out the status of the Nag Hammadi Codices, first in March 1966, and again in April, on the way to the Congress on The Origins of Gnosticism at Messina, Sicily. The meager information I had obtained in Cairo made me into an instant authority on such matters at the Congress. So I was appointed to a committee to compose a telegram to UNESCO endorsed by the Congress, urging UNESCO to complete the languishing photography. On passing through Paris shortly thereafter, I inquired if the telegram had been received and acted upon. I was told that the last 314 photographs had indeed arrived in Paris on June 6, 1966. And I was assured that publication would be completed by the end of 1968. I was of course pleased with such good news, but in more cynical retrospect realize that the publication timetable was at best wishful thinking, if not just an effective way to get me out of the office.

The German Archaeological Institute in Cairo had on my April trip given me access to Nag Hammadi photographs on file there, and I had worked twenty-four hours a day for a couple of days copying them. Then in June, I passed through Münster, Germany, to give a guest lecture at the University. In the process, I was lent some transcriptions by Martin Krause, which I stayed up all night copying by hand the night before my German lecture. On my return home, I obtained a modest NEH grant for three years, 1967-70, that made it possible to organize a small team to translate the few unpublished tractates to which I had by such unorthodox means obtained access. We stamped each with a note to the effect that they should not be published, since we had no publication rights to offer. But we did circulate them widely in mimeographed form.

During the three-year grant period, I wrote repeatedly to UNESCO, letters that all went unanswered. The official in charge of the Nag Hammadi matter, N. Bammate, was a member of a gourmet dining club in Paris, but otherwise was quite inactive. When I complained to his superior, I was told that he did not answer letters, since he came from an oral culture (Afghanistan).

I went back to Paris in January, 1968, to ask Bammate personally where things stood: for example, whether the fragments had been identified and placed on the leaves before photography, a prerequisite to using the UNESCO photographs for a facsimile edition that would put the material into the public domain available to all. Rather than bother with shuffling through the photographs to seek to answer my question, he said I could study them myself and write a report to him as to the status of the fragments. He even let me use a UNESCO office empty over the weekend for this purpose. He laid out for me about half of the glossy prints, and the negatives of the other half, no doubt so I could not abscond with a complete file.

Saturday morning, I found a photography shop in a Paris suburb willing to work straight through the weekend, and gave them some 600 negatives to make glossy-print enlargements in time enough for me to pick them and the negatives up by Sunday evening. Meanwhile in the UNESCO office, I laid the glossy prints one by one on the floor under my tripod and clicked away with my simple tourist's camera. Monday morning I turned in to Bammate the negatives and prints that he had lent me.

I also flew to Copenhagen and obtained from Søren Giversen microfilms he earlier had made in Cairo of Codices II, III and IX, which he however had not made available to others, on the grounds that Labib did not want the French to get them.

On returning to Claremont, I wrote the desired report and sent it to UNESCO. I now had photographs of all the Nag Hammadi codices.

We enlarged our American Nag Hammadi Project membership, ultimately to include some 38 persons. We assigned out all the Nag Hammadi tractates, and had produced draft transcriptions and translations of everything by 1970. This is what in effect broke the monopoly, in that we distributed widely our transcriptions and translations to the Nag Hammadi scholars who had been left out in the cold.

At the meeting of the Society for New Testament Studies in 1969 in England, I co-chaired with R. McLachlan Wilson a Nag Hammadi Seminar, to which I invited Henry Chadwick of Oxford, who had edited the Greek *Sentences of Sextus,* to discuss the Coptic translation in Codex XII that Frederik Wisse had just identified, and Alexander Böhlig of Tübingen to analyze the *Paraphrase of Shem* in Codex VII, on the basis of the transcriptions and translations we had sent them.

We arranged a lecture tour for Böhlig in America, so that he could work with our translators when lecturing on their campuses, and in turn gain access to our material. Böhlig made it possible for Wisse to go to Tübingen and co-edit with him *The Gospel of the Egyptians,* for which Böhlig held since 1963 the official assignment. This gave us for the first time some limited publication rights. Such mutually supportive collaboration characterized our procedures from the beginning.

I sent our transcriptions and translations to Kurt Rudolph of Leipzig in East Germany. His report about their contents, which he somewhat naively published in 1969,[15] motivated the very domineering head of the French monopoly, Henri-Charles Puech of the École pratique des Hautes Études and the Collège de France, to make a formal protest to UNESCO for having given me access to its photographs. Fortunately UNESCO told him that it was their responsibility to disseminate the cultures of its member states, not to restrict access. So they did not restrict my activity.

During the school year 1970-71, I lived in Paris but commuted once a week to Strasbourg as a Fulbright Professor at the University of Strasbourg. Each week, I gave a Nag Hammadi colleague, Jacques Ménard, our transcription and translation of a tractate, and the next week discussed it privately with him, while passing on to him another tractate for discussion the following week.

---

[15] K. Rudolph, "Gnosis und Gnostizismus, ein Forschungsbericht," *TRu* n. F. 34 (1969) 89-120, 181-231, 358-361. The third installment, with the subtitle "Nachträge," consists primarily of corrections I had sent him after reading proofs of the first two installments. He speaks quite openly, e.g. p. 359, of "the ongoing work of the editing team in Claremont (USA)" under my leadership.

By such means we saw to it that all interested scholars got access to the material. But we still lacked publication rights.

## 2. THE SECOND HALF OF THE FIFTY YEARS: THE PUBLISHING OF ALL THE NAG HAMMADI CODICES FROM 1970 TO 1995

We have already reached the half-way mark in the fifty years since the discovery, but the material was still not published and accessible to scholarship at large. In the first half of our fifty-year span only about a third of the discovery had been published. Only a fifth was available in English translation, no doubt because there had been no English monopoly. The history of a Nag Hammadi scholarship fully open to the whole academic community really began only in 1970.

During my sabbatical year 1970-71 in Paris, I worked in an office lent to me at UNESCO. At my urging, an "International Committee for the Nag Hammadi Codices" was not only nominated by UNESCO and appointed by the Arab Republic of Egypt, but even actually convened in Cairo in December 1970. Since I had long before arranged with Brill to publish the facsimile edition, Brill had made a plane reservation for their Dutch photographer to fly to Cairo and photograph the material as we restored it, if I could get the Committee to accept Brill (rather than some Egyptian firm) as publisher. I finally broke through the pomp and ceremony of the opening day of the Cairo meeting to get that much of the agenda acted on and a telegram off to Brill. This timing was crucial, for Brill's plane reservation was for the next day, and, due to the Christmas tourism, there were no plane seats left on later flights.

I proposed that a Technical Sub-Committee stay in Cairo after the formal meeting ended to reassemble the fragmentary leaves, so that a facsimile edition would be possible. I nominated for membership in the Technical Sub-Committee those who had long since had access to the material, and hence had some experience in working at least with photographs: the German delegate Martin Krause, the Swiss delegate Rodolphe Kasser, the Danish delegate Søren Giversen and myself, the American delegate and Permanent Secretary of the UNESCO Committee.

We worked some ten days, and again a fortnight in January, using as our point of departure the mimeographed transcriptions and translations the American team had prepared. Not only each day's results of reassembled leaves, but in fact all the Nag Hammadi materials, were photographed by the Brill photographer, so that complete photographic files came to Leiden and Claremont. But the job of placing fragments and establishing the sequence of leaves in each codex was far from complete. We returned once a year for a week or two as long as UNESCO would pay for the trips. But very many fragments still remained unplaced. I then took two of my students, Charles W. Hedrick and Stephen L. Emmel, for a semester to Cairo in 1974-75, and then left Emmel there for two more years to carry through the last fragment placements until the conservation project was really completed. The Institute for Antiquity and Christianity paid Emmel $100 per month for living expenses in Cairo during that period.

*The Facsimile Edition of the Nag Hammadi Codices* began publication in the Spring of 1972 with the appearance of *Codex VI*, less than a year and a half after we first got access in Cairo to the papyri themselves. The publication of the last of the thirteen codices, in two volumes of the *Facsimile Edition* containing *Codex I* and *Codices IX and X*, took place in 1977, in time to be announced in December in a plenary address at the AAR/SBL Annual Meeting in San Francisco.

To meet that deadline, we had an all-too-tight schedule: The last fragment had been placed on September 2 by Emmel in Cairo. This placement got the stamp of approval from our volume editor for the critical edition of the relevant codex, Birger Pearson, on September 30. Our placement was then phoned through to Frederik Wisse (whom we had, with Böhlig's help, stationed in Tübingen to work closely with the facsimile edition's printing firm in Stuttgart). He added a photo of the new fragment into the photograph of the correct leaf, which was then forwarded to Leiden in time to be bound and hand-carried to the AAR/SBL convention in December by the Director of Brill, W.C. Wieder, Jr. This meant that eight years after getting access to the originals in Cairo all thirteen codices had been put into the public domain. Hence we simultaneously published in December 1977 *The Nag Hammadi Library in English*,[16] our already-prepared English translation. Since then, it has appeared in three editions and become something of a best seller—over 100,000 copies sold.

---

[16] M. W. Meyer and J. M. Robinson eds., *The Nag Hammadi Library in English*, translated by members of the Coptic Gnostic Library Project of the Institute for Antiquity and Christianity (Leiden: E. J. Brill, 1977; paperback edition 1984; San Francisco: Harper & Row, 1977, paperback edition 1981); third, completely revised edition, R. Smith and J. M. Robinson, eds. (San Francisco: Harper & Row and E. J. Brill, 1988; paperback edition San Francisco: HarperCollins, 1990; unaltered fourth revised edition, Leiden: E. J. Brill, 1996).

A German New Testament scholar of distinction, Gerd Lüdemann of the University of Göttingen, has in a just-published book put in perspective this event at the 1977 SBL:[17]

> It was a truly historical moment when at the annual meeting of the Society of Biblical Literature in San Francisco in December 1977 this pioneering work of North American biblical scholarship was presented to the public. It made symbolically clear that the former predominance of German exegesis had come to an end forever.

Meanwhile our fourteen-volume critical edition, with introductions to each tractate, followed by transcripts, translations, notes and indices, had already begun to appear in 1975 with *The Gospel of the Egyptians* by Alexander Böhlig and Frederik Wisse.[18] The last two volumes, *The Apocryphon of John* by Frederik Wisse and Michael Waldstein,[19] and *Codex VII*, edited by Birger A. Pearson,[20] have both just appeared, to make this 1995 Annual Meeting of SBL not only the fiftieth anniversary of the Nag Hammadi discovery but also the celebration of the completion of the critical edition of all the Nag Hammadi texts.

Our translation team consisted in many cases of the same Americans who went with me to Cairo year after year to place fragments for the facsimile edition and who at the same time were preparing our critical edition. They continue to be prominent in the Nag Hammadi Section of SBL created at about that time, now the Nag Hammadi and Gnosticism Section chaired by John D. Turner. Two have become Project Directors at the Institute for Antiquity and Christianity, Birger A. Pearson and Marvin W. Meyer, directing projects that grew out of our Nag Hammadi experience. Several are members of the recently reorganized Brill monograph series, Nag Hammadi and Manichaean

---

[17] G. Lüdemann, *Ketzer: Die andere Seite des frühen Christentums* (Stuttgart: Radius, 1995) 232, n. 9. E.T. *Heretics: The Other Side of Early Christianity* (London: SCM; Minneapolis: Fortress, 1996).

[18] *Nag Hammadi Codices III,2 and IV,2: The Gospel of the Egyptians (The Holy Book of the Great Invisible Spirit)*, edited with translation and commentary by A. Böhlig and F. Wisse in cooperation with Pahor Labib (NHS 4; eds. M. Krause and J. M. Robinson, sub-series The Coptic Gnostic Library, ed. J. M. Robinson; Leiden: E. J. Brill, 1975).

[19] *The Apocryphon of John: Synopsis of Nag Hammadi Codices II,1; III,1 and IV,1, with BG 8502,2*, edited by F. Wisse and M. Waldstein (Nag Hammadi and Manichaean Studies 33, eds. J. M. Robinson and H.-J. Klimkeit, sub-series The Coptic Gnostic Library, ed. J. M. Robinson; Leiden: E. J. Brill, 1995).

[20] *Nag Hammadi Codex VII*, edited by B. A. Pearson, Nag Hammadi and Manichaean Studies 30, eds. J. M. Robinson and H-J. Klimkeit, sub-series The Coptic Gnostic Library, ed. J. M. Robinson; Leiden: E. J. Brill, 1996 [actually November 1995]).

Studies, whose original Editorial Board had only a small minority of Americans (Hans Jonas, George MacRae, Frederik Wisse and myself), but whose reorganized board has now a majority (Harold W. Attridge, Ron Cameron, Stephen L. Emmel, Charles W. Hedrick, Howard Jackson, Douglas M. Parrott, Birger A. Pearson and myself). This team has thus matured to give American scholarship an international prominence in Coptology and Gnosticism it never had before.

The copies of our original draft transcriptions and translations given to Jacques Ménard in Strasbourg in 1970-71 became his motivation for organizing at Université Laval in Quebec, Canada, the French-Canadian critical edition with commentary, directed by Paul-Hubert Poirier, *La bibliothèque copte de Nag Hammadi*. It began publication in 1977 at Peeters in Leuven and promises to complete its many-volumed edition before the end of the decade.

The *Berliner Arbeitskreis für koptisch-gnostische Schriften*, led by Hans-Martin Schenke, had obtained on loan the transcriptions and translations I had given to Kurt Rudolph, photographed them, and used this as the source material for their own translation activity. For they had already begun as early as 1958 publishing in the *Theologische Literaturzeitung*[21] translations of the few tractates that were already available in the meager volume of facsimiles Pahor Labib had published in Egypt in 1956. With all the material now in hand, their tempo escalated dramatically, and translations were followed by critical editions with commentaries, as dissertations were published. This Berlin group, though now somewhat scattered among the three centers, from Claremont to Quebec and Berlin, is currently working on a complete and definitive German translation to appear in the series *Die griechischen christlichen Schriftsteller der ersten Jahrhunderte*, as volumes 2 and 3 of the sub-series *Koptisch-gnostische Schriften*.

It is of some cultural-political significance, in terms of the sociology of knowledge, that a manuscript discovery originally monopolized by Western Europe, namely France and West Germany, with Denmark, The Netherlands and Switzerland playing supporting roles, is no longer dominated by Western Europe. Instead, the outsiders, rather than competing among themselves, have banded together to produce the comprehensive and definitive editions in English—not in England but in America, in French—not in France but in Canada, and in German—not in what was West Germany but in what was East

---

[21] J. Leipoldt, "Ein neues Evangelium? Das koptische Thomasevangelium übersetzt und besprochen," *TLZ* 83 (1958) 481-96.

Germany. What used to be considered in this area of research the outer fringes of the Western world have thus joined together to become a united cooperative undertaking. The three teams, representing the three scholarly language areas, have tended to merge into what has become the main strength of Nag Hammadi research in the world today. It is appropriately symbolic that the leaders of all three teams have planned to be here together to share in this celebration.

The coming of age of North American scholarship in this field can be illustrated by a cameo portrait of one of our members. I mentioned having taken two students with me to Cairo for seven months in 1974-75 to finish placing the many fragments that the Technical Sub-Committee of UNESCO's committee had not been able to place. One of them was Stephen L. Emmel. He had just begun Graduate School at Claremont, but gladly dropped out so as to be able to go along to Cairo and stay there a couple of more years to finish up the job. He then went to Yale for his doctorate with one of our team members, Bentley Layton, who had become America's leading Coptologist. Emmel is currently President Elect of the International Association for Coptic Studies, the kind of honor never before awarded to an American graduate student. By the way, he did get his doctorate, with a dissertation that is a *magnum opus* in its own right, making sense, in terms of an ancient organization of Shenoute's collected works, out of the chaos of thousands of leaves of Shenoute manuscripts from the White Monastery, scattered in museums and libraries throughout the Western world.[22]

But that is not all! Emmel, that home-town boy from Rochester, New York, has just accepted the Chair of Coptology at the University of Münster, Germany, upon the retirement of Martin Krause. When our team first started as unknown beginners, we tried to commend ourselves to the establishment, by conforming to their editing procedures. After all, Krause more than anyone else had the inside track at the Coptic Museum, where he had worked for years and acquired his own photographs and transcriptions. For Emmel now to become his successor in the only chair of Coptology in Germany, in fact in the world, is of course first of all a personal achievement for a really brilliant young scholar. But it also marks the coming of age of American scholarship in this field. One need merely compare the first critical editions of the Apocryphon of John[23] with the just-published

---

[22] See his "Shenoute's Literary Corpus" (Ph.D. dissertation, Yale University, 1993).

[23] M. Krause and P. Labib, *Die drei Versionen des Apokryphon des Johannes*; Søren Giversen, *Apocryphon Johannis: The Coptic Text of the Apocryphon Johannis in the*

critical edition in our Brill series,[24] a really superb achievement, to see the scholarly advance that has been made over the past generation.

### 3. THE NEW ETHOS FOR HANDLING MANUSCRIPT DISCOVERIES

The publication of the complete *Facsimile Edition,* just eight years after first getting access to the papyri themselves, has set an obvious standard for avoiding or overcoming monopolies in other manuscript discoveries. After all, we, though outsiders to the field, had shown that where there is a will there is a way. For the impossibilities ticked off by the insiders usually turned out to be excuses to justify their own self-interest, excuses that could readily be overcome if one really wanted to.

For example, the last bit of the Nag Hammadi monopoly had been the Jung Codex, Codex I, since it was not in Cairo, where we had achieved open access, but in a bank vault in Zürich belonging to the heirs of Carl Gustaf Jung. The heirs were the owners, but had agreed to return the codex to Cairo when the team of editors no longer needed it for their transcription. The spokesman for the editors, Rodolphe Kasser, was on our Technical Sub-Committee, and would still have unlimited access to it in Cairo, had it been returned. But then so could the rest of us! So he maintained that the heirs were not willing to return it because they knew it was worth a lot of money. But then the spokesman for the heirs told me the Jung family was ready to return it whenever the editors said they no longer needed it in Zürich. He even agreed to write the editors to inquire if he could return it. Thereupon he informed me that all who had responded (a postal strike had prevented the French from responding) had agreed to return it, except ... Rodolphe Kasser! Only when Kasser had sent the last volume of their edition to the publisher and thus insured that it would be the *editio princeps* did he agree to the return of the codex to Egypt.[25]

The most obvious comparison to the Nag Hammadi publication experience has been the abysmal publication record of the Dead Sea Scrolls, since both discoveries took place at about the same time and hence have all along been compared in various regards.

In the Fall 1979 issue of the *Biblical Archaeologist*, devoted exclusively to the Nag Hammadi discovery, Harry Thomas Frank, the editor of that issue, included a "Letter to the Readers" in which he

---

*Nag Hammadi Codex II with Translation, Introduction and Commentary* (Acta Theologica Danica 5; Copenhagen: Prostant apud Munksgaard, 1963).

[24] F. Wisse and M. Waldstein, *The Apocryphon of John.*

[25] See my review article, "The Jung Codex: The Rise and Fall of a Monopoly."

forcefully pressed home the invidious comparison with Qumran. And various Qumran scholars, from David Noel Freedman (University of Michigan and University of California at San Diego) to Stanislav Siegert (UCLA) and Zwi Werblowsky (Hebrew University), have appealed to me over the years to direct my energies to breaking the monopoly on the Dead Sea Scrolls. But I steadfastly declined the honor and privilege, and impossible chore, since, after all, that is not my field of competence. But then I was trapped into it by an odd kind of serendipity:

Hershel Shanks, who led the campaign to break the Qumran monopoly, mentioned with irony in his *Biblical Archeology Review* in 1989:[26]

> At least two sets of photographs of all Dead Sea Scroll texts—both published and unpublished—have been deposited in the United States for security reasons. But the agreements with the depositories—the Institute for Antiquity and Christianity in Claremont, California, and Hebrew Union College in Cincinnati—forbid their giving access to outside scholars.

I telephoned Shanks to correct his statement, by explaining that the photographs are not at the Institute but at our sister institution in Claremont, the Ancient Biblical Manuscript Center. Subsequently, Shanks made the correction:[27]

> Professor Robinson says he is as much an outsider as anyone. Were the Dead Sea texts under his jurisdiction, he would feel "morally obligated" to see that they were made available, as he did with the Nag Hammadi codices of which he was chief editor.

A few months later, Robert Eisenman of Long Beach State University invited me to participate in a day-long program he had scheduled there for April 28, 1990, on "Scrolls, Caves, and Hidden Manuscripts." He asked me to narrate how breaking a monopoly was done in the case of the Nag Hammadi texts.

Shortly thereafter, Eisenman visited me in Claremont. First he extricated from me a promise of the strictest confidentiality, which I honored, in spite of various awkward situations, for which I here apologize. He then broadly hinted that he had some photographs of unpublished Qumran material. On his next visit he conceded he had

---

[26] H. Shanks, "New Hope for the Unpublished Dead Sea Scrolls," *BAR* 15/6 (November-December 1989) 56.

[27] "Correction: Photographs of Unpublished Dead Sea Scrolls at Ancient Biblical Manuscript Center," *BAR* 16/1 (January-February 1990) 67.

photographs of all the unpublished fragments, and asked if I might use my know-how in publishing facsimile editions and my good offices with my publisher Brill to publish together with him a facsimile edition of the unpublished Qumran fragments.

Thereupon I talked to the Brill representative at the SBL International Meeting in Vienna, Austria, in August 1990. We agreed to meet at the Annual Meeting in New Orleans that November to work out a publication agreement. Before going ahead, I had lunch with my friend Frank Cross, to see if there really was any need for me to get involved at all. In New Orleans, Eisenman and I agreed to supply Brill with the front matter and the edited photographs by February, 1991. Brill agreed to produce a microfiche edition by the beginning of May. A formal contract with the Brill administration was signed on February 15-16, 1991.

I spent the Christmas semester break of 1990-91 writing the Introduction and Index, and labeling the thousands of glossy prints that Eisenman lent to me, only a small part at a time (lest I abscond with the whole), to choose the best of each of his several prints from each negative. Eisenman never told me what his connection in Israel was that had made it possible for him to get a copy of the negatives.

Our co-signed Introduction was particularly delicate, since my two conditions for participating were that the Introduction include no suggestion of criticism or polemic, and that Eisenman's views on Qumran, which I do not share, not be mentioned. I completed my chores in time for Eisenman to air-freight everything to Brill on time. Sample microfiche masters were produced in The Netherlands.

Just a month and a half before our publication date of May 3, 1991, Brill sent a staff member, Hans van der Meij, to a Qumran meeting at El Escorial, Spain, held on March 18-22, where overpowering pressure was put on the isolated Polish Qumran scholar Zdzislaw J. Kapera, to withdraw his offer to supply interested scholars with copies of the transcription by John Strugnell and Elisha Qimron of 4Q MMT, a Qumran text that they had heralded as sensational but that was still unpublished. Kapera crumbled.[28] For this and other

---

[28] The offer had been made by Z. J. Kapera, "An Anonymously Received Pre-Publication of the 4Q MMT," *The Qumran Chronicle* 2 (December 1990). The transcription itself was available as "Appendix 'A'." On March 12, 1991 General Amir Drori, at the request of Qimron, had written to Kapera, with a copy to the President of the Polish Academy of Sciences, Cracow Section, expressing "astonishment" at Kapera's offer. He had called on Kapera to "cancel your plans" and demanded an "immediate reply." At the congress in El Escorial, Kapera apologized to Qimron in the presence of Eugene Ulrich and Emanuel Tov (two of the troika that had succeeded John Strugnell as head of the Dead Sea Scroll cartel). On his return to Poland Kapera wrote on April 10, 1991 to

factors, on April 8, 1991 Brill canceled our signed contract and withdrew, but later published, once the monopoly had been broken, an
official microfiche edition edited by Emanuel Tov himself.[29]

Eisenman and I sought another publisher. After several well-
known houses would not touch the project with a ten-foot pole, we
turned by the end of the summer to Shanks, who eagerly agreed to
publish.

Without actually letting the cat out of the bag, Shanks published
his rationale for our facsimile edition in the issue of the *Biblical
Archaeology Review*[30] which was due to appear simultaneously with
our edition. His article was based on a telephone interview with me,
and was entitled "How to Break a Scholarly Monopoly: The Case of
the Gospel of Thomas." Here he pointed out that Pahor Labib's very
inadequate Egyptian facsimile edition of a few Nag Hammadi tractates including *The Gospel of Thomas*, published in 1956, led
promptly to a flood of translations, into Latin, German, French,
Danish, English and Swedish, which left the International Committee
of 1956 that had held the monopoly no choice but to publish a
"preliminary" excerpt of their *editio maior* in 1959, which is all they
ever published.[31]

Even they did not have official authorization for what they did
publish. For they had refused to put Pahor Labib's name on the title
page alongside their own names as editors, in view of the fact that he
had not actually been involved in the editing process. Labib then
never signed the authorization for them to publish an official edition.
Brill ultimately had to fall back on the same unofficial legitimacy that
the flood of competing translations had already used. Labib's facsimile edition, if nothing else, had, after all, put the text in the public
domain. Presumably we would still be waiting for their *editio maior*
as the *editio princeps* of *The Gospel of Thomas*, had not Labib's
little volume of facsimiles forced their hand! The moral of Shanks'

---

General Drori assuming full responsibility. He said he was "a frustrated scholar who had
been awaiting publication of the text 'soon' since April 1984 (not to say since 1952!)."
He quoted a statement by Strugnell and Qimran published in 1985 that "a preliminary
edition of the whole document will be finished within a year or so."

[29] *The Dead Sea Scrolls on Microfiche: A Comprehensive Facsimile Edition of the
Texts from the Judean Desert*, published under the auspices of the Israel Antiquities
Authority, ed. E. Tov (Leiden: E. J. Brill and IDC Microform Publishers, 1993).

[30] "How to Break a Scholarly Monopoly: The Case of the Gospel of Thomas," *BAR*
16/6 (November-December1990) 55.

[31] A. Guillaumont et al., eds., *The Gospel according to Thomas: Coptic Text Established and Translated* (Leiden: E. J. Brill, 1959); also Dutch, French, and German
editions appeared at Brill simultaneously.

article was that a facsimile edition, even a very inadequate one, can break a monopoly. That is all I hoped for, in the case of the Dead Sea Scrolls. After all, without access to the fragments themselves, we had to publish the photographs as they were.

Our two-volume *Facsimile Edition of the Dead Sea Scrolls* appeared in record time. The contract had been signed only on September 12, 1991, and, less than ten weeks later, our edition was presented at a press conference in New York on November 19, 1991, just a few days before the SBL Annual Meeting in Kansas City.

Shanks had not mentioned in our contract that he himself would insert his own Publisher's Foreword, including, in addition to a massive polemic, the transcription of 4Q MMT! Last-minute written efforts were undertaken by the President of The Claremont University Center, John D. Maguire,[32] and by the Chair of the Advisory Board of the Institute for Antiquity and Christianity, J. Harold Ellens,[33] to dissuade Shanks, but all to no avail.

Qimron sued for some $200,000 in damages for publishing his scholarship, the transcription of 4Q MMT. An Israeli court compelled Shanks to publish a second edition without the incriminating transcription of 4Q MMT, much to my relief. This legal procedure, incidentally, did not question in any way our right to publish the photographs themselves .

The urgency within the scholarly and lay public to bring the monopoly on the Dead Sea Scrolls to an end was documented by the fact that, unknown to me, two other efforts were underway at the same time to achieve the same goal. Ben Zion Wacholder and his computer-wise doctoral student Martin G. Abegg at Hebrew Union College in Cincinnati (where microfilms of the unpublished fragments were also on file, but equally inaccessible) had the ingenious idea of using a

---

[32] Maguire's letter of November 20, 1991 stated: "We do however have a major concern regarding the volumes as hand-bound and presented at the news conference: the inclusion of the lengthy and polemical foreword and its accompanying figures. Without exception, everyone at The Claremont Graduate School who has been apprised of the situation believes the foreword and figures should be removed from this historic work. ... The Claremont Graduate School feels strongly enough about this issue to agree to accept the cost of removing the inappropriate pages and repaginating where necessary. In the interest of retaining the enthusiastic support of the School in this project, we hope you will agree to the proposed changes."

[33] Ellens' letter of November 20, 1991, which I hand-delivered to Shanks at the SBL Annual Meeting in Kansas City, read in part: "To leave those elements in the volumes released for scholarly and popular consumption cheapens the objective scholarly quality of the volumes and makes us subject to just such unnecessary and unjust criticism from those scholars who will wish to find reasons to demean what we have accomplished here."

closely-guarded but nonetheless available card file of Qumran vocabulary that had been produced a generation ago, each card with a swath of text around the indexed word. One could put them end-to-end, so to speak, and thus reconstruct unpublished texts! Their first fascicle was published by Shanks on September 4, 1991.[34]

Meanwhile, on September 22, 1990, the Director of the Huntington Library, William A. Moffett, had announced that the negatives it had held in its vault for years were being made accessible to the scholarly public without any restrictions. He immediately—the same day—received a FAX from General Amir Drori, as Director, Israel Antiquities Authority, and Prof. Emanuel Tov, as Editor-in-Chief, The International Dead Sea Scrolls Project, urging him to reconsider and thus "save us the trouble of legal action." Moffett did not reconsider, and there was no legal action.[35] The invincible monopoly was broken by a simple common-sense decision of a decisive administrator.

At the Annual Meeting of SBL at Kansas City that same year, just a week after our *Facsimile Edition* had appeared, SBL President Helmut Koester convened a special called meeting of the society at 9 PM on the last evening, Nov. 25. The Chair of the Research and Publications Committee read a resolution that had just been officially adopted by SBL:[36]

> 1. *Recommendation to those who own or control ancient written materials*: Those who own or control ancient written materials should allow all scholars to have access to them. If the condition of the written materials requires that access to them be restricted, arrangements should be made for a facsimile reproduction that will be accessible to all scholars. Although the owners or those in control may choose to authorize one scholar or preferably a team of scholars to prepare an official edition of any given ancient written mate-

---

[34] B. Z. Wacholder and M. G. Abegg, *A Preliminary Edition of the Unpublished Dead Sea Scrolls: The Hebrew and Aramaic Texts from Cave Four*, fascicle 1 (Washington, D.C.: Biblical Archaeology Society, 1991).

[35] For the ethical issues involved, see my essay, "Ethics in Publishing Manuscript Discoveries: Panel Discussion," in *Methods of Investigation of the Dead Sea Scrolls and the Khirbet Qumran Site: Present Realities and Future Prospects* (Annals of the New York Academy of Sciences 722, eds. M. O. Wise, et al.; New York: New York Academy of Sciences, 1994) 468-71.

[36] On November 22, 1991 the Research and Publications Committee had (to quote its minutes) "directed that the statement on access be sent to funding agencies, publishers, primary repositories, be published in *RSN*, and be circulated through the American Council of Learned Societies to other learned societies interested in literary and artifactual remains (encouraging their participation in policy development). The Committee approved further distribution as widely as possible." I had it republished in the *Zeitschrift für Papyrologie und Epigraphik* 92 (1992) 296.

rials, such authorization should neither preclude access to the written materials by other scholars nor hinder other scholars from publishing their own
studies, translations, or editions of the written materials.

2. *Obligations entailed by specially authorized editions*: Scholars who are
given special authorization to work on official editions of ancient written
materials should cooperate with the owners or those in control of the written
materials to ensure publication of the edition in an expeditious manner, and
they should facilitate access to the written materials by all scholars. If the
owners or those in control grant to specially authorized editors any privileges that are unavailable to other scholars, these privileges should by no
means include exclusive access to the written materials or facsimile repro-
ductions of them. Furthermore, the owners or those in control should set a
reasonable deadline for completion of the envisioned edition (not more than
five years after the special authorization is granted).

There Emanuel Tov himself announced that all restrictions on free
access had been officially lifted.[37] You might as well unlock the barn,
once the horse is stolen.

I hope and trust, and in fact am convinced, that we have all learned
a lesson from this sad tale, for which we all bear some collective
responsibility, and that in the case of future important manuscript
discoveries a much more enlightened policy will be followed.[38] The
Nag Hammadi experience deserves some credit for having provided
positive incentives to such a better future, in helping to change the
ethos for handling important new manuscript discoveries.[39]

---

[37] As recently as October 1, 1995 Tov had reported by E-Mail to the "Judaios: First
Century Judaism Discussion Forum," denying rumors that the Israeli authorities had
"dropped their objection to the Huntington action" and affirmed that "all of us are still in
the middle of deliberations." On October 6, 1991 he wrote the Huntington proposing a
meeting to discuss the problem, and requested that the Huntington "delay all access to
the scrolls for one month, until the said meeting." The meeting never took place.

[38] By pure coincidence I presented an address proposing such policies the same weekend that the Huntington Library made its announcement. It has hence been widely
published: *Manuscript Discoveries of the Future* with an appendix containing the title
page, table of contents, introduction and sample plates from: *A Facsimile Edition of the
Dead Sea Scrolls*, Occasional Papers, The Institute for Antiquity and Christianity, ed.
J.L. Reed, 23 (Claremont: IAC, 1991); abridged by myself, "Avoiding Another Scrolls
Access Furor," *Los Angeles Times*, September 28, 1991, Section F, 13-14; abridged by
the editor, "Handling Future Manuscript Discoveries," *BA* (December 1991): 235-240;
abridged by H. Shanks, "What We Should Do Next Time Great Manuscripts Are Discov-
ered," *BAR* 18/1 (January-February 1992) 66-70; reprinted in unabridged form in
*Zeitschrift für Papyrologie und Epigraphik* 92 (1992) 281-96.

[39] In handling the 152 Sixth Century C.E. charred Greek documentary papyri rolls
from the Byzantine church in Petra, a conscious effort seems to have been made to
introduce clear new policies: "It will be recalled that all parties involved had signed an
access / publication agreement and we are hapy to report that the final division of the

I have moved in my own research from Nag Hammadi studies into reconstructing a critical text of the Sayings Gospel Q. The biggest problem with Q is of course the lack of any manuscript evidence, which has created the standard criticism that Q is only a hypothetical text. I must say that the absence of any Q manuscripts to be caught up in some Q monopoly was for me a strong positive incentive! We have made the results of our International Q Project promptly available, publishing each year in the *Journal of Biblical Literature* (the October issue) the preceding year's reconstructions, so that we in turn not be thought to be monopolizing the lost manuscript we are reconstructing. The final segment of our critical text of Q has just appeared.[40] We have already begun work on a revised edition to appear in book form and on CD-ROM, which we hope will become a standard tool in our discipline. The database has already begun publication in a multi-volume series.[41]

### 4. THE IMPACT OF THE NAG HAMMADI DISCOVERY ON THE SHAPE OF NEW TESTAMENT SCHOLARSHIP

Here it is not my purpose to itemize a series of specific details where the Nag Hammadi texts have influenced the understanding of New Testament texts.[42] Rather my intent is to maintain the focus on the shape of the discipline of biblical scholarship itself as a result of the Nag Hammadi discovery.

The forty-eight Nag Hammadi tractates would have commended themselves to biblical scholarship much more readily if they had been discovered in Palestine or Syria, where many of them were composed, rather than in Upper Egypt, where none of them was composed, and if they had survived not only in late fourth century copies of Coptic translations, but also in the original Greek in which the authors wrote in the first three centuries of the Common Era. Hence they caught us academically unprepared. Coptic was at that time only one of the

---

scrolls for publication purposes between the two groups was agreed to in late 1995." P. M. Bikai, "Update on the Scrolls," *ACOR Newsletter* 7.2 (Winter 1995) 11.

[40] M. C. Moreland and J. M. Robinson, "The International Q Project Work Sessions 23-27 May, 22-26 August, 17-18 November 1994," *JBL* 114 (1995) 475-485. An *addendum* will appear in the October 1997 issue.

[41] *Documenta Q: Reconstructions of Q Through Two Centuries of Gospel Research Excerpted, Sorted, and Evaluated. Q 11:2b-4.* (Louvain: Peeters, 1996).

[42] See H.-M. Schenke, "The Relevance of Nag Hammadi Research to New Testament Scholarship" (an unpublished paper presented at the Annual Meeting of the Society of Biblical Literature in Chicago, November 19, 1994).

more esoteric dimensions of textual criticism, and had been safely
ignored by all the rest of us. It can no longer be safely ignored.

Furthermore our traditional prejudices about Gnosticism had
dampened the interest of many. But some of the Nag Hammadi tractates are not Gnostic at all! For example, *The Teachings of Silvanus*
(VII,4) is Jewish wisdom literature (somewhat Christianized), and
indeed quotes (112.37-113.7) the *Wisdom of Solomon* (7:25-26) as
referring to Christ. Thus it involves a secondary Sophia Christology
that expands considerably the faint traces in the New Testament itself.

The bulk of the tractates are of course Gnostic, and that has been a
stumbling-block for many. After all, Gnosticism has commonly been
held to be unintelligible other-worldly and rather irrelevant mythology, a corruption of Primitive Christianity that abandoned the Old
Testament and its God—our God—in a Marcion-like perversion.
Hence, rather than, with an open mind, seizing upon this library, the
first really authentic early Gnostic texts that can speak for themselves, many in our discipline have simply left them to one side.
Therefore it is very important to communicate to a wider academic
public the surprising results that the specialists have thus far reached,
which should lead to a calming of such prejudices.

Rather than being a departure from the Old Testament as the basis
of our religious tradition, Gnosticism found there, rather than in
Homer or Zoroaster[43] or Gilgamesh, the inspiration for its mythology.
The book of Genesis is the favorite authority of Gnosticism! For
example, Gen 3 is retold detail after detail, even if with a typically
Gnostic twist, in *The Testimony of Truth* (IX,3). To be sure, the
Gnostics did interpret the Old Testament in a different way, as did,
however, also Philo, Josephus, the New Testament, Qumran and
Rabbinic Judaism. Hence Gnosticism stands in the biblical tradition
as well.

In effect, the roots of Gnosticism, previously sought all over the
ancient world, have become most visible in Judaism. Even the apoca-
lyptic literature of Judaism itself has been enriched with one Jewish
Gnostic apocalypse from Nag Hammadi, the *Apocalypse of Adam*
(V,5). George MacRae saw to its inclusion in the current edition of
*The Old Testament Pseudepigrapha.*[44] It narrates Adam's death-bed

---

[43] The tractate *Zostrianos* (VIII,1) concluded with an encoded subscript: "Zostrianos;
Oracles of Truth of Zostrianos, God of Truth; Teachings of Zoroaster." But the text is not
Zoroastrian, but Sethian, building on 2 Enoch.

[44] *The Old Testament Pseudepigrapha*, vol. 1: *Apocalyptic Literature and Testaments*,
ed. by J. H. Charlesworth (Garden City, NY: Doubleday, 1983) 707-11 (MacRae's
introduction), 712-19 (MacRae's translation).

testament to his son Seth, a kind of Gnostic *Heilsgeschichte*, narrating the three descents of the Gnostic Redeemer, Seth, to rescue the elect Sethians from flood, fire, and the final cataclysm.

Birger A.Pearson has summarized in his own Fiftieth Anniversary paper[45] the dependence of Nag Hammadi texts on Jewish apocryphal and pseudepigraphical literature: *The Apocryphon of John* (II,1; III,1; IV,1; BG 8502,2) builds on *1 Enoch*; *The Apocalypse of Adam* (V,5) builds on *The Life of Adam and Eve*; *Zostrianos* (VIII,1) builds on *2 Enoch*. Here one has before one's very eyes the source material of Gnosticism. All it took was the distinctive Gnostic twist, a powerful push from some kind of alienated Judaism, Samaritanism, or Proselytism, to engender the Gnostic movement and its distinctive literature.

A whole new Jewish sect, to add to the plethora already known to characterize Second Temple Judaism, has come into the clear light of day in the Nag Hammadi Codices. It is Hans-Martin Schenke who has brought into focus the Gnostic Sethians, who contributed the largest single cluster to the Nag Hammadi library, eleven of the forty-eight different texts. At the International Conference on The Rediscovery of Gnosticism held at Yale in 1978, one major section of the program, and one whole volume of its proceedings, were devoted exclusively to Sethianism.[46]

The Nag Hammadi Sethian texts can be subdivided into three groups, making it possible to discern roughly the history of Sethianism.[47] Some are only Jewish, with no Christian aspects: *The Three Steles of Seth* (VII,5), *The Thought of Norea* (IX,2), *Marsanes* (X), and *Allogenes* (XI,3), or at most with scant secondarily Christianizing interpolations: *The Apocalypse of Adam* (V,5) and *Zostrianos* (VIII,1). Others have a thin Christian veneer: *The Gospel of the Egyptians* (III,2; IV,2) and *The Trimorphic Protennoia* (XIII,1). Only a minority can be really called Christian Gnosticism: *The Apoc-*

---

[45] "From Jewish Apoclypticism to Gnosis" (a paper presented at the Fiftieth Anniversary of the Nag Hammadi Discovery: Copenhagen International Conference on the Nag Hammadi Texts in the History of Religions, September 19-24, 1995 at the Danish Academy of Sciences and Letters).

[46] *The Rediscovery of Gnosticism: Proceedings of the International Conference on Gnosticism at Yale, New Haven, Connecticut, March 28-31, 1978*, Vol. 2, *Sethian Gnosticism*, edited by B. Layton (SHR 41, NumenSup; Leiden: E. J. Brill, 1981). See especially H.-M. Schenke, "The Phenomenon and Significance of Gnostic Sethianism," 588-616, and also my contribution, "Sethians and Johannine Thought: The *Trimorphic Protennoia* and the Prologue of the Gospel of John," 643-62, as well as the "Discussion," 662-670, and the "Concluding Discussion," 671-685.

[47] See H.-M. Schenke, "Gnosis: Zum Forschungsstand unter besonderer Berücksichtigung der religions-geschichtlichen Problematik, *VF* 32 (1987): 2-22.

*ryphon of John* (II,1; III,1; IV,1; BG 8502,2), *The Hypostasis of the Archons* (II,4), and *Melchizedek* (IX,1). But this Christian Sethianism is the only kind previously known, having been attested by the heresiologists.[48] The relative rarity of Christian Sethian texts in the Nag Hammadi library is all the more surprising, when one considers that it is after all a Christian library, which can of course account for the secondary Christianizing of several of the Jewish Sethian texts. Most of the non-Christian Jewish Sethian texts represent instead a Neo-Platonic Gnosticism, as especially John D. Turner has worked out: *The Three Steles of Seth* (VII,5), *Zostrianos* (VIII,1), *Marsanes* (X) and *Allogenes* (XI,3). Thus one can see Sethianism evolving out of Judaism into early Christian and Neo-Platonic cultural contexts, much as did main-line Christianity itself. Indeed these history-of-religions trajectories of Sethianism and Early Christianity are even more parallel in that both emerged from Jewish baptismal sects.[49]

Nag Hammadi tractates also fill gaps in early Christian trajectories themselves. Half of the Pauline corpus presents us with authentic letters of Paul, the oldest Christian texts to have survived. Then the last half of the Pauline corpus shows how Paul was variously interpreted after his death. The latest letters in the Pauline corpus, the Pastoral Epistles, display a mild, "safe" Paul that reassured the canonizers to include him after all, in spite of the (mis)use of him being made by Gnostics and Marcionites. Acts tends to confirm this domesticated Paul.

But the earlier Deutero-Pauline Epistles, Colossians and Ephesians, had pointed in a more speculative, cosmic direction. Paul himself had emphasized that the believer is united with Christ, in baptism indeed dying with Christ. But Paul reserved one's resurrection with Christ for the eschatological future, what Ernst Käsemann drew to our attention as Paul's "eschatological reservation." Yet already Col 2:12 presents the believer as both dying *and* rising with Christ. And Eph 2:6 affirms God has thereupon enthroned the believer "in heavenly places" with Christ. Is not the believer's resurrection then past already?

The canonical texts hesitate actually to put it that way. For a Pastoral Epistle condemns the "godless chatter" of Hymenaeus and Phi-

---

[48] Irenaeus (*Adv. haer.* 1.29: "Barbelo-Gnostics"; 1.30: "Ophites" and "Sethians") and Epiphanius (*Panarion* 26: "Gnostics"; 39: "Sethians"; 40: "Archontics"), and *The Untitled Text* from the Bruce Codex.

[49] J.-M. Sevrin has worked out the baptismal dimensions of Sethianism, *Le dossier baptismal séthien: Etudes sur la sacramentaire gnostique* (BCNH, Section "Etudes" 2; Québec: Presses de l'Université Laval, 1986).

letus who "will lead people into more and more ungodliness, ... by holding that the resurrection is past already" (2 Tim 2:16-18). Here some kind of shadow-boxing is taking place, where the Pastorals are alluding to some otherwise unattested Christian leaders that clearly had gone too far. The only kind of resurrection for believers that this could be talking about is not physical, but purely spiritual. But if that spiritual resurrection has already taken place, an eschatologically future physical resurrection would have become quite superfluous. Hence the advocates of this "heresy" do not get an unbiased hearing in the New Testament.

But now, *The Treatise on Resurrection* (I,4) presents in a very appealing way precisely this spiritual resurrection that has taken place already, and indeed by appeal to the authority of *the* Apostle *par excellence*, Paul! Should not any objective historian trying to trace the Pauline school include this non-canonical Epistle as part of the left wing of that school alongside the Pastoral Epistles as documentation for the right wing? Or should we limit our knowledge of the left wing of the Pauline school to the smear by the right wing?[50]

*The Treatise on Resurrection* surely goes further than does Paul himself, indeed it would no doubt have been rejected by Paul, as is indicated by such texts as 1 Cor 4:8, where "already" is in effect branded as heretical, and Phil 3:11,20-21, where the believer's resurrection is clearly still future. But neither are the Pastoral Epistles and Acts written as Paul himself would have written. The fact that we are *their* heirs, rather than heirs of the spiritualized Gnostic option, makes them instinctively more congenial to us. But as critical historians we must analyze all the evidence, if we want to assess the full history of the Pauline trajectory or trajectories.

A somewhat similar debate may be behind the story of "Doubting Thomas" in John 20:24-29, who needed physical proof of the resurrection to believe. His more spiritual side of the debate may be reflected in the *Gospel of Thomas* and the *Book of Thomas (the Contender)*.[51]

Thus the Nag Hammadi codices have forced us to direct our attention to New Testament "apocrypha" to an extent never before realized. The current edition of Wilhelm Schneemelcher's standard *New*

---

[50] See Lüdemann, *Ketzer*, 133-49, E. T. *Heretics*, 120-142, for a full presentation of Colossians, Ephesians, the Pastoral Epistles, and *The Treatise on Resurrection* in this regard.

[51] G. J. Riley, *Resurrection Reconsidered: Thomas and John in Controversy* (Minneapolis: Fortress, 1995).

*Testament Apocrypha* contains eleven Nag Hammadi tractates.[52] What is even more significant, Helmut Koester's *Introduction to the New Testament* includes sixteen Nag Hammadi tractates![53] The field of Early Christian Literature has grown immensely, and we must grow with it!

Perhaps the most lively debate going on in New Testament scholarship as a result of the Nag Hammadi discovery has to do with whether *The Gospel of Thomas* is largely dependent on the canonical Gospels, in which case one might relax and seek to ignore it as purely secondary, or whether it is an independent source of information about the historical Jesus, in which case one should tighten one's belt, perhaps even learn Coptic, and bite the bullet.

Clearly *The Gospel of Thomas* does contain sayings that cannot be derived from the canonical Gospels, since they are not there to be found, yet sayings that in some cases are clearly not Gnostic, but have the same claim to being old, even authentic, as does the older layer of sayings in the canonical Gospels and Q. This can be illustrated by kingdom parables.[54] Saying 97: "The kingdom of the [father] is like a woman who is carrying a [jar] filled with flour. While she was walking on [the] way, very distant (from home), the handle of the jar broke (and) the flour leaked out [on] the path. (But) she did not know (it); she had not noticed a problem. When she had reached her house, she put the jar down on the floor (and) found it empty." Saying 98: "The

---

[52] *Neutestamentliche Apokryphen in deutscher Uebersetzung*, vol. 1, *Evangelien*, 5th edition, ed. W. Schneemelcher (Tübingen: Mohr [Paul Siebeck], 1989). English tr. *New Testament Apocrypha*, vol. 1. *Gospels and Related Writings*, ed. R. McL. Wilson (Louisville: Westminster/John Knox, 1992): *The Apocryphon of James* (I,2), *The Gospel of Thomas* (II,2), *The Gospel of Philip* (II,3), *The Book of Thomas (the Contender)* (II,7), *The Dialogue of the Savior* (III,5), *The (First) Apocalypse of James* (V,3), *The (Second) Apocalypse of James*, and *The Letter of Peter to Philip* (VIII,2); vol. 2, *Apostolisches; Apokalysen und Verwandtes*. English tr. *Writings Related to the Apostles, Apocalypses and Related Subjects: The Apocalypse of Paul* (V,5), *The Acts of Peter and the Twelve* (VI,1), and *The Apocalypse of Peter* (VII,3).

[53] H. Koester, *Introduction to the New Testament*, vol. 2, *History and Literature of Early Christianity* (Philadelphia: Fortress, 1982): *The Apocryphon of James* (I,2), *The Gospel of Truth* (I,3; XII,2), *The Apocryphon of John* (II,1; III,1; IV,1; BG 8502,2), *The Gospel of Thomas* (II,2), *The Hypostasis of the Archons* (II,4), *The Book of Thomas (the Contender)* (II,7), *The Gospel of the Egyptians* (III,2; IV,2), *The Letter of Eugnostos the Blessed* (III,3; V,1), *The Sophia of Jesus Christ* (III,4), *The Dialogue of the Savior* (III,5), *The (First) Apocalypse of James* (V,3), *The (Second) Apocalypse of James* (V,4), *The Apocalypse of Adam* (V,5), *The Paraphrase of Shem* (VII,1), *The Second Treatise of the Great Seth* (VII,2), and *The Three Steles of Seth* (VII,5).

[54] C.-H. Hunzinger, "Unbekannte Gleichnisse Jesu aus dem Thomas-Evangelium," in *Judentum, Urchristentum, Kirche: Festschrift für Joachim Jeremias* (Beiheft 26 zum *ZNW*, ed. W. Eltester; Berlin: Töpelmann, 1960; 2nd ed. 1964) 209-20.

kingdom of the father is like a person who wanted to kill a powerful person. He drew the sword in his house (and) stabbed it into the wall to test whether his hand would be strong (enough). Then he killed the powerful one." Such sayings are not Gnostic inventions, but simply part of the oral tradition of sayings ascribed to Jesus.

What is perhaps even more impressive is that *The Gospel of Thomas* contains some New Testament parables found in their pre-canonical form, that is to say, without Mark's secondary allegorical embellishments.[55] Saying 9: The Parable of the Sower, lacks the allegorical interpretation appended in Mark 4:13-20. Saying 65: The Parable of the Vineyard lacks the allegory of history with which the parable in Mark 12:1-11 is so permeated that even a rather conventional exegete, Werner Georg Kümmel, despaired of being able to disengage a non-allegorical core that could go back to Jesus.[56] But now *The Gospel of Thomas* presents us with just such a non-allegorical parable that may well go back to Jesus! Obviously *The Gospel of Thomas* was still in the flowing stream of oral tradition, and was not limited to canonical Gospels, themselves often secondary, and to Gnostic mythology as its sources.

The completely untenable position into which one can in all innocence flounder by ignoring *The Gospel of Thomas* is illustrated by an anecdote from the 1984 meeting of the Society for New Testament Studies in Basel, Switzerland. There Nikolaus Walter of the University of Jena presented a detailed analysis of all instances of Paul using sayings of Jesus, irrespective of whether one is to consider them authentic or not. Having been asked to be the respondent, I pointed out that all the sayings of Jesus that Walter listed were derived from the canonical Gospels, none of which had been written when Paul wrote. Obviously Paul was wholly dependent on oral tradition or non-canonical written sources. Hence sayings ascribed to Jesus outside the canon should be included.

Walter asked for an instance. What I came up with on the spur of the moment was 1 Cor 2:9: "But, as it is written, 'What no eye has seen, nor ear heard, nor the heart of man conceived, what God has prepared for those who love him.'" The nearest one had come to identifying the source is Origen's allusion to an *Apocalypse of Elijah*

---

[55] C.-H. Hunzinger, "Aussersynoptisches Traditionsgut im Thomas-Evangelium," *TLZ* 85 (1960) 843-46.

[56] "Das Gleichnis von den bösen Weingärtnern (Mark. 12.1-5)," *Aux Sources de la tradition chrétienne: Mélanges offerts à M. Maurice Goguel à l'occasion de son soixante dixième anniversaire* (Neuchâtel: Delachaux et Niestlé, 1950) 120-31.

(cited in the margin of the Nestle-Aland *Novum Testamentum Graece*).[57] But now it has cropped up as a saying of Jesus in *The Gospel of Thomas*, Saying 17: "I will give you what no eye has seen, and what no ear has heard, and what no hand has touched, and what has not occurred to the human mind." Should 1 Cor 2:9 not be included in a survey of Pauline verses parallel to sayings ascribed to Jesus?

Walter replied that Paul does not quote the words of 1 Cor 2:9 as a saying of Jesus. I reminded him that a whole section of his paper had been devoted to Pauline parallels not ascribed by Paul to Jesus, such as 1 Cor 13:2, about faith that moves mountains, but that are ascribed to Jesus in the canonical Gospels, in this case Matt 17:20; 21:21 // Mark 11:23. Should he not also include non-canonical instances?

Walter finally conceded the point. But when he published his revised paper, it was in this regard unaltered.[58] What could he do? After all, I had handed him a can of worms! Was he, in revising his paper for publication, to go through the whole *Gospel of Thomas*, not to speak of other non-canonical sources, looking for sayings ascribed to Jesus with Pauline parallels? It would be a rather hopeless undertaking for one whose scholarship up to that point had been limited to the canonical texts! Better just avoid the whole issue—and thus consign oneself to being part of the past of our discipline, rather than being part of its future!

A decade later, at the 1995 meeting of the Society for New Testament Studies in Prague, The Czech Republic, I succeeded in convincing Barbara Aland, who was currently preparing a revised fifteenth edition of Kurt Aland's *Synopsis Quattuor Evangeliorum*, not just to include a very good Greek retroversion of parallel sayings from the Coptic *Gospel of Thomas* that the *Berliner Arbeitskreis*, now under the responsibility of Hans-Gebhard Bethge, was preparing for her, but also at the back to include (instead of the Latin translation, and alongside new German and English translations, the later used in the quotations above) the Coptic text of *The Gospel of Thomas* itself. I

---

[57] See *The Books of Elijah, Parts 1-2*, collected and translated by M. E. Stone and J. Strugnell (SBLTT 18, Pseudepigrapha Series 8, ed. R. A. Kraft and H. W. Attridge; Missoula: Scholars Press, 1979) 41-73 for the many attestations for this saying. In Nag Hammadi it recurs in I,1: A,23-27 (pp. 58-59) and III,5: 140.1-4 (pp. 56-57), in the latter case also ascribed to Jesus, as it is also in other texts (pp. 50-53).

[58] N. Walter, "Paulus und die urchristliche Jesustradition," *NTS* 31 (1975) 498-522.

had cited to her as a North American instance John S. Kloppenborg's
*Q Parallels*[59]. She has subsequently written on a very positive note:[60]

> The stimulating discussion with you has brought me now to think over basi-
> cally once again the whole question of the revision of the *Synopse* and in this
> connection to study Kloppenborg. I am thoroughly impressed by the way he
> proceeds. To be sure, I would not like to offer a [Greek] translation for all
> parallel passages, but it is advisable no doubt in Coptic. ... The Aland *Syn-
> opsis* must be worked over in regard both to Nag Hammadi and to the Old
> Testament apocrypha.

The result is that not only Americans have to stare the Coptic text of
*The Gospel of Thomas* in the face when we use Kloppenborg's *Q
Parallels*, but that worldwide New Testament scholarship has to face
up to the Coptic text in using the standard four-Gospel *Synopsis* of
Aland.

North American New Testament scholarship has come a long, long
way, when the German establishment turns to an American publication as a role model! This coming of age of American biblical scholarship over the last half-century, in part due to the Nag Hammadi
codices, is itself well worth celebrating![61]

---

[59] J. S. Kloppenborg, *Q Parallels: Synopsis, Critical Notes and Concordance*
(Sonoma: Polebridge Press, 1988).

[60] In a letter of October 4, 1995.

[61] After the SBL presentation R. McLachlan Wilson listed to me distinguished American New Testament scholars of preceding generations, to relativize talk of the discipline
only now coming of age in America. But the scope of the presentation was that of the
sociology of knowledge, the structures of the discipline, not individuals, where one can
only agree heartily with Wilson. Among our predecessors my own role model is at least
for me preeminent, Ernest Cadman Colwell. Indeed a major part of his distinction
consisted in his involving himself actively in such a restructuring of the discipline, in his
specialization, New Testament textual criticism: He organized the International Greek
New Testament Project and implemented it by means of the ongoing Textual Critical
Seminar of SBL. His coming to grips with the restructuring called for in terms of the
sociology of knowledge would have been even more prominent, if it had not taken place
in the generation dominated by biblical theology on the right and demythologizing,
existentialistic hermeneutics on the left.

# RELIGIOUS TRADITION, TEXTUAL TRANSMISSION, AND THE NAG HAMMADI CODICES

*Stephen Emmel*
University of Münster

Our knowledge of religious traditions in the ancient world is largely dependent on textual transmission—not just on texts, but on the transmission of texts, an activity that was itself a symptom of vital religious traditions. In the case of the Nag Hammadi Codices (as well as many other ancient manuscripts, of course), the complexity of their textual history has a significant impact on our ability to interpret the texts, and so to understand the religious traditions that transmitted them ultimately to us. The Nag Hammadi Codices, as archeological artifacts, provide us with historical data that reach from the time of the codices' burial back through the circumstances of their manufacture, farther back through the circumstances under which the individual works in the codices were translated into and transmitted in Coptic, through the prior transmission history of these works in Greek, and finally back to the circumstances of their original composition (whatever that might mean in any given case) and the circumstances by which they came to be in Egypt. All along that long way, which in at least one case leads as far back as fourth century BCE Athens, we assume that the textual transmission coincided with social and religious realities, which it has been the goal of much Nag Hammadi research to try to reconstruct and describe. As we all know, what I am calling the "historical data" with which the codices provide us for this work of reconstruction and description are not the kinds of data that most historians would prefer to have, and hence extreme methodological clarity is needed both regarding investigation of the different stages in the history of the Nag Hammadi texts as such, and especially regarding the religious traditions that stand behind them.[1]

---

[1] A similar emphasis on methodological clarity was already enunciated by Bentley Layton in a speech to the Society of Biblical Literature fifteen years ago ("The Recovery of Gnosticism: The Philologist's Task in the Investigation of Nag Hammadi," *Second Century* 1 [1981] 92-99). See also A. Böhlig, "Die Bedeutung der Funde von Medinet Madi und Nag Hammadi für die Erforschung des Gnostizismus," *Gnosis und Manichäismus: Forschungen und Studien zu Texten von Valentin und Mani sowie zu den Bibliotheken von Nag Hammadi und Medinet Madi*, ed. A. Böhlig and C.

In his paper for this 50th Anniversary Commemoration,[2] Frederik Wisse inferred four phases in the transmission history of the *Apocryphon of John*. His outline can be generalized for the Nag Hammadi Codices in their entirety, his four phases corresponding to the salient parts of the complex textual history that I have just sketched briefly. Adopting Wisse's headings, which also trace the lines of transmission in reverse chronological order as I have done, we have to consider the following four phases: (1) "the Coptic monastic phase" of transmission as the most recent, (2) "the translation phase," (3) "the composition phase," and (4) "the pre-composition phase" as the earliest. Wisse emphasized that the information about the most recent phase is "by far the clearest," while "the earlier phases are increasing[ly] obscure and speculating about them runs the risk of leading to misunderstanding rather than enhanced understanding of the content of the document[s]," if I may alter his singular reference to the *Apocryphon of John* to a plural reference to all the Nag Hammadi texts.

Let me briefly characterize each of these four phases in the transmission history of the Nag Hammadi Codices. The most recent phase is, strictly speaking, whatever circumstance caused these particular books to be buried together in a sealed jar and their condition at that time. But more generally, this phase includes the entire history of each codex from the time of its manufacture to the time of its burial.[3] The only firm date we have here is still from Codex

---

Markschies (BZNTW 72; Berlin and New York: de Gruyter, 1994) 135-171, esp. 144-145.

[2] "After the Synopsis: Prospects and Problems in Establishing a Critical Text of the *Apocryphon of John* and in Defining Its Historical Location," in the present volume; cf. M. Waldstein and F. Wisse, *The Apocryphon of John: Synopsis of Nag Hammadi Codices II,1; III,1; and IV,1 with BG 8502,2* (NHMS 33; Leiden: E.J. Brill, 1995) 1-8.

[3] The exact content of the sealed jar (particularly whether or not it included Codex III, on which question see, e.g., A. Khosroyev, *Die Bibliothek von Nag Hammadi: Einige Probleme des Christentums in Ägypten während der ersten Jahrhunderte* [Arbeiten zum spätantiken und koptischen Ägypten 7; Altenberge: Oros Verlag: 1995] 22 and 3 n. 4; W.-P. Funk, "The Linguistic Aspect of Classifying the Nag Hammadi Codices," *Les textes de Nag Hammadi et le problème de leur classification: Actes du colloque tenu à Québec du 15 au 19 septembre 1993*, ed. L. Painchaud and A. Pasquier [BCNH, section "études" 3; Québec: Les Presses de l'Université Laval, Louvain: Éditions Peeters, 1995] 137 n. 23) is finally relevant only if we want to use the grouping of a given set of codices in the jar as a significant datum in the interpretation of a given work in one of those codices, e.g., interpreting that work as a part of a "library." Other such data (like the set of works within a given codex) are probably more significant, and certainly provide a more secure basis for historical reflection (M. A. Williams, "Interpreting the Nag Hammadi Library as 'Collection(s)' in the History of 'Gnosticism(s),'" *Les textes de Nag*

VII, whose cover was manufactured sometime after the middle of the
fourth century; but it must be recalled that Codex VII is linked with
Codices I and XI by shared scribal hands and other features, which
makes it likely that all three are to be dated to about the same time,
whenever that is. The typically fourth- or fifth-century pottery bowl
that was used to seal the jar in which the books were protected
indicates that probably the concealment occurred before the Arab
Conquest in the seventh century. While this very approximate
*terminus ad quem* is the same also for the remaining ten codices, the
manufacture of these ten could be dated earlier than the fourth century
(but probably not). Furthermore, since there is evidence to suggest
that the Nag Hammadi Codices comprise several sub-groups of
manuscripts, these groups might not have been brought together to
form the collection that we know until they were assembled for burial.
And hence the collection as a whole cannot necessarily be considered
a "library" in any historically meaningful sense.

The opinion that the collection is not necessarily a "library" runs
counter to the view that underlies Wisse's description of this most
recent phase of transmission as "the Coptic *monastic* phase," that is,
the view that "the Nag Hammadi Codices were produced and used ...
by monks in a Pachomian monastery." This view was first
propounded twenty years ago on the basis of a preliminary survey of
the scrap papyri (cartonnage) from the codices' covers, and since then
it has been argued on additional bases, by Wisse and others, and
widely accepted. But not by everyone. I myself share the opinion that
the evidence for this view does not add up to proof, or necessarily
even likelihood. For me it is a topic on which open-mindedness is still
called for. An opportunity to reexamine this topic has appeared
recently in the form of a book by Alexandr Khosroyev (of the Institute
of Oriental Studies in St. Petersburg, Russia), *Die Bibliothek von
Nag Hammadi*. The book includes a long chapter, "Zur Frage nach
dem vermutlichen Besitzer der Bibliothek," in which Khosroyev
systematically challenges each of the arguments in favor of a
Pachomian provenience.[4] What remains after such a critique—if it is
successful—is the entire diverse world of late antique Egypt, where a
solution is yet to be found—if it will ever be possible to find a

---

*Hammadi et le problème de leur classification: Actes du colloque tenu à Québec du 15
au 19 septembre 1993*, see n. 22 below).

[4] Cf. A. Khosroyev, "Bemerkungen über die vermutlichen Besitzer der Nag-Hammadi-
Texte," *Divitiae Aegypti: Koptologische und verwandte Studien zu Ehren von Martin
Krause*, ed. Cäcilia Fluck et al. (Wiesbaden: Dr. Ludwig Reichert Verlag, 1995) 200-205.

solution—to the question of who commissioned, manufactured, and owned the Nag Hammadi Codices. Clemens Scholten (in his 1988 article "Die Nag-Hammadi-Texte als Buchbesitz der Pachomianer") already showed the importance of approaching this problem on the basis of a broad assemblage of data, and this database should continue to be broadened by taking advantage of the increasing amount of work that is being done on late antique Egypt generally, especially on topics like literacy and its companion illiteracy or orality, education and bilingualism, magic and the survival of paganism. Identifying the sphere in which such books as the Nag Hammadi Codices were produced remains a primary desideratum.

The phase of transmission prior to the manufacture of the Nag Hammadi Codices was that of translating the individual texts from Greek into Coptic, followed by a history of recopying the Coptic texts. In no case do we have an autograph translation among the Nag Hammadi Codices. Based on what we know generally of the development of written Coptic, it is most likely that the translations were made sometime after the mid-to-late third century. Only for the works in Codices I, VII, and XI can we be relatively confident that they were already translated by the end of the fourth century. For each codex that lies hypothetically between the autograph translations of the texts in the Nag Hammadi Codices and the Nag Hammadi Codices themselves, we could ask the same questions that we asked before (who commissioned, manufactured, and owned them?), and to these questions we can add: what did these hypothetical codices contain? I assume that, at least to a very great extent, they contained differing groupings of works, including works of which we now have no knowledge at all. That is to say, for the most part we are dealing with the transmission of individual works—or parts of works—and not with the recopying of entire codices.[5]

More important (because perhaps more concretely ponderable) are the questions: Who translated these works? Why? How well did they do? And finally, what happened to the texts of these works in the course of their recopying in Coptic? A very interesting aspect of this phase of transmission has recently been investigated in a preliminary way by Wolf-Peter Funk, using numerical techniques for seriation, cluster analysis, and multi-dimensional scaling, according to specific

---

[5] Cf. W.-P. Funk, "The Linguistic Aspect of Classifying the Nag Hammadi Codices," 145-146; M. A. Williams, "Interpreting the Nag Hammadi Library as 'Collection(s),'" esp., e.g., 11-15.

linguistic variables in the "Sahidic" Nag Hammadi texts.[6] Scholars recognized early on that although most of the works in the Nag Hammadi Codices are written in the Sahidic dialect, the Sahidic of these texts is dialectally impure to varying degrees (and in varying ways). The commonly accepted explanation for this phenomenon has been that each of the works in question was translated into Sahidic by someone who was a native speaker of some other dialect.[7] The poorer a Sahidic translation they made, the easier it is now for us to discern features of their native dialect. The logic here is that Sahidic was becoming the prestige literary dialect in which people up and down the Nile might well aspire to write, if they wrote in Coptic. According to this model, the autograph translation was, in most cases, a linguistically peculiar, orthographically inconsistent text to begin with, and it then suffered the usual textual corruption at the hands of a series of an unknown number of copyists.

But Funk's tentative findings suggest a more complicated model, according to which the texts were originally translated in various parts of Egypt into different regional dialects, each translation thus being dialectally pure (so to speak) to begin with. Many of these non-Sahidic texts were then later "'translated' (or sometimes just superficially transcribed) into a kind of approximative Sahidic,"[8] a process of retranslation within the Coptic phase of transmission itself. But "in a number of these texts [in which some northern dialect is basically discernible, such as Bohairic] other dialects are clearly involved as well, and a certain superficial 'Southern' flavour, the trade-mark of the final production of the extant manuscripts, is omnipresent."[9] Thus a picture emerges, from a linguistic classification of the texts, of a history of transmission involving not just the usual sort of scribal corruption, but also purposeful alteration in linguistically, that is, dialectally, diverse circumstances, and we have no way of being sure about the length of time involved, nor about the

---

[6] W.-P. Funk, "Toward a Linguistic Classification of the 'Sahidic' Nag Hammadi Texts," *Acts of the Fifth International Congress of Coptic Studies: Washington, 12-15 August 1992*, vol. 2, *Papers from the Sections*, ed. D. W. Johnson (Rome: Centro Italiano Microfiches, 1993) 163-177; W.-P. Funk, "The Linguistic Aspect of Classifying the Nag Hammadi Codices," 107-147; cf. A. Khosroyev, *Die Bibliothek von Nag Hammadi*, 23-60.

[7] See, e.g., the references in B. Layton, "The Recovery of Gnosticism: The Philologist's Task," 94 n. 33; Khosroyev, *Die Bibliothek von Nag Hammadi*, 25-26.

[8] W.-P. Funk, "Toward a Linguistic Classification of the 'Sahidic' Nag Hammadi Texts," 172.

[9] Funk, "Toward a Linguistic Classification of the 'Sahidic' Nag Hammadi Texts," 179.

degree of such alteration. It might have been tantamount to redaction, such as scholars have already hypothesized in certain cases.[10] According to this model, then, the gulf between the Nag Hammadi Codices and the original Coptic translations on which they are ultimately based may be unbridgeable, except in some qualified sense.[11]

The two earliest phases of transmission distinguished by Wisse, the pre-composition phase and the composition phase, include transmission and redaction of the Greek texts down to the particular exemplars from which the Coptic translations were made.[12] I believe it is safe to say that the main interest of Nag Hammadi research has been focused on an effort to recover these two phases in the histories of the texts. From this point of view, it would be best if we could reconstruct the text of each work as it was originally composed, for we would then be in the best position to recover the intention of the author and reconstruct his or her environment. But the difficulties and risks of such work at any level of detail are—or should be—easy to recognize. It is even possible, as Karen King argued during this 50th Anniversary Commemoration with respect to the *Apocryphon of John*, that the very notion of a "work as it was originally composed" is misguided.[13]

I think I need only mention two important areas of Nag Hammadi research to remind us of what is at stake behind the assumption that we can press our texts back to the composition and pre-composition phases: *The Gospel of Thomas* and Sethianism. Both have been discussed extensively in one way or another at this conference already, so I will be brief. In order for *Gos. Thom.* to be used—as I am inclined to agree it should be used—as a source for the tradition of Jesus' sayings, we have to assume that the Coptic text gives us access to information that goes back to the first century. Frankly, I was dismayed to learn last evening from Jim Robinson's address that the next edition of the Aland gospel synopsis might include a Greek

---

[10] See the extensive list of opinions surveyed by L. Painchaud, "La classification des textes de Nag Hammadi et le phénomène des réécritures," *Les textes de Nag Hammadi et le problème de leur classification*, 53-72. Of course such redaction could have been carried out prior to the Coptic phases of transmission.

[11] The two models sketched here are not mutually exclusive. The initial translator might well have produced an "approximative Sahidic" text, which then might or might not have undergone subsequent "dialectal editing ... or inter-dialect translation." Cf. W.-P. Funk, "The Linguistic Aspect of Classifying the Nag Hammadi Codices," 143.

[12] Of course the continued transmission of the texts in Greek, or in versions other than Coptic, would also be of interest here, but for the most part we have no knowledge of it.

[13] "Approaching the Variants of the Apocryphon Of John," in the present volume.

retroversion of *Gos. Thom.* (even if it is the work of my very good friend Hans Bethge), but then I was delighted to hear that the synopsis might also include the Coptic text.[14] I myself would prefer that it include *only* the Coptic text, except where we have direct evidence for a Greek text, such as the Oxyrhynchus fragments. The Coptic text could be accompanied by a translation into a modern language, or into Latin—anything but a Greek retroversion, which would give the *impression* that we can reconstruct in detail some stage of the text's history prior to the translation phase, which I think we cannot do.[15]

The case of Sethianism is more complex, especially if it is true that the corpus of Sethian writings identified in the 1970s by Hans-Martin Schenke represents several centuries of literary history, as John Turner has reasonably argued.[16] Here our assumed ability to interpret these texts in third, second, and perhaps even first century contexts is the *sine qua non* for reconstructing a religious sect, with distinctive features and a long history. If Bentley Layton's recently published "Prolegomena to the Study of Ancient Gnosticism" are accepted,[17] this sect is in fact the only group in antiquity that used the term "gnostic" as a self-designation.

By now it must be obvious that what I am circling around is a problem of methodology: how do we account for the interpretive moves that we have to make in order to get from the evidence we have—a final Coptic phase of transmission—back to the composition phase, let alone to the pre-composition phase? For the most part, I think we take it for granted that the Nag Hammadi texts do bear some

---

[14] "Nag Hammadi: The First Fifty Years," in the present volume.

[15] In fact the 15th ed. of the synopsis (Stuttgart 1996) includes the complete Coptic text as an appendix, with new German and English translations as well as the Greek retroversion.

[16] H.-M. Schenke, "Das sethianische System nach Nag-Hammadi-Handschriften," *Studia Coptica*, ed. P. Nagel (Berliner byzantinische Arbeiten 45; Berlin: Akademie-Verlag, 1974) 165-172, with 1 plate; idem, "The Phenomenon and Significance of Gnostic Sethianism," *The Rediscovery of Gnosticism: Proceedings of the International Conference on Gnosticism at Yale, New Haven, Connecticut, March 28-31, 1978*, vol. 2, *Sethian Gnosticism*, ed. B. Layton, (SHR, Supplements to *Numen* 41.2; Leiden: E.J. Brill, 1981) 588-616; cf. idem, "The Problem of Gnosis," *Second Century* 3 (1983) 73-87; idem, "Gnosis: Zum Forschungsstand unter besonderer Berücksichtigung der religions-geschichtlichen Problematik," *Verkündigung und Forschung* 32 (1987) 7-11; and J. D. Turner, "Sethian Gnosticism: A Literary History," *Nag Hammadi, Gnosticism, and Early Christianity*, ed. C. W. Hedrick and R. Hodgson, Jr. (Peabody: Hendrickson, 1986) 55-86 (with bibliography xv-xliv passim).

[17] B. Layton, "Prolegomena to the Study of Ancient Gnosticism," *The Social World of the First Christians: Essays in Honor of Wayne A. Meeks*, ed. L. M. White and O. L. Yarbrough (Minneapolis: Augsburg Fortress, 1995) 334-350.

more or less close relationship to a hypothetical original composition, and we move back and forth between the Coptic text we have and the original we would *like* to have, keeping careful lookout for signs of corruption, mistranslation, redaction, and so on, in an effort to minimize being led astray by such a long and complex history of transmission.

But we move through a minefield. The Coptic phases of transmission pose nearly insurmountable barriers to recovering the translators' *Vorlagen*. It is not yet clear to what extent we can even recover the original texts of the Coptic translations. Except in the few cases where we have multiple copies or versions of a work, such as the *Apocryphon of John*, true textual criticism is all but impossible.

What, then, can be done? I want to give a two-pronged answer to this question, addressed to the two different halves of the textual transmission history. Regarding the composition phases, I was fascinated to learn during the present 50th Anniversary Commemoration that Michael Waldstein and Frederik Wisse had planned to include in their recently published *Apoc. John* synopsis (1995) a "critical translation" of the work with a "textual commentary" on the translation. If I understand their proposal correctly, this translation—which may yet appear, and of which Wisse provides a brief sample as an appendix to his paper in the present volume—would stand in place of a critical edition of the Coptic text with text-critical apparatus. Methodologically, this "critical translation" would be a relatively clean way to move from the Coptic texts we have, back to a representation of some form of the work in the composition phase, without having always to reconstruct a hypothetical Coptic and/or Greek text.

This procedure is reminiscent of what Bentley Layton proposed in his SBL speech fifteen years ago, and had already done, more or less, in his edition of *The Treatise on the Resurrection*,[18] namely, to "give a free ... translation of the [edited] Coptic archetype as though translated from the Greek, ... the free translation ... represent[ing] the Greek exemplar from which the Coptic archetype was [translated]," and given along with "a detailed commentary ... stressing Greek equivalents of main words or syntagms, especially technical terms; citing contemporary Greek texts to show typical usage; and

---

[18] B. Layton, "The Recovery of Gnosticism: The Philologist's Task"; idem, *The Gnostic Treatise on Resurrection from Nag Hammadi* (HDR 12; Missoula: Scholars Press, 1979); cf. T. Orlandi, *Evangelium Veritatis* (1992).

containing other kinds of practical criticism."[19] The purpose would be the same: to approximate an original composition without maintaining the fiction that we can actually reconstruct it in Greek or Coptic. Such commented translations would be based heavily on hypothesis and therefore would require extreme methodological clarity in order to be convincing and useful. That should be a *good* thing. So much for the first prong of my answer.

Regarding the Coptic phases of transmission, there is one obvious task that has not yet been carried out thoroughly and consistently, that is, to read the Nag Hammadi Codices as a part of *Coptic literature*. What I have in mind has partly already been expressed at this meeting, by Karen King in connection with *Apoc. John* and by others in connection with *Gos. Thom.*[20] The task is to read the texts exactly as we have them in the Nag Hammadi Codices in an effort to reconstruct the reading experience of whoever owned each of the Codices. This reading would have to be undertaken in full cognizance of contemporary Coptic literature, and the culture of Upper Egypt during, say, the third to the seventh centuries. It would be a primarily Coptological enterprise, with nothing directly to do with Christian origins, nor necessarily even with "Gnosticism," although the results of this Coptic reading would probably contribute insights that would be valuable for the more hypothetical investigation of the composition phase. A theory of Coptic reading and Coptic readers would have to be developed, especially to help us understand how an ancient reader of these books would have reacted to what we tend to judge to be obvious oddities ranging from "a certain negligence ... with regard to language detail as far as 'dialect norm' (not grammar as such) is concerned,"[21] to sometimes seemingly impenetrable obscurity of expression.

The attraction of what I am calling a "Coptic reading" of the Nag Hammadi Codices is that the codices are our primary data, and presumably they were read by someone—or at least they were laboriously created for that purpose. Hence such a "Coptic reading" takes us (in theory) the shortest distance into the minefield of the texts' complex history of transmission, and therefore it should provide us with more certain—albeit quite different—results than other

---

[19] B. Layton, "The Recovery of Gnosticism: The Philologist's Task ," 96-97.

[20] See Philip H. Sellew's paper published below; other relevant papers, by Ron Cameron and Stephen J. Patterson, are not published here.

[21] W.-P. Funk, "The Linguistic Aspect of Classifying the Nag Hammadi Codices," 146.

readings. It is, in a sense, the first task of investigation that such artifacts call for, now that the manuscripts have been fully conserved and the texts published. [22] Hand-in-hand with this task should go the kind of linguistic analysis that Wolf-Peter Funk has begun, because this investigation too is in a sense "primary" and liable to yield relatively reliable results that will have historical implications, as I noted earlier. Unfortunately, Funk was very likely correct when he wrote, "Full implementation of this [linguistic investigation] would probably necessitate substantial contributions from more people than we will ever have in Coptic linguistic research."[23] Here, there could well be at least another fifty years of work yet to be done.

---

[22] A move in this direction is Michael Williams's recent attempt to discover a rationale for the arrangement of the tractates in each of the Nag Hammadi Codices (and in the Codex Berolinensis Gnosticus), based on the fact that "rather than coming to us as a jumbled hodgepodge of traditions, the tractates come to us ordered." Arguing that the arrangements of the works in the respective codices "offer us the most direct clues about how the writings in these volumes were understood by their fourth century owners," Williams observes in conclusion that these writings' "hermeneutical contexts within their fourth century codices could be at least as interesting as contexts that we reconstruct for them in earlier centuries, and in most cases, much less hypothetical" (Williams, "Interpreting the Nag Hammadi Library as "Collection(s)," quotations taken from 39 and 41). See also T. Orlandi's approach to *The Gospel of Truth* (*Evangelium Veritatis* [1992]).

[23] W.-P. Funk, "Toward a Linguistic Classification of the 'Sahidic' Nag Hammadi Texts," 166.

# THE CGL EDITION OF NAG HAMMADI CODEX VII

*Birger A. Pearson*
University of California-Santa Barbara (Emeritus)

Nag Hammadi Codex VII[1] is the very last of the sixteen volumes comprising the "Coptic Gnostic Library" subseries of the "Nag Hammadi and Manichaean Studies" series[2] to be published by Brill in Leiden.[3] The volume contains a codicological introduction, and introductions, Coptic transcriptions, English translations, and textual notes to the five tractates contained in Codex VII. As Editor of the volume, I shall present in what follows a brief account of the history of its publication and some remarks on its various parts.

## 1. HISTORY OF PUBLICATION

Work on Nag Hammadi Codex VII began with the initiation in 1966 of the Coptic Gnostic Library project of the Institute for Antiquity and Christianity of The Claremont Graduate School, under the direction of Prof. James M. Robinson. Prof. Robinson had obtained photographs of the Nag Hammadi manuscripts as a result of a visit to the office of UNESCO in Paris—UNESCO was sponsoring a project to publish a facsimile edition of the manuscripts[4]—and these photo-

---

[1] B. A. Pearson, ed., *Nag Hammadi Codex VII* (NHMS 30; Leiden: E. J. Brill, 1996 [published 1995]). See J. M. Robinson, "Nag Hammadi: The First Fifty Years," in the present volume and in the series Occasional Papers of the Institute for Antiquity and Christianity 34; Claremont, CA, 1995.

[2] The series was formerly called "Nag Hammadi Studies," the first volume of which was published in 1971: D. Scholer, *Nag Hammadi Bibliography 1948-1969* (NHS 1; Leiden: E. J. Brill, 1971). The first volume of the renamed series is F. Williams, trans., *The Panarion of Epiphanius of Salamis, Books II and III (Sects 47-80, De Fide)* (NHMS 36; Leiden: E. J. Brill, 1994). The first volume of Williams' translation, *The Panarion of Epiphanius of Salamis, Book I (Sects 1-46)* is NHS 35 (Leiden: E. J. Brill, 1987).

[3] The number attached to this volume in the NHMS series (no. 30) reflects an earlier expectation that the volume would appear after no. 29 in the NHS series: M. A. Williams, *The Immovable Race: A Gnostic Designation and the Theme of Stability in Late Antiquity* (Leiden: E. J. Brill, 1985).

[4] For a complete account of this project and its results see *The Facsimile Edition of the Nag Hammadi Codices: Introduction* (prepared by James M. Robinson), published under the auspices of the Department of Antiquities of the Arab Republic of Egypt, in conjunction with The United Nations Educational, Scientific and Cultural Organization (Leiden: E. J. Brill, 1984). See now also J. M. Robinson, "Nag Hammadi: The First Fifty

graphs became the focus of study for doctoral students at Claremont and such other scholars with a knowledge of Coptic that could be brought into the project from elsewhere.[5] Planning began in Claremont for the publication of a critical edition of the unpublished Nag Hammadi manuscripts, and an agreement was concluded in 1969 with E. J. Brill in Leiden for a series of volumes to be called "The Coptic Gnostic Library." An announcement of the new monograph series, "Nag Hammadi Studies" (into which the CGL would be incorporated) was made in 1970.[6] Frederik Wisse (then a Ph.D. candidate at The Claremont Graduate School) was assigned as Editor for Codex VII.

A major milestone in the publication of the Nag Hammadi manuscripts was achieved toward the end of 1977 when, as a result of two publishing events, the entire "library" of Coptic Gnostic texts was finally in the public domain. These two events were the completion of the Facsimile Edition of the manuscripts with the publication of *The Facsimile Edition: Nag Hammadi Codices IX and X,*[7] and the co-publication by Brill and Harper & Row of all of the Nag Hammadi tractates in English translation: *The Nag Hammadi in Library in English.*[8] These two events were celebrated at the Annual Meeting of the Society of Biblical Literature in San Francisco in November, 1977.

*The Nag Hammadi Library in English,* first published in 1977,[9] consisted of English translations of all of the tractates in the Nag

---

Years," in the present volume and in the series Occasional Papers of the Institute for Antiquity and Christianity 34; Claremont, CA, 1995.

[5] My own involvement in the project began early in 1968, when I was an assistant professor in the Religion Department at Duke University, Durham, North Carolina. Proximity to the Claremont project was a major incentive in my accepting a position on the faculty of the then rather new Religious Studies Department at UC Santa Barbara, beginning in 1969. My first assignment in the project was Codex X, finally published in 1981: B. A. Pearson, *Codices IX and X* (NHS 15; Leiden: E. J. Brill, 1981). The work on Codex IX was done in collaboration with Søren Giversen of Aarhus University in Denmark.

[6] See J. M. Robinson, "The Coptic Gnostic Library," *NT* 12 (1970) 81-85. As first envisaged, "The Coptic Gnostic Library" series would consist of four volumes.

[7] Published under the auspices of the Department of Antiquities of the Arab Republic of Egypt, in conjunction with the United Nations Educational, Scientific and Cultural Organization (Leiden: E. J. Brill, 1977). The first volume, containing Nag Hammadi Codex VI, appeared in 1972, followed in the same year by the volume containing Nag Hammadi Codex VII.

[8] J. M. Robinson, General Editor, and M. W. Meyer, Managing Editor (Leiden: E. J. Brill; New York: Harper & Row, 1977).

[9] The most recent edition is the 3rd revised ed.: J. M. Robinson, General Editor, and R. Smith, Managing Editor (Leiden: E. J. Brill; San Francisco: Harper & Row, 1988).

Hammadi corpus, together with two tractates of the Berlin Codex.[10]
These translations reflected the on-going work of the Coptic Gnostic
Project of the Institute for Antiquity and Christianity, either already
published in the critical edition or in preparation for the critical
edition. Codex VII is represented as follows in the 1977 edition: *The
Paraphrase of Shem* (VII,*1*), introduced and translated by Frederik
Wisse (pp. 308-28); *The Second Treatise of the Great Seth* (VII,*2*),
introduced by Joseph A. Gibbons, translated by Roger A. Bullard,
edited by Frederik Wisse (pp. 329-38); *Apocalypse of Peter* (VII,*3*),
introduced by James Brashler, translated by Roger A. Bullard, edited
by Frederik Wisse (pp. 339-45); *The Teachings of Silvanus* (VII,*4*),
introduced and translated by Malcolm L. Peel and Jan Zandee, edited
by Frederik Wisse (pp. 346-61); and *The Three Steles of Seth* (VII,*5*),
introduced and translated by James M. Robinson, edited by Frederik
Wisse (pp. 362-67).

The revised edition of *The Nag Hammadi Library in English*[11]
contains for most of the tractates new and larger introductions and
revised translations. Codex VII is represented in that edition as
follows: *The Paraphrase of Shem*, introduced by Michel Roberge,
translated by Frederik Wisse (pp. 339-61); *The Second Treatise of
the Great Seth*, introduced by Joseph A. Gibbons, translated by
Roger A. Bullard and Joseph Gibbons (pp. 362-71);[12] *Apocalypse of
Peter*, introduced by James Brashler, translated by James Brashler
and Roger A. Bullard (pp. 372-78); *The Teachings of Silvanus*,
introduced and translated by Malcolm L. Peel and Jan Zandee (pp.
379-95); and *The Three Steles of Seth*, introduced by James E.
Goehring, translated by James M. Robinson (pp. 396-401).

The pressures of other commitments caused Frederik Wisse to
resign the editorship of the critical edition of Codex VII toward the
end of 1991. Professor Robinson asked me to assume this task, and I
agreed, with one condition: that the volume be composed at the
Institute in Claremont, with the aid of a computer, by someone other
than myself who would be capable of doing that work. The publishers
had asked for a substantial subvention for producing the volume, but

---

[10] Papyrus Berolinensis 8502 was brought to Germany from Egypt in 1896, but was
not published until 1955: W. C. Till, *Die gnostischen Schriften des koptischen Papyrus
Berolinensis 8502* (TU 60; Berlin: Akademie-Verlag, 1955; 2nd ed. by H.-M. Schenke,
1972). It contains the shorter version of *Ap. John* (BG,*2*; cf. NHC III,*1*), another version
of *Soph. Jes. Chr.* (BG,*3*; cf. NHC III,*4*), *Gos. Mary* (BG,*1*), and *Act. Pet.* (BG,*4*).

[11] Op. cit. n. 9.

[12] The introduction and the translation for this tractate are identical to those of the first
edition.

agreed to produce it without subvention from a "camera-ready" manuscript. Neal Kelsey, a doctoral candidate at The Claremont Graduate School, was engaged for this task and put all of the material on computer disk. The print-outs were sent to the respective contributors for revisions and up-dating. During the final stages of revision, the press of other duties prevented Kelsey from finishing his part of the project, and he resigned during the summer of 1995. Fortunately another Ph.D. candidate at Claremont was available to finish the job, Saw Lah Shein, who took charge of the final revisions and composed the entire volume in camera-ready copy for the press.

Meanwhile, plans were being made for the observance of the 50th anniversary of the discovery of the Nag Hammadi Codices (December, 1945) at the Annual Meeting of the Society of Biblical Literature in Philadelphia in November, 1995. The publishers of the critical edition were eager to have the two remaining volumes in the series[13] published in time for the anniversary observance, which would feature special lectures at the meeting and a reception sponsored by Brill.[14] During the last part of September I submitted the final corrections to the volume, the last ones by telephone in early October from my home in Escalon, California, and the camera-ready manuscript was sent from Claremont to Leiden on October 10. A half hour before his plane was to leave from Amsterdam on his way to Philadelphia, Dr. David Orton, Publisher for Brill of books in biblical and religious studies, received from Leiden two copies of the book, retrieved from the bindery on the same day. *Nag Hammadi Codex VII* was thus part of the Brill book display at the Philadelphia meeting, which began on November 18, and was featured at the Brill reception on November 20 as marking the completion of the sixteen-volume "Coptic Gnostic Library."

---

[13] The other volume in the series still unpublished at the beginning of 1995 was published during the summer, well in time for the November meeting: *The Apocryphon of John: Synopsis of Nag Hammadi Codices II,1; III,1 and IV,1 with BG 8502,2*, ed. F. Wisse and M. Waldstein (NHMS 33; Leiden: E. J. Brill, 1995).

[14] The papers published in this volume come out of that meeting and the special seminar held at Haverford College on November 17. Professor Robinson gave a plenary address on November 19, "Nag Hammadi: The First Fifty Years" in the present volume and in the series Occasional Papers of the Institute for Antiquity and Christianity 34; Claremont, CA, 1995. Another observance of the 50th anniversary of the Nag Hammadi find was held in Denmark in September 1995: "The Copenhagen International Conference on the Nag Hammadi Texts in the History of Religions, September 19-24, 1995," at the Royal Danish Academy of Sciences and Letters. The Proceedings from that conference will be published by the Academy.

The individual components of *Nag Hammadi Codex VII* represent in some cases revisions of work submitted earlier; in other cases completely new versions have been prepared. Thus, the list of contributors to the final volume differs somewhat from what would have been the case had the critical edition come out around the same time as *The Nag Hammadi Library in English*. The codex introduction and the edition of tractate *1: The Paraphrase of Shem*, by Frederik Wisse, represent final revisions of work earlier completed. In the case of tractate *2: Second Treatise of the Great Seth*, material had already been submitted in the early '70's by Joseph A. Gibbons, who had completed a dissertation at Yale on that tractate.[15] He had not been heard from for years, but when I finally located him he told me that he had left academia in the early '70's and had no further interest in the project. I then reassigned the tractate to a recently arrived colleague at Claremont, Gregory J. Riley, and gave him the choice of reworking Gibbons' material or redoing the entire thing himself. He chose the latter option.

In the case of tractate *3: Apocalypse of Peter*, an introduction had already been prepared for the critical edition by Michel Desjardins by the time that I took over the editorship. Desjardins revised his introduction, and I edited it to reflect the realities of the new translation, prepared by James Brashler. Brashler had earlier completed a dissertation on *Apoc. Pet.* at Claremont, which included a translation,[16] and he revised this translation substantially for publication in the critical edition.

The material in the critical edition on tractate *4: The Teachings of Silvanus* represents a very substantial revision by Malcolm Peel of work earlier submitted as a collaborative effort by him and Jan Zandee.[17] Indeed, Peel submitted a very extensive commentary to *Teach. Silv.*, such as would be appropriate for a monograph on that tractate,[18] material that I had to cut down for our volume's critical notes.

---

[15] J. A. Gibbons, "A Commentary on The Second Logos of the Great Seth" (Ph.D. dissertation, Yale University, 1972).

[16] J. A. Brashler, "The Coptic 'Apocalypse of Peter': A Genre Analysis and Interpretation" (Ph.D. dissertation, The Claremont Graduate School, 1977).

[17] Jan Zandee's own edition was published posthumously in The Netherlands in 1991: *The Teachings of Sylvanus (Nag Hammadi Codex VII,4): Text, Translation, Commentary* (Egyptologische Uitgaven 6; Leiden: Nederlands Instituut voor Het Nabije Oosten, 1991). He died in January of the same year.

[18] Peel and Zandee had earlier planned to publish for the NHS series such a monograph on *Teach. Silv.* Zandee's own posthumous work is more a collection of parallels than a real commentary. See Hans-Martin Schenke's review in *JAC* 36 (1993) 231-34.

The material in our volume on tractate *5: The Three Steles of Seth* represents revisions by James E. Goehring of material earlier submitted by him. He prepared the introduction and critical notes, and revised the translation, which is now attributed to him and James M. Robinson jointly.

The critical edition contains, as usual, indices of Coptic words, Greek words, and proper names. These indices were prepared by Clayton Jefford.[19]

The format of our volume represents editorial decisions taken by members of the Coptic Gnostic Library Project in 1969. Among other things, this format involves the printing of the facing text and translation according to the lines produced by the scribe in the manuscript, rather than imposing a paragraph format on the material, and presenting a single set of notes to both the text and the translation of each tractate. Word division in the Coptic transcriptions adhere to the practice used by Walter Till in his grammar.[20] The transcriptions to the respective tractates have been checked against the manuscript in the Coptic Museum in Old Cairo.[21]

## 2. NAG HAMMADI CODEX VII: CODICOLOGY AND LANGUAGE

Codex VII is the best preserved of all of the Nag Hammadi manuscripts; it is also inscribed in the most attractive hand, a round uncial script written by the same scribe who wrote NHC XI, *3* and *4*. Cartonnage found in the leather cover of the codex, consisting of inscribed papyrus pieces, includes receipts for grain dated 341, 346, and 348 CE, and letters and receipts with personal names and place names. These names and dates suggest a late 4th-century date for the codex, and a Pachomian monastic setting.[22]

In his introduction to Codex VII (pp. 1-13), Frederik Wisse gives a detailed account of how it was made.[23] NHC VII is a single-quire

---

[19] I had planned to include in the volume indices to ancient texts cited and modern authors, but the time pressures in the final stages of the work precluded the addition of these indices.

[20] W. C. Till, *Koptische Grammatik (Saïdischer Dialekt)* (2nd ed., Leipzig: VEB Verlag Enzyklopädie, 1961).

[21] Collations were done by Wisse in the early '70's, and by me in 1993.

[22] See esp. F. Wisse, "Gnosticism and Early Monasticism in Egypt," *Gnosis: Festschrift für Hans Jonas,* ed. B. Aland (Göttingen: Vandenhoeck & Ruprecht, 1978) 431-40; and A. Veilleux, "Monasticism and Gnosis in Egypt," *The Roots of Egyptian Christianity,* ed. B. A. Pearson and J. E. Goehring, (SAC 1; Philadelphia: Fortress, 1986) 271-306.

[23] Wisse was a pioneer in the codicology of the Nag Hammadi manuscripts in the early stages of the work of the Claremont project, beginning with detailed reconstructions of

codex containing 34 full and 3 partial sheets, cut from 4 rolls of papyrus. Apart from a single blank stub, which held one of the leaves (pp. 29/30) into the binding, the manuscript is completely preserved (except for some loss of text at the top of some of the last pages).

As part of his discussion of the handwriting, Wisse describes in some detail those aspects of the writing which reflect grammatical considerations: the "backstroke" or "serif" on the final *tau* of a syllable, and the rather uniform use of supralinear strokes to mark phonemes. Wisse also briefly reviews the notable grammatical features in Codex VII, especially dialectal differences among the tractates representing variations from standard Sahidic. Such dialectal features separate the five tractates into two identifiable groups: one with characteristics normally associated with the Bohairic and Fayyumic dialects (*Treat. Seth, Apoc. Pet.*, and *Steles Seth*) and the other with less variation from Sahidic, with characteristics normally associated with Achmimic or Subachmimic (=Lycopolitan) dialects (*Paraph. Shem* and *Teach. Silv.*). Variations among all five are such as to suggest that each of the tractates represents an independent translation of its Greek original.

### 3. NHC VII,*1*: *THE PARAPHRASE OF SHEM*

Our volume contains the first complete critical edition of *Paraph. Shem*[24] (pp. 16-127).[25] This tractate is an apocalypse containing a Gnostic revelation given by a heavenly being called "Derdekeas" to "Shem" (regularly rendered in the text as ϹΗΕΜ) in the course of a heavenly journey. In his introduction, Wisse argues that the curious term "paraphrase" in the title actually refers to only a small section of the text, 32.27-34.16, introduced by the sentence, "This is the paraphrase (παράφρασις):"[26] This section of the text consists of a commentary on the identity of some twenty mythological beings listed

---

codices VII and VIII. On the codicology of the Nag Hammadi Codices see Robinson's *Facsimile Edition: Introduction* (cit. n. 4). For a summary discussion of this and other aspects of the Nag Hammadi Codices, see my article, "Nag Hammadi Codices," in *ABD* 4:984-93.

[24] VII 1.1-49.9.

[25] The first published Coptic transcription is that of Martin Krause, in *Christentum am Roten Meer*, ed. C. Altheim and R. Stiehl (Berlin: de Gruyter, 1973) 2:2-105 (text and German translation). A transcription is also included in R. Charron, *Concordance des textes de Nag Hammadi; Le Codex VII* (BCNH, "Concordances" 1; Québec: Les Presses de l'Université Laval; Louvain: Éditions Peeters, 1992) 713-29.

[26] Apart from the prescript title (1.1) and the incipit (1.2) the term "paraphrase" occurs only here in the text.

in the previous context (31.4-32.5) in a passage referred to as a "testimony" (ὑπόμνησις) given by Derdekeas to Shem. This "testimony" (now called ὑπόμνημα) is reiterated in a later passage, pronounced by Shem to Derdekeas (46.1-47.7), but without the "paraphrase."

The title of *Paraph. Shem* invites comparison with *The Paraphrase of Seth* used by the "Sethian" Gnostics according to the testimony of Hippolytus (*Ref.* 5.19-22). Wisse describes the relationship between the two as follows:

> Apart from sharing the designation "paraphrase"[27] there is a remarkable agreement between the two in the description of the three primeval powers, but the common material does not extend in a significant way beyond the early pages of the tractate. Furthermore *Paraph. Shem* has at best only a few ambiguous Christian allusions, while *The Paraphrase of Seth* has many clearly Christian elements. Thus the relationship is at best distant; there are no indications that the one tractate depended upon the other. Perhaps both made use of a now lost document which had the designation paraphrase in the title. *The Paraphrase of Seth* also does not help in determining the *terminus ad quem* for *Paraph. Shem* since the one does not clearly presuppose the other. (p. 15)

That *Paraph. Shem* is a very difficult text is well known to anyone who has worked with it. Wisse ascribes the difficulties to a number of factors: textual corruption of the Coptic in the course of its transmission, incompetent translation from Greek to Coptic, and inherent weaknesses in the original Greek composition, such as inconsistencies in terminology and poor organization of the material. Wisse refers to the danger of "trying to make more sense and provide more order than the author intended or the tractate can support" (p. 20).

In terms of its religious-historical context, *Paraph. Shem* is clearly a "Gnostic" writing, though its affinities are hard to determine. Its three-principle system (Light-Spirit-Darkness), which it shares with Hippolytus' "Sethians" and their *Paraphrase of Seth*, has more affinities with Manichaeism than with any other Gnostic writing in the Nag Hammadi corpus. Indeed, the Manichaean comparison is suggested also by some of the mythological details in *Paraph. Shem*, including reference to a "dark lump (βῶλος)" into which the "forms of Nature" will be resolved "in the last day" (45.14-20). On the other hand, *Paraph. Shem* has almost nothing in common with the Nag

---

[27] The restricted meaning given to the term in *Paraph. Shem* 32.27, according to Wisse's analysis, does not seem to agree very well with its use in the title and the incipit, or its use in the title of the work in Hippolytus' account.

Hammadi tractates designated as "Sethian Gnostic" by some scholars,[28] or with patristic testimonies to "Sethian" doctrine aside from the
aforementioned passage in Hippolytus.[29]

As to any relationship between *Paraph. Shem* and Christianity, the
evidence is ambiguous. The tractate's rejection of water baptism, a
feature which it shares with Manichaeism, is not necessarily a
polemic against main-line Christianity. There is no clear reflection of
the use of Christian scripture. Wisse does suggest the possibility that
the "demons" referred to in 30.4-27 are Jesus and John the Baptist.
Of the second demon the text says, in Wisse's translation,

> For (γάρ) at that time (καιρός) the other demon (δαίμων) will appear upon
> the river to (ἵνα) baptize (βαπτίζειν) with an imperfect baptism (βάπτισμα)
> and to trouble the world (κόσμος) with a bondage of water. (30.21-27)

The "baptism" of this demon is referred to again at 31.14-22,
wherein the revealer (Derdekeas) announces that he will "appear in
the baptism of the demon to reveal with the mouth of faith a testimony
to those who belong to her." Wisse wisely refrains from attempting to
interpret this passage. He also seems tacitly to reject (rightly, in my
view) the suggestion by Michel Roberge[30] that the crucifixion of Jesus
is referred to at 39.30-31. The text, with its larger context, reads in
Wisse's translation as follows:

> Therefore I have appeared, being faultless, for the sake of the clouds, be-
> cause they are unequal, in order (ἵνα) that the wickedness (κακία) of Nature
> (φύσις) might be ended. For (γάρ) she wished at that time (καιρός) to snare
> me. She was about to establish (πήσσειν) Soldas who is the dark flame, who
> attended to the [completion] of error (πλάνη), that he might snare me.
> (39.24-40.1)

---

[28] These include *Ap. John* (II,*1*; III,*1*: IV,*1*); *Hyp. Arch.* (II,*4*); *Gos. Eg.* (III,*2*; IV,*2*);
*Apoc. Adam* (V,*5*; *Steles Seth* (VII,*5*); *Zost.* (VIII,*1*); *Melch.* (IX,*1*); *Norea* (IX,*2*);
*Marsanes* (X,*1*); *Allogenes* (XI,*3*); *Trim. Prot.* (XIII,*1*). On "Sethian" Gnosticism see esp.
Hans-Martin Schenke, "Das sethianische System nach Nag-Hammadi-Handschriften,"
*Studia Coptica*, ed. P. Nagel (Berlin: Akademie-Verlag, 1974) 165-72; idem, "The
Phenomenon and Significance of Gnostic Sethianism," *The Rediscovery of Gnosticism*,
ed. B. Layton (SHR 41; Leiden: E. J. Brill, 1980-81) 2:588-616; B. A. Pearson, "The
Figure of Seth in Gnostic Literature," ed. idem, *Gnosticism, Judaism, and Egyptian
Christianity* (SAC 5; Minneapolis: Fortress Press, 1990) 52-83.

[29] Esp. Epiphanius *Panarion* 39 ("Sethians") and 40 ("Archontics").

[30] See his introduction to *Paraph. Shem* in *NHLE* (3rd ed.) 341; also Roberge, "La
crucifixion du Sauveur dans la Paraphrase de Sem (NH VII,*1*), "*Actes du IVe Congrès
copte: Louvain-la-Neuve, 5-10 septembre 1988*, ed. M. Rassart-Debergh and J. Ries
(Louvain-la-Neuve: Université Catholique de Louvain, 1992) 381-87.

Roberge interprets the Greek word πήσσω (ⲡ̅ⲧⲩⲥⲥⲉ, 39.30-31), a late form of πήγνυμι ("stick, fix upon; fasten; make solid" —LSJ 1399b), to refer to the "fastening" of the earthly Jesus (=Soldas) to the cross.

It turns out that all of the supposed references to Christian scripture or tradition in *Paraph. Shem* are highly dubious. That does not mean, of course, that *Paraph. Shem* is a "pre-Christian" text. Wisse's own rough estimate of its date is late 2nd or early 3rd century (p. 22).[31]

## 4. NHC VII,2: *SECOND TREATISE OF THE GREAT SETH*

As mentioned above, Gregory Riley's edition of *Treat. Seth*[32] (pp. 129-99) is completely new, replacing an earlier version submitted by Joseph Gibbons.[33] Riley brings some interesting new insights into our understanding of this tractate. In his discussion (pp. 130-33) of the title[34] and identification of the tractate, Riley takes up the problem implicit in the title: Was there a "first treatise" of Seth, to which our tractate is a sequel? No such treatise is known, nor can the view first advanced by Henri-Charles Puech[35] and Jean Doresse[36] that *Treat. Seth* was composed as a continuation of *Paraph. Shem* in a two-volume work be sustained, since the two tractates are dramatically different in content. The solution to the problem comes in the realization that Derdekeas in *Paraph. Shem* and Jesus Christ in *Treat. Seth* can be understood as incarnations of the heavenly redeemer Seth. The name "Derdekeas" is based on an Aramaic word דַּרְדְּקָא, "male child," which is an epithet of the heavenly Seth in some Gnostic texts.[37] And

---

[31] Wisse had argued in an earlier work that *Paraph. Shem* contains evidence of the use of a pre-Christian redeemer myth, though he did not argue for a pre-Christian date for the tractate itself. See Wisse, "The Redeemer Figure in the Paraphrase of Shem," *NovT* 12 (1970) 130-40.

[32] VII 49.10-69.12.

[33] Our edition was preceded by that of the French Canadian project based at Université Laval in Québec: Louis Painchaud, *"Le Deuxième Traité du Grand Seth (NH VII,2)* (BCNH, Section "Textes" 6; Québec: Les Presses de l'Université Laval, 1982).

[34] The subscript title is preserved in Greek: ⲇⲉⲩⲧⲉⲣⲟⲥ ⲗⲟⲅⲟⲥ ⲧⲟⲩ ⲙⲉⲅⲁⲗⲟⲩ ⲥⲏⲑ (69.11-12).

[35] H.-C. Puech, "Les nouveaux écrits gnostiques découverts en Haute-Egypte (premier inventaire et essai d'identification)," *Coptic Studies in Honor of Walter Ewing Crum* (Boston: Byzantine Institute, 1950) 91-154, esp. 105, 123-24.

[36] J. Doresse, *The Secret Books of the Egyptian Gnostics: An Introduction to the Gnostic Coptic Manuscripts Discovered at Chenoboskion* (trans. P. Mairet; New York: Viking Press; London: Hollis and Carter, 1960) 149.

[37] See esp. G. G. Stroumsa, *Another Seed: Studies in Gnostic Mythology* (NHS 24; Leiden: E. J. Brill, 1984) 79.

Christian Sethians regarded Christ as an incarnation of the heavenly
Seth.[38] The title of *Treat. Seth* is secondary, attached to this tractate
during the transmission of *Paraph. Shem* and *Treat. Seth* by someone
who understood the redeemer figures in both to be avatars of Seth.[39]

In contrast to *Paraph. Shem*, *Treat. Seth* is clearly a Christian
Gnostic text. It does contain vestiges of typically "Sethian Gnostic"[40]
mythology: Yaldabaoth and his archons appear in the text (53.12-14;
68.28-29), with his vain claim to be the only God (53.28-31);[41] and
the Sethian Gnostic anthropogony is referred to (53.18-19), but the
main concern of the text is to defend a particular interpretation of the
person and work of Christ, particularly a docetic interpretation of his
passion and death. Riley takes issue with the view advanced by
Gibbons,[42] and passed on by others,[43] that *Treat. Seth* teaches a
"Basilidean" version of the crucifixion, i.e. that Simon of Cyrene was
crucified in Jesus' place.[44] The crucial passage reads as follows in
Riley's translation:

> For (γάρ) my death which they think happened, (happened) to them in their
> error (πλάνη) and blindness. They nailed their man up to their death. For
> (γάρ) their minds (ἔννοια) did not see me, for (γάρ) they were deaf and
> blind. But (δέ) in doing these things, they render judgment against them-
> selves. As for me, on the one hand (μέν) they saw me; they punished
> (κολάζειν) me. Another, their father, was the one who drank the gall and the
> vinegar; it was not I. They were hitting me with the reed; another was the
> one who lifted up the cross (σταυρός) on his shoulder, who was Simon.
> Another was the one on whom they put the crown of thorns. But (δέ) I was
> rejoicing in the height over all the riches of the archons (ἄρχων) and the off-
> spring (σπορά) of their error (πλάνη) and their conceit, and I was laughing at
> their ignorance. (55.30-56.20)

This passage does not state that Simon was crucified in the place of
Jesus, or crucified at all, only that he carried the cross of Jesus (Mark
15:20-21). Jesus' crucifixion happened to "their man," i.e. the earthly

---

[38] Pearson, "Figure of Seth" (cit. n. 28) 78.

[39] Such an explanation would account for the use of the name Seth, rather than Shem,
in the *Paraphrase of Seth* known to Hippolytus: it is really Seth who is the revealer, both
in that document and in *Paraph. Shem*.

[40] Cf. n. 28, above.

[41] See esp. N. A. Dahl, "The Arrogant Archon and the Lewd Sophia: Jewish Traditions
in Gnostic Revolt," *The Rediscovery of Gnosticism* (cit. n. 28) 2:689-712.

[42] "Commentary," 204

[43] E.g., K. Rudolph, *Gnosis: The Nature and History of Gnosticism* (Edinburgh: T. &.
T. Clark; San Francisco: Harper & Row, 1977) 168.

[44] Irenaeus *Adv. Haer.* I.24.4; Epiphanius *Panarion* 24.3.

body created by the archons. The real Jesus was beyond the fray, laughing at the folly of those who thought they were killing him. Thus, the interpretation of Jesus' passion in *Treat. Seth* is essentially the same as that found in *Apoc. Pet.* 82.1-6.[45]

## 5. NHC VII,*3*: *APOCALYPSE OF PETER*

Our volume contains the first complete critical edition of *Apoc. Pet.*[46] (pp. 201-47).[47] In his introduction (pp. 201-16) Michel Desjardins provides a close analysis of the tractate's literary structure, with a five-fold division of the text (A. Introduction, B. First Visionary Sequence, C. Central Revelatory Discourse, B$^1$. Second Visionary Sequence, A$^1$. Conclusion).[48] The central revelatory discourse, the longest section (73.10-81.3), receives the stress and contains vigorous polemic against false Christians ("the many," clearly the orthodox church) and true Christians ("the little ones," i.e. the Gnostics). The visionary sequences feature Peter in dialogue with the Savior watching the crucifixion of one whom the "priests and people" think is Jesus, while the real Savior is "laughing above the cross" (82.6). What is striking about this text is its appropriation of the figure of Peter and its use of Petrine traditions (including even 2 Peter), as well as its heavy reliance on the Gospel of Matthew. Desjardins sees in this tractate a reflex of early third-century disputes between a growing "orthodoxy" and Gnostic dissidents, the latter represented by the author of *Apoc. Pet.* and his constituency.

James Brashler's translation (pp. 218-47) differs considerably from earlier versions. I want to comment here on his interpretation of two particularly difficult passages. The first one, the passage with which the tractate opens (70.14-17), is particularly notorious. Here is Brashler's new translation:

---

[45] Cf. also *Act. John* 97-101.

[46] VII 70.13-84.14.

[47] The first published Coptic transcription is that of Martin Krause, *Christentum am Roten Meer* (cit. n. 25) 2:152-79. A transcription is also included in Charron's *Concordance*, 736-40.

[48] The recent studies by David Hellholm and Ulrich Schoenborn appeared too late to be considered in Desjardins' introduction: D. Hellholm, "The Mighty Minorities of Gnostic Christians," *Mighty Minorities: Minorities in Early Christianity—Positions and Strategies*, ed. D. Hellholm et al. (Oslo: Scandinavian University Press, 1995) 41-66; U. Schoenborn, *Diverbium Salutis: Literarische Struktur und theologische Intention des gnostischen Dialogs am Beispiel der koptischen 'Apokalypse des Petrus'* (SUNT 19; Göttingen: Vandenhoeck & Ruprecht, 1995).

As the Savior (σωτήρ) was sitting in the temple, in the inner part of the building at the convergence of the tenth pillar (στῦλος), and . . .

Compare the same passage as rendered in *The Nag Hammadi Library in English* (3rd ed.):

As the Savior was sitting in the temple in the three hundredth (year) of the covenant and the agreement of the tenth pillar, and . . .

The first problem has to do with the Coptic word rendered now by Brashler as "inner part," and in *NHLE* as "three hundredth."[49] Brashler now has in his transcription <ⲡ>ⲙⲉ𝒉ⲧ̄, emending what he takes to be the ms. reading ⲧⲙⲉ𝒉ⲧ̄. ⲙⲉ𝒉ⲧ̄ means something like "bowels," hence "inner part," and is masculine, requiring the masculine article ⲡ. In his note Brashler suggests that the word in the original Greek was κοιλία. The earlier reading "three-hundredth (year)" presupposes Coptic ⲧⲙⲉ𝒉ⲧ̄ <ⲛ̄ⲣⲟⲙⲡⲉ>, the numeral ⲧ̄ (=300) plus ordinal prefix ⲙⲉ𝒉-. ⲡⲓⲥ̄ⲙⲛⲉ, rendered by Brashler as "building," (vs. the earlier "covenant") is taken to render the Greek word σύνθεσις, which can mean "a combination of parts" (LSJ 1716b), hence a "building." ⲡⲓⲧ̄ ⲙⲁⲧⲉ, rendered by Brashler as "convergence" (vs. the earlier "agreement," which makes no sense), is understood in a spatial sense, and "literally refers to the coming together or convergence one would notice when looking up at the top of (a) column, 'the tenth pillar' in this imaginary temple where the Savior is at rest."[50]

Even more daring (if not desperate) is Brashler's solution to the problems posed by 71.25-33. The *NHLE* version reads,

having summoned you to know him in a way which is worth doing because of the rejection which happened to him, and the sinews of his hands and his feet, and the crowning by those of the middle region, and the body of his radiance . . .

Brashler now translates this passage as follows:

He summoned you to know him properly regarding the shedding (ἀποχή) (of blood) which tore him—even the sinews of his hands and his feet—and (regarding) the crowning by those of the middle region (μεσότης), and (regarding) the body (σῶμα) of his radiance.

---

[49] M. Krause (*Christentum am Roten* Meer 2:152) reads "fifth": ⲧ, "five," plus the ordinal prefix; R. Charron (*Concordance*, 736) preserves the *NHLE* reading.

[50] Note to 70.15, 218.

Brashler here takes †ⲀⲠⲞⲬⲎ (ἀποχή, lit. "rejection, renunciation") at 71.27 as a mistaken equivalent of ἀπόχυσις, related to the verb ἀποχέω ("pour out, shed"). In the following word ⲈⲦⲠⲎ2 (71.28), ⲠⲎ2 (a qualitative form of ⲠⲰ2) is construed as equivalent to ⲠⲰ2, "tear," instead of the homonym ⲠⲰ2, "reach, attain."

Whatever one might think of the "corrections" Brashler makes to the text, it has to be agreed that the passage as now rendered by him makes more sense.

## 6. NHC VII,4: *THE TEACHINGS OF SILVANUS*

As mentioned above, Malcolm Peel's edition of *Teach. Silv.*[51] is the culmination of work earlier done jointly by him and Jan Zandee.[52] His very extensive introduction (pp. 249-76) begins with a discussion of the title and colophon, and the tractate's literary form: "wisdom sayings literature," found in biblical and Jewish tradition and early Christianity. In terms of genre the closest parallel is *The Sentences of Sextus* (NHC XII,1), but *Teach Silv.* also shows an indebtedness to the Stoic-Cynic diatribe. Discussion of the content and an outline is followed by a discussion of the religious-historical setting of the tractate and the various influences that are reflected in it: biblical traditions; Hellenistic philosophy, especially Stoicism and Platonism; Alexandrian Jewish philosophy, especially Philo; and early Alexandrian Christian theology. There are no specific Gnostic features in *Teach. Silv.*; indeed, there are some indications in it of anti-Gnostic polemic (e.g. at 94.31-32; 116.5-9).

Peel takes fully into account in his introduction and notes the important work of Wolf-Peter Funk and Roelof van den Broek: Funk's discovery of two texts associated with St. Antony[53] and van den Broek's more recent discussion of the place of *Teach. Silv.* in the development of Alexandrian Christian theology.[54]

Funk discovered in the British Museum a tenth- or eleventh-century Coptic parchment sheet containing a parallel to *Teach. Silv.*

---

[51] VII 84.15-118.7 plus colophon, 118.8-9.

[52] Cf. discussion above, and note 17. Our edition was also preceded by that of the Laval project: Y. Janssens, *Les leçons de Silvanos (NH VII,4)* (BCNH "Textes" 13; Québec: Les Presses de l'Université Laval, 1983).

[53] W.-P. Funk, "Ein doppelt überliefertes Stück spätägyptischer Weisheit," *ZÄS* 103 (1976) 8-21.

[54] R. Van den Broek, "The Theology of the Teachings of Silvanus," *VC* 40 (1986) 1-23.

97.3-98.22 (BM 979) attributed to Antony. He also found that the same text occurs in an Arabic appendix to the *Rule of St. Antony*, translated into Latin in *PG* 40:1073-1080. Funk concluded from a study of the three texts that the passage in *Teach. Silv.* is an independent passage from an older wisdom text, that BM 979 is an independent translation of the original Greek, and that the Arabic version represents a monastic re-editing of the passage. The Coptic text of BM 979 also provides the possibility of reconstructing a lacuna in *Teach. Silv.* (at 97.35).

While early commentators have argued for a second-century date for *Teach. Silv.*, maintaining that it represents a stage in the development of Alexandrian Christian theology leading to Clement and Origen,[55] van den Broek asserts that it actually reflects in its content the work not only of Clement and Origen, but even the anti-Arians of the fourth century, around the time of the Council of Nicea. Peel takes issue with van den Broek's interpretation of some of the christological passages in *Teach. Silv.* (esp. 115.9-16) and argues instead for a pre-Nicene date for the tractate. Nevertheless, Peel does accept van den Broek's arguments that its author knows the work of Origen, and thus concludes that the tractate should be dated sometime between the death of Origen and the Council of Nicea (ca. 280-320). This in itself represents a relatively new departure in scholarly work on *Teach. Silv.*

Peel's translation contains many refinements and improvements of the Peel-Zandee translation in *NHLE*. I cite here one example, an important christological passage: 115.9-19. First, the *NHLE* version (3rd ed.):

> For he is always Son of the Father [end of paragraph]. Consider these things about God Almighty who always exists: this One was not always King for fear that he might be without a divine Son. For all dwell in God, (that is), the things which have come into being through the Word, who is the Son as the image of the Father.

Peel's new translation reads as follows:

> For (γάρ) he is always Son of the Father. Consider (νοεῖν) these things about God: the Almighty (παντοκράτωρ) who always exists did not always reign (as if) he might not (μήπως) be in need of the divine (θεῖος) Son. For (γάρ) all dwell in God, (that is), the things which have come into being

---

[55] The relevant works are too numerous to mention here; they are listed in Peel's bibliography (12 of them by Zandee alone).

through the Word (λόγος), who is the Son as the image (εἰκών) of the Father.

In the new translation a seeming anomaly (that "God was not always King") is resolved, and the co-eternality of the Son with the Father is underscored.[56]

## 7. NHC VII,5: *THE THREE STELES OF SETH*

In this new edition[57] of *Steles Seth*[58] James Goehring presents an introduction (pp. 371-85) wherein he discusses the tractate's title and identification, its religious-historical context (Sethian Gnostic), its content and use of sources, its ritual context, and its philosophical contacts, date (early 3rd cent.), and provenance (probably Alexandria). The most important features of the tractate taken up by Goehring are its contacts with Neoplatonism and its ritual context.

*Steles Seth* is one of four tractates in the Nag Hammadi corpus[59] that develops the triadic theology of earlier Sethian Gnosticism (Father-Mother-Son) in terms of categories derived from Middle Platonism (Numenius of Apamea is an important representative) and further developed in Neoplatonism.[60] The use and elaboration of the Existence-Life-Mind (ὕπαρξις-ζωή-νοῦς) triad[61] in this and related tractates is an example of such interaction with Platonic philosophy, and Goehring cites a number of other instances in *Steles Seth*, especially the use of technical terms derived from Platonism.

---

[56] Cf. also 113.6-20 and Peel's notes to the respective passages.

[57] Our edition was preceded by that of the Laval project: P. Claude, *Les trois stèles de Seth: Hymne gnostique à la triade (NHC VII,5)* (BCNH "Textes" 8; Québec: Les presses de l'Université Laval, 1983).

[58] VII 118.10-127.27 + colophon, 28-32.

[59] The others are *Zostrianos* (VIII,*1*), *Marsanes* (X,*1*), and *Allogenes* (XI,*3*).

[60] See the important article by J. M. Robinson, "The Three Steles of Seth and the Gnostics of Plotinus," *Proceedings of the International Colloquium on Gnosticism, Stockholm August 20-25, 1973*, ed. G. Widengren (Kungl. Vitterhets Historie och Antikvitets Akademiens Handlingar, Filologisk-filosofiska serien 17; Stockholm: Almqvist & Wiksell, 1977). Robinson did not mention *Marsanes* in his article; on that tractate and its relation to Platonism see my article, "Gnosticism as Platonism," *Gnosticism, Judaism, and Egyptian Christianity* (cit. n. 28) 148-64. See also J. D. Turner, "Gnosticism and Platonism: The Platonizing Sethian Texts from Nag Hammadi in their Relation to Later Platonic Literature," *Neoplatonism and Gnosticism*, ed. R. T. Wallis and J. Bregman (Studies in Neoplatonism: Ancient and Modern 6; Albany: State University of New York Press, 1992) 425-59.

[61] On this triad see the seminal article by P. Hadot, "Être, Vie, Pensée chez Plotin et avant Plotin," *Les sources de Plotin* (Entretiens sur l'antiquité classique 3; Geneva: Fondation Hardt, 1966) 107-41.

Especially interesting are the indications in *Steles Seth* of a ritual
context. The tractate consists essentially of three doxological hymns
purportedly inscribed on three steles by Seth, "the father of the living
and unshakable race" (118.12-13), as revealed to and transmitted by
one Dositheos. The hymns are addressed respectively in ascending
order to the three members of the (Sethian Gnostic) divine triad: the
Son Geradamas (father of the heavenly Seth) (118.24-121.17); the
Mother, Barbelo (121.18-124.15); and the ground of all being, the
Father (124.16-127.6). The hymns function in the liturgical setting of
a corporate ritual of ascent. The mythic ascent of Seth attested in
other Sethian Gnostic texts provides the paradigm for the communal
experience of an ascent to God on the part of a worshipping community. The hymns in *Steles Seth* are thus to be understood as a kind
of liturgy, celebrated not once but repeatedly in the community's
ritual life. Goehring points out that the hymns function as "a vehicle
through which the elect continually reaffirmed their salvation.
Continual participation in the liturgy made one 'the perfect among the
perfect' (127.6-11)" (p. 381). Even in this ritual dimension, *Steles
Seth* "shares fundamental perspectives with certain forms of Neoplatonism."[62]

The translation in our new edition is based upon one done by
James M. Robinson in the late '60's, but it has been substantially
revised by Goehring. A major aspect of this revision involves the
abandonment of archaic language in the doxologies in favor of a more
modern form of address (thus reflecting a recent tendency at work in
the worship life of English-speaking Christians and in newer translations of the Bible, e.g. the NRSV). Compare, for example, the
opening benediction in the first stele (118.25-31) as rendered respectively in *NHLE* (3rd ed.) and in the new edition:

> I bless thee, Father Geradama(s), I, as thine (own) Son, Emmacha Seth,
> whom thou didst beget without begetting, as a blessing of our God; for I am
> thine (own) Son.

> I bless you, father Geradama(s), I, as your (own) son, Emmacha Seth, whom
> you begot without begetting, as a blessing of our God; for I am your (own)
> son.

---

[62] P. 381. J. Goehring refers in a footnote to my article, "Theurgic Tendencies in
Gnosticism and Iamblichus' Conception of Theurgy," *Neoplatonism and Gnosticism* (cit.
n. 60) 253-75. On the rite of "cultic ascension" in Sethian Gnosticism see also Schenke,
"Gnostic Sethianism" (cit. n. 28), esp. 601-02.

There are some minor changes in the transcription in the new edition, mainly in the last few pages where the leaves are damaged, including the restoration of a lacuna at 126.4. But probably the most valuable part of our edition is the set of textual and interpretive notes that Goehring prepared for it.

## 8. CONCLUDING REMARKS

As Editor of this last volume in the CGL series I take great satisfaction, not only in seeing its completion but also in seeing the quality of the work reflected in it. While it is true, no doubt, that the last word has not been pronounced in our edition on the five tractates contained in Codex VII, its translations of the respective tractates can at least be said to supersede those found in *NHLE* and other translations currently available, and its introductions and textual notes reflect the latest stage of scholarship on them.

# THE WORK OF THE BERLINER ARBEITSKREIS: PAST, PRESENT, AND FUTURE

*Hans-Martin Schenke*
Humboldt University, Berlin

Under the circumstances I have to apologize for the topic that I chose for this occasion and which now stands somewhat isolated in the program. In any event, it was not my intention to feature especially our own research team and so to extol ourselves. Rather, it myselection of topic stems from my idea of what a commemorative speech concerning the Fiftieth Anniversary of the Discovery of the Nag Hammadi Library should be like. By the way, I discussed the problem of my present contribution earlier in Québec with Wolf-Peter Funk, who is one of the most important members of the *Berliner Arbeitskreis*, though living and working now at such a great distance from its center. So this topic has been our joint proposal. And we presupposed that J. M. Robinson and P.-H. Poirier would present something similar, passing in review the work of their respective teams, together with a preview of what has still to be done. On the other hand, it may pass for an excuse that I have already had my true speech of the day, a more objective one last year, in the form of a review of results—"The Relevance of Nag Hammadi Research to New Testament Scholarship"—having prepared it quite innocently and without any presentiment of the festival plans for this year.

## I. THE WORK OF THE BERLINER ARBEITSKREIS

The *Berliner Arbeitskreis*, which in the end learned to understand itself as the smallest of three groups including also the (larger) teams of the Coptic Gnostic Library project and the *Bibliothèque Copte de Nag Hammadi*, was never formally founded. It simply came into being and grew up around me in the department of New Testament Studies at Humboldt University, originating in a common interest in the religio-historical interpretation of The New Testament. Now, the main tool of this exegetical approach to the writings of the New Testament are the parallels from the spiritual environment of Early Christianity. And the usual dossier of parallels was so enormously increased by the Nag Hammadi discovery! And we wanted to help in applying these completely new materials to the problems of New Testament interpretation. As a sort of "Bultmannian" group, we were especially curious to see whether or not the religio-historical interpretation of the Gospel of John and other documents of the New Testament by our "figure-head," the famous and controversial scholar Rudolf Bultmann, proved to be right.[1] So at least the beginning was a practical one. But we learned very soon, in the process, that in order to make use of these parallels for the interpretation of the New Testament it was vital first of all to understand them in their own right.

Looking back beyond the real beginning, I see two essential roots for us in Berlin. We have as sort of a great-grandfather Carl Schmidt, who in his position as Professor of Church History in our faculty and as an officer (his main responsibility) of the so-called "Kirchenväterkommission," led by Adolf von Harnack at the Academy of Sciences of Berlin, practiced what I would like to call "applied" Coptology.[2] And we have as a grandfather Fritz Hintze, the former Egyptologist of Humboldt University, inasmuch as he was my personal teacher of Egyptology and "pure" Coptology.

But there is still a personal connection of another nature worth mentioning, also from a time when the *Berliner Arbeitskreis* did not yet exist, or was embryonic at best. There was an early cooperation with Johannes Leipoldt. But what brought us together was almost solely a common interest in a certain book that was out of reach. This was during that early phase of Nag Hammadi research when it was rumored in Europe that Pahor Labib in Cairo had edited the first (and only) volume of a facsimile edition of Nag Hammadi texts, including the *Gospel of Thomas* and the *Gospel of Philip*. But it turned out to be practically impossible to get this book in Europe. Leipoldt was interested in *Gos. Thom.*, and I myself in all the other purely Gnostic texts. In this "state of emergency" we "strictly bound ourselves by an oath" that whoever would receive the book first, would immediately send to the other a copy of those parts which were of interest to him.

---

[1] Cf. H.-M. Schenke, "Die Rolle der Gnosis in Bultmanns Kommentar zum Johannesevangelium aus heutiger Sicht, Protokoll der Tagung 'Alter Marburger'" *Hofgeismar* 2.-5. Januar 1991, 49-83. There is an abbreviated English version of this paper ("The Role of Gnosis in Bultmann's Commentary on the Gospel of John Reconsidered in the Light of Nag Hammadi Research," prepared for and read at a conference, "The Nag Hammadi Codices: Fifty Years of Scholarship (1945-1995)," organized by F. Bovon at Harvard Divinity School, April 22, 1995.

[2] Cf. *Carl-Schmidt-Kolloquium an der Martin-Luther-Universität 1988*, ed. P. Nagel (Halle: Wissenschaftliche Beiträge der Martin-Luther-Universität Halle-Wittenberg, 1990/ 23 (K 9) 1990.

It turned out that I was the happier one of us, because M. Krause, who was then an employee of the State Museums in East Berlin, brought back with him a copy of the book from an official trip to Cairo. I kept my oath and before casting a glance myself into the book, I had the *Gos. Thom.* copied and mailed to Ahrenshoop, the retirement home of Leipoldt at that time. In response I received the most extraordinary letter of my life. The letter contained only a reference to a scriptural passage: Mat. 25:40, reading thus: "Dear colleague, Matth. 25:40. Yours, Leipoldt." By the way, this poor facsimile edition became the (only) basis of our early translations.

A clearly marked second phase of the Berlin activity on Nag Hammadi texts is connected with the fact that J. M. Robinson had meanwhile entered the Nag Hammadi business and very soon became its manager, breaking former taboos and liquidating the monopolies of the time. And the two of us were acquainted with each other as theologians and New Testament scholars from the time before the Berlin wall. Through him we gained access to the transcriptions and translations of all the Nag Hammadi texts which his team had produced on the basis of photographs possessed by UNESCO. Besides, it was not for us in Berlin that Robinson sent copies of this material into the former GDR, but for K. Rudolph in Leipzig, a specialist on the Mandaean branch of Gnosis, from whom he expected to be provided with Mandaean parallels to the Nag Hammadi texts. But at least Robinson did not object to our making copies of the copies and studying them on the principle "for eyes only" in Berlin. This was the somewhat unofficial beginning of a fruitful cooperation between Claremont and Berlin—East Berlin.

The *Berliner Arbeitskreis* was an East Berlin group which accordingly had to work behind the Iron Curtain. And that means not only limited in its resources—the former GDR was a relatively poor country and for theologians money was especially scarce—but, above all, extremely restricted in its mobility. In a situation of this sort, in order to work satisfactorily and so to survive intellectually, one needs friends abroad. And we had such, not only in the far distant USA and in Canada, but also very near, in West Berlin. For there at the Free University of West Berlin, the Gnosis specialist Carsten Colpe and his school were at work, and it was possible to communicate most fruitfully "through the wall"—even in person. Although we were unable to go to West Berlin, the citizens of West Berlin were allowed to visit us in the East. And this they did, amply. Indeed, C. Colpe and his circle were virtual "corresponding" members of the East Berlin *Arbeitskreis*.

Let me now turn to the special way of work within our group. Our great advantage and our outstanding oppotunity was that all of us lived in one and the same town and studied at one and the same University and, additionally, that all of us came from the same theological school. In the first climax of our work, in the seventies, when we had the extraordinary possibility of working with all the Nag Hammadi texts, we met every week for at least three hours, and by and by translated and discussed linguistically and exegetically all the Nag Hammadi texts. During this period of work, I personally became aware (very late!) that ideas and realizations do not come only to a person sitting at the writing table, but can also be born in conversation. In addition, we met about once a month, on the weekend (Saturday mornings), in order to discuss more general aspects of Gnosis. We called these meetings irreverently "Gnosis palavers." And these palavers were quite regularly attended by the "Colpians" from West Berlin.

This extraordinarily intensive common work brought forth special results (so far) documented in German translations of many texts and in dissertations (printed or not) on selected Nag Hammadi writings. The (early) envisaged complete German translation, however, is only now in preparation.[3] In Berlin we "invented" the Gnostic variety of Sethianism. And also in Berlin two very special discoveries took place, namely that the writing without title, Codex VI,5, which was originally taken to be an unknown Hermetic tractate, is an excerpt of Plato's Republic,[4] and that there existed a parallel text of one of the most interesting passages of Silvanus (B.L. Or. 6003 or BM 979, respectively).[5]

When we were invited last year in Chicago by John Turner to make proposals for an appropriate celebration of this year's anniversary of the discovery of the Nag Hammadi library, one of my ideas was to use this opportunity also to publicly renounce and abjure our mistakes. There are such mistakes (widely unnoticed, it is true), not only achievements. The kind of things I have in mind may be illustrated by the example of two thrilling mistakes of the Berlin *Arbeitskreis*. An outstanding "monster" was the invention "Nebront" as the

---

[3] Cf. H.-M. Schenke, "Koptisch-Gnostische Schriften. Volumes 2 and 3," *Nag Hammadi and Gnosis, Papers read at the First International Congress of Coptology (Cairo, December 1976)*, ed. R. McL. Wilson (NHS 14; Leiden: Brill, 1978) 113-116.

[4] Cf. H.-M. Schenke, "Zur Faksimile-Ausgabe der Nag-Hammadi-Schriften: Nag-Hammadi-Codex VI," *OLZ* 69 (1974) 229-243 (especially 236-241).

[5] Cf. W.-P. Funk, "Ein doppelt überliefertes Stück spätägyptischer Weisheit," *ZÄS* 103 (1976) 8-21.

title of the second writing of NHC VI. We understood then the title as: ⲚⲈⲂⲢⲞⲚⲦ ⲏ: ⲚⲞⲨⲤ ⲚⲦⲈⲖⲒⲞⲤ = "Nebront or: Perfect Mind." However, this would not at all have taken place, if we had not relied on the proof sheets of Krause's edition, which he was so kind to place at our disposal, and it was he who gave the first letter not as Ⲧ, but as Ⲛ (or to put it more exactly, he had corrected an earlier reading of his: Ⲛ into: Ⲧ). We very soon afterwards renounced that. And this—more or less—silent abjuration may be publicly repeated here. ("Father, I have sinned"). Another blatant mistake is to be charged up to my own account. In the writing without title of Codex II, *Orig. World,* on p. 109.26, 30 there are the expressions ⲦⲂⲈ ⲚⲈⲖⲀⲀⲖⲈ and ⲦⲂⲈ ⲚⲈⲖⲞⲞⲖⲈ, respectively. Within the limits of my knowledge of Coptic "school grammar" back then, according to which I thought the syntagm "grapevine" would be in Coptic either ⲂⲰ ⲚⲈⲖⲞⲞⲖⲈ or ⲂⲈⲈⲖⲞⲞⲖⲈ, I took the element ⲦⲂⲈ to be a fayumicizing form of the numeral ⲦⲂⲀ = "ten thousand". And this was the way I came to the translation "ten thousand vines," which is wrong in more than one respect, but at all events it offered nine thousand nine hundred ninety-nine vines too many![6]

After mentioning the genuine intensity of our working together, I still have—in order to give a full picture—to hint at a certain ambition in relationship to, or competition with, the West German Nag Hammadi research of that time. For us it was personified in M. Krause, since, first as a member of the Deutsches Archäologisches Institut, Kairo, he was in charge of the Nag Hammadi texts in Cairo, and, afterwards, in Münster, had made his chair a center of German Coptology. Although in a more unfavorable situation, we in Berlin did not at all aim at reaching the scholarly standard in Münster, but at surpassing it. This was an essential part of our self-understanding. And our cooperation with North America was a *direct one*, skipping a possible mediation by the Federal Republic of Germany.

By the way, we also had a sort of foreign relation to the "farther" East, though in this direction the partnership was not one of mutual exchange, but practically of giving only. We kept a more or less close contact with interested scholars in Poland, Hungary, former Czechoslovakia, and the former USSR. "Our man" in Poland was Wincenty Myszor of Warsaw; in Hungary the contact-person was Petr Hubai of Budapest. In Czechoslovakia, we had some contact also in Nag Hammadi affairs with Petr Pokorny of Prague, and regarding the

---

[6] Cf. H.-M. Schenke, "Vom Ursprung der Welt, Eine titellose gnostische Abhandlung aus dem Funde von Nag-Hamadi," *TLZ* 84 (1959) 243-256 (especially 255).

USSR, we tried to keep Mrs. A. I. Elanskaja of the former Leningrad informed about what we knew and thought about the Nag Hammadi texts. But regarding generally foreign relations on a personal level, my most beautiful and fruitful experiences were the co-advisorship of the dissertations of Karen King,[7] formerly of Brown University in the USA, and of Henriette Havelaar[8] of the University of Groningen in the Netherlands. I have the very best recollections of the common work with both of them in Berlin. K. King had received a grant for study in West Berlin, and I had, in a sense, to act for C. Colpe, who was very sick at that time—at least it began that way. H. Havelaar came to Berlin for several shorter spaces of time.

It was just during the collaboration with H. Havelaar that the external conditions of scholarly work were fundamentally changed by the downfall of the Berlin wall and the following process of the unification of Germany—in various respects. A regeneration or several regenerations of the *Arbeitskreis* had already taken place earlier, perhaps a sort of re-vivification, for sometimes the *Arbeitskreis* seemed (to me at least) nearly moribund. And there was never a lack of interested students at our University. But now we are experiencing a completely new climax, or rather something like a "second spring." The new conditions of work—where there are no longer problems in getting literature, where we are being equipped with the newest computer technology, and where we can send, whenever we want, our students for collation work to Cairo—means to me a greater happiness than I feel able to express, at least here and in English. The new situation is also connected with the fact that the Berlin faculty of theology as the home and the basis of the *Arbeitskreis* is no longer the same as before. For the faculty of theology, the rearrangement of the political situation resulted in a double unification with other, formerly independent institutions for theological education, at first with the East Berlin so-called *Sprachenkonvikt*, a sort of *Kirchliche Hochschule* run by the church of East Germany, and afterwards with the traditional and well-known *Kirchliche Hochschule* of Zehlendorf in West Berlin. This means that the faculty of theology is now quite a gigantic institution with more than three times as many students than formerly, and—during the first period, at

---

[7] K. L. King, "The Quiescent Eye of the Revelation: Nag Hammadi Codex XI.3 'Allogenes', A Critical Edition," Ph.D. Diss., Brown University, 1984. See now her *Revelation of the Unknowable God, with Text, Translation, and Notes to NHC XI,3 Allogenes*, (Santa Rosa, CA: Polebridge, 1995).

[8] H. Havelaar, "The Coptic Apocalypse of Peter (Nag Hammadi Codex VII,3)," Theol. Diss., Groningen, 1993.

least—with three times as many professors as before. While formerly
we were ordered and had to take care not to distract our students from
their main task of being trained for their future ministry by offering
overly-specialized classes, we are now absolutely free to offer special
classes, which are taken by a relatively large number of students. So,
for example, during my last period in office, I was able to teach
classes like: Gnostic Sethianism; The Early Christian Tradition of the
Apostle Philip; The Nag Hammadi writing "Interpretation of Gnosis";
The Christian-Gnostic Apocalypse of Peter in the Context of Early
Christian Peter Traditions; "The Teachings of Silvanus" as an
Example of Gnostic Ethics. After my retirement, my last doctoral
student, U.-K. Plisch,[9] having received his degree, gave a class:
Introduction to Modern Gnosis Research with Special Consideration
of the Nag Hammadi texts (winter semester 1994/95).

For the present semester (winter semester 1995/96) my friend and
successor H.-G. Bethge prepared a class: "Fifty Years after the Nag
Hammadi Discoveries." The new stage of work of the *Berliner
Arbeitskreis* and the present situation of Nag Hammadi research at
Humboldt University is well characterized by the enormous scholarly
and organizing activity of H.-G. Bethge, who is now (one of the
many) professor(s) of New Testament studies at Humboldt University. So, since 1991, he has regularly been teaching Coptic for
doctoral and other students. Over a long period, five students have
acquired a good knowledge of Coptic. Two persons will make use of
this ability for a dissertation or *Habilitationsschrift*, respectively.
Two persons have been taught by him through a correspondence
course. He has been translating with his students the following Nag
Hammadi writings: *Hyp. Arch.*, *Orig. World*, *Exeg. Soul*, *Soph. Jes.
Chr.*, *Gos. Thom.*, *Ep. Pet. Phil.*, and *Dial. Sav.* His next topic will
be *Treat. Seth*. All these texts that have been translated in the group
are the responsibility of one or several members, in order to appear in
our German translation of the whole corpus of the Nag Hammadi
texts: "Koptisch-Gnostische Schriften, Volumes 2 and 3."[10]

Since 1994 an especially noteworthy project—the result of
Bethge's involvement in New Testament text criticism and his
personal and institutional connections to the *Institut für Neutestamentliche Textforschung* of Münster—is a revision of the *Gos. Thom.*

---

[9] The title of his dissertation is: "'Die Auslegung der Erkenntnis' (NHC XI,1) herausgegeben, übersetzt und erklärt," Theol. Diss., Berlin, 1994; meanwhile printed in *Texte
und Untersuchungen* 142 (Berlin: Akademie Verlag, 1996).

[10] Cf. n. 1 above.

for the *Synopsis Quattuor Evangeliorum*, 15th edition. In appendix I, there will be given the Coptic text together with a German and an English translation, and in addition, in the case of parallels only, a Greek retrotranslation, all this complemented by notes on text and translation. Mainly responsible for this project are, besides Bethge himself, Christina-Maria Franke, Judith Hartenstein,[11] and Uwe-Karsten Plisch. There are also plans—in future cooperation with the Münster Institute—for inclusion of other relevant Nag Hammadi materials in the *Synopsis Quattuor Evangeliorum*.

## II. REFLECTIONS ON THE GOSPEL OF PHILIP

Perhaps I may be allowed to conclude with a remark on something of my personal share in the work of the *Berliner Arbeitskreis*. During my year of guest-professorship at the Université Laval in Québec (1994/95), I really succeeded in finishing my long envisaged new and commented edition of the *Gospel of Philip*.[12] In a sense, I began my involvement in Nag Hammadi affairs with the Gospel of Philip. And therefore it was especially fascinating, near the end of my scholarly career, to return once more—and so intensively—to the topic of my youth. My point here is that during this year of final work on the *Gospel of Philip*, especially on the commentary, I felt always confronted with the phenomenon of "Fifty Years of Nag Hammadi Research" in a special, but important area.

It was such a long way from the beginning to our present state of knowledge! And I really enjoyed taking into consideration the enormous progress we made over the years. Let me pass in review some distinct stages and problems. There was the early edition of the text by W. C. Till (1963), prepared only on the basis of Pahor Labib's facsimile edition, and M. Krause's review of it with the correction of Till's readings based on his knowledge of the original in Cairo (1964). On the other hand, Till's edition was closely connected with a commentary written by R. McL. Wilson (1962). At almost the same time a parallel connection took place among two other pioneers of *Gos.*

---

[11] The topic of the hartenstein's dissertation, supervised by H.-G. Bethge, is Appearance Stories, especially from the Coptic material.

[12] Cf., as a preview of it, H.- M. Schenke, "Zur Exegese der Philippus-Evangeliums," *Coptology: Past, Present, and Future, Studies in Honour of Rodolphe Kasser*, ed. by S. Giversen, M. Krause, P. Nagel (Leuven: Orientalia Lovaniensia Analecta 61, 1994) 123-37. The title of the book itself will be, according to the pattern of our series: *Das Philippus-Evangelium (Nag Hammadi-Codex II,3) neu herausgegeben, übersetzt und erklärt von Hans-Martin Schenke* (TU; Berlin: Akademie-Verlag). It is already available on and from computers in Québec and Berlin, and in hard copy also in Claremont, CA.

*Phil.* research, C. J. de Catanzaro (1962) and J. Barns (1963). Afterwards a whole "chain" of dissertations was devoted to this fascinating document, with a special density in the late sixties and the early seventies, mostly coming from US universities:

| | | |
|---|---|---|
| G. L. Borchert | 1967 | Princeton Theological Seminary; |
| J.-E. Ménard | 1967 | Université de Strasbourg; |
| W. W. Isenberg | 1968 | University of Chicago; |
| H.-G. Gaffron | 1969 | Universität Bonn; |
| W. J. Stroud | 1971 | The Iliff School of Theology, Denver; |
| J.-M. Sevrin | 1972 | Université Catholique de Louvain; |
| E. T. Revolinski | 1978 | Harvard University, Cambridge, Mass.; |
| M. L. Turner | 1994 | University of Notre Dame. |

And finally, of course, we have to emphasize the presentation of the Coptic text by B. Layton in his edition of Nag Hammadi Codex II (1989) as an outstanding milestone in the history of research on *Gos. Phil.* Perhaps this milestone does not mark the end of the way, as many users seem to think, but certainly a point very near the end. The basic problems were the deciphering of mutilated letters on the fringes of the many lacunae of the papyrus leaves, under normal and black light, and the handling of these lacunae themselves, under the question whether or not it was possible to restore the text there. An additional problem was the analysis of the special kind of Sahidic Coptic in which *Gos. Phil.* and Codex II in general have been written .

Now, regarding my commentary on *Gos.Phil.*, future readers will be confronted with a general curiosity. The same person who has been blamed by many for having cut this text to pieces will be seen at work putting these pieces together again and so searching for the line, or lines, of thought running through the document. But there will also be found many single and minute curiosities, all resulting in the impression that "my *Gos.Phil.* is not yours." So, then, to conclude, I would like to give three examples.

1. Layton thought I was right, and I was not. P. 73, 23-27, corresponding to my #93b, reads in Isenberg's translation: "It was from that place that Jesus came and brought food. To those who so desired he gave [life, that] they might not die." My point here is the reconstruction of the text in the lacuna of the second sentence. It only seems to be plausible. But taken seriously, this reconstruction presents higher theological nonsense. So, instead of Layton's (and my earlier): ⲁϥϯ ⲛⲁⲩ [ⲛ̅ⲟⲩ]ⲱ[ⲛϩ], we should better read: ⲁϥϯ ⲛⲁⲩ [ⲉⲟⲩ]ⲱ[ⲙ̅]. This would result in the following modification

of Isenberg's translation of this second sentence: "To those who so desired he gave [something to eat, that] they might not die."

2. I (already) thought Layton was right, and (it finally turned out that) he was not. The passage 66.23-29 (= #64) can, in my opinion at least, only be understood as a diatribic homily on the Parable of the Two Sons (Mt 21:28-31a [that is, still without the answer which takes the one son to be better than the other one]). And this general understanding concerns especially the very last sentence, which reads according to Layton: ⲁⲩⲱ ⲡⲟⲩⲱϣ ⲁⲛ [ⲡⲉ] ⲛ̄ⲡⲉⲓⲣⲉ ⲁⲛ, and is understood according to Isenberg's translation, which is, however, practically identical with Layton's own in his *Gnostic Scriptures*: "and [it is] always a matter of the will, not the act." But this means a distortion of the text in more than one respect. Instead, L. Painchaud and I, returning to an old idea of Ménard, prefer to read and understand: ⲁⲩⲱ ⲡⲟⲩⲱϣ ⲁⲛ [ⲙ]ⲛ̄ ⲡⲉⲓⲣⲉ ⲁⲛ = "And (accordingly) it is not the will (alone) [a]nd not the act (alone) (that counts)" as the elliptical conclusion of the discussion.

3. An experiment in a hopeless case. The case I have in mind is the name of Sophia in the passage p. 59.31-60.1 (= #36). It is so difficult to understand, although there are only three letters missing at the beginning. The name/designation reads: [--- . . . ]ⲥⲉ ⲡⲉⲓ ⲛ̄ϩⲙⲟⲩ. So, my last and desperate attempt was to analyze what we have backwards from the end of the phrase. By this procedure we find: ϩⲙⲟⲩ "salt" preceded by ⲛ̄- (attributive particle) preceded by ⲡⲉⲓ "kiss" (noun) preceded by ⲥⲉ- "drink" (infinitive in the *status nominalis*). Taking all this together we arrive at "(to) drink kisses of salt". In order to transform this predicative expression into a denominative (Polotsky's "Benennung"), we only need to reconstruct as its basis in the lacuna a nominalizing element like: [--- ⲣⲉϥ] or: [--- ⲧ-ⲉⲧ]. But is the linguistic result [--- ⲣⲉϥ]ⲥⲉ ⲡⲉⲓ ⲛ̄ϩⲙⲟⲩ = "She who drinks salty kisses" also meaningful on the level of semantics? Is it a real possibility (for a woman) to drink salty kisses? I refuse to say, I don't know! For, at least, Hannah did so (1 Sam 1:1-18).

# THE ISSUE OF PRE-CHRISTIAN GNOSTICISM REVIEWED IN THE LIGHT OF THE NAG HAMMADI TEXTS

*Edwin M. Yamauchi*
Miami University

## INTRODUCTION

One of the first problems with a study of Gnosticism is agreeing upon a definition of Gnosticism.[1] Hans-Martin Schenke has defined Gnosticism as "a religious salvation movement of late antiquity in which the possibility of a negative attitude towards self and world is taken up in a special and unmistakable way and consolidated into a consistently world-negating world view, which expresses itself in characteristic word usage, metaphorical language, and artificial myths."[2] There are, however, problems with such a "broad" or vague definition, in particular if a trait like docetism[3] is used to infer the full Gnostic system.

A more detailed or "narrow" definition is preferable. Birger A. Pearson offers a list of ten characteristics, of which the first five are most significant: 1) "first, that adherents of Gnosticism regard *gnosis* ... as requisite to salvation. 2) "second, a characteristic *theology* according to which there is a transcendent supreme God beyond the god or powers responsible for the world in which we live." 3) "Third, a negative, radically dualist stance vis-à-vis the cosmos involves a *cosmology*, according to which the cosmos itself, having been created by an inferior and ignorant power, is a dark prison in which human souls are held captive." 4) "fourth, an *anthropology*, according to which the essential human being is constituted by his/her inner self, a divine spark that originated in the transcendent divine world and, by means of gnosis, can be released from the cosmic prison and can return to its heavenly origin." 5) "an *eschatology*, which applies not only to the salvation of the individual but to the salvation of all the

---

[1] See E. M. Yamauchi, *Pre-Christian Gnosticism,* 2nd ed. [hereafter *PCG*] (Grand Rapids: Baker Book House, 1983) 13-19.

[2] H.-M. Schenke, "The Problem of Gnosis," *SecCent* 3 (1983) 76.

[3] See E. Yamauchi, "The Crucifixion and Docetic Christology," *CTQ* 46 (1982) 1-20.

elect, and according to which the material cosmos itself will come to its fated end."[4]

## HISTORY OF RELIGIONS SCHOOL

The concept of a pre-Christian Gnosticism was first proposed by W. Anz in 1897, and then forcefully promoted by the *religionsgeschichtliche Schule* or "History-of-Religions School," most notably by Wilhelm Bousset (d. 1920) and Richard Reitzenstein (d. 1931).[5] Inspired by their works as well as by the publication of Mandaic texts by Mark Lidzbarski, Rudolf Bultmann outlined the classic model of the pre-Christian Gnostic Redeemer myth in a celebrated article published in 1925.[6] He and his influential students have interpreted many of the New Testament books such as the Pauline letters and the Gospel of John as both reacting against and being influenced by a pre-Christian Gnosticism.

Scholars such as Karl Wolfgang Tröger[7] continue to assume the existence of a pre-Christian Gnosticism which influenced the New Testament. The most thorough-going interpreter of the New Testament texts on the basis of a pre-Christian Gnosticism has been Walter Schmithals. He stresses the need of reasoning on the basis of a "hermeneutical circle," but surprisingly dismisses the Nag Hammadi texts as "einen relative späten Gnosis."[8]

A scholar who has reinterpreted Christianity on the basis of a pre-Christian Gnosticism is Jean Magne. He believes that he can demonstrate "how the Gnostic movement evolved into the Christian religious movement through a gradual rejudaization."[9] Among those who have recently interpreted Paul on the basis of a pre-Christian Gnosticism is Hyam Maccoby, who considers Paul's views a "moderate Gnosti-

---

[4] B. A. Pearson, "Introduction," in B. A. Pearson, ed., *Gnosticism, Judaism, and Egyptian Christianity* (Minneapolis: Fortress, 1990) 7-8.

[5] *PCG*, 21-24. See also E. Yamauchi, "History-of-Religions School." *New Dictionary of Theology*, ed. S. B. Ferguson and D. F. Wright (Leicester/Downers Grove, IL: InterVarsity Press, 1988) 308-09.

[6] R. Bultmann, "Die Bedeutung der neuerschlossenen mandäischen und manichäischen Quellen für das Verständnis des Johannesevangeliums," *ZNW* 24 (1925) 100-46.

[7] K. W. Tröger, "Christianity and Gnosticism," *TD* 34 (1987) 219-25, an article written in honor of Rudolf Bultmann's 100th birthday.

[8] W. Schmithals, *Neues Testament und Gnosis* (Darmstadt: Wissenschaftliche Buchgesellschaft, 1984) 11.

[9] J. Magne, *From Christianity to Gnosis and from Gnosis to Christianity* (Atlanta: Scholars Press, 1993) 6; cf. ch. 6.

cism."[10] He concludes, "Whether Colossians was written by Paul himself or by a disciple, its alignment is with the Gnostics, not against them."[11] To Maccoby, "Thus, Paul is basically a Gnostic thinker in his view of God, Satan and the Torah, though he has distinctive traits that differentiate him from other Gnostics."[12]

## THE DEAD SEA SCROLLS

In the initial excitement of the discovery of the Dead Sea Scrolls from Qumran in 1947 and their subsequent publication, some scholars sought to find evidence of a pre-Christian Gnosticism reflected in these texts. K.-G. Kuhn in an early article published in 1950 found evidence for Gnosticism in the scrolls' reference to "knowledge" and "mysteries": "This Gnostic structure of the new text can scarcely have sprung up from Jewish tradition."[13] André Dupont-Sommer, who was the first to suggest the Qumran community's identification with the Essenes, exclaimed, "As a matter of fact, the idea of Knowledge, Gnosis, impregnates the whole of Qumran thought and mysticism...."[14] Bultmann himself in the 1950's hailed the Dead Sea Scrolls as vindicating his views.[15]

But upon further study, it is quite clear that the dualistic world view of the Qumran community is quite different from the dualism of Gnosticism. The ethical dualism of Qumran and John's Gospel contrasts sharply with the cosmological dualism of the Gnostics.[16]

---

[10] H. Maccoby, *Paul and Hellenism* (London: SCM Press and Philadelphia: Trinity Press International, 1991) 37.

[11] Maccoby, 45.

[12] Maccoby, 52.

[13] K. G. Kuhn, "Die in Palästina gefundenen hebräischen Texte und das Neue Testament," *ZTK* 47 (1950) 211, cited by W. S. LaSor, *The Dead Sea Scrolls and the New Testament* (Grand Rapids: Eerdmans, 1972) 89.

[14] A. Dupont-Sommer, *The Essene Writings from Qumran* (Cleveland: World Publishing Co., 1962) 332.

[15] See my discussion in *PCG*, 151-52.

[16] See J. H. Charlesworth, "A Critical Comparison of the Dualism in 1QS 3:13-4:26 and the 'Dualism' Contained in the Gospel of John," *NTS* 15 (1968-69) 389-418; reprinted in J. H. Charlesworth, ed., *John and the Dead Sea Scrolls* (New York: Crossroads, 1991) 76-106; W. F. Albright, *New Horizons in Biblical Research* (London: Oxford University Press, 1966), ch. 3, "New Testament Research after the Discovery of the Dead Sea Scrolls"; see also E. Yamauchi, "Qumran and Colossae," *BSac* 121 (1964) 141-52.

## THE NAG HAMMADI TEXTS

The Nag Hammadi texts were discovered in 1945 only two years before the discovery of the Dead Sea Scrolls. Whereas the full publication of the latter, in part because of their fragmentary nature, has lagged and been embroiled in controversy, all of the Nag Hammadi texts were available in an English translation in 1977, thanks to the leadership of James M. Robinson and his team of translators. In the Introduction, Robinson pays tribute to his mentor, Rudolf Bultmann, Hans Jonas, and the History of Religions scholars: "One cannot fail to be impressed by the clairvoyance, the constructive power, the learned intution of scholars who, from limited and secondary sources, were able to produce working hypotheses that in fact worked so well."[17]

Robinson and likeminded scholars such as Douglas M. Parrott, George W. MacRae, Birger Pearson, Frederik Wisse, Charles W. Hedrick, and Gesine (Schenke) Robinson have adduced the following Nag Hammadi tractates as possible evidence of pre-Christian Gnosticism and its Redeemer Myth: a) *Eugnostos* (NHC III,3 and V,1), b) the *Apocalypse of Adam* (NHC V,5), c) the *Paraphrase of Shem* (NHC VII,1), and d) the *Trimorphic Protennoia* (NHC XIII,1). Now it should be noted that when some scholars use the term "pre-Christian" they do not use it in the expected chronological sense, but rather in a logical sense of what is prior to its later Christianization. C. W. Hedrick avers, "Hence, while there may currently exist no Gnostic text that can conclusively be dated into the first century CE so as to allow an argument for pre-Christian Gnosticism in a temporal sense, there is ample evidence for a "pre-Christian" Gnosticism in a logical sequential sense."[18]

### Eugnostos

One of the earliest scholars to have access to the Nag Hammadi texts, Jean Doresse, called attention as early as 1948 to the appropriation of

---

[17] J. M. Robinson, ed., *The Nag Hammadi Library in English* (New York: Harper & Row, 1977) 25.

[18] C. W. Hedrick, "Gnosticism," *Mercer Dictionary of the Bible*, ed. W. E. Mills et al. (Macon, GA: Mercer University Press, 1990) 335. Cf. C. W. Hedrick, "Introduction," *Nag Hammadi, Gnosticism, and Early Christianity*, ed. C. W. Hedrick and R. Hodgson, Jr. (Peabody, MA: Hendrickson, 1986) 9: "While there may be no extant gnostic manuscripts from the early first century CE to show that there existed a pre-Christian gnosticism in a chronological sense, these texts clearly demonstrate the existence of pre-Christian gnosticism."

*Eugnostos* by the *Sophia of Jesus Christ* (NHC III,4 and BG 8502).[19]
Here we seem to have an actual example of a non-Christian Gnostic
text which has been reused in a Christian Gnostic text, thus illustrating the priority of non-Christian Gnosticism.

Douglas Parrott believes that there is no significant evidence of
Christian influence in the composition of *Eugnostos*. He does not
believe that Eugnostos is to be identified with the copyist of the
*Gospel of Egyptians*, who clearly identifies himself as a Christian.
Parrott favors a date in the first century CE.[20] On the other hand, M.
Tardieu detects Christian influences and dates *Eugnostos* to the end
of the second century.[21] D. Trakatellis observes, "All the above,
without proving any direct literary dependence on the biblical texts,
render possible the assumption that Eugnostos is writing in a period
of time and a place where biblical vocabulary and Christian ideas
were widely circulated .... At any rate, the existence of christian [*sic*]
elements of whatever origin in the *Letter of Eugnostos* seems to
contradict the theory of its possible pre-christian origin."[22]

But leaving aside the issue of *Eugnostos'* date and of possible
Christian allusions, we may still ask about the nature of its Gnosticism. Parrott notes that *"Eugnostos,* then, cannot be considered
gnostic in any classic sense."[23] Elsewhere, while stressing the contributions of Egyptian religion to the document, Parrott observes, "As
has been noted, *Eugnostos* is in a sense a transition, or bridge
document. Its Gnosticism is an 'add on.'"[24] Pearson comments, "Its
presentation of the unknown God and the heavenly world, based in
large measure on speculative interpretations of Genesis, could easily
belong to a 'Jewish Gnostic' document."[25] Deirdre Good begins her
study with the following statement: "The present work assumes that
*Eugnostos* is a Gnostic writing: its apophatic theology (denial of

---

[19] See *PCG,* 104-07.

[20] D. M. Parrott, "Eugnostos and the Sophia of Jesus Christ," *ABD, vol. 2,* ed. D. N.
Freedman (Nashville: Abingdon Press, 1992) 668-69.

[21] M. Tardieu, *Écrits Gnostiques: Codex de Berlin* (Sources gnostiques et manichéennes 1; Paris: Éditions du Cerf, 1984) 66.

[22] D. Trakatellis, *The Transcendent God of Eugnostos,* trans. C. Sarelis (Brookline:
Holy Cross Orthodox Press, 1991) 17.

[23] D. M. Parrott, "Eugnostos the Blessed (III,*3* and V,*1*) and The Sophia of Jesus
Christ (III,*4* and BG 8502,*3*)," *The Nag Hammadi Library in English,* 3rd ed., ed. J. M.
Robinson (San Francisco: Harper & Row, 1988) 220.

[24] D. M. Parrott, "Gnosticism and Egyptian Religion," *NovT* 29 (1987) 91.

[25] B. A. Pearson, "Jewish Sources in Gnostic Literature," *Jewish Writings of the
Second Temple Period,* ed. M. E. Stone (Assen: Van Gorcum; Philadelphia: Fortress,
1984) 477.

qualities that can be ascribed to God in order to stress absolute otherness) is characteristic of Gnosticism, as is its criticism of a philosophical understanding of God. It does not, however, contain what many scholars see as the central myth of Gnosticism: ... In *Eugnostos*, there is no tragedy in the divine world with which Sophia/Ennoia or any other entity can be associated."[26]

But since when is an apophatic view of God an identifying mark of Gnosticism, rather than of Middle Platonic philosophy? Much of *Eugnostos'* teachings can be explicated in terms of Platonism as Roelof Van Den Broek points out.[27] *Eugnostos* is not radical in its rejection of the world, as the created world truly reflects the upper aeons, so that the invisible things can be known from the visible world (*Eugnostos* 74).[28] As Good has argued, there is no Fall of Sophia in *Eugnostos*, although the Sophia of Jesus Christ does have such a concept. Jerry L. Sumney after commenting, "At this point we may wonder whether anything in Eug makes it a particularly Gnostic work,"[29] cites the following elements: 1) the multiplication of beings in the higher aeons, 2) the personalization of the divine powers, and 3) the creation of the world by a creature. But although these elements might conceivably allow for a later radicalization, they do not serve as evidence for "a revolt against the cosmos as the primary motivator of earliest Gnostic speculation," as Sumney contends.[30] In other words, *Eugnostos* does not measure up to the definition of Gnosticism established by Pearson; it can only be held to be Gnostic in a Procrustean manner.

## Apocalypse of Adam

George W. MacRae believes that the *Apocalypse of Adam* is "independent of Christian influence, and believes that it can be dated between the first and the fourth centuries CE, probably earlier rather than later." As to its polemic against baptism, he suggests, "Since nothing in the text clearly suggests Christian baptism, it is possible that the document reflects an encounter between Jewish practitioners

---

[26] D. J. Good, *Reconstructing the Tradition of Sophia in Gnostic Literature* (Atlanta: Scholars Press, 1987) 1.

[27] R. Van Den Broek, "Jewish and Platonic Speculations in Early Alexandrian Theology: Eugnostos, Philo, Valentinus, and Origen," *The Roots of Egyptian Christianity*, ed. B. Pearson and J. Goehring (SAC; Philadelphia: Fortress, 1986) 190-203.

[28] One is reminded of Rom 1:20 and Heb 11:3.

[29] J. L. Sumney, "The Letter of Eugnostos and the Origins of Gnosticism," *NovT* 31 (1989) 179.

[30] Sumney, 181.

of baptism and sectarian gnostics who diverge from them on this issue in particular."[31] Likewise Kurt Rudolph asserts, "This document works together very skilfully several traditions and is certainly a witness of early Gnosis, since it still stands very near to the Jewish apocalyptic literature and has no Christian tenor."[32] After listing several possible parallels between the Illuminator and Christ, Parrott in a new introduction in the third edition of the *Nag Hamadi Library in English* concludes: "It is difficult to see any compelling reason to identify the figure with Christ."[33] Hedrick and other scholars regard the theme of the illuminator's punishment as having no necessary reference to Christ, but explain this on the basis of "pre-Christian Jewish traditions of the persecution and subsequent exaltation of the righteous man as reflected in Wis 1-6 and Isa 52-53."[34]

As to the date of the *Apocalypse of Adam* and its composition, Hedrick has analysed the *Apocalyspe* as originally based on two sources, the first standing near the border between Jewish apocalypticism and Gnosticism, and the second reflecting a developed Gnostic mythology. Hedrick believes that the two sources were edited perhaps in the Transjordan sometime prior to the beginning of the second century.[35]

Of the *Apocalypse of Adam* Pearson concludes, "Typologically it is a 'pre-Christian' text inasmuch as it adheres to a very early type of Gnosticism, in which Jewish features are clearly displayed, and no positive Christian influence is clearly present. Nevertheless, it may be a comparatively late document (second or third century?) ...."[36] Pearson also holds, "Even if the *Apocalypse of Adam* were chronologically late, it would represent a form of Jewish Gnosticism which

---

[31] G. MacRae, "Apocalypse of Adam," in J. H. Charlesworth, ed., *The Old Testament Pseudepigrapha* (Garden City, NY: Doubleday, 1983) I, 709.; idem, "The Apocalypse of Adam," *Nag Hammadi Codices V,2-5 and VI with Papyrus Berolinensis 8502,1 and 4*, ed. D. M. Parrott (Leiden: E. J. Brill, 1979) 152. Cf. H. Koester, *Introduction to the New Testament II: History and Literature of Early Christianity* (Philadelphia: Fortress, 1982) 211.

[32] K. Rudolph, *Gnosis* (tr. R. McL. Wilson; San Francisco: Harper & Row, 1983) 135.

[33] *NHLE*, 278.

[34] C. W. Hedrick, "Adam, Apocalypse of," *ABD*, vol. 1, 11.

[35] C. W. Hedrick, *The Apocalypse of Adam: A Literary and Source Analysis* (SBLDS 46; Chico, CA: Scholars Press, 1980).

[36] Pearson, "Jewish Sources in Gnostic Literature," 473-74.

resisted the kind of Christianization we have noted in the case of the *Apocryphon of John*."[37]

Source B contains a remarkable passage of thirteen numbered kingdoms which are faulty explanations of the Illuminator. Hedrick suggests that this is "traditional material that was later incorporated into the present document."[38] Parrott suggests that it originated in an Egyptian milieu.[39]

Not all scholars agree that the *Apocalypse of Adam* is an early representative of non-Christian Gnosticism.[40] Françoise Morard believes that it is a Sethian Gnostic text which has been influenced by Christianity.[41] She maintains that though the allusions are veiled, nonetheless there are certain references to Christianity.[42] She believes that the passage about the punishment of the flesh of the Illuminator (77.16-18) is a clear reference to Christ.[43]

The first editor, A. Böhlig, discerned references to Mithras in the series of kingdoms. Böhlig finds such references in kingdoms seven, eight, ten, and eleven.[44] A scholar who has recently highlighted the Iranian elements, both from Zoroastrianism and Mithraism, in the tractate is Andrew Welburn.[45] Welburn suggests that the frequent references to the "virgin birth of the Illuminator" (Kingdoms 3, 4, 6, and possibly 1) are best explained as allusions to the stories of the

---

[37] B. A. Pearson, "The Problem of 'Jewish Gnostic' Literature," *Nag Hammadi, Gnosticism, and Early Christianity*, ed. C. Hedrick and R. Hodgson, Jr. (Peabody, MA: Hendrickson Publishers, 1986) 33.

[38] Hedrick, "Adam, Apocalypse of," 11.

[39] D. M. Parrott, "The Thirteen Kingdoms of the Apocalypse of Adam: Origin, Meaning and Significance," *NovT* 31 (1989) 67-87.

[40] See *PCG*, 109-11, 218-19. See especially G. M. Shellrude, "The Apocalypse of Adam: Evidence for a Christian Provenience," *Gnosis and Gnosticism*, ed. M. Krause (Leiden: E. J. Brill, 1981) 93-94.

[41] F. Morard, *L'Apocalypse d'Adam (NH V,5)* (BCNH, Section "Textes" 15; Québec: Les Presses de l'Université Laval, 1985).

[42] Morard, 7, "Quant au traité lui-même, notre commentaire montrera, je l'espère, qu'il n'est pas possible de le considérer comme une oeuvre préchrétienne et que, pour être voilés, les allusions au christianisme n'en sont pas moins certaines."

[43] Morard, 99: "C'est ici un des passages du texte qui paraît postuler le plus ouvertement une origine de l'écrit contemporaine de l'éclosion—ou de peu postérieure à la première diffusion—du christianisme." Cf. 100, "Le châtiment de l'Envoyé dans sa chair ne peut donc être, à nos yeux, qu'inspiré par l'événement chrétien, sans que pour autant l'auteur soit lui-même un chrétien—du moins un chrétien de la Grande Église d'alors."

[44] A. Böhlig, "Die Adamsapokalypse aus Codex V von Nag Hammadi als Zeugnis jüdisch-iranischer Gnosis," *OrChr* 48 (1964) 47-48.

[45] A. Welburn, "Iranian Prophetology and the Birth of the Messiah: the Apocalypse of Adam,"*ANRW* II.25.4 (1988) 4752-94.

Saoshyants or "redeemers," who were born from Zoroaster's seed, which had been hidden in a lake.[46]

In a more general monograph, which is informed by the ideas of Rudolf Steiner,[47] Welburn also discerns such Iranian influence in the reference to the Magi episode in Matthew.[48] According to Welburn, "At any rate, the eschatological star-child was in some circles also the reappearing Zarathushtra, and in Christian versions he becomes Jesus."[49]

Welburn prefers to see the incarnations of the thirteen kingdoms in the *Apocalypse of Adam* as those of the prophet Zarathushtra (Zoroaster) rather than Mithra, by noting the assimilation of Zarathustra to Mithra in Parthian times. He refers to the tradition of "Zaratas, who appeared in Babylonia[50] and was honoured as the founder of the Mithraic cult in its syncretistic form...."[51]

But there are many things amiss with Welburn's use of Iranian traditions to explicate Matthew and the *Apocalypse of Adam*. First of all, though the word *magos* was originally an Iranian word, it came to mean "astrologer" and is clearly used in this sense in Matthew.[52] To support his comments on the connection between the magi and Iran, he appeals to the medieval Syrian *Chronicle of Zuqnin*. The earliest reference to Zoroaster as the source of the prediction about the star and savior is found in Theodore bar Konai (9th cent. CE).[53] The view that Zoroaster was the founder of Mithraism is found in Porphyry (3rd cent. CE).[54] The traditions about Zoroaster's seed giving rise to the Saoshyants are taken from late Pahlavi works which were not

---

[46] Ibid., 4757.

[47] A. Welburn, *The Beginnings of Christianity: Essene Mystery, Gnostic Revelation and the Christian Vision* (Edinburgh: Floris Books, 1991) 26-29.

[48] Welburn, 86.; idem, "Iranian Prophetology," 4785: "On the other hand, a certain stratum of Christian tradition held on to Zoroastrian connections, as is shown by the visit of the Magi in Matthew ..."

[49] Welburn, "Iranian Prophetology," 4789.

[50] On this Pythagorean tradition, see M. Boyce and F. Grenet, *A History of Zoroastrinaism, Vol. 3: Zoroastrianism under Macedonian and Roman Rule* (Leiden: E. J. Brill, 1991) 523-24.

[51] Welburn, "Iranian Prophetology," 4774.

[52] See my *Persia and the Bible* (Grand Rapids: Baker Book House, 1990), ch. 13; see also my "The Magi Episode," *Christos, Chronos, and Kairos*, ed. J. Vardaman and E. Yamauchi (Winona Lake, IN: Eisenbrauns, 1989) 15-39.

[53] Boyce and Grenet, *A History of Zoroastrinaism III*, 450.

[54] Ibid., 548.

composed until the 9th-10th centuries CE![55] Though there are Greek traditions about Zoroaster, who appeared as Zaratas, there has been no evidence of Zoroastrianism found in Mesopotamia.[56]

I agree with Böhlig that there is at least one clear allusion to a Mithraic motif in the eighth kingdom: "A cloud came upon the earth. It enveloped a rock. He originated from it" (80, 21-25). The rock birth of Mithras is a common feature of Mithraic reliefs. Though Mithra(s) was an ancient Indo-Aryan god, who is attested as early as a treaty between the Hittites and the Hurrians (14th cent. BCE), it was not until the late first century CE that we have evidence of the Roman mystery religion, which we call Mithraism. No mithraea were found, for example, at Pompeii or Herculaneum, which were buried by Mt. Vesuvius in CE 79. There is an allusion to Mithras dragging a bull into a cave in Statius (CE 80). Some Mithraic scholars do not believe that the development of a Roman Mithraism antedates the reign of Hadrian.[57] Though we have numerous examples of Mithraic rock birth motifs attested in Europe, we have none from Egypt. Robert Bull found a mithraeum at Caesarea, which is dated to the fourth cent. CE.[58] The only Mithraic site in the Near East which attests the rock birth motif is Dura-Europos, where the mithraeum is dated to CE 168.

What are the implications of this evidence for the dating of the *Apocalypse of Adam*? It would appear to me that such a reference to Mithras' rock birth cannot be dated before the late second century CE, which in turn would date the composition of the *Apocalypse* even later. Scott Carroll has also pointed out that the Solomonic tradition reflected in the *Apocalypse of Adam* belongs to what he calls the "third stage of development (late second through the fourth century)."[59] Now though some scholars would maintain that the late date of the *Apocalypse* does not matter, it does make more probable the

---

[55] On the lateness of many key Zoroastrian documents see E. Yamauchi, "Religions of the Biblical World: Persia," *ISBE*, vol. 4, rev. ed, ed. G. W. Bromiley (Grand Rapids: Eerdmans, 1988) 123-29; idem, *Persia and the Bible*, ch. 12. On the complete dearth of Persian religious texts from the critical Parthian Era (250 CE - 225 CE) see my review of E. Yarshater, ed., *The Cambridge History of Iran III: The Seleucid, Parthian and Sasanian Periods* in *American Historical Review* 89 (1984) 1055-56.

[56] Boyce and Grenet, 357.

[57] See E. Yamauchi, "*The Apocalypse of Adam*, Mithraism, and Pre-Christian Gnosticism," *Études Mithraiques* (Leiden: E. J. Brill, 1978) 555-56.

[58] L. M. Hopfe and G. Lease, "The Caesarea Mithraeum," *BA* 38 (1975) 1-10.

[59] S. T. Carroll, "*The Apocalypse of Adam* and Pre-Christian Gnosticism," *VC* 44 (1990) 273.

argument that references to the suffering of the Illuminator are indeed allusions to Christ.

## Paraphrase of Shem

Though he does not assert that the Paraphrase of Shem is chronologically a pre-Christian document, Frederik Wisse claims that "there is no obvious Christian material" in the tractate.[60] Its sharp polemic against water baptism can be interpreted as a polemic not against Christians but against some Jewish baptismal sect. Well, we do have clear evidence of a Jewish "baptismal" sect in the Jordan Valley. We have the Dead Sea Scrolls from Qumran, whom most but not all scholars identify with the Essenes described by Josephus, and Philo. But it is rather difficult to frame the anti-baptismal polemic of the Nag Hammadi texts with respect to the ritual lustrations of Qumran, so we must think of some other Jewish sect who valued "baptism" in a more central salvific role.

Several scholars have noted that the passage about the baptism of Soldas (30.32f.) appears to be a clear reference to the baptism of John the Baptist.[61] Wisse's non-Christian interpretation of the *Paraphrase of Shem* is opposed by other scholars such as Barbara Aland[62] and Jean-Marie Sevrin.[63] Sevrin states, "The description of the baptism of the savior Derdekeas in the river by the demon Soldas (clearly inspired by the synoptic narratives of the baptism of Jesus [Mark 1:19]), furnishes the key of this virulent antibaptismal polemic."[64] Christopher Tuckett agrees with this interpretation: "There are also some striking references to baptism in this text. 37.19ff.... looks very

[60] F. Wisse, "Shem, Paraphrase of," *ABD*, vol. 5, 1196.

[61] J.-M. Sevrin, "À propos de la 'Paraphrase de Sem,'" *Le Muséon* 88 (1975) 90; K. Rudolph, "Coptica-Mandaica," *Essays on the Nag Hammadi Texts in Honour of Pahor Labib*, ed. M. Krause (Leiden: E. J. Brill, 1975) 210; J.-D. Dubois, "Contribution à l'interprétation de la Paraphrase de Sem (NH VII.1), *Deuxième Journée d'Études Coptes*, ed. Jean-Marc Rosenstiehl (Louvain: Éditions Peeters, 1986) 155-56.

[62] B. Aland, "Die Paraphrase als Form gnostischer Verkündigung," *Nag Hammadi and Gnosis*, ed. R. McL. Wilson (Leiden: E. J. Brill, 1978) 90, n. 43: "Zur Frage, ob die Paraphrase des Sêem christlich ist oder nicht, nur so viel: Mir scheint keinerlei Schwierigkeit zu bestehen, sie als aus christlichen Milieu erwachsen zu verstehen ...."

[63] J.-M. Sevrin, "À propos de la 'Paraphrase de Sem,'" *NovT* 12 (1970) 130-40.

[64] J.-M. Sevrin, "Les rites et la gnose, d'après quelques textes gnostiques coptes," *Gnosticisme et Monde Hellénistique*, ed. J. Ries et al. (Louvain-la-Neuve: Institut Orientaliste, 1982) 441.

much as if it is directed against 'orthodox' Christian claims about water baptism."[65]

What should be noted is the addendum by Michel Roberge to Frederick Wisse's introduction to the tractate in the third edition of the *Nag Hammadi Library in English* [hereafter *NHLE*].[66] In contrast to Wisse's interpretation, Roberge speaks of "the baptism of the Savior and his ascent on the occasion of his crucifixion (30.4-40.31)."[67] In a study of the anthropology of the tractate, Roberge identifies the symbolism of the Intellect as a fish, as a clear reference to Christianity.[68] In a detailed study Roberge interprets the entire tractate as an interpretation of the crucifixion from a docetic perspective, focusing especially on 39.24b-40.3. He notes that a key word, the verb πήσσειν, which Wisse translated "to establish," is regularly used for affixing victims to the cross. He interprets the demon Soldas as representing the earthly Jesus who is in opposition to the heavenly Christ, i.e. Derdekeas. The decapitation of Rebouel (40.4-31a) then represents a polemic against the Great Church.[69] Roberge concludes, "This part of the tractate contains a harsh antibaptismal polemic, probably directed against the Great Church."[70]

J.-D. Dubois agrees in many respects with Sevrin, though the lack of New Testament citations inclines him to view the tractate's polemic as aimed not against the Great Church but against a sect of Jewish-Christian baptists, shedding light on the antecedents of Manichaeism.[71] Rather than a polemic against a Jewish baptismal sect, it is indeed easier to compare the anti-baptismal rhetoric of the *Paraphrase of Shem* with the protestations of Mani against the Elchasaites, a Jewish Christian sect, as now revealed in the Cologne

---

[65] C. M. Tuckett, *Nag Hammadi and the Gospel Tradition* (Edinburgh: T. & T. Clark, 1986) 18.

[66] James M. Robinson, ed., *The Nag Hammadi Library in English* (San Francisco: Harper & Row, 1988).

[67] M. Roberge, "The Paraphrase of Shem (VII,*1*)," *NHLE*, 339.

[68] M. Roberge, "Anthropogonie et anthropologie dans la *Paraphrase de Sem* (NH VII,1), *Le Muséon* 99 (1986) 244.

[69] M. Roberge, "La crucifixion du sauveur dans la Paraphrase de Sem (NH VII,1)," *Actes du IVe Congrès Copte*, ed. M. Rassart-Debergh & J. Ries (Louvain-la-Neuve: Université Catholique de Louvain, Institut Orientaliste, 1992) 381-87.

[70] Roberge, *NHLE*, 341.

[71] Dubois, "Contribution," 160: "Par delà la polémique baptismale, l'esquisse de ces quelques perspectives suffisent à indiquer la caducité des positions de F. Wisse dans son article sur la figure du Sauveur dans la *PSem*. La *PSem* constitue un document unique, mais significatif de polémiques contre des milieux, judéo-chrétiens baptistes. À ce titre c'est un document neuf qui jette une lumière sur les antécédents du manichéisme."

Mani Codex, published in 1970.[72] A. Henrichs reports that Mani reacted against their baptisms as follows, "The daily baptisms are equally useless. In fact, they attest to a daily defilement of the body.... The only true purity is that through Gnosis."[73]

Several other Nag Hammadi tractates contain Gnostic polemic against mere water baptism, which is clearly indicated as the Church's rite. Why should the polemic of the *Paraphrase of Shem* and of the *Apocalypse of Adam*, despite their veiled language, be any different and be understood as a polemic against a Jewish baptismal sect whose attestation is as murky as pre-Christian Gnosticism itself?[74]

### Trimorphic Protennoia.

As we have the text of the *Trimorphic Protennoia* today, there can be no question but that it is a text of Christian Gnosticism, but a number of scholars have argued that this represents only a later redaction. Gesine (Schenke) Robinson interprets the *Trimorphic Protennoia* as basically a document of non-Christian Gnosticism. She would "postulate an identical gnostic world of thought for *Trim. Prot.* and the Logos hymn lying behind the Prologue of John."[75] She maintains, "For it is not the last, extant copy of *Trimorphic Protennoia* with its redactional interpolations that is important, but rather its basic substance, which is no doubt pre-Christian, if not perhaps in a chronological sense, at least in terms of the history of tradition."[76]

John D. Turner suggests a four-stage development: 1) the first stage is represented by the *Grundform* of the non-Christian Pronoia hymn found in the ending of the longer version of the *Apocryphon of John,* 2) long aretalogies of self-predication were added, 3) the expanded version was accomodated to the developed cosmogonical myth of the Sethians, 4) finally the polemical Christian Sethian

---

[72] A. Henrichs, "Mani and the Babylonian Baptists: A Historical Confrontation," *Harvard Studies in Classical Philology* 77 (1973) 50.

[73] Ibid., 57. See R. Cameron and A. J. Dewey, trans., *The Cologne Mani Codex* (SBLTT 15; Chico: Scholars Press, 1979).

[74] Cf. F. Morard, "L'Apocalypse d'Adam du Codex V de Nag Hammadi et sa polémique anti-baptismale," *RevScRel* 51 (1977) 214-33.

[75] G. Robinson, "Trimorphic Protennoia," *ABD*, vol. 6, 663-64.

[76] G. Robinson, "The Trimorphic Protennoia and the Prologue of the Fourth Gospel," *Gnosticism & the Early Christian World*, ed. J. E. Goehring, et al. (Sonoma: Polebridge, 1990) 45.

material which draws on Johannine language was added.[77] More succinctly, Turner summarizes his view as follows: "My own position is that *Trimorphic Protennoia* underwent superficial Christianization in its second stage of redaction, but specific and polemical Christianization in its third stage of redaction. The superficial resemblances to the Johannine prologue scattered throughout *Trimorphic Protennoia* are to be explained by the emergence of both texts from gnosticizing oriental sapiental [*sic*] traditions at home in first-century Syria and Palestine."[78] Craig Evans also believes that both the Prologue and the *Trimorphic Protennoia* drew from a common Jewish Wisdom tradition.[79]

In contrast to the position of Gesine Robinson and James M. Robinson, a number of scholars have concluded that the parallels between the *Trimorphic Protennoia* and the Prologue of John are best explained on the basis of the latter's priority. Yvonne Janssens in her editions of the *Protennoia* in 1974 and in 1978 insisted that the parallels indicated a dependence of the *Protennoia* upon John.[80] However, in her 1983 contribution to the R. McL. Wilson Festschrift, she is willing to leave the last word to specialists in the Fourth Gospel.[81] But she does raise an important point for those who accept a later Christianization: "But it is precisely in the 'Christian' passages that the 'kinship' with the Johannine Prologue is most marked!"[82]

A recent study which has challenged the advocates of the view that the *Trimorphic Protennoia*, when divested of later Christian layers, preserves evidence of pre-Christian Gnosticism, has been contributed by Alastair H. B. Logan. Instead of verbal parallels, Logan compares the myth of the *Trimorphic Protennoia* as a whole with the Gnostic systems reported in Irenaeus, *Adversus haereses* 1.29 and the

---

[77] J. D. Turner, "Trimorphic Protennoia: Introduction and Translation," *Nag Hammadi Codices XI, XII, XIII*, ed. C. W. Hedrick (NHS 28; Leiden: E. J. Brill, 1990) 511-522.

[78] J. D. Turner, "Sethian Gnosticism: A Literary History," *Nag Hammadi, Gnosticism, and Early Christianity*, ed. C. W. Hedrick and R. Hodgson, Jr., 65, n. 4.

[79] C. A. Evans, "On the Prologue of John and the *Trimorphic Protennoia*," *NTS* 27 (1981) 395-401.

[80] Y. Janssens, "Le Codex XIII de Nag Hammadi," *Le Muséon* 7 (1974) 341-413; idem, *La prôtennoia trimorphe (NH, XIII,1)* (BCNH 4; Québec: Laval University Press, 1978); idem, "Une source gnostique du Prologue," *L'Evangile de Jean: sources, redaction, théologie*, ed. M. de Jonge (BETL 44; Gembloux: Duculot, 1977) 355-58.

[81] Y. Janssens, "The Trimorphic Protennoia and the Fourth Gospel," *The New Testament and Gnosis*, ed. A. H. B. Logan and A. J. M. Wedderburn (Edinburgh: T. & T. Clark, 1983) 229-43.

[82] Ibid., 242.

*Apocryphon of John* as well as the Johannine Prologue. His conclusion is that "the *Protennoia* is not Bultmann's hypothetical pre-Christian Gnostic *Grundschrift* for the Prologue but in fact presupposes and develops the form of the Christian Gnostic myth found in the *Apocryphon* which is itself dependent on John...."[83]

Advocates of a pre-Christian core to the *Trimophic Protennoia* have pointed out parallels with the concluding Pronoia hymn in the Apocryphon of John. But Michel Tardieu, editor of a recent synoptic version of the *Apocryphon of John*, believes that the Pronoia hymn is itself not a pre-Christian document but derives from a dissident esoteric circle within the Johannine community ca. 120 CE. Tardieu believes that the Pronoia hymn is a Gnostic pastiche of the Prologue adopted by the redactor of the *Trimorphic Protennoia*.[84]

## CONCLUSIONS

The Nag Hammadi texts have hardly settled the question of the origin of Gnosticism, though they have led many scholars to recognize their undeniable Jewish elements. James M. Robinson in his 1981 presidential address to the Society of Biblical Literature conceded: "pre-Christian Gnosticism as such is hardly attested in a way to settle the debate once and for all."[85] In a similar fashion George W. MacRae declared, "And even if we are on solid ground in some cases in arguing that the original works represented in the (Nag Hammadi) library are much older than the extant copies, we are still unable to postulate plausibly any pre-Christian dates."[86] Birger Pearson maintains, "Although it is true that we do not have any *primary* textual evidence for Gnosticism earlier than the second century, it need not be concluded that Gnosticism could not have existed as early as the first century."[87]

Scholars who have assumed the pre-Christian origin of Gnosticism have failed to present a plausible scenario of its beginnings. Helmut Koester, for example, writes: "Was there an original Gnostic religion with its original pre-Christian myth? The answer to this question must

---

[83] A. H. B. Logan, "John and the Gnostics," *JSNT* 43 (1991) 59.

[84] As reported by Logan, 58.

[85] J. M. Robinson, "Jesus: From Easter to Valentinus (Or to the Apostles' Creed)," *JBL* 101 (1982) 5.

[86] G. W. MacRae, "Nag Hammadi and the New Testament," *Gnosis: Festschrift for Hans Jonas*, ed. B. Aland (Göttingen: Vandenhoeck & Ruprecht, 1978) 146-47.

[87] B. A. Pearson, "Philo, Gnosis and the New Testament," in Logan and Wedderburn, *The New Testament and Gnosis*, 85, n. 5.

be negative."[88] Elsewhere he admits, "The history of Gnosticism in its early stages during the period of early Christianity cannot be identified with the history of a tangible sociological phenomenon."[89] Hans-Martin Schenke, who has been the chief advocate of a pre-Christian Sethian Gnostic system, has now conceded: "Almost two decades ago, these general considerations were my starting point in a special attempt to trace the majority of the gnostic systems back to a single system or point of origin that could be understood as the primitive gnostic system. Such an attempt now has to be abandoned."[90] Michael Williams after surveying various theories which have been proposed for the origins of Gnosticism concludes that with regard to the demonizing of the demiurge, "the cumulative evidence seems actually to be pointing away from the probability that we will ever find some single socio-political or socio-economic 'smoking gun' that constituted the 'crisis' responsible for this innovation."[91]

Since the Mandaic, Manichaean, Syriac, Hebrew, New Testament, Patristic, and even the Coptic texts, to which scholars have appealed for evidence of pre-Christian Gnosticism, have not yielded convincing evidence of a developed Gnosticism prior to Christianity, I may be perhaps pardoned for wondering if pre-Christian Gnosticism is not just a phantom figure which was created by brilliant German scholars who let loose a will-o'-the wisp chimaera, which many have sought and which some believe they have seen reflected in the ambiguous evidence of the Nag Hammadi texts. Despite the important new evidence provided by these texts not a few scholars[92] have remained

---

[88] H. Koester, "The History-of-Religions School, Gnosis, and Gospel of John," *StTh* 40 (1986) 131.

[89] Koester, *Introduction to the New Testament*, vol. 2, 207.

[90] Schenke, "The Problem, " 86.

[91] M. A. Williams, "The Demonizing of the Demiurge: The Innovation of Gnostic Myth," *Innovation in Religious Traditons*, ed. M. A. Williams et al. (Berlin: de Gruyter, 1992) 95.

[92] See for example: O. Betz, "Das Problem der Gnosis seit der Entdeckung der Texte von Nag Hammadi," reprinted in his *Jesus, der Herr der Kirche* (Tübingen: J. C. B. Mohr [P. Siebeck], 1990) 361-85; U. Bianchi, "Le gnosticisme et les origines du christianisme," *Gnosticisme et monde hellénistique*, ed. J. Ries et al., 228; idem, "Some Reflections on the Greek Origins of Gnostic Ontology and the Christian Origin of the Gnostic Saviour," in Logan and Wedderburn, *The New Testament and Gnosis*, 43; I. P. Culianu, "The Angels of the Nations and the Origins of Gnostic Dualism," in *Studies in Gnosticism and Hellenistic Religions*, ed. R. van Den Broek and J. Vermaseren, 79-80; I. P. Culianu, *The Tree of Gnosis* (San Francisco: HarperSan Francisco, 1990) 8, 29, 51; J. Duchesne-Guillemin, "Gnosticisme et Dualisme," *Gnosticisme et monde hellénistique*, ed. J. Ries et al., 89-101; idem, "On the Origin of Gnosticism," *A Green Leaf: Papers in Honour of Professor Jes P. Asmussen*, ed. J. Duchesne-Guillemin and D. Marcotte (Leiden: E. J. Brill, 1988) 349-63; G. Filoramo, "Sulle Origini dello Gnosticismo," *Rivista*

unconvinced that they demonstrate the existence of a full-fledged Gnosticism with a redeemer myth prior to Christianity.

di Storia e Letteratura Religiosa 39 (1993) 493-510; S. Pétrement, A Separate God: The Christian Origins of Gnosticism (tr. C. Harrison; San Francisco: HarperSan Francisco, 1990); Alan F. Segal, Two Powers in Heaven: Early Rabbinic Reports about Christianity and Gnosticism (SJLA 25; Leiden: E. J. Brill, 1978); idem, The Other Judaisms of Late Antiquity (BJS 127; Atlanta: Scholars Press, 1987) 1-40; M. Simonetti, "Alcune riflessioni sul rapporto tra gnosticismo e cristianesimo," Vetera Christanorum 28 (1991) 337-74.

# THE THOUGHT PATTERN OF GNOSTIC MYTHOLOGIZERS AND THEIR USE OF BIBLICAL TRADITIONS

*Gerard P. Luttikhuizen*
University of Groningen

In his paper "The reign of John Hyrcanus as the Seedbed for Sethian Gnosticism" read at the 1994 meeting of the Nag Hammadi and Gnosticism Section, Douglas Parrott recalled that it was then the 30th anniversary of the famous SBL exchange between Gilles Quispel and Hans Jonas over the origins of Gnosticism.[1] Whereas Quispel wished to make it clear that the Gnostic religion originated within Judaism, Jonas, while conceding that the Gnostics made ample use of Jewish materials, emphasized the anti-Jewish spirit of this use and at least wondered whether Jews themselves could have had such a motivation and have originated such a movement.

## I

In his paper Parrott takes the side of Quispel, although he appears to have been inspired above all by a remark made by Jonas. (Jonas concluded his response with the observation that, if Gnosticism could be shown to have been engendered within Judaism, this would add the last touch to the kind of violent and defiant impulse he saw at work behind this religious movement. I come back to Jonas's characterization of the Gnostic religion below.)

Parrott observes that the issue whether Gnosticism began within Judaism, as a revolt against Judaism, has never been resolved. His paper is an attempt to find a period in Jewish history when such a revolt could have occurred. He focuses on the persecution of Hellenized Jews during the reign of John Hyrcanus I and deems it possible that in this period a group of Jews revolted against the traditional formulation of their faith. In Parrott's view, this revolt of Jews against Jews might have been the seedbed of Sethian Gnosticism.

---

[1] G. Quispel, "Gnosticism and the New Testament," *The Bible in Modern Scholarship*, ed. J.P.Hyatt (Nashville: Abingdon Press 1965) 252-71; H. Jonas, "Response to G. Quispel's 'Gnosticism and the New Testament,'" ibid., 279-93.

It is not my intention to enter into a direct argument with Parrott's paper, which, I hope, will soon be published, and which I expect will receive due attention. The question of whether or not the Gnostic religion originated within a Jewish milieu has been an important and much-debated issue during the past 50 years and still remains a vexing question. In this respect, the issue fits well, too, within the theme of the Nag Hammadi and Gnosticism Section of the SBL this year.

In his attempt to remove doubts on the side of Jonas, Parrott actually strengthens the view put forward by Quispel. I would like to contribute to this discussion by more clearly taking the other side. Although it will appear that I have some serious problems with Jonas's argument and, besides, that I approach the issue from a different point of view, I agree with him that a Jewish origin of the Gnostic religion is highly doubtful.

My paper is called "The Thought Pattern of Gnostic Mythologizers and Their Use of Biblical Traditions." As may be apparent from this title, my interest is focused on Gnostic mythologizers not only as producers of texts but also, and even more so, as users and *readers* of texts (biblical texts or, for that matter, second- and third-hand interpretations of biblical texts, but also post-biblical Jewish and early Christian texts and traditions). In fact I was confronted for the first time with a specifically Gnostic use of earlier tradition—in this case New Testament texts or, more precisely, early Christian texts that were later to become parts of the canonical New Testament—when, some years ago, I studied *The Letter of Peter to Philip* in Codex VIII. The passage in question still seems to me most relevant.

I will first briefly discuss this short section of *The Letter of Peter to Philip* and juxtapose it to interpretations of early Christian traditions in a few other Christian Gnostic writings. Next I will pose the question of how we should explain this utilization of earlier traditions and confront the results of this examination to the use of Jewish scripture and tradition by Gnostic mythopoets. It is my contention that their adoption and adaptation of Jewish materials can be explained in basically the same way as the Gnostic use of early Christian traditions.

## II

*The Letter of Peter to Philip* includes a sermon by Peter addressed to "his disciples." The body of this short speech is a citation of early kerygmatic formulae relating to the passion of Jesus. The traditional profession of faith is followed by a Gnostic interpretation. I quote:

And he (Peter) was filled with holy spirit and spoke in this way:
"Our illuminator, Jesus, [came] down
And he was crucified.
And he wore a crown of thorns
And he put on a purple robe
And he was [crucified] upon a cross
And he was buried in a tomb
And he rose from the dead.
My brothers, Jesus is a stranger to this suffering. But we are the ones who have
suffered through the transgression of the mother" etc. (139.14-23).

The remarkable thing of course is that a traditional Christian creed is cited and, thereupon, radically re-interpreted, if not turned upside down. Jesus is not a victim of the transgression of Sophia. As we are told elsewhere in this text, he came down into the world voluntarily in order to illuminate "the fallen seed," "his own" (cf. 136.17f and 22f). During his descent he had put on a mortal body, a product of the cosmic rulers, so as not to be recognizable to these powers (136.20-22). Although the saviour descended into the lower world and, in that sense, suffered, his suffering is not comparable to that of the Gnostics. Therefore Peter says in the same text that they, the apostles, as representatives of the Gnostics, have to suffer more than Jesus: "If he, our Lord, suffered, how much must we (suffer)?" (138.15-16). Obviously, the Gnostic author cannot believe that Jesus, who is called "our God" (133.7f), should have been subjected to physical suffering.

What we find here is that the contents of an early Christian creed testifying to the passion of Jesus are subsumed entirely into a Gnostic mythical thought pattern. In this mythical transformation, Christ is viewed as the illuminator from the transcendent world. The idea that he could suffer as a physical being is rejected explicitly.

A comparable use of early Christian traditions can be found in *The Apocalypse of Peter* in Codex VII.[2] We find in this text numerous echoes of writings that were to become part of the New Testament. In all likelihood the *Apocalypse* distinguishes three manifestations of Christ: the pleromatic Christ who forever remains in the transcendent world, the saviour who, apparently at different times, descends into

---

[2] Cf. H. W. Havelaar, *The Coptic Apocalypse of Peter. Text Edition with Translation, Commentary and Interpretative Essays* (Dissertation, University of Groningen, 1993; scheduled to appear in *Texte und Untersuchungen zur Geschichte der altchristlichen Literatur*, Berlin: Akademie-Verlag, 1997).

the world to enlighten the Gnostics, and, finally, "the Living Jesus" or the "incorporeal body," the light body that was temporarily united with a mortal body. The physical body is designated as the "servant" or "substitute" of the "Living Jesus." It is also called ironically "the son of their (*i.e.* the archons') honour." The text tells how the Living Jesus withdrew from his substitute before the arrest and crucifixion (NHC VII 81.4-10; 82.1-3, 28-30; 83.4-7). This entails that the one who was tortured and put to shame was not the Living Jesus, but his fleshly substitute, a "son" of the cosmic rulers. In a vision, Peter sees the Living Jesus glad and laughing near the cross.[3]

By correlating the Gospel accounts with a complicated Gnostic Christology, a wholly new meaning is generated. In effect the Gospel accounts of Jesus' suffering are supplanted by a different understanding of the person and the mission of the Christian saviour.

I refer to a third text: *The Acts of John* cc. 97-102 with its vision of the cross of light. This section of the Johannine *Acts* (probably dating from the second half of the second century) shows a few Valentinian features.[4] Interestingly, it makes a distinction between "the wooden cross in Jerusalem" and the cross of light which is revealed to John in a vision on the Mount of Olives. Apparently the cross of light is imagined as having the shape of the capital T. The horizontal bar which is "firmly established" (98.1f; because it is fixed on the main bar?) separates the lower world from the world above, and thus seems to be identical with the putative boundary between the two worlds.

In the horizontal bar the "members" of "the one who came down," i.e., Christ, the divine Saviour, are assembled (100.2-7). The idea seems to be that eventually all these members or light particles belonging to Christ will be lifted up (as one body) to the place above the boundary, where Christ (i.e., the true, transcendent being of Christ) is located.

Also in this section of *The Acts of John*, the relation to the Gospel accounts, especially the Fourth Gospel, is oppositional: in clear contrast to the Gospel, Christ (the descended saviour) reveals to John, who had fled from the crucifixion scene unto the Mount of Olives, that he, Christ, is not the one who is crucified on the wooden cross in

---

[3] Cf. *The Second Treatise of the Great Seth* in the same codex, esp. 51.20-52.3 and 55.16-56.20.

[4] E. Junod and J.-D. Kaestli, *Acta Johannis* (Corpus Christianorum, Series Apocryphorum 1-2; Turnhout: Brepols, 1983) esp. 581-677. Cf. my article "A Gnostic Reading of the Acts of John," *The Apocryphal Acts of John*, ed. J. Bremmer (Kampen: Kok-Pharos, 1995) 119-52.

Jerusalem. What the ones who believe this say about Christ is "humble" and "unworthy" of him (99.6f). John is summoned by the saviour to disdain the people who believe that he is crucified. Accordingly, the story concludes with the report that John laughs at the people around the cross in Jerusalem.

Again, specifically Gnostic conceptions of Christ and of the cross of Christ are imposed on New Testament traditions about the crucifixion of Jesus. Just as in the two aforementioned texts, it is denied that the Christian saviour was hanged on the cross and died, although this is clearly told in the Gospels. The true meaning of the cross is not revealed in the Gospels but in an esoteric revelation to John, the beloved disciple of Jesus. Those who keep to the literal meaning are despised and ridiculed.

### III

How should we explain this radical transformation of meaning in Gnostic texts? For one thing, the above reading of Gospel accounts through the lens of Gnostic Christology can be viewed as an extreme instance of something quite normal and legitimate. Readers (with the possible exception of scholarly interpreters) of philosophical or religious texts are facing the task of integrating the information of the text into their own system of values and into their own life experience.

The German literary theorist Hans Robert Jauss introduces the concept of "horizon of expectations" (a concept borrowed from Karl Popper) to elucidate the reception of texts by readers.[5] He makes it clear that the horizon of expectations plays the role of a frame of reference, without which the text is bound to remain meaningless. An important component of the horizon of expectations, particularly if we are concerned with religious or philosophical texts, is one's familiarity with other written and oral texts: readers assign meaning to a given text in the light of what they know from other texts, especially those texts that have normative value to them or otherwise are held in high esteem.[6] It should be clear, then, that *the response of Gnostics to the Gospel accounts of Jesus' suffering was determined by the relationship of these texts to the Gnostic esoteric tradition.* The intertextual

---

[5] *Literaturgeschichte als Provokation* (Frankfurt: Suhrkamp, 1970). Cf. e.g., D. W. Fokkema and E. Kunne-Ibsch, *Theories of Literature in the Twentieth Century* (London: C.Hurst & Comp., 1977) ch. 5: "The Reception of Literature: Theory and Practice of 'Rezeptionsästhetik.'"

[6] See my "Intertextual References in Readers' Responses to the Apocryphon of John," *Intertextuality in Biblical Writings: Essays in Honour of Bas van Iersel*, ed. S. Draaisma (Kampen: J.H. Kok, 1989) 117-26.

tension between the Gospel accounts and the above Gnostic writings reveals that on essential points the information of the Gospel stories differed from the Gnostic horizon of expectations.

Readers of religious and philosophical texts are likely to focus on those meanings in the text that are crucial within the frame of their own pattern of thought. In many cases—not only in the event of Gnostics encountering a biblical text—the reader's frame of reference has revisionary power. This could be illustrated with several interesting examples. I have to confine myself here to just mentioning the free and highly creative use of Old Testament Scripture by the apostle Paul,[7] to Martin Luther's reading of what in his understanding are key passages in Paul's epistles to the Galatians and to the Romans[8] and to feminist and (other) liberation theology approaches to biblical texts. It is highly significant that Elisabeth Schüßler Fiorenza should call her emancipatory reading of the New Testament a "hermeneutics of suspicion."[9] In all these cases we are dealing with readers interpreting their own Scripture. For that matter, the use of biblical materials in the Quran is a better parallel.[10]

Returning to the above Gnostic writings: the Gospel accounts of Jesus' passion acquired a profound, new symbolic meaning when they were connected with the frame of reference of Gnostic mythology. The suffering and vulnerable Jesus of the Gospel stories was transposed into the purely spiritual and therefore impassible illuminator from the divine world and, in Valentinian speculation, the cross was seen as the place where the light particles scattered in the world of darkness are assembled before they return to the divine world. This new view of the Christian saviour involved a negative evaluation and, eventually, the complete rejection of the Gospel tradition. The canonical Gospel accounts of Jesus' teaching activity and of his suffering were believed to contain superficial and even erroneous information about the redemptive activity of Jesus Christ. What remained was the allegorical interpretation as a means to unearth the truth allegedly hidden beneath the canonical Gospel texts and accessible only to enlightened readers.

---

[7] Cf. R. Hays, *Echoes of Scripture in the Letters of Paul* (New Haven and London: Yale University Press, 1989).

[8] See esp. the seminal essay by Krister Stendahl, "The Apostle Paul and the Introspective Conscience of the West," *Paul Among Jews and Gentiles*, ed. K. Stendahl (Philadelphia: Fortress, 1976) 78-96.

[9] *In Memory of Her: A Feminist Theological Reconstruction of Christian Origins* (New York: Crossroad, 1984) 56.

[10] Cf. J. Jomier, *Bible et Coran* (Paris: Ed. du Cerf, 1959).

## IV

I now proceed to the use of Jewish traditions by Gnostic mytho-logizers. The problem can be summarized as follows: on the one hand we find that in surviving versions of the Gnostic myth of origins, massive use is made of biblical and post-biblical Jewish materials, from the Genesis stories about the creation of the world and the early history of humankind and traditions about the part played by a hypostatized form of wisdom to Jewish names and Semitic puns. On the other hand, many elements of the Gnostic myth are utterly incompatible with the Jewish religion. By far the most striking feature of course is the identification of the biblical God with the ignorant, arrogant and wicked creator of the cosmic prison in which the Gnostics are forced to live.

In his reponse to Quispel, Jonas strongly—perhaps too strongly—emphasizes the hostile relationship with Judaism. Although I share his doubts about the Jewish origin of the Gnostic religion, I wonder whether Jonas is right in assuming that the use of Jewish traditions by Gnostic mythologizers was motivated by an anti-Jewish animus, or, in Jonas's biting terminology, by a "spirit of vilification, of parody and caricature, of conscious perversion of meaning, wholesale reversal of value-signs, savage degrading of the sacred—of gleefully shocking blasphemy."[11]

To begin with, we have to account for what John Turner terms the literary history of Gnosticism.[12] *The Apocryphon of John, The Hypostasis of the Archons*, and similar writings quite likely are relatively late and indeed artificial and highly complex literary artefacts. We are not witnessing in these texts the birth process of the Gnostic myth. I fully agree with Karl-Wolfgang Tröger when he points to the phenomenon of "anti-Judaist *topoi* already handed over from one generation of Gnostics to the other as frozen traditions without any living and direct attitude and polemics against Judaism." Tröger adds that this "at least applies to the topos of the arrogant and ignorant demiurge."[13]

---

[11] Art. cit. n. 1, 287.

[12] "Sethian Gnosticism: A Literary History," *Nag Hammadi, Gnosticism, and Early Christianity*, ed. C. W. Hedrick and R. Hodgson, Jr. (Peabody, MA: Hendrickson, 1986) 55-86.

[13] "The Attitude of the Gnostic Religion towards Judaism as Viewed in a Variety of Perspectives," *Colloque international sur les textes de Nag Hammadi*, ed. B. Barc (Québec: Les Presses de l'Université Laval, 1981) 86-98, esp. 91.

My next observation is in the same line. It should be clear that the Gnostic stories about the ignorance of the creator-god, about his failed creation, his deceptive instructions and his repressive rule over the cosmos are burdened with anti-Jewish connotations only if these elements of the Gnostic myth are connected with a frame of reference in which the Jewish Bible is a dominant factor. This must be presupposed in Jewish readers (and pagan sympathizers with the Jewish religion) in the ancient world as well as in any modern reader who is brought up in Western civilization, but the horizon of expectations of ancient Gnostics may well have been quite different.[14] The determining factor in their frame of reference was not the Jewish Bible but their own esoteric tradition. The stories about the arrogance and the ignorance of the creator-god and about his failed creation first of all confirmed Gnostic readers and hearers in their *gnosis*. To them, these stories illustrated their superiority over the demonic creator of the material world. The stories made it clear that Gnostics had basically nothing to fear from the cosmic demiurge and his devices, and so on.

## V

What then of the *first* use of biblical and Jewish materials by Gnostic mythopoets? I must confess that I would prefer not to go into this question at all, for we run the risk here of entering the domain of pure historical speculation. In any case, the attempts below are tentative and hypothetical.

I start from the well-known fact that Gnostics seem to have been convinced that, as enlightened persons, they had immediate access to the full truth about God, the world, and humankind. This conviction, however, did not prevent them from finding inspiration in non-Gnostic religious and philosophical writings and traditions, but of course they interpreted the information in these texts from their own distinctive horizon of expectations. Viewed from this perspective, it is only in a concealed and misleading way that in other traditions reference is made to the definite truth. Consequently, their *gnosis* not only enabled but also forced Gnostic mythmakers to use non-Gnostic materials critically and creatively.

Critical, selective, and revisionary interpretation of earlier texts is likely to indicate that there is a gap between the information in the texts and the horizon of expectations of the reader or interpreter. Parrott and others explain the strained intertextual relationship

---

[14] See my article mentioned above, n. 6.

between Jewish and Gnostic texts as the result of a "hermeneutical shift" (Pearson) which would have occurred at some time and place within Judaism. But this striking phenomenon can also, and I surmise in a more natural way, be explained as *a consequence of the integration of biblical and Jewish materials within the frame of a basically different, i.e. a pagan, mythical thought pattern.*[15]

We can trace the thought pattern of Gnostic mythologizers—the frame of reference within which they interpreted Jewish and other non-Gnostic materials—by analyzing their texts. (But some caution is in order here since, as we have noted, the extant versions of the classic Gnostic myth of origins may represent later stages in the history of the Gnostic religion). Actually a very clear example of such an analysis can be found in Birger Pearson's article "Jewish Elements in Gnosticism and the Development of Gnostic Self-Definition."[16] But Pearson's observations do not necessarily lead to the conclusion he is drawing. Pearson alleges that one of the most characteristic notions of the so-called Sethian Gnostics is their self-definition as the "seed," "race" or "children" of Seth and proposes that these ideas concerning Seth and his Gnostic posterity are ultimately based on a sophisticated exegesis of Gen. 4.25 (p. 131).

But then Pearson makes the quite pertinent observation that the Gnostic use of the term "seed" and "race" includes other ideas, "by which it is possible to arrive at a deeper understanding of the Gnostic self-definition" (ibid.). For the Gnostics see themselves ultimately, Pearson affirms, as nothing less than the "seed," "race," or "generation" of the highest God himself. He rightly argues that with these and similar expressions "we are confronted with the heart and core of the Gnostic religion, the idea of the consubstantiality of the self with God" (p. 132).

I fully agree with these observations, but what Pearson does not consider—and here my doubts begin—is that the self-definition "the race of Seth" might be a secondary and contingent translation of what he correctly calls the heart and core of the Gnostic religion, or, in my terminology, one of the elements of its coherent thought pattern. This is not unimportant, for the biblical materials lead Pearson to the conclusion that *in the earliest history* of the Gnostic religion, much of

---

[15] I reckon with the possibility that Gnostic mythmakers had no direct knowledge of the Jewish Bible but, instead, disposed of compilations of second-hand allegorical interpretations.

[16] In *Gnosticism, Judaism, and Egyptian Christianity*, ed. B. A. Pearson (Minneapolis: Fortress, 1990) 124-35.

its mythology was based on Jewish scripture and tradition. If it is correct to make a distinction between the basic pattern of Gnostic convictions and its expression or actualization in Jewish language, this conclusion is not a matter of evidence.[17] It is indeed obvious that the self-definition "the race of Seth" has a Jewish connection,[18] but it is hard to see why this should also hold true of the more basic idea of the consubstantiality of the self with God (the idea of being "essentially divine," p. 133).

Later in his essay, Pearson points to what he identifies as another central feature of the Gnostic religion: the necessity for the divine seed to be awakened through *gnosis*. He makes it clear that in the Sethian system, Seth functions as a redeemer figure, the one, that is, who reveals the true gnosis. Pearson does not, however, explicitly account for the possibility that the role played by Seth is a secondary implementation of a more fundamental idea which is not necessarily or exclusively Jewish, that is the idea of the soteriological function of revelatory knowledge.

Pearson's observations at least imply that it makes sense to distinguish basic assumptions from secondary expressions (in this case expressions in Jewish vocabulary).[19] The basic premises even of the Sethian group of mythological writings (which, I repeat, may represent a later development in the history of the Gnostic religion) point to a pagan rather than to a Jewish environment. I am not the first to think in particular of an origin in philosophical circles inspired by (allegorical interpretations of) Plato's *Timaeus*.[20]

---

[17] Cf. M. A. Williams, *The Immovable Race. A Gnostic Designation and the Theme of Stability in Late Antiquity* (NHS 29; Leiden: E.J. Brill, 1985) 203-9.

[18] It may have an anti-Jewish connotation if we understand "the offspring of Seth" in contrast to "the offspring of Abraham."

[19] Cf. my "Johannine Vocabulary and the Thought Structure of Gnostic Mythological Texts," *Gnosisforschung und Religionsgeschichte, Festschrift für Kurt Rudolph*, ed. H. Preißler and H. Seiwert (Marburg: Diagonal-Verlag, 1994) 175-181. Here I make a distinction between the surface structure of mythological texts (vocabulary, narrative items) and the underlying mythical thought structure (with reference to the structural study of myths by Claude Lévi-Strauss).

[20] Cf. A. D. Nock's well-known statement "Gnosticism is Platonism run wild" ("Gnosticism," *HTR* 57 [1964] 266) and John Dillon's designation "the underworld of Platonism" (*The Middle Platonists: 80 B.C. to 220 A.D.* [London: Duckworth, 1977] 398). Of special importance is B. Layton, *The Gnostic Scriptures* (Garden City, NY: Doubleday, 1987) 5-12. See further the reviews and discussions by K. Rudolph (*Theologische Rundschau* 36 [1971] 33-48) and H. J. Krämer, *Der Ursprung der Geistmetaphysik. Untersuchungen zur Geschichte des Platonismus zwischen Platon und Plotin* (Amsterdam: B.R. Grüner, 1964) 223-64.

This is not the place to make a plea in favour of a Platonist connection with the basic thought pattern of the classic Gnostic myth of origins. But it may be observed that studies of the possible (Jewish or non-Jewish) antecedents of isolated Gnostic motifs or narrative ingredients are not of much help. The real question is where we should locate the emergence of the basic pattern of mythical convictions underlying Gnostic mythology. This thought pattern quite probably could be expressed by means of diverse and heterogeneous materials.

## VI

As I suggested above, the highly liberal and, in a sense, disparaging use of Jewish texts by Gnostic mythopoets might be the result of attempts to read these texts through a Gnostic lens and to make Gnostic stories out of non-Gnostic materials.

This explanation gives rise to the question of whether Jonas is right in seeing an anti-Jewish spirit at work behind the radical revisions of the first chapters of Genesis and other Jewish traditions, and whether it is correct to characterize this utilization of biblical traditions as "protest exegesis." Probably we cannot entirely exclude this possibility, but the anti-Jewish connotations at least are not as obvious as Jonas and others assume. I would supplement my remarks on this question above by adding: to possible early Gnostic mythologizers of Platonist provenance, the very story of the creation in Genesis combined with the anthropomorphic properties ascribed to the biblical God might well have been reason enough to identify this God not with their supreme, transcendent Godhead but with the demiurge of the material world. This adaptation to their pattern of thought does not necessarily presuppose a living controversy with the Jewish religion or with Jewish people.

It is not difficult, by the way, to see why Platonist mythmakers took an interest in the biblical stories about the creation of man in the image and likeness of God, about the forbidden fruits of the tree of knowledge, etc. (stories which they might have known through second-hand collections). By means of (further) allegorical interpretation they used these stories to give more detailed expression to their own preconceived ideas.[21]

---

[21] Occasionally the Gnostic texts reveal that they were composed out of heterogeneous narrative materials. For instance, it is curious to find that precisely the material body (or in the version of the Gnostic myth in *The Apocryphon of John*, the psychic body) of man should bear likeness to the image of the invisible highest God in a myth that stresses that the sole God-like element in man is his *pneuma*. See further my article "The Jewish Factor in the Development of the Gnostic Myth of Origins," *Text and Testimony. Essays*

The hypothesis of a Platonist origin helps us to understand the specific use of biblical traditions in the surviving variants of the Gnostic myth of origins. For the rest, the search for a Platonist connection is not likely to be an easier task than the search for a Jewish connection. In either case we have to account for a missing link. Actually, Parrott's paper is an advanced attempt to find the missing link in the history of Judaism. If we connect the earliest development of Gnostic mythology with the (largely unknown) history of Platonist schools of thought we have to postulate a change in the way philosophers in late antiquity felt and thought about God, the world and the demiurge.[22] Obviously, the above hypothesis entails that the massive and at the same time revisionary utilization of biblical and Jewish materials represents a secondary stage (or a surviving sideline?) in the history of the Gnostic religion.

In the first part of this paper I drew attention to the use of early Christian traditions about the passion of Christ in a few Gnostic writings. The relevant Gospel accounts are thoroughly revised and brought into conformity with the mythical thought systems of Gnostic mythopoets. Apparently, the Jewish and the early Christian traditions are treated in basically the same way. Yet the situation or context is different. For the critical interpretations of early traditions about Jesus Christ in the Christian Gnostic texts discussed above function in an explicitly polemical scheme: they are meant to contrast the esoteric views of a specific Gnostic Christian group with the supposedly superficial and inferior ideas of other Christian groups.[23] These writings bear witness to an actual controversy between Christian communities about the person and the mission of Jesus Christ.

I have not found clear indications that the critical revision of Old Testament and Jewish texts and traditions belongs to a direct polemic

---

*in Honour of A.F.J. Klijn*, ed. T. Baarda et al. (Kampen: J.H. Kok, 1988) 152-61. Cf. M. Goulder, "Colossians and Barbelo," *NTS* 41 (1995) 601-19, esp. 605f.

[22] Cf. A. H. Armstrong, "Gnosis and Greek Philosophy," *Gnosis. Festschrift für Hans Jonas*, ed. B. Aland (Göttingen: Vandenhoeck & Ruprecht, 1978) 67-124, esp. 99. With respect to the above missing link, Armstrong makes the interesting conjecture that it is not among Jews persecuted by Jews but among pagan peoples persecuted by Jews that the Gnostic religion originated: "The wild suspicion ... has sometimes crossed my mind that it might be plausible to look for the origins of Gnosticism (if any evidence was available) among the peoples forcibly Judaized by John Hyrcanus and Aristobulus in the 2nd century B.C., the Idumaeans, Ituraeans or Peraeans" (92, n. 7).

[23] For an elaboration of this view see my "Early Christian Judaism and Christian Gnosis, and their Relation to Emerging Mainstream Christianity," *Critical Scholarship and the New Testament: A Dialogue with Willem S. Vorster (Neotestamentica. Journal of the New Testament Society of South Africa* 28.3 [1994]) 219-34.

*against Judaism.* It is noteworthy that the most violent attacks against the Old Testament and its heroes are found in Gnostic writings that are purportedly addressed to other groups of Christians, Christian believers, that is, who still held the Old Testament revelation in high esteem (*The Second Treatise of the Great Seth*, NHC VII,*2*, and *The Testimony of Truth*, NHC IX,*3*).[24] It is evident that in these texts, the rejection of the Old Testament was not prompted by anti-Jewish feelings. As far as the attacks against the Old Testament involve a rejection of Judaism, it is a symbolic Judaism rather than a living Judaism connected to Jewish contemporaries and their faith.

---

[24] B. Pearson, "Use, Authority and Exegesis of Mikra in Gnostic Literature," *Mikra: Text, Translation and Interpretation of the Hebrew Bible in Ancient Judaism and Early Christianity*, ed. M. J. Mulder and H. Sysling (CRINT, Section Two: The Literature of the Jewish People in the Period of the Second Temple and the Talmud, 1; Assen/Maastricht: Van Gorcum; Philadelphia: Fortress, 1988) 635-52, esp. 640-41.

PART TWO

THE *APOCRYPHON OF JOHN*

# APPROACHING THE VARIANTS OF
# THE *APOCRYPHON OF JOHN* [1]

*Karen L. King*
Occidental College

The fifty years since the discovery of the Nag Hammadi Codices in Egypt have seen a profound deepening of our understanding of the phenomena of Gnosticism and early Christianity. Chief among the works that have contributed to this understanding is the *Apocryphon of John*.[2] It is known to us in three tractates, each from a separate Nag Hammadi codex (II,1; III,1; and IV,1), and a copy is also inscribed in the Berlin Codex (Codex Berolinensis 8502,2).[3] In addition, the second century church father Irenaeus knew a work related to the first part of the *Apocryphon of John* and cited from it in his heresiological work, *Against Heresies* I.29.[4]

While this plentitude probably indicates something about the significance of the work in antiquity (as well as its simple good fortune to have been so well preserved), the plethora of textual variants in the manuscripts has presented scholars with complex problems relating to the composition and transmission of the work, editorial labor on the different versions, and identifying sources. Answers to all of these

---

[1] An earlier version of this paper was read at a conference on "The Nag Hammadi Codices: Fifty Years of Scholarship (1945-1995)" organized by François Bovon at Harvard Divinity School, April 22, 1995. I would like to thank the organizer and participants of this conference for their helpful questions and criticisms. In particular I offer my appreciation to Louis Painchaud and Jorunn Jacobsen Buckley for their constructive criticism and bibliographical suggestions. I would also like to thank the participants of the Haverford Seminar for their constructive and engaging responses, especially for the careful, formal responses and critiques by Birger Pearson and Michael Williams.

[2] A synoptic edition: *The Apocryphon of John. Synopsis of Nag Hammadi Codices II,1; III,1; and IV,1 with BG 8502.1*, ed. F. Wisse and M. Waldstein (Nag Hammadi and Manichaean Studies 33, Leiden: E. J. Brill, 1995) is now available. I want to thank Michael Waldstein for generously providing an advance working copy of this edition. All Coptic citations from the Nag Hammadi Codices used in this paper are from the Brill edition. For the Berlin Codex, the edition of W. Till and H.-M. Schenke (*Die gnostischen Schriften des Koptischen Papyrus Berolinensis 8502* [Berlin: Akademie Verlag, 1972]) is consulted as well.

[3] Hereafter abbreviated BG.

[4] See M. Krause, "The *Apocryphon of John*" in W. Foerster, *Gnosis: A Selection of Gnostic Texts*, Vol. 1 (Oxford: Clarendon Press, 1972) 100-103.

issues are integral to larger interpretive questions about the work's historical, social, and religious meanings. My own approach, as a projected contribution to this larger interpretive project, is to locate and analyze the particular tendencies and interests of the variants of the *Apocryphon of John* in order to further our understanding of Sethian Gnosticism.

This essay is, however, not yet an analysis of the variants in the *Apocryphon of John*, but a prolegomenon to such a study. A prolegomenon is necessary because recent work on orality and writing in chirographic cultures has called for scholars to reassess many of our suppositions about "the medium status of texts, the use of sources, and the organization of thought negotiated in ancient texts, with renewed attention to oral proclivities."[5] Although the *Apocryphon of John* is intrinsically and characteristically a literary composition, in the first section of this essay I want to examine the ways in which *the oral/aural sensibilities of the practice of writing itself* might be operative in its composition and transmission practices. This approach eschews a sharp dichotomy between orality and writing as misleading[6] and focuses instead on ways in which oral sensibilities are at work in literary practices. The point is to understand more clearly ancient literary conventions, sensibilities, and attitudes so as to understand better how conventions of oral speech are entangled in the literary composition of the *Apocryphon of John,* and to gauge better the significance of both stability and fluidity in transmissional processes.

A second, related issue is aroused by the modern preoccupation with determining the original form of the *Apocryphon of John*. The indelibility of the printing process seems to have marked scholars'

---

[5] W. H. Kelber discussing the work of Paul Achtemeier, "Modalities of Communication, Cognition, and Physiology or Perception: Orality, Rhetoric, and Scribality," *Orality and Textuality in Early Christian Literature*, ed. J. Dewey, *Semeia* 65 (Atlanta, Ga.: Scholars Press, 1995) 206.

[6] Although studies in orality began by making a sharp distinction between oral and written cultures (see, for example, Walter Ong, *Orality and Literacy*), more recent studies have come to explore how writing operates and what roles it plays in cultures that nonetheless remain primarily oral and illiterate. Kelber, for example, summarizes: "Separating one modality of communication as a distinct entity from every other is likely to distort linguistic realities. It is more advisable to attend to phenomena such as residual oral traces or orality filtered through textuality, transformation of voice and the rhetorical outreach of texts, cooperation and tension between oral and textual drives, the engagement of oral and visual, or audio-visual aids in the work of perception, the tangled interfaces of speech with writing, the gradual dominance of one medium over other media, and the reabsorption of a prior heritage into a culture shaped by new media technologies" ("Orality, Rhetoric, and Scribality," 194).

imaginations with the conception that manuscript variants are to be perceived as corruptions. Persons within a chirographic culture, marked more by oral sensibilities, might imagine the situation quite differently, however. Variants might be seen as improvements, useful additions, or corrections. In short, our "corruption" might be their "correction." In the second part of this essay, I want to examine the value of considering the textual variants, not as corruptions of some imaginary pure original, but as evidence that can be used for writing a dynamic history of Sethian Gnosticism.

## ORAL SENSIBILITIES IN THE LITERARY PRACTICES OF THE *APOCRYPHON OF JOHN*

Oral sensibilities are evident in several aspects of the literary practices of the *Apocryphon of John*: the work's own explicit (surface-level) attitude, which understands writing in terms of speech and hearing; the entanglement of writing with oral practices; oral features of composition/transmission; and stability and fluidity in the transmission process. Each of these topics will be taken up in turn.

### *Attitudes toward writing in the Apocryphon of John.*
The main point of departure for recent studies of orality and writing in chirographic cultures is the observation that it is anachronistic to import our print culture attitudes toward writing into the ancient context.[7] William Graham, for example, sharply contrasts ancient sensibilities about writing with contemporary print sensibilities:

> Writing[8] ... was inseparable from speaking. In turn, a written text was something conceived as realizable only in the vocal act of reading aloud:

---

[7] The classic study on how the orientation to writing in a print culture differs significantly from that of chirographic cultures is W. J. Ong, *Orality and Literacy. The Technologizing of the Word* (New York and London: Routledge, 1993; reprint of 1982 edition). Among other things, he argues that the modern Western understanding of writing has been determinedly shaped by the invention of the printing press and mass print culture. It is anachronistic to read this relatively late and relatively rare sensibility onto other cultures.

[8] Graham is specifically discussing the comments of an Egyptian scribe given in a papyrus from the Egyptian New Kingdom, "a scribal culture that we associate automatically with passionate attachment to the written word and the production of diverse writings consciously intended for posterity." The papyrus reads: "A human being perishes, and his body becomes dirt; all his fellows dissolve to dust. But writings let him live on in the mouth of the reader. A book is more useful than the house of a builder, than chapels in the west; it is better than a solidly walled castle and a monument in the temple. Is there any here [today] like Jedef-Hor or another like Imhotep?....What these wise men proclaimed, occurred, and what came from their mouths was realized. It was discovered

The *reader* was inevitably a *lector*, one who gives life to the written work by voicing it. The associations of writing in his mind were instinctively aural rather than visual in the first instance—exactly the opposite of our own ingrained response, which would be to think of the fixity of the 'black and white' page, the calligraphed image, not the sound of the words of the text, as the enduring monument to the author's memory.[9]

Graham goes on to define a book in such chirographic cultures as "something to be read aloud or recited from, an *aide-memoire* and repository of the vocal words of an author—in short, a transmitter of speech where voice cannot carry and memory cannot suffice."[10] Such a definition corresponds remarkably well to the *Apocryphon of John's* description of writing. All four extant versions concur in depicting writing as essentially the repository of the spoken word. For example, at the conclusion of the revelation, the revealer says to John:

> "I am speaking these things to you so that you might write them down and give them to your fellow spirits in secrecy" (BG, 75.15-19).[11]

> "I have completed all things for you in your ears.[12] For I have spoken all things to you in order that you might write them down and give them to your fellow spirits secretly" (II 31.26-30).[13]

Or again at the Savior's departure, the texts say:

> "I will teach you about what will occur. For indeed I gave these things to you to write them down and make them secure" (BG 76.5-9).[14]

> "And the Savior gave these things to him in order that he might write them down and make them secure" (II 31.32-34).[15]

---

as a saying, it was written in their books....They have gone, their names would have been forgotten, but writings keep their memory alive" (cited in W. A. Graham, *Beyond the Written Word. Oral Aspects of Scripture in the History of Religion* [Cambridge: Cambridge University Press, 1987] 32).

[9] Graham, *Beyond the Written Word*, 32.

[10] Graham, *Beyond the Written Word*, 39.

[11] The version of III is quite similar, except it uses the perfect tense: "I have spoken these things to you" etc.

[12] At the beginning of the text, the Pharisee, Arimanios, tells John that the Nazarene "filled your ears with lies" (II 1.15; III 1.12-13; BG 19.19). Here, too, the speech of the Savior is depicted aurally.

[13] IV shows only orthographic variants in comparison with II here.

[14] III 39.24 uses the Greek ἀσφαλεία rather than the Coptic ⲧⲁϫⲣⲟ. The implications are only slightly different.

[15] IV shows only orthographic variants in comparison with II here.

After the Savior departs, John did not, however, sit down and write a book. Instead, the texts tell us:

> "And he went to his fellow disciples. He began to tell them the things that had been told to him by the Savior" (BG 76.18-77.4).[16]

> "And he went to his fellow disciples. He recounted[17] to them the things that the Savior had told to him" (II 32.4-5).

At two other places not in BG or III II/IV mentions books. The first case suggests readers consult "the Book of Zoroaster" if they want additional information about the demons who control the passions.[18] In the second instance, the speaker refers to Moses' book: "It is not the way Moses wrote while you were listening. For he said in his first book ...."[19] Here, even in citing from a written text, the sensibilities are still oral (Moses *said* in his book) and aural (you *heard* what Moses wrote).

It is clear from these passages that the *Apocryphon of John* understands writing primarily in terms of speech and hearing. "The things" that are passed on to the disciples are not written books, but the spoken message of the revealer. In particular, the phrase, "I have completed all things for you *in your ears*," vividly indicates that the reception of the message is understood to be aural.

Why then write anything down at all? The *Apocryphon of John* gives us two clues. First of all, writing makes speech secure.[20] It is, in other words, a function of reliability, probably aimed at guarding against lapses in memory.[21] Second, writing extends the range of

---

[16] III says that John "stood" before his fellow disciples; this variant may reflect the theme of stability (see M. A. Williams, *The Immovable Race. A Gnostic Designation and the Theme of Stability in Late Antiquity* [NHS 29, Leiden: E. J. Brill, 1985]) but does not indicate a differing attitude toward the text's view that revelation is promulgated through speech, not writing.

[17] IV 49.25 has ϫⲱ ("speak") here rather than II's ⲧⲉⲟⲩⲱ ("recount," "utter").

[18] II 19.8-10.

[19] II 19.8-10.

[20] The two terms used are: ἀσφάλεια which means immovable, stable or assured from danger, safe; and ⲧⲁϫⲣⲟ which means strong, reliable, firm.

[21] In answer to a question about Manichaeism's attitude toward writing, Manfred Hutter has suggested that the high valuation given to books in this tradition reflects Mani's view that true religion begins with a pure oral revelation, but then falls into decline due to the imperfections of the oral transmission process. Writing helps fix the tradition in its original purity. Thus it is an advantage for the founder himself to have written down his teaching; such a practice is superior to those traditions in which teaching is passed down only by followers, as for example in Christianity. (Summarized from a conversation at the International History of Religions Conference, Mexico City, August, 1995).

speech beyond the immediate audience. While, in the fictive situation of the *Apocryphon of John's* frame narrative, John can pass such speech on directly to his fellow disciples, in actual practice the audiences of the *Apocryphon of John* have to rely on writing. The reference to "the Book of Zoroaster" may indicate that writing was also considered to be a repository where one could get additional information not otherwise available.

Nor are writing and speech here in competition with each other.[22] Writing can exist and be highly valued, and at the same time be flexible in its oral/aural expressions[23] insofar as "sacred writings were primarily oral in function and aural in impact, rather than written or visual."[24] The *Apocryphon of John*, for example, would always have been read aloud.[25]

---

[22] Graham, *Beyond the Written Word*, 62: "The power of scripture as holy writ has been prominent in all traditions in which scripture has figured at all prominently. Nevertheless, this power is not at odds with the power of the scriptural word that is read aloud or recited. The written and spoken aspects of the text complement and augment each other, and hence to speak of competition between the two has little meaning. Any comprehension of what scripture is must include awareness of its role and function as written text, just as of its role and function as spoken text." Or again, 65: "Whatever the primordial power and significance of the spoken word or formula, it does not evaporate with the coming of writing and reading, in religious or other spheres of life. The book and none more so than the holy book of scripture is, or was, first the vehicle of the living, spoken word, then an object of veneration. Where spoken word and written word have met most fully was likely first in scripture, in holy texts that sought to fix and hold the spoken word of sacred truth and power in the most tangible way possible." His view here stands in sharp contrast to W. Kelber's argument in *The Oral and the Written Gospel. The Hermeneutics of Speaking and Writing in the Synoptic Gospel Tradition, Mark, Paul, and Q* (Philadelphia: Fortress, 1983). which sees the two in sharp competition.

[23] For example, Graham, *Beyond the Written Word*, 139, writes about the early Pachomians (my emphasis): "In this monastic discipline, the life of faith striven for was envisioned as a scriptural life pure and simple: This meant a life permeated and paced, as well as directed and governed, by the living, lively words of scripture. The sources indicate that sacred writings were primarily oral in function and aural in impact, rather than written or visual. In these writings, God spoke through the voices of the biblical writers in the timeless and transforming speech of divine revelation. Literalism does not seem to have been the necessary corollary of scripturalism among the Tabennesiots. *Their oral citation of scriptural passages appears to have been an effort to capture allusively the correct sense without adhering word for word to one particular linguistic or textual version generally recognized as authoritative.* The important fact for these persons was that God spoke to them through the voices of the biblical writers in the timeless speech of divine inspiration or revelation. The total commitment of the life they chose to pursue and their visceral sense of the immediacy of the divine presence were mirrored in the intensity of their preoccupation with scripture and the vividness with which they heard God's voice in its words."

[24] Graham, *Beyond the Written Word*, 139. This statement can be qualified by noting the ways in which speech and writing ask the hearer to internalize certain images (see Kelber, "Orality, Rhetoric and Scribality," 202-5).

[25] See G. L. Hendrickson, "Ancient Reading," *Classical Quarterly* 25 (1929) 182-96.

The degree to which oral sensibilities are present in ancient texts, where and how such sensibilities are operative, and the interplay of oral and written practices will vary from text to text, and especially across various genres. Moreover, we must reckon with a range of attitudes toward writing in antiquity that would vary based on geographical area, education and literacy rates, local practices, scribal professionalism, availability of writing materials, and other related factors.[26] But we can predict that attitudes, such as those of the *Apocryphon of John*, will still be located within a limited range of chirographic sensibilities.

It appears that oral/aural sensibilities are fundamental to attitudes toward the written work in the *Apocryphon of John*. Indeed the *Apocryphon of John* would be an exceptional case if this were not so. It remains now to describe more precisely how and where such sensibilities are operating.

*Writing and oral practices*

An intersection between writing and oral practices can be seen: in the oral reading and hearing of the written work; in its use in oral settings; and in the genre of the work as dialogue.

Given the relatively low literacy rates in antiquity, particularly among non-elite classes, it is probable that many persons became acquainted with the contents of the *Apocryphon of John* solely or primarily through aural experience and oral performance.[27] Even the study of the written text would have had oral/aural aspects, such as reading aloud, discussion, or pedagogical exposition of a teacher to students. The work itself refers to several situations where speech is

---

[26] An excellent analysis of differing attitudes toward writing and speech in Greek and Egyptian magical practice is given by D. Frankfurter, "The Magic of Writing and the Writing of Magic: The Power of the Word in Egyptian and Greek Traditions," *Helios* 21.2 (1994) 190-199. In the second half of his paper, Frankfurter explores the ways in which these relatively different attitudes converged uniquely in later Hellenistic and Roman periods (199-211). Part of the original difference is attributed to the fact that writing in Egypt in pre-Hellenistic times was the exclusive provenance of the priesthood (196), whereas in Greece writing was practiced across a wider range of domains, as it came to be in Egypt in Hellenistic and especially Roman times.

[27] This is especially true if we assume that persons to which this material was aimed were not all of the elite upper classes, who would have been mostly literate. Outside of this class, literacy was extremely limited (see W. V. Harris, *Ancient Literacy* [Cambridge, MA: Harvard University Press, 1989]). We need to reckon here also with the variety of audiences indicated by the complex transmission history of the *Apocryphon of John;* literacy rates may have been higher among the audiences that collected and hid the Nag Hammadi Codices than among audiences that used the work in earlier versions, especially among Sethian Gnostic groups.

important: baptismal ritual and anointing,[28] magical healing, and preaching or teaching.[29]

The case of healing is particularly interesting. It is my contention that the *Apocryphon of John*'s "theory of names" and the extensive lists of names of the demons that control various parts of the psychic body and the passions[30] were used for magical purposes of healing. There are several reasons for this proposal: The demons are clearly said to be in charge of the various parts of the body and the passions. Yet the extensive length of the catalogue and the detailed care with which each demon's name is given suggest that the list has a purpose and utility beyond merely pointing out that all is not well with the human body. There is considerable evidence that knowing the name of a demon gave one power over it.[31] Plotinus explicitly attests to such practice among Gnostics:

> "For when they (Gnostics) write magic chants, intending to address them to those powers, not only to the soul but to those above it as well, what are they doing except making the powers obey the word and follow the lead of people who say spells and charms and conjurations? ... But when they say they free themselves from diseases, if they meant that they did so by temperance and orderly living they would speak well, just as the philosophers do; but in fact they assume that the diseases are evil spirits, and claim to be able to drive them out by their word.[32]

---

[28] See the *Apocryphon of John* II 31.22-25; J.-M. Sevrin, *Le dossier baptismal sé-thien. Études sur la sacramentaire gnostique* (BCNH, Section Études 2; Québec: Les Presses de l'Université Laval, 1986) 9-48; J. Turner, "Ritual in Gnosticism," *Society of Biblical Literature Seminar Papers*, ed. E. H. Lovering (Atlanta: Scholars Press, 1994) 139-147, 157.

[29] See the *Apocryphon of John* BG 76.18-77.5; III 40.6-9; II 32.4-5.

[30] See BG 40.19-41.12; II 11.26; 12.26-34.

[31] For a discussion on widespread practices of magic for healing, see R. Kotansky, "Incantations and Prayers for Salvation on Inscribed Greek Amulets," *Magika Hiera. Ancient Greek Magic and Religion.*, ed. C. A. Faraone and D. Obbink (New York and Oxford: Oxford University Press, 1991) 107-37; examples from Coptic Christianity can be found in M. Meyer and R. Smith, *Ancient Christian Magic. Coptic Texts of Ritual Power* (San Francisco: Harper and Row, 1994) 79-145.

[32] *Ennead* II,9.14.1-15. See also the discussion by B. Pearson, "Theurgic Elements in Gnosticism and Iamblichus's Conception of Theurgy," *Neoplatonism and Gnosticism*, ed. R. T. Wallis and J. Bregman (*Studies in Neoplatonism: Ancient and Modern 6*, International Society for Neoplatonic Studies, Albany: SUNY Press, 1992) 253-54, 267; M. A. Williams, "Psyche's Voice: Gnostic Perceptions of Body and Soul," manuscript of paper distributed for discussion at the Nag Hammadi and Gnosticism Section/Platonism and Neoplatonism Group joint session, AAR/SBL Annual Meeting, Kansas City, November 24, 1991.

Plotinus here gives us an example of precisely what I believe to be the function of the list of demons in the longer version of the *Apocryphon of John*: to drive out diseases from the body through magical performances involving control of the demons who rule various parts of the body and cause disease. While we can say little about precisely what such performance would have looked like, it is highly probable that the healing involved oral invocation of the demons. Hence, in this case, writing is used to preserve names used primarily for oral practices.

The most prominent use of the *Apocryphon of John*, however, would probably have been as a resource for teaching and preaching, oral recitation from memory or reading aloud. Its use as a resource for prayer or other ritual practices (baptism and anointing) is possible, but much less clear. As the audiences of the *Apocryphon of John* shifted throughout the course of its transmission history,[33] the contexts in which it was read and used would change as well, so we need to be careful not to identify the *Apocryphon of John* with one situation or one function. Teaching, however, was quite likely one use of the *Apocryphon of John* with some audiences during its history. The use of books in teaching provides a good example of the complexity of the interaction between the written and the oral. Rosalind Thomas notes that books were increasingly used in the Roman period for teaching purposes, but she also notes that the value of books for teaching continued to be questioned. She writes:

> Galen and his contemporaries were primarily concerned about the utility of the book for teaching. It might be grossly inadequate unless backed up by the help of the teacher himself: 'I order that these notes should be shared only with those who would read the book with a teacher,' he says. So a text might be regarded more as an aid to memorization of what had been passed on orally by a teacher, as a reminder to those who know: this is strongly reminiscent of Plato's strictures in the *Phaedrus* (274b-279b) on the slight value of a written text for real knowledge. So while written texts were certainly not forbidden in the philosophical schools, they might be seen as subordinate to the oral methods of teaching. One interesting corollary of this attitude is that the true teachings of a founder of a philosophical school (like that of Epicurus) might be thought to reside in the traditions continued by the school rather than in the original written texts left by the founder, and this might even entail the interpolation of the texts....[34] But there is an apparently much more fluid process of interpretation and tradition in the

---

[33] See the discussion below, p. 128.

[34] It may be that Mani's emphasis upon writing as a tool of fixity is made precisely in reaction against such common practices (see above note 21). In this case, Mani is the exception that proves the rule.

schools, even interpolation of the philosophical texts, which eschews a strict regard for verbatim accuracy or individual intellectual copyright.[35]

This perspective is extremely helpful in trying to imagine one kind of situation—there were almost certainly others—in which the *Apocryphon of John* may have been written, copied, and read.[36] Scribes may have incorporated their own interpretations or those of other teachers when making new copies or translations, as well as have incorporated additional material. For example, the long list in II 15.29-19.10 correlating parts of the psychic body with specific demons could have been added in just this fashion. Scribes may very well have entered "corrections" or "improvements" as well, both of which would reflect the particular interests and emphases not only of the scribe or teacher, but of his or her audience as well. Indeed insofar as scribes were free from the constraints of an ideal of verbatim transmission and authorial "copyright," they were able to function as editors and even authors. While the categories of author, editor, and scribe are still useful, the clear distinctions among these categories in print culture can obscure the fluid practices of ancient chirography, if they are employed too statically. Such fluidity also had its limits, however, as will be discussed below.

The oral/aural nature of writing is also emphasized by the genre of the text as a revelation dialogue. Here the authority of the text (as divine revelation) is tied to its imagined oral performance (as speech in dialogue). Modern sensibilities, in contrast, often understand printed writing to be more authoritative than speech because of print's reliability in passing on (massive amounts of) information accurately. According to Ong,[37] the modern Western attitude to writing is based on the invention of printing and the mass production of identical copies. This technological innovation fostered an attitude that grants authority to the printed text precisely on the basis of typography's capacity to reproduce a work consistently, and the reader's capacity

---

[35] R. Thomas, *Literacy and Orality in Ancient Greece* (Cambridge: Cambridge University Press, 1992) 161-62.

[36] It is crucial to stress here that I am not arguing for a return to form criticism. The analysis is still focused on the *written text*, not on an attempt to get behind writing to its "original" oral form and context (*Sitz im Leben*). Nor does the analysis here presuppose an easy movement from oral to written text, or from written text to social situation. Rather the point is to understand *the oral/aural sensibilities of the practice of writing itself*. A sharp dichotomy between orality and writing is what is misleading. Insofar as we understand these sensibilities more fully, we are in a better position to understand the continued intermingling of oral sensibilities with scribal practices.

[37] Ong, *Orality and Literacy*, 117-38.

to analyze the coherence of complex information beyond the vagaries of memory (even the extraordinary memory of some members of oral cultures). Writing also fixes memory in ways that limit the social adaptation of traditional materials to new situations through the "flexible memories" of oral performers. We expect words and ideas in printed texts to be uniform, consistent, and coherent. The sensibilities that reign in the *Apocryphon of John*, however, are closer to those of oral and chirographic cultures in which the logic of practice often predominates over that of narrative consistency.[38] In the *Apocryphon of John,* the authority of writing may derive less from its reliability *in contrast to* the spoken word, than from its reliability *in relating* the spoken word. It is the connection to speech, not the contrast between the unreliability of speech and the reliability of writing, that makes writing of value. Here again, cross-cultural comparison may be illuminating.[39] Graham tells us that:

---

[38] Gregory Nagy, "Literary and Cultural Studies Today. Tenth Anniversary Celebration of the Center for Literary and Cultural Studies," Harvard University, October 21-22, 1984, noted that it was Aristarchus who set the precedent for the modern task of recovering the original form from multiformity in his work on Homeric manuscripts. Aristarchus' work was highly "bookish" and not oriented toward performance but toward uniformity and authority. Yet it is possible for scribes to be seeking the *one* authoritative version of a text (like Homer or a biblical work) without necessarily losing their perspective on writing as the transmission of speech. Certainly attitudes toward the standardization of written texts were not uniform in the ancient Mediterranean. And in any case, the invention of the printing press and mass production provide the basis for modern sensibilities in ways that could not have existed in a chirographic culture.

[39] Graham discusses the possible link between the idea of a heavenly book and the rise of sacred scriptures in "Semitic" monotheisms: "The motif of a celestial book or tablet of divine wisdom goes back to ancient Mesopotamia and Egypt and recurs in almost all subsequent Near Eastern traditions, apparently as an expression of divine omniscience. Geo Widengren has argued further that such a book was coupled in the ancient Near East, Judaism, and finally Islam to a messenger figure to whom the book is given in a personal encounter with God or who is verified through such an encounter (e.g., Moses at Sinai, Muhammad on his Ascension, or *Mi'raj.)*" (*Beyond the Written Word,* 50). "The appearance of many elements of these ideas in Jewish, Christian, and Muslim scripture reflects the persistence and strength of the notion of a written book as the repository of divine, suprahuman knowledge or divine, heavenly decrees. The book emerges in these traditions as a physical symbol of divine as opposed to human knowledge, and hence as a tangible symbol of authority and truth" (*Beyond the Written Word,* 51).

But Graham also discusses the way in which oral and written aspects of Torah are both emphasized in a complementary fashion on p. 51-52. The Rabbis' conception of Torah as passed down both as writing and as speech is a great example of the way the two can exist side-by-side. Martin Jaffee has defined this interaction with more precision: "Understanding, under the aspect of tradition, is thus a collective enterprise, a conversation continually under construction. And it is just this conversation under construction which constitutes the historical meaning of the text. Its meaning is the history of its reading and interpretation. To the degree that post-mishnaic sages engaged precisely in such a conversation regarding their own texts and traditions, they too were constructing

"Nevertheless, it is especially in traditional cultures around the world that the fundamental link between the spoken word and truth is all but indissoluble—not because oral transmission and communication are practically or technically superior to written forms, but because most traditional cultures see the loci (but not necessarily the origins) of both truth and authority primarily in persons and their utterances, not in documents and records. In such contexts, the teacher who knows the sacred text by heart and has devoted his or her life to studying and explicating it is the one and only reliable guarantor of the sacred truth. The power of the holy word is realized only through the human word of the seer, prophet or spiritual master, not through a manuscript, even where the latter is also important. However exalted its status in a particular tradition, the written text alone is typically worthless, or at least worth little, without a human teacher to transmit both it and the traditions of learning and interpretation associated with it. To be reckoned as scripture, whether in its written or oral form, any text must be perceived in some sense as a prime locus of verbal contact with transcendent truth, or ultimate reality.[40]

Certainly this claim is at the heart of the *Apocryphon of John's* generic claim to be the repository of spoken revelation. It is the word of the divine revealer and the prophetic seer that guarantees the truth of the work as revelation. It may be the case, then, that reliability is guaranteed by appeal to spoken revelation, not through logical consistency or stable transmission. So, on the one hand, logical consistency is less important to chirographic sensibilities than to ours, but the dialogue form may be even more crucial and less expendable to the ancients than modern sensibilities might feel.

The genre of the work as a revelation dialogue[41] also raises issues about the intermingling of attitudes toward speech with literary

---

an oral hermeneutic, an oral tradition, and, ultimately, an Oral Torah. But the text lying at the basis of the Oral Torah, the Mishnah, is a conventional literary product. The self-evident ideological and jurisprudential *function* of the concept of Oral Torah, therefore, is not to be confused with its origins. Rather, the conception emerges quite directly and uncontroversially out of the technology of rabbinic tradition as a *written* tradition. *The oral interpretive culture generated by the text is the primary referent of the term Oral Torah"* ("How Much Orality' in Oral Torah? New Perspectives on the Composition and Transmission of Early Rabbinic Tradition," *Shofar* 10.2 [1992] 72). For our purposes, the significant point here is the careful admonition not to confuse oral function (or *Sitz im Leben*) with the processes of production ("origin"). Attention to oral sensibilities in writing, however, is crucial for understanding the formation of the work as "a conventional literary product."

[40] Graham, *Beyond the Written Word*, 68. A good example of this phenomenon is the Vedic tradition in India.

[41] See P. Perkins, *The Gnostic Dialogue. The Early Church and the Crisis of Gnosticism* (Studies in Contemporary Biblical and Theological Problems, New York: Paulist Press, 1980), esp. 25-73.

practice. The claim of the work to derive its contents from revelatory speech and vision functions to authorize its teachings. Most of the passages that explicitly indicate an understanding of writing as speech are located in the frame narrative. This location suggests a linkage between certain attitudes toward writing as speech and the genre of the work as a revelation dialogue.[42] The dialogue form is essential in creating a fictive impression of the mythic origins of the work's content in divine speech, and even in creating a vivid sensual image in the minds of the hearers by asking them to visualize the theophany of Christ to John.[43] The imitation of speech in writing serves not only to indicate a conceptuality of writing as the repository of speech, but also brings the conventions of speaking into writing. Antoinette Clark Wire discusses the impact of introducing such conventions of speech into literary activity in her consideration of Paul's letters:

> "Then what do we call the orality of Paul's letters spoken and delivered in the churches, which is not the orality of a traditional oral literature first shaped among the non-literate? Here I find Havelock's classic *Preface to Plato* suggestive for his contrast between Homer's oral traditional literature and Plato's dialogues. Socrates always appears provoking people orally and the dialogues were certainly read aloud, but the evocation of story in Homer has given way in Plato to the dialectic of question and answer and the critique of so much that is traditional (in spite of some arguments from tradition). This kind of orality speaks for a particular individual and, like Paul's letters, uses a genre allowing a very polemical address with the intent to disrupt and persuade. Such dialogues and speeches are and continue to be oral genres, but in classical practice they become staples of Greek higher education in rhetoric and are often used by literary people to enter the broader public sphere of communication. By writing speeches, dialogues, or letters, one could extend the impact of one's critical thinking through the mouths of others and—if Havelock is right—put in question thereby the rule of traditional stories and customs over the popular mind."[44]

---

[42] Graham, *Beyond the Written Word*, 65, writes: "Thus it bears repeating that, in many senses, speech always precedes writing, cosmically and anthropologically as well as historically. If there is anything that can be called protoscripture, it is surely the utterances of ecstatics, prophets, and seers, in which it is commonly held to be not they but the divinity who speaks through them as their chosen mouthpieces." Such sensibilities may have been at work in compositions like the *Apocryphon of John* which, although clearly literary works, claimed nonetheless to be the repository of spoken revelation.

[43] Kelber, "Orality, Rhetoric, and Scribality," 205, in discussing the work of Nathalie King, writes that "a fundamental strategy of the ancient art of persuasion (was) to bring auditors to see what was being said, so that the images they visualized were vivid to the point of being indistinguishable from actuality."

[44] A. C. Wire, "Performance, Politics, and Power: A Response," *Orality and Textuality in Early Christian Literature*, ed. J. Dewey (*Semeia* 65, Atlanta, GA: Scholar's Press, 1995) 133-34.

Wire argues that the persuasive and critical aspects of speech can be brought to a broader audience through writing. This implies, however, not just speech written down, but the development of a literary practice through the importation of rhetorical conventions into the processes of writing itself. Moreover, attention to the interactions of writing and oral practices also helps take the interpretation of the *Apocryphon of John* beyond ideological reification and imagine it in a context in which human activity and human senses have a place in cognition.[45] Here a human social world appears in which auditory, visual, and other sensual experiences function in the processes of cognition: people speaking, the sound of voices, their inflections, the gestures and postures that accompany their speech, hearing, reflection, the physical acts involved in writing and book production.[46] The economic factors of publication, and the class implications of literacy also appear as factors that aid in sociological description. Looking at writing in this manner moves us away from seeing writing in terms of a single moment of origin, which reifies and essentializes the processes of writing, to understanding writing as a set of historical acts involving movement and change.

## Oral features of composition/transmission

Until the work of Lord and Parry,[47] analysts of Homeric epic treated the poems as the result of stages of literary activity involving various kinds of editorial labor, interpolation, and revision. Lord and Parry changed all that. They argued in a succession of studies that the poem was the result of oral composition, shown by its use of repeated formulas, type-scenes or themes, and story patterns. Further analysis has shown that these works incorporated the voices of a wide variety of preexisting smaller genres, such as prayers, hymns and laments, brief stories of the gods and heroes, love poetry, genealogies, exhor-

---

[45] As Kelber, "Orality, Rhetoric, and Scribality," 212, puts it: "In all instances, attention to the modalities of communication and physiology of perception will be a rewarding task that can liberate us from our historical, ideational reading that has banished the senses from cognition. More generally, see M. Johnson, *The Body in the Mind. The Bodily Basis of Meaning, Imagination, and Reason* (Chicago and London: The University of Chicago Press, 1987).

[46] For a description of book production and inscription, see H. Gamble, *Books and Readers in the Early Church. A History of Early Christian Texts* (New Haven and London: Yale University Press, 1995) 42-81.

[47] See, for example, A. B. Lord, "Homer as Epic Poet," *Harvard Studies in Classical Philology* 72 (1967) 1-46 and M. Parry, "Language and Characterization in Homer," *Harvard Studies in Classical Philology* 76 (1972) 1-22.

tation, and so on. By drawing upon traditional materials and incorporating smaller complexes, the bard shapes traditional materials toward some end.[48]

Unlike Homeric epic, the *Apocryphon of John* is firmly in the realm of literary composition, and the four versions of the work give ample demonstration of editorial labor, interpolation, and revision. At the same time, however, it is possible to note that the conventions of oral composition did not immediately disappear with the advent of writing. Two features in particular illustrate this point: the incorporation of smaller generic units and the use of oral techniques. *These features appear in the Apocryphon of John as literary practices, but literary practices that have been shaped by oral sensibilities.* Here again, we do not have "pure" orality or "pure" literary activity, but an entanglement of practices and sensibilities.

Composition is not a matter of unique *creatio ex nihilo*; rather it involves the incorporation of a variety of smaller generic units into a larger, more stable narrative frame. The narrative order of the *Apocryphon of John* is typical for ancient myth: theology (theogony), anthropology (anthropogony), ethics (a narrative of the origins of evil), and eschatology (the final destiny of humanity). Into this mythic frame, the *Apocryphon of John* has incorporated a variety of smaller generic units: a cosmogony (also known to Irenaeus),[49] a melothesia

---

[48] Here, however, it is important not to import a naively reflective view of art or static functionalism into the discussion. Peter Rose, *Sons of the Gods, Children of Earth: Ideology and Literary Form in Ancient Greece* (Ithaca and London: Cornell University Press, 1992) 44, argues that "form most profoundly mediates any relation between those ideas (of the *Iliad*) and any recoverable reality giving rise to those ideas," but at the same time "there is a dynamic of radical change at work...(which) opens a gap between medium and message and fosters a new level of consciousness" (*Sons of the Gods*, 53).

[49] One of the first problems to be addressed, subsequent to the discovery of the Berlin Codex, was whether Irenaeus knew and used a copy of the *Apocryphon of John* in writing his work. Schmidt's first report on the discovery of the *Apocryphon of John* (BG,2) argued that the beginning of the text was cited by Irenaeus (*Adv. Haer* I.29; see C. Schmidt, "Ein vorirenäisches gnostisches Originalwerk im koptischer Sprache," *Sitzungsberichte der preussischen Akademie der Wissenschaften zu Berlin* (Berlin: Verlag der Akademie der Wissenschaften, 1896) 839-47 and idem, "Irenäus und seine Quelle *in adv. haer. I,29*," *Philotesia: Paul Kleinert zum LXX Geburtstag*, ed. A. Harnack et al. (Berlin: Trowitzsch & Sohn, 1907) 317-336. This view was at first widely accepted (see, for example, Harnack, "Nachschrift" to Schmidt, "Ein vorirenäisches gnostisches Originalwerk"). R. Liechtenhan, "Die pseudepigraphe Literatur der Gnostiker," *ZNW* 3 (1902) 229, assumes that Irenaeus knew and excerpted the *Apocryphon of John*, and suggests that the heresiologists may often have created their accounts of Gnostic "Theologumena" from such revelatory writings without our realizing it. But later Schmidt's position came under criticism. While there are important similarities between the two accounts, divergences seem to preclude a direct literary relationship. H.-M. Schenke, "Nag Hammadi Studien I: Das literarische Problem des

(only in II/IV), a dialogue on the fate of souls, and the Pronoia hymn (only in II/IV). In addition, the midrash on Genesis 1-7 reflects a generic type, which appears in related works such as the *Hypostasis of the Archons*, whether or not it ever existed as an independent document. The processes of combining these materials within the larger mythic narrative have left many literary traces, shown especially by comparison of the various manuscripts, including Irenaeus, and by internal inconsistencies.

Editorial labor also shows clear evidence of oral techniques, such as performancial variation, substitution, elaboration or expansion, abridging, and retelling. By performancial variation, I mean a rephrasing of materials that does not essentially alter meaning.[50] For example:

BG 74.5-10:

ⲀⲨⲰ ⲘⲠⲞⲨⳐⲘⲀⲧⲉ ⲚϢⲞⲣⲠ ⲀⲨⲉⲓ ⲉⳕⲢⲀⲓ ⲉⲨϢⲞⲬⲚⲉ ⲦⲎⲢⲞⲨ
ⲉⲦⲀⲘⲒⲞ ⲘⲠⲀⲚⲦⲒⲘⲒⲘⲞⲚ ⲘⲠⲚⲀ ⲉⲨⲢ ⲠⲘⲉⲉⲨⲉ ⲘⲠⲉⲠⲚⲀ ⲚⲦⲀϥⲉⲓ
ⲉⲠⲉⲤⳈⲦ

("And they did not first succeed. They all came to a plan to create a counterfeit spirit, for they remembered the spirit which had come down.")

III 38.15-20:

ⲀⲨⲰ ⲘⲓⲠⲞⲨⳐⲘⲀⲦⲉ ⲘⲓⲠϢⲞⲣⲠ ⲚⲤⲞⲠ ⲀⲨⲰ ⲓⲚⲦⲉⲢⲞⲨ-
ⲦⲘⳐⲓⲘⲀⲦⲉ ⲀⲨϢⲀⲬⲓⲚⲉ ⲘⲚ ⲚⲉⲨⲉⲢⲎⲨⲓ ⲉⲦⲢⲉⲨⲦⲀⲘⲒⲞ ⲓⲘⲠⲉⲠⲚⲀ
ⲚⲀⲚⲦⲒⲘⲒⲓⲘⲞⲚ ⳕⲚ ⲞⲨⲘⲓⲘⲎⲓⲤⲒⲤ ⲘⲠⲉⲠⲚⲀ ⲉⲓⲢⲉⲓ ⲉⲠⲉⲤⳈⲦ

("And they did not succeed the first time. And when they did not succeed, they planned with one another to cause the creating of

---

Apocryphon Johannis," *Zeitscrift für Religions- und Geistesgeschichte* 14 (1962) 58, see also 63, argues that: "Nicht unser AJ selbst—mit geringfügigen Abweichungen im Text— ist die Quelle des Irenäus, sondern nur eine diesem AJ verwandte Schrift." So also, N. Petersen, "The Literary Problematic of the *Apocryphon of John*," Ph.D. dissertation, Harvard University, 1967, 69-74. M. Krause, in Foerster, *Gnosis*, 103, concludes that: "We may assume that Irenaeus for his description of the Barbelognostics had at his disposal a source which was indeed not identical with the cosmogony and the fall of Sophia in the *Apocryphon* (BG 26.6-44.19), but yet was similar to it." See Krause for a list of significant differences (in Foerster, *Gnosis*, 100- 103).

[50] See J. D. Crossan, *In Fragments. The Aphorisms of Jesus* (San Francisco: Harper and Row, 1983) 37-66, for a nuanced discussion of the distinction between performancial and hermeneutic variations.

the counterfeit spirit in imitation of the spirit which had come down.")

II 29.20-26:

ⲁⲩⲱ ⲉⲧⲉ ⲙ̄ⲡⲟⲩⲙⲁⲧⲉ ⲙ̄ⲡϣⲟⲣⲡ` ⲛ̄ⲧⲁⲣⲟⲩⲧⲙ̄ⲙⲉⲧⲉ ϭⲉ ⲁⲩⲥⲱⲟⲩϩ ⲉϩⲟⲩⲛ ⲟ̄ⲛ ⲙⲛ̄ ⲛⲟⲩⲉⲣⲏⲩ ⲁⲩⲉⲓⲣⲉ ⲛ̄ⲟⲩϣⲟϫⲛⲉ ϩⲓ ⲟⲩⲥⲟⲡ` ⲁⲩⲧⲁⲙⲓⲟ ⲛ̄ⲟⲩⲡ̄ⲛ̄ⲁ̄ ⲉϥϣⲏⲥ ⲙ̄ⲡⲉⲓⲛⲉ ⲙ̄ⲡ̄ⲛ̄ⲁ̄ ⲉⲧⲁϩⲉⲓ ⲉϩⲣⲁϊ ϩⲱⲥⲧⲉ ⲉⲃⲟⲗ ⲛ̄ϩⲏⲧϥ` ⲁⲥⲱⲱϥ ⲛ̄ⲙ̄ⲯⲩⲭⲏ

("And they did not succeed at first. When they did not succeed, they gathered with each other again; they made a plan together. They created a despicable spirit in the image of the Spirit which had come down in order to pollute the souls through it.")

Here one sees a variety of differences that may be ascribed to different factors. The meaning of the first sentence remains essentially the same; only the expression is different, probably due to independent translation from the Greek. The next sentence provides an example of performancial variation: "They all came to a plan to create a counterfeit spirit," (BG); "And when they did not succeed, they planned with one another to cause the creating of the counterfeit spirit" (III); or "When they did not succeed, they gathered with each other again; they made a plan together; they created a despicable spirit" (II).[51] While these variations could result from independent translation, it is more probable that these expressions are simple performancial variations. A common type of performancial variation is the expansion of the number of stichs in the verbal core. III and II show an expansion of the single-stich core structure ("they did not at first succeed"); II additionally shows an expansion of the single-stich core structure ("they made a plan together").[52] To see the differences as due to independent translations from the Greek or translations of different versions would be to read too much literary quality into a simple variation of expression.

The final phrases, however, clearly interpret the relation of the counterfeit spirit to the true spirit and its purpose quite differently in each of the three versions. Here we have to do with not a performan-

[51] Birger Pearson has convincingly suggested that the difference between the terms "counterfeit" (BG, III) and "despicable" (II) is due to a textual corruption in the Greek (II reading ἄτιμον for ἀντίμιμον; ἄτιμον is translated into the Coptic ϣⲏⲥ. Here BG and III have preserved the earlier reading, and we are firmly in the realm of scribal activity not oral performance.

[52] See Crossan, *In Fragments*, esp. 37-40.

cial, but a hermeneutical variation due to editorial/authorial labor. Significant differences in meaning are achieved by the substitution of concepts: for example in determining whether the counterfeit spirit is created *by remembering* the true spirit (BG) or it is created *in imitation* of the true spirit (III);[53] or by elaboration: II adds that the purpose of the despicable spirit is to pollute souls.

The examples of elaboration or expansion that are most clear are the major additions of the melothesia and the Pronoia hymn, but there other minor cases of expansion or elaboration as well, such as that just discussed above.

Some scholars understand the absence of the melothesia and the Pronoia hymn from BG and III to be examples of abridgment rather than expansion.[54] There are other cases as well. It appears, for example, that II/IV may have deleted the phrase ("if anything exists beside him") in BG 26.10-11[55] in order to remove the confused implication that the supreme being might in some way be limited.[56]

It is also common for different versions of the same episode to occur as retellings, another kind of hermeneutical variation. For example, the story of God cursing Adam and Eve is told with quite different intents in II 23.37-24.2 compared with BG 61.7-18. The version in Codex II portrays Eve as a seductress and understands man's authority over woman to be part of the holy decree, while BG understands woman's subordination to man to be an ignorant and wicked plan of the Demiurge in contrast to the will of the holy height.[57] Such examples could be multiplied.

All these types of variants, with the exception of performancial variations, significantly affect the meaning of the work and demonstrate important interpretive tendencies. While such variants are textual, they reflect the sensibilities of oral performance, which makes

---

[53] Michael Williams has suggested that the difference here may be due to an error in translation, where the translator of BG mistook μίμησις for some form of μιμνήσκω or μνήμη. While this explanation is plausible, the difference in the Coptic still constitutes a hermeneutical variation, whether intentional or not. In either case, intentional or unintentional variation, the example does not constitute a simple practice of oral variation.

[54] See, for example, M. Tardieu, *Écrits gnostiques: Codex de Berlin* (Sources Gnostiques et Manichéennes 1; Paris: Les Éditions du Cerf, 1984) 42.

[55] Codex III contains a similar phrase at III 6.23-24.

[56] In this case, I would argue that the more difficult reading of BG and III indicates an earlier version in comparison to that of II/IV.

[57] See K. L. King, "Sophia and Christ in the *Apocryphon of John*," *Images of the Feminine in Gnosticism*, ed. K. L. King (Studies in Antiquity and Christianity, Philadelphia: Fortress Press, 1988) 169-71.

room for the views of the performer, as well as the needs and interests of the audience. This flexibility in oral performance is an important aspect of tradition's capacity to adapt to and to address changing circumstances and intellectual interests. By fixing tradition, writing tends to limit this kind of flexibility; but as long as oral sensibilities are still operative in writing itself, variations in the textual repositories have the potential to provide information about changing circumstances and interests.

There are also variants that belong to more strictly literary aspects of the transmission process: independent translations from the Greek,[58] translation from differing Greek recensions,[59] differing scribal/orthographic conventions,[60] or scribal errors.[61]

It is often the case that writing promotes a tendency toward increased narrative and logical consistency.[62] One characteristic of II/IV compared with BG and III seems to be its tendency to such bookish[63] sensibilities, that is, the tendency to avoid contradiction and ambiguity. The text of II/IV is not of course without contradiction and its own difficulties of interpretation, but in comparison with BG and III, there is a greater sensitivity to clarity and consistency of internal presentation.[64] This may indicate relatively more influence of literate sensibilities.

---

[58] Variants here are apparent both in vocabulary and syntax. For example, in comparing BG 74.11-12 with III 38.20-21, one can postulate that III has kept the Greek term μετασχηματίζειν while BG has translated the term into the Coptic ϣⲓⲃⲉ.

[59] The most significant differences here lie between the shorter version (BG and III) compared with the longer version (II and IV).

[60] The differences between II and IV seem to have arisen at the stage of copying a common Coptic tradent. The differences are primarily orthographic (for example, II 9.29 reads ⲁⲭⲙ̄ where IV, 15.14 reads ⲉⲭⲛ̄.

[61] Occasionally a difference is due to scribal error, for example, dittography at IV, 11.913; II 23.17-20; IV, 20.18 has deleted two letters compared with II 13.4-5; or haplography of II compared with IV 4.9-10.

[62] See J. Goody and I. Watt, "The Consequences of Literacy," *Comparative Studies in Society and History* 5 (1963) esp. 321.

[63] Codex II twice mentions books (first book of Moses, *Book of Zoroaster*) in contrast to BG and III.

[64] The best example is that the lists of powers at II 12.15-25 and II 15.14-23 are consistent, while in BG 43.11-44.4 and BG 49.11-50.4 the lists differ. Other less extreme examples include the following: II 2.4-15 in comparison with BG 21.5-22.5 gives three forms/faces (child, old man, and servant) while BG gives only two (child and old man); II 3.4-5 in comparison with BG 23.11-12 states that the transcendent deity is "total perfection" in contrast to BG's statement that "it cannot be perfected." Moreover, if we hypothesize that the Greek *Vorlage* of BG was in some form known to II, it may be that II omits BG 26.2-6 (which limits knowledge of the transcendent God) and 29.17-18 ("of the unbegotten father") because they are problematic. That BG 29.17-18 is also not in III may indicate that the problem was widely felt.

*Transmission history: stability and fluidity*

It is possible to trace at least some aspects of the transmission history of the *Apocryphon of John* with relative certainty. All four manuscripts are copies of translations from Greek into Sahidic Coptic.[65] The four versions of the *Apocryphon of John* represent three independent translations from Greek (II/IV, III, and BG).[66] II/IV and BG/III were translated from different recensions of the Greek, and it may be that some differences between BG and III also go back to differences in the Greek recensions of which they are translations. II and IV represent a common Coptic *Vorlage*[67] and show primarily orthographic variants or differences due to scribal errors. Further variations among the texts were probably introduced in the processes of Coptic transmission, although these are difficult to distinguish from variants in the Greek recensions. II/IV, BG, and III all contain special material of varying length and significance, as well as significant overlap in content, form, conceptuality, and language. Each of the manuscripts evinces occasional scribal error.

It is therefore possible to identify several distinct states in the transmission history of the *Apocryphon of John*. There were at least two recensions in Greek (long and short) and possibly three (represented by II/IV, III, and BG), three independent translations into Coptic, and copies of all three Coptic versions. The *Apocryphon of John* was inscribed in four separate codices, three of which came to belong to the same collection, and were hidden together in a jar. The fact that all four scribal hands and the covers of the four codices are all different indicates that they were probably not originally intended to be part of the same collection. Indeed Codex IV contains only two works, both of which are also in Codex III, an unusual and expensive duplication.

This analysis results in the following diagram (where G=Greek version; C=Coptic version):

---

[65] So also, for example, F. Wisse, *ABD* III, ed. D. N. Freedman et al. (New York: Doubleday, 1992) 899: "All four copies of *Ap. John* are written in Sahidic with IV,1 conforming more closely to the standardized spelling of this Upper Egyptian dialect."

[66] So also, for example, Wisse, *ABD* III, 899.

[67] So also Wisse: "II,1 and IV,1 are copies of the same Coptic translation of a long recension" (*ABD* III.899).

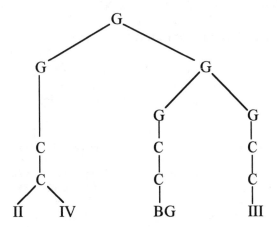

While useful, this linear diagram is an oversimplification of the transmission history. It lacks the complexity needed to provide a full accounting for all the textual variants among the extant versions, since it is unable to account for the agreements of III with II against BG;[68] of II with BG against III;[69] or where II, III, and BG all differ).[70]

---

[68] Examples include:

III 6.22-23 adds: "for his goodness supplies all the aeons." This phrase is completely absent in BG, but II 4.14-15 and IV read: "and it is he who gives them strength in his goodness." It is possible the omission in BG is due to haplography, as Michael Williams has suggested.

BG 27.11 says that Barbelo is the *perfect* Pronoia; III and II don't have "perfect. "

III 9.18 reads "father" with II 6.19 against the "spirit" of BG 30.8.

III 10.10 agrees with II 6.33 and IV 10.13 in reading that noyc is called for as a "fellow worker" for whoever is asking (is it the Son?), while BG 31.5-6 says only "a single thing." Here it is likely that "fellow-worker" is earlier, and BG has changed it.

III 10.17 agrees with II 7.5 against BG in placing the phrase "though a/the word" at this spot; BG has it later and the others repeat it.

III 13.18 agrees with II 9.12-13 in saying that Seth was placed with regard to "the second aeon with the second light Oriel." BG omits "the second aeon." On the other hand, BG 36.1 and II agree against III in saying that Seth is *over* rather than *in* the second light.

III 18.17 agrees with II 12.6 and IV ,19.4 in saying that Yaltabaoth was *lord* (xoeic) over them because of the Mother's light within him, while BG 42.19 says he became *Christ* (xc) over them. Compare BG 49.13 with III 22.21.

Both III 21.7 and II 14.6 (IV 22.8) say the Invisible Spirit poured a/the *holy* spirit over the Mother; BG 47.2-3 simply says "Spirit" (not holy).

III 24.11-12 agrees with II 19.29-30 against BG in stressing that the spirit went out of the chief archon/Yaldabaoth.

Note, however, that there are no clear cases where the differences between II and IV cannot be accounted for by scribal error or linguistic preferences, indicating a close linear relationship between these two manuscripts. The relationships among II/IV, III, and BG are more complex. These problems have a variety of possible resolutions, some of which are more significant than others for transmission history, but, taken as a whole, they make it clear that a linear model

---

III 26.23-25 agrees with II 21.12-13 in reading that in this way, man became mortal; not in BG.

III 27.11 and II 21.22 agree against BG 56.6-7 in reading *trees* instead of *tree*.

III 30.5-6 and II 24.8 say *they* were clothed in darkness; BG 62.2-3 says *he* was clothed in a *dark mist*.

III 33.12 reads "from now on"; II 25.31 (and IV) read "from here on"; no phrase in BG.

III 33.15 and II 25.34 the *hypostasis* (state) of being in the flesh; BG 65.,19 has only the flesh.

BG 73.6-7 says that *she* (Epinoia) sheltered him and *some* people; III 37.25-38.2 says that *they* sheltered themselves and *some other* people; II 29.7-10 says that *they hid* themselves and *many other* people.

III,38.16-17 and II 29.21 both have "when they did not succeed"; not in BG.

BG 75.7 has *he* (the counterfeit spirit) closed their hearts; III 39.8 and II 30.9 have they (the angels) closed their hearts. Michael Williams suggests this difference may be due to scribal error, BG reading ⲁϥ for ⲁⲩ.

[69] Examples include:

At BG 27.9-10 and II 4.31, the text reads that Barbelo came forth/appeared, a phrase absent in III.

BG 30.12 and II 6.21 read "which first appeared"; III lacks "first."

BG 31.3-4 and II 6.31-32 / IV 10.10-11 read "with the perfect Pronoia"; not in III.

BG 39.5 agrees with II 10.26 in reading that the chief archon produced by copulating (BG)/joining (II) with his *arrogance* against III 15.7 which reads he copulated with his *ignorance*.

BG 42.1-3 and II agree against III in saying that the fourth is named Yao and has seven heads; III also adds that the fourth is lion-faced in addition to being serpent-faced.

BG 56.5-6 and II 21.21 agree against III 27.10-11 in reading "delight" (τρυφή) rather than "food" (τροφή) as the bitter deception of paradise. While this difference could easily be due to scribal error, it might also be a conscious interpretation of the "food" as sexual "delight."

BG 57.20-58.1 agrees with II 22.9 against III 28.17 in saying that *they* (Adam and Eve) ate instead of *he* (Adam) ate.

BG 60.13 and II 23.15 (IV) agree against III 30.11 in saying that the consort of the Mother *will* be sent forth instead of *was* sent forth.

BG 66.7 and II 26.2-3 describe the eternal life as "imperishable"; not in III.

BG 67.3 says all the souls will *live*; III 34.5-6 and II 26.11 say they will *be saved*.

BG 71.7-8 and II 27.35 call the Holy Spirit merciful; not in III.

[70] BG 27.17-18 says that Barbelo "contemplates" (νοεῖ) It; III reads "she glorified It"; and II lacks any comparable phrase.

of textual transmission alone is inadequate to account for the variations among the versions.

This complexity is not surprising in the face of publication practices in antiquity. Publication in antiquity differs in almost every way
from contemporary publication of printed books.[71] Recent work by
Gamble stresses that once an edition leaves the hands of the author,
he or she loses control over the work:

> "In providing copies of a work to friends an author effectively surrendered
> further personal control over the text. A recipient might make her copy
> available to another, who could then make a copy in turn. No expense was
> involved to her than the cost of materials, and, if need be, the services of a
> scribe. In this way copies multiplied and spread seriatim, one at a time, at
> the initiative of individuals who lay beyond the author's acquaintance. Since
> every copy was made by hand, each was unique, and every owner of such a
> copy was free to do with it as he or she chose. In this way a text quickly
> slipped beyond the author's reach. There were no means of making authori-
> tative revisions, of preventing others from transcribing or revising it as they
> wished, of controlling the number of copies made, or even of assuring that it
> would be properly attributed to its author. In principle the work became
> public property: copies were disseminated without regulation through an in-
> formal network composed of people who learned of the work, were inter-
> ested enough to have a copy made, and knew someone who possessed the
> text and would permit it to be duplicated. Thus a text made its way into gen-
> eral circulation gradually and for the most part haphazardly, in a pattern of
> tangents radiating from the points, ever more numerous, where the text was
> available for copying."[72]

The transmission of the *Apocryphon of John* seems to have followed
a very complex pattern. The number and kind of variants among the

---

[71] H. Marrou, "La technique de l'édition a l'époque patristique," *VC* 3 (1949)
208-224, argued that books were published in the patristic period by copying from a
principal unique exemplar of a work authorized by the author. The primary example he
cites is the publication of the works of Augustine. There are two problems with
generalizing this process for the *Apocryphon of John*: First, there is no clear "author"
who can disseminate and approve exemplars for copying. Secondly, his thesis provides no
help in discovering how differences among the versions of the *Apocryphon of John* could
have come about. What Marrou usefully contributes is to note that it is anachronistic to
identify an "edition" with many identical copies (such as the printing press can produce);
rather an "edition" is the exemplar used for copying. Sometimes two exemplars might
have equal status (p. 221, n. 48), but both would have been approved by the author.

[72] Gamble, *Books and Readers,* 85. Gamble's description refers to the production of
literature among a literate elite, where "publication took place in the context of social
relations between persons interested in literature, and subsequent copies of the work
circulated along paths of friendship or personal acquaintance." During the empire,
however, a commercial book trade arose which "operated more or less independently of
social relations."

four versions clearly demonstrate that such a work was disseminated without the sort of copyright and plagiarism regulations we are used to.

The complexity of the publication and transmission processes also indicate that we need to reckon with a variety of audiences, represented by the stages of the work. The interests of these audiences may be indicated in part by patterns in the secondary editorial labor on each of the versions. Moreover each copy of the *Apocryphon of John* would have been read in conjunction with the other works in the same codex, giving clues about how the work would have been interpreted and what the interests of each codex's audience might have been.

|  NHC II  |  Berlin Codex  |
| --- | --- |
| *Apocryphon of John* | *Gospel of Mary* |
| *Gospel of Thomas* | *Apocryphon of John* |
| *Gospel of Philip* | *Sophia of Jesus Christ* |
| *Hypostasis of the Archons* | *Acts of Peter* |
| *On the Origin of the World* | |
| *Exegesis on the Soul* | |
| *Book of Thomas the Contender* | |

|  NHC III  |  NHC IV  |
| --- | --- |
| *Apocryphon of John* | *Apocryphon of John* |
| *Gospel of the Egyptians* | *Gospel of the Egyptians* |
| *Eugnostos the Blessed* | |
| *Sophia of Jesus Christ* | |
| *Dialogue of the Savior* | |

The tendencies of the variants, as well as the placement of the *Apocryphon of John* in the four codices, provide some indications of similar or changing views over a period of about three centuries (dating the Greek versions to the end of the second century to the fifth century date of the Berlin Codex).

The many variations in the manuscript tradition attest abundantly that writing in this case has not functioned to "fix" the content into an absolutely set form. Nor can we reckon with a single function, situational context, literary context, or audience for the work.

The extent of the variants would seem to indicate that other values are at work in writing than textual stability, or rather that other notions of stability itself are operative. It is important to locate what aspects of the work remain stable and which are fluid. Stability and fluidity may be governed to some degree by ancient generic conventions,[73] so we need to be aware of these in order to assess the meaning of similarities as well as differences. Christine Thomas' work on the *Acts of Peter* suggests that there is evidence that scribes felt more free to alter works circulating in the names of culture heroes (like Peter or John) than those circulating in the names of known authors. Hence works ascribed to a specific author are likely to demonstrate less transmissional fluidity than those ascribed to a culture hero, like John.[74] She also suggests that other factors, such as genre and generic conformity, imaginative content, and whether a work was written in a 'high' or 'low' style, may also contribute to ancient attitudes toward the relative fixity or fluidity of a work.[75]

Moreover, it is quite possible that a different notion of stability is at work in ancient writing than in modern print. Kelber, in discussing Lord's work on Homeric composition, notes that oral poets:

> actualize the legacy of tale-telling with a consistently conservative urge to preserve essential themes and story patterns. On the face of it, stability arises from the pragmatics of communication as it seeks to serve the performers' needs and to accommodate their audiences. But it is not reducible to utilitarian principles. The tenacity with which tradition holds on to building blocks and thematic complexes springs from that deeper conviction that the story provides 'the very means of attaining life and happiness.' Stability in this sense, however, is not the same as the modern preoccupation with literal fixity and logical consistency. Oral performers are bound by

---

[73] I am indebted to the work of Christine Thomas on the *Acts of Peter* for this insight (see especially C. Thomas, *The Acts of Peter, the Ancient Novel, and Early Christian History*, Ph.D. dissertation, Harvard University, 1995, 117-69).

[74] See, for example, C. Thomas, 103, 104: "Works such as Esther, Daniel, *Joseph and Aseneth*, the Acts of Peter, and the Alexander romance, however, evidence a degree of textual instability that, when compared with the five late Greek erotic novels, is a difference in degree constituting a difference in kind. Each of these texts was issued in several revisions, each was translated more than once, and all except *Joseph and Aseneth* had significant portions added to them over the course of their history. All of these works, moreover, are arguably anonymous, and most do not even have fixed titles in the manuscript tradition. The five late Greek erotic novels, on the other hand, all carry the names of their authors...A direct relationship seems to hold, then, between anonymity and transmissional fluidity among ancient novelistic texts. Perhaps ancient scribes perceived less obligation to protect the *ipsissima verba* of texts unsanctioned by the name of an author. Yet, as noted, there seems to be also a slight degree of flux even for some of the five late Greek erotic novels, so other features may play a role: the fact that these works do not belong to a recognized genre, as well as their imaginative nature, may have also offered the scribe greater license. In Greek style, literary conventions, and generic affinities, the Acts of Peter, the Alexander romance, and even the five Greek novels are a far sight less sophisticated than the 'highbrow' literary products of a Polybios, or even a Philostratos."

[75] See the summary of C. Thomas, *The Acts of Peter*, 104.

tradition, but not as something sacrosanct; no single feature of the tradition is frozen in position. Lord's theory of oral composition allows for ceaseless fluctuations, which entail "saying the same thing in fewer or more lines," "expansion or ornamentation," "changes of order in a sequence," "addition of material," "omission of materials," "and substitution of one theme for another." To such a degree is variation practiced in oral tradition that no two singers can be said to use the traditional repertoire in exactly the same way.[76]

There are two points here that are relevant for our consideration of the *Apocryphon of John*. First, the conservative impetus to preserve materials, whether or not they any longer fit, belongs to a deeply rooted sensibility that tradition is not to be changed lightly, that it embodies what is wise and true (and hence salvific). This can be seen in the *Apocryphon of John's* tendency to keep older views even when they conflict with its changed perspective.[77] Second, the work seems to take the view that stability is not compromised by summarizing, elaborating, adding, deleting, or retelling. These practices belong to the sensibilities of oral stability of performance, not the textual stability of print.

In conclusion, it has been possible to suggest ways in which oral sensibilities are at work in the literary practices of the transmission history of the *Apocryphon of John*. Insofar as we understand the oral aspects and practices of writing and reading more fully, we are in a better position to account for the variants.

## APPRECIATING THE MANY VERSIONS

At a recent conference, the Shakespeare scholar Patrick Ford noted that currently the mission of textual editing is generally seen as the restoration of sense and coherence, damaged by the hazards of transmission and time, a definition that applies well to current approaches to the composition and transmission history of the *Apocryphon of John*. But in Ford's view, such methods, which reduce the existing textual variety to a set of intelligibly related texts, have nothing to do with how literature was perceived and used by ancient people. He suggests that we move away from a focus on the author and text to reader perspectives, in order to give an appropriate and

---

[76] Kelber, "Orality, Rhetoric, and Scribality," 197-98.

[77] The tendency to incorporate a wide variety of materials, without strict regard for coherence, may also be tied to the work's constant appeal to traditional cultural materials (such as Genesis and the *Timaeus)* in conveying its own very different perspectives. It claims to be *restoring* the true meaning of those materials, a meaning which has been corrupted and distorted by the actions of the counterfeit spirit.

useful indeterminacy to the texts. They can then be seen as instances of scribal performance.[78] From this perspective, the archetype itself has no privileged evidentiary value. Every performance of the work is valuable.

It seems to me that the point to this kind of criticism is that the focus on establishing the "original" text can have the (unintended?) effect of erasing the history of the work, a history inscribed precisely in the tendencial particularities of the many versions. Attempting to establish earlier versions or even the earliest version of a work is not wrong-headed *per se,* when it is part of the attempt to establish the full history of the work. It is also clearly the case that some stages in the transmission history are not only easier to construct than others, but are for specific purposes also more important.[79] But an overemphasis upon the value of the "original" over every other version can become problematic: 1) insofar as the attempt to establish an original erases and devalues the significance of the actually existing exemplars, in all their variety, and with it information that is potentially significant for establishing a history of Sethian Gnosticism; 2) insofar as our imagination of such an original is grounded upon expectations of originality, coherence, and uniformity that might be unfounded; and 3) insofar as such an original is always hypothetical and very difficult

---

[78] The comments of Patrick Ford (and those of Gregory Nagy below) are here reproduced from my notes taken at a conference on "Literary and Cultural Studies Today. Tenth Anniversary Celebration of the Center for Literary and Cultural Studies" (Harvard University. October 21-22, 1994). These notes themselves form an exemplar of scribality, since they are neither an exact reproduction of the oral performance of these speakers nor the composition of the hearer/note-taker either. Rather they reproduce the oral experience through the written cipher of the scribe. They tell us "about" both the performance and the interests of the scribe, but not "purely" one or the other.

[79] The question, raised at the conference discussion, of whether all moments in the evolutionary history of the work are equally significant raises the concomitant question of "significant for what?" For different purposes, different recensions will be more significant. The addition of the names of the demons that control various parts of the body, for example, would be extremely significant to someone interested in magical healing.

Another comment that the "original creation of a work" might be a "far more significant act than relatively slight modifications by a later scribe" raises two separate issues. First of all, insignificant changes are of no interest at all, except insofar as they provide evidence for textual stability, so the contrast between the two somewhat skews the issue at hand. The issue concerns the effects of granting an exclusive, privileged status to a hypothetical, reconstructed original over significant existing manuscript versions. A complementary resistance to loosening the distinction among author, editor, and scribe (in the face of good evidence that such loosening better reflects actual practices) may show an investment in "authorial originality" tied to Romanticism's ideals of creativity, uniqueness, and feeling. Why else do we have so much interest in an imagined "original, creative act"?

to establish with any degree of certainty, especially in the details; in the case of the *Apocryphon of John* the original Greek text in all its detail surely lies beyond our grasp.

Rather than see the tendencies of a version as the distortion of the hypothetical "original," tendencies[80] can be analyzed as evidence of the meaning and practices (the social and intellectual history) of the audiences who knew the *Apocryphon of John*. In this approach, the "tendencies" of the texts are no longer perceived as "corruptions" or "distortions" that must be removed in order to reveal the original practices of the "circles" around the *Apocryphon of John*;[81] they are instead important keys to understanding the history of such "circles." Privileging the "original" with regard to "reliability" effectively erases

---

[80] The term "tendency" is often used to imply that a perspective is "tendentious," that is, an example of biased, prejudiced, or self-interested partisanship and advocacy, in contrast to objective, impartial, impersonal, neutral, and just judgment. But by "tendency" here I mean only the direction toward some purpose which reflects the social and political interests that the work implicitly or explicitly purveys. The analysis of the tendencies of all the versions presupposes the view that all literary works have purposes and interests that can be discerned through analysis.

[81] Many differences among the versions are understood to be due to editorial labor under the influence of "tendencies." The tendencies of these editors are often termed "deviation," "distortion," etc., and in general their work is said to diminish the "reliability" of the version. For example, S. Giversen, *Apocryphon Johannis. The Coptic Text of the Apocryphon Johannis in the Nag Hammadi Codex II with Translation, Introduction and Commentary*, (Acta Theologica Danica 5; Copenhagen: Prostant Apud Munksgaard, 1963) 277-78, concludes: "In C II it is possible to detect a distinct tendency towards emphasizing the sublime and playing down anthropomorphic elements; for this reason BG and also C III must at times be regarded as somewhat more reliable in terms of content." Giversen says explicitly that in shortening II, "no change seems to have been made in the tendency of their teaching ... (rather) the alterations are of an editorial nature" (*Apocryphon Johannis*, 279). Giversen's point is that the original *should* be a reliable witness to the teaching of the "circles" in which AJ originated. "Tendencies" reduce this reliability: "It does not follow from this that the AJ of C II presents an account of the teaching which these circles round Epicurus had taught from the very beginning, nor does it follow that the tradition of the teaching has been expounded in a less distorted form than the didactic exposition of BG and C III. For it must be remembered that the AJ of C II contains a clear tendency towards a distinct didactic system, a tendency which repeatedly turns out to represent an innovation in the tradition of AJ" (*Apocryphon Johannis*, 279). As an example of tendentious editing, Giversen describes the following: "This tendency of the *Apocryphon of John* of C II is a tendency towards detracting from the anthropomorphic character of the high beings and towards stressing the lofty. A clear example of this was disclosed by linguistic analysis, e.g., when we examined C II 61.32-- 62.15; by examining C II 61.33 and the parallel accounts we noted that the text of C II had been subjected to a tendentious change in relation to BG, where Ialtabaoth in BG is referred to as the abortion of darkness, whereas C II had changed it into 'a veil of darkness'." (*Apocryphon Johannis*, 280). Another example he gives is the description of Sophia's distress: in BG as moving to and fro in the darkness (BG 45.14-15) whereas in II 61.24-25 it says oblivion came forth for her in the darkness of ignorance (*Apocryphon Johannis*, 280).

or at least devalues the text's history and performances, which are keys to social and intellectual history. The identification of a primary exemplar is not useful if and insofar as the process erases that history.

Moreover, in attempting to restore the "original" coherence of the work, we may be in danger of giving the *Apocryphon of John* a coherence it in fact never had.[82] It may not be useful in some cases to analyze inconsistencies as literary problems. For example, rather than be taken as indications of sloppy editorial labor (or lack of group cohesiveness),[83] inconsistencies might indicate tensions within the logic of a system,[84] or they may be evidence of an attitude in which being comprehensive or meeting changing needs is more important than complete logical consistency. In antiquity, persons are probably used to hearing narratives told in a variety of versions, as is shown for

---

[82] The attempt to resolve every issue of contradiction or difficulty by positing literary additions, omissions, editions, etc., may go too far and work to give the *Apocryphon of John* a coherence it may never have possessed and certainly doesn't possess now. An example is provided by Krause in Foerster, *Gnosis*, 101: "We learn in the Apocryphon further details about their origin (i.e., that of five aeons), which are in part self-contradictory; the first aeon to come into being is Ennoia (BG 27.2-8), who has various names, for example the 'perfect Pronoia of the All' (BG 27.10-11), Barbelo (BG 27.14), 'the First Ennoia' (BG 27.18). According to this, Ennoia and Pronoia are two names of the same aeon, but later (BG 28.9-10, 18; 29.12) Barbelo and Ennoia are different beings, and here (BG 29.12) Ennoia came into being after Barbelo. Thus the account of the origin of this Ennoia must have been omitted in all four versions of the *Apocryphon of John*." The operative assumption here is that the "original" was a logically coherent, literary composition, disturbed by later editorial omission. There is, however, no textual evidence for such an "omission." The only "evidence" is provided by the logic of the critic, who judges the text to be inadequate measured against the standard of an ideally logical narrative, an ideal that is not articulated (and hence functions normatively and uncritically). Here it may be that the analysis is less useful framed as a literary analysis, than it would be as an insight into the work's logic.

[83] Wisse, *ABD* III, 900, says: "*Ap. John* shares a number of themes and mythologumena" with other Nag Hammadi texts, but he insists that any similarities are not due to a common sectarian background. Rather: "Literary borrowing would explain both the common traditions and the different uses to which these are put.... The fact that the details of the myths proved to be very unstable and were readily corrupted in the translation and copying process indicates that they were not intended as objects of belief and held little importance in themselves." In my view, this perspective misunderstands the relationship of texts and practices. Wisse's presupposition is that logical coherence of texts and among texts is necessary to group formation. However, this perception may have more to do with contemporary (Christian?) notions that presume literalism and that privilege belief over practice than with ancient social formation or the uses of traditional materials in practice and performance (see P. Bourdieu, *Outline of a Theory of Practice* (Cambridge Studies in Social Anthropology; Cambridge: Cambridge University Press, 1977); C. L. Briggs, *Competence in Performance. The Creativity of Tradition in Mexicano Verbal Art* (Philadelphia: University of Pennsylvania Press, 1988).

[84] I have the impression that many studies framed as literary analyses function rather as logical analyses (as above note 82).

example in the fluidity of the Jesus parable tradition. It may be the case that people listen for truth in these teachings, less with a mind to literal repetition than for the meaning conveyed. Persuasiveness operated less with a view to logical consistency than to making sense of and giving meaning to the (often inconsistent) world of human experience. It might be, then, that the impulse to comprehensiveness and inclusiveness was often more decisive than the desire for logical consistency. It is possible that the determination to find a place for all ideas within its system was such a central and fixed tenet that it led to sometimes serious, if not impossible tensions among elements which simply didn't fit together very well.

A particularly glaring example of inconsistency lies in the different names for the powers in BG 43.11-44.4 and 49.11-50.4. Such blatant internal inconsistencies are extremely jarring to modern print sensibilities. Yet they can be answered in other ways than by positing editorial oversight. The written variants may keep intact variant traditions; the conservative desire not to lose anything or the desirability of inclusiveness and flexibility may have been more important than consistency.

Moreover, the establishment of an "original" text of the *Apocryphon of John* may not be possible, either because there is not sufficient evidence[85] or because there never was an "original text."[86] Wisse

---

[85] Yet such an "original" remains an ideal goal even where it is recognized as impossible to obtain. For example, Wisse, *ABD* III, 899, writes: "In spite of the presence of three independent translations of the Gk., it is often difficult if not impossible to determine from the original reading where they differ. It appears that all three translators had serious difficulties understanding and/or rendering the complexities of the Gk. text. Thus a dependable critical edition that reflects the original Gk. seems out of reach." The word "dependable" here conveys the sense of loss.

[86] A similar approach is taken by Christine Thomas in her study of the *Acts of Peter*. She concludes, 81: "Students of the Acts of Peter are thus faced with the remarkable lack of anything resembling an 'original text.' Precisely this absence is significant in assessing the genre of the Acts of Peter, that is, the type of written work it was considered to be by its ancient audience; and that the process of excerpting, abridging, redacting, and translating that led to its variegated manuscript tradition, usually held to be so problematic, is in fact not problematic at all, but meaningful in itself. For, though the audience of the Acts of Peter remains difficult to reconstruct, it is patently clear that at least the individuals who excerpted, translated, and re-edited the text also read the Acts of Peter with singular care. Their actions on the text, which resulted in our manuscript tradition, reflected their attitudes toward it. And the attitudes of the ancients are valuable for any treatment of the genre and purpose of the Acts of Peter."

There is clear evidence in antiquity both of cases where a principal exemplar was approved by an author for publication, and of cases where there was no such archetype. As an example of a literary work which was published in a "final edition" by the author, see the discussion of Augustine's practice by Marrou, "La technique de l'édition a l'époque patristique," 208-224. Examples where there would not have been an "original"

concludes that in the case of the *Apocryphon of John*, it is not possible to resolve the manuscript tradition into a dependable reflection of a common Greek *Vorlage*.[87] Why not?

The matter is more complicated than just resolving the question of which variants are more "original" than others. At stake is the question of the identity of the *Apocryphon of John*. As Peter Schäfer notes, the determination of an "original" is often really an "arbitrary choice of one form of the text as a zero point on the continuum: all versions before it are source documents, those after it are redactions."[88] This observation is particularly pertinent to the *Apocryphon of John*, since most of its content can be relegated to different literary sources (the cosmogony, the midrash on Genesis, the melothesia, the dialogue on fate, and the Pronoia hymn). If we take away those sources and regard the frame narrative and Christianizing elements as secondary, not much remains. At least nothing one would call the *Apocryphon of John*. The identification of an original work with authorial originality does not fit ancient literary sensibilities and practices.

Do we then define some minimal content necessary for identifying a work as the *Apocryphon of John*? Can a work be the *Apocryphon of John* that does not contain the frame narrative? Is the title to be taken as the distinguishing marker of self-identification? Does the work need to be Christianized to be the *Apocryphon of John*? At what point does locating the "sources" of the work become irrelevant for identifying the work as the *Apocryphon of John*? What criteria should be employed in making such a decision?

Another issue is that where one locates the "original" on the continuum and how the source materials are understood and characterized have been used to classify the work as "Gnostic" or "Christian." For example, without the frame narrative, the dialogue form, and other Christian elements, the *Apocryphon of John* is no longer

---

exemplar include cases where an orator's speech may have been taken down in notes by several hearers and published by them in different versions. In this case, R. Thomas, *Literacy and Orality*, 160-61, writes: "One incidental but important result of the primacy of the oral version is that there might be no single written text which could be regarded as the author's own 'authorized' version." But the *Apocryphon of John* has more characteristics of a composite literary composition than an oratorical performance inscribed through notes, although it was probably known primarily through speech. There is, as R. Thomas stresses, "obviously a complicated relationship between the oral nature of the performance and the use of writing" (*Literacy and Orality*, 160). It is this complexity that needs investigation.

[87] Wisse, *ABD* III, 899.

[88] Cited in C. Thomas, *The Acts of Peter*, 112.

"Christian." Or again, Hauschild questions the Gnostic character of the work by arguing that the *Apocryphon of John's* doctrine of the two spirits is not specifically Gnostic since it shows similarities with Qumran teaching.[89] But the different contexts in which shared materials might be located does not determine the identity of the *Apocryphon of John*, any more than the use of Jewish apocalyptic in Mark 13 makes the *Gospel of Mark* "non-Christian." No one disputes that the *Apocryphon of John* draws upon "non-Gnostic" and "non-Christian" materials. Examples range through Jewish Genesis midrash and Wisdom teaching, middle-Platonic cosmology, astrology, Stoic anthropology and ethics, and probably other traditional materials as well. The acceptance of common, shared tradition[90] more likely

---

[89] W.-D. Hauschild, *Gottes Geist und der Mensch. Studien zur frühchristlichen Pneumatologie* (Beiträge zur evangelischen Theologie 63; München: Chr. Kaiser Verlag, 1972) 224-72. M. Waldstein, "On the Relation Between the Two Parts of the *Apocryphon of John*," *Der Gottesspruch in der Kopt. Literatur. Hans-Martin Schenke zum 65. Geburtstag*, ed. W. Beltz (Hallesche Beiträge zur Orientwissenschaft 15; Halle: Druckerei der Martin-Luther-Universität, Halle-Wittenberg, 1995) 107, uses this as evidence to indicate that the dialogue on the soul was secondarily added.

[90] Comparative studies aimed at determining the sources of the *Apocryphon of John* keep pointing toward "common tradition" rather than direct literary dependence. For example: W. van Unnik, "A Formula Describing Prophecy," *NTS* 9 (1963) 93, on the opening of heavens, and the use of the past-present-future formula; W. J. Blackstone, "A Short Note on the 'Apocryphon Johannis," *VC* 19 (1965) 163, on the encounter between an apostle and a Jewish priest in *Acts of Philip* and the *Apocryphon of John*; Hauschild, *Gottes Geist und der Mensch*, 224-72, on the opposition of spirits in the *Apocryphon of John* and Qumran; M. Waldstein, "The Providence Monologue in the *Apocryphon of John* and the Johannine Prologue," *JECS* 3.4 (1995) 369-402, on Jewish wisdom tradition in Gos. John, *TrimProt*, and the *Apocryphon of John's* providence monologue; Tardieu, *Écrits gnostiques*, 39-40, 250-51, on negative theology sections in *Allogenes* and the *Apocryphon of John*. Even with regard to Genesis, the *Apocryphon of John* is not so much providing a direct interpretation of the text (already LXX), but stands within a complex tradition of interpretation (see B. Pearson, "Jewish Sources in Gnostic Literature," *Jewish Writings of the Second Temple Period: Apocrypha, Pseudepigrapha, Qumran Sectarian Writings, Philo, Josephus*, ed. M. E. Stone [Assen: Von Gorcum; Philadelphia: Fortress Press, 1984] 443-481). Similar arguments can be made regarding the use of Middle Platonic and Stoic conceptuality and terminology (see T. Onuki, *Gnosis und Stoa. Eine Untersuchung zum Apokryphon des Johannes* [Novum Testamentum et orbis antiquus 9; Göttingen: Vandenhoeck & Ruprecht, 1989]), and astrological materials (see R. van den Broek, "The Creation of Adam's Psychic Body in the *Apocryphon of John*," *Studies in Gnosticism and Hellenistic Religions presented to Gilles Quispel on the Occasion of his 65th Birthday*, ed. R. van den Broek and M. J. Vermaseren [Études préliminaires aux religions orientales dans l'Empire romain 91; Leiden: E. J. Brill, 1981] 38-57. The mention of the *Book of Zoroaster* might also imply that the *Apocryphon of John* excerpted material from it (or it could just be a reference to one place where more material of the same type could be found). Tardieu, *Écrits gnostiques*, 39-40, has pointed toward an original Chaldaean apocalypse as the base text underlying the *Apocryphon of John*. The question under debate, however, is not whether

indicates a sociological attitude of universalizing identity formation, rather than non-Christian or non-Gnostic origins. Determination of source materials and comparison with related cultural traditions are essential to the analysis of the historical meaning and usages of the *Apocryphon of John*. The danger lies in misunderstanding what the evidence is evidence of. Here again the desire for an "original" can be misleading, both with regard to determining and categorizing the identity of the *Apocryphon of John*.

An alternative is to regard all the versions of the work as equally the *Apocryphon of John*. In this case the synoptic edition prepared by Wisse and Waldstein is precisely what is called for.[91] The preserved tradition of the *Apocryphon of John* is small enough to make this approach practical.

CONCLUSION

The purpose of this essay was to provide a prolegomenon for the study of the particular tendencies and interests of the variant recensions of the *Apocryphon of John* by assessing the impact of oral sensibilities in ancient writing on the composition and transmission processes of the *Apocryphon of John*. The results caution us toward critical reflection about our imagination of how writing was conceived by those who read and used the *Apocryphon of John*; about the adequacy of our comprehension of literary processes in antiquity (including uncritical projection of print sensibilities); and about the appropriateness of applying our values (such as creativity, originality, and logical consistency) in historical reconstruction. Attention to the oral sensibilities of the practice of writing serves to highlight the work's own attitude toward writing, the entanglement of writing with oral practices, the "oral" features of composition and transmission, and the values implied by the stability and fluidity in transmission. At the same time, this examination also highlights the degree to which the *Apocryphon of John* is a literary composition, whose variants are largely accounted for by literary processes. In the end, the most significant point here is that the variants are valuable in and of themselves as witnesses to the history of Sethian Gnosticism, and they should not be discounted or erased in the process of seeking a hypothetical original text.

---

the *Apocryphon of John* has drawn upon other materials (it clearly has), but how are we to interpret the use of common tradition with regard to literary composition?

[91] See note 2.

# AFTER THE *SYNOPSIS*:[*]
## PROSPECTS AND PROBLEMS IN ESTABLISHING A CRITICAL TEXT OF THE APOCRYPHON OF JOHN AND IN DEFINING ITS HISTORICAL LOCATION

*Frederik Wisse*
McGill University

Upon completing the difficult restoration work of one of the Manichaean codices from Medinet Mahdi, the great German papyrologist Hugo Ibscher is reported to have remarked that in view of the fact that the scientific part of the study of the document was now finished, he was happy to leave the rest to others. Given his great achievement, Ibscher may be forgiven for having a somewhat inflated opinion of his own contribution, but he was correct in sensing that there is a kind of hierarchy in the various scholarly tasks that are part of a full study of an ancient codex. Compared to the other tasks, the restoration of the pages is indeed the most fundamental of all and the only one that limits itself to the purely physical aspects of a codex. That was, no doubt, why Ibscher considered the papyrological stage the only truly scientific one.

Restoration and preservation are much like laboratory-based research in that they require instruments and techniques for separating pages, putting fragments in their proper place on the basis of the color and continuity of fibers, preserving the result between Plexiglas, providing a precise physical description of the codex as reconstructed on the basis of the surviving evidence, and, ideally, publishing the results in a facsimile edition. If done correctly, this task needs to be done only once. I have had the pleasure of having been involved in the papyrological phase of the Nag Hammadi codices and can attest to the high demands and great charm of this task. Ideally everyone studying ancient texts should have some direct familiarity with the physical aspects of the study of manuscripts. This will help to provide a better framework to put the other scholarly tasks in proper perspec-

---

[*] M. Waldstein and F. Wisse, *The Apocryphon of John: Synopsis of Nag Hammadi Codices II,1; III,1; and IV,1 with BG 8502,2* (NHMS 33; Leiden: E. J. Brill, 1995).

tive. As in the case of seeing how sausages are made, the "eating" will never be quite the same.

The hierarchy of tasks, in which the papyrological study comes first, suggests on the one hand a chronological order in that some tasks necessarily presuppose others, but more important, as Ibscher implied, it involves an order in degrees of certainty in which the stages are increasingly dependent on subjective judgments and speculative hypotheses. Ibscher was a bit mischievous by reserving the term science (*Wissenschaft*) only for his own work, for the other tasks are not less scholarly for being dependent on hypotheses. They only become less than scientific if that dependence is not sufficiently recognized and taken into account in the methods used. It is this recognition and its methodological consequences that will be the focus of these reflections on the future study of the *Apocryphon of John* (*Ap. John*).

The editions of the text of the four MSS of *Ap. John* published prior to the *Synopsis* were made before the restoration work was completed, and thus they were premature and at best tentative. Establishing the text comes, of course, chronologically second in the hierarchical sequence in that it can only be done properly when the papyrological phase has been finished. For very fragmentary manuscripts, however, such as Codex IV, the placing of fragments often depends on the correct reconstruction of the text, and thus in such a case, restoration and establishing the text depend on each other and have to be done simultaneously.

If only one copy of a text survives, establishing the text consists of providing an accurate transcription. The choice of conventions for word division is a pragmatic one, and is to be judged in terms of helpfulness to the reader and the editor's awareness of options in the rare cases when a different word division presents an alternate sense reading. Editors also have a choice of conventions for suggesting emendations when the text appears to be corrupt. One can present the manuscript reading in the transcription and suggest emendations in the textual notes, or present the emended text and put the manuscript reading in the notes. It is not uncommon to follow a hybrid form in which all clearly necessary emendations are entered in the edited text and less certain ones are relegated to the notes. At stake is finding a balance between confronting the reader with the text as found in the manuscript and the need to indicate textual corruptions. Early in the editing process of the *Ap. John* versions, I tended to be quite liberal in suggesting emendations. Later I questioned the need of some of them and moved closer to a minimal emendation policy, but in the end we restored most of the earlier emendations. Of course, in the case of *Ap. John*, the fact that the parallel versions often support the emendation allowed for a more liberal emendation policy.

For fragmentary manuscripts, establishing the text involves reconstructing, in so far as is possible and desirable, the lacunae in the text. It is a task which I particularly enjoy and thus am in some danger of overdoing. The focus must remain on the purpose of reconstructing text, i.e., to make full use of the clues provided by the parts of words and letters that are visible, and to draw, as far as that is possible, inferences about the length and nature of the lost text. By doing too little the editor deprives the user of the edition of a judgment which would normally be superior to the user's own guess, and by doing too much the user is tempted to draw unwarranted conclusions on the basis of the reconstructed text. In the case of *Ap. John* IV, which represents the same Coptic version as *Ap. John* II, it made sense to reconstruct all lines that were at least partially preserved. As a matter of fact, the value of *Ap. John* IV is largely restricted to that of a witness to the much better preserved text of *Ap. John* II. A careful reconstruction of the lacunae in *Ap. John* IV made it possible to ascertain with a high degree of certainty whether it had more, the same, or less text than the parallel in *Ap. John* II. Since copying errors due to homoioteleuton are relatively common, the reconstructed text can indicate whether textual variation occurred, and often also the nature of the variation.

The reconstruction of lacunae in *Ap. John* III, *Ap. John* BG, and *Ap. John* II (when the parallel in *Ap. John* IV was also lost) was in most cases aided by the parallel in one or more of the other versions. The parallel version can, however, only give a clue as to the probable sense, but not to the Coptic wording. A major weakness in textual reconstructions in the earlier editions of *Ap. John* was the failure to stay within the confines of the space available.[1] Another major weakness was the mistaken assumption that the lost text was more or less identical to the Coptic wording found in one of the parallel versions, rather than conforming to the grammar, syntax, idioms, use of Greek words, and spelling convention attested in the surviving part of the text itself. Thus the proper reconstruction of lacunae in the text

---

[1] The reconstruction should always be tested by carefully imitating the scribal hand in the space available (for example in a facsimile edition). One should never assume in a lacuna unusual spacing, scribal errors, and forms or constructions that are at variance with those attested in the surviving text. When the lacuna extends into the left or right margin, the reconstruction must observe the confines of the writing column. Any reconstruction which does not observe these restrictions is without value.

requires a provisional index of all Coptic and Greek words attested in the text. For the *Synopsis* it is likely that there is still room for improvements in the reconstruction of lacunae,[2] but we believe that this does not compromise the text as presented in the edition. Our aim was to present a definitive text and we deserve blame if we fell short. Unless more pages or fragments of *Ap. John* are discovered, there should not be a further need to establish the text of the two short and the long version of *Ap. John*.

Normally when more than one copy of a text survives, the task that follows upon establishing the text of each copy is the production of a critical text on the basis of all the available evidence. In the case of *Ap. John* this applies only to the long version of which two copies are extant in Coptic. A critical text could have been constructed from this without difficulty,[3] but since there was a primary need for accurate transcriptions of II and IV, this took precedence.[4] A critical Coptic text of the long version is, however, readily apparent from the composite translation of II/IV and the textual notes presented in the *Ap. John Synopsis*.

Since the four known Coptic manuscripts of *Ap. John* represent two independent translations from the Greek text of the short version, as well as a translation of the long version, it is impossible to provide a critical Coptic text which would represent all three versions. The best one can do is produce a synopsis of the Coptic versions which can serve as the basis of a critical modern language translation that

---

[2] Particularly in the very fragmentary pages 1-4 of *Ap. John* II, where the parallel text in III and IV has suffered even greater loss, and also BG has significant lacunae.

[3] It would be advisable for such an edition to ignore the very frequent differences in spelling.

[4] The differences between *Ap. John* II and IV are with few exceptions limited to matters of orthography. *Ap. John* II shares with the other tractates in Codex II the characteristic of having been written in Sahidic but with many spellings that betray a Subachmimic vocalization. The scribe of II, however, is very inconsistent, for he uses both the Subachmimic and the standard Sahidic form of many words. The scribe of IV, on the other hand, uses with few exceptions the most common Sahidic form of words. A likely explanation for this is the general shift to standard Sahidic, evident also in Coptic biblical manuscripts from the fourth century, of which II would represent the beginning and IV an advanced stage. This phenomenon should not be mistaken for an attempt to adapt texts written in non-Sahidic dialects for use by Sahidic speakers. Rather what appeared to have happened was that texts, which had been translated by various individuals into their native Coptic dialects, were adapted in monastic scriptoria to an apparently new and artificial form of Coptic which was accessible to all Coptic speakers. Without the rapid spread of cenobitic monasticism in fourth century Egypt, the shift to and quick success of standard Sahidic becomes inexplicable. Only the scriptoria of the monasteries could assure the remarkable degree of uniformity achieved in Sahidic orthography and scribal conventions during the second half of the fourth century.

combines the short and long versions, and makes reasoned choices
when there is a difference in meaning. Such a critical modern translation is actually an attempt to bypass the Coptic translations to get as
close as possible to the common Greek text behind the them. Less
than a year ago we still intended to produce for the *Ap. John Synopsis*
such a critical English translation based on the two short and the long
version accompanied by a textual commentary that justified the
choices made among the variants. Time constraints forced us to
abandon this ambitious project. It remains a crucial next step in the
study of *Ap. John*.[5] If done successfully, such a critical translation
would accomplish the primary scholarly task, i.e., expressing in a
modern language what the ancient text says.[6]

The process leading to a critical translation of *Ap. John* is a particularly difficult one.[7] For the differences between the versions in the
parts held in common are not only very numerous but are often
substantial. A critical translation, if it is to be of scholarly value,
cannot be based on arbitrary choices. The assumptions about the
transmission history of the text and the principles that guide the
choice between variants must be exposed and justified. Before
mentioning my specific assumptions about the text and the hierarchy
of explanations that guide my choice among variants, I must expose
the basic canon on which my approach rests. It is one that I consider
fundamental in all historical research, including the attempts at
recovering the sense of the original Greek text of *Ap. John* as well as
recovering the historical circumstances of its composition, redac-
tion(s), translations into Coptic, and inscription in the four codices
that survive. Following the traditional formulation of the canons of
textual criticism—to which it is closely related—it could be stated as:
*explicatio simplicior potior*.[8] As reasonable as this rule may sound
when formulated this way, there is a powerful scholarly bias against
it, and particularly in historical studies it is violated with impunity.
No one did a better job of exposing the scholarly bias against the

---

[5] See the Appendix to this paper for an attempt at a critical English translation of the
*Ap. John Synopsis*, 1-4.

[6] Though it often tries to do more, a commentary on the text is an extension of such a
translation. Its main purpose is to clarify to a modern reader (who would not be privy to
the knowledge or experience that the ancient author assumed to share with the intended
reader) what the text says. Thus a commentary would normally have been unnecessary
for the intended ancient reader.

[7] The four translations presented in the *Ap. John Synopsis* are a modest step towards a
critical translation in that they have been made to conform to one another in wording as
much as the Coptic would appear to allow.

[8] This is of course, a form of Occam's Razor.

*simplicior potior* rule than Charles Dickens in his delightful account of "the Pickwick controversy" (*The Pickwick Papers*, The Penguin English Library 1972, pp. 216-217; 227-9). It think it is worth quoting in full:

It was at this very moment that Mr. Pickwick made that immortal discovery which has been the pride and boast of his friends. and the envy of every antiquarian in this and any other country.... Mr. Pickwick's eye fell upon a small broken stone, partially buried in the ground, in front of a cottage door. He paused.

'This is very strange,' said Mr. Pickwick.... 'There is an inscription here, ... I can discern,' continued Mr. Pickwick, rubbing away with all his might, and gazing intently through his spectacles: 'I can discern a cross, and a B, and then a T. This is important,' continued Mr. Pickwick, starting up. 'This is some very old inscription, existing perhaps long before the ancient alms-houses in this place. It must not be lost.'

He tapped at the cottage door. A labouring man opened it.

'Do you know how this stone came here, my friend?' inquired the benevolent Mr. Pickwick.

'No, I don't sir,' replied the man civilly. 'It was here long afore I war born or any of us.'

Mr. Pickwick glanced triumphantly at his companion.

'You - you - are not particularly attached to it, I dare say,' said Mr. Pickwick, trembling with anxiety. 'You wouldn't mind selling it, now?'

'Ah! but who'd buy it?' inquired the man, with an expression of face which he probably meant to be very cunning.

'I'll give you ten shillings for it, at once.' said Mr. Pickwick, 'if you would take it up for me.'

The astonishment of the village may be easily imagined, when (the little stone having been raised with one wrench of a spade) Mr. Pickwick, by dint of great personal exertion, bore it with his own hands to the inn, and after having carefully washed it, deposited it on the table.

The exultation and joy of the Pickwickians knew no bounds, when their patience and assiduity, their washing and scraping, were crowned with success. The stone was uneven and broken, and the letters were straggling and irregular, but the following fragment of an inscription was clearly to be deciphered:

+

BILST
UM
PSHI
S.M.
ARK

Mr. Pickwick's eyes sparkled with delight as he sat and gloated over the treasure he had discovered. He had attained one of the greatest objects of his ambition. In a county known to abound in remains of the early ages; in a village in which there still existed some memorials of the olden time, he—he, the Chairman of the Pickwick Club—had discovered a strange and curious inscription of unquestionable antiquity, which had wholly escaped the observation of the many learned men who had preceded him. He could hardly trust the evidence of his senses.

'This – this,' said he, 'determines me. We must return to town, to-morrow.'

'To-morrow!' exclaimed his admiring followers.

'To-morrow.' said Mr. Pickwick. 'This treasure must be at once deposited where it can be thoroughly investigated, and properly understood.' (pp. 216-217)...

It appears from the Transactions of the Club, then, that Mr. Pickwick lectured upon the discovery at a General Club Meeting, convened on the night succeeding their return, and entered into a variety of ingenious and erudite speculations on the meaning of the inscription. It also appears that a skillful artist executed a faithful delineation of the curiosity, which was engraven on stone, and presented to the Royal Antiquarian Society, and other learned bodies—that heart-burnings and jealousies without number were created by rival controversies which were penned upon the subject and that Mr. Pickwick himself wrote a pamphlet, containing ninety six pages of very small print, and twenty-seven different readings of the inscription.... That Mr. Pickwick was elected an honorary member of seventeen native and foreign societies, for making the discovery; that none of the seventeen could make anything of it; but that all the seventeen agreed it was very extraordinary.

Mr. Blotton, indeed—and the name will be doomed to the undying contempt of those who cultivate the mysterious and the sublime—Mr. Blotton, we say, with the doubt and caviling peculiar to vulgar minds, presumed to state a view of the case, as degrading as ridiculous. Mr. Blotton, with a mean desire to tarnish the lustre of the immortal name of Pickwick, actually undertook a journey to Cobham in person, and on his return, sarcastically observed in an oration at the club, that he had seen the man from whom the stone was purchased; that the man presumed the stone to be ancient, but solemnly denied the antiquity of the inscription—inasmuch as he represented it to have been rudely carved by himself in an idle mood, and to display letters intended to bear neither more nor less than the simple construction of—'BILL STUMPS, HIS MARK;' and that Mr. Stumps, being little in the habit of original composition, and more accustomed to be guided by the sound of words than by the strict rules of orthography, had omitted the concluding 'L' of his christian name.

The Pickwick Club, as might have been expected from so enlightened an Institution, received this statement with the contempt it deserved, expelled the presumptuous and ill-conditioned Blotton, and voted Mr. Pickwick a pair of gold spectacles, in token of their confidence and approbation; in return for which, Mr. Pickwick caused a portrait of himself to be painted, and hung up in the club room.

Mr. Blotton though ejected was not conquered. He also wrote a pamphlet, addressed to the seventeen learned societies, native and foreign, containing a repetition of the statement he had already made, and rather more than half intimating his opinion that the seventeen learned societies were so many 'humbugs.' Hereupon the virtuous indignation of the seventeen learned societies, native and foreign, being roused, several fresh pamphlets appeared; the foreign societies corresponded with native learned societies; the native learned societies translated the pamphlets of the foreign learned societies into English; the foreign learned societies translated the pamphlets of the native learned societies into all sorts of languages: and thus commenced that celebrated scientific discussion so well known to all men, as the Pickwick controversy. (pp. 227-9)

The *simplicior potior* rule implies that one should conclude that the Greek exemplars behind the three versions differed only when all attempts to explain the difference on the basis of a shared Greek text fail. Only the following distinctions are needed to account for differences *in sense* between the versions:

G = the sense of the original Greek of *Ap. John*. It is established by the agreement in sense between the long version and at least one of the short versions.

S = the sense of the Greek of the short version, i.e. when *Ap. John* III and *Ap. John* BG agree in sense against the long version. Since all indications are that L is a redaction of S, one may assume that S = G. If *Ap. John* III and *Ap. John* BG differ in sense and neither is supported by the long version, the sense of G can be argued only on the basis of internal considerations.

S-III = the text of *Ap. John* III when it differs in sense from the agreement between *Ap. John* BG and the long version. S-III may be due to a Greek exemplar which differs from G, but it is simpler to assume that it is due to the Coptic translator.[9]

---

[9] It is not possible to distinguish between the Greek exemplar behind any of the Coptic versions and their Coptic translators. The nature of the differences in sense between *Ap. John* III and *Ap. John* BG make it likely that some and possibly all were introduced inadvertently or deliberately by the translators.

S-BG = the text of *Ap. John* BG when it differs in sense from the agreement between *Ap. John* III and the long version. S-BG may be due to a Greek exemplar which differs from G, but it is simpler to assume that it is due to the Coptic translator.

L = the Greek of the long version when it differs in sense from S. L may be due to the Coptic translator, but it is simpler to assume that it represents the Greek redactor of the long version.

Special attention must be given to the not infrequent instances in the versions of *Ap. John* where the expected sense is lacking. These apparent nonsense readings go well beyond corruptions that appear to be due to scribal errors. This raises the question what kind of sense is appropriate for an esoteric text like *Ap. John*. It should be noted that in most cases *Ap. John* does make sense in a way similar to that found in non-esoteric religious writings of the period. This would permit the important assumption that the Greek text behind the Coptic versions made sense throughout, and that if the expected sense in a Coptic version of *Ap. John* is lacking this is most likely due to mistranslation.

This poses a dilemma to the modern translator. Normally one can expect a text written originally in Coptic to make sense within the framework of the author's intent and thought world. If, for example, in a writing of Shenoute the expected sense appears to be lacking, this would normally be due—except in the rare instances when the text has suffered corruption during its transmission—to the modern translator's ignorance of Coptic idiom, or ignorance of the peculiarities of Patristic monastic rhetoric. In such a case pressing on for sense can normally be expected to lead to the sense appropriate to the context. This is not the case for the Coptic versions of *Ap. John*. Not only is textual corruption due to scribal errors a far greater problem than for the much more carefully copied writings of Shenoute, but the original sense appears not infrequently to have been obscured by faulty translation. For all three Coptic versions this happens particularly when the sentence structure or argumentation is complex. In such cases one cannot be sure that the original sense is preserved in any of the versions, and pressing on for sense would be counterproductive. Thus the editor of a critical translation must, at the risk of exposing his own ignorance of Coptic idiom or of appropriate sense, designate readings as probable mistranslations. This has no serious implications for the establishment of G, if two versions agree against a suspected nonsense reading in the third version. If, however, one version has a likely nonsense reading and the other two differ in sense, the sense of G can be argued only on the basis of internal considerations.

If the author of *Ap. John* were well known, the successful construction of a critical translation might well be the end of the scholarly task. In the case of a pseudonymous text, however, important questions about the historical location of the text remain open. Unfortunately, it is in the very nature of such a text that it will include no unambiguous clues about its real author, the date, and the circumstances of its composition. Thus any scholarly attempt to speak to these issues must not only be very modest in its claims, but must also be careful to observe the *explicatio simplicior potior* rule. The best clues available are about the transmission history of *Ap. John*. Four phases can be inferred. The clues about the last phase are by far the clearest. The earlier phases are increasingly obscure and speculating about them runs the risk of leading to misunderstanding rather than enhanced understanding of the content of the document.

### 1. The Coptic Monastic Phase

There are strong indications that the Nag Hammadi Codices were produced and used, not by a Gnostic sect, as was first assumed, but by monks in a Pachomian monastery located near the discovery site. Documents used as cartonnage to stiffen the leather cover of Codex VII include monastic letters among which is one from Pachomius to Paphnoute. Among these are several dated documents from the middle of the fourth century which prove that Codex VII was written after 348 C.E. The three scribal colophons that survive at the end of Codices I, II and VII conform to the pious scribbles found in monastic manuscripts. The Coptic dialect in which most of the tractates were written is standard Sahidic, the orthographic convention created in fourth century monastic scriptoria. The generally ascetic outlook of this diverse collection of tractates also fits the monastic setting. Thus the most direct significance of the Nag Hammadi Codices is the light it sheds on early cenobitic monasticism in Upper Egypt.

The production and use of heterodox Christian, Gnostic, and even some pagan writings by Pachomian monks during the early years of the cenobitic monastic movement is not altogether surprising. Pachomius' own documented involvement in language mysticism would indicate that interest in esoteric literature was the rule rather than the exception in the early decades of the movement. What unified the monks was a shared dedication to the ascetic life rather than to orthodoxy. It took quite some time before the orthodox hierarchy in Alexandria was able to exert some control over the rapidly growing monastic movement. We know of a purge of heretical books under abbot Theodore, the successor of Pachomius, in response to Athanasius' anti-heretical Paschal letter of 367 C.E. This may well have been the occasion of the burial of the Nag Hammadi codices at some distance from the monastery, perhaps in the hope of recovering them at a later time. It is likely that the monks cherished these unorthodox books, and particularly *Ap. John*, mainly for their ascetic and esoteric value.

## 2. The Translation Phase

The scribal mistakes in the *Ap. John* versions indicate that they were copied from Coptic exemplars. Thus the translation from Greek to Coptic must have happened sometime before the mid- to late fourth century date of the Codices. Though we do not have direct evidence for the translation phase, a probable case can be made that it took place in the late third and early fourth century among Graeco-Egyptian ascetics. The most famous of these is St. Antony, but more likely candidates would be persons like Hierakas of Leontopolis who wrote in both Greek and Coptic and was known for his radical encratism and heterodox views. The earliest known biblical translations into various Coptic dialects appear to come from the same time and setting, and they are similarly idiosyncratic and flawed as translations.[10] These translations were most likely intended for private use by unilingual Copts who were joining the increasingly popular anchoritic monastic movement. These hermits would have brought esoteric books like *Ap. John* into the cenobitic communities which some of them joined during the first half of the fourth century. The minority of Nag Hammadi tractates written in the Subachmimic dialect, such as *Ap. John* II, are probably closer to the translation phase than the Sahidic ones.

If this reconstruction of the translation phase is correct it would indicate that third and early fourth century Christian ascetics in Egypt operated outside orthodox control and were attracted to Gnostic and other esoteric literature which reflected their ascetic outlook.

---

[10] F. Wisse, "The Coptic Versions of the New Testament," *The Text of the New Testament in Contemporary Research: Essays on the Status Questionis*, ed. B. D. Ehrman and M. W. Holmes (Studies and Documents 46; Grand Rapids: Eerdmans, 1995) 131-141.

### 3. The Composition Phase:

It is impossible to be specific or even generalize about the date, place and circumstances of the composition and major redaction of *Ap. John*. It would appear that several mistaken assumptions have guided the scholarly reconstruction of the composition phase of the Nag Hammadi tractates. The first is the tendency to work on the basis of the earliest possible date of a text. In view of the date of the codices, however, and the translation phase some decades earlier, composition could have been as late as the early fourth century. Since the estimated date of composition often has far reaching implications, proper historical method (based on the *simplicior potior* rule) demands that one starts with the latest possible date and move to an earlier one only if there is sufficient internal or external evidence to warrant this.[11] For none of the Nag Hammadi tractates are there compelling reasons to date them before the third century C.E.. though it is certainly possible that some were composed earlier. Even in the case of *the Gospel of Thomas*, which some scholars date as early as the late first or early second century, the earliest external attestation in Hippolytus, *Refutatio* 5.7.20 and the earliest Greek fragments do not necessitate a date earlier than about 200 C.E. Nothing in the content of *the Gospel of Thomas* requires an earlier date. Some scholars have taken the absence of Christian elements in a tractate to be indicative of an early date, or the absence of the influence of the "great" second century Gnostic systems, but there was no necessity for third century authors to include such elements. There is no apparent reason to date the composition and redaction of *Ap. John* before the late third century, though it is possible that it happened a century earlier.

A second mistaken assumption in much of Nag Hammadi scholarship is that the tractates were composed in and for distinct Gnostic sects. This was also the conjecture of the Christian heresiologists, beginning with Irenaeus, who thought that the Gnostic writings known to them incorporated the teachings of distinct sects, though they did not have direct evidence for this. They conceptualized the Gnostics behind the text as sectarians who, like orthodox Christians, defined themselves in terms of a set of doctrines. This, however, is highly

---

[11] M. J. Edwards, "The Epistle to Rheginus: Valentinianism in the Fourth Century," *NovT* 37 (1995) 76-91, points out the mistake of previous commentators in assuming the earliest possible date, assuming Valentinian identity on the basis of the other tractates in the Jung Codex, and interpreting the tractate in a heretical way when an orthodox reading is more probable. Edwards correctly reverses the burden of proof to where it should be.

unlikely, for the Gnostic tractates look more like the creations of visionaries who would rebel against the orthodoxy of any group, and who were open to ideas from a variety of religious traditions as long as it served their ascetic and esoteric interests. Even the Valentinian tractates do not appear to adhere to any community "orthodoxy," though there is no doubt about the existence of Valentinian communities in late antiquity. *Ap. John* may have found use in Gnostic religious communities, but nothing in it suggests that it was composed in and for a specific Gnostic sect.

The third questionable assumption is that the apostolic names assigned to pseudepigraphical writings, such as *Ap. John*, were not arbitrary but point to the specific community which produced these pseudepigrapha and assigned them to a particular apostle with whom they identified. Thus the writings assigned to the Apostle Thomas are thought to originate in Edessa in northern Syria, though their contents has little in common, and it is assumed that tractates attributed to the Apostle James have a Jewish Christian connection. Unfortunately such speculations are beyond proof and disproof. As far as is known, the Apostles were revered in all areas and by all factions of the church, and the reason for choosing one name rather than another, if there was one, is in most cases obscure.

## 4. The Pre-Composition Phase

Much of the interest in the Nag Hammadi texts, especially from the side of New Testament scholars, is in the earlier traditions which may have been incorporated in them. There can be no doubt that at least some of the tractates are based on earlier traditions and were subject to later redaction. *Ap. John* is our best example of this; it is difficult to say whether it is typical. *Ap. John* is extant in a short and a long version, and its first part is based on a Gnostic document known to Irenaeus in about 180 C.E., while the longer version has interpolated a major section which it claims to have taken from "the Book of Zoroaster." Apart from these documented cases of the use of sources and redaction in *Ap. John* it is impossible to specify further ones with any degree of certainty. The same mythological themes appear in a number of writings, and the eclectic adaptation of material from other texts appears to be the rule rather than the exception. Attempts to isolate the sources and redactional material are frustrated by the vulgar nature of most of the tractates. The authors appear to have made little effort to plan their treatises and thus the many awkward shifts and anomalies are more likely weaknesses in the original composition rather than evidence of incorporation of sources or of later redaction.

## APPENDIX: *An Attempt At A Critical Translation Of Ap. John (Synopsis Pages 1-4)*[12]

The teaching [of the] savior (σωτήρ), and [the revelation] of the mysteries (μυστήριον), [and the] things hidden in silence, [even these things which] he taught John, [his] disciple (μαθητής).

And (δέ) it happened one day, when John, the brother of James—they are the sons of Zebedee—had gone up to the temple, that a Pharisee named Arimanius approached him and said to him. "Where is your master whom you used to follow?" He said to him. "He has gone to the place from which he came." The Pharisee said to him. "With deception (πλάνη) did this Nazarene deceive (πλανᾶν) you (pl.), and he filled your ears with [lies], and closed [your hearts] **2** (and) turned you from the traditions (παράδοσις) of your fathers."

"When I, [John], heard these things, I turned away from the temple (ἱερόν) to a desert mountain. And I grieved (λυπεῖν) greatly in my heart saying, "How (πῶς) [then was] the savior (σωτήρ) appointed (χειροτονεῖν), and why was he sent into the world (κόσμος) by his Father, and who is his Father who sent him, and of what sort is that aeon (αἰών) to which we shall go? For (γάρ) what did he [mean (when)] he said to us. 'This aeon (αἰών)[to which we shall go] is of the type (τύπος) of that imperishable aeon (αἰών),' but he did not teach us concerning the latter of what sort it is."

Straightway, while I was contemplating these things, behold, the heavens opened and the whole creation (κτίσις) **3** which is below heaven was illuminated by a light, and the [whole] world (κόσμος) was shaken. I was afraid and I looked, and behold, a child [who stood] by me appeared to me in the light. And (δέ) [it changed] in likeness to an old man. And it [changed its] likeness (again) to become like a servant. [As I looked] at it I did not [understand (νοεῖν)

---

[12] Text found only in L (= the long version) has been put in italics. Square brackets are used only if the text is uncertain in all three versions. Greek has been added if it occurs in at least one of the versions. Bold numbers correspond to the pages of the *Ap. John Synopsis*. Where L and S (= the short version) have variant readings only the preferred reading (defended in the commentary) is used.

the] miracle whether there was a [likeness (ἰδέα)] with multiple forms (μορφή)in the light - (since) its forms (μορφή) appeared through each other - or (οὐδέ)] whether it was a single [likeness (ἰδέα)] with three faces.

He said to me "John, why do you wonder (διστάζειν), and (ἤ or εἶτα) why [are you] afraid? Surely (γάρ) you are not (μή) unfamiliar with this likeness (ἰδέα)! Do not [be] faint-hearted! **4** I am the one who is with [you (pl.)] always. I am [the Father], I am the Mother, I am the Son. I am the eternal One. I am the undefiled and incorruptible One. [Now I have come to teach you] what is [and what was] and what will come to [pass], that [you may know the] things which are not revealed [and those which are revealed, and to teach you] concerning the [unwavering race (γενεά) of] the [perfect (τέλειος) Man]. Now [therefore, lift up] your [face, that] you [may receive] the things that I [shall teach you] today, [and] may [tell them to your fellow] spirits (πνεῦμα) who [are from] the [unwavering] race (γενεά) of the perfect (τέλειος) Man."

## *Textual Commentary to the Ap. John Synopsis 1-4:*

1.2-4: The descriptive title supplied by L is not a superscript but an incipit. It was created on the basis of the opening and closing scenes; the reference to silence may reflect 9.14.

1.6: both S and L probably read ἐγένετο δὲ μιᾷ τῶν ἡμερῶν (cf. Lk 8:22; 20:1).

1.14: L starts the first person narrative earlier than S, where it begins in 2.3.

2.3: Π added "John" in apposition (cf. Rev. 1:9).

2.5: The Gk. probably read εἰς τὸ ἔρημον.

2.9-10: BG put the ⲉⲛⲧⲁϥⲧⲛⲟⲟⲩϥ mistakenly with the first occurrence of ⲡⲉϥⲉⲓⲱⲧ.

2.13-15: The statement in S that clarifies the preceding question has been turned by L into a further question that specifies the preceding one.

2.20: L has omitted "by a light," perhaps because it seemed redundant, but its presence is presupposed in the next sentence.

2.19: BG has misplaced the participial (or adjectival) phrase perhaps by following the Gk. word order too closely . The Gk. may have read: πᾶσα ἡ κτίσις ἐφώτισεν οὖσα ὑποκάτω τοῦ οὐρανοῦ (or ὑπὸ τὸν οὐρανόν).

3.3: For the position of ἰδού (behold) BG conforms to the pattern in Rev. 6:2; 14:1,14, and L conforms to Acts 7:56; it is hard to say which reflects S.

3.3-12: The lacunae obscure some of the differences between S and L. If S had only two appearances, as the reconstruction of BG suggests, then L has added one (by using also the other meaning of παῖς) to make it conform to the number three in 3.12. L has changed John's uncertainty about the vision he saw (which is also reflected by the "wonder" in 3.14) into a descriptive statement which leaves the reference to wonder in 3.14 unmotivated. BG may have misplaced the phrase in 3.6.

3.16: BG probably reflects S correctly in presenting an explanation why there was no need for John to be afraid of the vision (the point is that he can be expected to be familiar with the savior both as child [παῖς] and as old[er] person). L has changed this to a rhetorical question. L has awkwardly connected the imperative "Do not be faint-hearted" to the preceding sentence.

4.5: skipped by L due to homoioteleuton.

4.6: Gk. behind ⲁⲧⲙⲟⲩⲭϭ and ⲁⲧⲭⲱϩⲙ was probably ἀκέραιος; the latter is used as loan word in 8.11.

4.11-12: Gk. was probably ἀφανής and φανερός.

4.14: L added "the unwavering race" on the basis of 4.19.

4.15: L omitted "listen" probably because it appeared redundant.

4.17: ϩⲱⲱⲕ in BG probably translated καί.

# THE PRIMAL TRIAD IN THE *APOCRYPHON OF JOHN*

*Michael Waldstein*
International Theological Institute

The object of this paper is to analyze the intersection of Platonic and Jewish motifs in the account of the primal divine triad given by the *Apocryphon of John* (5.3-17.6).[1] *Ap. John*'s heavenly world combines features of a Middle-Platonic system of emanations with features of a Jewish heavenly court. The tensions which arise in this combination partly explain why *Ap. John* (and the traditions behind it) "split" the inherited Hellenistic-Jewish God into a good and merciful upper God who is personally identified as the Middle-Platonic transcendent deity but retains central features of the God of Israel, and an evil lower God who is personally identified as the God of Israel and the devil but also possesses features of the Platonic demiurge.[2]

## 1. THE FATHER

Jesus' revelation in *Ap. John* begins with a rather mainstream philosophical account of the first principle.[3] Particularly close parallels can be found in Aristides[4] and Alcinous. Philo, Irenaeus and Clement, among others, stand in the same tradition.[5]

---

[1] The text of *Ap. John* is quoted by page and line number in Michael Waldstein and Frederik Wisse, *The Apocryphon of John: Synopsis of Nag Hammadi Codices II,1 III,1 and IV,1 with BG 8502,2* (NHS 33; Leiden: E. J. Brill, 1995). The English translation offered below is composite: it is substantially a translation of BG, corrected by III and II/IV.

[2] The paper develops a suggestion made by B. Pearson, "Gnostic theology actually splits the biblical God into a transcendent, 'unknown' God and a lower creator deity" ("Jewish Elements in Gnosticism and the Development of Gnostic Self-Definition," *Jewish and Christian Self-Definition*, ed. E. P. Sanders, 2 vols. [Philadelphia: Fortress, 1981] 1.151-60, notes 240-45; here 1.154; see also B. A. Pearson, "Philo and Gnosticism," *ANRW* II.21.1 (1984) 295-342; esp. 338-39.

[3] See J. Mansfeld, "Compatible Alternatives: Middle Platonist Theology and the Xenophanes Reception," in, ed., *Knowledge of God in the Graeco-Roman World*, ed. R. van den Broek, T. Baarda, and J. Mansfeld (EPRO 112; Leiden: E. J. Brill, 1988) 92-117; discussion of *Ap. John* in particular 116-17.

[4] See W. C. van Unnik, "Die Gotteslehre bei Aristides und in gnostischen Schriften," *ThZ* 17 (1961) 168-74, here 167-68; A. Werner, "Das Apokryphon des Johannes in seinen vier Versionen synoptisch betrachtet und unter besonderer Berücksichtigung

## 1.1. A Treatise in Negative Theology

Jesus' main account of the Father (*Ap. John* 5.3-9.6) is followed by two brief sections (the difficulty of revealing the Father: *Ap. John* 9.7-10.4; and the Father's reflection in luminous water: *Ap. John* 10.5-17) which function as a transition to the discussion of Barbelo, the Mother. The main account itself falls into seven sections distinguishable by their syntax and contents. The argument moves, quite logically, from the *via negativa*, through the *via eminentiae*, to a particular account of the *via positiva*.

### 1.1.1. Introduction: List of Attributes (Ap. John 5.3-11)

The account of the first principle begins with a brief introductory statement followed by a list of seven attributes.

> [The Monad,] since he is a unitary rule and nothing rules over him,
> (1) [is] the God and Father of the All,
> (2) [the] holy One,
> (3) the invisible One,
> (4) who is above the All,
> (5) who [exists as] his incorruption,
> (6) [existing in] the pure light into which no light of the eye can gaze.
> (7) He is the Spirit (*Ap. John* 5.3-11).

The first designation, the substratum to which all subsequent attributes are applied, is "Monad." "Monad" emphasizes that the first principle is utterly one, by himself and alone. This foundational designation is followed by a clause which gives a reason for the subsequent attributes. It is because the Monad is a μοναρχία, a unitary or solitary beginning, rule or cause which has nothing before him or ruling over him, that the subsequent seven attributes are applied to him.

### 1.1.2. Arguments for Absolute Priority (Ap. John 5.12-6.7)

At *Ap. John* 5.12 the syntax shifts from a list of attributes to a series of arguments. The same stylistic transition from a list of attributes to

---

anderer Nag-Hammadi Schriften in Auswahl erläutert" (Th.D. dissertation, Humboldt Universität Berlin, 1977) 20.

[5] See D. T. Runia, "Themes in Philonic Theology with Special Reference to the *De mutatione nominum*," *Knowledge of God in the Graeco-Roman World*, ed. R. van den Broek, T. Baarda, and J. Mansfeld (EPRO 112; Leiden: E. J. Brill, 1988) 67-91, analyzing *Mut.* 1-38; R. van den Broek, "Eugnostos and Aristides on the Ineffable God," *Knowledge of God* 202-18, 207-8, citing Justin, *II Apol.* 6.1-2; Tatian, *Or. ad Graec.* 4.1; Theophilus, *Ad Autol.* I.3-4; Clement, *Strom.* V.83.1; Mansfeld, "Middle Platonist Theology," 112-55, citing Irenaeus, *Adv. Haer,* I.12.2; 2.13.3; 2.13.8; 2.28.4-5; 4.11.2; Clement, *Strom.* V.81.4-82.4.

a series of reasoned statements can be observed in Aristides and Alcinous.[6] Four claims are made and each is followed by a subordinate clause with γάρ.

> (1) It is not right to think of him as divine or something similar,
>    for (γάρ) he is more than a god.
> (2) He is a rule over which nothing rules,
>    for (γάρ) there is nothing before him.
> (3) Nor does he need them. He does not need life,
>    for (γάρ) he is eternal.
> (4) He does not need anything,
>    for (γάρ) he cannot be completed,
>    as if he were lacking so that he might be completed.[7]
> (5) Rather he is always completely perfect.
> (6) He is light (*Ap. John* 5.12-6.7).

The concern of the first four statements is the *priority* of the first principle over everything else: the Father is not one among other gods, he is the first ruling principle, not in need of anything. The fifth statement draws the comprehensive conclusion, the Father is completely perfect.

### 1.1.3. Arguments in the Via Negativa (Ap. John 6.8-19)

In *Ap. John* 6.8 the text continues with claims followed by subordinate clauses which give reasons for the claims. However, claims are not expressed in the form of sentences, but in a series of single terms. With the exception of the fifth term (eternal), all seven terms are grammatically negative.[8] The seven clauses which follow the seven terms do not use the conjunction γάρ, but probably ὅτι, translated variously by BG and II as ⲉⲃⲟⲗ ϫⲉ and ϫⲉ.

> (1) He is illimitable
>    since there is no one prior to him who sets limits to him;
> (2) the unexaminable One
>    since there exists no one prior to him to examine him;
> (3) the immeasurable One
>    since no other one measured him, as if being prior to him;

---

[6] See Alpigiano, ed., *Aristide, Apologia* 1.4..57; John Dillon, ed., *Alcinous: The Handbook of Platonism* (Clarendon Later Ancient Philosophers; Oxford: Clarendon, 1993) 10.3; John Whittaker and Pierre Louis, ed., *Alcinoos, Enseignement des doctrines de Platon* (Budé; Paris: Belles Lettres, 1990) H 164.31-165.3.

[7] Cf. Aristides, "Perfect, means that there is no lack in him and he does not need anything." Alpigiano, ed., *Aristide, Apologia* 1.4.57.

[8] It could be argued that the fifth adjective, "eternal" is negative conceptually, even if not grammatically. Conceptually it is a particular case of "unlimited" derived from limited time, the only form of duration known to human experience.

(4) the invisible One
   since no one saw him;
(5) the eternal One
   since he exists always;[9]
(6) the ineffable One
   since no one comprehended him so as to speak about him;
(7) the unnamable One
   since there is no one prior to him to give a name to him (*Ap. John* 6.8-19).

Negations are found already earlier in the text. What is distinctive in the present section is the consistent rhythmic application of negation. It is a more systematic exercise in the *via negativa*. All but the fifth statement involve some reference to the activity of someone other than the Father: (1) limiting, (2) examining, (3) measuring, (4) seeing, (6) speaking and (7) naming. These activities, which can be applied to beings in the cosmos, are impotent in the case of the Father. The Father is utterly beyond them.

*1.1.4. Summary List of Attributes (Ap. John 6.20-7.3)*
In *Ap. John* 6.20 the regular rhythm of Section Three is replaced by a grammatical structure encountered already in Section One, a list of attributes.

This One is the light immeasurable,
the pure One
   who is [holy (and) immaculate ;
the ineffable One
   who is perfect (and) incorruptible (*Ap. John* 6.20-7.3).

The section appears to be a recapitulation of the argument up to this point. Each of the seven attributes listed is present in the preceding sections. However, the recapitulation is not *complete*. Not every claim present in the preceding sections reappears, perhaps because the author wanted to produce a list with seven members.

| the light | (1) immeasurable | cf. *Ap. John* 6.8 |
| | (2) pure | cf. *Ap. John* 5.9 |
| | (3) holy | cf. *Ap. John* 5.6 |
| | (4) καθαρόν | Greek not present, but see *Ap. John* 5.9 |
| | (5) ineffable | cf. *Ap. John* 6.16 |
| | (6) perfect | cf. *Ap. John* 6.6 |
| | (7) incorruptible | cf. *Ap. John* 5.8 |

---

[9] In BG 24.2 the subordinate clause is relative. The translation "since" is adopted on the basis of the circumstantial preserved in IV. The original Greek may have been a participle.

*1.1.5. Arguments in the* Via Eminentiae *(Ap. John 7.4-17)*

A new syntactic pattern appears in Section Five (*Ap. John* 7.4-17), negative statements followed by a "but" clause, either triple, "he is neither ... nor ... nor ..., but he is..." or double, "he is neither ... nor, but he is..." or single, "not ... but he is..."

> (1) He is neither perfection, nor blessedness, nor divinity,
>     but he is something far superior to them.
> (2) He is neither unlimited nor limited,
>     but he is something superior to these.
> (3) For he is not corporeal, he is not incorporeal.
> (4) He is not large, he is not small.
> (5) He is not a quantitfiable— for he is not a creature— nor is he qualifiable,[10]
>     nor can anyone know him at all.[11]
> (6) He is not someone who exists,
>     but he is something superior to them,
> (7) not as being superior,
>     but as being himself (*Ap. John* 7.4-17).

In this section, attributes of the Father serve not only as affirmations or negations, but as springboards for seeing the Father as more excellent or eminent above them. This kind of argument, the *via eminentiae*, was already used in Section Two: "It is not right to think of him as a god or something similar, for he is *more than* a god" (*Ap. John* 5.12-14). The form of the argument in Section Five is more complex. The first five arguments are based on exhaustive sets of concepts, each of which is denied of the Father. The principle is clearest in arguments two to five: (2) unlimited—limited; (3) corporeal—incorporeal; (4) large—small; (5) quantifiable—qualifiable. The triad of concepts in the first argument, perfection—blessedness—divinity, is less obviously exhaustive. It is probably an alternate formulation of the exhaustive existence—life—intelligence triad found in Neo-Platonic sources.[12]

The sixth argument offers the most general formulation of the *via eminentiae*. The most general notion by which objects of human knowledge are encompassed is the notion "something" or "something

---

[10] The reading "nor is he qualifiable" is found only in III 5.12-14. It forms a standard pair with "not quantifiable." It was probably omitted inadvertently in BG.

[11] BG reads the adverb ὅλως, "at all," with the next clause: "He is not at all someone who exists" (BG 24.20-21).

[12] "See John D. Turner, "Notes to Text and Translation: NHC XI,3: *Allogenes*," *Nag Hammadi Codices XI, XII, XIII*, ed. C. W. Hedrick (NHS 28; Leiden: E. J. Brill, 1990) 243-67, here 263; Ruth Majercik, "The Existence-Life-Intellect Triad in Gnosticism and Neoplatonism," *Classical Quarterly* 42 (1992) 475-88.

that exists." The fifth argument insists that the Father is not something that exists; he is not one among other beings, a member in a cosmos, subject to an encompassing whole. The point is similar to Socrates's statement about the Good in the *Republic*, "it is not a being but still beyond being (ἔτι ἐπέκεινα τῆς οὐσίας), surpassing in dignity and power."[13]

The seventh argument concludes the section by excluding a possible misunderstanding of the *via eminentiae* itself. One could understand the *via eminentiae* as a positive form of knowledge. Being greater or superior is a relation truly present as an attribute in beings which are part of a larger whole. It is one of the attributes by which such beings can be known in positive terms. The Father, by contrast, lies beyond membership in a larger whole. His superiority is not a relation inherent in him as a positive attribute. He is superior simply by being himself. He is a principle which is *summus exsuperantissimus*,[14] "superior," not in degree, but beyond and outside all that might encompass it.[15]

### 1.1.6. Aeon, Time, Self-Sufficiency and Activity (Ap. John 7.18-8.12)

A thematic shift occurs at *Ap. John* 7.18. The *via eminentiae* is left behind and attention turns to time and activity.

(1) He does not partake in an aeon.
(2) Time does not exist for him,
    for he who partakes in an aeon, others prepared (it) for him.
(3) And time was not apportioned to him,
    since he does not receive from another who apportions.
(4) And he is without want.
(5) There is no one at all before him that he might receive from him.[16]
(6) He desires himself alone in the perfect light.
(7) He will contemplate the pure light, the immeasurable majesty (*Ap. John* 7.18-8.12).

---

[13] Plato, *Republic* 6.19 (509b); the broader context of this passage and its insistence on eminence is spelled out in Alcinous, *Handbook* 10.5; H 165.21-26.

[14] This dense formulation of the *via eminentiae* is found in Apuleius, *De Platone* 1.12; Siniscalco 37-8, cf. A.-J. Festugière, *La Révélation d'Hermès Trismégiste* IV: *Le Dieu inconnu et la gnose* (Études bibliques; Paris: J. Gabalda, 1954) 4-5.

[15] The pattern of alternatives deployed in *Ap. John* is reminiscent of the "first hypothesis" in Plato's *Parmenides* (137c-142a). *Ap. John* derives the argument probably not directly from the *Parmenides*, but from Middle Platonic reinterpretations of the *Parmenides*. See Dillon, ed., *Alcinous, Handbook*, commentary, 109; cf. the doctrinal understanding of *Parmenides* 137-42 in the anonymous commentary on the *Parmenides* attributed by Hadot to Porphyry; Pierre Hadot, *Porphyre et Victorinus*, 2 vols. (Paris: Études Augustiniennes, 1968) 2.64-104.

[16] The phrase "that he might receive from him" is absent in BG but attested in III 6.2 and II 3.35.

Of the seven claims made in this section, the first three address the question whether aeons and time apply to the Father.

In his discussion of "aeon" as a central concept in Hellenistic-Roman texts Festugière points out a multivalence important for understanding the point made by *Ap. John*.[17] In ancient astronomy the heavenly spheres are arranged in spatial order, but they also measure time. Accordingly, "aeon" can be a temporal concept (the measure of time provided by a particular heavenly sphere) as well as a spatial concept (a sphere that has a certain content). It can also be a personal concept (the intellect or divine mover that moves a particular heavenly sphere). Working with such an understanding of aeon and time, *Ap. John* argues that sharing in an aeon presupposes something prior that prepares the measurement by submitting the measured to a measure. Since there is nothing prior to the Father, aeons and time do not apply to him.

Statements four and five form a transition from the theme of time to that of the Father's twofold intellectual activity. The Father's complete self-sufficiency implies not only that he does not share in aeons or time, but also that his activities, his desire and knowledge, are entirely self-directed.[18]

A possible misunderstanding should be avoided: the Primal Deity, the Father, according to *Ap. John* and other Middle-Platonic sources, is not one among other beings, but utter plenitude beyond any specific instance of being. There is nothing "outside" the Father which could cause him to conceive new desire for or new knowledge of something not yet possessed. The statements, "He desires himself alone in the perfect light. He will contemplate the pure light, the immeasurable majesty," do not, therefore, imply that the Father is limited to himself, indifferent to and ignorant of everything in the cosmos. Rather, since the cosmos is not something outside the Father and additional to him, the Father's desire and knowledge of himself contains his desire and knowledge of all, including the cosmos.

### 1.1.7. An Account of the Via Positiva (Ap. John 8.14-9.6)

A new syntactic pattern begins in *Ap. John* 8.14, namely, a series of positive predicates with the definite article, each followed by a substantivized relative clause in apposition (III and BG) or a circumstantial (II), which characterizes the Father as the giver of the

---

[17] Festugière, *Hermès Trismégiste* 4.152-99.
[18] Cf. Alcinous, *Handbook* 10.3; H 164.27-31.

immediately preceding attribute. The discussion of the Father in sections one through six included a number of positive predicates, for example, holy (*Ap. John* 5.6), pure light (*Ap. John* 5.9), completely perfect (*Ap. John* 6.6; cf. 7.3). The argument of *Ap. John* 8.14-9.6 explains how such positive statements are compatible with the claim that the Father is unknowable and unutterable. The *via positiva*, it argues, is ultimately reducible to the *via negativa* and the *via eminentiae*.

| | |
|---|---|
| (He is) the eternal One, | the One who gives eternity; |
| the light, | the One who gives the light; |
| the life, | the One who gives life; |
| the blessed One, | the One who gives blessedness; |
| knowledge, | the One who gives knowledge; |
| the always good One, | the One who gives good, |
| | the One who does good; |

—not on the basis that he possesses, but on the basis that he gives—

| | |
|---|---|
| the mercy | that gives mercy; |
| the gift | that gives a gift, |

the immeasurable light (*Ap. John* 8.14-9.6).

The underlying principle of this section is formulated in the seventh statement. Positive attributes are applied to the Father "not on the basis that he possesses (these attributes) but on the basis that he gives (them)."[19] To say that the Father is eternal, light, living, blessed, knowing, and good does not mean that these attributes belong to the Father in the primary sense. It means that the Father causes them in the beings of the cosmos. Only the particular beings of the cosmos possess the attributes in the primary sense; the Father does not. The point is not that the Father is defective, that he lacks eternity, light, life, blessedness, knowledge and goodness, but that his plenitude is more eminent than all particular instances of these attributes. The *via positiva* is, therefore, a particular instance of the *via negativa*.

## 1.2. Overview: Genre, Provenance and Historical Place

The little treatise in negative theology which opens Jesus' secret revelation (*Ap. John* 5.3-9.6) is a sophisticated and disciplined piece of philosophic writing in the mainstream of Middle-Platonic philosophy. It does not present its arguments as discursively as one of its closest parallels, Alcinous's *Handbook*, but proceeds more by simple assertion. Nevertheless, carefully worked out arguments stand

---

[19] A similar argument is found in Alcinous, *Handbook* 10.5; H 165.20-26; Philo, *De Mut. Nom.* 14; see Runia, "Themes in Philonic Theology," 80.

behind it. This combination of assertory form and reflected foundation suggests that the treatise belongs to the genre of philosophical school writing, designed to offer an introductory overview of negative theology for novices, later to be unfolded or glossed by argument.

When one compares this treatise with the image of the heavenly world that immediately follows it in *Ap. John*, one finds numerous points of difference and disagreement. The strict limits imposed on knowledge and speech about the first principle are quickly overstepped as one moves from the darkness of negative theology into a brightly lit heavenly court whose sovereign and subjects interact in petitionary prayer, gracious responses and liturgical glorification. One way of explaining these differences and disagreements is the hypothesis that the treatise is derived from a source, perhaps from a handbook like Alcinous's *Didaskalikos*, in which a philosophical perspective is expressed that was not entirely and organically integrated into *Ap. John*.[20]

### 1.3. Transition to the Mother (Ap. John 9.13-19; 10.5-17)

At *Ap. John* 9.13 the language shifts away from the language used in the preceding account of the Father. Abstract philosophical terminology gives way to a more sensual and imaginable way of speaking.

*The text sandwiched between the two first-person passages (see note 20):*

> His aeon is indestructible,
> at rest, reposing in silence,
> the One who is prior to everything.
> He is the head of every aeon,
> because his goodness provides for every aeon,[21]
> if there exists anything beside him (*Ap. John* 9.13-19).

*Continuation of the text after the first person plural passage:*

> It is he who contemplates himself in his own light which surrounds him,
> namely, the spring of living water,
> the light full of purity;
> [and] the spring of the Spirit,

---

[20] *Ap. John* 9.7-12 and 9.20-10.4 contain remarks in the first person (singular in the first text; plural in the second) about the ignorance of the one speaking or writing. These remarks are difficult to imagine on the lips of Jesus. They may be remnants of a form of the text in which it was not yet placed on the lips of Jesus.

[21] The clause "because his goodness provides for every aeon" (III 6.22-23) is lacking in BG. It is attested in II 4.14-15.

which poured forth living water from itself.[22]
And he provided all aeons and worlds.
In every direction he perceived his own image
by seeing it in the pure light-water which surrounds him (*Ap. John* 10.5-17).

The earlier account had stated explicitly that the Father "does not partake in an aeon" (*Ap. John* 7.18). Now the Father dwells and rests in an indestructible aeon as the head of many aeons and provides for them all.

Luminous spiritual water gushes forth from him and surrounds him on all sides like a mirror. In whatever direction he turns, he sees a reflection of himself. As Plato's "receptacle" receives the imprint of forms, so the luminous waters receive the Father's image.

An important parallel to the water/mirror passage appears later in the scene in which a luminous human image is projected from above on to the waters of chaos below, leading Yaldabaoth and his archons, who see the image in the waters, to decide, "Come, let us create a man in the image of God and the likeness" (see *Ap. John* 38.1-18). Several motifs found in Genesis 1 are recast and combined in this scene: the waters of chaos correspond to the waters of Gen 1:2 ("and God's spirit moved about over the waters"); the projected luminous image is reminiscent of the first beginning of light, "Let there be light;" (Gen 1:3; cf. 1:4-5); and the decision of Yaldabaoth and his archons to create Adam is a quote of God's words in Gen 1:26 ("Let us make man in our image and likeness").

The same three motifs are combined in the projection of the Father's image on to the luminous waters surrounding him, the end-result of which is Barbelo, "the first Human" or "the first Man" (*Ap. John* 12.2). Genesis motifs appear thus on two levels. They are played out first in a completely positive mode at the beginning of *Ap. John*'s theogony and then in a partly negative mode at the beginning of *Ap. John*'s anthropogony. The literary contacts with Genesis are fully explicit on the lower level. The relation to Genesis is recognizable on the higher level primarily in the parallel between the two levels.

## 2. THE MOTHER

*Ap. John*'s account of the Mother, Barbelo, is strikingly different from its account of the Father. The Father is shrouded in mystery, named with great conceptual rigor in strictly negative terms. The passage on

---

[22] The translation follows the construction of III 7.6-7.

the luminous waters (*Ap. John* 9.13-19; 10.5-17) already adopts more sensory language. The transition is complete in the account of the Mother.

## 2.1. Barbelo Comes Forth and Glorifies (Ap. John 10.18-12.11)

Barbelo's entry into and activity in the heavenly court is described in two steps, each followed by a list of attributes.

> And his thought became actual[23]
> (and) came forth
> (and) attended him in the brilliance of his light.[24]
>> She is the power who is before the All,
>> who came forth.
>> She is the Providence of the All,[25]
>> who shines in the light,[26]
>> the image of the invisible One,
>> which is the perfect power,
>> Barbelo,
>> the perfect aeon of glory.
> It is him that she glorifies,
> since she had come forth because of him.
> And it is him that she contemplates.
>> She is the first thought,
>> his image.
>> She became a first Man
>> who is the virginal Spirit,
>> the thrice-male,
>> the thrice-powerful,[27]
>> the thrice-named,
>> the thrice-begotten,
>> the androgynous aeon
>> who does not grow old,
>> who came forth from his Providence (*Ap. John* 10.18-12.11).

---

[23] Both III and BG have the Coptic ⲣ̄ ⲟⲩϩⲱⲃ; II and IV have a lacuna here, but the available space in II 4.26-27 suggests ⲁⲩⲱ [ⲧⲉϥⲉⲛⲛⲟⲓⲁ ⲁⲥϣⲱⲡⲉ ⲛⲟⲩ]ϩⲱⲃ. ⲣ̄ ⲟⲩϩⲱⲃ should thus not be understood in the usual sense as "do work" (Crum 654a) but as "becoming a thing."

[24] Following the text of III 7.14, ϩⲙ ⲡⲉϥⲗⲁⲙⲡⲏⲇⲟⲛⲟⲥ ⲛ̄[ⲟⲩⲟⲉⲓ]ⲛ, but moving the possessive from ⲗⲁⲙⲡⲏⲇⲟⲛⲟⲥ to ⲟⲩⲟⲉⲓⲛ. The original Greek phrase may have been ἐν τῇ λαμπηδόνι φωτός αὐτοῦ.

[25] BG 27.10-11 adds the term "perfect". "She is the perfect Providence of the All" ⲉⲧⲉ ⲧⲁⲓ̈ ⲧⲉ ⲧⲡⲣⲟⲛⲟⲓⲁ ⲉⲧϫⲏⲕ ⲉⲃⲟⲗ ⲛ̄ⲧⲉ ⲡⲧⲏⲣϥ̄. II has a lacuna here, but there is not enought room for ⲉⲧϫⲏⲕ ⲉⲃⲟⲗ.

[26] Following the text of III 7.17, ⲉⲧⲣ̄ⲟⲩⲟⲉⲓⲛ ϩⲙ ⲡⲟⲩⲟⲉⲓⲛ, instead of BG's "the light, the likeness of the light" ⲡⲟⲩⲟⲓ̈ⲛ ⲡⲉⲓⲛⲉ ⲙ̄ⲡⲟⲩⲟⲉⲓⲛ.

[27] III 8.1-2 reads [ⲡϣⲟⲙⲛⲧ] ⲛ̄ϩⲩⲙⲛⲟⲥ, the thrice-praised. The reading of BG is supported by II.

## 2.1.1. Emergence, Attendance and Glorification (Ap. John 10.18-11.1; 11.14-17)

Barbelo comes forth as the reality of the invisible Spirit's thought (ἔννοια) of himself, already contained in the power of that thought, but actualized in its exercise: "And his thought became actual." The distinction between the Monad, which lies beyond thought, and its thought of itself shows that *Ap. John* belongs to the group of metaphysical systems which emphasize the distinction between a transcendent One (ἔν) and the realm of thought (νοῦς).[28]

Having come forth as an actual entity, Barbelo takes her stand before the invisible Spirit.[29] One connotation of this "standing" is stability and immutability.[30] Another is "standing" as a ceremonial or liturgical act, as attendance upon a king or god.[31] In three passages similar to BG 27.6-7 (ⲁⲥⲁ2ⲉⲣⲁⲧⲥ ⲙ̄ⲡⲉϥⲙ̄ⲧⲟ ⲉⲃⲟⲗ, lit.: "stood before him") the Greek παράστασις and παρίστημι are preserved in one of the three versions.

| III 11.5 | BG 32.6-7 | II 7.18; |
|---|---|---|
| ⲉⲩⲡⲁⲣⲁⲥⲧⲁⲥⲓⲥ | ⲭⲉ ⲁϥⲁ2ⲉⲣⲁⲧ[ϥ] ⲉⲣⲟϥ | ⲁⲧⲣⲉϥⲁ2ⲉⲣⲁⲧϥ ⲉ- |
| III 11.19 | BG 33.3-4 | II 7.34—8.1 |
| ⲉⲩⲡⲁⲣⲁⲥⲧⲁⲥⲓⲥ | ⲭⲉ ⲉⲩⲉⲁ2ⲉⲣⲁ[ⲧⲟⲩ] | ⲁⲧⲣⲟⲩⲱ2ⲉ ⲉⲣⲁⲧⲟⲩ |
| ⲛⲁϥ | ⲉⲣⲟϥ | ⲉⲣⲟϥ |
| III 12.18-19 | BG 34.10 | II 8.22-23 |
| ⲉⲧⲁ2ⲉ ⲉⲣⲁⲧⲟⲩ ⲉ- | ⲉⲧⲡⲁⲣ2ⲓ̈ⲥⲧⲁ ⲉ- | ⲉⲧⲁ2ⲉⲣⲁⲧⲟⲩ ⲁ- |

Barbelo comes forth and immediately turns back toward her source in ceremonial-liturgical attendance. This sequence of emanation–attendance is a regular pattern in the unfolding of the heavenly world

---

[28] The origin and development of the ἔν-νοῦς schema before Plotinus is analyzed by H. J. Krämer, *Der Ursprung der Geistmetaphysik: Untersuchungen zur Geschichte des Platonismus zwischen Platon und Plotin*, 2nd ed. (Amsterdam: B. R. Grüner, 1967) 193-292; on Gnostic systems that adopt the ἔν-νοῦς schema, see 223-64; on *Ap. John* in particular, see 254, note 227; 255 note255.

[29] ⲁⲥⲁ2ⲉ ⲉⲣⲁⲧⲥ̄ ⲙ̄ⲡⲉϥ[ⲙ̄ⲧⲟ] ⲉⲃⲟⲗ (III 7.13-14); ⲁⲥⲁ2ⲉⲣⲁⲧⲥ ⲙ̄ⲡⲉϥⲙ̄ⲧⲟ ⲉⲃⲟⲗ (BG 27.6-7); the parallel II 4.28-29 is poorly preserved, but in conjunction with IV 7.3-4 one arrives at the text ⲧⲁⲓ̈ ⲉⲧⲁ2ⲟ[ⲩⲱⲛ]2 ⲉⲃⲟⲗ ⲙ̄ⲡⲉϥⲙ̄ⲧⲟ ⲉⲃⲟⲗ.

[30] The Platonic tradition speaks of "standing" ideas or emanations to express their immunity from change and corruption; see M. A. Williams, *The Immovable Race: A Gnostic Designation and the Theme of Stability in Late Antiquity* (NHS 29; Leiden: E. J. Brill, 1985) 103-111.

[31] For παράστασις see Liddell-Scott I.5; II.1 (1325a) and especially Lampe B 1-2 (1025b); for παρίστημι, Liddell-Scott B.I (1340b) and Lampe B.1-2 (1041a). The verb παρίστημι in the ceremonial-liturgical sense is frequent in the LXX. See Hatch-Redpath, 1070c-71a.

in *Ap. John* (thirteen times). It is even found in the emergence of the aeons subordinate to Yaldabaoth (see *Ap. John* 41.2).

Barbelo's primary activity in her attendance upon the invisible Spirit is praise and glorification. And the primary reason for this glorification, solidly rooted in Jewish theology, is the invisible Spirit's role as the origin of all things, "since she had come forth because of him" (see Job 38:6-7; *Jubilees* 2:2-3; 11Q5 26:11-12; Rev 4:11). The use of † ⲉⲟⲟⲩ (=δοξάζειν), points clearly to a *Jewish*-Greek setting in which the characteristic Septuagint sense of δόξα—δοξάζειν had already developed.[32]

In coming forth from the Father and taking her stand before him in ceremonial-liturgical attendance, Barbelo thus combines features of a Middle-Platonic hypostasis and of a Jewish angel engaged in the characteristically Jewish liturgical activity of glorifying (δοξάζειν).

The theme of Barbelo as the invisible Spirit's self-knowledge is an important element in *Ap. John*'s account of salvation. Salvation through self-knowledge is ultimately a return to the invisible Spirit's self-reflection. In the call of awakening Barbelo exhorts the initiate in her role as Providence: "follow your root, which is I, the merciful One!" (*Ap. John* 81.11-12). The listener's movement of tracing his inner root in self-reflection can terminate only at the ultimate depth of that root, which is Barbelo herself, the invisible Spirit's thought of himself. The same concepts have thus two uses.

> In the first place, there are the ontological and metaphysical problems shared with Middle and Neo-Platonism. In addition, there is a soteriological, archetypal use. On this point, what the first principle does with itself...is what the individual does in attaining illumination.[33]

### 2.1.2. Barbelo's Titles (Ap. John 11.2-12; 11.17-12.10)
Barbelo's titles are set forth in two series:
*The first series of titles, following emergence and attendance:*

> She is the power who is before the All,
> who came forth.
> She is the Providence of the All,
> who shines in the light,
> the image of the invisible One,
> which is the perfect power,

---

[32] See Gerhard Kittel, "δοκέω, δόξα, δοξάζω, κτλ," *TDNT* 2 (1964) 232-55; for δοξάζω, see 253-54.

[33] Harold Attridge, in John Whittaker, "Self-Generating Principles in Second-Century Gnostic Systems," *The Rediscovery of Gnosticism, 1: The School of Valentinus*, ed. Bentley Layton (SHR 41; Leiden: E. J. Brill, 1980) 176-89; discussion 189-93, here 193.

Barbelo,
the perfect aeon of glory (*Ap. John* 11.2-12).

*The second series of titles, following glorification*

She is the first thought,
his image.
She became a first Man
who is the virginal Spirit,
the thrice-male,
the thrice-powerful,
the thrice-named,
the thrice-begotten,
the androgynous aeon
who does not grow old,
who came forth from his providence (*Ap. John* 11.17-12.10).

The list of titles and attributes begins with Barbelo's role as a mediator between the invisible Spirit and the All. Although she is such a mediator, she is not, the text insists, less than the invisible Spirit. She is not a first dimming of the invisible Spirit's light. Such dimming is affirmed only of the third member of the heavenly Triad, the Son (see *Ap. John* 15.12). Although she comes forth from the invisible Spirit's thinking, she is his very thought of himself. Although she comes forth from the invisible Spirit's providence (πρόνοια), she does so as his very own providence for the All. The immediacy of the invisible Spirit's presence in her implies that she is "the perfect power" and "the perfect aeon of glory." For this reason she can receive one of the invisible Spirit's own distinctive attributes, "virginal Spirit."

At the same time she is distinct from the invisible Spirit. Although she is the invisible Spirit's thought of himself, she is a Thought that becomes a distinct knower who can "contemplate" the invisible Spirit (*Ap. John* 11.17). Although she is the invisible Spirit's own providence, she becomes Providence in person. In this distinctness from the invisible Spirit she later conceives a Son from him. In her distinctness she is the "...ideal wife and mother."[34] However, the text is quite careful to qualify these feminine traits. Barbelo is also "thrice-male" (*Ap. John* 12.4) and "androgynous" (*Ap. John* 12.8). "This description of Barbelo, the 'Mother' figure and consort of the

---

[34] Michael A. Williams, "Variety in Gnostic Perspectives on Gender," in , ed., *Images of the Feminine in Gnosticism* (SAC 4; Philadelphia: Fortress, 1988) 2-22, 17.

Father, makes it clear that 'she' is not unambiguously feminine."[35] As the Father's thought and providence, she *is* the Father, a male principle, "a first Man" (*Ap. John* 12.2) or "the first Man" (*Ap. John* 14.14).[36] And yet she faces him as his feminine counterpart. Her/his identity can be described only in paradoxical terms that join identity and distinction. "She is both the Father *and* herself."[37]

## 2.2. Barbelo Unfolds
### 2.2.1. The Triad (Ap. John 12.12-14.4)
Already in the section on her emergence Barbelo appeared as a principle of multiplicity whereby the monadic Father unfolded himself. She was introduced as the Father's reflection in luminous waters, a description reminiscent of the Platonic "receptacle," a principle of multiplicity. Triadic expansion was hinted at in some of her titles: "the thrice-male, the thrice-powerful, the thrice-named, the thrice-begotten" (*Ap. John* 12.4-7).

Triadic expansion now becomes explicit as Barbelo asks for and receives Foreknowledge (πρόγνωσις); Indestructibility (ἀφθαρσία); and Eternal Life. Clearly, she does not "need" these attributes, as if she were lacking in foreknowledge, incorruptibility and eternal life. Just as the Father overflowed into Barbelo and doubled himself in this self-reflection, not because of any need, but because he is "the always good One, the One who gives good, the One who does good" (*Ap. John* 8.19-20), so Barbelo asks him to grant her a Triad as superabundant gifts.

---

[35] Karen L. King, "Sophia and Christ in the *Apocryphon of John*," *Images of the Feminine in Gnosticism*, ed. Karen L. King (SAC 4; Philadelphia: Fortress, 1988) 158-76, here 162.

[36] Although "First Man" is not mentioned as an attribute of the Father in the negative theology section, it does appear as one of his distinctive attributes later in *Ap. John*. "First Man" (*Ap. John* 37.19) is explicitly applied to the Father when he appears "in the form of a man" (*Ap. John* 37.20) and projects his appearance onto the waters below. Consequently, when Yaldabaoth and his archons make a "man" (*Ap. John* 38.16) they do so in the image of the Father, "the one who is from the beginning, the Perfect Man" (*Ap. John* 39.10-11). "Perfect Man" may refer to the Father already in Jesus' formulation of the subject of his revelation "the race of the perfect Man" (*Ap. John* 4.14) and in the parallel formulation "the race of the perfect Man of eternal light" (*Ap. John* 74.8). The verbal revelation which precedes the projection of the Father's image onto the waters refers to the Father simply as "the Man." "The Man exists and the Son of Man" (*Ap. John* 37.8). See H.-M. Schenke, *Der Gott "Mensch" in der Gnosis: Ein religionsgeschichtlicher Beitrag zur Diskussion über die paulinische Anschauung von der Kirche als Leib Christi* (Göttingen: Vandenhoeck & Ruprecht, 1962) 6-7; 34-37; 41-43.

[37] Jorunn Jacobsen Buckley, *Female Fault and Fulfilment in Gnosticism* (Chapel Hill: University of North Carolina Press, 1986) 41.

Barbelo establishes a pattern of three elements: emergence, ceremonial—liturgical attendance, and glorification. The appearance on the scene of each of the Triad's members follows the same pattern, preceded by two new elements: Barbelo makes a request and the invisible Spirit graciously consents.

(1) Barbelo requests an attribute;
(2) the invisible Spirit consents;
(3) the attribute comes forth as a distinct divine figure, feminine like Barbelo;
(4) the new figure takes her place in ceremonial attendance with Thought (ἔννοια);
(5) she glorifies the Invisible One and Barbelo.

| And Barbelo requested from him to grant <her> foreknowledge, | Again she[38] requested to grant her indestructibility, | She requested to grant her eternal life, |
|---|---|---|
| (and) he consented. | and he consented. | and he consented. |
| When he had consented, Foreknowledge came forth | When he had consented, Indestructibility came forth | And when he had consented, Eternal Life came forth |
| and she stood in attendance with Thought, which is Providence, | (and) she stood in attendance with Thought and Foreknowledge. | and they stood in attencance |
| while glorifying the invisible One and the perfect power, Barbelo, since they had come into being because of her. | She glorified the Invisible One and Barbelo since she had come into being because of her. | and glorified him and Barbelo, since they had come into being because of her, from the coming-forth of the invisible Spirit (*Ap. John* 12.12-14.4) |

Two distinct strands of thought appear to be united in the Barbelo—Triad, one of them Platonic, the other distinctly Jewish. On the one hand, Barbelo's unfolding shows her to be a locus of ideas, exemplars for the lower world, corresponding to the Middle-Platonic thesis that the Platonic ideas are located in the mind of the first or second divine

---

[38] BG expands the subject of this clause by adding ⲛ̄ϭⲓ ⲧⲉⲉⲓϭⲟⲙ "Again this power asked" (BG 28.13-14). The phrase is absent from II and III which are well preserved here.

principle.[39] On the other hand, these ideas share features of Jewish angels engaged in the heavenly liturgy.[40]

### 3. THE SON

*Ap. John*'s account of the Son, usually called the Self-Generated (αὐτογενής), straddles an important point of division in the unfolding of the heavenly world. The sentence, "And all these came into being in silence and thought" (*Ap. John* 17.5-6), marks the end of the section that deals with the primal Triad of Father, Mother and Son. The immediately following section deals with the creation of the All, the Self-Generated's installation as god over the All and the organization of the All into four lights (*Ap. John* 17.7-23.12). The first of the Self-Generated's three attendant aeons, the Mind, comes forth before the boundary between the primal Triad and the All is crossed (*Ap. John* 17.2); the other two, the Word and the Will, come forth after it, in the course of the creation of the All (*Ap. John* 17.9-13). The point of transition at *Ap. John* 17.4 is thus not hard and fast, but there is some interlacing between the unfolding of the primal Triad and the creation of the All.

The Self-Generated's appearance on the stage of *Ap. John* can be divided into six scenes. The transition from the primal Triad to the All occurs at the beginning of the fourth scene.

1. The Self-Generated is born.
2. He is anointed as Christ.
3. He receives his first attendant aeon, the Mind.
4. He creates the All through the Will and the Word.
5. He is installed as God over the All
6. He organizes the All in four Lights

### 3.1. The Self-Generated is Begotten and Born (Ap. John 15.5-17)

Barbelo gazed intently into the pure light.[41]
She turned to him,
and gave birth to a spark of light
resembling the blessed light,[42]

---

[39] See Krämer, *Ursprung der Geistmetaphysik*, 242, on the similarity between Gnostic systems of aeons and lists of Platonic forms or ideas.

[40] *Ap. John* 14.13-15.4 is a difficult passage describing the development of a female pentad and a female-male decad.

[41] Following the text of III 9.10-12.

[42] Following the text of III 9.13-14 which is supported by II 6.14-15.

but he (the spark) is not equal in greatness.[43]
This is the only-begotten One who came forth from the Father,
the divine Self-Generated,
the first-born Son of all the Father's (sons),[44]
the pure light[45] (*Ap. John* 15.5-17).

The begetting of the only-begotten Son closely resembles Barbelo's own emergence as a distinct figure. She emerged as the Father's thought of himself. The Son emerges as Barbelo's vision of the Father. Yet there is a difference. In the emergence of Barbelo, the Father acts within himself. Barbelo, by contrast, gazes into the light of another, the Father. The Father's light shines actively into her and forms her knowledge so that her offspring comes forth "from the Father" (*Ap. John* 15.14) and can be called his "son" (*Ap. John* 15.16). In contrast to Yaldabaoth, the Self-Generated is therefore an authentic image. It is apparently only when the female knows the male and the action of begetting proceeds actively from the male, that authentic new male offspring comes into being as a result.[46]

While Barbelo is equal to the Father, their Son is not. While the male's self-reflection produces a feminine image which is equal to him, the female's knowledge of the male produces a male image which, though an authentic image, is less than both herself and her

---

[43] Following the text of III 9.14-15. The readings of BG and II probably arose as attempts to specify the term of comparison. BG specifies it in one way, "not equal to *her* (i.e., Barbelo) in greatness" (BG 30.3-4); II in the other, "not equal to *his* (i.e., the Father's) greatness."

[44] Following the text of III 9.18-19. BG seems to have misunderstood the grammatical function of the word "all" in the Greek original, "ⲡϣⲏⲣⲉ ⲛϣⲣ̄ⲡ ⲙ̄ⲙⲓⲥⲉ ⲙ̄ⲡⲧⲏⲣϥ ⲛⲧⲉ ⲡⲉⲡⲛ̄ⲁ, the first-born son of the All of the Spirit."

[45] Following the text of III 9.19 which understands "the pure light" as an appositive to Son. BG links the phrase with its preceding erroneous translation, "... All of the Spirit of pure light." Light is one of the Son's main attributes.

[46] II inverts the direction of knowledge, perhaps in order to align divine begetting more closely with human sexual begetting in which the male actively enters the female: "And he (i.e., the invisible Spirit) looked into Barbelo in the pure light which surrounds the invisible Spirit and his spark and she conceived from him. He begot a spark of light" (II 6.10-13). The passage is strange. There seem to be two sparks, one at the origin, surrounded by light, another begotten in Barbelo. The formulation, "He looked... in the light which surrounds *the invisible Spirit*," sounds as if the invisible Spirit were distinct from the one who looks. This problem would disappear if one inserted the feminine pronoun instead: "*She* looked... in the light which surrounds the invisible Spirit." The use of the masculine pronoun might be a translation or transcription error rather than an androcentric rethinking of metaphysical relations between male and female.

male.[47] The male remedies this defect in the immediately following scene by anointing the Self-Generated with Christhood-goodness.

The Son receives three titles associated with his relation to his Father and Mother:

> only-begotten;
> Self-Generated;
> first-born.

The first of these, only-begotten, μονογενής (*Ap. John* 15.13), ογϣρογωτ, an only son (II 6.15), probably picks up one of Jesus' titles in the Johannine Prologue,[48] μονογενὴς θεός (John 1:18), πνογτε πϣнρε ñογωτ (Horner). Platonic-philosophical resonances may be present as well: μονογενής is one of the attributes of the one heaven of the single universe fashioned by the demiurge in Plato's *Timaeus* (31b). His third title, πϣнρε ñϣрπ ммісе, the first-born son (*Ap. John* 15.16) of all the Father's sons, probably picks up Col 1:15, πρωτότοκος πάσης κτίσεως, πϣрπ ммісе ñсωñт νιμ (Horner), the first-born of all creation.

The two titles, only-begotten and first-born appear to clash. Is he the *only* son or the *first of many*? Perhaps *Ap. John* envisages different levels of sonship: the first-born is the only-begotten, because his sonship is unique. No insurmountable barrier is thereby erected, however, because in the movement of ἐπιστροφή "all the Father's sons" reach the Father's own self-reflection.

The second title "Self-Generated, αὐτογενής" is situated in a different context, namely, Neo-Pythagorean and Middle-Platonic discussions of secondary divine hypostases. Sources that attest these discussions suggest that the concept of self-generation was used for two main reasons. First, the coming forth of a divine hypostasis is the self-externalizing of a power already inherent in the origin; no causality foreign to or outside of the emerging figure is at work. Second, to speak of "begotten" hypostases implies the activity of "begetting" in the first principle which compromises its complete rest and immobility. The "self-generating" speaking of the self-begetting

---

[47] King ("Sophia and Christ," 162) argues that the Son's defect stems in part from Barbelo's failure to solicit the Father's assent before her conception. However, there is no indication of any self-willed action parallel to Wisdom's attempt to conceive without her consort. The Father is involved as the ultimate active principle.

[48] The entire passage on the Son is permeated by Christian elements, so that a use of the Johannine Prologue is not a-priori unlikely. See Schenke, "Gnostic Sethianism," 609-612.

of secondary hypostases avoids this difficulty.[49] The only section which suggests that the divine immobility is a concern of *Ap. John* is the negative theology section. As soon as the text moves on to the Mother, it does not hesitate to attribute to the Father a number of activities that imply movement. The Father wells up as a spring of living spiritual water. He gazes out and sees himself reflected. He presides in the heavenly court, graciously receiving and granting petitions addressed to him. The first reason, the active emergence of divine figures from their origin, is probably more pertinent. *Ap. John* may use the term αὐτογενής to underline that the Son does not passively receive himself from his origin, but actively comes forth from the origin.

### 3.2. The Self-Generated is Anointed (Ap. John 15.18-16.17)

And the invisible Spirit rejoiced over the light
who had come into being,
he who had come forth first from the first power,
which is his Providence, Barbelo.
And he anointed him with his Christhood/goodness
. so that he became perfect
and not lacking anything of Christ/good,
because he had anointed him with the Christhood/goodness of the invisible
    Spirit[50]
which he poured out for him.
And he received the anointing by the virginal Spirit.
And he attended him,
glorifying the invisible Spirit and the perfect Providence,
because of whom (ref. Spirit) he had come forth (*Ap. John* 15.18-16.17).

The invisible Spirit welcomes the Self-Generated as an authentic member of the divine Triad and compensates for his lack of perfection by anointing him. A similar sequence is described by Philo:

The Divine Word (λόγος) ... is the child of parents incorruptible and wholly free from stain, his father being God, who is likewise Father of all, and his mother Wisdom, though whom the universe came into existence; because, moreover, his head has been anointed with oil, and by this I mean the ruling faculty is illumined with a brilliant light ... (*Fuga* 109-110).

---

[49] See John Whittaker, "Self-Generating Principles in Second-Century Gnostic Systems," *The Rediscovery of Gnosticism, I: The School of Valentinus*, ed. Bentley Layton (SHR 41; Leiden: E. J. Brill, 1980) 176-89; discussion 189-93; here 176-77.

[50] Following the text of III 10.3-4, ⲙⲡⲁϩⲟⲣⲁⲧⲟⲛ ⲙ̄ⲡ̄ⲛ̄[ⲁ].

All the major elements of *Ap. John*'s portrayal of the Self-Generated are present in this text, though the order of light and anointing differs. Nevertheless there is reason to think that the anointing scene in *Ap. John* presupposes a specifically Christian setting, evident above all in a pun on χρηστός—χριστός. The pun appears three times in the three versions with some variation of forms:

|           III            |        BG         |          II           |
| :----------------------: | :---------------: | :-------------------: |
|      M̄N̄TX̄P̄C̄       |     M̄N̄TX̄C̄    |     M̄N̄TX̄P̄C̄     |
|         X̄P̄C̄          |      X̄C̄        |    MN̄T[X]P̄[C]     |
|    [M]N̄TXP̄HCTOC      |     M̄N̄TX̄C̄    |    [M]N̄Ṭ[X]P̣C̄    |

In Greek manuscripts of the first five centuries A. D., Christ is *the* most stable *nomen sacrum:* χριστός almost never appears written in full, but almost always as X̄P̄C, X̄C̄ and related forms; conversely, X̄P̄C and X̄C̄ always refer to Christ.[51] The few texts in which X̄P̄C, X̄C̄ and related forms appear to signify something other than Christ are OT passages on the Lord's anointed,[52] or quotations of a phrase found frequently in the LXX version of the Psalms: "χρηστὸς ὁ κύριος, the Lord is good."[53] Psalm 33:9, for example, reads, "γεύσασθε καὶ ἴδετε ὅτι χρηστὸς ὁ κύριος, taste and see that the Lord is good." 1 Peter 2:3 alludes to this text, transposing it into the past, "ἐγεύσασθε ὅτι χρηστὸς ὁ κύριος, you have tasted that the Lord is good." In Papyrus 72 the text reads OTI X̄P̄C O K̄C̄.[54] In accord with the solidity of X̄P̄C as a nomen sacrum, the apparatus of Nestle-Aland interprets this reading as, "ἐγεύσασθε ὅτι χριστὸς ὁ κύριος, you have tasted that Christ is the Lord." This reading, which is followed by a number of manuscripts, is probably not a mere scribal error but an allegorical interpretation of Psalm 33:9 expressed

---

[51] See Ludwig Traube, *Nomina Sacra: Versuch einer Geschichte der christlichen Kürzung* (Darmstadt: Wissenschaftliche Buchgesellschaft, 1967) 113-16; Anton H. Paap, *Nomina Sacra in the Greek Papyri of the First Five Centuries A. D.: The Sources and some Deductions* (Papyrologica Lugduno-Batavia 8; Leiden: E. J. Brill, 1959) 94; 109-111; José O'Callaghan, *Nomina sacra in papyris Graecis saeculi III neotestamentariis* (AnBib 46; Rome: Pontifical Biblical Institute, 1970) 68-70; 80-81.

[52] See Paap, *Nomina Sacra*, 55.

[53] See Paap, *Nomina Sacra*, 37.

[54] See O'Callaghan, *Nomina sacra*, 38.

in the form of a pun on χρηστός—χριστός.[55] This pun is well attested in early Christian literature.[56]

The paleographic evidence makes it virtually certain that x̄p̄c̄ and x̄c̄ in *Ap. John* should be read as forms of the *nomen sacrum* Christ. The *nomen sacrum* was most likely present already in the two Greek versions of *Ap. John* since it is found independently in all three Coptic translations. The abstract noun ⲘⲚⲦⲬ̄Ⲣ̄Ⲥ̄, Christhood, probably translates the Greek χριστότης, which is rare, but attested.[57] On the other hand, the reading of III 10.3, [Ⲙ]ⲚⲦⲬ̄Ⲣ̄ⲎⲤⲦⲞⲤ, suggests that another Greek word is involved as well, namely, the abstract noun χρηστότης, goodness. Χρηστότης is an important divine attribute in the LXX, Philo, the New Testament and early Christian writings: God's mercy, goodness and liberality in giving.[58]

Both data, the *nomen sacrum* x̄p̄c̄ -x̄c̄ and the Jewish-Hellenistic notion of God's χρηστότης, are probably involved in the Self-Generated's anointing. The invisible Spirit completes his Son by liberally anointing him with his own Christhood-goodness, thereby establishing him as the Christ par excellence who lacks nothing of Christ—good or Christhood—goodness.[59] It is possible that the pun was first introduced by a scribe who replaced part of the text's original ⲬⲢⲎⲤⲦⲞⲦⲎⲤ and ⲬⲢⲎⲤⲦⲞⲤ with the *nomen sacrum* x̄p̄c̄— x̄c̄, just as the scribe of Papyrus 72 or its *Vorlage* replaced ⲬⲢⲎⲤⲦⲞⲤ in 1 Peter 2:3 with x̄p̄c̄ . Yet, the insistent threefold repetition of the ⲬⲢⲎⲤⲦⲞⲤ motif in an *anointing* scene, resulting in an *anointed* one, a ⲬⲢⲒⲤⲦⲞⲤ, suggest that the pun is more deeply rooted in the text. "This passage seems to me to try to explain the name Χριστός in a double way: by 'anointing' and by χρηστός."[60]

The emergence of the Self-Generated follows the pattern already observed in the emergence of Barbelo and her co-aeons: coming forth is followed by ritual—liturgical attendance and glorification. Yet, in

---

[55] Paap, *Nomina Sacra*, 110. Even without the reading x̄p̄c̄ the passage applies the terms χρηστός and κύριος to Christ; see Konrad Weiss, "χρηστός," *TDNT* 9 (1974) 483-92, here 488.

[56] See the presentation and discussion of the evidence in Antonio Orbe S. J., *La Uncion del Verbo: Estudios Valentinianos - Vol III* (AnGreg 113; Rome: Università Gregoriana, 1961) 73-82; Orbe quotes and discusses in particular: Justin, *Apol.* 1.4.5; Tertullian, *Apol.* 3; *Nat.* 1.3; Theophilus, *Autol.* 1.12.

[57] See Lampe, s.v., 1532b.

[58] Psalm 24:7; 30:19; 118:65,66,68; 144:7; Psalms of Solomon 5:13-15; 18:1. Philo, *Leg. Alleg.* 3.73; *Vit. Mos.* 2.132. Rom 2:4; 11:22; Eph 2:7; Titus 3:4-5. Letter to Diognetus 9:1-2; 10:4; 2 Clement 15:5; see Weiss, "χρηστός," 490-91.

[59] See Orbe S. J., *Uncion del Verbo*, 108-112.

[60] Walter C. Till, "The Gnostic Apocryphon of John," *JEH* 3 (1952) 14-22, here 17.

the case of the Self-Generated, attendance and glorification occur only after *two* processes: the Self-Generated comes forth as Barbelo's thought of the Father and the Father makes up for the defect of the resulting offspring by anointing him as χρηστός/χριστός. His birth from Barbelo is not enough; he is completed by the Father and it is in this completeness that he takes his place in the heavenly court.

There are three closely related father-son pairs in *Ap. John:* (1) the invisible Spirit and his son, the Self-Generated, begotten in his "likeness, ЄΙΝЄ" in his mother Barbelo (III 9.13-14); (2) the heavenly Adam and his son, the heavenly Seth;[61] (3) the terrestrial Adam, created by Yaldabaoth "in imitation (μίμησις) of the one who exists from the beginning, the perfect Man" (BG 49.4-6), and his son, the terrestrial Seth, begotten in Eve in "the likeness of the Son of Man" (II 24.36-25.1). In these three father-son pairs, the invisible Spirit is "the first Man" (*Ap. John* 37.19), Adamas is "the first (Man) who came forth, ΝΤΑϤΟΥⲰΝϨ ЄΒΟλ" (*Ap. John* 21.18), "the perfect and true Man" (*Ap. John* 21.17), and the terrestrial Adam is the first earthly (rather than perfect and true) Man. The Self-Generated is the first Son of Man, the heavenly Seth the second Son of Man and the terrestrial Seth (*Ap. John* 65.20) the final and third Son of Man, forefather of the entire human race.

|  | *Man* | *Son of Man* |
|---|---|---|
| Primal Triad | the invisible Spirit<br>the first Man | the Self-Generated, Christ<br>the first Son of Man |
| The All | Adamas<br>the first Man to come forth | the heavenly Seth<br>the second Son of Man |
| The lower world | Adam<br>the first earthly Man | the earthly Seth<br>the third Son of Man |

This system of Men combines aspects of the archetype—image relation in Platonic philosophy, and of the father—son relation in biblical genealogies. The two traditions are easily merged here because Seth (according to Genesis 5:3) is begotten in the likeness and image of Adam, just as Adam (according to Genesis 1:26) is created in the image and likeness of God. The terms εἰκών and ἰδέα

---

[61] No mother is mentioned here. The text's silence need not, however, be interpreted as implying, "Evidently, no female mate is needed to give birth to Adam's (i.e., Adamas's) son." Buckley, "Sophia, Adam, and Yaltabaoth," 42. The absence of Seth's mother *does* emphasize, however, that the central paradigmatic figures are the male father and son figures.

used by the Septuagint in the translation of these two passages lend themselves particularly well to the combination of the two traditions.

|          | Adam (Gen 1:26)        | Seth (Gen 5:3)          |
|----------|------------------------|-------------------------|
| LXX      | Ποιήσωμεν ἄνθρωπον      | καὶ ἐγέννησεν           |
|          | κατ' εἰκόνα ἡμετέραν    | κατὰ τὴν ἰδέαν αὐτοῦ     |
|          | καὶ καθ' ὁμοίωσιν       | καὶ κατὰ τὴν εἰκόνα αὐτοῦ |

The three father-son relations just traced form the metaphysical and soteriological backbone of *Ap. John*. The metaphysically descending series of Man—Son of Man relations can be traced back, soteriologically, up to its origin. The "race of Seth" (*Ap. John* 22.19) reaches its completion when it realizes its Sethian, therefore Adamic, therefore Human, and therefore Divine identity, moving on all three levels from Son to Father and through all three levels from image to paradigm, all the way up to the "first Man" who completes his Son by anointing him with his Christhood-goodness. The anointing of the Self-Generated, the first Son of Man, provides a model of completion for Seth's offspring, the human race.[62] Anointing, perhaps associated with the five seals of baptism, imparts to the descendents of Seth the invisible Spirit's goodness so that they can become χρηστός—χριστός, images assimilated to the first Son of Man, the first Seth, Christ.

### 3.3. The Self-Generated Receives the Mind (Ap. John 16.18-17.6)

And he requested to give him a fellow worker, the Mind,[63]
and the invisible Spirit consented.
The Mind came forth.
He stood in attendance together with Christ
glorifying him and Barbelo.
Now, all these came into being in silence and thought[64] (*Ap. John* 16.18-17.6).

The request for a fellow worker introduces the topic of the immediately following section, the work of creating and organizing

---

[62] "The account of the perfection of the Son above also provides a complete model of salvation for those lower beings who will be created below." King, "Sophia and Christ," 162. The term "salvation" is perhaps too strong since the Son is already an authentic image begotten by the Father. The notion of "completion" is the one deployed in the text.

[63] Following the text of III 10.9-10, ⲛ̄ⲟⲩϣⲃ̄ⲣⲣⲉϥⲣ̄ ϩⲱⲃ, a fellow worker, which is supported by II 6.33-34, ⲛ̄ⲟⲩϣⲃ̄ⲣⲣ ϩⲱⲃ. BG 31.5-6 reads, ⲛⲟⲩⲓϩⲓⲱⲃ ⲛ̄ⲟⲩⲱⲧ, one thing.

[64] Following the text of III 10.15, ϩⲛ̄ ⲟⲩⲥⲓⲅⲏ ⲙ̄ⲛ ⲟⲩⲉⲛⲛⲟⲓⲁ instead of BG 31.10-11 ϩⲛ ⲟⲩⲕⲁⲣⲱϥ ⲛⲟⲩⲉⲛⲛⲟⲓⲁ, in silence of a thought.

the All. Of the Triad of powers associated with the Self-Generated, the Mind is the most fundamental. It is later followed by the Will and the Word, its more outward-directed movements. Although the Mind comes on stage as an agent involved in the creation of the All, his primary activity at this point is that of all preceding members of the heavenly court, attendance and praise.

The final sentence, "Now, all these came into being in silence and thought," marks an important boundary between two spheres of being, and anticipates, by contrast, the emergence of the All through the Will and the Word.

| THE DIVINE TRIAD | THE ALL |
|---|---|
| comes into being in *silence* | comes into being through *word* |
| comes into being in *thought* | comes into being through *will* |

The first sphere is that of the divine Triad proper, Father, Mother and Son with their attendant aeons, all of whom come to be, not through a creative word, but in the silence of thought.[65] The second is that of the spiritual All, the four lights and the inhabitants of the aeons belonging to these lights, who come to be, not in the silence of thought, but in the outward-directed movements of will and of word (λόγος προφορικός). It is not surprising, therefore, that the Will and the Word are introduced only later, after the boundary between the primal Triad and the All has been crossed.[66]

## 4. A CURIOUS EDDY IN THE STREAM OF HELLENISTIC JUDAISM

The passage on the primal triad in *Ap. John* can now be placed in its history of religions context. It represents a curious turbulent eddy in the broad stream of Jewish Platonizing thought.

### 4.1. Metaphysics of Mind from Plato to Plotinus

Hans Joachim Krämer has argued persuasively that Gnostic speculations about the divine world, such as that of *Ap. John*, can be seen as witnesses to the development of a metaphysics of mind (νοῦς) from Plato's unwritten doctrine through the early Academy and Middle-Platonic philosophy to Plotinus.[67] To judge from the extant

---

[65] See MacRae, *Some Elements of Jewish Apocalyptic and Mystical Tradition and their Relation to Gnostic Literature*, 2 vols. (Ph.D. dissertation, Cambridge University, 1966) 1.187.

[66] See Werner, "Apokryphon des Johannes," 46.

[67] See Krämer, *Ursprung der Geistmetaphysik*, 223-64.

texts and heresiological summaries, he argues, Gnostic literature was not itself a protagonist of such philosophical development, but made use of it in painting its imaginative pictures of the unfolding divine world.[68]

The unfolding of the primal unity into multiplicity, according to the metaphysics received in *Ap. John*, is a process of mental reflection by which the first ground externalizes itself and grasps itself both for itself and for an other. "In the γνῶσις θεοῦ established in this way God is thus both subject and object: by externalizing himself he mediates himself to himself *and* to others, knows himself *and* is known."[69]

The Father-Mother-Son triad elaborated by *Ap. John* in this context appears to be ultimately rooted in Plato's *Timaeus*.[70] Having discussed the material universe fashioned by the demiurge after the pattern of the forms (27d-47e), Timaeus makes a new beginning (αὖθις ἀρχή) in his argument and turns in 47e to a principle implicit in this discussion, namely, a "receptacle (ὑποδοχή)" or "nurse (τιθήνη)" (49a) which is the substratum, "the this and that, τὸ τε τοῦτο καὶ τὸ τόδε" (50a) to which characteristics derived from the forms belong. In this context he enumerates a triad of principles, leaving aside the demiurge, who would be a fourth:

> ...that which comes to be, that in which it comes to be and that by imitation of which that which comes to be is born. We may fittingly compare the receptacle (τὸ δεχόμενον) to a mother, that from which to a father, and the natural being (φύσις) to a child (*Timaeus* 50c-d).

In the *Timaeus*, the father-mother-son triad does not serve to articulate a metaphysics of mind, but an account of the material universe. In Plato's late ontology, by contrast, a similar triad appears on a higher level:

(1) the One, which is a principle of unity and identity
(2) the (feminine) indefinite Dyad which acts as a principle of multiplicity

---

[68] See Krämer, *Ursprung der Geistmetaphysik*, 253. Krämer did not yet have access to the more philosophically reflective Nag Hammadi texts, e.g., the *Tripartite Tractate* and *Allogenes*. His judgment certainly applies to *Ap. John*.

[69] Krämer, *Ursprung der Geistmetaphysik*, 254-55.

[70] For a detailed discussion of the development from Plato to the Sethian texts, see John Turner, "The Virgin that Became Male: The Feminine Principle in Platonic and Gnostic Metaphysics," manuscript (1995) 1-45.

corresponding to the "receptacle" of the *Timaeus*;
(3) the realm of ideas which comes to be from these two.[71]

Plato does not appear to apply the father-mother-son image to this higher triad. The *Republic* speaks of the Good as "the Father" (506e) of an intelligible light which proceeds from him as his "child," ἔκγονος (506e; 507a),[72] but a mother is lacking.

Plato's successor Speusippus, further elaborated the feminine principle of diversity by distinguishing various levels on which it comes into play. On the lowest level, that of sensible things, the receptacle is no longer completely mastered by the principle of form; "the result is the emergence of evil."[73] The same distinction between a higher and a lower feminine principle, the latter responsible for evil due to insufficient formation by the male, reappears in *Ap. John* as the distinction between Barbelo and Wisdom (Reflection, ἐπίνοια occupies a position between them).

In several passages Philo alludes to the father-mother-son triad of the *Timaeus* and casts it variously as God-Wisdom-Logos, God-Wisdom-world, or God-Wisdom-sense perception.[74] It is not clear how much metaphysical weight he gives to these triads: there are other competing patterns, e.g. the θεός-κύριος pair (reflected in *Ap. John* 64.8-19). The God-Wisdom-Logos version is structurally identical to *Ap. John*'s triad.

An important step appears to have been taken first by Neo-Pythagoreans such as Moderatus of Gades (late First Century A.D.): while Plato's One and Indefinite Dyad were coeval, Moderatus derived the Dyad from the Monad—a derivation found also in Sethian and Valentinian texts and, later, in Plotinus.[75] In fact, Sethian and Valentinian texts are important as witnesses to an otherwise unattested Middle-Platonic schema later unfolded by Plotinus. The root of Plotinus's system, as Krämer has shown, is the triad of the

[71] See Kenneth M. Sayre, *Plato's Late Ontology: A Riddle Resolved* (Princeton: Princeton University Press, 1983); Turner, "Virgin that Became Male," 3-5.

[72] On the use of this passage in Philo, see Runia, "Themes in Philonic Theology," 75 with note 22.

[73] Turner, "Virgin that Became Male," 6 with note 10.

[74] See esp. *Leg. Alleg.* II.49; *Det.* 115-16; *Ebr.* 30-31; *Fug.* 108-109; *Somn.* II, 70; *Spec. Leg.* III, 180; see David Winston, *Logos and Mystical Theology in Philo of Alexandria* (Cincinnati: Hebrew Union College Press, 1985) 20-21; Turner, "Virgin that Became Male," 7-8.

[75] See Krämer, *Ursprung der Geistmetaphysik*, 323; Turner, "Virgin that Became Male," 8-13.

One, the indefinite Dyad and the Mind (νοῦς).[76] This foundational triad tends to be obscured, because Plotinus conceives the Dyad as life, movement or impetus,[77] rather than as a separate hypostasis comparable to the Mind (νοῦς) and the World-Soul. Although it is not cast as a Father-Mother-Son triad, Plotinus's foundational triad of dynamically unfolding principles is the closest attested parallel to the Sethian Father-Mother-Son triad.[78]

### 4.2. The Religious Impetus

The metaphysics of mind sketched above posits a double movement: the movement of self-explication (πρόοδος or προβολή) of the divine principle and the movement of reflection (ἐπιστροφή) in which derived levels of being tend back to their origin. This double movement gives a characteristic religious form to human consciousness: rooted in the self-explication of the divine ground, human consciousness inclines back into this ground, longing for vision.[79]

According to Plotinus, the way of reflection (ἐπιστροφή) leads inward, into a center of the soul that never descended.[80] The details of the relation between this innermost center of the human soul and the One need not be discussed here.[81] At the very least, when the soul achieves its inward reflection, the boundaries between it and the highest level of reality disappear: "there is nothing in between, nor are there still two but both are one; nor could you still make a distinction."[82] This final goal is already anticipated in some way in the nature of the soul: the innermost part of the soul and its divine origin are of one kind; they are "consubstantial."[83]

---

[76] See Krämer, *Ursprung der Geistmetaphysik*, 337 with note 532; cf. Turner, "Virgin that Became Male," 17 with note 33.

[77] See Krämer, *Ursprung der Geistmetaphysik*, 313-14.

[78] Excepting Valentinian speculations which are probably dependent on Sethian texts.

[79] Krämer, *Ursprung der Geistmetaphysik*, 312-37 unfolds the highly sophisticated account which Plotinus gives of this double movement and of a third element implied in it, the self-definition and self-limitation of derived levels.

[80] Plotinus, *Enneads* 4.8.8. The underlying principle is stated in the brief and clear synthesis *Enneads* 5.2.1 (23): "Nothing is separated or cut off from that which is before it."

[81] See the texts adduced by Krämer, *Ursprung der Geistmetaphysik*, 317, note 469, in which Plotinus equates the ἐπιστροφή of νοῦς to the One with its ἐπιστροφή into itself.

[82] Plotinus, *Enneads* 6.7.34 (13-14).

[83] See Plotinus, *Enneads* 4.7.10.

On this point there is agreement between Plotinus and his opponents called Γνωστικοί by Porphyry.[84] In fact, Plotinus criticizes his opponents for a certain excess in their claim to inner divinity. He does so, not because such a claim is false, but because he considers his opponents too facile in making it and too haughty in raising themselves over souls found in other parts of the material cosmos.[85] Whether Plotinus's critique of his opponents is just or not, one thing is clear: they stand in a similar religious tradition inscribed in a similar metaphysics of mind. In this respect Porphyry's Γνωστικοί closely resemble the intellectuals behind *Ap. John*.

### 4.3. Splitting the Inherited Hellenistic-Jewish Deity

There are a number of distinctive elements in *Ap. John* in comparison with Middle- and Neo-Platonic accounts of the intelligible world. Already the manner in which Platonic motifs are deployed is distinctive: they are not argued philosophically but employed imaginatively to paint a picture in which other and more sensual colors are used as well. Even the strict negative theology which opens *Ap. John*'s account of the Godhead plays a more imaginative than conceptual role. It suggests the depth of the first principle without ruling out sensual representations (e.g. the representation of the Father as looking at himself reflected in surrounding waters). Plotinus puts his finger on this sensual element, though he seems to be unable to understand where it comes from and what role it plays since he maps his Gnostic opponents strictly within his own philosophical framework.

> And in general they falsify Plato's account of the manner of demiurgy and many other matters, and degrade the man's teachings, as if they had understood the *intelligible nature*, but he and the other blessed philosophers had not. And by giving names to a multitude of *intelligible* realities they think they will appear to have discovered the exact truth, though by this very multiplicity *they bring the intelligible nature into the likeness of the sense-world*.[86]

Plotinus is correct in pointing out the sensual character of the heavenly world painted by his opponents. Had he been more familiar with Jewish religious literature and experience, or more willing to enter into it as an ancient and venerable tradition, he would have seen

---

[84] Porphyry, *Vita Plot.* 16.11.

[85] See Plotinus, *Enneads* 2.9.5 (1-14); 2.9.9 (46-51).

[86] Plotinus, *Enneads* 2.9.6; emphasis added.

that the elements of sensual imagination, including the multiplication of names, are not a mere corruption of Plato's teachings or products of intellectual vanity.

*Ap. John*'s Middle-Platonic transcendent deity gazes around himself into the primal waters of Genesis 1 and discerns in them his own reflection, Barbelo-Wisdom, the effulgence of his own light. This scene is closely linked to *Ap. John*'s reading of Genesis 1:3 (light shining forth) and 1:26 (appearance of the luminous human image on the waters of chaos). The later creation of Adam after the luminous image on the waters has its archetypal counterpart in the mirroring of the transcendent deity in the waters surrounding it. The system of personal aeons with abstract names appears to be the result of the conflation of a list of Platonic ideas and orders of Jewish angels.[87] The overall image of *Ap. John*'s upper world is that of a Jewish heavenly court. The members of the court not only contemplate, as Middle-Platonic hypostases do, but they participate in a heavenly liturgy described in the language of the Septuagint: they stand in attendance (παριστάναι) before God and glorify (δοξάζειν) him in songs of praise. The dialogue of prayer flashes back and forth between him and them. They ask him for favors; he graciously grants them; they respond with praise. Jewish genealogy (Adam, Seth and the descendents of Seth) is found on the various levels of being with higher genealogies acting as Platonic paradigms for lower ones. The multiplication of beings required for a heavenly court of angels expands the coupling of Middle-Platonic masculine (or neuter) principles of unity and feminine principles of diversity into a system of syzygies. Christian themes are present as well, particularly in the anointing of the Self-Generated, but they do not play as architectonic a role in the very structure of the heavenly world as Middle-Platonic and Jewish elements do.

It is remarkable that the formative presence of Jewish elements in *Ap. John*'s account of the Primal Triad goes hand in hand with a complete silence of the Biblical text itself. *Ap. John*'s overall story partly explains this silence. The theogonic and cosmogonic section (*Ap. John* 5.3-34.12) portrays what happened *before* Genesis 1:1—realities and events, therefore, about which the Biblical text has nothing to say explicitly. Yet this explanation raises the question of Jewish elements even more sharply. Why should they be present in

---

[87] Among all the members of the upper world, only Harmozel is explicitly called an "angel" ἄγγελος (*Ap. John* 19.16); the term "angel" is more frequently used for the evil archons of the lower world.

*Ap. John*'s account of beings and events *before* Genesis 1:1? Who is the God presiding in *Ap. John*'s heavenly court? On the basis of the distinctly Jewish features listed above one could suppose that he is the God of Abraham, Isaac and Jacob.

Yet Yaldabaoth's vain claim "I am a jealous God; there is none beside me" (*Ap. John* 34.6-7) clearly indicates that *he* possesses this identity. His vain claim is a quotations reflecting claims made by the God of Israel in a number of passages in Exodus, Deuteronomy, Hosea, Joel and Isaiah (LXX) some of which appear to have been regularly used in Jewish liturgy.[88]

| | | |
|---|---|---|
| ἐγὼ γάρ εἰμι | κύριος ὁ θεός σου, | θεὸς ζηλωτὴς (Exod 20:5) |
| ὁ γὰρ | κύριος ὁ θεὸς ζηλωτὸν ὄνομα, | θεὸς ζηλωτής ἐστιν (Exod 34:14) |
| ὅτι ἐγώ εἰμι | κύριος ὁ θεός σου, | θεὸς ζηλωτὴς (Deut 5:9). |
| οὗτος | θεός ἐστιν, καὶ | οὐκ ἔστιν ἔτι πλὴν αὐτοῦ (Deut 4:35) |
| ἐγὼ δὲ | κύριος ὁ θεός ... καὶ | θεὸν πλὴν ἐμοῦ οὐ γνώση (Hos 13:4) |
| ἐγὼ | κύριος ὁ θεὸς ὑμῶν, καὶ | οὐκ ἔστιν ἔτι πλὴν ἐμοῦ (Joel 2:27) |
| ἐγώ εἰμι, καὶ | | οὐκ ἔστιν θεὸς πλὴν ἐμοῦ (Deut 32:39) |
| ἐγὼ | κύριος ὁ θεός, καὶ | οὐκ ἔστιν ἔτι πλὴν ἐμοῦ θεός (Isa 45:5) |
| ἐγὼ | κύριος ὁ θεός, καὶ | οὐκ ἔστιν ἔτι (Isa 45:6) |
| ἐγώ εἰμι | ὁ θεός, και | οὐκ ἔστιν ἔτι πλὴν ἐμοῦ (Isa 46:9) |

Dahl has shown that the scene of Yaldabaoth's jealous hubris occupies a relatively fixed place in the plot of a number of Sethian texts.[89] The scene is usually placed at the end of the lower cosmogony and it is usually followed by a sequence of events that play on a set of passages selected from Genesis 1-2: the movement of the Spirit on the waters (Gen 1:2b); the disclosure of the exemplary Man in word and light (Genesis 1:3) and the proposal, "Let us make Man" (Gen 1:26-27) leading to the blowing of luminous divine power (or spirit) into Adam (Genesis 2:7).[90] The plot developed by means of these texts is the creation of the human race. The passage of luminous power from the demiurge into human beings is the central event of this creation.

---

[88] See Schenke, *Der Gott "Mensch" in der Gnosis*, 87; George W. MacRae, "The Ego-Proclamation in Gnostic Sources," *Studies in the New Testament and Gnosticism*, ed. D. J. Harrington and Stanley B. Marrow (Wilmington: Michael Glazier, 1987) 203-17; here 206; on the liturgical use of such formulae, see ibid. 209.

[89] See Nils A. Dahl, "The Arrogant Archon and the Lewd Sophia: Jewish Traditions in Gnostic Revolt," *The Rediscovery of Gnosticism, II: Sethian Gnosticism*, ed. Bentley Layton (SHR 41; Leiden: E. J. Brill, 1981) 689-712, here 693-94. The texts analyzed by Dahl include the *Apocryphon of John, On the Origin of the World, Hypostasis of the Archons, Gospel of the Egyptians* and Irenaeus, *Adv. Haer.* 1.29-30.

[90] See Dahl, "Arrogant Archon," 695-97.

Yaldabaoth plays the role of the impotent fool in this plot. He claims to be the only God precisely at the beginning of a series of events in which, the reader knows, he is tricked out of his divinity and inadvertently passes it on to the human race. As it is placed in the overall plot, the scene is stinging in its irony.[91]

The function of the "jealous hubris" scene in the overall plot of texts classified as Sethian suggests a possible reason for splitting an inherited Hellenistic-Jewish deity into two figures, one good and the other evil. When the religious impulses of a Middle-Platonic metaphysics of mind as articulated in *Ap. John* intersect with the impulses of Jewish piety, tensions arise and movement is bound to follow. Philo resolves such tensions by choosing to be primarily an interpreter of the biblical text who deploys Middle-Platonic motifs as they appear useful in reading the text. His primary loyalty is a loyalty to the God of Abraham, Isaac and Jacob as mediated by Moses. This God has moved far toward the Middle-Platonic transcendent deity. One may wonder whether the resulting image of God is cohesive, but there is no doubt that Philo *sees* it as cohesive and *intends* to remain loyal to Moses.[92]

*Ap. John* represents a different choice open to Hellenistic Jewish intellectuals. Rejecting the claim, "I am a jealous God; there is none beside me" (*Ap. John* 34.6-7) and choosing to place their foothold decisively and radically in a Middle-Platonic metaphysics of mind and the God=Man identification, the intellectuals behind *Ap. John* took the logical step of splitting the inherited Hellenistic Jewish deity in a curious Platonic-Jewish criss-cross-pattern into an upper God who was personally identified as the Middle-Platonic transcendent God, but retained some central features of the God of Israel, and a lower God who was personally identified as the God of Israel, but was cast in the role of the Platonic demiurge.

Despite the complication introduced by this criss-cross-pattern there is no doubt that the Jewish side drew the shorter stick. The portrayal of the God of Israel as the impotent fool who would keep divinity from human beings reflects this choice. What is particularly objectionable, but ultimately impotent, in the God of Israel is his insistent claim, "I am a jealous God; there is none beside me" (*Ap. John* 34.6-7).

---

[91] See Dahl, "Arrogant Archon," 697.

[92] See David T. Runia, "Was Philo a Middle Platonist? A Difficult Question Revisited," *Studia Philonica Annual* 5 (1993) 112-40.

Gnostic texts and heresiological summaries contain images of the demiurge which can be arranged in a spectrum of increasing vilification from demiurgic angels not at war with the highest deity to *Ap. John*'s Yaldabaoth, who is the devil, Samael, the blind god (see *Ap. John* 29.20-30.8). It is a dangerous temptation to equate this phenomenological spectrum with the "deposit" of development, like the gradually changing life-forms deposited in geological strata that follow each other in time.[93] According to Fossum, "(T)he *Apocryphon of John* ... shows us the last step in the development of Gnostic dualism."[94] The "splitting" of the Hellenistic Jewish deity suggests the opposite hypothesis. It suggests that Ialdabaoth, the negative "part" of the Hellenistic Jewish deity, was not born in a gradual development of increasingly evil demiurges, but in a single fall from the utmost heights to the utmost depths. When the claim to sole existence is rejected, the "part" of the original deity identified with that claim changes its identity without intermediaries from positive to negative. The historical position of Valentinian speculation confirms this hypothesis. Valentinus recast ideas encountered in *Ap. John* in the direction of a much more positive image of the demiurge. In addition, the roles played by the demiurge of various Gnostic texts differ not only in degree of vilification but in the *kinds* of concern expressed in them.[95] In Ptolemy's *Letter to Flora*, for example, the demiurge serves, among other things, to define the relation between the law passed down in the books of Moses and the new and more perfect moral teaching of Jesus.[96] This function is quite foreign to *Ap. John*'s Yaldabaoth.

The writers and editors of *Ap. John* in its final form were certainly Christians. Was there a pre- or non-Christian version of *Ap. John*, a purely Jewish/Platonic version? The importance of this question should not be exaggerated. It does not touch upon the *Ap. John*'s central concerns. The issue in *Ap. John* is not, as in Marcion, a perceived clash between a facet of the God of Israel (his role as the God of law and punitive justice) and the God of Jesus Christ (the

---

[93] Williams, Michael A. "The Demonizing of the Demiurge: The Innovation of Gnostic Myth," *Innovation in Religious Traditions*, ed. M. A. Williams, C. Cox and M. S. Jaffee (Berlin: Mouton de Gruyter, 1992) 73-107, here 81-83.

[94] Jarl Fossum, *The Name of God and the Angel of the Lord: Samaritan and Jewish Concepts of Intermediation and the Origin of Gnosticism* (WUNT 36; Tübingen: J. C. B. Mohr [P. Siebeck], 1985) 219.

[95] See Williams, "Demonizing of the Demiurge," 82-83.

[96] See Epiphanius, *Panarion* 33; Ptolemy identifies the divine law-giver of the Pentateuch as the demiurge in *Panarion* 33.7.4 (Williams 203).

forgiving "Pauline" God of grace), but a perceived clash between another facet of the God of Israel, namely, the God jealous of his identity as the only God, and the God of the Middle-Platonists, the Monad-Father who emanates his divinity without envy. This clash does not arise from concerns specific to a Jewish-Christian religious setting; it arises as a curious turbulent eddy in the stream of Platonizing Jewish thought.

# SOPHIA-MÊTÊR:
# RECONSTRUCTING A GNOSTIC MYTH*

*Sergio La Porta*
Harvard University

The myth of the "fall of Sophia," one of the central elements of gnostic mythology, is used in many gnostic texts to explain the origin of this world of darkness. Although the origin and development of this myth is obscure, George MacRae has argued effectively for its Hellenistic Jewish background.[1] However, much work remains to be

---

* I would like to thank Prof. G. Stroumsa of the Hebrew University, my tutor, for his guidance and his patience.

[1] G. W. MacRae, "The Jewish Background of the Gnostic Sophia Myth," *NovT* 12 (1970) 86-101. Most scholars seem to be in agreement that the underlying force of the *Ap. John* was some form of Alexandrian/Hellenistic Judaism which was later Christianized. For other Hellenic Jewish influences in the *Ap. John* , cf. R. van den Broek, "Autogenes and Adamas: The Mythological Structure of the *Apocryphon of John*," *Gnosis and Gnosticism: Papers Read at the Eighth International Conference on Patristic Studies (Oxford, September 3rd-8th 1979)*, ed. M. Krause (NHS 17; Leiden: Brill, 1981) 16-25; R. van den Broek, "Creation of Adam's Psychic Body in the *Apocryphon of John*," *Studies in Gnosticism and Hellenistic Religions Presented to Gilles Quispel*, ed. R. van den Broek and M. J. Vermaseren (*EPRO* 91; Leiden: Brill, 1981) 38-57; N. A. Dahl, "The Arrogant Archon and the Lewd Sophia: Jewish Traditions in Gnostic Revolt," *The Rediscovery of Gnosticism: Proceedings of the International Conference on Gnosticism at Yale, New Haven, Connecticut, March 28-31, 1978*, Vol. 2, *Sethian Gnosticism*, ed. B. Layton (Suppl. to *Numen* 41; Leiden: E. J. Brill, 1980-1981) 689-712; I. Gruenwald, "Aspects of the Jewish-Gnostic Controversy," *Rediscovery* 2.713-723; B. Pearson, "Biblical Exegesis in Gnostic Literature," *Armenian and Biblical Studies*, ed. M. Stone (Jerusalem: St. James, 1977) 70-80; G. Quispel, "Ezekiel 1:26 in Jewish Mysticism and Gnosis," *VC* 34 (1980) 1-13; G. Stroumsa, *Another Seed: Studies in Gnostic Mythology* (Leiden: E. J. Brill, 1984); G. Stroumsa, "Polymorphie divine et transformations d'un mythologème: l'*Apocryphon de Jean* et ses sources," *VC* 35 (1981) 412-434; G. Stroumsa, "Form(s) of God: Some Notes on Metatron and Christ," *HTR* 76 (1983) 269-288. On the later Christianization of the *Ap. John*, cf., K. King, "Sophia and Christ in the *Apocryphon of John*," *Images of the Feminine in Gnosticism*, ed. K. King (Studies in Antiquity and Christianity; Philadelphia: Fortress, 1988) 158-176 and H.-M. Schenke, "The Phenomenon and Significance of Gnostic Sethianism," *Rediscovery* II, 588-616. Quispel has sought to remove the Hellenization of Gnosticism and picture it rather as "a religion of its own, with its own phenomenological structure," though "it owes not a little to Judaism" ("Gnosticism and the New Testament," *VC* 19 [1965] 65-85, esp. 73). By contrast, James Goehring has argued that the sexual cause of Sophia's "fall," that is, her desiring to produce offspring without a consort, most closely parallels and most probably originates from the classical myths of Typhaon and Hephaistos ("A Classical Influence in the Gnostic Sophia Myth," *VC* 35 [1981] 16-23). And recently

done in piecing together a clearer picture of its growth. The important treatise called the *Apocryphon of John*,[2] in which the fall of Sophia plays a prominent part, may provide a key in helping us understand it. As the myth unfolds in the *Ap. John*, certain discrepancies and obscurities become apparent within the text. These include: the simultaneous occupation of the twelfth aeon by Phronesis and Sophia; the confusing roles and identities of the Epinoia of light and Zoe; and the overlapping functions and attributions of Sophia and the Barbelo. It is my contention that through analyzing these problematic features of the text we are able to find traces of the development of the myth of Sophia and possibly to reconstruct the development of the mythic account of her fall.

## I. SOPHIA: THE TWELFTH AEON?

We may begin by summarizing the text's narration of events concerned with the emanation of Sophia. After the creation of the Barbelo and the divine Autogenes (Christos), Christos and Aphtharsia, an aeon of the Barbelo, produce four emanations or powers.[3] It continues:[4]

---

Simone Pétrement has defended a purely Christian explanation for this myth (*A Separate God*, San Francisco: Harper, 1990).

[2] Four versions of the *Ap. John* are in existence today: The first tractate of the second Nag Hammadi Codex (NHC II, *1*); the first tractate of the third Nag Hammadi Codex (NHC III, *1*); the first tractate of the fourth Nag Hammadi Codex (NHC IV, *1*); and the second tractate of the Papyrus *Berolinensis* 8502 (BG). NHC II and NHC IV are the longer versions of the treatise while NHC III and BG are the shorter versions. NHC II is the better representative of the longer versions, while the BG is the better representative of the shorter. For a description and history of the various codices, cf. K. Rudolph, *Gnosis: The Nature and History of Gnosticism* (San Francisco: Harper and Row, 1983) 34-53.

[3] This is based on Irenaeus' account in his *Adversus Haereses* in Irénée de Lyon, *Contre les hérésies*, Book I, 2 vols, ed. A. Rousseau and L. Doutreleau, (*Sources Chrétiennes*; Paris: Cerf, 1979) 1.29.2. Thelema, Ennoia, and Zoe should probably be read as Thelema and Aeonia Zoe: "et de Thelemate rursus et Aeonia Zoe quatuor emissiones factas ad subministrationem quatuor luminaribus." This is most likely due to a scribal error; see R. Van den Broek, "Autogenes and Adamas," 18, n. 6; and S. Giversen, ed. and trans., *Apocryphon Johannis. The Coptic Text of the Apocryphon Johannis in the Nag Hammadi Codex II with Translation and Commentary* (Acta Theologica Danica 5; Copenhagen: Munksgaard, 1963) 180-181.

[4] I provide the two better of the four versions of the text: BG and NHC II. Cf. n. 2 above. All italics in the text are my own to indicate emphasis. All translations of *Ap. John* are mine unless otherwise noted. Translation for NHC II is based upon Giversen's edition. Translation for BG is based upon W. C. Till, ed. and trans., *Die gnostischen Schriften des koptischen Papyrus Berolinensis 8502* (TU 60; Berlin: Akademie, 1955). All other translations of Nag Hammadi texts from *The Nag Hammadi Library in English*, ed. J. M. Robinson and M. W. Meyer (New York: Harper and Row, 1977).

And the four are: Grace, Understanding, Perception, and *Phronesis*.[5] And Grace is with the first luminary, Armozel, who is the angel of light over the first aeon. And with him there are three aeons with him: Grace, Truth, and Form. [6] The second luminary is Oroiael who is set over the second aeon. And there are three aeons with him who are: Forethought, Perception, and Memory.[7] The third luminary is Daveithe who is set over the third aeon. And there are three aeons with him who are: Understanding, Love, and Idea.[8] And the fourth aeon is Eleleth who is set over the fourth aeon. And there are three aeons with him who are: Perfection, Peace, and *Sophia*[9] (BG 33.6-34.8).

And the four powers are: Understanding, Grace, Perception, and *Phronesis*.[10] And Grace is with the light aeon Armozel, who is the first angel. And with that aeon there are three other aeons: Grace, Truth, and Form.[11] And the second light is Oriel, who is set up over the second aeon. And with him there are three other aeons: Afterthought, Perception, and Memory.[12] And the third light is Daveithai, who is set up over the third aeon. And with him there are three other aeons: Understanding, Love, and Idea.[13] But the fourth aeon is established over the fourth light, Eleleth. And with him are three other aeons: Perfection, Peace, and *Sophia*[14] (NHC II 8.2-8.21).

From two versions of this passage, it is clear that Sophia appears as the twelfth and the last in a series of aeons. This pattern is roughly the same in all four versions of the myth we possess. However, if we look closely at the text we notice something peculiar. In the case of the first

---

[5] Coptic: ⲧⲭⲁⲣⲓⲥ, ⲧⲥⲩⲛⲍⲉⲥⲓⲥ, ⲧⲉⲥⲑⲏⲥⲓⲥ, ⲧⲉⲫⲣⲟⲛⲏⲥⲓⲥ.

[6] Coptic: ⲧⲭⲁⲣⲓⲥ, ⲧⲙⲏⲉ, ⲧⲙⲟⲣⲫⲏ.

[7] Coptic: ⲧⲡⲣⲟⲛⲟⲓⲁ, ⲧⲉⲥⲑⲏⲥⲓⲥ, ⲡⲣⲡⲙⲉⲉⲩⲉ.

[8] Coptic: ⲧⲥⲩⲛⲍⲉⲥⲓⲥ, ⲧⲁⲅⲁⲡⲏ, ⲧⲍⲓⲇⲉⲁ.

[9] Coptic: ⲧⲙⲛ̅ⲧⲧⲉⲗⲓⲟⲥ, ϯⲣⲏⲛⲏ, ⲥⲟⲫⲓⲁ.

[10] Coptic: ⲧⲙⲛ̅ⲧⲣⲙⲛ̅ϩⲏⲧ, ⲧⲭⲁⲣⲓⲥ, ⲧⲉⲥⲑⲏⲥⲓⲥ, ⲫⲣⲟⲛⲏⲥⲉⲓⲥ. F. Wisse in his translation of the NHC II version of the *Ap. John*, *NHLE* 109, renders these: "understanding, grace, perception, and prudence." B. Layton (*The Gnostic Scriptures*, [Garden City: Doubleday, 1987] 33) renders them: "intelligence; loveliness; perception; prudence." Giversen (*Apocryphon Johannis*, 61) translates them: "wisdom, Charis, Aisthesis, Phronesis." However, his translation maintains the distinction, which is apparent in the Coptic, between ⲙⲛ̅ⲧⲣⲙⲛ̅ϩⲏⲧ and ⲥⲟⲫⲓⲁ by rendering ⲥⲟⲫⲓⲁ simply as Sophia. ⲙⲛ̅ⲧⲣⲙⲛ̅ϩⲏⲧ only occurs in NHC II. In BG, NHC III, and Irenaeus, "Synesis" (ⲥⲩⲛⲍⲉⲥⲓⲥ) occurs instead. Since Crum (*A Coptic Dictionary*, 715a), lists ⲙⲛ̅ⲧⲣⲙⲛ̅ϩⲏⲧ as synonymous with σύνησις, the argument is unaffected and each text remains consistent.

[11] Coptic: ⲧⲭⲁⲣⲓⲥ, ⲧⲙ̅ⲏⲉ, ⲧⲙⲟⲣⲫⲏ.

[12] Coptic: ⲧⲉⲡⲓⲛⲟⲓⲁ, ⲧⲉⲥⲑⲏⲥⲓⲥ, ⲡⲣⲡⲙⲉⲉⲩⲉ.

[13] Coptic: ⲧⲙⲛ̅ⲧⲣⲙⲛ̅ϩⲏⲧ, ⲧⲁⲅⲁⲡⲏ, ϯⲇⲉⲁ.

[14] Coptic: ⲡⲭⲱⲕ ⲉⲃⲟⲗ, ϯⲣⲏⲛⲏ, ⲧⲥⲟⲫⲓⲁ.

three light-aeons or luminaries, their power is also an aeon, but not so with the fourth:

| Luminary: | Armozel | Oriel | Daveithai | Eleleth |
|---|---|---|---|---|
| Power: | Charis | Aisthesis | Synesis | Phronesis |
| Aeons: | Charis | Aisthesis | Synesis | Sophia (!) |
| | Aletheia | Epinoia | Agape | Perfection |
| | Morphe | Mneme | Idea | Eirene |

The first luminary is Armozel, the power given to him is grace (Charis), and the three aeons with him are Charis, Aletheia (truth), and Morphe (form). Charis is both his power and one of the aeons along with him. So it is, by analogy, with the other luminaries: Oriel's power is Aisthesis (perception) and Aisthesis also appears as one of his aeons; Daveithai's power is Synesis (understanding or wisdom) and Synesis also appears as one of his aeons. Following the preceding pattern one would expect the fourth luminary, Eleleth, whose power is Phronesis (prudence), to possess perfection, Eirene (peace), and Phronesis as his aeons. Instead, he possesses perfection, Eirene, and Sophia![15]

This peculiarity in the text has been noted by S. Giversen, Y. Janssens, and M. Tardieu.[16] Giversen explains it by stating that Sophia and Phronesis possess rather similar meanings.[17] He notes that this switch might have been accidental, but as Sophia plays such an important role in the overall myth, it seems more probable that it was an intentional move. The reason for Sophia's location, according to Giversen, was to place her "in a position in the system of aeons which makes her subsequent failure to appear understandable, namely, in the last place among the twelve aeons,"[18] as far away as possible from the Father. As Phronesis is semantically similar to Sophia, it was a reasonable replacement. Tardieu cites the shared, even interchangeable, meaning of Sophia and Phronesis and also states that it was not

---

[15] It might also be of some significance that the first three luminaries are established over their aeons while, by contrast, Eleleth's aeon is established over him.

[16] Giversen mentions that "the circumstances concerning the fourth power are different," (*Ap. John*, 182). Y. Janssens, "L' *Apocryphon de Jean*," *Le Museon* 84 (1971) 43-64, 403-32, follows Giversen's explanations. Tardieu comments that the Coptic versions "écrivent *sophia* comme dernier élément de la triade du quatrième luminaire. Le flottement de la terminologie peut s'expliquer," *Écrits Gnostiques: Codex de Berlin* (Sources Gnostiques et Manichéennes 1, Paris: Cerf, 1984) 271.

[17] Giversen, *Ap. John*, 182.

[18] *Ibid.*, 182.

a random interchange.[19] However, he adds a rather different explanation based on the concept that, for the redactor of the *Ap. John*, or at
least this part of it,[20] the essence of God was Wisdom and Aeon:
"l'Aion que révèle l'essence du Père est aussi Sagesse."[21] He then
posits that these sections, which describe the Aeon of the Father, are
enclosed by the two terms that define the Father: section 11 begins
with "Aeon" and section 23 ends with "Sophia."[22] It cannot be
disputed that Phronesis and Sophia are semantically interchangeable
and that Sophia's position is consistent with the role attributed to her
by the theogony of *Ap. John*. However, neither Giversen nor Tardieu
explain Sophia's earlier placement in the myth. Sophia's replacement
by Phronesis suggests that the latter most probably preceded her as
the twelfth aeon, while the former occupied a different position. This
may be evidenced by Irenaeus who, in *Adversus Haereses* I.29.2,
describes the emission of the four luminaries and their aeons. As
expected, Phronesis is the fourth luminary's aeon: "Phronesin autem
quarto, quem nominant Eleleth."[23] But, in contrast to the *Ap. John*,
Irenaeus does not mention Sophia as one of Eleleth's aeons. Instead,
he identifies Sophia with the Holy Spirit and indicates that she was
emitted from "the first Angel who remains near to the Only-
begotten."[24] Thus it seems Irenaeus is the recipient of a different
tradition which does not place Sophia as the last of the aeons. Before
proceeding to the question of Sophia's position, I shall put forward
another reason, overlooked by both Giversen and Tardieu, for
Sophia's replacement of Phronesis.

## II. Sophia Erupta

In positing another reason for the replacement of Phronesis by
Sophia, I would like to call attention to a more general feature of
gnostic myth, a feature first noted by François Sagnard. In his *La
Gnose Valentienne*, Sagnard coined the term, "envelopment," to
describe one of the usual forms of the "loi d'extension" of the divine
expansion.[25] Its basis is that an emanating aeon includes within itself

---

[19] M. Tardieu, *Écrits*, 271.
[20] That is sections 11-23 according to Tardieu's division.
[21] Tardieu, *Écrits*, 271
[22] *Ibid.*, 271.
[23] *Adv. Haer*, I.29.2 .
[24] *Adv. Haer*, I.29.4.
[25] F. Sagnard, *La Gnose Valentienne et le Témoignage de Saint Irénée* (Paris: J. Vrin,
1947) 242-3. His discussion revolves around "«l'économie» de l'Incarnation": how "Le

all its emanations and is thus an example of divine economy. John Sieber, discussing the treatise *Zostrianos* (NHC VIII, 1), shows how the Barbelo is also subject to this principle in that treatise.[26] Other scholars have noticed it within the *Ap. John* itself. For example, Bentley Layton in the notes to his translation of the *Ap. John* states that the Barbelo is part of the Pentad of the Father while simultaneously being the Pentad of the Father.[27] A. J. Welburn uncovered such a principle lying behind some of the cosmological names of the Archons in *Ap. John*.[28] And Simone Pétrement has formulated the idea that the four luminaries represent Christ as angels and that their names are able to evoke certain characteristics of the "anointed one."[29] These examples should suffice in order to apply this principle to the four luminaries and their aeons as well. We may state, then, that within the power Charis are enveloped Charis, Aletheia, and Morphe. This is a particular type of envelopment, in which the enveloping subject is one of the enveloped. Thus, the power Charis envelops the aeon Charis, the power Aisthesis envelops the aeon Aisthesis, the power Synesis envelops the aeon Synesis.[30] However, as noted above, Sophia causes a break in the expected pattern as the power Phronesis does not envelop the aeon Phronesis. This break emphasizes the disruptive character of Sophia's appearance

Although Sophia and Phronesis may be almost synonymous and semantically interchangeable, there is one quality of Sophia which distinguishes her completely from Phronesis: the title *Prouneikos*.[31]

Christ-Logos est inclus dans le Sauveur, et celui-ci à son tour s'enveloppe du Christ psychique," 243.

[26] J. Sieber, "The Barbelo Aeon as Sophia," *Rediscovery*, II, 788, writes: "the Barbelo Aeon of *Zostrianos* contains within herself the other three aeons."

[27] B. Layton, *The Gnostic Scriptures*, 31, n. 6a. M. A. Williams, *The Immovable Race: A Gnostic Designation and the Theme of Stability in Late Antiquity* (NHS 29, Leiden: E. J. Brill, 1985) 107, n.5, also points out this reading.

[28] A. J. Welburn, "The Identity of the Archons in the *Apocryphon Johannis*," *VC* 32 (1978) 241-254. Especially note his conclusions that "the doctrine [of the seven-foldness of the fourth archon] seems to be that the several powers which govern separately in the various spheres are all contained in essence in the unity of the most powerful and glorious planet, the Sun," 246.

[29] S. Pétrement, "Les quatres «illuminateurs»: sur les sens et l'origine d'un thème gnostique," *Rev. Et. Aug* 27 (1981) 1-23.

[30] Notice the same pattern in two of the preceding examples of envelopment: the Barbelo is simultaneously the Pentad of the Father and a member of the Pentad; the Sun (n. 28 above), represented by the seven-headed fourth Archon Iao, is simultaneously one of the powers of the Archons and the one that contains the others.

[31] Sophia is labeled *Prouneikos* in BG 32.10-11; 51.1-2; NHC III 15.3-4; 23.19-21. The term is also used by Irenaeus, *Adv. Haer.* 1.29.4. Cf. A. Pasquier, "Prouneikos: A Colorful Expression to Designate Wisdom," *Images of the Feminine in Gnosticism*, 47-

While Sophia and Phronesis may both roughly refer to "wisdom," only Sophia is *Prouneikos*, usually rendered by sexual terms such as "lewd" and "whore." Anne Pasquier has recently illuminated other possible meanings of *Prouneikos*. She concludes that *Prouneikos* may also describe someone who is untamable, impetuous, disruptive as well as promiscuous: "In a few words, it means 'somebody who cannot be held back (untamable or indomitable) because he is eager to spread as a peddler (his Power), thus provoking discord.'"[32] Sophia's designation *Prouneikos* amplifies her disruptive nature which is first exemplified by her appearance instead of Phronesis as the twelfth aeon. Sophia's nature finally manifests itself in an act of self-will—an action without a consort—which produces the abortion, Ialdabaoth. Here, her restless and disruptive character is most poetically displayed. This portrayal is analyzed in detail by Michael Williams who states that the "*ApocryJn* presents a *developed etiology* of instability or movement by means of the version of the Sophia myth found in this work."[33] This eruption of self-will causes Sophia to descend into darkness and, upon reflection, to move "to and fro" or to "rush around" in shame.[34] This characterization of Sophia resembles in many ways that of the figure who contrasts true wisdom in Proverbs and is described as a "whorish woman" (Prov 6:26).[35]

Overall, the author or redactor of the *Ap. John* was at pains to present Sophia's fall as the result of her own character flaws. He did this in three ways: 1) labeling her *Prouneikos* or furnishing her with an "Invincible Power" to procreate; 2) describing her in terms representing instability and appropriate to an anti-wisdom figure; and 3) placing her as the last aeon, breaking the expected pattern of emanation.

---

66. In NHC II she does not possess this title but rather is said to possess an "Invincible Power" (Coptic: Ⲧϭⲟⲙ ⲛ̅ⲁⲧⲭ̅ⲣⲟ ⲉⲣⲟⲥ). Giversen, *Apocryphon Johannis*, 194-95, explains that this is the power given to all who come forth from the Invisible Spirit, although the only other example he can cite is Christ. Therefore, this is a special power given to Sophia, "which makes it possible for her thought to become reality" (*Ibid.* 195). More important than whether she is explicitly called *Prouneikos* is that she contains an overwhelming urge or power to move, procreate, and disrupt.

[32] Pasquier, "Prouneikos," 56-7.

[33] Williams, *Immovable Race*, 103; (Williams' italics). Cf. also his article, "Stability as a Soteriological Theme in Gnosticism," *Rediscovery*, II, 819-29. Pasquier also touches upon this in "Prouneikos," 58-60.

[34] NHC II 13.13-26; BG 44.19-20. Cf. Williams, "Immovable Race", 112-13. Note also Irenaeus' description of Sophia's attempt to find a consort: "she struggled and strained forward" (*Adv. Haer.* 1.29.4).

[35] Cf. also Prov 2:16-19; 5:1-23; 6:20-29.

### III. SOPHIA SYZYGOS

The question of Sophia's original place within the myth still remains. A rather different position for Sophia—that of the first emanation, the Barbelo, itself—seems to have been her earlier station.[36] A key to this answer may be provided by NHC II 23.20-25. This passage allows us to link Sophia with the designations "holy spirit" and "mother of the living" as well as with the function of revealer/redeemer, three characteristics attributed to the Barbelo. These lines proclaim: "And our sister Sophia came down in innocence so that she might correct her deficiency. Therefore she was called "Zoe" (life)—that is the mother of the living—by the Pronoia of the Authenteia."

Giversen interprets the "she" (ϵρος) in 23.23 as referring to the woman who had just been created instead of to Sophia.[37] According to him, if "one refers the word ϵρος to the nearest preceding feminine being, Sophia, neither the assertion that she became the mother of all living, nor its reference to C II 58,18 [= NHC II 10.18] and to Genesis 3,20 receives its due importance."[38] NHC II 10.18 discusses the concealment of Ialdabaoth by Sophia in a luminous cloud so that none may be able to see it except for "the holy spirit who is called the mother of the living." Giversen, from the above commentary, perceives the holy spirit to be the Barbelo labeled as such when it was emanated.[39] For Giversen, then, the phrase "the mother of the living" should be ascribed to the Barbelo in this instance. However, it would be more sensible to understand the designation, "holy spirit," as

---

[36] This seems the case in other texts as well. For example, in the second conclusion of the *Gospel of the Egyptians* (NHC III 68.10-69.5), Sophia is included in the list of the divine hierarchy and equated with the Barbelo. According to F. Wisse and A. Böhlig, *Nag Hammadi Codices III,2 and IV,2: The Gospel of the Egyptians (The Holy Book of the Great Invisible Spirit)*, ed. A. Böhlig and F. Wisse (*NHS* 4; Leiden: Brill, 1975) 206, the list should be read in the following manner: "1) the great invisible Spirit; 2) his only begotten Son, the eternal light; 3) his great consort the incorruptible Sophia, the Barbelo; 4) the pleroma. Listed this way the trinity and the pleroma are the initiators of redemption." In *Eugnostos the Blessed*, Sophia is the feminine aspect of the androgynous Immortal Anthropos who is the first creation of the Father (NHC III 76.14-77.4).

[37] By contrast, Wisse (*Ap. John*), Layton (*Gnostic Scriptures*), and Tardieu (*Écrits*) all translate NHC II 23.20-25 as referring to Sophia. However, Giversen's objections should be addressed.

[38] Giversen, *Apocryphon Johannis*, 263.

[39] NHC II 5.7. Giversen does not supply a specific commentary on II 10.18, merely stating: "58.7-19. Sophia places her offspring, concealed from the rest of the world of light," *Apocryphon Johannis*, 199. However, his comment, "In C II 58,18, the holy spirit is mentioned as 'the mother of the living', and undoubtedly, here the living meant the beings in heaven in the kingdom of light" (ibid., 263), allows us to assume that he understands the holy spirit as the Barbelo.

referring to Sophia.[40] Irenaeus seems to have possessed a version of the myth which expressly says so, as he writes that they call the "holy spirit" both Sophia and Prouneikos.[41] Moreover, the context of II 10.18 is Sophia's concealing her abortion from the rest of the world of light. It would therefore be senseless to allow the Barbelo, the primary emanation of the Father, to see it. Rather, it would be more logical to understand this statement as meaning that Sophia is concealing her creation from everything but herself. Giversen's objection, then, that the referent of the "holy spirit" in II 10.18 must be a higher being than Sophia can be refuted and Sophia may be regarded as being the holy spirit.

Giversen's other objection is based upon Gen 3:20b, in which Eve is called "the mother of all living," a designation which he thinks belongs only to the Barbelo. Although I agree that an allusion is being made to this verse, I disagree with Giversen's interpretation of this allusion. In *Ap. John* and many other gnostic texts, Eve is more closely associated with Sophia than she is with the Barbelo. It is Sophia and Eve who share the characteristics of rebellion: improper sexuality and desire for forbidden knowledge. MacRae sees the fall of Eve, and especially Gen 3:20, as the principle source of the fall of Sophia.[42] Even if I would not put it as strongly as MacRae, I do think that his overall suggestion is valid and that the fall of Eve played a large role in the myth of the fall of Sophia. I also share his sentiment that "one would miss an essential insight into the Gnostic myths if he failed to realize that a close correspondence is intended there between the celestial world of the Pleroma and the material world of men."[43]

---

[40] In Jewish wisdom literature Sophia is identified with a (holy) spirit (Wis 7:7; 7:22-3; 9:17). MacRae, "Jewish Background," 90, sees the *Ap. John* as an "excellent example" of Sophia's identification with the Spirit of God in Gen 1:2b "and the Spirit of God was moving over the face of the waters." However, in the *Ap. John* Sophia does not move to and fro over the waters; rather, her moving to and fro is interpreted as a sign of her shamefacedness and desire for repentance. Of course, Gnostics were partially motivated in their connection between Sophia and spirit by the fact that רוח is feminine in Hebrew. MacRae also cautiously advances the idea that the holy spirit may be Sophia ("Jewish Background," 89).

[41] *Adv. Haer.* 1.29.4.

[42] He cites the following as evidence: 1) both are women; 2) the motivation for the falls are the same; and 3) the close association between Sophia and Zoe ("Jewish Background," 100). Stroumsa provides a detailed examination of the figure of Eve in gnostic literature and arrives at the conclusion—with which I concur—that the myth of Sophia is best understood through taking into consideration the fall of Eve (*Another Seed*, 171).

[43] "Jewish Background," 99. We might note as well that in the apocryphal Adam and Eve books, the fall of Satan has been modeled upon that of Adam and Eve in order to present it as the prototype of their fall, thus stressing the correlation between heavenly and earthly events.

This intimate connection would be lost if Eve were to be linked with the Barbelo instead of with Sophia. This may be seen in other texts as well. In *Orig. World* Sophia and Eve are closely related: Eve is referred to as the daughter of Sophia (NHC II 115.31-33) and "the first virgin, the one who without a husband bore her first offspring" (NHC II 114.5). In *Exeg. Soul* (NHC II 6), although the connection between Sophia and Eve is not expressly made, parallels between the journey of the soul and the tribulations of Sophia are evident.[44] *Thund.* (NHC VI,2) may also highlight the close association between Eve and Sophia. Though not named, a female revealer of knowledge is certainly the narrator and it is highly probable she is the double personality Sophia-Eve/Zoe.[45] For example, we may note the similarities between the monologue delivered in *Thund.* with the declaration of Eve in *Orig. World*.

Furthermore, Sophia is often referred to as a mother in gnostic myth. In the *Ap. John* she is referred to as the mother in NHC II 20.29. In the *Ep. Pet Phil* (NHC VIII,2), Sophia alone is called the mother (NHC VIII 135.10-21). In *Eugnostos* she appears as the "All-Begettress" and one of her aspects is called the "All-Mother Sophia" (NHC III 82.5; NHC III 82.21). In the *Ap. John*, of course, she is also a negative mother in that she is the mother of Ialdabaoth.[46] But even here the imagery used has been appropriated from more positive descriptions in Jewish wisdom literature. Wisdom's role as co-creator at the beginning of the creation (Prov 3:19; 8:27-31) now becomes the negative creation of the demiurge. Upon creating Ialdabaoth she conceals him and a throne within a luminous cloud, again conjuring up images of Jewish Wisdom: "I [Wisdom] dwelt in high places, and my throne was in a pillar of cloud" (Sir 24:4); "Who has gone up into heaven, and taken her [Wisdom], and brought her down from the clouds?" (Bar 3:29). Wisdom is also associated with God's throne or

---

[44] Cf. M. Scopello's introduction to *Exeg. Soul* in *NHLE* 191; and J.-M. Sevrin in *L'Éxégèse de l'Âme (NH II, 6): Texte établie et présenté,* (BCNH 9; Québec: Université Laval; Louvain: Peeters, 1983) 40.

[45] For a different opinion, cf. Layton's introduction to his translation, *Gnostic Scriptures*, 77-8, and his article "The Riddle of the Thunder," *Nag Hammadi, Gnosticism, and Early Christianity*, ed. C. W. Hedrick and R. Hodgson Jr. (Peabody, MA: Hendrickson, 1986) 37-54.

[46] An interesting contrast is provided by Epiphanius, who states it is the Barbelo who is called Ialdabaoth's mother (*Panarion* 25.3.4).

is herself enthroned: "give me the wisdom that sits by thy throne" (Wis 9:4; also 1 Enoch 84:3; Sir 24:4).[47]

Indeed, the ЄΡΟϹ cannot refer to the created woman because of her function within the myth. Ialdabaoth creates woman in order to capture the power of Sophia in the material world. This power of Sophia is what was referred to above as *Prouneikos* or the power "to make her thoughts a reality."[48] Ialdabaoth steals that power from her (NHC II 10.20). In order to retrieve it, the Barbelo sends luminaries in the guise of the angels of Ialdabaoth to deceive him into blowing that power into Adam in order to make Adam move (NHC II 19.15-33). To further help the retrieval of Sophia's power, the Barbelo sends an Epinoia of light to help Adam (NHC II 20.9-27). Ialdabaoth eventually realizes the purpose of this Epinoia and tries to counteract this by clothing Adam in a mortal body (NHC II 20.28-21, 13). When this fails, he tries to steal it from Adam after putting him to sleep. Yet he is still not able to grasp the Epinoia and can only retrieve part of the power—Sophia's power to procreate—that Adam has within him. From it Ialdabaoth is able to create woman (NHC II 22.18-23.3). Since he cannot remove the Epinoia, Ialdabaoth's original plan was to divide Sophia's power between Adam and Eve and to keep it in the material world through reproduction. However, the Epinoia makes her countermove by awakening Adam and saving him from the devices of Ialdabaoth, removing "the veil which was over his [Adam's] mind; and he became sober out of the drunkenness of darkness" (NHC II 23.4-8). Following this appears the above-quoted passage NHC II 23.20-25. The role of the created woman in the myth is to help keep the power which has been placed in Adam in the world, not to help Sophia correct her deficiency.

In order to fully appreciate Sophia as the referent of Zoe, mother of the living, we must realize that the redemptive Epinoia of light appropriated a function previously carried out by Sophia.[49] Sophia's association with Epinoia is borne out by 20.15-29 where the Epinoia of light as revealer/redeemer first appears:[50]

---

[47] In addition, in the *Sayings of Ahikar*, vi. 95, wisdom may be associated with a throne, for "the kingdom is [hers]," (J. B. Pritchard, ed., *The Ancient Near East: An Anthology of Texts and Pictures*, [Princeton University Press: Princeton, 1958] 428).

[48] Giversen, *Apocryphon Johannis*, 195; cf. NHC II 10.2.

[49] Irenaeus states that Sophia was emitted from the first Angel, Armozel, who was believed to be the Savior: "hunc autem esse Sotera volunt et vocant Armozel" (*Adv. Haer.* 1.29.2.).

[50] Epinoia is mentioned twice before in the NHC II but in a different role. First as an emanation in 8.11, and then in an obscure statement in 9.26 in which Sophia is said to

And he (Barbelo) sent, through his beneficent Spirit and his great mercy, a helper to Adam, luminous Epinoia which comes out of him (Barbelo), who is called Life (Zoe). And she assists the whole creature, by toiling with him and by restoring him to his fullness and by teaching him about the descent of his seed (and) by teaching him about the way of ascent, (which is) the way he came down. And the luminous Epinoia was hidden in Adam, in order that the archons might not know her, but that the Epinoia might be a correction of the deficiency of the mother (Sophia).[51]

In this passage it is clear that Sophia is to be linked with the Epinoia.[52] First, the Epinoia is sent through the spirit, which I have demonstrated to be Sophia. Second, the Epinoia shares many characteristics with Wisdom in Jewish wisdom and apocalyptic literature: 1) Wisdom is commonly a revealer; 2) Wisdom appears as a redeemer (Wis 10); 3) Wisdom descending into the created world is also a common theme (1 Enoch 42: 2; Bar 3: 37); 4) Wisdom is depicted as a tree (1 Enoch 32: 3-6),[53] somewhat as the Epinoia is referred to as the tree of knowledge of good and evil in NHC II 22.3-8.

How the Epinoia appropriated the role of the revealer/redeemer of the myth is, I think, partly due to an ambiguity in the text. I first thought that the longer version in NHC II preserved an earlier version of the myth in which the Epinoia was originally the ninth aeon. However, Michael Williams has suggested that the shorter versions might be more original in placing Pronoia as that aeon. The problem of Sophia's simultaneously being the creator of this world of evil and the saving revealer/redeemer was overcome by stripping her of the

---

belong to her. I will discuss this reference later. She also appears indirectly in 14.10-14. In this passage, Sophia has just repented and she is taken up into the ninth (aeon) in order to correct her deficiency. If we count upwards from the twelfth aeon, the ninth aeon is that of Epinoia. See Layton, *Gnostic Scriptures*, p. 39, n. 14c. In this context she seems to be acting as redeemer, but I will discuss how this occurred later as well. Note, in the BG version of the text no passage similar to 9.26 is present and Pronoia is emanated rather than Epinoia. When Sophia is brought up to the ninth aeon, she is therefore brought to the aeon of Pronoia.

[51] Trans. Wisse, *NHLE*, 116.

[52] In the *Trim. Prot.* Sophia is also referred to as the "Light's Epinoia"(NHC XIII 39.30). Cf. Y. Janssens, ed., *La prôtennoia trimorphe (NH XIII,1): Texte établie et présenté* (Bibliothèque Copte de Nag Hammadi, Section 'Textes' 4, Québec: Presses de l'Université Laval; Louvain: Peeters, 1978) 69-70. Layton, in his translation, also considers Sophia to be a holy spirit who is "also called life (Zoe), and referred to as "an afterthought" (*Gnostic Scriptures*, 25). However, he never gives a full explanation for why he thinks such, only indicating that Wisdom is sent back into the world by the Barbelo, Pronoia ("forethought") and "as an envoy of forethought is called forethought's afterthought" (*Gnostic Scriptures*, 44, n. 20b).

[53] MacRae also notes these similarities ("Jewish Background," 91-2).

latter function. This left a gap which the Epinoia, a later addition to
the story, filled. As an emanation from the Barbelo (Ennoia), the title
*epinoia*, "afterthought," was quite a logical one for this figure, for she
was sent after the creation of Ialdabaoth and Adam.. The two earlier
appearances of the Epinoia (NHC II 8.11, where she replaces Pronoia
as the ninth aeon, and NHC II 9.26 where Sophia is said to belong to
Epinoia) were probably even later additions based on a misreading of
NHC II 14.10: here, Sophia is brought back up to the "ninth" in order
to restore her deficiency.

But the text does not specify to what "ninth" it refers. Layton assumes that the ninth refers to the ninth aeon from the bottom, which
would be that of Epinoia;[54] I think a redactor of the text did the same
thing. However, the original reference was most probably to the ninth
*heaven*,[55] the pleroma.[56] This misreading would explain the awkward
passage NHC II 9.26. This redeeming function of the Epinoia was
then carried to the rest of the myth. We should therefore regard the
task of revelation and redemption as being solely a property of
Sophia.

This much can be adduced from the NHC II version of the *Ap.
John*. However, the BG version differs from the Codex II version by
presenting the entire episode as an exegesis of Gen 3:20,[57] and it does
not possess a passage equivalent to NHC II 23.20-22 ("our sister
Sophia ... innocence"). However, Sophia conceals Ialdabaoth in a
similar manner and here also none can see him except the holy spirit
who is the mother of the living.[58] Moreover, the Barbelo sends "son
souffle bienfaisant et sa grande miséricorde"[59] *as* an aide to Adam
rather than sending an aide *by means of* its spirit and mercy. This aide
is the Epinoia of light which Adam calls Zoe. Thus we have here a
more direct linkage between Sophia, the Epinoia, and Zoe.[60] Overall, I

---

[54] Layton, *Gnostic Scriptures*, 39, n. 14c.

[55] Giversen, *Apocryphon Johannis*, 236-37.

[56] Tardieu in his commentary interprets the ninth as the ninth heaven (*Écrits*, 297). He
also further adds that the ninth or "l'ennéade est le lieu normal de la Mère" (*Écrits*, 97).
However, Tardieu still maintains that the twelfth aeon is the proper place for Sophia. Note
as well that Norea is taken back into the pleroma in order to correct her deficiency
(*Norea*, NHC IX 28.24-30).

[57] Cf. Tardieu, *Écrits*, 325.

[58] BG 38.7-12. Accordingly, Tardieu's comment: "L'identification de l'Esprit saint et
de la mère des vivants provient d'une exégèse associant Gn 1,2 et Gn 3,20. La *ruah*
divine (pneuma) est mère (ici Sophia)" (*Écrits*, 276).

[59] Tardieu's translation, *Écrits*, 134.

[60] This, necessarily, challenges Tardieu's view that Sophia and Epinoia are diametrically opposed to one another (*Écrits*, 273-4).

would argue that BG has altered an older version of the myth that portrayed Sophia's descent as one of salvific revelation in order to explain how Eve came to be called the mother of the living in *Genesis*. This is not to say that BG altered the longer recensions of the *Ap. John*; rather it altered a common source adopted by the longer version. In doing so, however, it further distorted the salvific function of Sophia.

This identification of Sophia as revealer/redeemer would also clarify our understanding of the hymn at the end of the NHC II/IV version of the *Ap. John*. Here, the Pronoia, the Barbelo, is depicted as the revealer/redeemer who descends into the world three times to awaken humanity. However, if we understand that it is Sophia, rather than the Barbelo, who is descending and awakening, the connection to the previous awakening passages becomes clear. For it is Sophia who has descended three times, not the Barbelo.[61] The first descent occurred upon her creation of Ialdabaoth. Although no descent is expressly stated, one may be presumed to have happened, as it says that she was "taken back up" after she repented (NHC II 14.9). Sophia's second descent occurred when she was sent as a helper to Adam (NHC II 20.15-18). Sophia's third and final descent, possibly in the form of Norea,[62] was for Seth's benefit, so that the process of salvation may begin once more (NHC II 25.2-7).

To summarize, Sophia, at one level of the transmission of this myth was the holy spirit, the mother of the living, Life (Zoe) as well as the revealer of redemption, characteristics the present version of the *Ap. John* attributes to the Barbelo. It thus seems reasonable to speculate that previously Sophia may have been the first emanation of the Father.[63] This is true for other texts as well. In the *Tri. Trac.* (NHC I,5), Thought (Ennoia, a cognomen of Barbelo in *Ap. John*), Silence (Sige, who is normally the partner of the Father in the Valentinian primary dyad), Wisdom (Sophia), and Grace are equated (57.3-8).[64] In the *Exeg. Soul*, the soul, whose journey is parallel to

---

[61] Jewish Wisdom as a descending figure has been mentioned above; however, one should particularly note the similarity between this hymn and Wis 10 where Wisdom is a revealer/redeemer.

[62] In *Norea*, the figure of Norea greatly resembles that of Sophia. She, too, cries out to be brought back up into the pleroma in order to correct her deficiency. Also cf. Layton, *Gnostic Scriptures*, 47, n. 25d.

[63] MacRae, "Jewish Background," 88, remarks that "there is also a sense in which the Gnostic Sophia is, *at least originally*, linked with the supreme Aeon, the Father, even though she appears in some versions of the myth to be the lowest of the Aeons." Italics mine.

[64] Note that in this text the Logos, not Sophia, commits the error.

that of Sophia, is conceived of as originally being with the Father. In *Orig. World*, Sophia's image appears in the waters and she is the figure who reprimands Ialdabaoth for thinking that he is the only God.[65] And in the *Hyp. Arch.*, although the identity of the speaker who first contests Ialdabaoth's claim is unclear, the speaker of this challenge may be connected, or even identified, with Sophia, since it is her finger that stretches forth into the darkness in order to disprove Ialdabaoth's statement that nothing existed before him. Moreover, the speaker of the second reprimand is identified as Sophia's daughter, Zoe, whose connection to Sophia was elucidated above.[66] These two functions, appearing in the waters and reprimanding Ialdabaoth, are assigned to the Barbelo in the *Ap. John*[67] but clearly belong to Sophia in *Orig. World* and *Hyp. Arch.*[68]

The distinction between Sophia and a Barbelo-like figure is also murky in the *Gos. Truth*, which presents the introduction of error into the universe not as the fault of a particular aeon but rather as the pleroma's ignorance of the Father: "When the totality went about searching for the one from whom they had come forth ... ignorance of the Father brought about anguish and terror.... For this reason error became powerful."[69] The pleroma is analogous to the Barbelo in *Ap. John* and the error here resembles the one committed by Sophia in many versions of her fall. It is also worth noting that Error (πλανή) is feminine. It is quite possible that the redactor of this Valentinian tractate knew a version of the Sophia myth in which Sophia was still closely associated with the Barbelo and so equated Sophia with the feminine πλανή of the entire pleroma.[70]

---

[65] NHC II 103.16-32.

[66] NHC II 94.20-95.13.

[67] NHC II 14.13-15.

[68] Note, however, that in the *Ap. John* Ialdabaoth thinks that it is his mother Sophia who calls out to him. This statement might be regarded as a polemic against an older reading of the myth in which Sophia was the one who called to Ialdabaoth. Cf. Quispel, "Valentinian Gnosis and the Apocryphon of John," *Rediscovery* 1:118-127, who mentions that Sophia mirrors herself in the waters in *Orig. World* and *Hyp. Arch.* but not in *Ap. John*. He further notes, however, that Irenaeus says that Valentinus taught this as well. Quispel thus assumes that "Valentinus was familiar with a 'Gnostic' myth as contained in the actual *Apocryphon of John*, but preserving certain primitive features that are absent from the existing versions" (ibid., 120).

[69] NHC I 17.5-15.

[70] The similarities between this passage and the myth of Sophia have also been noticed by J.-E. Ménard, ed. and trans., *L'Evangile de Vérité* (Leiden: Brill, 1972) 80-1, and by H. Attridge and G. MacRae, "Introduction," to *The Gospel of Truth* in *NHLE* 39, who write: "A mythological account, like that of the fall of Sophia, ... no doubt underlies this description of Error."

Further evidence for this may be found in other parallels between the Barbelo and Wisdom in Jewish apocalyptic and wisdom literature.[71] First, the Barbelo and Wisdom are the first emanations or creations of God. In Proverbs, Wisdom is the first of His creations (Prov 8:22; also Sir 1:4,9; 24:8-9; Wis 7:25; 9:9). Second, as the first of His creations, they represent stability and praise God (Prov 8:23;30-1).[72] Third, the Barbelo is referred to as the "first thought" and God's "image" (NHC II 5.5-6). In the Wisdom of Solomon Wisdom is his breath, emanation, reflection, and image (7.25-6). Fourth, the Barbelo is an androgynous figure. It is called "the Mother-Father," "the first man," "the thrice-male," "the male-female," and "the thrice-androgynous named one"[73] In *de Fuga* (51), Philo mentions that Wisdom is called "Bethuel" because she is the daughter of God. However, Wisdom is simultaneously called Rebecca's father. In order to explain how Wisdom can be the daughter of God and a father Philo declares that "all the virtues bear the names of women, but have the powers and actions of fully-grown men, since whatever is subsequent to God, even if it be the most ancient of all other things, still has only the second place when compared with that omnipotent Being, and appears not so much masculine as feminine."[74]

## IV CONCLUSION

Following the examination of the role of Wisdom in the *Ap. John* above it becomes apparent that two types of wisdom are presented,

---

[71] These parallels are so striking that Quispel concluded that it was the Barbelo, and not Sophia, which most closely resembled the Jewish figure of Wisdom. He further speculated that: "There [in the *Ap. John*] Barbelo, the female counterpart of God, is called the 'first idea'…and understandable as a title of Wisdom; but the last of the aeons, who falls because of her lascivity, is called Sophia. And it would seem that this is a complication of the more simple concept, that Wisdom herself falls" ("Gnosticism and the New Testament," 74).

[72] Michael Waldstein successfully demonstrates how the Barbelo's attendance and glorification of the Father are "solidly rooted in Jewish theology," see "The Primal Triad in the *Apocryphon of John*," Paper for the Haverford Seminar on the Apocryphon of John, November 17, 1995, p. 21 (= p. ??? in the present volume).

[73] NHC II 5.6-9. BG does not mention the *Metropator* (BG 27.22-28.3). Note that Sophia in other Gnostic texts is also conceived of as androgynous. In the *Exeg. Soul*, the soul is also simultaneously considered as androgynous and feminine. The first 3 lines of the tractate read: "Wise men of old gave the soul a feminine name, Indeed she is female in her nature as well" (NHC II 127.19-21). And in line 24 it says that she "is androgynous in form." And as mentioned above, Sophia in *Eugnostos* is the feminine aspect of the androgynous Immortal Anthropos who in many ways resembles the Barbelo (NHC V 76.14- 77.4).

[74] Philo, "De Fuga et Inventione," *The Works of Philo*, trans. C. D. Yonge (Peabody, Mass: Hendrickson, 1993) 321-340, 325.

one positive and one negative. The former is represented by the Barbelo and the latter by Sophia. We may schematize this dichotomy in the following manner:

| Positive Wisdom Characteristics | Negative Wisdom Characteristics |
|---|---|
| Glorifying and Stabilizing Emanation | Disobedient and Destabilizing Emanation |
| Mother of Living | Mother of Ialdabaoth |
| Descent with Revelatory Effects | Descent with Disruptive Effects |

However, the imagery of both these representations stem from the same source: the figure of Wisdom within Jewish tradition. The development of this dichotomy is, of course, ultimately a matter of speculation, but we may be able to get an idea of its early stages through ideas circulating in Jewish apocalyptic literature. The myth of Sophia has its roots in an adapted wisdom myth which saw Wisdom in a positive, even salvific, role. This myth was subsequently transformed into one in which its values were partially inverted. To my knowledge, the closest parallel to this idea of inverting Wisdom's value is found in 1 Enoch 6-11, in which the origin of evil is described. These chapters present two reasons for the birth of evil in this world, both of which are the result of a revolt against God. The former ascribes the origins of evil to sexual intercourse between the sons of God—who descend to earth—and humans; the latter to teaching humans about certain forbidden knowledge.[75] Here, of course, are the basic ingredients of the negative myth of Sophia: a revolt against God, a descent which causes an impure mixture, improper sexual conduct, and the desire for forbidden knowledge. A possible objection to relating the myth of Sophia and 1 Enoch 6-11 is that in the myth of Sophia, Sophia creates Ialdabaoth, the Jewish God, while in 1 Enoch, no such event occurs. However, in 1 Enoch we see already the process of moving the origins of sin away from the human into the divine sphere. In Gen 6:5 it is clearly mankind who is evil and not the angels. But, as Nickelsburg points out, in 1 Enoch the

---

[75] G. Nickelsburg, "Apocalyptic and Myth in I Enoch 6-11" *JBL* 96 (1977) 383-405, analyzes these chapters in terms of two separate traditions based upon these two explanations of evil. He also indicates the similarities between the account concerning the instruction of mankind in fire, metalwork, etc. and the myth of Prometheus and Prometheus Bound. Stroumsa also sees this account as a reversal of a myth in which "the heavenly figures bringing knowledge and culture to humans were seen as 'héros civilisateurs' rather than as negative figures" (*Another Seed*, 20). As evidence for this he cites *Jubilees* 4:15, in which it is written that the angels of the Lord descended in order to "instruct the children of men, and that they should do judgment and uprightness on the earth" (*Another Seed*, 22).

blame falls on the angels, who revolt against God, and the giants, their offspring.[76] Additionally, in 1 Enoch 9:5, 10-11, there is the plea of the archangels on behalf of mankind, which is very accusatory towards God. This may possibly indicate a certain amount of frustration with a strict monotheism. Having heard the cries of humanity they exclaim to God:

> And now behold, the spirits of the souls of the dead make their complaint, And their groaning has come up to the gates of heaven, And it is not able to cease from the presence of the iniquities that are taking place on the earth. And you know all things before they happen, And you see things and you allow them, And you do not tell us what we ought to do about them.[77]

Even if we do not wish to go as far as Nickelsburg in stating that this is "the bitter and desperate cry of *our author's own people*,"[78] it is nonetheless a passionate expression of the problematic contradiction posed by the existence of evil in a world supposedly made by a God who is Good.

The story in Enoch may also witness a turning point in the conception of wisdom which led to a distinction between types of Wisdom. The opening and closing sections of 1 Enoch suggest that the composers of this text believed in an Enochic wisdom which surpassed, or at least equaled, Mosaic wisdom.[79] In 81:6 the holy ones tell Enoch that they will let him live with his son for another year so that "you may teach your children another law and write it down for them and give all of them a warning." And when Enoch gives this to Methuselah, his son, he says, " I have revealed to you and given you the book concerning all these things. Preserve, my son, the book from your father's hands in order that you may pass it to the generations of

---

[76] The angels are provided with a leader: Shemihazah in one tradition and 'Asha'el in the other (Nickelsburg, "Apocalyptic and Myth," 383). Could there also be a connection with Enoch's translation into Metatron, also known as Lesser YHWH, who is held responsible for the dualistic thinking of R. Elisha' ben Abuya (BT Hag. 15a)? Cf. G. Scholem, *Major Trends in Jewish Mysticism*, 3 ed. (New York: Schocken, 1974) and G. Stroumsa, "Aher: A Gnostic,"*Rediscovery*, II, 808-818.

[77] Nickelsburg, "Apocalyptic and Myth," 387.

[78] *Ibid.*, 389. Italics his.

[79] R. A. Argall, *1 Enoch and Sirach: A Comparative Literary Analysis of the Themes of Revelation, Creation and Judgment* (Atlanta: Scholars Press, 1995) 18, shows how the opening passages of 1 Enoch parallel Deuteronomy 33. He writes that these parallels "suggest from the start that the revealed wisdom imparted by Enoch stands on a par with its Mosaic counterpart. Enoch is a figure of Moses-like significance, who predates Moses! His blessing on the righteous and chosen presupposes that they are in possession of Enochic Torah." Cf. also G. Nickelsburg, "Wisdom and Apocalypticism in Early Judaism: Some Points for Discussion" *SBL Seminar Papers* (1994) 715-732, 720.

the world. I have given wisdom to you, to your children, and to those who shall become your children" (82:1-2). It is also noteworthy that the nature of the wisdom imparted by Enoch is a promise of salvation (5:5-9).[80]

It must be emphasized that I do not think Gnosticism to have originated from apocalyptic circles; that is, I do not think the negative myth of Sophia stems from 1 Enoch or any other work. Rather, it seems that this myth appeared in a similar intellectual, spiritual, and possibly even historical setting as 1 Enoch.[81] The circles that propagated this myth obviously possessed a heightened feeling of frustration compared to their apocalyptic counterparts, but nonetheless shared many similar concerns, such as the problem of evil within a monotheistic theology and the insufficiency of the Torah to satisfy all the needs of a changing society. Against this theory, Simone Pétrement in her recent book, *A Separate God*, has argued that the Gnostic phenomenon arose within Christianity. Although Pétrement assembles a wealth of information and makes many insightful observations, I cannot agree with her premise that "if Gnosticism is not explained by Christianity, it is difficult to see it as anything but a collection of bizarre doctrines, seemingly arbitrary and more or less absurd."[82] In fact, I think Pétrement's book tells us more about early Christianity and the theology of Paul and John than it does about the origins of Gnosticism.[83] Rather, I would agree with Quispel's statement: "Gnosticism is not a late chapter of the history of Greek philosophy and therefore a Christian heresy, an acute Hellenization of the Christian religion. Nor is it a fossilized survival of Old Iranian or even Indian religious concepts....It is rather a religion of its own, with

---

[80] Cf. Argall, "1 Enoch and Sirach," 97.

[81] N. A. Dahl, "Arrogant Archon," 691, argues that "at least one main branch of radical gnosticism originated in some syncretistic Jewish fringe group."

[82] Pétrement, *A Separate God,* 4.

[83] In fact one might suggest that part of Christ's image as revealer/redeemer was seen to be directly inherited from Sophia! J. M. Robinson, "Jesus as Sophos and Sophia: Wisdom Tradition and the Gospels," *Aspects of Wisdom in Judaism and Early Christianity*, ed. R. L. Wilken (Notre Dame, IN: University of Notre Dame Press, 1975) 11, notes that Luke 49:11, "Therefore also the Wisdom (Sophia) of God said, 'I will send them prophets and apostles,'" is edited by Matthew (23:34) to: "Therefore I send you prophets and wise men and scribes." Robinson comments, "it is not enough to say Matthew simply eliminates the reference to Sophia. Rather one must recognize that he identifies Sophia with Jesus, by attributing to Jesus not only a saying previously attributed to Sophia, but by attributing to Jesus the content of the saying, namely Sophia's role as the heavenly personage who throughout history has sent the prophets and other spokesmen."

its own phenomenological structure."[84] The mode of expression of this religion was inherently mythological and greatly indebted to Judaism.

A hypothetical schematization for the development of the myth of Sophia in the *Ap. John* might look like this: 1) A Wisdom myth in which Wisdom appeared as a positive revealer/redeemer figure much as she does in Proverbs and Wisdom of Solomon. Considered the consort of God and his assistant in the creation of the universe, she developed into an independent androgynous emanation. 2) Through a similar and contemporaneous set of historical or intellectual factors that influenced apocalyptic literature, a dichotomy appeared within Wisdom, marking the introduction of a distinction between a higher, salvific wisdom and a lower wisdom associated with the Torah. Simultaneously, the responsibility for the origin of evil shifted away from human to celestial beings (ca. $2^{nd}$ to $1^{st}$ c. BCE). 3) The mythic account of the origin of evil and the idea of a higher and a lower wisdom were harmonized with Neopythagorean concepts of the creation of the universe, such as Numenius' doctrine of *proschrêsis*. These negative features of Wisdom were attributed to a purely female wisdom figure, Sophia. She, however, interacted with the world in the capacity of a revealer/redeemer figure. The Barbelo, on the other hand, retained the androgynous character of the first created being and was the Ennoia of the Invisible Spirit. It was this stage of the tradition that Irenaeus inherited. 4) The tension suggested by a revealer/redeemer figure who was also the creator of evil brings about the final separation of the Barbelo and Sophia. Sophia's positive interaction with the world is omitted and she is placed as the lowest of the aeons. The Epinoia sent by the Barbelo then replaced her as the instrument of redemption and revelation to fill the gap left by Sophia's absence.

---

[84] Quispel, "Gnosticism and the New Testament," 73.

# RESPONSE TO THE PAPERS OF
# KAREN KING, FREDERIK WISSE, MICHAEL
# WALDSTEIN AND SERGIO LA PORTA[1]

*Michael A. Williams*
University of Washington

Our presenters have offered us a set of papers that are very useful due to their collective coverage of a wide range of issues about *Apocryphon of John*. The papers by Karen King and Frederik Wisse direct us to some fundamental questions regarding how we should go about imagining what *constitutes* the text of *Apocryphon of John*, before we get to the issue of interpreting it. The papers by Michael Waldstein and Sergio La Porta draw us more into issues of the religio-historical meaning of the text. If Prof. King would have us be more patient and cautious about ruminating, almost at a tactile stage, on the significance of the plurality of identities for *Apocryphon of John*, Prof. Waldstein and Mr. La Porta are both pressing beneath the surfaces of the texts as we have them, to possible earlier underlying mythic, intellectual and social traditions as they *might have been*, and the significances of the latter. Some of these differences among the four papers are merely the result of diversity in focus, but it also seems to be the case that there is some divergence in methodological philosophy. I express my gratitude to each of these presenters for what I have learned in reflecting on their papers, and I offer the following comments and questions to each:

## K. L. KING'S "APPROACHING THE VARIANTS OF THE *APOCRYPHON OF JOHN*"

Prof. King's observations constitute an extremely helpful theoretical caution against our anachronistically treating chirographic cultures as though they were like our own. Her general emphasis on the attention that we probably ought to pay to all of the several stages in a document's growth involves a healthy heuristic exercise that is

---

[1] This response was originally delivered in the course of the seminar on the *Apocryphon of John* at Haverford College, November 17, 1995, part of the Society of Biblical Literature's commemoration of the 50th anniversary of the discovery of the Nag Hammadi Library.

good for the intellectual souls of scholars in a field such as ours, where our tendency traditionally has been to equate rather too facilely or thoughtlessly the "text" of a given writing only with what is after all our own modern text-critical "guess-timate" about the "original," skipping past on our way perfectly real, physical copies of that writing that someone did use. Prof. King speaks of the large number of "audiences" for *Apocryphon of John* that we ought to keep in mind, "almost a dozen difference audiences," by her count (p. 24). This insistence on the greater attention we should give to other "audiences" than just the proverbial (and hypothetical) "original readers," is excellent advice. This is especially true in the case of those audiences for whom we have the most tangible evidence— namely, the audiences who used the four codices in which *Apocryphon of John* appears. For example, Prof. King's paper directs our attention to the issue of oral performance, and picking up her emphasis here we might ask what we are to make of the implications of the selection and arrangement of tractates within BG, II, III, and IV for the issue of the "performances" of *Apocryphon of John* in the fourth century? If we ought to imagine fourth century users reading aloud from such codices, should we imagine the possibility of the reading or performance of an entire codex? If so, the "sound" of *Apocryphon of John* in BG will have differed from the version in II not only because the former is a shorter recension, but also because of difference in positions of the work within the two codices and combination with entirely different sets of tractates.

From her theoretical reflections, Prof. King formulates a rather radical challenge: *Apocryphon of John*'s identity cannot be limited to the shape it has in any one of its manuscripts, or limited to some hypothetical "original" version, but rather one should "regard all the versions of the work as equally the *Apocryphon of John*" (p. 33).

As I think about the implications of this challenge, I cannot help but reflect upon analogies from other literature of the same general period. An example that comes to mind is the Gospel of Mark, in its longer and shorter versions. Is the Gospel of Mark with the long ending in 16:9-20 somehow "*not* the Gospel of Mark," in a way that the Gospel of Mark from 1:1-16:8 is? I think most of us might admit that the Gospel of Mark with the long ending *was* one ancient "version" of this writing. Prof. King's challenge with respect to the identity of *Apocryphon of John* would seem, by extrapolation, to suggest that the longer version of Mark is not ordinarily sufficiently appreciated as an achievement, as an important meaning of the text, as a significant moment in its social history. Indeed, we would have to admit that the long version of Mark with 16:9-20 has been far more historically significant than what many or most scholars today would consider the more "original" shorter version, simply because it has been the longer version that has been used by most readers down through history—by a *huge* majority. And yet how many of us are in the habit of teaching a course on the New Testament or the gospels in which we spend far more time, or as much time, or even *any* time, discussing the meaning of Mark in its longer form? A similar case, though perhaps with fewer literary consequences, might be the longer version of the Gospel of John, inclusive of the story in 7:53 - 8:11 about the woman caught in adultery.

I take it that Prof. King's theoretical and methodological position would have to be that we should, to paraphrase her wording with respect to *Apocryphon of John*, "regard all the versions of the work as equally [the Gospel of Mark or Gospel of John]," including not only the various Greek manuscript versions of these gospels but also translations into languages such as Coptic, Latin, Syriac, and so forth. But though this way of thinking about such ancient works offers some helpful balance to an exclusive focus on a hypothetically reconstructed "original" as the only legitimate version, I would pose the following questions:

First of all, granted that for each stage in the transmission of such writings as *Apocryphon of John* we should allow theoretically for a different audience, how many of these audiences can we realistically know much about in theological, not to speak of social-historical, terms? For example, for the "audience" of the Codex II text of *Apocryphon of John*, we do have at least the evidence of Codex II itself—the choice of other tractates, their arrangement, the colophon at the end of the codex, decoration on the leather cover, and so forth. Such evidence, though not as informative as having, say, a fourth century commentary on the work, still reveals to us something about this particular reading of *Apocryphon of John*. But by comparison, how much social or theological information can we squeeze out about the "audience" for the Coptic translation *underlying* the Codex II text of *Apocryphon of John*, especially since we do not have direct access to the Greek text from which it would have been made?

But beyond these purely practical limitations, I have reservations about the theoretical position that one ought to regard *all* versions of a work as "equally" that work. Even though Prof. King is correct that we may need to give much more attention to various stages in the history of an evolving work like *Apocryphon of John*, is *every* moment in that evolutionary history equally significant? To take an extreme example: Isn't the original creation of a work usually a more significant cultural act for us than the relatively slight modifications of it made in the course of one copy produced by a later scribe? Do we really want to abandon all distinction between author, editor and scribe? Admittedly, these roles sometimes overlap to a significant degree. Authors of ancient texts like these were often doing something more like what today we might call "editing" (i.e., of their sources), and scribes did frequently act like editors in altering the content of exemplars. Nevertheless, is there no value in maintaining these distinctions in principle?

It seems to me that Prof. King herself concedes the special importance of certain stages in the evolution of a work, when she makes her point about genre as a criterion for defining the minimal content *Apocryphon of John* (pp. 31, 38)—she sees the creation of the frame and question-and-answer format as the step that made *Apocryphon of John* an identifiable whole, the step in which *Apocryphon of John* was "created." Now that is a very plausible position, but it seems to depend precisely on the assumption that all moments in the evolution of a work are *not* in fact equal.

In a related vein: I would like Prof. King to comment further on her point (pp. 27-28) about obstacles being created by a text-critical search for the "original" version of a writing. I well understand part of what she is saying here—i.e., that labeling and dismissing characteristic "tendencies" in a particular version as later "corruptions," and limiting our interest only to the hypothetical "original," overlooks important information that we might gain about the ongoing social and intellectual history underlying the work's continuous use. However, I am a bit confused as to how far Prof. King would push this. She *seems* to be arguing that all efforts to identify the order of stages in literary evolution are obstructive in this sense. The question I have is that, if our interest here is supposedly in social and intellectual *history*, doesn't social history, ideally, have a *movement* to it? A history? A story? And how are we to have a "social *history*" of a work like *Apocryphon of John* if we do not make *attempts* at discriminating layers and *orders* of layers.

Now I would be the first to concede the problems here. And indeed, I have not myself been so optimistic about reconstructing *in any detail* the textual history of *Apocryphon of John*—except to regard some elements in the longer recension as probably not belonging to the oldest stage in the story of the text (e.g., the melothesia section and the Pronoia hymn). And perhaps what Prof. King is claiming is that *because* one cannot be certain of the order of some of the various stages, then one must treat the different versions of *Apocryphon of John* as (1) different performances of "Sethianism," (2) which we cannot with certainty order into a story of development, but (3) which as a plurality of performances shows us that at least there *was* a social history here. In other words, the multiple versions may not give the tools for reconstructing a social history in the narrative sense, but nevertheless they should be appreciated on their own and not homogenized, since they do provide evidence that there *was* underlying development.

But it seems to me to be one thing to suggest that all stages were important or "legitimate" or worthy of study in their own right, and another to say that the very notion of reconstructing the history of a text somehow violates its natural character as a product of a chirographic culture. I can't quite understand Prof. King's claim (p. 40) that "the fixity we assume in printed materials limits the ability of materials to respond flexibly to changing situations." I might understand it better if she had said "the fixity we assume in printed materials *mistakenly assumes a limitation in the ability of authors and editors to respond flexibly to changing situations*" ("Materials," it seems to me, do not themselves "respond to situations.").

In sum, Prof. King has pressed some important theoretical questions on us that can bring a much better balance to our analysis of an ancient work like *Apocryphon of John*. Yet at the same time, I wonder if she may not be swinging the theoretical pendulum too far in the other direction, in dismissing the theoretical importance of distinguishing between author and scribe, between original work and modified copy.

As a final note, I could add some specific observations about her lists in footnotes 65-68, of instances of agreement of various versions against one another. I concur that some of the textual variants involve something more than merely scribal errors or alternate translations. But I do think that the list she provides should be pared down considerably, since many of these are surely only instances of error or different translation. In one place, Prof. King speaks of performancial and hermeneutical variation (pp. 15-16). While I concede that these are important concepts, I wonder about the choice of examples she provides there. At least as far as the difference between the ⲉⲩⲣ̄ ⲡⲙⲉⲉⲩⲉ in BG 74.5-10 and the ϩⲛ ⲟⲩⲙⲓⲙⲏ[ⲥⲓⲥ] in III 38.15-20 is concerned, don't we more likely have a translator's mistaking of μίμησις for some form of μιμνήσκω or μνημή? Using Prof. Wisse's rules, we would say that S-BG differs from an agreement between S-III and L here, and therefore the difference does come from the Coptic translator and not from a different Greek exemplar. But is the Coptic translator's role really a hermeneutical variation, or merely mistake? And in the first part of the passage, do we call this performancial variation, or simply different translation?

My overall point is that while variations in "performance" are present in these manuscripts of *Apocryphon of John*, we are justified in distinguishing between more and less *significant* innovations in performance.

## F. WISSE'S "AFTER THE *SYNOPSIS*"

Like Prof. King, Prof. Wisse gives attention to the various social locations of *Apocryphon of John*, beginning with the most concretely attested, the Coptic monastic owners whom he posits for the manuscripts, and moving back through the development to the "pre-composition phase." I found his summary in this portion of the paper clear and helpful, but I would raise the following questions:

In what he labels the "translation phase," Prof. Wisse contends that such translations were most likely made in the third and early fourth centuries, by heterodox ascetics, and that these translations were "most likely intended for private use by unilingual Copts" (p. 8). I wonder if Prof. Wisse could clarify a bit more precisely what he has in mind by "private use"? Is he searching only for some description that would rule out an organized community or sect? Or does he literally mean use by only one individual, for private reading? Or would he allow the centrality of "oral performance" that Prof. King has argued, and if so, does "oral performance" entail a social situation that would be better described in terms other than "private use"? It seems to me that Prof. King has raised some very good issues about chirographic culture that would suggest that few books were ever produced for "private use," at least in our modern sense of the term.

In what Prof. Wisse calls the "composition stage," he argues that there is no evidence that *Apocryphon of John* was composed for a specific sect, but rather was more likely the work of "visionaries" who were open to ideas from a variety of religious traditions. I would want to ask Prof. Wisse if his own canon of *explicatio simplicior potior* ought not to be invoked here? When you have a text transmitting a rather elaborate esoteric mythic tradition such as is found in *Apocryphon of John*, encompassing theogony, cosmogony, anthropology and soteriology, a paradigmatic portrait of conversion, and a severe warning that the only people who will go to a permanent place of punishment, "where there is no repentance," are the ones who

accept the knowledge revealed in the book but then later become
apostates (Ap. John II 27.24-33), a text expressing in this last and
other aspects a "paraenetic concern," as Norman Petersen long ago
observed in his Harvard dissertation on *Apocryphon of John*—I
wonder if the *simplest* explanation is not that such a writing makes
most sense as something composed for readers with some consciousness of community defined by their shared acceptance of the revelation? We don't have to label this a "gnostic sect" or even a "Sethian"
sect. But I would tend to say that we *do* have to think of a *community*, if we are looking for the *simplest* hypothesis. The notion of some
kind of history of communal audiences for *Apocryphon of John* is in
my view also the simplest explanation for its relatively rich manuscript tradition. Prof. Wisse's resistance to any talk of communal
provenance seems to me to be an *over*correction for the famous
heritage of heresiological pigeonholing according to specific "gnostic"
sect. To insist that we are justified only in speaking vaguely about
texts copied for some kind of "private use," or of writings composed
in the first place by "visionaries" who were open to all ideas, seems to
me to be resisting unnecessarily a much simpler kind of thesis.

In his discussion of the composition phase, Prof. Wisse does invoke the *simplicior potior* canon when he deals with the dating of
tractates. In his view, the simplest thesis is the latest possible date,
unless other evidence warrants a move earlier. I understand his
caution here, and I think that he is quite correct to criticize the
opposite approach that is so often seen these days, where the earliest
possible date (for texts like the *Gospel of Thomas*) is often too
eagerly accepted. But while I understand the point, I would have to
disagree with the rule that Prof. Wisse articulates, in the case of
*Apocryphon of John* or any other ancient work. In my view, the more
appropriate rule is to speak, where we can, of a range between earliest
and latest possible dates. Actually, to stick with such a range is
*simplicior potior*. The "latest possible date" should remain exactly
that, and not somehow be given privilege as the hypothetical date.

Finally a couple of comments about Prof. Wisse's canons on pp.
6-7. In general, these are sensible criteria, but I would suggest one
qualification:

His third and fourth rules argue that when the long recension
agrees in sense with one of the shorter versions, BG or III, against the
other shorter version, it is simpler to assume that the diverging short
reading is due to that Coptic translator rather than to a difference at
that point between underlying Greek exemplars of the short texts. It
seems to me that this general rule does not quite take account of

instances such as that in III 14.23 par (one of Prof. King's cases of III/II agreement against BG), where the difference between III (ⲥⲩⲛⲍⲩⲅⲟⲥ) and BG (ⲥⲩⲙⲫⲱⲛⲟⲥ) involves a different *Greek* term. A similar instance is in III 23.15, where that text has the Greek term [ⲟ̅ⲩ]ⲡ`ⲟ`ⲗⲅⲉ, "become/be slack," while BG and II/IV have ⲁⲣⲅⲟⲛ, "inactive." Other examples of this would be III 26.19 (ⲁⲛⲧⲓⲙⲓⲙⲟⲛ, agreeing with ⲱⲃⲃⲓⲁⲉⲓⲧ in II?) vs. BG 55.8-9 (ⲁⲛⲧⲓⲕⲉⲓⲙⲉⲛⲟⲛ); or III 26.21 (ⲁⲛⲁⲡⲗⲁⲥⲓⲥ, agreeing with II/IV) vs. BG 55.10-11 (ⲡⲗⲁⲥⲙⲁ). Of course, Coptic scribes or translators used terms of Greek origin and it is possible that such differences (sometimes involving mistakes) were introduced at the Coptic stage. But is it really true that that is always the simpler explanation in these instances? It is simpler only in the sense that it involves a few number of actors than if one assigns the differences to the activity of earlier scribes copying and modifying a short Greek recension, producing somewhat difference versions of it. However, I doubt that anyone wishes to argue that there was no history of scribal transmission of the shorter version(s) of the *Apocryphon of John* prior to the first Coptic translations of it. If we have such a series of Greek copies before the first Coptic translations, I see no reason why those scribes should be imagined as having made fewer alterations in the text than later Coptic translators and scribes. Thus, when we have cases like those above, where the Coptic text shows us at least the very good possibility that the underlying Greek could have been different, then it seems to me that the simpler, more "conservative" thesis would be that there was a difference in the Greek texts underlying BG and III.

## M. WALDSTEIN'S "THE PRIMAL TRIAD IN THE *APOCRYPHON OF JOHN*"

Essentially, Prof. Waldstein questions whether Hans Jonas was correct to view myths such as that in *Apocryphon of John* as true intellectual ancestors of modern existentialist nihilism, and therefore to ascribe to those ancient myths a tendency toward world-negation (*Entweltlichung*) that achieves full development only in later nihilism. Prof. Waldstein answers in the negative, and he rejects Jonas' thesis that modern existentialism is the correct hermeneutical key for understanding texts such as *Apocryphon of John*. Prof. Waldstein's argument is that there is a qualitative and fundamental difference between the *Entweltlichung* of nihilism and what might be termed the cosmic perfectionism of *Apocryphon of John*. The latter is interested in withdrawal to a more perfect, transcendental order or cosmos, not

in rejecting "all definite being, all definite order" (p. 40). The difference is so fundamental, Prof. Waldstein implicitly argues, that Jonas
is not justified in seeing the *Entweltlichung* of nihilism present even *in
nuce*, as it were, in *Apocryphon of John*'s mythic speculation. The
difference is qualitative, like the difference between a complete
vegetarian and one who only eats the best cuts of meat.

Prof. Waldstein offers another hermeneutical approach, reading
*Apocryphon of John*'s basic myth as the creation of Jewish intellectuals who simply opted for one alternative solution to the difficulties
generated by the intersection of Jewish piety with the religious
impulses of Middle-Platonic metaphysics. The rather sensual colors in
which metaphysical reality is portrayed in *Apocryphon of John*'s
myth are not, as one ancient critic (Plotinus) charged, crude corruptions of Plato's teachings, but rather are better understood as the
intentional contribution of a tradition (Judaism) rich in concrete
imagery.

I find his critique of Jonas compelling, and I would have to agree
completely. What is important about Prof. Waldstein's study here is
that he is showing that the most "usual" of the "usual suspects"
ordinarily rounded up as examples of "gnosticism," the *Apocryphon
of John*, does *not* in fact seem to qualify with respect to some of the
most central elements in Jonas' classic phenomenological construction
of "gnosticism"! To my mind, this exercise succeeds in demonstrating
how different *Apocryphon of John* can look when we approach it
freed from the prevailing paradigm (the construct "gnosticism") that
would have pressed us to read all sorts of things into it that are *not*
there, and overlook crucial things that *are*. Working from within what
is surely one of the citadels of alleged "gnostic anticosmism," Prof.
Waldstein challenges us to see in *Apocryphon of John* what, he
claims, is actually a form of "cosmic piety."

His argument, based especially on the centrality of "sensual images" of heavenly courts, is a subtle one. I would augment it in at
least one way, by underscoring the significance of the family imagery
in the transcendent realm. The heavenly world is not only a court but
a family, the ideal family, and we have to ask ourselves, in Geertzian
terms, whether such a divine model may not only be a "model *of*"
(i.e., the divine world taking its shape from the social experience of
the mythmakers) but also a "model *for*" (i.e., the divine world
presenting ideal patterns that are in some sense to be imitated).
Although it does seem fairly clear that *Apocryphon of John* as we
have it would have readers spurn sexual desire and procreation as an
archontic device, do we really have the situation where *Apocryphon*

*of John* has transferred the theme of ideal family entirely to the transcendent realm, so that it has no relevance whatsoever, except in the negative, for the actual social lives of intended readers?

Finally, related to my last comments: Prof. Waldstein has called attention to intersecting "dimensions" in the myth—so that there is both Platonic metaphysics and Jewish heavenly court and other myth. I have just suggested that there might even be another dimension of intended significance: the portrait of the ideal family. But in any event, I would like to have Prof. Waldstein comment further about his contentions at different points in the paper that one of these dimensions or another is the "more prominent." For example, at one point (pp. 19f), he discusses what aspect of the "standing" imagery is "more prominent." Is it so easy to tell this? What exactly do we mean by more prominent? A similar point is made at the end of the paper, where he argues that it would be a mistake to categorize these people as (Middle-) Platonists, because Jewish traditions play a central architectonic role (p. 44). I would like him to elaborate on how we measure such things?

## S. LA PORTA'S "SOPHIA MÊTÊR"

Sergio La Porta's fundamental hypothesis is that underlying the myth confronting us in *Apocryphon of John* was a mythic tradition in which Wisdom was more positively portrayed, and with less ambivalence. Mr. La Porta argues that in the earlier stages Wisdom played a leading role to an extent that has been partially effaced in the evolution of the myth, with dimensions of her original role increasingly assigned to other figures such as Barbelo and Epinoia. This evolution took place, Mr. La Porta contends, due to a developing "frustration with a strict monotheism" (p. 16). This much of Mr. La Porta's position is broadly similar to Prof. Waldstein's hypothesis about the emergence of a "curious eddy" in Hellenistic Judaism from the marriage of Middle Platonic metaphysics with Jewish myth, because both Prof. Waldstein and Mr. La Porta stress the role of issues of theodicy and problematic portraits of God. And I have great sympathy with the general shape of this part of Mr. La Porta's thesis.

Now the special case that Mr. La Porta defends in this paper is that we can identify specific evidence for moments in this evolution of Sophia's role in differences among the manuscript recensions. It will be noted that some important parts of this case depend on assumptions about textual development that contrast strikingly with those laid out by Frederik Wisse. I am talking about his contention that

aspects of the myth in the shorter recensions are secondary modifications of what is found in the long recension. I will mention two key
examples, and in both instances I do have some problems with his
reconstruction of the direction of evolution:

His explanation on pp. 11-12 of Sophia's identification with Epinoia is interesting, but should be revised: According to Mr. La Porta's
model, Epinoia is "originally" an emanation among the twelve
distributed in the four luminaries, the ninth from the bottom. Epinoia's connection with Sophia would have resulted from a misunderstanding of II 14.10, where Sophia is restored not to her own aeon but
to the one above her offspring, the "ninth." That would have led to a
(mistaken) connection between Sophia and Epinoia, and that mistaken
connection would then have led to Epinoia's redeeming function in the
rest of the myth. However, this approach leaves two things unexplained: (1) why then would Epinoia have been replaced later by
Pronoia in the shorter recensions, and (2) why would the redactors in
the shorter recensions have also changed the phraseology in II 9.25
(Sophia of Epinoia) into an expression that happens to be more
reminiscent (as Mr. La Porta points out, p. 8, n.40) of the wisdom
tradition in Proverbs ("our sister" Wisdom; Prov. 7:4)? Naturally,
neither change would be impossible. But wouldn't a simpler hypothesis be to assume that the shorter recensions are more original in
having Pronoia in that aeon? The explanation for Epinoia's redeeming
function in the myth might be better explained simply in terms of this
word itself, "reflection, intellective faculty, etc.," as a natural term to
express the experience of enlightenment. (Under Mr. La Porta's
hypothesis, we would actually have a rather amazing coincidence: that
there just *happened* to be in that ninth-from-the-bottom position a
term that then lent itself to the mythic role of illumination.) If there is
a connection between Epinoia's "ninth" position in II/IV and what is
said of Sophia in II 14.10 par, perhaps it is instead that Sophia was
already connected with Epinoia's redeeming function, and the
redactor of the long recension drew the conclusion that (1) the "ninth"
meant not simply a ninth heaven above the "eighth," but still outside
the pleroma, but rather the ninth aeon up in the four-luminary group,
and (2) therefore the Pronoia in that slot should be changed to
Epinoia.

The other example is from his argument on pp. 12-13. Mr. La
Porta views BG as less primitive than II in the story of Eve's appearance to Adam. He suggests that the reference in II 23.20- 21 to
Sophia coming down to rectify her deficiency has been effaced in BG,
so that Eve, not Sophia, becomes the one called "the Mother of the

living." As supporting evidence, he argues that in spite of this alteration so as to have Eve "sent to Adam for redemptive purposes," the remainder of the myth in BG does make it clear that "it is, as in NHC II, Ialdabaoth who creates Eve and sends her to Adam, not any divinity" (p. 13; cf. p. 10). But it seems to me that *Apocryphon of John's* myth of Eve's creation—in any of the MSS, actually—is constructed with some ironic intent and needs to be read accordingly. Ialdabaoth does indeed create Eve in order to attempt to "keep the power which has been placed in man in the world" (p. 10). Yet in spite of this intent, the woman's creation has an opposite effect. Eve's appearance to Adam is a positive moment of (self-) revelation, somehow parallel to Barbelo's appearance from the Invisible Spirit. In other words, I am not sure that there is enough *internal inconsistency* in the short recensions here to push us toward explaining them as secondary at this point. If they are secondary here, I think that would have to be demonstrated on grounds other than the ones Mr. La Porta has presented.

Finally, I would like to add a comment about Mr. La Porta's intriguing discussion of "Sophia erupta," and the way in which her appearance in the list of aeons in the fourth group seems to be a sudden and unexplained replacement of Phronesis. I think his argument here about the way in which Sophia seems to "break the pattern" by her very appearance, even before her subsequent act, is quite ingenious. The one objection I would raise may in fact not be a very substantial or convincing one, but I think that at least it should be considered:

Though I do think that a good case has been made that Phronesis was originally in the fourth aeon, I wonder if it is necessary to assume that it is *Sophia* who has replaced Phronesis in the list. We normally conclude this only because it seems to be the term in this group of three most closely related semantically to Phronesis. However, could that be a false clue. What intrigues me is that in general there seems to be a pattern of having each time three terms ending in -σις, -η, and -α. That could mean that Sophia, like Aletheia, Pronoia, and Idea, might *originally* have been the -α member in the last set. That would then shift the problem to explaining why Phronesis would have come to be replaced by "Perfection" (perhaps τελείωσις?). If, on the other hand, we assume that Sophia is indeed the item that has replaced Phronesis, then we need to ask whether ⲘⲚⲦⲦⲈⲖⲈⲒⲞⲤ or ⲠⲬⲰⲔ ⲈⲂⲞⲖ must translate some -α word, (τελείωμα? But wouldn't we expect τελείωσις or τελειότης?). If not, would we want to maintain that this term was the only exception to the pattern noted above, where each set had an -α term? If Phronesis were replaced by "Perfection," then perhaps this was prompted by reflection on the theme of Sophia's departure from and eventual return to a condition of perfection. I offer these observations only to draw more attention to the issue of whether we really should so quickly assume that Sophia is the obvious interloper here.

PART THREE

THE *GOSPEL OF PHILIP*

# ON THE COHERENCE OF
# THE *GOSPEL ACCORDING TO PHILIP*

MARTHA LEE TURNER
University of Notre Dame

In comparison with certain other documents deriving from the "tamer" side of the gnostic world, the *Gospel according to Philip* has been somewhat neglected. In some respects, this is easily understandable. Apart from a dozen or so cameo appearances, it lacks the superstar billing which catapulted the *Gospel according to Thomas* to instant fame. Nevertheless, the potential of the *Gospel according to Philip* to illuminate the fascinating and diverse muddle of intersecting gnosticisms and Christianities in the first centuries C.E. is perhaps even higher. Some key seems to be missing.

The nature of the document itself remains in question. Is it some sort of collection? And if so, what are the sources of its components, what principles govern their organization? Is it an original composition, reflecting the perspectives of a single author or community? These questions cannot be set aside in favor of questions of interpretation, because they are foundational for interpretation. Their answers, even if they remain on a tacit level, determine the practice of interpretation, including whether, when, and how any of its passages can be used to illuminate any other.[1] Multiple answers to these questions have been proposed, and multiple interpretive approaches pursued, but no general consensus has emerged, nor even much explicit discussion of the issues involved. The study of the *Gospel according to Philip* has been becalmed, in a significant degree, by a lack of any clear sense of how to proceed.

---

[1] This includes interpretation which seeks to link the meaning of a passage to its present literary context. To play, anachronistically and for purposes of illustration, with a modern tradition of subtitles: imagine the effects on interpretation if another ancient manuscript were found, identical in all respects except bearing, after the title, as a subtitle: *An Anthology of Diverse Voices*; or *The Evolution of My Opinions from Darkness to Light*; or *The Illuminated Teachings of the Divine Master*; or *Heretical Excerpts For Refutation*; or *A Pocket Edition of the Old Catechism*. The possibilities sketched by each of these subtitles so radically flavors the idea of the present literary context that each would transform the process of interpretation—and hypotheses roughly corresponding to most of them have been proposed.

This paper seeks to present, from a more theoretical orientation, one type of methodological perspective which guided and informed work on the *Gospel according to Philip* which I have presented elsewhere at greater length and with far more support than can be offered in this brief format.[2] I will here present a typology and evaluation of previous hypotheses about the nature of the document, with some reflection on the kinds of evidence on which each type of assessment has been based.

## THE NATURE OF THE QUESTION

The data presented by our document is, in its raw form, confusing. Any hypothesis about the coherence of the *Gospel according to Philip* must attempt to account for (at least) these features:

• short units which seem capable of functioning independently of each other, including both those which seem to be non-sequiturs in their present setting, and those with assorted links to surrounding material;

• apparent connections between units in sequence: catchword associations, both simple and sophisticated, and analogous developments;

• irregularly recurring and metamorphosing themes.

Alongside these, I would introduce:

• sectarian terminology, conflicting usages, and distinctive features which are concentrated in (or wholly restricted to) certain portions of the document.

Moreover, viable hypotheses should also be consistent with:

• the conditions of writing in late antiquity;

• the conventions of some genre (or generic context);

• plausible motivations and commitments on the part of all agents.

Hypotheses can be evaluated on the basis of their success in explaining these (and perhaps other) features of the text and its relation to a larger context.

The alternatives are not simply those of unity or diversity. Various types and degrees of unity are possible, each posing different ap-

---

[2] M. L. Turner, *The Gospel according to Philip. The Sources and Coherence of an Early Christian Collection* (NHMS 38; Leiden: E. J. Brill, 1996).

proaches to and constraints on interpretation. The extent to which an integrated interpretation of any issue within the document is justified depends on these questions.

There are a number of types of coherence which a document like this might possess: a uniform and recognizable style, a set of metaphors consistently deployed, an overall plan or structure of the document as a whole, a genre (or, at least, a generic context), an identifiable provenance (usually conceived in terms of linguistic milieu or group affiliation and intergroup conflict), a single purpose or function, a coherent set of liturgical practices and interpretations (such as might derive from a single community), theological or doctrinal consistency. Moreover, each of these types of coherence could exist at several levels. For example, a recognizable literary or rhetorical style might be seen in a few editorial insertions within a collection of otherwise untouched material, or in thoroughgoing redactional reworking of all or of any portion of a collection's components, or as the product of original literary composition rather than of collecting or editing activity. Alternatively, a recognizable style might be the distinguishing feature of material derived from one specific source. As another example, a coherent Christology might run through every passage relevant to such issues, or might be seen in clumsy, contradictory Christological statements revised in partial harmony with a redactor's views, or diverse and even mutually exclusive Christologies might be found.

As in these examples, implications about the document's compositional process and/or redactional history lurk beneath every possible assertion about its unity or literary nature, and vary with the degree of coherence postulated as well as with its kind. It is important for clear thinking that we notice where our observations cease and our speculations about the processes that could account for them begin. Nevertheless, a fully satisfactory understanding of the document should involve the explicit postulation of process(es) by which it could have come into existence. Such hypotheses should account for the observable features of the text, and should be plausible in the world of late antiquity and more or less gnostic Christianity.

Any such hypothesis will also have implications beyond the characteristics it was meant to explain, and these implications must be in harmony with the observed characteristics of the text. Teasing the maximum number of implications out of each hypothesis, and then checking as many of them as possible against the text itself and its context, is the only type of control we have over our speculations— but it is a fairly rigorous one.

Unfortunately, the scholars who have addressed themselves to this issue have not usually carried their speculations far enough to make much use of this check. Many assessments have either stopped with a description of the features of the text, or have postulated a compositional process on the basis of a few features, and then moved on to whatever sort of interpretation that process would warrant. The problem is not, however, that investigators have been too speculative, but that their speculations have been neither carefully (enough) framed nor carefully (enough) tested. A satisfactory theory about the formation of the *Gospel according to Philip* should:

- be based on very carefully observed characteristics of the text;
- hypothesize a process or processes by which such characteristics could have come about;
- explore the implications of that process, and test each implication against the observed characteristics of the work and as many external factors as possible.

Is it premature for such a theory? It will seem premature until one is proposed that fits these criteria and wins a significant degree of acceptance.

## A TYPOLOGY OF PROPOSED SOLUTIONS

The typology of solutions that follows is organized according to the major characteristics of the document which must be accounted for. I will concentrate on theories that have been rather more fully developed, and that present representative ways of handling the issues involved. The following is neither a history of scholarship on the *Gospel according to Philip*[3] nor a comprehensive evaluation of the contribution to the study of the *Gospel according to Philip* of any of the scholars discussed.

### Quasi-Independent Units and Sequential Continuities (and Discontinuities)

One of the most easily observed characteristics of the text is that it seems discontinuous (whether it truly is or not). Apparent non-sequiturs interrupt the flow of thought frequently; between such discontinuities, the material often looks like the kind of unit that could

---

[3] For such a history of scholarship, with respect to the issue of the work's unity only, see chapter 2 of M. L. Turner, *The Gospel according to Philip*.

function independently, or like a small group of such units.[4] A satisfactory understanding of the document must include some explanation of this appearance. It is very difficult to discuss this feature, however, without continual reference to the appearance of myriad connections between such potentially independent units. Themes, issues, and images often appear to form bridges between statements that lack syntactic or logical connections. Sometimes the nucleus of a unit seems clear enough, but that nucleus is surrounded by shorter, potentially free-standing, units, which can be interpreted as making the same or an analogous point (often in either more abstract or more concrete and mythological terms). At other times, only a single common word eases the abruptness of transition.[5] Still other short units follow each other with no discernible connection whatsoever. A few units start so abruptly that something essential appears to be missing.

Since most of the connections between one unit and the next are not made explicit (as by means of commentary or transition), one must proceed with caution, continually asking how many of the connections that one sees are "really there," and to what extent one is reading them into the text. At one end of the spectrum of possibilities, apparent continuities between passages would result from random collecting or casual grouping around a word or theme. Under such an hypothesis, sharply opposing opinions on the same theme might appear side by side, but neither their inclusion in the work nor their juxtaposition would warrant any attempt at synthesis. At the other end of the spectrum, an individual writer's abrupt and telegraphic style might be responsible for the appearance of discontinuity; in this

---

[4] Our document's position in Codex II directly following the Gospel according to Thomas, and the widespread use of "saying" or "paragraph" numbers as a handy means of reference, has tended artificially to strengthen this impression, of course.

[5] The term "catchword association" is a label which has led to misunderstandings, because (1) it covers a number of different phenomena, and (2) it carries with it, at least for some readers, a prejudgment about the nature of these phenomena, namely, that items so joined have no other connection with each other. The same kinds of linkage that tend to be called "catch word associations" when they occur in a multi-source wisdom collection (the *Sentences of Sextus*, for example) are more likely to be identified as rhetorical devices when they appear in an original work. Curiously, though, the same specific names for such phenomena are applied in both cases: anaphora, chiasmus, climax, sorites, and the like. The deployment of these devices ranges from the crudely mechanical to the subtly sophisticated. We need a term for the group of rhetorical devices that involve the repetition of one or more words, and "catch word association" can serve, if we remember to see in it neither a judgment about the origins of the material in which it appears, nor an observation that no other link is present , nor yet that only a crude kind of verbal association is being made.

case, every possible linkage between contiguous (and non-contiguous) texts should be searched out and examined, as the secret key left by the author. Some positions in the middle are also logically possible: passages from disparate sources on originally unrelated topics (or conflicting doctrines) might be placed side by side, without any modification, because someone saw a potential relevance between them, some provocative combination of images deemed worthy of offering for contemplation. Alternatively, a single longer and more discursive document could have been excerpted or epitomized to produce the extant document, in which case the outline of some narrative or conceptual order might perhaps remain discernible.

Evaluations of the *Gospel according to Philip* as a collection or florilegium are based primarily on this appearance of potentially independent units, taken together with the absence of the syntactic and logical connections which we might expect in a single continuous writing, however terse. The ease with which these features can be observed, and the historical circumstance that much of the early work on the document was done in the shadow of the *Gospel according to Thomas*, have combined to give hypotheses of the "florilegium" type the feeling of something obvious and self-evident. Those who have subscribed to this view have not generally felt that it needs much explicit support or defense, nor that its implications were extensive and capable of being tested.

Early in the study of the *Gospel according to Philip*, R. McL. Wilson raised the question of the document's seeming lack of coherence. He wrote, "to speak of 'structure' or 'composition' in relation to such a document as the Gospel of Philip may appear at first sight to be a misuse of these terms,"[6] and asserted that "it cannot be contended that Philip is a single coherent text, composed according to normal standards of writing."

Nevertheless, Wilson cautioned that modern standards of continuity may be inappropriate:

> This rambling and inconsequential method of composition is not without parallel in the writings of the Fathers, or in the Bible itself. Clarity is sometimes introduced by modern chapter divisions, and if the texts were written out as in Philip without these aids to comprehension we should be faced with the same bewildering movement, as of a butterfly flitting from one theme to the next.[7]

---

[6] R. McL. Wilson, *The Gospel of Philip* (London: Mowbray, 1962) 7.

[7] Wilson, *Gospel of Philip*, 8-9.

He also observed that the material on the first few pages can be blocked together under headings: contrasts relating to modes of human existence, the mission of Christ, the nature of truth.[8] Despite his characterization of the document as "an extreme case," he urged that this "does not justify us in abandoning the effort to discover how its author (or compiler) went to work." Wilson focused on independent units and discontinuities (as well as recurring themes, treated below), but was aware that much material by individual authors presents similar problems, if in considerably milder forms. Wilson wrote sometimes about an author (or, on occasion, an 'author'), sometimes about a compiler, but did not take a definite stand about the document's unity.

Jacques E. Ménard focused particularly on the catchword links between units.[9] Ménard believed that these were far mechanical and superficial way of linking otherwise unrelated units. Rather, they present a guide provided by the author to help the reader understand the continuity and the progression of his thought.[10] Although he wrote of an author, Ménard's estimate of this continuity must be seen, however, against the backdrop of earlier commentators who saw the work as "chaotic," a "florilegium" "without any definite plan of composition."[11] Ménard saw these catchwords as guiding us to group together two, three, four, five or even more "sayings" for interpretation—a relatively modest claim, in terms of the unity of the document as a whole.[12] Nevertheless, he made a convincing case for the impor-

---

[8] Wilson, *Gospel of Philip*, 9-10.

[9] J. É. Ménard, *L'Évangile selon Philippe. Introduction, texte, traduction, commentaire* (Paris: Letouzy & Ané, 1967) 2-6. This publication, Ménard's 1967 Strasbourg dissertation, differs little in its interpretation of the nature of the *Gospel according to Philip* from his 1964 publication, *L'Évangile selon Philippe* (Montréal: Université de Montréal, 1964; Paris: P. Lethielleux, 1964). (The 1967 work adds a Coptic text facing the translation, a commentary, and detailed indices.) While Ménard rejected the validity of Schenke's division of the *Gospel according to Philip* into "sayings," he kept Schenke's numbering system for purely practical purposes.

[10] Ménard, *L'Évangile selon Philippe* (1967) 3.

[11] The often quoted oxymoron 'chaotic arrangement' was introduced into the discussion by Robert M. Grant in his presidential address to the SBL in 1959 when he characterized the work as "materials arranged chaotically, if one can speak of chaotic arrangement." See R. M. Grant, "Two Gnostic Gospels," *JBL* 79 (1960) 2. Hans-Martin Schenke even earlier had characterized the document as a florilegium: H.-M. Schenke, "Das Evangelium nach Philippus," *Koptisch-gnostische Schriften aus den Papyrus-Codices von Nag Hammadi*, ed. J. Leipoldt and H.-M. Schenke (Hamburg: Herbert Reich, 1960) 33. Eric Segelberg referred to it as "a collection of 'sayings' without any definite plan of composition." See E. Segelberg, "The Coptic-Gnostic Gospel According to Philip and its Sacramental System," *Numen* 7 (1960) 191.

[12] Ménard, *L'Évangile selon Philippe* (1967) 3-6.

tant point that the sequence of the material—whatever else may be
true of it—is neither completely random nor the result of a mindlessly
mechanical juxtaposition based on catchword association alone.
Writing about an author and his theology, but also in terms of sources
and collecting, Ménard did not combine his observations and insights
into an overall theory of the document.

More recently Bentley Layton put forward a view of the *Gospel
according to Philip* based largely on the appearance of independent
units with relatively weak connections between them. Layton's
analysis was cautious, but explicit. He described the document as "a
Valentinian anthology containing some one hundred short excerpts
taken from various other works," which included "sermons, treatises,
or philosophical epistles ... as well as collected aphorisms or short
dialogues with comments."[13] Although he observed that not all parts
of the text can be securely identified as deriving from the Valentinian
movement, he suggested that some material might perhaps have been
written by Valentinus himself. Based on this assessment, Layton
warned against working from multiple passages to produce a holistic
understanding of the document's position on any given matter:

> Because probably more than one Valentinian theological perspective is rep-
> resented in *GPh*, it would be misleading to reconstruct a single theological
> system from the whole anthology. Rather, individual groups of excerpts can
> profitably be studied in isolation, with comparison of other works or frag-
> ments of Valentinianism or of classic gnosticism.[14]

Layton included in his introduction an index of key words and themes
in the *Gospel according to Philip*. "With due caution," he wrote,
"they can be used to identify excerpts that belong together." It
remains unclear, however, what procedures would constitute "due
caution" or what kind of "belonging together" Layton had in mind.
There are few (or even, perhaps, no) terms in the document which
were the exclusive property of the Valentinian movement, much less
of any given school or stage within it.[15]

---

[13] B. Layton, *The Gnostic Scriptures: A New Translation with Annotations and
Introductions* (Garden City, NY: Doubleday, 1987) 325.

[14] Layton, *Gnostic Scriptures*, 326.

[15] E.g.: "truth," "light," "paradise," "Adam," "animal," "slave," "Mary," "virgin,"
"garment, nakedness," "soul," "leave the world," "inherit," "mystery," "baptism, water"-
-to cite only the first two items from each section of his index. See Layton, *Gnostic
Scriptures*, 326-7. For the possibility that some of the document's "bridal chamber"
references may come from a non-Valentinian source, see below.

In the same year, Hans-Martin Schenke published a revised translation of the *Gospel according to Philip* along with a new introductory essay.[16] He continued to insist that the *Gospel according to Philip* is a *florilegium* or collection of excerpts, some without connecting links, some linked only by association of ideas or by catchwords, and considered that this theory was on the brink of becoming the scholarly consensus. His understanding of the component units of the work, however, had long since shifted from 'sayings' to 'paragraphs'—which implies less, perhaps nothing, about their current state of connection or isolation—and he continued to readjust his estimation of their parameters, mostly by subdivision.[17]

Schenke, like Layton, pointed out that the materials compiled as the *Gospel according to Philip* represent more than one school of Valentinianism (and perhaps sources beyond Valentinianism), and that therefore one cannot meaningfully talk of the theology of this text.[18] He included a listing of references to a number of key themes, and referred the reader to Layton's index of 45 concepts and themes.[19] The production of thematic indices, however, does not address the main problem inherent in a collection of excerpts: whether and when they can be used to interpret one another.

At the other end of the conceptual spectrum from collections lie hypotheses in which these same, seemingly independent units of text are seen as pointing to an extremely terse, gnomic style, employed by an individual author, or by a redactor who massively recast collected materials, but left implicit the connections by which they could be assembled into a world view.

Hans-Georg Gaffron based his understanding of the unity of the *Gospel according to Philip* primarily on its use of catchword and idea associations, especially complex and sophisticated catchword patterns involving multiple pairs of opposites.[20] The absence of explicit connections and the athematic order were seen by Gaffron as evidence that diverse sources lie behind the text, but the dense interweaving of materials found in passages such as 51.29-52.18

---

[16] H.-M. Schenke, "Das Evangelium nach Philippus," *Neutestamentliche Apokryphen, vol. I. Evangelien*, ed. W. Schneemelcher (Tübingen: J. C. B. Mohr [P. Siebeck] 1987) 148-154 introduction, 155-173 translation.

[17] Schenke, "Das Evangelium," 152.

[18] Schenke, "Das Evangelium," 154.

[19] Schenke, "Das Evangelium," 153-154.

[20] H.-G. Gaffron, "Studien zum koptischen Philippusevangelium unter besonderer Berücksichtigung der Sakramente" (Th.D. dissertation: Friedrich-Wilhelms-Universität, Bonn, 1969).

show a highly individual and distinctive manner of thinking and expression. He rejected the label "florilegium," and saw the text as the work of a strong and skillful redactor who everywhere rewrote his material in a highly individual, even idiosyncratic, manner.[21] Under the hypothesis of such a thorough rewriting of source materials, one could assume that the text in its present form presents a single viewpoint in any matter of importance to its redactor—and Gaffron went on to treat it accordingly.

Gaffron's evidence for such a thorough rewriting consisted principally of the large number of catchword and idea associations that bind together portions of the *Gospel according to Philip* In their dominance, and particularly in the distinctive nature of some of the antithetical pairs, he saw the distinctive expression of an individual author. Gaffron thought that many such pairs go beyond gnostic commonplaces (such as light–dark, good–bad, right–left, dead–living, above–below, here–there, male–female): hidden–revealed, beget–create, night–day, Hebrew–Christian, slave–son/free, winter–summer, sow–reap, dissolve–indissoluble, established–not established, child of Adam–child of the perfect human, nature–spirit, Echamoth–Echmoth, blind–sighted, loan–gift, fallen woman–virgin, agriculture of God–agriculture of the world, marriage of pollution–unpolluted marriage, glorious strength–contemptible weakness.[22]

Gaffron was particularly impressed by the opening passage (51.29 to 52.18), which is extremely tightly interwoven with such pairs of opposite catchwords—too tightly interwoven, he judged, to be a compilation of material excerpted from a variety of gnostic sources. Instead, he saw this passage as forming a single thought complex which could only have been shaped by a single author. But if this is true, he argued, the same individual must have left a strong impress upon the entire work, since such pairs of opposites recur throughout the document.[23]

Most of these pairs of oppositions are not idiosyncratic enough to warrant such a conclusion, however. Many of them are not distinctive at all, but are the commonplaces of gnostic, or Christian, or even pagan expression.

The *Gospel according to Philip* does, however, open with an extremely complex and elegant example of the interweaving of multiple "catchwords," many of which appear as antithetical pairs in the

---

[21] Gaffron, "Studien," 14-15

[22] Gaffron, "Studien," 14-15 and 231 (notes).

[23] Gaffron, "Studien," 14-15.

subject and predicate positions of the first several statements. The pattern is kept up for over a page, though with slightly less density, and is then abruptly dropped at the last line of page 52. Although the paired oppositions involved are mostly commonplaces, the way in which they are intertwined (whether originally or secondarily) is quite remarkable—but also uncharacteristic of the document. The only other passage offering something similar to the opening section's density of antitheses is also found early on, in a remarkably sophisticated passage about language and its complex relations to truth. That section, from 53.14 to 54.18, relates an entire group of oppositions— citing four of those considered generically gnostic by Gaffron—to the "worldly" pole of the world–eternal realm polarity, and then lines that opposition up with the oppositions: not established–established, deceptive–creative, and multiple–unitary. Anyone who could write, or assemble, this passage could certainly have written, or assembled, the opening sequence as well. Nevertheless, the section on language possesses an explicit logical continuity which is not present between the components of the opening catena. Paired opposites are frequent in the material contained in the rest of the *Gospel according to Philip*, but these two sections are exceptional in the density with which they are deployed. More typically, a passage reflects on a single pair, or relates one opposition to another, in a way that is not especially remarkable for gnostic works—certainly nothing like the use made of antitheses in *Thunder*!

David Tripp, in a paper for the 1979 Oxford Patristics Conference, also denied that the *Gospel according to Philip* could be "merely a collection of extracts;" rather, it displays "a continuity of argument which a *florilegium* could not provide."[24] He saw it as an original work, the "jottings of the author in person"; "when there are quotations, they are usually marked as such."[25] This estimate of the work was based primarily on his discernment of a single dominant theme, to which other themes were related. With respect to the impression of brief units mostly without clear, logical connections, Tripp saw the *Gospel according to Philip* as a loosely organized but original composition, comprehensible in its form as sermon-notes. Tripp wrote:

---

[24] David H. Tripp, "The 'Sacramental System' of the Gospel of Philip," *Studia Patristica* 17, part 1, ed. E. A. Livingstone (Oxford: Pergamon Press, 1982) 251-267. See especially 251.

[25] These clarifications were expressed to me by Tripp in a conversation on October 2, 1993.

> The method of arrangement chosen is that which in our day would be called
> the 'retreat–address' style: concentrated exposition of major points, inter-
> spersed with substantial pauses for reflection, and moving across the terrain
> to be traversed in a zig-zag fashion, rather than with the order demanded by
> formal logic.[26]

Tripp attempted to describe the *Gospel according to Philip* in action,
with some relation to a social function.[27] The work is indeed liberally
sprinkled with "concentrated exposition of major points," but these
are embedded in a matrix of briefer materials, not "pauses for
reflection."[28] On occasion, a terse or enigmatic statement is followed
by something which may be an explanation or illustration—but the
latter is often also densely stated, and ambiguous in its relevance to
the original statement. Unambiguous alternation between these two
modes is rarely seen.

Tripp's remark that the *Gospel according to Philip* displays "a
continuity of argument which a *florilegium* could not provide" raises
an important question: "What kinds of continuity do florilegia
typically provide?" Gaffron's belief that the dense interweaving of
pairs of antithetical terms could only be attributable to the distinctive
style of an individual writer seems to be based on assumptions about
the degree of sophistication possible in unrelated units strung together
through the use of repeated-word rhetorical devices.

Passages analogous to 51.29-52.35 occur in various sorts of collections, although they are not common. The *Sentences of Sextus*
begins with a chain of propositions linked by common terms, which
takes the form of a sorites or chain syllogism: "A faithful person is an
elect person. An elect person is a person of God. A person of God is
worthy of God. One worthy of God does nothing unworthy of God.
Therefore, if you wish to be faithful, do nothing unworthy of God."[29]
The next several statements develop the same general ideas. Nevertheless, this document is a Christianized revision of a preexisting
collection of materials; Henry Chadwick considered that this opening

---

[26] Tripp, "Sacramental System," 252.

[27] Tripp wrote that his model was the published lectures of W. Herrmann, *Systematic
Theology (Dogmatik)*, Eng. trans., N. Micklem and K. A. Saunders (London: G. Allen &
Unwin, Ltd.; New York: Macmillan, 1927). He quoted: "It was his habit when lecturing
to dictate a paragraph to his audience and then to expatiate upon it ex tempore."

[28] It may also be that Tripp's impression has been influenced by the lacunose state of
the text, especially the periodically recurring lacunae at the bottom of the pages.

[29] *Sentences of Sextus*, 1-5.

sequence contains both originally Pythagorean statements and originally Christian ones.[30] That is, the "chain syllogism," which serves as an introduction to the work, was woven together from unrelated statements from divergent sources. A similar chain appears in the demotic Egyptian *Instruction of Ankhsheshonqy:* "Do not insult a common man. When insult occurs beating occurs. When beating occurs killing occurs. Killing does not occur without the god knowing. Nothing occurs except what the god ordains."[31]

A closer analogy, albeit one which is not used to introduce a collection, is also found in *Ankhsheshonqy*. Like the opening passage of the *Gospel according to Philip*, this passage makes use of antithetical pairs of terms which knit each statement to the next:

> The friend of a fool is a fool, the friend of a wise man is a wise man. The friend of a stupid man is a stupid man. The mother [mw.t] gives birth, the way [my.t] makes a friend. Every man acquires property; it is a wise man who knows how to protect it. Do not hand over your property to your younger brother, so as to let him become your elder brother thereby. Do not prefer one of your children to another; you do not know which of them will be kind to you. If you find your wife with her lover, get yourself a worthy bride. Do not acquire two voices. Speak truth to all men; let it cleave to your speech. Do not open your heart to your wife; what you have spoken to her goes to the street. Do not open your heart to your wife or to your servant. Open your heart to your mother; the woman is discreet. A woman—her affairs is what she knows. Instructing a woman is (having) a sack of sand whose side is split open.[32]

This instruction, too, is a composite document of monostichs which were assembled and arranged, not an original work. Other portions include both sequences of wholly unrelated materials and materials arranged by topic, first word, or situation. The passage above differs from the opening of the *Gospel according to Philip* in the brevity of its elements and in their mundane concerns, but it shows the same type of web woven from multiple catchwords, many of which are antithetical pairs. It also shows some statements linked by analogy, and a pun (*mw.t* and *my.t*).

---

[30] See H. Chadwick, *The Sentences of Sextus. A Contribution to the History of Early Christian Ethics* (Cambridge: Cambridge University Press, 1959) 138-140.

[31] Instruction of Ankhsheshonqy 22.21-25, *Ancient Egyptian Literature: A Book of Readings, vol. 3, The Late Period*, ed. M. Lichtheim (Berkeley: University of California Press, 1980) 176-177.

[32] See Miriam Lichtheim's analysis of this passage in M. Lichtheim, *Late Egyptian Wisdom Literature in the International Context: A Study of Demotic Instructions* (OBO 52; Freiburg: Universitätsverlag; Göttingen: Vandenhoeck & Ruprecht, 1983) 64.

Another type of hypothesis can be based on the appearance of potentially independent units bound by an asyntactic web of recurrent imagery. A once coherent document (of whatever kind) might acquire the appearance of extreme disorganization and disunity by violent rearrangement. Mechanical means (such as the chance disorganization of loose pages) could effect such a rearrangement, but to my knowledge no one has pursued this possibility in relation to the *Gospel according to Philip*. A deliberate rearrangement which separated coherent units is also a possibility—perhaps with the intent to obscure the point, prevent understanding, or create an aura of mystery.

Wesley William Isenberg attempted to explain the extreme abruptness of some of the materials in the *Gospel according to Philip* by elaboration of this possibility.[33] He considered the work to be a compilation of excerpts primarily from an Christian gnostic sacramental catechesis, perhaps with the addition of some material taken from a gnostic gospel.[34] Like many others, Isenberg noted that the *Gospel according to Philip* is not logically arranged—but proposed that the apparent disorder of the text derives from someone's deliberate choice to obscure an order which was once clear (or at least, clearer).

> That the author intended to arrange some material systematically is attested by the several catenae of passages, which use either an association of ideas or catchwords as links. At the same time there is evidence to suggest that the author purposely dissected paragraphs of thought and rather haphazardly placed the pieces in various parts of the work. One of the results of the use of this curious technique has been the impression that there is a planned recurrence of thought in the gospel. But no logically consistent plan has yet been discovered, and it is difficult to escape the thought that *Philip*'s structure is to some extent, at least, simply the result of coincidence and accident.[35]

At one point, Isenberg suggested a possible motive for this "curious technique":

---

[33] W. W. Isenberg, "The Coptic Gospel According to Philip" (Ph.D. Dissertation, University of Chicago, 1968), 24-53. Isenberg's remarks on the form, structure and content of the *Gospel according to Philip* are paralleled, in somewhat condensed form, in his introduction to the work in *Nag Hammadi Codex II,2-7*, ed. B. Layton (Leiden: E. J. Brill, 1989) 131-9.

[34] Isenberg, *Nag Hammadi Codex II,2-7*, 134. Compare "Coptic Gospel," 47-51, when he considered the material derived from a gnostic gospel to include 57.28-58.10; 63.30-37; 59.23-27; 63.37-64.5; 55.37-56.3; 64.10-12; 74.24-75.2; 75.2-14; 71.3-15; 64.10-12; 60.10-15; 73.9-14.

[35] Isenberg, "Coptic Gospel," 34-35.

Presumably to heighten the effect of the mysterious, the compiler-editor chose to arrange this material strangely: sometimes logically, by means of association of ideas and catchwords, and sometimes illogically, by sprinkling ideas here and there in incoherent patches. The result is something of a literary curiosity—a "gospel" which has almost none of the obvious "gospel" characteristics.[36]

Isenberg presented three types of passages as evidence that such dissection had occurred: 1) passages which, for grammatical reasons, must have been linked to contexts other than those in which they are now found, 2) passages similar to each other in expression and concept and therefore once joined, and 3) passages with "strikingly similar" thematic content.

Isenberg's sole example of the "grammatical" type of evidence involves the passages 70.5-9, 76.22-77.1, 66.7-29.[37] The second and third of these begin with indefinite subjects ("they" and "he") which are difficult to relate to the actors in the immediately preceding passages, and all of them, particularly the first and third, show little continuity with the material which now surrounds them. In Isenberg's analysis, the subject of the first sentence of 76.22-77.1—"they"— cannot refer to anything in the preceding material but makes sense if seen as a continuation of 70.5-9, as a continuation of the discussion there of the powers' inability to see or seize one who has put on the perfect light: "Not only will they not be able to seize the perfect man, but they will not be able to see him."[38] Unfortunately, this "they" could also be understood as a pseudo-passive, e.g.: "The perfect

---

[36] Isenberg, "Coptic Gospel," 53.

[37] Isenberg, "Coptic Gospel," 31. See also *Nag Hammadi Codex II,2-7*, 133. The reconstructed passage, in Isenberg's translation, reads: "As for those who have clothed themselves with the perfect light, the powers do not see them and are not able to seize them. But one will clothe himself with this light in the mystery, in the union" (70.5-9). "Not only will they not be able to seize the perfect man, but they will not be able to see him, for if they see him they will seize him. In no other way will one be able to acquire this grace for himself [unless] he clothe himself with the perfect light [and] he [himself] become perfect. Every [one who will put it] on will go [without being seen]. This is the perfect [light. Thus it is necessary] that we become [perfect men] before we come forth [from the world]. He who has received the all [without being master] over these places, will be [unable to be master over] that place, but he will [go to 'the Middle' (?)] as imperfect. Only Jesus knows the end of this one" (76.22-77.1). "Either he will be in this world or in the resurrection or in the places which are in the middle. May it not be that I should be found therein" (66.7-29).

[38] ΟΥ ΜΟΝΟΝ ΠΡⲰΜⲈ ⲚⲦⲈⲖⲈⲒⲞⲤ ⲤⲈⲚⲀϢⲈⲘⲀⳘⲦⲈ ⲀⲚ ⲘⲘⲞϥ ⲀⲖⲖⲀ ⲤⲈⲚⲀϢⲚⲀⲨ ⲈⲢⲞϥ ⲀⲚ.... The translation given above is from Isenberg's 1968 translation ("Coptic Gospel," 31 and 386), but his 1989 translation does not differ significantly: "Not only will they be unable to detain the perfect man, but they will not be able to see him." (*Nag Hammadi Codex II,2-7*, 195)

human being not only cannot be restrained, but also cannot be seen."[39]
Passive constructions are routinely constructed this way in Coptic,
which lacks a true passive voice. If "the perfect human being" is
understood as the real subject, there is no jarring transition from the
sentence immediately preceding it in the manuscript, which contrasts
those who do not know themselves with those who do.[40] In 66.7-29,
the third unit in Isenberg's proposed sequence, the subject (again,
"he") could as easily be seen as a resumption of the discussion about
"the one who comes out of the world" begun at 65.28, interrupted by
a small digression about an erroneous opinion (65.36-66.4) and an
exhortation (66.4-6). While grammatical evidence sounds promising,
Isenberg's lone example of it is not very convincing.

Isenberg's second group of passages, those purporting to show
similarity of sentence structure and thought content, involved a theme
or analogy presented in the first segment which he understood to be
logically necessary to the second segment.[41] The material in Isenberg's examples, and the type of situation envisioned by his theory in
the abstract, could also be seen as simply depending on familiar
teachings. The same is true of the proposed sequences based on a
strong similarity of theme or teaching.[42]

Isenberg conjectured that the dissection which resulted in the present shape of the *Gospel according to Philip* would have come more

---

[39] Trans. Layton, *Gnostic Scriptures*, 348.

[40] Moreover, the amount of repetition of the first text in the second makes the idea that
the passages were once continuous a little suspect.

[41] He gave three examples in 1968: 75.13-14 plus 61.36-62.5, 63.5-11 plus 70.22-29,
and 59.6-11 plus 63.32-64.9. The first two of these, together with the sole example of the
first category, were the only three examples given in Isenberg's 1989 introduction to the
*Gospel according to Philip* in *Nag Hammadi Codex II,2-7*. A) In 75.13-14 and 61.36-
62.5, both passages use "receive" and "give," in the same order. B) In 63.5-11 plus
70.22-29, the first passage describes how glass jars, but not earthenware ones, can be
remade if broken, because they "came into being through a breath." The second passage
begins, "The soul of Adam came into being by means of a breath." These clearly depend
on the same or similar traditions, but this need not imply anything more than that. C)
Taking 63.32-64.9 as following 59.6-11 both allowed Isenberg to group together material
referring to Mary Magdalene but also gave him a warrant for separating 63.30-32 on the
barren Sophia from the discussion of Mary Magdalene. These two passages on 63 may
well represent distinct traditions, but Isenberg's dissection and rearrangement theory is
not the only way in which they could have come to be juxtaposed. See Isenberg, "Coptic
Gospel," 31-33 and *Nag Hammadi Codex II,2-7*, 133.

[42] His examples of this third category, based on "strikingly similar thematic content,"
were: 52.2-6 plus 60.1-6; 60.34-61.12 plus 78.12-25; 68.22-26 plus 70.9-22; 56.15-20
plus 73.1-8; 54.31-55.5 plus 62.35-33.4; 55.14-19 plus 59.18-27; and possibly 51.29-
52.2 plus 52.21-24 plus 62.5-6. See "Coptic Gospel," 34.

naturally to an editor working on compiled materials than to the original author of the passages involved.

> ... it is ... irregular and unnatural for an author intentionally and frequently to dissect the very thought he has put together into a continuity and to distribute the pieces here and there in his work, especially when it is apparent that an isolated segment of thought may sometimes make little or no sense in the context in which it finds itself. It would be more likely that a compiler who was also editing his material to serve his own purposes would find use for this technique. The diversity of content in *Philip*, drawn as it appears from more than one source, also commends the conclusion that a compiler-editor is responsible for this text.[43]

Thus, Isenberg attributed some of the abrupt transitions and apparent non-sequiturs in the *Gospel according to Philip* to an excerpting and collecting process, while others had their genesis in the dissection and violent dispersal of the text.

As curious as this appeared to Isenberg, such procedures turn out to be neither unusual nor necessarily esoteric in their motivation. Other collections of diverse materials from late antiquity did sometimes break up and redistribute blocks of source material, though mostly in accordance with comprehensible motives and aesthetics.[44]

The *Sentences of Sextus*, a Christianized version of a lost Pythagorean collection, and Porphyry's *Letter to Marcella*, along with some smaller collections, present a kind of synoptic problem illustrating just this procedure. Occasionally, Porphyry and the other collections give an unusually complex sentence with several clauses, which are present in the *Sentences of Sextus*—but at widely separated places. Chadwick remarks that "the first impression made by this evidence might be that Sextus has consistently and deliberately split up sentences which were originally united."[45] In a few cases, material which might offend a Christian reader has been left out. In most cases, it seems that the divisions were prompted only by an attachment to brevity and mystery.[46] We seem to have had an editor who

---

[43] Isenberg, "Coptic Gospel," 35.

[44] For a survey of this (and other) organizing principles in some collections from late antiquity, see M. Turner, *Gospel according to Philip*, chapters 3 and especially 4.

[45] Chadwick, *Sentences*, 147-153.

[46] Chadwick left open the possibility that the Sentences of Sextus may depend on a slightly different version of the lost Pythagorean collection than do Porphyry and the later small collections. The possibility leads to similar problems, however: at some stage, someone either sundered what once was joined, or brought together what once was far apart.

was not only proficient in stringing together extremely terse statements into fairly large and coherent mosaics, but who actively favored the gnomic over the discursive. In any case, these divisions were done in such a way that the isolated parts all make sense on their own. Did the manuscripts not present a synoptic problem, we would never have guessed that the dispersed members were once part of a more discursive whole.

The oldest constituent epigram collections which went to make up the *Greek Anthology* show a much more comprehensible tendency to divide up source material. Insofar as uninterrupted sequences of the material assembled by Meleager and by Philip of Cos can be identified, these editors regularly split up contributions by their more prolific authors, and interspersed them with those of others. They were motivated, it seems, by an aesthetic that favored the presentation of excerpts in similar sized blocks, and the alternation of authorial voices. They also regularly grouped epigrams by theme and motif—even when the result juxtaposed sharply contrasting material in a way that might seem incongruous or frivolous.[47]

Yet another analysis of the *Gospel according to Philip*, also based on the connections made within the text, viewed the admittedly slippery individual units which have been our main concern so far as themselves composite.

In 1970, Rodolphe Kasser presented, as part of an introduction to his translation of the *Gospel according to Philip*, a sketch of what a source analysis of the document might look like.[48] He did not make his criteria specific enough to show why he selected precisely the passages he did for each source, and no others.

Kasser identified four original sources: "source A," "source B," a "Philip' source," and an "etymological" source."[49]

Kasser characterized the passages of his source A as possessing a very sober character, and as referring to Christ simply as "Christ;" he stated that they may have formed a small collection for "usage sacramental."[50] The name "Christ," however, appears in only three of the ten passages he included in "source A," and is also found in numerous passages not included in "source A." Kasser did not

---

[47] For analysis of the constituent subcollections of the Greek Anthology, see A. Cameron, *The Greek Anthology from Meleager to Planudes* (Oxford: Clarendon, 1993).

[48] R. Kasser, "Bibliothèque Gnostique VIII: L'Évangile selon Philippe," *RTP*, ser. 3, 20 (1970), 12-20 (introduction), 21-35, 82-106 (translation).

[49] Kasser, "L'Évangile," 16-17.

[50] Kasser, "L'Évangile," 16.

elaborate on what he meant by sacramental usage, nor on what its identifying marks might be, but numerous passages in the text have been identified, by one investigator or another, as being or depending on some sort of sacramentally oriented catechism. While some of the passages he included in this source deal, more or less directly, with sacramental matters, not all of them can be so read, and many others dealing with such affairs are not included—especially the material found from page 67 to about 75, none of which was included by Kasser in "source A."

Kasser's "source B" consisted of "sentences isolées, et d'un caractère assez énigmatique."[51] He listed its contents, but had nothing further to say about it as a whole.

The third source, the "Philip" source of fragments supposedly from an apocryphal gospel, was rather more coherent. He limited this source to passages including both a saying and a narrative frame (he took the latter always to be redactional), and to those which refer to Jesus simply as "the Lord."[52] These—along with several other passages much like them—might quite plausibly stem from an apocryphal gospel (or gospels).

Kasser's fourth source consisted of explanations of sacred names, principally by means of etymology. The passages he included (along with a few others) do demonstrate an approach which might be called etymological exegesis. This type of unit, however, can occur in a variety of generic settings: gospels, homilies, letters, treatises, catechetical material, and (probably) other contexts. The passages in question need not come from the same source nor even the same kind of source.

To these, Kasser added a list of further elements he conjectured were also represented: a first apologetic element, a second apologetic element, an archontic element, a "powers" element, and some catechetical elements. He gave no information about how he identified these elements, much less how their chronological order might begin to be determined.

Kasser imagined that the document's redactional history was extremely complex. Beyond the somewhat hazy source analysis outlined above, he described the redactional layers of a few units. His method there was to look for a central, very concise kernel, which he identified as the original or most primitive level. Explanations, clarifications, limitations, contextualizations, and applications were then

---

[51] Kasser, "L'Évangile, 16.

[52] The latter restriction does protect his "source A." Kasser, "L'Évangile," 17.

assigned to layers of redaction. This is, of course, familiar from gospel criticism—but there, the original sought is a saying passed down orally, gradually acquiring accretions in the process of its oral transmission, in its first shaping into a written work, and (sometimes) in the process of a later reworking.[53] The relevance and the rationale of the approach becomes cloudy when one begins to dealing with either original authors or excerptors of others' works, original or not.

Kasser's article was offered as an exploration: "Une étude plus approfondie permettra peut-être de pénétrer dans la préhistoire du texte actuel de l'Evangile selon Philippe; nous ne pouvons que l'esquisser ici."[54] Its value lies more in its provocative potential than in its concrete working out. If, indeed, the *Gospel according to Philip* is a composite of materials from diverse sources, then the identification of those sources would be extremely valuable for interpretation.

### Recurring and Metamorphosing Themes

The connections between individual units and the material before and after them has not been the only sort of coherence sought, and sometimes found, in the *Gospel according to Philip*. An overarching theme, or themes, or a thematic progression have been found by some investigators, and have been cited both as evidence of the work of an original author and as evidence of a redactor who rearranged collected materials. Such hypotheses are based on apparent connections which are not sequential.

As before, some early investigators made observations along these lines without developing a clear hypothesis. Two of Wilson's observations belong under this heading: certain characteristic themes recur repeatedly throughout the work, and the references to the important term "bridal chamber" do not begin until almost halfway through the document.[55] Wilson suggested that these observations together "suggest a sort of spiral movement, gradually approaching the central and deepest mystery."[56] Ménard, following a similar vein, went on to suggest that these form "une pareille continuité dans le texte, une semblable pensée en forme de spirale,"[57] but he did not map such links onto any specific spiral structure.

---

[53] It would seem that Kasser's "Philip" source is an exception to this rule, for he recognized its elements by their conjunction of a saying attributed to Jesus plus a narrative frame.

[54] Kasser, "L'Évangile," 16.

[55] Wilson, *Gospel of Philip*, 9-10.

[56] Wilson, *Gospel of Philip*, 10.

[57] Ménard, *L'Évangile selon Philippe* (1967) 6.

One type of hypothesis offered in explanation of such recurring themes involves the careful arrangement of materials. A collector might have assembled material from diverse sources and, while making relatively few changes in its wording, arranged it very carefully into a pattern to communicate his or her own message. It is possible that such materials might retain many of their own stylistic features, including oblique and perhaps misunderstood references and allusions irrelevant to their new context. The result would look superficially like a collection of disparate materials, but an overall plan would also be apparent to careful scrutiny, presenting a single, coherent viewpoint—at least, on all matters of much importance to the collector-arranger.[58] Such a conjecture is loosely related to Gaffron's rewriting redactor, but postulates only a redactor strong at rearrangement, and is based on recurring, non-sequential themes rather than sequential links of repeating words.

Gerald Leo Borchert framed an argument along these lines.[59] Unlike Gaffron, he saw no clear stylistic cohesion in the *Gospel according to Philip*, but saw, instead, a clear thematic progression in its materials. Borchert considered the work to have been "constructed from fragments and assembled without adequate connectives," "a mixed collection" including "narrative materials, apothegmata, beatitudes, exhortations, indirect dialogue, parables, at least one vision, pithy sayings which are on the order of maxims or epigrams, analytical treatments of names and various parallel constructions."[60] He noted that these fragments were assembled from both canonical and extra-canonical sources, such as "homiletical, catechetical, apologetical and perhaps hymnical materials."[61] He observed, however, that calling the text "florilegium," while not incorrect, has discouraged scholars from investigating its arrangement.[62]

Borchert set out to challenge the idea that a collection must have a random or "chaotic" organization, and to consider the possibility that the *Gospel according to Philip* might be "a *grouping* of materials (some collected and some perhaps written by the editor), which are organized (and even altered) to suit his purposes but left without

---

[58] Conflicting viewpoints on unimportant matters might perhaps survive.

[59] G. L. Borchert, "An Analysis of the Literary Arrangement and Theological Views in the Gnostic Gospel of Philip" (Th.D. dissertation, Princeton Theological Seminary, 1967).

[60] Borchert, "Analysis," 4 , 35, and 43.

[61] Borchert, "Analysis," 43.

[62] Borchert, "Analysis," 4-5.

connectives."[63] He concluded that the text "gives the external appearance of being a disjointed collection of literary fragments but . . . contains a discernible organizing scheme."[64] While expressing doubt that the motivations of the collector could be certainly discerned, he considered that "it is possible that the editor may have intended to develop a treatise which would give an external appearance of confusion, yet offer to the one who searched behind the external appearance a hidden organization."[65] For the rest of his study, Borchert developed this possibility:

> as a clever maze-maker, the editor assembles sayings, parables, recorded incidents and semantic arguments to produce a work which twists and turns the mind of the reader as it confronts him with the fundamental differences in the "ways of being" and leads him by steady manipulation of words to consider the meaning of Gnostic salvation.[66]

He tended to attribute most gnosticizing interpretations to the document's redactor rather than to already gnostic sources,[67] although he did not argue against the existence of such, and briefly postulated a gnostic commentary on the opening chapters of Genesis as one of the sources of material.[68]

Borchert believed he had found not only the overarching theme of the *Gospel according to Philip*, but also the plan on which it is organized. The theme is salvation—Borchert proposed *"De salvatione"* as an alternate title. He unfolded the plan he saw by dividing the work into seven very unequal segments, each with a subtheme. There is, of course, no redundancy in the text of the *Gospel according to Philip* that can support or refute such a division's appropriateness: any argument of this kind can only rest on the fidelity of the proposed themes to the materials in each section, and on the cogency of the proposed progression of themes.

The bulk of Borchert's work deals with his thematic division of the *Gospel according to Philip* into 7 main sections (each also further subdivided):

---

[63] Borchert, "Analysis," 36 (emphasis his).

[64] Borchert, "Analysis," 36-37.

[65] Borchert, "Analysis," 36.

[66] Borchert, "Analysis," 46.

[67] Borchert, "Analysis," 23-26, 37-38. He sometimes seemed to reflect an assumption that 'orthodox' materials are prior to 'heretical' ones, which must have been generated from the 'orthodox.' His use of the term 'Philip' to refer both to the collector-redactor and to the work as we have it may also have led him to sometimes equate the two.

[68] Borchert, "Analysis," 26-28.

I.   Introduction: The "Basic "Ways of Being" in the World (51.29-52.35)
II.  The Conflict: the Godhead and the Archon-Dominated World
III. The Message: The Illumination of Three Great Mysteries (56.15-59.6)
IV.  The Resolution of the Conflict: The Attaining of Salvation (59.11-62.17)
V.   The Significance of Salvation: The Great Contrast (62.17-66.29)
VI.  The Sacramental Role in Salvation (66.29-77.15)
VII. The Life of Salvation: The Way of Knowledge (77.15-86.18)[69]

These sections vary from about one and one-third manuscript pages to about ten and one-half pages. Borchert's proposed structure is an attempt to get behind the apparent jumble of themes to a level of abstraction not given by the text itself, but understood to be inherent in it. He warned against an exclusive dependence on reason in attempting to understand a work based on experience and intuitive insight.[70]

A number of the main sections have themes so broad that many other passages, randomly chosen from the text, would fit as well as the material of the section. Examples of especially broad themes proposed for the main divisions are: "The Conflict: The Godhead in the Archon-Dominated World," "The Resolution of the Conflict: The Attaining of Salvation," and "The Significance of Salvation: The Great Contrast." Many of Borchert's categories seem superimposed on the text. They can certainly be read into it, but only somewhat arbitrarily. On the other hand, one of his divisions may amount to a more durable insight.

A work by an original author, as well as a skillful compilation, would also probably have an overall theme or group of themes. If this work were found to center on a single theme, or on a small group of distinctive themes, this would indicate a strong interest behind the text, whether of an original author or of a collector.

Søren Giversen presented an argument for considerable unity in the document, based primarily on the continued recurrence of certain key themes.[71] Jorunn Jacobsen Buckley has more recently called Giversen "the most convincing advocate of Gos. Phil.'s approach."[72]

---

[69] This outline can be extracted from Borchert's table of contents or from the section headings in his exegesis. For a briefer survey of his seven sections and their contents, see Borchert, "Analysis," 49-58.

[70] Borchert, "Analysis," 47-48.

[71] S. Giversen, *Filips Evangeliet. Indledning, studier oversaettelse og noter* (Copenhagen: G. E. C. Gads Forlag, 1966) 9-38.

[72] J. J. Buckley, "Conceptual Models and Polemical Issues in the Gospel of Philip," *ANRW II.25.5* (Berlin: de Gruyter & Co., 1988) 4167-4194.

Giversen considered that the *Gospel according to Philip* does contain some small, originally independent units of traditional material—e.g., the narratives and similes on pages 64 and 65. Small, independent units appear in other ancient and patristic writers as well, he observed.[73] Nevertheless, he stressed the sequential continuities involving as much as a page or more of text— simple catchwords, complex verbal linkages with repeating pairs of antithetical terms, material seemingly related only through similar imagery, material seemingly related only through analogous developments. His points are well taken, but mostly illustrate the different approaches to dividing the text into parts for study and easy reference. The thematic groupings Giversen favored give a small number of rather large divisions, in contrast to Kasser's numbering of four hundred of the smallest possible sense units, with Layton's and Schenke's numerations (109 and 127, later revised to 175) falling in between. Such numbering systems are mostly compromises between the division of sense units and the production of an unambiguous reference system. Giversen showed that a number of Schenke's paragraphs appear together in larger thematic groups, a possibility which Schenke does not seem to have ever denied.[74]

Giversen's saw the *Gospel according to Philip* as revolving around three interlocking themes: paradise and its events, modes of creation, and the bridal chamber with its rich web of associations.[75] These themes are not expounded or explored in any organized way, but the very fact that so much of the text concentrates on these themes itself constitutes a plan, in Giversen's opinion. Nevertheless, these are very broad topics: the first could be paraphrased as creation and related topics, and (given what we seem to be able to deduce about the meaning of bridal chamber in Valentinian circles) the third, salvation and, perhaps, the sacramental mediation and/or depiction of salvation. The second—modes of creation—involves a distinctive way of approaching and imaging the potentialities of human beings, and the failure to attain them. It is built on a broadly gnostic base, which may also be observed in the elaborate systems of aeons and their emanations. Giversen correctly notes that our failure to understand much of the imagery in the *Gospel according to Philip* puts us in a poor position to evaluate its coherence. The fact that certain themes come up again and again does not, by itself, guarantee that the statements

---

[73] Giversen, *Filips Evangeliet*, 28-29.

[74] Giversen, *Filips Evangeliet*, 23-26.

[75] Giversen, *Filips Evangeliet*, 35-37.

of them are from the same source, or are even compatible, but it does delineate the limit of the diversity of the text: these interests have at least partially guided whatever process was responsible for the whole. These themes do not account for the whole contents of the document, and might disclose a collector's dominant interests as cogently as a distinctive theologian's system.

The center of David Tripp's argument for an original author lay in an overall thematic continuity, too.[76] Most of his remarks related to the document's unity were based on its use of imagery and metaphors, and his perception that the final quarter of the document could be seen as the culmination of the first three quarters. Tripp's phrase "moving across the terrain to be traversed in a zig-zag fashion" describes approximately the characteristic described by several other scholars as a "spiral progression." Themes are abandoned or shift their meanings, but often earlier themes and perspectives are picked up again later, creating a tantalizing impression of an elusive order. In the hands of a skilled author, such an approach clearly could be deployed effectively—though the result might not look quite like the *Gospel according to Philip*.

Tripp saw this zig-zagging (or spiraling) of themes as centered around the presentation of one dominant concept: "Life, and the transmission of life." Images and metaphors of life are luxuriously abundant. References to sprouting, growing, bearing fruit, ripening, harvesting, taking root, eating and being eaten, begetting, conceiving, bearing offspring, and the like are rife throughout the document, and function there as metaphors for spiritual realities. The theme of life, however, and this mode of expression for it, are central to many strands of Valentinianism—as, to give a single example, in the hymn preserved as Valentinus' own composition.[77] Many of them, particularly those involved with plant life, are abundant in the canonical gospels as well.[78] Their dominance in the pages of the *Gospel according to Philip* could be the work of an author for whom such a mode of expression was congenial—but it could equally well have resulted from the labors of a collector working with source material already rich in these features, or a collector and/or epitomizer who concentrated such expressions from sources (or a single source)

---

[76] D. H. Tripp, "Sacramental System," 251-267.

[77] See *Quellen zur Geschichte der christlichen Gnosis*, ed. W. Völker (SAQ, n.s. 5; Tübingen: J. C. B. Mohr [P. Siebeck], 1932) 59 (= Fragment 8).

[78] "Food chain" and "life cycle" metaphors are less common there.

originally less rich in them, or an editorializing collector or redactor who contributed some or all of them.

Tripp claimed that the bulk of the *Gospel according to Philip* is ordered to the concluding sections 110-127 (77.15 to the end), and that these final portions expound on both the effect which the life of believers can have on others, and on the qualities of spiritual life which are necessary for that effect. Sections 110-115 (=77.15-79.30), he wrote, discuss the quality of spiritual life, chiefly in terms of generous and outreaching love; 116-127 (=79.31 to the end) then explore ways in which such spiritual life affects others and generates similar life in them. Tripp correctly observed that from 77.15 on the text is more tightly structured; similar observations have been made by many others. Tripp's characterization of the second subsection of that block, however, seems somewhat arbitrary: the generation of similar life in others occupies most of page 78, while much of the text from 79.31 on continues to dwell on ethics and spiritual purity, with a shift from a more "philosophical" mode of discussion to eschatological imagery in the final two pages (85 and 86).

A thematic arrangement of the material, whether by an author or a collector, could easily account for the impression of recurring themes. Certain subjects would appear again and again, viewed from different perspectives. The concern for the overall message that is implied by either an author or a redactor who has orchestrated a muddle of different extracts into a coherent work would, however, lead us to expect certain things: (1) Topics would come up again and again, not irregularly but under broad theological headings. Borchert has proposed that this is in fact the case, while Tripp has cited the zig-zag/retreat address style as the reason why it is not the case. (Giversen conceded that there was no clear thematic arrangement, but contended that a continued preoccupation with a few broad themes demonstrates a single perspective, even without a thematic arrangement; metaphors of "zig-zagging" or "spiraling" sidestep the issue.) (2) Any "metamorphosing" of these themes should be of the sort involved in moving between the different areas of a single coherent theology (rather than the shift between different and possibly conflicting theologies). (3) We would expect only slight traces of divergent sectarian affiliations to have survived a rearrangement such as Borchert had in mind, and none in an original work such as envisioned by Giversen and Tripp.

## SUMMARY AND PROSPECTS

As we have seen, many assessments of the nature of the *Gospel according to Philip* have been based on features which have been seen by reasonable and perceptive scholars in radically different—even diametrically opposed—ways. Even when there is some agreement as to observable phenomena, divergent and sometimes incompatible deductions have been made from the observations agreed upon. While many scholars feel secure in the rightness of their own assessment of the document, it would be instructive to try to understand the conditions which have made this scholarly muddle possible.

The condition which I take to be key to the situation is that many of the characteristics of the text (at least if taken individually) are compatible with multiple hypotheses about their origin. Sequential discontinuities and the potential of some passages for self-sufficient coherence can be, and have been, made to support the propositions that the document is an unorganized collection of diverse excerpts, that it is the work of a single somewhat unmethodical thinker, that it has undergone violent rearrangement, that it was deliberately structured as an insight-provoking meditation, and that it has undergone an complex redactional history. Sequential links, including those involving repeated terms or images, have generated theories that its contents were strung together mindlessly by the use of catchwords, that collected materials have been massively rewritten by someone with a recognizably idiosyncratic style, that someone has left these words as keys to an otherwise cryptic meaning, and that the document possesses the flow normally expected from original writing, despite our incomprehension of its referential world. Non-sequential continuities—the reappearance of themes and ideas at multiple points in the text—have been presented as evidences of the general interests of a collector, the style of theologizing of an original author, the tight thematic arrangement of collected materials, the violent disarrangement of the text, and of an intended homiletic use.

This assessment opens several possibilities: (1) A larger number of the agreed upon characteristics might be accounted for by theory, although most of the assessments referred to above do account for multiple features of the text. (2) A search might be made for other features, not yet observed or not yet considered in this way, which might shed light on the text's origin, use, history, or the like. (3) Historical information and assumptions which underlie hypotheses—for example, assumptions about the process of writing and/or collect-

ing in the ancient world—might be formulated in a way that would
allow their testing or refinement.

I have elsewhere attempted to make contributions in categories (2)
and (3) above, which cannot reasonably (or convincingly) be summarized in a paper of this length.[79] But those contributions, even if right,
can hardly be the last word. It is my hope that readers of this essay
will be challenged by it to reconsider their manner of approaching
these questions, and extend rigorous lines of thought into areas as yet
unimagined.

---

[79] Specifically, I have argued that some sectarian jargon is used in incompatible ways
in the *Gospel according to Philip*—my candidate as a less ambiguous piece of evidence—
—and that there are numerous differences in style and concerns, on the basis of which a
source analysis can be made—i.e., further new evidence, albeit of a corroborative rather
than decisive nature. I have also made inquiries into the historical background of
collections and the editorial practices commonly applied to them, along with some
questions about the motivations of gnostic speculators, which might be validly extended
to gnostic collectors. The original  version of this article contained some condensed
sampling of these results, since no other form of them was then easily available. See M.
Turner, *Gospel according to Philip*.

# HOW VALENTINIAN IS *THE GOSPEL OF PHILIP*?

*Einar Thomassen*
University of Bergen

In his pioneering 1959 study of *Gos. Phil.*,[1] Hans-Martin Schenke concluded "daß das Philippus-Evangelium valentinianischen Ur-sprungs ist."[2] At the same time, however, Schenke reflected on the difficulties that the composite character of *Gos. Phil.* presented to a hypothesis of provenance, and therefore modified his statement as follows:

> Das gilt mit der Einschränkung, die durch den Sammlungs-Charakter der Schrift gegeben ist. Man muss von vornherein damit rechnen, daß sie Gedankengut verschiedener gnostischer Richtungen enthält. So können wir nur sagen wollen, daß die Mehrzahl der Stücke valentinianisch ist und daher vermutlich die Sammler Valentinianer waren, ohne daß die Festlegung auf eine bestimmte Schule möglich wäre.[3]

Thus Schenke assumed that *Gos. Phil.* in all likelihood contained sections or passages of non-Valentinian origin which had been joined together with the Valentinian sections by the Valentinian compilers or redactors of *Gos. Phil.*. However, Schenke did not specifically identify any non-Valentinian passages in the tractate, nor did he offer any arguments in support of his contention that the Valentinian "collectors" would have been intrinsically predisposed to mix non-Valentinian material with the Valentinian. Schenke's reservations against accepting *Gos. Phil.* in its entirety as Valentinian have not been substantiated by subsequent research either. They nonetheless reappear in recent scholarship. Thus, for example, Wesley W. Isenberg, in his introduction to the latest edition of *Gos. Phil.*, in the

---

[1] H.-M. Schenke, "Das Evangelium nach Philippus. Ein Evangelium der Valentinianer aus dem Funde von Nag-Hamadi," *TLZ* 84 (1959) 1–26; reprinted, with revisions, in J. Leipoldt and H.-M. Schenke, *Koptisch-gnostische Schriften aus den Papyrus-Codices von Nag-Hamadi* (Theologische Forschung 20; Hamburg-Bergstedt: Herbert Reich, 1960) 31–65, 81–82. References to "Schenke I" in the following are to this latter publication.

[2] Schenke I, 34.

[3] Schenke I, 34..

series *The Coptic Gnostic Library*,[4] describes the tractate as being "generally Valentinian in theology."[5]

The lack of progress on this question is illustrated by the fact that when Schenke introduces *Gos. Phil.* a generation later for the most recent revised edition of Schneemelcher's *New Testament Apocrypha*,[6] he more or less repeats what he said in 1959:

> However, although thus of a Valentinian character, the Gos. Phil. (in keeping with its nature) cannot be traced back to, or identified with, a particular Valentinian school. Its Valentinian excerpts may have been brought together from works of different schools. Again, all the gnostic elements which are found in it need not be Valentinian. We must rather from the outset reckon with the possibility that material from other gnostic movements has also flowed into the Gos. Phil., since indeed it could very early be used by non-Valentinian gnostics too.[7]

But this time, the syncretistic character of *Gos. Phil.* as well is asserted as an *a priori* assumption on the basis of the composite form of the tractate, and not on the basis of observations on specific passages of the text.

As long as evidence to the contrary is not forthcoming, however, it seems preferable to work on the hypothesis that *Gos. Phil.* contains a coherent doctrine representing a single form of Valentinianism. A distinction should be made between the question regarding the coherence of *Gos. Phil.* as a text, on the one hand, and the internal consistency and homogeneity of the theological notions it contains, on the other. The textual incoherence of *Gos. Phil.* is an indisputable fact. It is less evident how this incoherence should be explained. At least three different situations may be conceived as having contributed to the present state of the text. A process of excerpting and compilation from older written sources is only one possible factor. A second possibility is that *Gos. Phil.* should be interpreted as a series of personal notes made by an individual writer, either for the purpose of oral expansion in a sermon or a teaching situation, or as materials for

---

[4]W. W. Isenberg, "Introduction, Tractate 3: The Gospel according to Philip," *Nag Hammadi Codex II,2–7 Together with XIII,2\*, Brit. Lib. Or. 4926(1), and P. Oxy. 1, 654, 655*, ed. B. Layton, vol. 1 (Nag Hammadi Studies 20; Leiden: E. J. Brill, 1989) 129–217.

[5]W. Isenberg, "Introduction," 131.

[6]*Neutestamentliche Apokryphen in deutscher Übersetzung*, ed. W. Schneemelcher, 5th ed., vol. I, Tübingen: J. C. B. Mohr [Siebeck], 1987, 148–173; Eng. tr. ed. R. McL. Wilson, *New Testament Apocrypha*, vol. I, Cambridge 1991, 179–208. This English version is cited below as "Schenke II."

[7]Schenke II, 186.

a written work.[8] Thirdly, there is the distinct likelihood that the text has been rearranged at a stage subsequent to its original composition by a redactor, or even by a scribe arbitrarily displacing passages in the text. Wesley Isenberg has rather convincingly pointed to several instances where such "disjoining" has taken place with no apparent motive.[9] Moreover, these three explanations are not mutually exclusive. Indeed, it may well be that the text which presents itself to us as *Gos. Phil.* is the outcome of several successive stages of excerpting, collecting, independent note-composition, redaction and scribal confusion, and that the history of its textual transmission is so complex that we can never hope to reconstruct it with any degree of confidence.

But the textual incoherence of *Gos. Phil.* should not be confused with the question about the homogeneity of its theological ideas. For it might well be the case that all the rambling pieces of the text have their origin in the same sectarian milieu. Methodologically, too, this seems to be a more economical and more testable working hypothesis than the assumption of an unknown number of sources. Such a hypothesis will make it necessary to undertake a systematic interpretation of *Gos. Phil.* from the specific point of view of Valentinian doctrine. Only thus may we be able to identify possibly non-Valentinian elements in the present text which may form the basis for considerations concerning its transmission. Moreover, Valentinianism existed in diverse forms. About this diversity we have some, albeit far too little, information, the central building-block here being the evidence about the Eastern and the Italian "schools,"[10] and their different doctrines about the body of the Savior.[11] We therefore also need to ask again, in spite of Schenke's pessimistic statements on the subject, the question about which particular form of Valentinianism *Gos. Phil.* represents.

It lies outside the scope of this paper to provide a full Valentinian commentary on *Gos. Phil.* All we shall do here is to offer a limited number of observations on the Valentinianism of *Gos. Phil.*, as well as on the resistance given by some passages against a consistently Valentinian interpretation.

---

[8]This possibility was pointed out to me by Karen L. King in a private communication.

[9]W. Isenberg, "Introduction," *Nag Hammadi Codex II,2-7*, 133–134.

[10]This division is attested independently by three sources: Tertullian, *Adv. Val.* 4.1–3, 11.2; Clement of Alexandria, *Exc. Theod.* superscript; Hippolytus, *Ref.* VI.35.5–7.

[11]Hippolytus, *Ref.* VI.35.5–7.

## I

Valentinian texts generally deal with three main themes: salvation in history, redemption in ritual, and protology. A basic method of Valentinian theology is to establish patterns of parallelism between these three themes, so that for instance the mediator figure of the Son may be represented as operating in analogous ways in his historical incarnation, in his ritual presence, and in his function in protological manifestation. *Gos. Phil.* does not deal with protology. Its focus lies instead on the two other themes, salvation in history and ritual redemption. These themes are handled as parallel expressions of a transition from one state to another, from the old to the new, from "before" to "now," or "after." In this respect *Gos. Phil.* is similar to the document underlying the final part of the *Excerpts from Theodotus* (66–86). In both texts that transition is conceived as a salvation-historical event taking place with the advent of the Savior, and at the same time as effected in ritual acts of redemption. This general perspective can be illustrated by *Gos. Phil.* 52.21–25:

> When we were Hebrews we were orphans and had (only) our mother, but when we became Christians we got both father and mother,

and compared with *Exc. Theod.* 68 and 79:[12]

> As long as we were children of the Female only, as of a dishonourable union (συζυγίας), we were incomplete, childish, without understanding, weak and without form, brought forth like abortions: we were children of the Woman. But once we were given form by the Savior, we became children of a Man and of a bridal chamber (ἀνδρὸς καὶ νυμφῶνος τέκνα). (68)
>
> As long, then, as the seed is still unformed, it is a child of the Female. But once it is formed, it is changed into a man and becomes a son of a Bridegroom (υἱὸς νυμφίου). No longer is it weak and subjected to the visible and invisible cosmic (powers), but having become a man it becomes a male offspring. (79)

Both texts presuppose the Valentinian Sophia myth. According to all known Valentinian versions of this myth, the fallen, separated and suffering aeon successively produces the substances of matter, soul and spirit. The last of these, the spiritual, which chiefly interests us here, is brought forth in the form of images of the Savior and his angels, who are the manifestation of the Pleroma sent forth by it to the

---

[12]The two passages should be read together, taking into account that the section about the astral powers in *Exc. Theod.* 69–78 clearly has been inserted from a separate source.

suffering Sophia.[13] The notion of "image" (εἰκών) is used in this context with reference to Gen. 1:26–27: The multiple unity of the Savior and his entourage of angels provides the paradigm for the generation of the spiritual seed which will later be inserted into the first human. But "image" also implies a deficiency, since the seed of the Female, Sophia, originates only from a vision by one, and not from a union of two.[14]

These notions are attested elsewhere in *Gos. Phil.*:

> He said that day in the prayer of thanksgiving: 'O you who have joined the perfect light with the holy spirit, unite also the angels with us, the images.' (58.10–14)

Also, the section 65.1–26 describes how the souls of men and women are promiscuously mingled with unclean spirits of the opposite sex, but, the section concludes, "if the image and the angel join with one another, none can dare to make advances to the male or the female."

The moment of salvation occurs when the "image" is united with the angel which served as model for its generation by the Mother. This moment of unification took place, from the salvation historical point of view, with the advent of the Savior and his incarnation in this world, while from the ritual point of view it is effected through the mystery of the bridal chamber. But the notion of salvation through unification implies a number of other ideas which are tied together in a complex dialectic. We need, for instance, to consider the following additional elements:

- The relationship between the historical act of salvation and the ritually accomplished act of redemption.
- The joining of "the perfect light" with "the holy spirit" in 58.11–13, which serves as the paradigm for the unification of images and angels.
- The double character of the redemption, which is conceived partly as a rebirth arising from the unification of the father and the mother, and partly as itself being the unification in the bridal chamber.

---

[13]*Tri. Trac.* 90.31–91.6, 91.32–92.4, 93.25–29, 94.10–95.16, 96.17–97.27; Irenaeus, *Haer.* I.4.5, 5.6; *Exc. Theod.* 21.1.

[14]ὅσα οὖν ἐκ συζυγίας, φασί, προέρχεται, πληρώματά ἐστιν· ὅσα δὲ ἀπὸ ἑνός, εἰκόνες, *Exc. Theod.* 32.1 (the same formula is found in Clement of Alexandria, *Strom.* IV.90.2). *Tri. Trac.* for this reason calls the spiritual seed a kind of passions (95.2–7).

*

The historical event of salvation is described in the following passage:

> Jesus revealed [...] Jordan, the fullness [of the] kingdom of heavens. The one who [was born] before all things was reborn; the [one who] was anointed in the beginning was reanointed; the one who was redeemed redeemed (others) in turn.

> Indeed, it is right to speak of a mystery! The Father of the Totality joined with the virgin who came down, and fire illuminated him. On that day he revealed the great bridal bedroom. It was for this purpose that his body came into being. On that day it came forth from the bridal bedroom as something which has come into being from the bridegroom and the bride. In this way Jesus made the Totality firm in it through these (acts?), and it is right for each of the disciples to proceed into his rest. (70.34–71.15)

There is a parallelism between the description of Jesus' saving acts during his cosmic presence and the redemptive ritual. This is why Valentinian soteriology in general emphasizes the importance of the baptism of Jesus. The Savior saves not simply by virtue of his coming to rescue his own kin lost in the cosmos, but also by himself undergoing and prefiguring a process of salvation which is to be re-enacted in ritual acts. This soteriological parallelism between the Savior and the *salvandi* entails the notion that the Savior redeems by being himself redeemed. Thus *Exc. Theod.* 22.6–7 speaks about

> ... the redemption of the Name which descended upon Jesus in the dove, and redeemed him. For Jesus as well was in need of redemption in order that he might not be detained by the thought of deficiency in which he had been placed as he came forth through Sophia.

*Tri. Trac.* asserts that

> even the Son, who is laid down as a model (ΤΥΠΟC) of redemption for the Totality, [need]ed the redemption as well, he who became human—because he submitted himself to all things needed by us, we who in the flesh are his Church.[15] After he, then, had received the redemption first, through the *logos* which came down upon him, all the others who have received him have received the redemption through him. For those who have received the one who has received have also received that which existed in him. (124.25–125.11)

---

[15]Or: "his churches" (ⲀⲚⲀⲚ ϨⲚ ⲤⲀⲢⲜ ⲈⲦⲞⲈⲒ Ⲛ̄ⲚⲈⲔⲔⲀⲎⲤⲒⲀ Ⲛ̄Ⲧⲉϥ); but ⲈⲔⲔⲀⲎⲤⲒⲀ is not used in the plural elsewhere in the tractate (or in other Valentinian documents).

On this logic, the Savior redeems because he has provided the *typos* of redemption through being himself redeemed in baptism. What effects this redemption is described variously in the sources. In the two texts just quoted it is the "Name," or a certain *"logos,"* which descends upon the Savior at his baptism in the Jordan; in *Exc. Theod.* 16 it is "the Spirit of the Father's Thought," while *Exc. Theod.* 61.6 just speaks about "the Spirit."[16]

In the passage quoted above (70.34–71.15), *Gos. Phil.* offers its own interpretation of this theme, emphasizing the anointing element in the baptismal ritual, and the union of the bridal chamber. A union took place "on that day" between "the Father of the Totality" and "the virgin who came down." There is an illuminating fire, which is an allusion to the working of the ointment, as can be seen from other passages in *Gos. Phil.*, where the association of fire and chrism is explicitly made,[17] and at the same time "the great bridal bedroom" (ⲠⲚⲞϬ ⲘⲠⲀⲤⲦⲞⲤ) is manifested through the union taking place.[18]

But if this refers to the event at the Jordan, as the typological pre-figuration of the redemptive ritual of baptism, how are we to identify the "Father" and the "virgin" in the passage? One might at first be inclined to interpret "the Father of the Totality" as referring to the Savior, as the "bridegroom" in the union of the bedroom, whereas the "bride" would be the collective symbol of the spirituals who are saved through the union—in other words, of Sophia. The Savior and Sophia are of course steady marriage partners in Valentinian mythology. However, if Jesus is to be understood in this context as a paradigm of the baptizand, will we not, on the contrary, have to interpret him as "the virgin who came down" (ⲦⲠⲀⲢⲐⲈⲚⲞⲤ ⲚⲦⲀϨⲈⲒ ⲀⲠⲒⲦⲚ̄), and who is (re)united with the Father (and with the Pleroma) at the moment of his baptism?

In fact, it would be unusual for the Savior in his role as Sophia's bridegroom to be referred to as "the Father of the Totality"—this designation more properly belongs on higher levels in the Valentinian system (the transcendent Father himself, or his manifestation in the Son). Moreover, the phrase "the virgin who came down" can hardly be understood to refer to anything other than the incarnation of Jesus.[19] But can Jesus really be represented as a female virgin? A

---

[16]For other variants, cf. n. 26.

[17]Cf. 57.22–28, 67.2–9.

[18]The word παστός, attested in Valentinianism only by *Gos. Phil.*, is apparently used as a synonym for νυμφών.

[19]κατέρχεσθαι is used in Valentinianism to refer either to the descent-incarnation of

simple solution to this problem is to assume a textual irregularity, i.e. that we should actually read ⲡⲡⲁⲣⲑⲉⲛⲟⲥ. This assumption of an error would also explain the fact that the pronouns in the immediate context are masculine, and in particular in the phrase "fire illuminated him" (ⲁⲩⲕⲱⲧ ⲣ̄ ⲟⲩⲟⲉⲓⲛ ⲉⲣⲟϥ). The virginity of Jesus could then be interpreted as referring to the undefiled nature of his conception and birth.[20]

Although such a solution cannot be definitively excluded, there exists another way of considering this problem which may allow us to overcome the assumption of a choice between two mutually exclusive alternatives. Both interpretations may in fact be true: Jesus can be seen as bride and bridegroom both at the same time.

This paradoxical suggestion can be made plausible, I believe, through an analysis of the the notion of the "body" referred to in the passage. The significance of this characteristic Valentinian notion is to express a consubstantiality of the Savior and the *salvandi*, which in turn rests on a soteriology of mutual participation between them. At the moment of his descent into the cosmos, it is thought that the Savior assumes as his body the spiritual seed of Sophia which he will redeem, and which constitutes the Church. This notion can be explained in the following way: insofar as the Savior redeems by being himself redeemed, and this redemption is shared in through the ritual re-enactment of it by its recipients, these recipients can, paradoxically, also be conceived as participating in the descent that the Savior performs as the agent of salvation. Because the Savior performs roles of both agent and recipient of redemption, and these roles are linked by means of a salvifically efficient symbolic parallelism with the recipients of redemption acting in ritual, both of these roles may in turn also be assumed by the recipients. In the present passage from *Gos. Phil.*, we may thus infer that the body of Jesus represents the totality of those whom his incarnation purports to save, i.e. the "images" who are the spiritual seed of the Female and whom he assumed as his body at the moment of his descent and incarnation into the world. Through the unification taking place in the bridal chamber and revealed at the Jordan, the "body" too is redeemed; that

---

the Saviour, or to the Spirit which came down upon him at baptism; cf. G.W.H. Lampe, *A Patristic Greek Lexicon*, s.v. 1; F. M.-M. Sagnard, *La gnose valentinienne et le témoignage de Saint Irénée* (Paris: Vrin, 1947) 644.

[20] Cf. 55.27–28: "Mary is the virgin whom no power defiled"; 71.19–21: "Christ was born from a virgin so that he might rectify the fall which occurred in the beginning"; *Tri. Trac.* 115.15–17: "... it was without sin, defilement and impurity that he allowed himself to be conceived."

is to say, the notion of the body is the symbolic expression of the soteriological relationship between Jesus and the redeemed; the idea that they are redeemed through his typological prefiguration of their ritual redemption is expressed by saying that his body takes part in the unification he attains in the bridal chamber.

Now before we try to analyse further the dialectics of this soteriology in *Gos. Phil.*, we may take a closer look at the unification with the angels and how this idea is articulated in the Valentinian sources.[21] The best known occurrence of this idea is the one in Irenaeus, *Haer.* I.7.1 which says that "when the whole seed is perfected," Achamoth will receive the Savior as her bridegroom in the Pleroma, and the spiritual humans will similarly divest themselves of their souls and be bestowed as brides on the angels surrounding the Savior. In this text, the unification in the bridal chamber is conceived as an eschatological event. *Exc. Theod.* 64 has a similar version.[22] On the other hand, the version in Hippolytus asserts that Sophia and the "Joint Fruit" of the Pleroma, i.e. the Savior, were united already at a pre-cosmic stage, and that seventy *logoi* were thus produced which at a later stage were sown into human souls pure from the influence of demons.[23] In that version there is no need of a redemption of the spirituals, since the unification has already taken place, the realm above has already been set right (VI.36.3), and the spiritual souls on earth are unaffected by the evil spirits. In fact, only the psychic sons of the Demiurge are the object of the mission of the Savior according to Hippolytus (VI.35.2–3, 36.3).

The latter point is also made in Irenaeus' version: "The Savior is said to have come to the psychic, since it possessed free will, in order to save it" (Irenaeus, *Haer.* I.6.1). At the same time, however, this source states that "he received the first-fruits of those whom he intended to save; from Achamoth he acquired the spiritual, from the Demiurge he put on the psychic Christ ..." (Irenaeus, *Haer.* I.6.1). There is an inconsistency here in Irenaeus' source, which may be explained as resulting from an attempt to harmonize two different soteriologies: According to the first of these, the incarnated Savior is consubstantial and concorporeal with the ones he comes to save;

---

[21] An investigation in this direction was began already in Schenke I, 35–38.

[22] I fail to see that *Exc. Theod.* 44.1, 53.2–3, 64 speaks about two unifications, as Schenke I, 36 asserts. These excerpts, which go back to the same source as Irenaeus, *Haer.* I.1–8, seem to assume, as that text, that the impregnation of Sophia took place through a vision, not a union.

[23] Hippolytus, *Ref.* VI.34.3–4.6; also cf. 32.4, 36.4.

according to the second the salvation of the spiritual is a pre-established reality, and only the psychics remain as an object of cosmic salvation history. The difference which can be perceived here seems to fit well the distinction between the Oriental and the Italian "schools" as described by Hippolytus:[24] The former postulated a spiritual body for the Savior which took part in his redemptive incarnation in the cosmos, whereas the latter taught that only a psychic Savior was born here, who had to be redeemed by a spiritual Savior. It is the first of these theories that is properly a soteriology of mutual participation in incarnation and redemption between the Savior and the spirituals, and which entails a notion of a redeemed redeemer, whereas in the second the soteriological mutuality is broken up: The spirituals do not need redemption, the Savior does not need to assume flesh himself in order to redeem them—only what is psychic is affected by the material, and the spiritual, retaining only the role of agent of redemption, is sent to the cosmos to instruct and liberate the psychic, or for its own education.[25]

It seems that *Gos. Phil.* adheres to the first of these soteriologies, the one which may be labelled "Oriental," but which also appears to be the older and more primitive one in the history of Valentinian theology.[26] As was mentioned above, *Gos. Phil.* says that the souls are seduced by unclean spirits, who mingle promiscuously with them, until "the image and the angel join with one another" (65.1–26). Similarly, in 53.11–12 the soul deposited in the world is said to have fallen into the hands of brigands.[27] This is a theme which, within Valentinianism, goes back to Valentinus himself, who in a fragment preserved by Clement of Alexandria likens "the heart" to an inn ravaged by strange visitors, meaning unclean spirits.[28] The theme is taken up by Hippolytus' treatise, but is given a notably different turn:

---

[24]Hippolytus, *Ref.* VI.35.5–7.

[25]It is within this soteriological type too that we find the interpretation of the baptism at Jordan as the descent of the spiritual Saviour upon the psychic Christ (Irenaeus, *Haer.* I.7.2), or of the spiritual Christ upon the psychic Jesus (Irenaeus, *Haer.* I.15.3, 21.2).

[26]Tertullian attributes in *De carne Chr.* 10.1 the doctrine of a psychic body of the Saviour to the Valentinians, but in 15.1 that of a spiritual body to Valentinus himself. In *Val.* 4.3 he says that Axionicus in Antioch was more faithful to Valentinus' original teachings than were Ptolemaeus and others (in the West).

[27]Similarly 83.25–28.

[28]*Strom.* II.114.3–6 = fr. 2, W. Völker, ed. *Quellen zur Geschichte der christlichen Gnosis* (Sammlung ausgewählter kirchen- und dogmengeschichtlicher Quellenschriften, n. s., 5, Tübingen: J. C. B. Mohr [Siebeck], 1932).

> This material man, in their view, is like an inn, or residence, either of the soul alone, or of the soul and demons, or even of the soul and *logoi*—which *logoi* have been sown from above, from the Joint Fruit of the Pleroma and from Sophia, into this world and they dwell in the earthly body if no demons reside with the soul. (VI.34.6)

Thus according to Hippolytus the souls which dwell in the body together with the *logoi* are immune from the attacks of the demons. These *logoi* are the outcome of the already consummated union of Sophia and the Joint Fruit-Savior, and their presence in the cosmos is not a condition from which they need to be saved. *Gos. Phil.*, on the other hand, holds that the soul "had fallen into the hands of brigands, and they had taken it captive. But he (sc. Christ) saved it" (53.11–13). This theme is also found in Heracleon,[29] in *Exc. Theod.* 69–78,[30] in *Gos. Truth*,[31] *Tri. Trac.*,[32] and in *Val. Exp.*[33] These texts form one group[34] over against the ones which state that the spirituals are not affected by evil spirits, or passions: the treatises of Hippolytus and Irenaeus,[35] *Exc. Theod.* 43.2–65,[36] and the fragment in Irenaeus, *Haer.* I.7.2. The treatise of Irenaeus, and the section *Exc. Theod.* 43.2–65, which derives from the same source, retain the unification of the spirituals with the angels as an eschatological idea, but since the spirituals are in the world at most to be trained and do not actually need to be saved from it, this unification no longer has the significance which it no doubt originally had as a soteriological notion, describing the redemption from a situation characterized by separation from spiritual fullness and by subjection to passions and ignorance.

Consequently, *Gos. Phil.* should be grouped with those Valentinian texts which consider that a redemption of the spirituals takes place in the world. It takes place from one point of view with the histori-

---

[29]Especially frgs. 13, 18 Völker. Heracleon is normally placed in the Italian "school," but seems to have preserved the doctrine of Valentinus himself on this point, in spite of what Hippolytus says in *Ref.* VI.35.6.

[30]Also cf. 80.3, 81.1, 83–85.

[31]Cf. 17.33–36, 20.35–38, 22.16–21, 28.24–30.15, etc.

[32]105.10–21, 114.30–39, 116.18–27, 126.9–37.

[33]This is clearest in the first of the appendices to this treatise, *On Bap. A* 40.14–18.

[34]The list is not intended to be exhaustive, only to establish the existence of the two groups in principle.

[35]Cf. Irenaeus, *Haer.* I.6.2: "they themselves cannot suffer any injury or lose their spiritual substance, whatever material actions they may engage in."

[36]Cf. 56.3: "saved by nature"; 61.3–4 only the psychic is ἐμπαθής; 61.8 only the psychic is saved through the resurrection, also cf. 62.

cally unique advent, baptism, passion and resurrection of the Savior, and from another point of view in indefinitely repeatable ritual. According to this type of soteriology, the redemption is conceived in terms of a joining of what is separate through the fact of cosmic existence, and at the same time as a dialectic of mutual participation between the Savior and the *salvandi*. The Savior himself needs to be redeemed, having become present in the world, and the spirituals share in his redemption through ritual acts. What is especially notable with *Gos. Phil.*, in comparison with the other texts in the group, is the insistence on the bridal chamber as a motif of redemption. In *Exc. Theod.* 76.1 the paradigmatic redemption of the redeemed redeemer is expressed in the following way,

> Just as the birth of the Savior takes us away from birth and Fate, so also his baptism removes us from the fire, and his passion from passion, so that we may follow him in all things.

whereas *Gos. Phil.*, as we saw, makes the Savior proclaim:

> O you who have joined the perfect light with the holy spirit, unite also the angels with us, the images,

and interprets this joining as the mystery that took place at the Jordan (70.34ff).

An implication of this soteriology of symbolic parallelism is that the roles of redeemer and redeemed become highly ambiguous. For whereas we would expect "the perfect light" to be the Savior, and "the holy spirit" to represent Sophia, in accordance with the notions about the marriage of these two figures that we are familiar with from other sources, it appears that when the event at Jordan is interpreted as the Savior's own paradigmatic redemption, and that redemption is described in terms of the unification of the bridal chamber, the Savior himself has to play the role otherwise attributed to Sophia. That is to say, the Savior seems here to be the same as the "body" consisting of the spiritual seed of Sophia (and which in a sense is the same as "Sophia" herself), which is redeemed through his own redemption. Consequently, if we return at this point to the section 70.34–71.15, and the statement about the unification of "the Father of the Totalities" with "the virgin who came down," we may now ask ourselves whether this should not most appropriately be seen as a statement of the general *principle* of the unification in the bridal chamber, where there is a female and human, and a male and divine partner. The question about the precise identity of each of these partners then only arises on a different and further level of specification, and at that level it will be correct both to say that Jesus, as corporeally co-extensive with Sophia and as the model of the saved human, represents the female part in the union, *and* that, as the saving manifestation of the fullness of the Father, and the personified unity of all the angels, he is the male bridegroom in the bridal chamber.

Indeed, it seems that this double role of the Savior is an important component of what *Gos. Phil.* calls "a mystery":

> The Christ has everything in himself, whether man or angel or mystery, and the Father (56.13–15).

And, to complete this logic of mutual inversions by one more observation: If Christ can be cast in the role of redeemer and that of man needing redemption at the same time, the reverse is equally true. Through the ritual identification with the redeemed redeemer the person who is initiated through the anointing does not simply remain in the role of the redeemed spiritual human—s/he "is no longer a Christian but a Christ" (67.26–28).

*

It seems that the underlying logic of these mutual identifications may be described as the interplay of two "joinings." The first of these is the joining of human and angel in the bridal chamber—which is closely related to the baptism/anointing ritual, and most probably not performed as a distinct ritual from it (see below). The other is the parallelism which joins this ritual act itself with its model, the redemption of the redeemer, which is not only a singular historical act of redemption, but also a symbol with salvation-efficient power in its ritual re-enactment. In both cases *Gos. Phil.* employs the term "image." The double usage of the term is shown by the following passage:

> Truth did not come into the world naked, but it came in types (ΤΥΠΟC) and images (ϨΙΚШΝ). The world will not accept it in any other way. There is rebirth as well as an image (ϨΙΚШΝ) of rebirth. It is truly necessary to be reborn by means of the image (ϨΙΤÑ ΤϨΙΚШΝ). Which image? Resurrection. The image must rise again by means of the image. The bridal chamber[37] and the image must enter into truth by means of the image; this is the resto-

---

[37]Most editors and commentators prefer to treat ΝΥΜΦШΝ as an error for ΝΥΜΦΙΟC. It should be pointed out however that in the usage of *Gos. Phil.* νυμφίος is joined with νυμφή, whereas the partner associated with εἰκών is ἄγγελος.

> ration. Not only must those who produce (ⲭⲡⲟ) the Name of the Father and
> the Son and the holy spirit do so, but also <those who> have produced them
> for you (?).[38] If one does not acquire (ⲭⲡⲟ) them, the Name will also be
> taken away from him. But one receives them in the anointing of the [...] of
> the power of the Cross. This power the apostles called 'the right and the
> left.' For this person is no longer a Christian but a Christ. (67.9–28)

On the one hand, εἰκών in this passage refers to the spiritual person
who will be reborn and resurrected. On the other hand the word is
also used to designate that by which this takes place, the image of
rebirth and resurrection. What is this latter εἰκών? Unfortunately the
text does not seem to have been well transmitted, and cannot be
translated with exactitude at all points. But it seems reasonable to
interpret the εἰκών referred to in the latter sense as the symbolic ritual
acts by which rebirth and resurrection are effected. The symbolism of
these acts, however, is related to the resurrection of the Savior as their
paradigm. At this point we need to make the following considerations:
(1) the relationship of the immateriality of symbolism and the physi-
cality of acts in ritual; (2) the relationship of historical event and
transferable symbolism in the narrative about the Savior's redemptive
work; (3) the relationship of (1) and (2); and (4) the joining and
disjoining of spirit and matter in the redemptive process itself.

*Gos. Phil.* seems to identify a paradox in the redemptive efficacy
of ritual. Ritual is symbolic action, but its efficacy as action depends
on its ability to transform the physical acts it consists of into the
immaterial symbolism they represent. What takes place in ritual is
desired to be something real (rebirth and resurrection), but this reality
is only achieved by eliminating the reality of the physical acts
performed in the ritual and by affirming the reality of the non-
physical symbolism of which these acts are the bearers. This seems to
be the problematic which the passage quoted circles around: Rebirth,
resurrection and truth can only be attained through an "image," i.e.
through symbolic acts, but they are nevertheless attained through it.
Thus the "Name" mentioned in the text is affirmed to be something
real, not just the sound of a word, and the "anointing" contains a
power, it is not merely a symbolic gesture.

Valentinian reflections about the efficacy of ritual are found especially in *Exc. Theod.*:

---

[38]This is Isenberg's (above, note 4) translation, but the sentence cannot be restored
with confidence. Schenke II 196: "(So) it is fitting for those who have not only obtained
the *names* of the Father, the Son and the Holy Spirit, but have obtained *these very things*
<for themselves>."

The power which brings about the transformation of the baptised is not a matter of the body, for it is the same person who ascends (from the baptismal water), but of the soul. (77.2)

It is not, however, the bath alone that makes free, but knowledge too: who we were, what we have become, where we were, where we have come to be placed, where we are tending, what birth is, and what rebirth. (78.2)

As far as fire is concerned, there is one part which is corporeal and attacks all bodies, and another one which is pure and incorporeal, and attacks what is incorporeal, such as demons, angels of wickedness, and the Adversary himself. Thus the celestial fire has a double nature, being partly intelligible, partly sensible. And baptism is double in a similar way, being partly sensible through the water, which extinguishes the sensible fire, and partly intelligible through the Spirit, which protects from the intelligible fire. And the corporeal spirit nourishes and inflames the sensible fire, as long as it is weak, but extinguishes it when it gets stronger. The Spirit which is given us from above, however, which is incorporeal, not only prevails over the elements, but the powers and the wicked rulers as well.

And the bread and the oil are consecrated by the power of the Name of God. In their external appearance they are just as they have been taken; but with regard to their power they are transformed into a spiritual power. In the same way the water, both that which has been exorcized and that which has become baptism, not only separates what is inferior, but also acquires consecration. (81–82)

Here too there is a δύναμις, associated with the Name, or with the Spirit, which transforms the physical acts and elements of the ritual into an immaterial reality. The double character of ritual is also a concern in *Gos. Phil.*:

Through water and fire the whole place is purified—the visible by the visible, the hidden by the hidden. There are hidden things in the visible ones: water within water, fire within ointment. (57.22–28)

If one goes down into the water and come up without having received anything and says, 'I am a Christian,' he has borrowed the Name. But if he receive the holy spirit he has the Name as a gift. (64.22–27)

From water and fire the soul and the spirit have come into being, from fire and light the son of the bridal chamber. The fire is the ointment, the light is the fire. I do not speak about that fire which has no form, but about the other, whose form is white, which is bright and beautiful, and which gives beauty. (67.2–9)

Through the holy spirit we are indeed reborn. But we are born through Christ by means of two things. We are anointed through the Spirit. Once we were born we were joined. None can see himself either in water or in a mirror without light. Nor again can you see by the light without water or a mirror. For this reason it is necessary to baptize with two things: light and water. And light means ointment. (69.5–14)

Baptism is the "the holy" building. Redemption is "the holy of the holy." "The holy of the holies" is the bridal chamber. Baptism contains resurrection and redemption; redemption is in the bridal chamber. But the bridal chamber is in what is above [.... (69.12–18)

The anointing is superior to baptism. For because of the anointing (ⲡⲭⲣⲓⲥⲙⲁ) have we been called Christians, not because of baptism. ... Whoever has been anointed possesses everything: resurrection, light, cross, holy spirit. The Father gave him this in the bridal chamber, and he received. (74.12–22)

The mysteries of truth are manifest as types and images. The bedroom, however, remains hidden. It is the holy in the holy. (84.20–23)

(*The person who has received the light in the bedroom:*) When he leaves the world he has already received the truth as images, and the world has already become Aeon. (86.11–13)

The efficacy of the ritual depends on the successful joining of its visible and hidden aspects. *Gos. Phil.* stresses that it is necessary to "receive" "in" ritual something that is different from its outward form, referred to by the notions of "light" and "bridal chamber." But at the same time the indispensability of the "image" is emphasized; in this world, the outward form cannot be dispensed with. (In semiotic terms we might perhaps say that there can be no signification without a signifier.) Thus there must take place a joining of the inward and the outward, but one which produces a reversal: what is enacted in the outward acts is the inward signification of these acts. The performance of water baptism and anointing is the same as an actual rebirth and a resurrection. In order to make this identification, the significance of water baptism and anointing must first be abstracted from the acts themselves, in order to be subsequently reaffirmed as being identical with and accomplished through them.

From this point of view the notion of the "image" may be seen to refer simultaneously to the visible ritual acts and to the empirical person performing these acts. If this person is joined with the angel or with the bridegroom/bride in these acts, this is because the acts themselves are joined with their symbolic inward significance, and this double joining is expressed by terming the inward and hidden aspect itself of the ritual "the bridal chamber." With regard to the structure of this conception, an unevenness may nevertheless be observed: The "bridal chamber" represents the joining itself as well as one of its two joining parts. In fact, the performance of the ritual acts assimilates the performer to the non-empirical ideality of the acts in order to make possible the joining of the empirical person with the angel representing his/her ideal identity. Thus the joining takes place simultaneously between the angel, on the one hand, and the empirical person *and* the ritually idealized person, on the other. On this logic, the bridal chamber must be both *in* the baptismal ritual as its inward meaning, and at the same time identical with it, in the sense that the outward acts of water immersion and anointing are necessary enactments of the bridal chamber. The general principle is explicitly recognized by *Gos. Phil.*, which lets the Savior state:

> I have come to make [the lower] like the up[per, and the ou]ter like the in[ner], and to join them in th[at] place [... the]se places by means of types. (67.31–35)[39]

It may also be observed, however, that although there is said to be a joining where each of the joined parts is equally necessary, there is also a hierarchy. The inner is superior to the outer, just as the angel is to the image. It is not just a joining of equal partners, but also that of an inferior part with a superior one. This creates an ambiguity which is transferred to the level of the outward ritual, where the anointing part can be valorized above the water baptism part (74.12–22). The bridal chamber, i.e. the "inward" of the ritual, is from one point of view above the "outward," the water and the ointment, but from the point of view that the outward is joined with the inward through being a necessary vehicle for the redemption process, and thus from one perspective is elevated to the rank of an equal partner in this process, its hierarchical subordination to the inward is relocated to the outward ritual sequence of acts as a relationship between water baptism and anointing.[40]

*

---

[39] As is well known, this saying occurs in many other contexts too: *2 Clem.* 12:1–2, *Gos. Thom.* log. 22, etc.; cf. *New Testament Apocrypha*, ed. R. McL. Wilson, vol. I, 210–211, 212–14. But *Gos. Phil.* seems to link the saying specifically to its theory of ritual, which can also be inferred from the immediately preceding context.

[40] It appears that anointing would have followed water immersion in the actual performance of the initiation, as in early Christian "Western" practice.

Now we may relate these observations on the redemption effected in ritual to the redemptive function of the Savior's "coming." As we saw, an important aspect of his redemptive work is associated with his own baptism and anointing at the Jordan (70.34–71.15). This is connected with the notions of rebirth and the bridal chamber. But it is also connected with resurrection:

> Those who say that the lord first died and then arose are in error, for he first arose and then died. If one does not first acquire resurrection, one will not die. (56.15–19)

> While we exist in the world we must acquire resurrection. (66.16–18)

> Those who say they will die first and then arise are in error. If they do not first receive resurrection while they live, when they die they will receive nothing. So also when speaking about baptism they say, 'Great is baptism!' For if one receives it one will live. (73.1–8)

We have already seen how both rebirth and resurrection are associated with the baptismal ritual. But Jesus' own resurrection is also identified with his baptism. This can be explained by the fact that the Valentinians identified the baptism of Jesus as the soteriologically crucial event during his earthly life, and this in turn is due to the paradigmatic role of his baptism vis-à-vis the Valentinians' own ritual of redemption. The complex of ideas is elegantly compressed in the following passage:

> Philip the apostle said: Joseph the carpenter planted a garden because he needed wood for his trade. It is he who made the cross from the trees which he planted. And his seed hung on that which he planted. His seed was Jesus, and the plant was the cross. But the tree of life is in the middle of the garden, and from the olive-tree comes ointment, and from the ointment resurrection. (73.8–19)

Joseph is the earthly father of Jesus, who is also alluded to in 55.33–36: "The lord [would] not have said, 'My [father who is in] heaven' unless [he] had another father, but he would have said simply, ['My father']." Undoubtedly, Joseph in the first passage also means the Demiurge, the garden the cosmos and the trees matter (note the explicit reference to "wood" [ϣⲉ <*ὕλη]). But the focus here is on the earthly birth of Jesus as a human with a material body. According to the soteriology of mutual participation characteristic of an important strand of Valentinianism, the Savior shares in the condition of the spirituals he comes to save by assuming a material body. It is this incarnation which is the crucifixion, as is clear in the passage above: "his seed hung on that which he planted. His seed was Jesus, and the plant was the cross." In the logic of this soteriology, the Savior lets himself be incarnated in order that the spirituals on their part may be released from the body. There is thus a symmetrically inverted joining and disjoining: When the Savior is joined to matter, the spirituals are disjoined from it. Or, in other words, his crucifixion is their resurrection; thus the cross which is matter is also the olive-tree which produces ointment, i.e. resurrection.

But there is not only a logic of inversion here, but also one of symbolic parallelism. Having been incarnated, the Savior himself needs to be redeemed. This, as we have seen, takes place at the Jordan. Here, the "virgin" is joined with the Father, revealing the bridal chamber in an act which not only redeemed Jesus himself, but also the spirituals by being a paradigm which is salvifically efficient through its ritual re-enactment. Both of these logics of salvation work together at the same time, however, so that incarnation, crucifixion, resurrection and baptism/anointing become inseparable aspects of the same redemptive act, where the joining of spirit and matter in the Savior effects the disjoining of the two in the spirituals, partly by a logic of substitutive inversion, partly by one of parallelism. Thus, the crucifixion is not only a joining but also a disjoining:

> '[My] God, my God, why, O lord, have you forsaken me?' He spoke these words on the cross; for he had separated himself (ⲁϥⲡⲱⲣⲝ) from that place. (68.25–26)

The words spoken on the cross (Matt. 27.46) are taken by *Gos. Phil.* to refer to the separation of the spiritual Savior from his material body.[41] The crucifixion represents the incarnation of the Savior in a material body as a substitutive redemptive act, but at the same time it signifies the liberation of spirit from matter as a paradigm of salvation. The baptism of Jesus is also simultaneously a joining and a disjoining. The incarnate Savior is united with the Father (the Spirit coming down), and at the same time (though we must extrapolate this) released from matter. Crucifixion/resurrection and incarnation/baptism are aspects of the same act, but at the same time there is a structurally inverted relationship between them: In resurrection, the Savior is the active agent of a disjoining, whereas in baptism he is the passive partner in an act of joining.

---

[41]Cf. L. Painchaud, "Le Christ vainqueur de la mort (EvPhil NH II 68,17b–29a): une exégèse valentinienne de Mt 27,46," *NovTest* 38 (1996) 1–11.

These dialectics reflect the function of the narrative of the Savior
in the redemptive ritual, in which the performing agent is at the same
time the passive recipient of the redemptive power. The Savior is
portrayed in the narrative as redeemer and redeemed at the same time
because he is both the agent of and the paradigm for redemption. But
these roles are intricately tied together. The historical saving advent of
the Savior is at the same time a concrete singular act and a repro-
ducible symbol. The ritual re-enactment of the symbol is conceived,
however, as a re-instantiation of the original act. Sign and event are
thought to coincide. But in this process an inversion takes place. In
the transformation of the original act-event into symbol, and from
symbol again into the act-event of ritual, the roles of redeemer and
redeemed become mingled, along with the double identification of sign
and event. Turning the acting Savior into a symbol implies that he
must share in the same condition as the ones whom his salvific act
purports to save; he is incarnated, he becomes himself an object of
redemption. At the other end, ritual acts performed by incarnate
humans are transformed into disembodied symbols through the
identification with the Savior. Just as he had to become incarnate and
"crucified" in order that they might be released from their bodies, so
he became a symbol in order that their ritual acts might acquire a
symbolic reference. His sharing in the human condition by assuming a
body corresponds to their sharing in him by means of symbolic ritual
acts.

It is in this way that the outward act of baptism/anointing acquires
a symbolic significance which is said actually to turn the initiate into
not only a Christian but a Christ (67.26–27)—the symbolism is
thought to effect a virtual identification. On the way to this identification, however, there has taken place a double identification of symbol
and performed act, with the consequence that the agent and the object
of the act become in some respects interchangeable. Just as the Savior
can be represented in both active and passive roles in the redemption,
so the ritual acts have both an active and a passive aspect: what takes
place in the redemptive ritual is described as a "receiving"—the term
is so common, not only in *Gos. Phil.*, but in Valentinianism generally,
that it must be regarded as technical. Just as there is an "outward"
and an "inward" aspect of ritual, there is also an active and a passive
one: "If one goes down into the water and come up without having
received anything and says, 'I am a Christian,' he has borrowed the
Name. But if he receive the holy spirit he has the Name as a gift"
(64.22–27). The active character of the ritual act ("going down") thus
relates to its interpretation as a passive event ("receiving") in a way

which is analogous to how the "outward" relates to the "inward." It may be noted that the different valorization of the latter also applies to the active/passive aspects of the ritual. (It might even be possible to interpret the hierarchy of anointing/water baptism in this light: The immersion in water is an act essentially performed by the baptizand himself, whereas the anointing must be executed by a second person, and puts the initiand even physically into the position of a passive receiver.)

*

We may now return to one of the issues which were posed at the outset, how we are to understand the fact that the redemption is conceived partly as a rebirth, arising from the unification of the father and the mother, and partly as itself being the unification in the bridal chamber. *Gos. Phil.* in fact links the two ideas in the following passages:

> The heavenly man has many more children than the earthly man. If the children of Adam are many, although they die, how much more the children of the perfect man, who do not die but are always being born. The father makes a child, but the child is unable to make a child. For he who has been born is unable to give birth; instead, the child acquires brothers, not children. All those who are born in the world are born from nature (ⲉⲩⲭⲡⲟ ⲘⲘⲟⲟ[ⲩ] ⲉⲃⲟⲗ ⲀⲚ ⲦⲪ︦ⲨⲤⲓⲤ), and all the rest [take nour]ishment from [that] whence they have been born. ... For the perfect conceive and give birth through a kiss. For this reason we also kiss one another. We receive conception from the grace which is in one another. (58.17–59.6)

> There is the son of man and there is the son of the son of man. The lord is the son of man, and the son of the son of man is the one who creates through the son of man. The son of the son of man received from God so that he might create: he possesses so that he may give birth. He who has received so as to create is a creature. He who has received so as to give birth is an offspring. He who creates is unable to give birth. He who gives birth has power to create. Of course, one who creates is said to give birth, but his offspring is a creature. [...] birth, they are not his children, but they are [...]. Whoever creates works openly and is visible himself too. But whoever gives birth gives birth [secretly] and is himself hidden [...] image. (81.14–30)

Near the beginning of the text it was said that "when we became Christians we got both father and mother" (52.24–25). This introduced the theme of rebirth: at the advent of the Savior, the spirituals were reborn as the children of the Male. In this context, the Savior plays an active role, he unites with the Mother and causes their common children to be born. This theme is what recurs in the two

passages above, which portray the spirituals as the children of the
perfect man. On the other hand it was said in the section 70.34–71.15
that at the Jordan Jesus was himself reborn, and the virgin united with
the Father, revealing the bridal chamber. Here, the Savior is cast in
the role of the passive, or receiving, partner in the unification event,
and, more than that, even as the reborn child itself. Thus in a sense he
is both Father, Mother and child all at once.

These multiple roles of the Savior may be explained from the logic
of the symbolic parallelism of redemption. Both in his roles as the
receiving part in the unification and as the reborn child he typifies the
spiritual redeemed through the ritual of initiation. But in addition to
that it may also be observed that even the role of begetter is assumed
by the redeemed. In the bridal chamber they are not only reborn, or
act as the passively receiving part in the union, but they also copy the
perfect man whose children they are by themselves giving spiritual
birth. Thus we are to understand the spiritual life which has been
realized with the advent of the Savior as one in which the redeemed
are simultaneously children, partners in a spiritual marriage, and
fathers of spiritual offspring, in a mode of being where there is no
distinction between these roles:

> It is not possible for anyone to see anything of those things that really exists
> unless he becomes like them. The situation of human beings in the world,
> who see the sun without being the sun, and who see the heaven and the earth
> and everything else without being them, is not how it is in the realm of truth.
> Rather, you have seen something from that place and you have become those
> things: Having seen the Spirit you have become the spirit; having seen the
> Christ you have become Christ; having seen the Father you shall become
> father. Thus [here below], seeing everything you do not [see] yourself, but
> when you see yourself in the other [realm], what you see you shall
> be[come]. (61.20–35)

Spiritual existence means that there is no distinction between active
and passive, between the agent of the act, the object of it, the act
itself, and its result. The grammatical categories of human language
do not apply, just as the words themselves are no longer separated
from their referents: "in the Aeon there is a different sort of joining"
(76.8–9).[42]

It is this spiritual mode of being of the reborn which is contrasted
from the beginning of *Gos. Phil.* with the state of the Hebrews, of the
ones who can create but not give birth, of the fornicators and of the

---

[42]In this context belongs of course also the many reflections in *Gos. Phil.* on real and
unreal names (cf. the indexes s.v. ⲣⲁⲛ).

slaves, a state whose fundamental characteristic is its lack of the self-procreative unity residing in spiritual consubstantiality.

## II

While the preceding section was concerned with outlining the soteriological logic of *Gos. Phil.* and to argue both for its internal coherence and for its fundamental agreement with Valentinianism, I would here like to add some specific observations which also indicate a Valentinian provenance for *Gos. Phil.*.

1. One such observation concerns the relatively optimistic cosmology of *Gos. Phil.*. It is well known that Valentinianism generally adopts a more positive view of the cosmos and of its ruler(s) than can be found in other forms of gnostic dualism, for instance in the Sethian documents. This more positive cosmology can be found in *Gos. Phil.* 55.14–19:

> The rulers thought that it was by their own power and will that they were doing what they did, but the holy spirit was secretly accomplishing everything through them as it wished.

The idea that the cosmic powers are invisibly moved by a higher, rational, active cause, i.e. Sophia after she has been freed of her passions by the Savior, is well known from Valentinian sources.[43] The basic notion here is that the cosmos is the result of the demiurgic action of rationality on the irrationality of matter. *Gos. Phil.* links this theme with its characteristic epistemology of naming: The cosmic rulers have usurped the names of the truly good transcendent realities (54.18–32, 53.23–54.5), a theme which can also be found in *The Tripartite Tractate*.[44] On the other hand it is consistent with the relatively optimistic cosmology of Valentinianism when the names in the world nevertheless are considered a vehicle of truth: "Truth brought names into existence in the world for our sakes because it is not possible to learn it without these names" (54.13–15); "Truth, which existed from the beginning, is sown everywhere" (55.19–20). This is further linked to the theory of the "images," which was discussed above (67.9ff, 84.14ff; 86.11–15), and it also gives the opportunity to expound the hidden meaning of various names, which we find scattered in several places in *Gos. Phil.*.

---

[43]*Tri. Trac.* 100.30–36, 101.3–5, 104.30–105.2; Irenaeus, *Haer.* I.5.1.3.6; *Exc. Theod.* 47.2, 49.1, 53.4; Hippolytus, *Ref.* VI.33, 34.8.

[44]70.37–71.7, 79.7–9.29–30, 97.30–32.

2. To this might be added Schenke's observation about "the relative redemption of the psychic Demiurge,"[45] in 84.29–85.1. In fact, *Gos. Phil.* never refers to a specific "Demiurge"; instead it apparently prefers to speak about "rulers" or "gods" in the plural. It also never uses the word "psychic." But in principle the observation is sound: The "all of deity" which will be unable to enter into the holy of the holies, but will dwell under the wings of the cross, as in an ark when the eschatological flood comes, is in line with characteristic ideas found elsewhere in Valentinianism, where the psychic powers of the cosmos are thought to attain a special kind of salvation below the Pleroma[46]—the cross no doubt refers to the Limit encircling the Pleroma and protecting its spiritual purity.

3. A further topic commented on in *Gos. Phil.* is the Eucharist. A eucharistic meal is well attested for at least some of the Valentinians.[47] *Gos. Phil.* apparently interprets it as an element in the ritual of redemption,[48] since it applies to it the same logic of substitutive mutual participation as in baptismal initiation. The meal consists of bread and a cup of wine mixed with water, representing the flesh and blood of Jesus, which are described as the Logos and the holy spirit respectively (57.1–8, 75.14–22).[49] Partaking of the bread and the wine means sharing in the flesh (57.4.6) or body (75.22) of Jesus as the perfect man. This is quite consistent with the soteriological notions which were discussed above in connection with baptism: The Savior assumes a material body in order to free the spirituals from their dependence on the body. Through his incarnation they on their part are enabled to rise "naked," i.e. with the spiritual body of the perfect man.

There is a characteristically Valentinian allusion to the incarnation in 63.21–24:

> The Eucharist is Jesus. For it is called in Syriac 'Pharisatha,' which means 'what is spread out.' For Jesus came to crucify the world.

As we have seen above, the crucifixion typifies the incarnation. But what does it mean to crucify the world? We have to assume that what

---

[45]Schenke II, 186; cf. already Schenke I, 35.

[46]Cf. Irenaeus, *Haer.* I.7.1.5; *Exc. Theod.* 34.2; *Tri. Trac.* 122.12–27. See also, however, *Exc. Theod.* 63.2, and E. Thomassen and L. Painchaud, *Le Traité Tripartite* (BCNH 19; Québec: Les Presses de l'Université Laval, 1989) 448–449.

[47]Cf. NHC XI,*2de* = *On Euch. A/B*; *Exc. Theod.* 82.1; Irenaeus, *Haer.* I.13.2.

[48]Cf. the sequence baptism, anointing, Eucharist, in 67.28–29.

[49]The Eucharist is also alluded to in 55.6–14, 63.21–24, 75.1, 77.2–7.

is crucified is the body of the Savior, which stands for matter in general, i.e. the world. So what is crucified in the end is the Savior's body, while his spiritual self is thereby being released from its conjunction with matter, and by implication all the spirituals too, who are freed from cosmic existence, and who by the partaking of the flesh and the blood of the Savior in the Eucharist also, as his spiritual body, share in the redemptive separation of the spiritual from matter on the cross. In addition to this, however, the notion of the "spreading out" (ⲡⲉⲧⲡⲟⲣϣ ⲉⲃⲟⲗ) is highly significant. It refers of course to the spreading out of the Savior's arms on the cross. But the word is also a technical term used by the Valentinians to express the abstract notion of an emanation from unity to plurality. Thus in *Tri. Trac.*, for instance, the Son is said to extend and spread himself out[50] for the sake of the Totality when it is brought into being from the Father. The use of this term represents a characteristic Valentinian synthesizing of protology, salvation in history, and redemption in ritual. The "spreading out" means that the unitary source of being submits itself to the condition of the multiple in order that those who exist under that condition may share in the unitary—this is what takes place through the Savior's incarnation in the empirical world and through the partaking of the one Savior in repeatable and multiple ritual performances, as well as in the protological unfolding of the divine oneness into a plurality of aeons.

4. The notion of the Son as the Name of the Father (54.5–13) is also characteristically Valentinian, familiar from *The Gospel of Truth* (38.6–41.3) and other sources.[51] *Gos. Phil.* relates this theme to that of the epistemology of the "names," which is a somewhat original twist, but, as we have seen, is clearly within the parameters of Valentinian thought.

5. The metaphors of sowing in winter and reaping in summer (52.25–35) are part of the Valentinian tradition history, as is shown by Heracleon, frr. 32–36 Völker; cf. especially the end of fr. 36.[52]

---

[50] ⲥⲁ ⲩⲧⲛ̅ ⲁⲃⲁⲗ < *ἐκτείνεσθαι, and ⲡⲁⲣⲉϣϥ ⲁⲃⲁⲗ < *πλατύνεσθαι, *Tri. Trac.* 65.4–11. These terms are technical Neo-pythagorean vocabulary, taken over by the Valentinians; cf. Thomassen and Painchaud, *Le Traité Tripartite*, 305; and E. Thomassen, "The Philosophical Dimension of Gnosticism: The Valentinian System," in *Understanding and History in Arts and Sciences*, ed. R. Skarsten et al. (Acta Humaniora Universitatis Bergensis 1; Oslo: Solum Forlag, 1991) 69-79.

[51] Cf. E. Thomassen, "Gnostic Semiotics: The Valentinian Notion of the Name," *Temenos* 29 (1993) 141–156. The first to point out the connection with *Gos. Truth* was, I think, R. McL. Wilson, *The Gospel of Philip* (London: A. R. Mowbray, 1962) 76.

[52] Cf. Wilson, *op. cit.* 70.

6. It was noted above how 53.11–12 and 65.1–26 echo one of the few fragments preserved from Valentinus himself. There seem to be other instances of this. Thus 70.26–28, which says that Adam, because of the spirit imparted to him, uttered words superior to the powers, has a fairly close parallel in another fragment.[53] Another idea found in the same fragment, that the gods human beings worship are the creations of their own hands, is paralleled in 72.1–3. Finally, the passage describing how the holy person makes holy even his body and the nourishment he takes (77.2–7) is comparable to the fragment from Valentinus about the incorruptibility of food in the body of Jesus.[54] It is not improbable, as Bentley Layton has suggested,[55] that other quotations from and allusions to the lost writings of Valentinus are contained in *Gos. Phil.*, but, of course, we shall not be able to confirm this.

A final remark here may be added concerning the names Echamoth and Echmoth in 60.10–15. Schenke suggested, in his first work on *Gos. Phil.*, that this refers to the two Sophias known from the system in Irenaeus, where the lower one is named Achamoth.[56] However, the distinction of two Sophias is known only from the tradition of the treatises of Irenaeus, Hippolytus, and *Exc. Theod.* 43.2–65, and, as was suggested above, *Gos. Phil.* belongs to a different strand of Valentinianism than those texts. In fact, in the passage cited, *Gos. Phil.* merely comments on the Aramaic form of a commonly used term, just as it does elsewhere with several other items of theological vocabulary. Thus the distinction between "simply Wisdom" and "the Wisdom of death," or "the little Wisdom," which also does not correspond very well with the way the two Sophias are described in the texts mentioned, is probably better interpreted in terms of *Gos. Phil.*'s general concern with expounding the true and spiritual meaning of certain names, as against their apparent and cosmic significance: The Echamoth who is the Mother, and, when united with the Savior, the holy spirit, is different from the wordly wisdom which only leads to death.

---

[53]Clem. Alex. *Strom.* II.36.2–4 = fr. 1 Völker. Cf. Schenke I, 53n8.

[54]Clem. Alex. *Strom.* III.59.3 = fr. 3 Völker.

[55]Cf. B. Layton, *The Gnostic Scriptures* (Garden City, N.Y. and London: Doubleday, 1987) 325.

[56]Schenke I, 35. In Schenke II, 186, however, this interpretation is mentioned as only one possibility.

## III

Now to return to the question which was raised at the beginning of this paper: Are there any non–Valentinian elements in *Gos. Phil.*? On this point we can only offer a couple of remarks.

One important question in this respect concerns the category of the psychic, on which *Gos. Phil.* is remarkably non-explicit. As was already mentioned, the term "psychic" does not occur in connection either with human beings, or with the cosmic powers. But although the specific terminology is missing, something which is not unparalleled in Valentinian writings,[57] *Gos. Phil.* does presuppose a tripartition of human beings. In the first sections of the tractate (51.29–52.24), it takes the form of a distinction between Gentiles, Hebrews, and Christians,[58] an idea which is also attested elsewhere.[59] Moreover, the following passage makes a distinction between two categories among the ones saved by the Savior:

> The Christ came to ransom (TOOY) some, to save (NOY2M) others, and to redeem (CⲰTE) others. Those who were strangers he ransomed and made his own. And he brought back his own, whom he had laid down as a pledge in accordance with his will. (52.35–53.6)

The distinction between the strangers, whom he ransomed, and "his own" who were saved, seems to correspond to that between the "slaves" and the "children," or "free men" (52.2ff, 69.1–4, 80.29–31.12–14). The "children," who are "his own," refer to the consubstantiality of the Savior and the spirituals, whereas the ones who are strangers, but nevertheless able to be saved, can only be the psychic offspring of Sophia, produced before her vision of the Savior.[60] The "slaves" may in turn be distinguished from the "animals" (80.23–81.14).[61] As we have seen (II.2. above), a lower-level, extra-

---

[57]For instance *Gos. Truth,* or *Val. Exp.* (for the latter in this regard, cf. E. Thomassen, "The Valentinianism of the *Valentinian Exposition* (NHC XI,2), *Le Muséon* 102 (1989), 233–234.

[58]Also cf. 62.5–6.26–32, 75.25–76.6.

[59]*Tri. Trac.* 109.24–113.5; Heracleon, fr. 20 Völker.

[60]For the term "strangers" (ἀνοίκειος, ἀλλότριος) cf. Heracleon, frr. 11, 40 *in fine,* 43 Völker; *Gos. Truth* 31.1–4, *Exc. Theod.* 33.3.

[61]The anthropological tripartition is made rather more complex by the fact that "Hebrews," "captives," and "enslaved" also designate the spirituals in their cosmic existence before the advent of the Saviour. Thus there is a problem in distinguishing between the ones who because of their innate and potential spirituality make the transition from psychic to spiritual existence at the encounter with the Saviour, and the ones who are psychic by nature and must remain so. *Gos. Phil.* does not seem to resolve this ambiguity.

pleromatic salvation is also envisaged for cosmic deity, though not explicitly for a certain class of humans.

One feature is, however, unusual in a Valentinian context: *Gos. Phil.*'s use of the term "the middle":

> Whoever receives all things [...] hither, can [...] that place, but he will [the mid]dle (ⲦⲘⲈⲓϬⲞⲦⲎⲤ) as being imperfect. Only Jesus knows the end of that person. (76.33–77.1)

> And so he dwells either in this world or in the resurrection or in the places in the middle (ϨⲚ̄ Ⲛ̄ⲦⲞⲠⲞⲤ ⲈⲦϨⲚ̄ ⲦⲘⲎⲦⲈ). God forbid that I be found there! In this world there is good and evil. Its good things are not good, and its evil things not evil. But there is evil after this world which is truly evil— what is called "the middle" (ⲦⲘⲈⲤⲞⲦⲎⲤ). It is death. While we are in this world we need to acquire the resurrection, so that when we strip off the flesh we may be found in rest and not walk in the middle. For many go astray on the way. (66.7–21)[62]

"The middle" is clearly a term with highly negative connotations. It refers to a situation after death which is described as utterly evil, and as wandering astray. The wider contexts of both passages describe how the redeemed person leaving the world is clothed in the perfect light of the perfect man, and is unassailable to the powers that have to be passed on the way to the truly good existence of the *anapausis*. Ending up in the "middle" apparently means that the dead person is unable to make the passage, and will remain restlessly at midpoint between this world and the transcendent realm.

In extant Valentinian sources, on the other hand, the term "the middle" is used as a rather neutral term designating the intermediary region between the visible cosmos and the Pleroma, though with two distinct references: (1) the Demiurge/the Hebdomad: Ptolemy, *Ep. Flora,* in Epiphanius, *Pan.* 33.7.4; Heracleon, fr. 40 Völker; Hippolytus, *Ref.* VI.32.7–9; (2) Sophia/the Ogdoad: Irenaeus, *Haer.* I.5.3–4, 7.1; cf. also *Tri. Trac.* 92.26. The treatise of Irenaeus also says that the Demiurge and the righteous psychics will find their repose in the region of Sophia, the middle (I.7.1.5; cf. *Exc. Theod.* 34.2). Evidently *Gos. Phil.* is closer to the first of these two usages: in topological terms it would probably situate "the middle" in the

---

[62] According to Wesley Isenberg, who introduced and translated *Gos. Phil.* for *The Coptic Gnostic Library* series (op. cit. [n. 4], 133), these two passages originally formed a continuous whole. Bentley Layton, however, who is responsible for the critical edition of the Coptic text in the same publication, links the second passage with the preceding text in the manuscript, interpreting the 3. sg. masc. pronoun as referring back to ⲠⲈⲦⲚ̄ⲚⲎⲨ in 65.27. For present purposes we do not need to take sides on this issue.

Hebdomad. But the very negative view of this region as the dreaded place of sojourn for the unredeemed soul, is unparalleled in the Valentinian sources, and invites an explanation. Does it perhaps indicate a polemical stance against catholic Christianity, i.e. a criticism of the sacraments of the Catholics as being inefficient for complete redemption, just as *Gos. Phil.* also criticises the Catholic belief in a post-mortem resurrection of the body (56.26ff, etc.)? Here one might think of a situation where strong confrontation with non-Gnostic Christians has motivated a reinterpretation of the notion of "the middle," which originally seems to have served a more accommodating purpose, into a topic of polemics. There is then still a question, however, how this depreciation of the notion of the middle fits in with the traces of the traditional Valentinian soteriology of the psychics that were noted above. In any case, *Gos. Phil.* contains an anomaly on this point, with regard to the known forms of Valentinianism.

Finally might be mentioned the puzzling remark in 55.29–30: "the Hebrews, who are the apostles and the apostolic men" (ⲚϨⲈⲂⲢⲀⲒⲞⲤ ⲈⲦⲈ ⲚⲀⲠⲞⲤⲦⲞⲀⲞⲤ ⲚⲈ ⲀⲨⲰ [Ⲛ]ⲀⲠⲞⲤⲦⲞⲀⲒⲔⲞⲤ). This apparent depreciation of the "apostles" is not only in conflict with Valentinian usage,[63] but also with the several other passages in *Gos. Phil.* where the apostles are described as transmitters of knowledge and of initiation, for instance 74.16–18: "The Father anointed the Son, the Son anointed the apostles, and the apostles anointed us." It thus would seem that the relative clause in 55.29–30, if not a larger segment of the text, is an interpolation. But who put it there, and for what purpose, remains a mystery.

Apart from its idiosyncratic use of the term "the middle," and this last instance of a likely interpolation, however, *Gos. Phil.* conforms to known patterns of Oriental Valentinian teaching. Although it appears to draw on older materials and traditions, it expresses a reasonably coherent system of thought, which can have represented the shared beliefs of a community, and is hardly adequately described as an unmethodical collection of disparate quotations.

---

[63]Cf. e.g. *Exc. Theod.* 3.2, 25.2, 66, 76.3; *Tri. Trac.* 116.17.

# RITUAL IN THE *GOSPEL OF PHILIP*

*Elaine Pagels*
Princeton University

Even now, fifty years after the discovery of the Nag Hammadi library, certain patristic scholars still use "gnosticism" as shorthand for all that is false, a foil for everything genuine and authentic. Perhaps this should not surprise us; but I confess I was disappointed to see that Peter Cramer's recent book on baptism (Cambridge, 1993) merely repeats the ancient heresiologists' charges and ignores the Nag Hammadi texts along with decades of secondary research. Following the pattern of ancient polemic, Cramer traces the origins of baptismal ritual against what he calls gnostic Christians' "intellectualist and elitist belief."[1] "What is wrong with gnostics," Cramer declares, is that they believe that "the vision of divine reality ... can be translated into the language of objective knowing"[2]; he concludes, predictably, that such intellectualizers have scant use for baptism, and no under-standing of sacraments.

Those of us who work on the Nag Hammadi texts grew up on such sweeping generalizations about gnosticism and sacraments, generali-zations ranging from Bousset's claim that "the gnostic religion is entirely dominated by sacraments,"[3] to Schmithal's insistence that "sacramental piety is alien to gnosticism."[4] After fifty years of Nag Hammadi study we are finally learning (as Michael Williams' recent monograph reminds us)[5] to drop generalizations about whatever it is we thought we meant by the term "gnosticism" and speak instead about specific texts.

As we look again at sacraments in the Gospel of Philip, let us remind ourselves that it also is misleading to generalize about what is "Valentinian." Doing so often has led us to read into whatever text we

---

[1] P. Cramer, *Baptism and Change in the Early Middle Ages* (Cambridge: Cambridge University Press, 1993) 20.

[2] Ibid., 45.

[3] See W. Bousset, "Gnosis," *PW* VII.2,1503-1534, especially 1521.

[4] W. Schmithals, *Die Gnosis in Korinth* (FRLANT 66; Göttingen: Vandenhoeck & Ruprecht, 1965) 233.

[5] M. A. Williams, *Rethinking "Gnosticism": An Argument for Dismantling a Dubious Category* (Princeton, NJ: Princeton University Press, 1996).

are investigating generalizations based on other sources. I suggest, too, that we leave aside certain questions raised by those scholars who pioneered this discussion, including Hans-Martin Schenke[6] and Eric Segelberg,[7] such as how many sacraments Philip presupposes, and what is the function of each. Most scholars today agree that the author of Philip is obviously no Hippolytus; instead of detailed description of ritual acts he interprets them impressionistically.[8] And while the Gospel of Philip no doubt was compiled from various sources, I agree with Schenke that "the whole is governed by a quite specific spirit,"[9] so that we may speak of the author's viewpoint (as we do of, say, the Gospel of Mark, which, of course, also is compiled from various sources).

Much of what we find in Philip, Schenke reminds us, the author shares in common with many of his Christian contemporaries. Like perhaps the majority of other Christians, the author of Philip sees the primary transactions of religious life taking place in the community through ritual means—above all in baptism, chrism, and eucharist. Sacramental transactions occur, Philip says, when one who *is* God's "image" uses water, oil, bread, and wine as "types and images" (85.16), that is, as means of receiving divine reality.

Does Philip have in mind some form of ritual separate from those practiced by the majority of his Christian contemporaries? A well-known passage in Irenaeus' *Adversus Haereses* tells us that certain followers of Valentinus distinguish between water baptism and forms of ritual they call ἀπολύτρωσις, and apparently regard as a kind of second baptism, citing the words of Jesus ("I have another baptism with which to be baptized, and I eagerly hasten toward it," Luke 12:50). Irenaeus tells us that by contriving prayers and rituals that allegedly surpass baptism, such Valentinians deprecate—even, in effect, deny—baptism.[10]

---

[6] H.-M. Schenke, "Das Evangelium nach Philippus. Ein Evangelium der Valentinianer aus dem Funde von Nag-Hammadi," *TLZ* 84 (1959) 1-26.

[7] E. Segelberg, "The Coptic-Gnostic Gospel according to Philip and its Sacramental System," *Numen* 7 (1960) 189-200.

[8] Cf. M. A. Williams, "Realized Eschatology in the Gospel of Philip," *Restoration Quarterly* 3 (1971) 14: Philip "employs sacramental imagery with a great deal of freedom, as though viewing the initiation process as a continuous whole, rather than insisting upon analytically isolating the precise contribution of each sacrament."

[9] See H.-M. Schenke, "Das Evangelium nach Philippus," *Neutestamentliche Apokryphen in deutscher Übersetzung*, ed. W. Schneemelcher, 5th ed., 2 vols. (Tübingen: J. C. B. Mohr [Siebeck], 1987) 1.148–173.

[10] *Libros Quinque Adversus Haereses*, ed. W. W. Harvey (Cambridge: Typis Academicis, 1857) I.21.1-4.

In the past, when scholars routinely used all the texts we had available to interpret any one of them, I shared the view, then widely held, that, in effect, all Valentinians followed such practices.[11] The otherwise unattested eucharistic prayer for union with the angels that Philip attributes to Jesus (58.11-17) might be taken to support the view that Philip, too, knows ritual forms that differ from those shared by most Christians.

Yet closer analysis of Philip indicates, as Michel Desjardins points out, that its author neither denigrates "first baptism" nor indicates any knowledge of a "higher" or even a distinct baptismal ritual.[12] When Philip speaks of baptism, he seems to have in mind no separate ritual, but, so far as we can tell, the kind of rite generally referred to in sources as diverse as the *Didache*, Justin's *Apology*, and Hippolytus' *Apostolic Constitutions*. On the basis of the sparse and varied evidence available we cannot, of course, assume uniform baptismal practice among second and third century Christians. And although we cannot say what precise ritual form Philip may have in mind, he does mention divestiture of clothing (75.20-26), descent into water (64.24; 72.30-73.1; 77.10-15), and immersion as the threefold name ("father, son, and holy spirit") is pronounced over the candidate (67.20-22) apparently followed by chrismation (69.5-14; 67.4-9), and the kiss of peace (59.1-6), and concluded by participation in the eucharist. Nothing in Philip's allusive and poetic references to these ritual elements is incompatible with the ritual that Hippolytus, describing what is probably a conservative form of Roman practice some 70 to 80 years later, relates in detail. (Philip, however, does not mention— but may presuppose—the repeated acts of exorcism that Hippolytus describes as preceding baptism, nor does he mention "laying on of hands.")

Much of Philip's interpretation of the anticipated effects of baptism is commonplace as well. Justin Martyr, for example, repeatedly characterizes baptism as regeneration, citing the third chapter of John's gospel, which promises spiritual rebirth "from water and the

---

[11] E. Pagels, "A Valentinian Interpretation of Heracleon's Understanding of Baptism and Eucharist and Its Critique of 'Orthodox' Sacramental Theology and Practice," *HTR* 65 (1972) 153-69; for a more recent perspective, see J. Jacobsen Buckley, "Conceptual Models and Polemical Issues in the Gospel of Philip," *ANRW* II/25.5, ed. W. Haase and H. Temporini, 4188: "Orthodox, ineffectual baptism is likened to a transaction in which the recipient unwittingly remains in debt." Here Buckley contrasts orthodox baptism, regarded, in her view, as ineffective, with the effective rites Philip advocates.

[12] M. Desjardins, "Baptism in Valentinianism," paper delivered at the Annual Meeting of the SBL, Boston, 1987, especially 18-22.

holy spirit" (John 3:5; 1 Apol. 61). Hippolytus will agree that baptism conveys "regeneration from the holy spirit." Besides rebirth, Philip associates baptism and chrism with resurrection, a well-known theme attributed to Paul (Rom 6:3-11; perhaps also Eph 5:14; Col 3:1). Philip rejects, however, the—equally Pauline—theme that baptism involves ritual death as well as (or prior to) rebirth.[13] But Philip agrees with Justin and Hippolytus on the primary theme—that the holy spirit is expected to descend upon the baptismal candidate and effect regeneration.

What concerns Philip, however, is the awareness that ritual performance of baptism does not always effect these anticipated transactions. Consequently Philip—unlike any of the church fathers from Justin to Tertullian or Hippolytus[14]—raises what is for him an urgent question: How is it that one person, receiving baptism, receives the holy spirit, while another may undergo the same ritual "without receiving anything" (64.24)? Klaus Koschorke observes that Philip does not regard the sacrament as working *ex opere operato*,[15] but I suggest that our understanding of Philip is better served if we refrain from casting his views into language developed in Catholic/Protestant debate over a thousand years later. The doctrine of *ex opere operato* involves distinctions between objective operation of the sacrament and the recipient's subjective state—neither of which concerns this author.

Instead, Philip considers sacramental efficacy in the context of religious convictions he shares with his Christian contemporaries and near contemporaries, including, for example, Justin, Tatian, Tertullian, Athanagoras, and Origen; namely, that baptism engages human beings with spiritual forces hidden from ordinary perception—forces both diabolical and divine.[16] For Philip, as for his fellows, supernatural malevolence has much to do with human alienation from the true God. He agrees with Justin and Athanagoras that invidious spiritual powers, masking as pagan gods, use deceit to snare their prey into pagan worship, since they "do not wish (humanity) to be saved" (55.32-55.7).

---

[13] Cf. Buckley, "Conceptual Models and Polemical Issues," 4191.

[14] According to Lampe's analysis, among patristic writers it is Origen who first raises this question. Origen may, of course, have been prompted by Valentinian Christians.

[15] K. Koschorke, *Die Polemik der Gnostiker gegen das Kirchliche Christentum* (NHS 12; Leiden: E. J. Brill, 1978) 142-143.

[16] See, for example, the incisive discussion by H. Wey, *Die Funktionen der bösen Geister bei den griechischen Apologeten des zweiten Jahrhunderts nach Christus* (Wintermur: Keller, 1957).

But Philip takes this common conspiracy theory one giant step farther. He—and apparently many of his fellow Valentinians—goes far beyond the majority of his fellow Christians: he declares that certain lower spiritual powers not only deceive people by luring them into *pagan* worship, but actually insinuate deceit into *Christian* worship as well, subverting its power. Philip insists that even *Christian worship*, once sabotaged by powers who "want to enslave (humanity) to themselves forever," itself may become means not of deliverance, but of enslavement. Philip warns, then, that baptism, that transformer of spiritual energies, commonly understood to expel evil spirits and charge the initiate with God's spirit, may have its circuits changed, so to speak, by invidious spiritual powers.

How could such sabotage happen? The Valentinian teacher Theodotus had warned that evil spirits "often" steal into the water with baptismal candidates, and receive the baptismal "seal" with them, and so become inseparably bound to their human captives (*Exc. ex Theod.* 83). But Philip attributes not to *demons* but to the *archons* a far more sophisticated form of deception. According to Philip, the archons subvert the sacrament by *stealing the language* that forms an essential element of Christian sacraments and Christian teaching. For, Philip explains, divine truth "brought names into the world for our sake, since it was not possible to show (or: teach) truth without (names)" (54.15-16). By introducing language, truth acted "out of love" for humanity, for whom language would become the indispensable means of learning truth. But those malevolent lower powers who seized upon truth's gift and stole the "names," intended to transform them from a means of disclosing truth into an instrument of deception:

> The archons wanted to deceive humanity, since they saw that he had a kinship with what is truly good; and they took the names of those things that are good and gave them to those that are not good (ⲚⲚⲈⲦⲚⲀⲚⲞⲨ ⲀⲨⲦⲀⲀϥ ⲀⲚⲈⲦⲚⲀⲚⲞⲨⲞⲨ ⲀⲚ, 54.19-31).

> Names given to those (ⲈⲦⲞⲨϯ ⲘⲘⲞⲞⲨ) in the world have a great deception (ⲚⲞⲨⲚⲞϬ ⲘⲠⲖⲀⲚⲎ) for they separate the heart from what is established to what is not established. Thus the one who hears the name "God" does not perceive what is established, but what is not established. So also with the "father" and the "son" and the "holy spirit" and "life" and "light" and "the resurrection" and "the church" and all the other names—people do not perceive the things that are established, but they perceive the things that are not established (53.25-36).

Such sabotage threatens to reverse the effects of baptism. Because the archons have "switched the names," the very terminology of Christian instruction, instead of enlightening catechumens, may deceive them. Instead of releasing the initiate from bondage to lower powers, such baptism may bind the candidate to malevolent archons. Tertullian, speaking for the majority of believers, expresses confidence that baptism "releases us from demons ... and leaves their prince (the devil) drowned in the water."[17] Theodotus sees baptism as offering release from bondage to the astral and planetary powers ("until baptism, the astrologers are right ...").[18] But according to Philip, the archons plan to use the very media of redemption in order to "take the free man and enslave him to themselves forever" (54.29-31).

Philip, following Johannine and Pauline theology, as we noted, often characterizes the effects of baptism as *rebirth* and *resurrection*. But, he warns, the archons attempting to subvert the effects of the sacrament also have deceived many—perhaps a majority—of baptized Christian into "error" concerning Christ's divine birth and his resurrection. For Philip, these are anything but theoretical issues; they involve much more than theological speculation. Instead they constitute the central story—the myth, so to speak,—underlying sacramental action. "Myth is the mother of ritual,"[19] Gerschom Scholem once said, and Philip wholeheartedly would have agreed. For Philip, how one understands Jesus' birth and his resurrection are *practical* matters, religiously speaking; they interpret what happens to the initiate in baptism.

Let us take a moment to see how this works. First, Philip declares, "some say that Mary conceived through the holy spirit; they are in error" (55.24-25). Philip castigates those who believe that Jesus' birth was an event that derived its significance from its uniqueness, a miraculous event in which a woman conceived by parthenogenesis. Philip insists instead that Jesus, while born as we are from earthly parents, was born *spiritually* from the holy spirit and from the Father in heaven. In this μυστήριον, "the Father of all united with the virgin who descended," that is, with the spirit (71.5-6), generating Christ's "body" (71.9-10), that is, the church. Thus the paradigm was established, so that we, too, following Christ, likewise are sacramentally "born again through the image" (67.12-15; 71.19-20). Although we, like Jesus, were born first of human parents, Philip says, "we are

---

[17] Tertullian, *De Bapt.* 9.9.

[18] Exc. ex Theod. 78.1-2.

[19] G. Scholem, *On the Kabbalah and Its Symbolism*, (New York: Schocken, 1969) 132-133, quoted in M. Idel, "Rabbinism versus Kabbalism: On G. Scholem's Phenomenology of Judaism," *Modern Judaism* 11 (1991) 284.

indeed reborn through the holy spirit" (69.5), as the Gospel of John confirms (cf. 3:5), so that, "when we became Christians we had both father and mother" (52.24-25)—both holy spirit and heavenly father.

Philip declares that "the apostles and the apostolic ones" err in remaining oblivious of—or offended by—the holy spirit's actions. Such people apparently interpret Jesus' birth and resurrection as if they happened only to *him* and not to *ourselves* as well. Philip indicates that his perspective differs from that of many other Christians, who regard Jesus' divine birth as a unique, revelatory historical event—instead of an event that becomes, as it has for Philip, a sacramental paradigm.

When Philip turns to the second dispute—the dispute over resurrection—again he takes for granted a direct analogy between Christ's experience and that of the initiate. "Those who say the Lord died first and [then] rose up err; for he first arose and then died." Philip makes the analogy explicit: "If one does not first attain the resurrection, he will not die" (56.15-19). Taking up the topic later, he adds that:

> Those who say they will die first and then rise err. If they do not first receive the resurrection while they live, when they die they shall receive nothing. So also, speaking about baptism, they say, "Baptism is a great thing, because if people receive it they shall live" (73.1-7).

As others have noted, Philip takes issue with Christians who take Paul's words to mean that in baptism we undergo ritual death[20] (cf. Rom 6:3-4: "Do you not know that all of us who have been baptized into Christ Jesus were baptized into his death? Therefore we have been buried with him by baptism into death ..."). Philip declares that, on the contrary, "when we go down into the water [of baptism] we do not go down into death" but are reborn. Then, through chrism, (apparently the anointing that completes the baptismal ritual) we receive resurrection. Here again, Christ's paradigm is fulfilled in the initiate: "for the Father anointed the son, and the son anointed the apostles, and the apostles anointed us" (74.17-18). Saying 67 seems to indicate that baptism, chrism and eucharist (which may also be characterized as bridechamber) convey, respectively, rebirth, resurrection, and reunion, or "entrance into the truth which is the restoration." What matters to Philip is less to delineate the action of each sacrament than to show that the initiate first reenacts Jesus' divine birth, then his resurrection, and, finally, his reunion with his *syzygos*.

---

[20] Cf. Buckley, "Conceptual Models and Polemical Issues in the Gospel of Philip" 4186-4190.

(Philip's allusive style does not allow us to specify precisely the action of each ritual element; as indicated above, I agree with Williams, Sevrin, and others who see all of these as elements of the complete initiation.)

Philip's theology does involve identification mysticism, as Ménard says; but not, as Ménard suggests, identification "de l'ame à son moi"[21]—that is, identification between the soul and some sort of 'given,' essentially divine self. (On this basis, Ménard concludes that this gospel, for all its "Semitic" overlay, essentially consists of a confluence of Neoplatonist and Stoic elements.[22]) Philip clearly regards his teaching as Pauline sacramental theology, which centers on the identification between the initiate and Christ—an identification evinced in Philip's characterization of Christ as ⲡⲧⲉⲗⲓⲟⲥ ⲣ̄ⲣⲱⲙⲉ (55.14), and of the initiate, conversely, as having the potential to become, through sacramental transformation, a Christ (ⲟⲩⲭ̄ⲣ̄ⲥ̄, 67.27).

Philip's sacramental theology shares much in common, then, with the majority of his Christian contemporaries; as we noted, sacramental transactions occur, Philip says, when one who *is* God's "image" uses water, oil, bread, and wine as "types and images," that is, as means of receiving divine reality. Far from rejecting visible sacraments, Philip, as we have seen, regards them as the indispensable means of receiving reality. Philip does acknowledge that types and images share in some of the same ambivalence as does language: both involve a hidden element as well as a manifest one (cf. 57.25-29). So, Philip explains, the "cup of prayer containing wine and water is a type of the blood which is eucharized (ⲉⲧⲟⲩⲣ̄ⲉⲩⲭⲁⲣⲓⲥⲧⲉⲓ); and it is full of the holy spirit" (ϥⲙⲟⲩ⳿ ⲉⲃⲟⲗ ⳿ⲙ ⲡ̄ⲡⲛ̄ⲁ̄ ⲉⲧⲟⲩⲁⲁⲃ). This similarity has led Karl Koschorke (and Bernard Barc, following him) to argue that types and images share in the same provisional, ambivalent relationship to divine reality as does language.[23] Conse-

---

[21] Ménard, *L'Évangile selon Philippe. Introduction, texte, traduction, commentaire* (Paris: Letouzy & Ané, 1967) 12 ff.

[22] Ménard, *L'Évangile selon Philippe*, 35: "Ces divers rapprochements nous amè amèneront aussi à conclure que, malgré toutes les influences sémitiques qu'il a pu subir, *L'Évangile selon Philippe* demeure ou ouvrage de gnose de type hellénistique. Il se situe au confluent des deux grandes philosophies greques, le néo-platonisme et le stoïcisme."

[23] The otherwise excellent article by Klaus Koschorke suggests this: see "Die 'Namen' im Philippusevangelium. Beobachtungen zur Auseinandersetzung zwischen gnostischen und kirchlichen Christentum," *ZNW* 64 (1973) 307-322; B. Barc, "Les Noms de la Triade dans L'Évangile selon Philippe," *Gnosticisme et Monde Hellénistique*, ed. J. Ries (Louvain-la-neuve: Université catholique de Louvain, Institut orientaliste, 1982) esp. 361-363.

quently, where Philip characterizes the sacramental elements as
ЄYϢHC, Koschorke translates the term as 'wertlos,' thus characterizing types and images as 'worthless.'[24] But Schenke has given us here
a more accurate translation of ЄYϢHC:[25] not 'wertlos,' but
'verachtate,' that is, 'despised,' a term which Philip immediately
qualifies as "despised, as compared with the perfect glory." Sevrin
observes from the context that Philip characterizes "types and
images" as simultaneously *precious* and despised, *strong* and *weak*,
depending upon whether one sees them in relation to the divine truth
itself, or to this world. But the whole passage demonstrates, as Sevrin
notes, the enormous grace such images convey: "It is thanks to the
contemptible types and the weak things that we enter ... into the secret
of the truth."[26]

For while Philip's discussion of *names* is equivocal and ambivalent, when he discusses "types and images"—the sacramental elements[27]—he does not equivocate. While "names" are necessary to
teach truth, Philip notes that, when implicated in deception, they may
also teach error. But "types and images" do much more than *words*;
they do more than *teach*; instead they—and they alone, Philip says,—
*convey* divine reality. We recall the famous passage: "truth did not
come into the world naked, but it came in types and images; *the world
will not receive truth in any other way*." The passage continues:

> There is rebirth and an image of rebirth. It is necessary, truly, that we be
> reborn through the image. What is the resurrection and the image? Through
> the image, one must rise up. The bridal chamber and the image? Through the
> image, one must enter into the truth, which is the restoration.[28]

Unlike words, then, which only *teach about* or *symbolize* divine
reality,[29] the sacramental elements *convey* it. (Philip, one gathers, is
not a low church Protestant!) Philip uses the action verb ЄIPЄ (Greek

---

[24] "Die 'Namen,'" 312.

[25] H.-M. Schenke, "Das Evangelium nach Philippus," *TLZ* 84.1 (1959); Wesley W.
Isenberg translates ЄYϢHC as "lowly," *Nag Hammadi Codex II.2-7*, ed. B. Layton
(Leiden: E. J. Brill, 1989) 211.

[26] J.-M. Sevrin, "Les Noces Spirituelles dans L'Évangile selon Philippe," *Le Muséon*
87 (1974) 179.

[27] While Sevrin regards the terms as synonymous ("Les Noces," 143-193), Barc wants
*typos* to refer to the elements, and *eikones* to the spiritual realities *within* the elements
("Les Noms de la Triade" 361-363.

[28] In this passage, notoriously difficult to translate, I follow Sevrin's reading; for his
rationale, see "Les Noces" 172f.

[29] As Janssens puts it, in "L'Évangile selon Philippe," *Le Muséon* 81 (1988).

ποεῖν) to characterize their efficacy: "The Lord *did* everything in a mystery: baptism, chrism, eucharist, redemption, and bridechamber" (67.29-30). Philip repeatedly says that one who participates in sacraments "receives" divine reality: "When we drink [the eucharistic 'cup of prayer'] *we shall receive* for ourselves the wholly perfect man" (75.15-20, see note for other references).[30] The author takes for granted that baptism, chrism, and eucharist effect transformation ("from water and fire the soul and the spirit came into being; from water and fire the son of the bridal chamber came into being") (67.4-6). In fact, as we have seen, it is precisely this conviction about the efficacy of the sacraments that raises for Philip that question so central to his concern—how it happens that some people participating in these sacraments, nevertheless "receive nothing"—or, at best, a name to which they cannot truly lay claim. For those who receive only the "names" (Father, Son, Holy Spirit) without receiving the divine realities they signify will find out that the name they received in baptism ("Christian") will be taken away from them as well (67.20-21).

Is Philip saying, then, what several distinguished commentators generally have taken him to mean—that Christian sacraments which effectively transform and redeem some recipients remain only empty vessels—or, worse, deceit—for the rest? Noting the contrast Philip draws between those who already have "received truth in the images" and those who hold the name "Christian" only provisionally, such commentators as Jacques Ménard have assumed that this contrast spells out essential and permanent division between the pneumatic elect and psychic believers.[31] Yet Philip's concern is not so much—and certainly not only—with the spiritual elite as he is with those whom David Tripp calls the "weaker brethren,"[32] those who call themselves Christians, but are unwittingly implicated in error. For Philip does not see the irreconcilable distinction between psychic and pneumatic Christians that many commentators have inferred from the

---

[30] 57.9; 59.5-6; 64.24-31; 67.10; 73.2-6, 17-19; 74.22; 86.6-10.

[31] See, for example, Ménard, *L'Évangile selon Philippe*, 20-25, 230-46. All of these commentators, pioneers in the study of the Gospel of Philip, ventured into this difficult text in the traditional way, as we all learned to do, by assembling all possible clues from every text that might have relevance, from the polemics of the heresiologists to the *Apocryphon of John* or *Pistis Sophia*. In doing so, they seem to have adopted the conviction basic to the heresiologists' accounts—that Valentinian Christians concern themselves above all with the spiritual destiny of the elect, while expressing either indifference or contempt for that of ordinary believers (cf. Irenaeus, *Adv. Haer.* I.6.1-5).

[32] D. H. Tripp, "The 'Sacramental System' of the Gospel of Philip," *Studia Patristica* 17, part 1, ed. E. A. Livingstone (Oxford: Pergamon Press, 1982) 251-267.

heresiologists' accounts (and, all too often, have read into such works as the Gospel of Philip). Instead, as Michel Desjardins notes, Philip invokes the distinction he finds in Paul's letters (cf. 1 Cor 2:14-15) between Christians whom Paul calls "psychics" and those he calls "pneumatics." And Philip, like Paul, expresses concern, not contempt, for those who, although baptized, have not yet attained *gnosis*, who have not yet received "the truth in the images"[33] (86.14).

When Philip considers the future prospects of such "weaker brethren," he expresses great hope. For although he has told how malevolent archons conspired "to take the free man and enslave him to themselves forever," Philip never says their plan *succeeded*—at least not for long. On the contrary, the archons soon found their plans foiled. Immediately after describing how the archons conspired to deceive humankind by switching the names, Philip goes on to say that:

> *Afterward*, what a favor (OYϨMOT for χάρις, literally, what *grace*) they do for them! They make [the names] be removed from the things that are not good, and place them among the good (54.25-29).[34]

While the latter sentence is simple enough to translate, Robert McL. Wilson acknowledges that he has difficulty accepting what it says: "It is difficult to think of the archons causing men to remove what is not good to the good (in the 'true' sense)."[35] Ménard, confronted with the same difficulty, concludes that the archons set the names not on what is *truly* good, but only what is "good" in a *worldly* sense.[36] Both Wilson and Ménard rightly feel that it is out of character for the archons, who "wanted to make [the free man] a slave to themselves forever" now to reverse the effects of their malevolence.

Philip explains, however, that the archons do this not, as they imagine, on their own volition, but only as the holy spirit uses them as her unwitting agents:

> The archons thought it was by their own power and will that they were doing what they did, but the holy spirit secretly was accomplishing everything through them as it wished.

---

[33] Desjardins, "Baptism in Valentinianism," 1, 25-6, 34.

[34] Note that the verb tenses change in midsentence, suggesting that the archons' *past* deception is being undone in the *present*, with *future* consequences.

[35] R. McL. Wilson, *The Gospel of Philip* (London: Mowbray & Co., 1962) 77.

[36] Ménard, *L'Évangile selon Philippe*, 133.

So, Philip says, the spirit "shepherds everyone and rules every power, both tame and wild" (60.30-31).[37] At present, Philip continues, evil prevails, even among "the seed of the holy spirit," some of whom remain, he says, "the slaves of evil." His characterization may find a parallel in Theodotus' account of Valentinian Christians who say that "the finest emanation of Sophia"—her seed, apparently—consist both of those who are "called" as well as those who are "chosen" (cf. Matt 22:14; *Exc. ex Theod.* 21.1). While Philip does not makes this same distinction, he does, throughout the body of his work, characterize some Christians as free, and others as slaves. But Philip concludes his gospel with a vision of the time of consummation, when finally "the perfect light will pour out upon everyone; and all those who are in it will receive (the chrism); then the slaves will be free and the captives delivered" (85.25-30).

Philip offers, then, a view of the Christian community presently divided between those who have gnosis, and those entangled in erroneous beliefs, who remain, unwittingly—but only temporarily—subject to the archons. Philip envisions their final inclusion with the "free" in the deliverance Christ offers. But to participate in the eschatological consummation requires that they have participated in the church's sacraments; for no one, Philip warns, will receive (the perfect light) in the consummation who has not already received it here in "types and images" (86.6-7), that is, apparently, in baptismal ritual.

Philip offers, then, a rare glimpse of the Christian community as this Valentinian Christian perceives it—a community divided between the few who have *gnosis*, and the many who remain caught in what he regards as erroneous beliefs concerning Christ's birth and resurrection (beliefs that seem to echo what Bultmannian church historians call "the kerygma"). Philip offers, too, a glimpse of Christian baptismal theology as we have rarely seen it—a baptismal theology based upon both the Johannine view of baptism as rebirth and the Pauline view of baptism as resurrection.

---

[37] Earlier Philip had explained that when Christ came into the world, he found the soul "subject to the robbers, and taken captive. But he saved it—those who were good in the world, *and the evil*" (53.11-13). This last phrase, which also has baffled commentators, makes sense only when we see that the holy spirit's power ultimately prevails over that of the archons to offer deliverance to those who are still slaves. Their ultimate deliverance is neither automatic nor universal; but, Philip declares, "The one who is enslaved *against his will* will be able to become free" (79.15).

PART FOUR

THE *GOSPEL OF THOMAS*

# THE WRITINGS ASCRIBED TO THOMAS AND THE
# THOMAS TRADITION *

*Paul-Hubert Poirier*
Université Laval, Québec

The history of the apocryphal traditions regarding the apostle Thomas is rather singular.[1] These traditions apparently owe nothing to the evangelical scene of which Thomas is the central figure, and which has contributed most to fashion his image in Christian memory, that is his doubt about Christ's resurrection and his ensuing encounter with the risen Jesus (John 20:24-29). On the contrary, it is a three-word comment in the *Gospel of John* on the name of Thomas which seems to be the genesis of the rich Thomasian literary tradition. This comment "Θωμᾶς ὁ λεγόμενος δίδυμος—Thomas called the twin", occurs three times in John in an identical manner, viz. in 11:16; 20:24, and 21:2. Formally speaking, this explanation of Thomas's name is a typical double name, even if, according to G. H. R. Horsley,[2] the phrase "*A ho legomenos B* = A spoken of [as] B" is not common as a double name formula.[3]

The most usual interpretation[4] of the Johannine gloss "ὁ λεγόμενος δίδυμος—called the twin" understands it as the Greek translation of the Aramaic word meaning "twin" (*tā'mā'*, תאמא, ܬܐܡܐ), of which John would have given a Greek transcription under the form Θωμᾶς, *Thomas*. Whatever may be the value of this

---

* I wish to thank Ann Henderson, M.A., for her careful revision of my English.

[1] On these traditions, see R. Kuntzmann, *Le symbolisme des jumeaux au Proche-Orient ancien. Naissance, fonction et évolution d'un symbole* (Beauchesne, Religions 12; Paris: Beauchesne, 1983) 164-182 and S. Mimouni, "1. Thomas (apôtre)," in *Dictionnaire de spiritualité*, tome XV (Paris: Beauchesne, 1991) 708-718.

[2] *New Documents Illustrating Early Christianity. A Review of the Greek Inscriptions and Papyri Published in 1976* (North Ride N. S. W. [Australia]: The Ancient History Documentary Research Centre, Macquarie University, 1981) 89-96 (§ 55), and "Names, Double," *The Anchor Bible Dictionary*, vol. 4, ed. D. N. Freedman (New York: Doubleday, 1992) 1011-1017.

[3] "Names, Double," p. 1013.

[4] Cf. *En quête de la Gnose. II. Sur l'Évangile selon Thomas. Esquisse d'une interprétation systématique* (Paris: Gallimard, 1978) 213-214, and B. Layton, *The Gnostic Scriptures* (Garden City, N. Y.: Doubleday, 1987) 359. See also U. Monneret de Villard, *Le leggende orientali sui magi evangelici* (Studi e testi 163; Città del Vaticano: Biblioteca Apostolica Vaticana, 1952) 46, n. 1.

296

explanation, it is clear that the Johannine double name is one of the main sources of the Thomasian apocryphal traditions, all of which portray Thomas as Christ's double, or twin, and, consequently, as Christ's privileged spokesperson.

Although the problems related to Thomas's name deserve a fresh examination, this is not the place to conduct it. The purpose of this paper is much more limited, and will be confined to the three main representatives of the Thomas literary tradition and their relationship. It has been agreed that these three works, the *Gospel According to Thomas* (hereafter *Gos. Thom.*),[5] the *Book of Thomas* (*Book Thom.*),[6] and the *Acts of Thomas* (*Acts Thom.*),[7] could be placed along a trajectory which would reflect the linear and consistent growth of the Thomas tradition. It has also been proposed that these writings are close enough to one another to be considered as the products of the same "School of St. Thomas." But when one considers the use each of these works makes of the name of Thomas and the emphasis they place on the apostle's twinship with Jesus, one is led to question the homogeneity of the tradition these works have been ascribed to.

## I. A SURVEY OF THE HISTORY OF RESEARCH

The first scholar to have posited that a relationship could be established between the *Gos. Thom.* and the *Acts Thom.* was Henri-Charles

---

[5] Edition of the Coptic version (Nag Hammadi Codex II,2) by B. Layton and English translation by T. O. Lambdin in *Nag Hammadi Codex II, 2-7 together with XIII, 2*, Brit. Lib. Or.4926(1), and P.Oxy. 1, 654, 655*, vol. 1, ed. B. Layton (NHS 20; Leiden: E. J. Brill, 1989) 50-93; edition and English translation of the Greek fragments by H. W. Attridge, ibid., 95-128.

[6] Edition of the Coptic version (NHC II,7) by B. Layton and English translation by J. D. Turner in *Nag Hammadi Codex II, 2-7 together with XIII, 2*, Brit. Lib. Or.4926(1), and P.Oxy. 1, 654, 655*, vol. 2, ed. B. Layton (NHS 21; Leiden: E. J. Brill, 1989) 179-205. The usual title for this tractate (The Book of Thomas the Contender) is a mistranslation and should be avoided; see H.-M. Schenke, *Das Thomas-Buch (Nag-Hammadi-Codex II,7)* (TU 138; Berlin: Akademie-Verlag, 1989) 193-194.

[7] Edition of the Syriac version and English translation by W. Wright, *Apocryphal Acts of the Apostles. Edited from Syriac Manuscripts in the British Museum and others Libraries with English Translations and Notes* (London and Edinburgh: Williams & Norgate, 1871; reprint Amsterdam: Philo Press, 1968); edition of the Greek Version by M. Bonnet in R. A. Lipsius and M. Bonnet, *Acta Apostolorum Apocrypha* (Leipzig: Hermann Mendelssohn, 1903; reprint Darmstadt: Wissenschaftliche Buchgesellschaft, 1959) 2:99-288; English translation of the Greek version by G. Bornkamm, "Acts of Thomas," *New Testament Apocrypha*, vol. 2, *Writings relating to the Apostles, Apocalypses and Related Subjects*, ed. E. Hennecke and W. Schneemelcher, English trans. ed. R. McL Wilson (London: SCM Press Ltd, 1965) 442-531.

Puech in the late 1950s.[8] He expressed this view on the basis of the occurrence, in both works, of the name Judas Thomas, or Thomas Didymus, and on certain features common to the *Gos. Thom.* and the *Acts Thom.* Relying on these elements, Puech concluded that the *Gos. Thom.* must have been composed prior to the *Acts Thom.*, and that the *Acts Thom.* were dependent upon the *Gos Thom.* As for the *Book Thom.*, Puech was not able at that time to submit it to a careful examination. Nevertheless, he established a connection between the *Book Thom.*, 138.1-21, and the *Gos. Thom.*, saying 13,[9] as propounding a similar interpretation of the intimacy between Jesus and Thomas, Thomas being truly Jesus' brother and companion because, through Jesus, he has come to know the truth.[10]

Under the title "A New Link in the Syrian Judas Thomas Tradition,"[11] John D. Turner proposed, first in 1972 and more fully in 1975, a new hypothesis in order to elucidate the situation of the *Book Thom.* in the Thomas literary tradition. According to Turner, the *Book Thom.* is "the sum of two originally separate works," designated by him as "section A" and "section B":

> One work, section A, was a dialogue between Thomas and the Savior, perhaps entitled "The Book of Thomas the Contender writing to the Perfect." The other work, section B, was a collection of the Savior's sayings gathered into a homiletical discourse (introductory apocalypse, woes, blessings, final admonition), perhaps entitled "The Hidden Words which the Savior spoke, which I wrote down, even I, Mathaias." A redactor has prefixed section A to

---

[8] See *En quête de la Gnose*, II.75-76 (originally published in 1957-1958), and "Gnostic Gospels and Related Documents" (originally published in German in 1959), in *New Testament Apocrypha*, vol. 1, *Gospels and Related Writings*, ed. E. Hennecke and W. Schneemelcher, English trans. ed. R. McL Wilson (London: SCM Press Ltd, 1963) 286-287.

[9] Here is T. O. Lambdin's translation of saying 13: "Jesus said to his disciples, 'Compare me to someone and tell me whom I am like.' Simon Peter said to him, 'You are like a righteous angel.' Matthew said to him, 'You are like a wise philosopher.' Thomas said to him. 'Master, my mouth is wholly incapable of saying whom you are like.' Jesus said. 'I am not your master. Because you have drunk, you have become intoxicated from the bubbling spring which I have measured out.' And he took him and withdrew and told him three things. When Thomas returned to his companions, they asked him, 'What did Jesus say to you?' Thomas said to them, 'If I tell you one of the things which he told me, you will pick up stones and throw them at me; a fire will come out of the stones and burn you up.'"

[10] *En quête de la Gnose* II.237 (originally published in 1970-1971).

[11] In *Essays on the Nag Hammadi Texts in Honour of Alexander Böhlig*, ed. M. Krause (NHS 3; Leiden: E. J. Brill, 1972) 109-119. Turner has developed his hypothesis in *The Book of Thomas the Contender from Codex II of the Cairo Gnostic Library from Nag Hammadi (CG II, 7). The Coptic Text with Translation, Introduction and Commentary* (SBLDS 23; Missoula, Montana: Scholars Press) 1975.

section B, and prefaced the whole with an *incipit* title composed on analogy with the original title to section B, and designating Mathaias as the scribe of the whole. The subscript title, designating Thomas as the scribe of the whole was borrowed from the original title to section A, and suffixed to the newly-formed whole.[12]

According to Turner's hypothesis on the literary composition of the *Book Thom.*, its first section alone is to be ascribed to the Thomas tradition, in which it occupies "a median position" between the *Gos. Thom.* and the *Acts Thom.*, and this, from a triple point of view, "in (1) date of composition, (2) relative dominance of the role played by Thomas in these works, and (3) in terms of the development from a *sayings collection* preserved by Thomas (*Gospel of Thomas*) to an actual dialogue between Jesus and Thomas (*The Book of Thomas the Contender*) to a full-blown romance centered on the missionary exploits of Thomas (*Acts of Thomas*)."[13] To these considerations, Turner adds that the theme of sexual asceticism becomes increasingly more pronounced from the *Gos. Thom.* through the *Book Thom.* to the *Acts Thom.* On the basis of these observations, Turner concludes that "these three works, then, reflect a growing tradition centered on the Apostle Thomas, twin of Jesus and recipient of his secret words, and which increasingly understands him as a contender and missionary for the cause of abstinence from all that is wordly, especially sex."[14] Therefore, if the *Book Thom.* must be situated between the *Gos. Thom.* and the *Acts Thom.* in the growth of the Thomas tradition, the composition of section A of the *Book Thom.* could be placed at *ca.* 200 AD, shortly before the *Acts Thom.* [15]

In his well known anthology of gnostic literature,[16] Bentley Layton has brought together, as pertaining to one and the same "School of St. Thomas," three texts, viz. the *Hymn of the Pearl* incorporated in the *Acts Thom.* (chap. 108-113), the *Gos. Thom.*, and the *Book Thom.* According to Layton, these writings share two characteristics calling for their inclusion in a common doctrinal trend. The first of these characteristics is the model of divine twinship, which, in the Thomas

[12] *The Book of Thomas the Contender*, 215.

[13] "Thomas the Contender, Book of," in *The Anchor Bible Dictionary*, vol. 6, ed. D. N. Freedman (New York: Doubleday, 1992) 529.

[14] "A New Link in the Syrian Judas Thomas Tradition," 118.

[15] Ibid. See also "Thomas the Contender, Book of," 529: "The Book of Thomas the Contender (...) was likely composed in the first half of the 3d century A.D. Two products of this tradition have been dated with fair certainty: the *Gospel of Thomas*, composed ca. A.D. 50-125, and the *Acts of Thomas*, composed ca. A.D. 225."

[16] *The Gnostic Scriptures* (Garden City, N. Y.: Doubleday, 1987) 357-409.

tradition, "far from being only a romantic exaggeration" based on the name "Thomas the twin," is "a profound theological model for the reciprocal relationship of the individual Christian and the inner divine light or 'living Jesus': to know oneself was to know one's divine double and thence to know god; to follow the living Jesus was to know and integrate one's self."[17] The second element is a myth of origins, best exemplified in the *Hymn of the Pearl*, but also apparent in the *Book Thom.* and the *Gos. Thom.* According to this myth, the individual true self, sent from the Kingdom of light, "now resides within a realm, or state, of 'sleep, darkness, and death',"[18] of which it is delivered by the will of the Father and the intervention of a savior, who teaches it to recognize itself and distinguish between light and darkness. Although Layton acknowledges that "the order in which the three works ... were composed" is a "crucial factor" in his reconstruction of a Thomas School,[19] he doesn't propose a definite hypothesis as to their sequence. Nevertheless, he seems to give chronological priority to the *Hymn of the Pearl*, whether or not it was composed in Edessa. In the first case, the *Hymn* "could have provided the model, even if it were a non-Christian one, on which the Thomas tradition was based." In the second, it "would have been imported to Edessa and secondarily adopted by the School of St. Thomas to its own purposes."[20]

The most recent contribution to the history of the Thomas tradition has been offered by Gregory J. Riley in a paper presented in 1991 and in a book published in early 1995.[21] In both of them, Riley advocates the existence of a Thomas community "which looked to this apostle for inspiration and spiritual legitimacy and created the Thomas tradition originated in the period prior to the writing of the canonical Gospels." The same Thomas community "produced the Gospel of Thomas and the Book of Thomas (the Contender), and evoked from the community of the Beloved Disciple the Doubting Thomas pericope in John 20."[22] Whereas the *Gos. Thom.* and the *Book Thom.*

---

[17] Ibid., 359.

[18] Ibid., 360.

[19] Ibid., 369.

[20] Ibid.

[21] "Thomas Tradition and the Acts of Thomas," *Society of Biblical Literature 1991 Seminar Papers, One Hundred Twenty-Seventh Annual Meeting. November 23-26, 1991, Kansas City, Missouri*, ed. E. H. Lovering (SBLSP 30; Atlanta: Scholars Press, 1991) 533-542, and *Resurrection Reconsidered. Thomas and John in Controversy* (Minneapolis: Fortress, 1995).

[22] "Thomas Tradition and the Acts of Thomas," 533.

both agree in rejecting the body, denying physical resurrection, and emphasizing knowledge (*gnôsis*) and enlightenment instead of faith, the *Gospel of John*, on the other hand, would, on each of these points, correct the image of the apostle put forward by the Thomas community: "Thomas touches the physical resurrected body of Jesus (thus confirming resurrection of the flesh), 'believes,' and submits to Jesus as Lord and God."[23] As for the *Acts Thom.*, they are in deliberate continuity with this tradition, of which they keep the essential components: the name Thomas, the theme of the twinship of the apostle with Jesus, and the polemic against the body and its dangers. At the same time, the *Acts Thom.* bespeak the influence of the canonical figure of Thomas: the apostle addresses Jesus as his Lord and God, and calls him his master. As Riley says, "the author of the Acts shows that Thomas has learned his Johannine lesson."[24] Therefore, the *Acts Thom.* are "in the midst of the battle," halfway between "the *kerygma* of the flesh" proclaimed by the Church, and the spiritual tradition represented by the *Gos. Thom.* and the *Book Thom.*[25]

## II. THE LITERARY WITNESSES OF THE THOMAS TRADITION

After this brief survey of the research devoted to the Thomas tradition, let us consider its three chief literary representatives, and ask the following questions: How and to what extent do they appeal to the twin motif associated with the name of Thomas and its traditional etymological rendering, and what kind of relationship does exist between these writings?

### 1. The Gospel According to Thomas

Despite the lack of consensus concerning the date of the *Gos. Thom.*, it appears that this writing is, besides or shortly after John, the earliest product of the Thomasian literature.[26] That the *Gos. Thom.* belongs to this "corpus" may be established, on the one hand, by the occurrence of the name of the apostle in the prologue, saying 13, and the final title, and, on the other hand, by the fact that some of its sayings have been taken up by a highly Thomasian text, the *Acts Thom.* However, when the occurrences of the name of Thomas in the

---

[23] Ibid.

[24] Ibid., 536.

[25] *Resurrection Reconsidered*, 68.

[26] See F. T. Fallon and R. Cameron, "The Gospel of Thomas: A Forschungsbericht and Analysis," *ANRW*, Teil II: *Principat*, Band 25.6, ed. W. Haase and H. Temporini (Berlin: W. de Gruyter, 1988) 4224-4226.

*Gos. Thom.* are closely scrutinized, they reveal a paradoxical situation for a document of such antiquity. These occurrences: five in the Cairo manuscript (Nag Hammadi Codex II) and one in the Oxyrhynchus papyrus, can be divided as follows:

— Prologue:
  1. NHC II 32.12-13 ⲆⲓⲆⲨⲙⲟⲥ ⲓ̈ⲟⲨⲆⲁⲥ ⲑⲱⲙⲁⲥ
  2. P. Oxy. 654.2-3 Ἰούδα ὁ ] καὶ Θωμᾶ
— Saying 13:
  3. NHC II 35.2      ⲑⲱⲙⲁⲥ
  4. NHC II 35.8-9    ⲑⲱⲙⲁⲥ
  5. NHC II 35.11     ⲑⲱⲙⲁⲥ
— Final title:
  6. NHC II 51.28     ⲑⲱⲙⲁⲥ.

Of these occurrences, only the first two belong to the form typical of the Thomas tradition, that is the designation of the apostle by the name Ἰούδας Θωμᾶς or ܬܐܘܡܐ ܝܗܘܕܐ. Strictly speaking, only the second comes under this tradition. Indeed, the form offered by the prologue, in the Cairo manuscript, is a hybrid, a kind of *lectio conflata*, reflecting at the same time the early Syrian tradition (ⲓ̈ⲟⲨⲆⲁⲥ ⲑⲱⲙⲁⲥ) and the Johannine formulation (Θωμᾶς ὁ λεγόμενος δίδυμος), but in a sequence (ⲆⲓⲆⲨⲙⲟⲥ ⲓ̈ⲟⲨⲆⲁⲥ ⲑⲱⲙⲁⲥ instead of ⲓ̈ⲟⲨⲆⲁⲥ ⲑⲱⲙⲁⲥ ⲆⲓⲆⲨⲙⲟⲥ) which is both an hapax and an aberration. Inasmuch as it places the nickname first, the Coptic *Gos. Thom.* seems to have no longer known the precise meaning and function of δίδυμος. In any case, it can't be maintained that the name Didymus Judas Thomas is "a phenomenon characteristic of and restricted to early Syriac literature."[27] On the other hand, if the Oxyrhynchus Papyrus witnesses the Syrian wording of the apostle's name, it renders it in a form usual in Greek double names (Ἰούδα ὁ καὶ Θωμᾶ).[28]

Therefore, only the Greek version of the *Gos Thom.* can clearly be ascribed to the early Syrian tradition, while the Coptic version attests to a mixed and secondary tradition. As to the twin motif, so characteristic of the Thomas tradition, it doesn't appear as such in the *Gos.*

---

[27] As H. J. W. Drijvers writes in "Facts and Problems in Early Syriac-Speaking Christianity," *SecCen* 2 (1982) 158.

[28] See G. H. R. Horsley, "Names, Double," 1012: "*A ho (hos) kai* (...) is by far the most common formula used to indicate a byname, nothwithstanding that it occurs only once in the NT (Acts 13:9, Saul/Paul)."

*Thom.*, even if saying 13 asserts a unique intimacy between Thomas and Jesus. In any case, the fact that the *Gos. Thom.* introduces the apostle as the privileged recipient of Jesus' secret and living words suffices to establish him as the disciple *par excellence*.

## 2. *The Acts of Thomas*

It is a well known fact that the *Acts Thom.* display a precise knowledge of the *Gos. Thom.*, from which they take many sayings.[29] On the other hand, the *Acts Thom.* developed on the basis of Thomas's name, a full-fledged twin symbolism, which is absent from the *Gos. Thom.* The omnipresence of this symbolism is the main thread of the narrative of the *Acts Thom.* There are many instances of a clear identification of Thomas with Jesus, in chap. 11-12, 31, 39, 54-57. But, more striking than these is the fact that the *Acts Thom.*, as a whole, are built upon a network of subtle analogies drawn between Jesus and his apostle, to the point that Thomas's destiny appears as a mirror image of his Lord and master's fate.[30] Therefore, it is all the more surprising that, at the peak of the narrative, when Thomas delivers a final exhortation before his martyrdom, he overtly repudiates his twinship with Jesus: "I am not Jesus," says Thomas to the women converted by him, "but a servant of Jesus. I am not Christ, but I am a minister of Christ. I am not the Son of God, but I pray to be counted worthy with him" (chap. 160). Rather than an orthodox revision of the identification of Thomas with Christ, Thomas's recantation reveals the true nature of the twinship put forth by the *Acts Thom.*: it has to be conceived of as a spiritual rather than physical twinship.

By their reworking of traditional data borrowed from the *Gos. Thom.*, by the way they develop and systematize the twinship symbolism, and by their recourse to romance, the *Acts Thom.* are ultimately responsible for the production of the Thomas Didymus figure which later apocryphal literature, and Christian tradition in general, were to inherit. In this creative process, the *Acts Thom.* are indebted to a tradition of which the *Gos. Thom.* is the earliest witness, but which ultimately goes back to John, or the tradition echoed by John.

---

[29] See H.-Ch. Puech, "Gnostic Gospels and Related Documents," 286-287.

[30] See R. Kuntzmann, *Le symbolisme des jumeaux au Proche-Orient ancient*, 176, who gives data.

## 3. The Book of Thomas

As we have seen above, John D. Turner proposed situating the *Book Thom.* halfway between the *Gos. Thom.* and the *Acts Thom.* Although Turner brings in valid arguments, this hypothesis seems less convincing when one considers the way the *Book Thom.* exploits the Thomasian theme. The following are those passages of the *Book Thom.* which presuppose the knowledge of specific elements of the literary Thomas tradition:

i.   The *incipit* of the *Book Thom.* (138.1-4: "The secret words that the savior spoke to Judas Thomas which I, even I Mathaias, wrote down, while I was walking, listening to them speak with one another") is obviously a pastiche of the opening lines of the *Gos. Thom.* (32.10-12: "These are the secret words the living Jesus spoke and which Didymus Judas Thomas wrote down.")

ii.  The prologue of the *Book Thom.* (138.4-21) expounds the Thomasian theme with a vocabulary found nowhere else except in the *Acts Thom.*: brother (chap. 11-12); twin (31, 39); friend or companion (56). Furthermore, it appears that the *Book Thom.* uses this theme in a secondary manner, to accredit the dialogue it claims to report: "Brother Thomas, while you have time in the world, listen to me, and I will reveal to you the things you have pondered in your mind. Now *since it has been said* that you are my twin and true companion, examine yourself and learn who you are, in what way you exist, and how you will come to be. *Since you will be called* my brother, it is not fitting that you be ignorant of yourself. ... *So then,* you, my brother Thomas, have beheld what is obscure to men, that is, what they ignorantly stumble against." The use in this passage of conjunctions like ⲉⲡⲉⲓ and ⲉⲡⲉⲓⲆⲏ, or of a formula like ⲉⲧⲃⲉ ⲡⲁⲓ̈, gives a justificatory value to the elements they introduce.

iii. As to the main body of the text, it doesn't contain any specific Thomasian ingredients, except for one occurrence (142.7-8) of the name Thomas, in a form which is reminiscent of the Syrian tradition (with ⲑⲱⲙⲁⲥ instead of ⲆⲓⲆⲩⲙⲟⲥ), but is closer in its wording to the Johannine Gospel, as a comparison between (a) the *Book Thom.*, (b) John (11:16; 20:24; 21:2), and (c) the Sahidic version of John shows:

(a) ⲓⲟⲩⲆⲁⲥ ⲡⲁⲓ̈ ⲉⲧⲟⲩⲙⲟⲩⲧⲉ ⲉⲣⲟϥ ϫⲉ ⲑⲱⲙⲁⲥ

(b) Θωμᾶς ὁ λεγόμενος δίδυμος

(c) ⲑⲱⲙⲁⲥ ⲡⲉⲧⲉϣⲁⲩⲙⲟⲩⲧⲉ (v.l. ⲡⲉϣⲁⲩⲙⲟⲩⲧⲉ) ⲉⲣⲟϥ ϫⲉ ⲆⲓⲆⲩⲙⲟⲥ.

iv.  Otherwise, there is in the *Book Thom.* no indisputable parallel to the *Gos. Thom.*, with the exception of a probable allusion to saying 2, but in a damaged passage (140.41-141.2).

In his edition of the *Book Thom.*, Hans-Martin Schenke[31] has expressed the view that the author of the *Book Thom.*, although well acquainted with the Thomas tradition, stood outside of it. Without going as far as Schenke, it is nevertheless obvious, on the basis of the observations which have been made, that the author appeals to this tradition in a literary way, in order to authenticate the revelatory dialogue he is handing down, which means that the *Book Thom.* belongs only secondarily to the Thomas tradition. At any rate, the *Book Thom.* cannot be numbered with the *Gos. Thom.* and the *Acts Thom.*, two works, especially the latter, which are indisputably Thomasian.

## III. THEIR RELATIONSHIP AND INTERDEPENDENCY RECONSIDERED

After this analysis of the three main literary witnesses of the Thomas tradition, what is to be said of their connection? First, it appears that they cannot be placed along the same Thomasian trajectory, the linear development of which would require a direct dependency on one another. No longer is it possible to explain their common traditional stratum by the hypothesis of a School of St. Thomas, as Bentley Layton has proposed. Indeed, the myth of origins, which Layton sees as one of the major characteristics of this school, is best exemplified, according to him, by the *Hymn of the Pearl*. It has been established that this piece, although incorporated in the *Acts Thom.* and known only through them, is adventitious to them.[32] Therefore, it would be hazardous to impose upon it a formative role in the reconstruction of a hypothetical Thomas school.

Actually, when one considers the three works examined so far, one is faced with a tradition less articulate than has been thought. In the case of the *Gos. Thom.* and the *Acts Thom.*, if it is evident that the *Acts Thom.* are indebted to the *Gos. Thom.*, their mutual relationship can only be established backwards, from the *Acts Thom.* to the *Gos.*

---

[31] *Das Thomas-Buch*, 65.

[32] On this question, see P.-H. Poirier, "L'Hymne de la Perle des Actes de Thomas: étude de la tradition manuscrite," *Symposium syriacum 1976* (Orientalia christiana analecta 205; Rome: Pont. Institutum Orientalium Studiorum, 1978) 19-29, and *L'Hymne de la Perle des Actes de Thomas* (Homo religiosus 8; Louvain-la-Neuve: Centre d'histoire des religions, 1981) 171-184.

*Thom.* While the *Gos. Thom.* offers a relatively meagre Thomasian substance—chiefly the ascription of the work to the apostle, his status as recipient of the secret words of Jesus, and the praise he receives in saying 13—the *Acts Thom.* borrows significant material from the *Gos. Thom.* which is integrated into the orchestration of the Thomasian symbolism. That means that the author of the *Acts Thom.* knew of the *Gos. Thom.* as belonging to the tradition he was systematizing. Therefore, the *Acts Thom.* played a decisive role in the emergence and development of the Thomas tradition. It can even be affirmed that, if they had not been available, the identification of a consistent Thomas tradition in the *Gos. Thom.* and the *Book Thom.* would hardly have been possible. This is particularly clear in the case of the *Book Thom.* On the one hand, it exhibits nothing more than a literary rehashing of the twin symbolism in order to confirm a revelatory discourse; on the other hand, the ideas it develops were too widely spread in Late Antiquity to be considered as strong evidence of its indebtedness to the *Gos. Thom.* or the *Acts Thom.*

The chronological frame devised by Turner, that is: *Gos. Thom.* – *Book Thom.* – *Acts Thom.*, has been widely accepted. But, in the view of the present writer, it needs a slight correction. If the priority of the *Gos. Thom.* over the *Acts Thom.* is self-evident, that is far from being the case for the *Book Thom.* Indeed, the *Book Thom.* takes for granted a twin symbolism which must have been already familiar to its readers. The *Acts Thom.* are the only text where such a symbolism is elaborated. Moreover, when the *Book Thom.* calls Thomas the brother of Jesus, it uses a title coined by the *Acts Thom.* Therefore, considering that the *Book Thom.* is indebted to the *Gos. Thom.* by its *incipit*, and to the *Acts Thom.* by its prologue, it must be later than both of them, and dependent on both of them. Consequently, instead of a single Thomas trajectory, there are at least two, one leading from the *Gos. Thom.* to the *Acts Thom.*, another from the *Gos. Thom.* and *Acts Thom.* to the *Book Thom.* Furthermore, it must be assumed that the *Acts Thom.* had access, in addition to the *Gos. Thom.*, to another expression of the Thomas tradition, closer to John (or the pre-Johannine tradition) than to the *Gos. Thom.* Otherwise, it would be difficult to explain the pervasiveness of the twin symbolism in the *Acts Thom.*, when this symbolism is virtually absent from the *Gos. Thom.*

*          *          *

This inquiry into the Thomas tradition has so far been limited to a specific phase of its history, namely the portion which remains accessible through literary documents. Is it possible to go back in time, to the origin of the Thomas theme, that is, specifically, the twin symbolism attached to the apostle's name? The most obvious candidate, or, at least, the earliest witness of this symbolism remains the *Gospel of John*. Even if it is probable that the saying tradition embedded in the *Gos. Thom.* is earlier than John, it doesn't imply that the Thomas theme itself is earlier than John. However, the traditional tinge of the Johannine gloss ("Thomas *called* the twin") suggests that the evangelist was already relying on an accepted etymology or equivalence. Moreover, all early and extra-Johannine attestations of a double name for Thomas, although close to John, are divergent enough for modern scholars to hypothesize the existence, at the very least, of a tradition regarding the form of Thomas's name, if not of a full-blown Thomas tradition. And John might well have been echoing such a tradition.

In his *Resurrection Reconsidered*, Gregory J. Riley has proposed a brilliant reconstruction of Thomas Christianity in its controversy with the community of John. According to Riley, this controversy expresses itself most notably in the Doubting Thomas pericope (John 20:24-29). In Riley's hypothesis, this pericope has been intended as "a recasting of the character of an historical disciple much like the recasting of the character of John the Baptist"[33]: "As John had used the character of John the Baptist to speak to the community of the Baptist, so he uses the character of Thomas to speak to the community of Thomas."[34] Therefore, "the Doubting Thomas pericope is evidence within the Gospel of John for the prior existence of the community of Thomas."[35] Riley's hypothesis is an interesting attempt to elucidate the prehistory of the Thomas community and tradition. Unfortunately, his undertaking suffers a major drawback in that he takes for granted the existence of a pre- or extra-Johannine Thomas community. It is difficult, under such a presupposition, to avoid circularity in argument. The Doubting Thomas pericope is considered as evidence of a community. Then, the existence of this community is a prerequisite for the interpretation of the said pericope. Another difficulty is that Riley doesn't take into consideration the function of the Doubting Thomas pericope within John. To mention only one

---

[33] *Resurrection Reconsidered*, 99.

[34] Ibid., 107.

[35] Ibid., 178.

point, Anton Dauer[36] has established that the Thomas pericope corresponds precisely to the Nathanael pericope in John 1:45-51.

In spite of these reservations, Riley has opened a new avenue for the research on the Thomas tradition. At the same time, he has shown that the lack of reliable sources still impairs our knowledge of the early history of the Thomas tradition, and will probably continue to do so for some time. But, lamentable as this situation is, it certainly contributes to the unceasing fascination this tradition exerts on us.

---

[36] "Zur Herkunft der Tomas-Perikope Joh 20, 24-29," *Biblische Randbemerkungen. Schülerfestschrift für Rudolf Schnackenburg zum 60. Geburtstag*, ed. H. Merklein and J. Lange (Augsburg: Echter-Verlag, 1974) 56-76.

# THE *GOSPEL OF THOMAS* 76.3 AND CANONICAL PARALLELS: THREE SEGMENTS IN THE TRADITION HISTORY OF THE SAYING

*Steven R. Johnson*
The Claremont Graduate School

## INTRODUCTION

New Testament and Nag Hammadi scholarship has been hampered at times in the last forty years by the tendency of scholars to approach the relationship of the *Gospel of Thomas* to the canonical gospels as though Thomas as a text-in-whole represents a sayings tradition that can be fixed in one general place and time. For this reason, the discussion often polarizes as an either-or choice: either Thomas contains sayings of an early body of tradition, a tradition that represents a trajectory of transmission independent of the development of the canonical traditions; or Thomas is at best a second century document and all parallel sayings are derived from the canonical gospels, whether in Greek or Coptic, and subsequently "gnosticized." Yet, it has often been recognized that the tradition history of Thomas is much more complex than this.[1] For this reason, Oscar Cullman stated in 1962 that "As far as the possibility of an independent tradition is concerned, that is, a tradition which would not have been earlier than the Synoptic tradition, in this respect each Logion must be tested; and in each case we must be warned against premature generalizations, either positive or negative." Bruce Chilton argued several years ago that "each saying in Thomas must be typed in respect of redaction and tradition before the possibility that it is authentic can reasonably be considered."[2] I would agree with Chilton, but I would equally emphasize both sides of the coin: each saying

---

[1] The history of the debate and all of its permutations does not need to be rehearsed here – an excellent and up-to-date history of research on this topic exists in English: S. J. Patterson, "The Gospel of Thomas and the Synoptic Tradition: A Forschungsbericht and Critique," *Forum* 8 (1-2; March-June, 1992) 45-97.

[2] B. Chilton, "The Gospel According to Thomas as a Source of Jesus' Teaching," *Gospel Perspectives, Vol. 5: The Jesus Tradition Outside the Gospels* (ed. D. Wenham; Sheffield: JSOT, 1985) 164. O. Cullmann, "The Gospel of Thomas and the Problem of the Age of the Tradition Contained Therein," *Int* 16 (1962) 434-5.

should be carefully analyzed before the possibility of its authenticity *or* its derivation from the canonical gospels can be considered.[3]

The purpose of this study is to investigate the tradition and redaction-history of the saying of Jesus commonly referred to as "Treasure in Heaven," especially as it has been utilized in three first or second century CE gospels: Thomas 76.3, Luke 12:33, and John 6:27.[4] The outline is as follows: 1) establishing John 6:27 as a version of the "Treasure in Heaven" saying; 2) addressing problems engendered by assuming Thomas' relative isolation from or direct dependence on the canonical gospels, and proposing an alternative solution, one that argues for more interaction between tradent communities; 3) clarifying relationships between the three gospels with respect to their treatment of this saying. This study assumes work already undertaken by myself and others on the reconstruction of the Q version of this saying.[5] Hence, it assumes evidence of a number of redactional modifications of Q in the Lukan version of the saying.[6]

## JOHN 6:27

Identifying John 6:27 as a highly modified version of the Treasure in Heaven saying is problematic since the Johannine version does not contain the words "treasure" or "heaven." However, the potential hermeneutical thrust of the saying does not depend on the inclusion of these specific words, as the Thomas version ("which abides"; com-

---

[3] More recently, C. Hedrick ("Thomas and the Synoptics: Aiming at a Consensus," *SecCent* 7 [1, 1989-90] 56) has said something of the same: "What I am suggesting here is that we drop advocacy for dependence/independence of the compiled text of Thomas as it now exists in its Coptic and fragmentary Greek versions, and focus attention on individual logia. What is clear and beyond question is that if Thomas did use the Synoptic Gospels as sources, it also drew on an independent Synoptic-like source or sources. And it is that conclusion that forces us initially to treat every logion in the *Gospel of Thomas* as if it reflected an independent sayings tradition, since we cannot know *a priori* from which source the saying derives."

[4] See also Matt 6:19-20. James 5:2-3 may reflect knowledge of the Q/Matthew version of the saying: so P. J. Hartin, *James and the Q Sayings of Jesus* (JSNTSup 47; Sheffield: JSOT Press, 1991) 180; cf. M. Dibelius, *James: A Commentary on the Epistle of James,* rev. H. Greeven; ed. H. Koester; trans. M. A. Williams (Hermeneia; Philadelphia: Fortress, 1976) 28-29, 236-237.

[5] For the history of scholarship on the Q saying, see S. R. Johnson, "Q 12:33-34 Database," in the forthcoming *Documenta Q,* series ed. J. M. Robinson et al. (Louvain: Peeters). This International Q Project database is currently available by contacting the Institute for Antiquity and Christianity in Claremont, CA. The IQP reconstruction of Q 12:33 can be found in "The International Q Project: Work Sessions 23-27 May, 22-26 August, 17-18 November 1994," *JBL* 114/3 (1995) 475-485.

[6] For my own reconstruction compared to the decision of the IQP, see the addendum to this paper.

pare Q's "in [the] heaven[s]") indicates, and several points argue in favor of this identification.

First, there are indications that John 6:27 is a traditional saying of Jesus which the author has adapted in the composition of a Johannine-style discourse. John 6:27 stands out as the first synoptic-like wisdom admonition used in John. The Gospel of John uses very few general wisdom admonitions of Jesus as it is.[7] This admonition, however, is then used as part of the introduction to the Bread of Life Discourse (John 6:35-58): In fact, it is the keystone for the construction of the entire sixth chapter of John. John 6:26 connects 6:27 to the previous Feeding of the 5,000 (6:1-5) and sets up the comparison of perishable vs. abiding food, the guiding theme for the rest of the chapter.[8] Verses 28-33 begin the interpretation of 6:27 by defining the main verb and its object: "Working" is defined in 6:28-29 as "believing"; "food" is defined in 6:30-33 as the "true bread from heaven" which "gives life to the world" (unlike manna that lasts for a day and gets worm-eaten overnight).

The subsequent Bread of Life Discourse is an extended commentary on especially these two issues. While there are a number of ways to break down the structure of the Discourse into constituent parts in order to analyze its thematic and theological development,[9] here I would simply note how 6:35-47 focuses on the concept of believing, while 6:48-58 develops the bread motif. Verses 51-55 in particular return to the previous definition of "food" as the "bread from heaven" and provide further definition: the bread from heaven is Jesus' flesh. Hence, the saying of Jesus in John 6:27 is the starting point of an extended theological exposition on the power and efficacy of partaking of the eucharistic elements.

Yet, while John 6:27 is most likely a traditional saying of Jesus, the more specific question, whether or not it is a modified version of the treasure saying, remains. The following table compares John 6:27 to the other gospel versions:

---

[7] Other examples include John 7:24; (12:26;) 12:35; 14:27; and 16:24.

[8] John 6:26-27: "...you seek me... because you ate of the loaves and were filled. Do not work for the food which perishes..."

[9] See R. E. Brown, *The Gospel According to John (I-XII)* (AB 29; Garden City, NY: Doubleday, 1982) 293-294.

| Q 12:33 | Matt 6:19-20 | Luke 12:33 | Gos. Thom. 76:3 | John 6:27 |
|---|---|---|---|---|
| (... | Μὴ θησαυρίζετε ὑμῖν θησαυροὺς ἐπὶ τῆς γῆς, ὅπου σὴς καὶ <u>βρῶσις</u> ἀφανίζει καὶ ὅπου κλέπται διορύσσουσιν καὶ κλέπτουσιν· | Πωλήσατε τὰ ὑπάρχοντα ὑμῶν καὶ δότε ἐλεημοσύνην· | | ἐργάζεσθε <u>μὴ τὴν</u> <u>βρῶσιν τὴν</u> <u>ἀπολ-</u> <u>λυμένην</u> |
| ...) | | | Ⲛ̄ⲧⲱⲧⲛ̄ ϨⲰⲦ ⲐⲎⲨⲦⲛ̄ ϢⲒⲚⲈ Ⲛ̄ⲤⲀ | ἀλλὰ |
| θησαυρίζετε δὲ ὑμῖν | θησαυρίζετε δὲ ὑμῖν | ποιήσατε ἑαυτοῖς βαλλάντια μὴ παλαιού-μενα, | | |
| θησαυροὺς | θησαυροὺς | θησαυρὸν <u>ἀνέκλειπτον</u> | Ⲡ(ⲈϤ)ⲈϨⲞ ⲈⲘⲀϤ- ⲰⲬⲚ̄ ⲈϤⲘⲎⲚ ⲈⲂⲞⲖ | τὴν βρῶσιν τὴν μένουσαν εἰς ζωὴν αἰώνιον, |
| <u>ἐν</u> <u>οὐρανοῖς,</u> | <u>ἐν</u> <u>οὐρανῷ,</u> | <u>ἐν τοῖς</u> <u>οὐρανοῖς,</u> | | |
| ὅπου οὔτε σὴς οὔτε <u>βρῶσις</u> ἀφανίζει | ὅπου οὔτε σὴς οὔτε <u>βρῶσις</u> ἀφανίζει | ὅπου κλέπτης οὐκ ἐγγίζει | ⲠⲘⲀ ⲈⲘⲀⲢⲈ ⲬⲞⲞⲖⲈⲤ ⲦϨⲚⲞ ⲈϨⲞⲨⲚ ⲈⲘⲀⲨ ⲈⲞⲨⲰⲘ | |

| Q 12:33 | Matt 6:19-20 | Luke 12:33 | Gos. Thom. 76:3 | John 6:27 |
|---------|--------------|------------|-----------------|-----------|
| καὶ ὅπου | καὶ ὅπου | οὐδὲ | ΟΥΔΕ | |
| κλέπται | κλέπται | σὴς | ΜΑΡΕ | |
| οὐ | οὐ | | (ϥ)ϥN̄Τ | |
| διορύσσουσιν | διορύσσουσιν | διαφθείρει· | ΤΑΚΟ. | |
| οὐδὲ | οὐδὲ | | | |
| κλέπτουσιν· | κλέπτουσιν· | | | |

Lucien Cerfaux once asked: "Is it by chance that Matthew 6:20 and John 6:27 have in common the Greek word βρῶσις, which is rather rare and which signifies 'the eating worm' in Matthew and 'the food' in John?"[10] I would argue that it is not. Both sayings involve a contrast between working for or storing up earthly, material goods and working for or storing up what is heavenly and eternal. This concept is fundamental to Q 12:33, Luke 12:33, and Thomas 76.3 as well. All five versions of this saying are wisdom admonitions in the second person imperative form. All use the clausal form: imperative—object—object qualifier. Like Matthew, John consists of two antithetically parallel admonitions, though the use of earthly images in the saying and thus the implicit contrast between earthly and heavenly, or perishable and imperishable, lends itself to an expansion of the saying into parallel admonitions, as I will argue has happened with John independent of Matthew.[11]

John is similar to Luke and Thomas in the use of two object qualifiers pertaining to the contrast between perishability and nonperishability. Like Thomas, John understands this saying to be metaphorical. In Thomas, one is told to seek the treasure, but one is not told what the treasure is. Thomas 76.3 is prefaced with images of selling cargo and buying a pearl (Gos. Thom. 76.1-2), but the imagery is embedded in a parable, and thus is not to be understood concretely. The parabolic form leaves one to divine or discover just what the treasure is that is to be sought. John, on the other hand,

---

[10] L. Cerfaux & G. Garitte, "Les Paraboles du Royaume dans l'Evangile de Thomas," Mus 70 (1957) 313: "est-ce par hasard qui Mt., vi, 20 et Jo., vi, 27 ont en commun le mot grec βρῶσις, plutôt rare et qui signifie 'le ver rongeur' en Mt. et 'la nourriture' en Jo.?"

[11] The implicit contrast is found in the Lukan and Thomasine versions as well. The IQP has voted that Q contained the negative imperative. Luke then changed this negative demand, "Do not store up treasures," to a positive demand, "Sell your possessions and give alms." Cf. Col 3:1-2 for a concept similar to the gospel versions, but with little common vocabulary (ζητεῖτε (Gos. Thom. 76:3); ἐπὶ τῆς γῆς (Matt 6:19)).

spends most of the rest of chapter six unpacking the metaphorical images of 6:27 ("work," "food"), eventually leading the reader to understand that this saying is really a rationale for why one should partake of the eucharist: "Work" is belief in the Christ, and the "food which endures" is his body, the "bread from heaven," which gives eternal life to those who eat of it.

The abundance of similarities between Q 12:33, its redacted versions in Matthew and Luke, Thomas 76.3, and John 6:27 are simply too numerous to dismiss as coincidence: John 6:27 is a modified version of the Treasure in Heaven saying.

The fact that βρῶσις is used in John in a manner different from Matthew or Thomas is understandable. John found "food" to be more valuable than "treasure" as the object of one's striving when developing the Bread of Life Discourse and its introduction around this saying. It also provided a connection to John 6's sister passage, the Woman at the Well Discourse in John 4, with its initiatory "Give me a drink!" command and its subsequent discussion about "living waters." That John 6:27 uses the imperative form but lacks the two adversary clauses of the other versions is understandable if John wanted to focus on the imperative, its object, and their interpretation, which is precisely what John does in 6:28-58. John replaced the adversary clauses in 6:27 with the assurance "which the Son of Humanity will give to you. For it is on him that God the Father has set his seal." This addition also assures the observant reader that subsequent interpretation of this saying is going to focus specifically on Jesus. Yet, if βρῶσις originally belonged in the first adversary clause of this saying, then its presence in John 6:27 is evidence that John knew of a fuller version of the saying and chose to abbreviate it.

John's implied second imperative, "(work) for the food which abides," is supplemented by the favorite Johannine expression "into eternal life" (εἰς ζωὴν αἰώνιον).[12] At first glance, the relative clause "which abides" would appear to be Johannine, μένω being a favorite Johannine term. But the form and meaning of the word as it is used here differ from its use anywhere else in the Johannine corpus.[13] Most

---

[12] Cf. the addition of the comparable εἰς ζωὴν αἰώνον to the likewise-modified traditional saying of Jesus in John 12:25: "Those who love their life shall lose it, and those who hate their life *in this world* will keep it *into eternal life*." Cf. also John 4:14: "But those who drink of the water I will give them will never thirst (οὐ μὴ διψήσει εἰς τὸν αἰῶνα). The water that I will give will become in them a spring of water gushing up into eternal life (εἰς ζωὴν αἰώνον)."

[13] Only here is μένω used as an accusative participle. Only here is the participial form of μένω used with a relative pronoun preceding it. This is, in fact, one of the few times

important, it is not used here in the familiar way of furthering John's christology of immanence.

Even with all of these changes made to the form and content of the saying in John, both the basic concept behind the Treasure in Heaven saying and significant vocabulary shared with other versions are clearly identifiable in John 6:27.

One other difficulty should be addressed: Why does the author risk modifying the saying so much as to make it virtually unrecognizable in order to fit it into the author's larger theological schema? Part of this answer is simply that the author felt the freedom to do so. Every generally known and accepted traditional saying of Jesus in John (that is, ones that have synoptic parallels) has been modified to fit the Johannine pericope into which it is embedded. Helmut Koester has found this to be true when trying to identify non-canonical parallels as well.[14] But this may not be the final answer to the question. John may also be consciously modifying the saying away from its implied meaning or interpretation in John's source, or from its expressed interpretation in tradent communities that John is in contact with.

## THOMAS 76.3

The *Gospel of Thomas* has this saying attached to the Parable of the (Pearl) Merchant (76.1-2).[15] Thomas 76.3 serves as a summary admonition: "So you also, seek the treasure..."[16] The many verbal

---

μένω is used adjectivally, in a relative clause. This is also one of the few places where μένω is not connected with a preposition of immanence (ἐν, ἐπι, or παρά).

[14] H. Koester, "Gnostic Sayings and Controversy Traditions in John 8:12-59," *Nag Hammadi, Gnosticism, and Early Christianity*, ed. C. W. Hedrick & R. Hodgson, Jr. (Peabody, MA: Hendrickson, 1986) 109. In attempting to identify a sayings source behind John 8:12-59 that is different in nature from synoptic sources, Koester achieved varying degrees of success in different parts of John 8, and two of his concluding comments explain why: "In most of the gnostic texts traditional sayings are already embedded in dialogue and discourse. It is difficult to isolate them, and the exegete's eyes are not sufficiently trained for this task." And, in John, "There seems to be little respect for the original 'form' of a saying; i.e., basic formulations ('There is light within a man of light, and he lights up the whole world') can be transformed into I-sayings ('I am the light of the world')."

[15] Cf. Matt 13:45-46.

[16] R. Cameron ("Parable and Interpretation in the Gospel of Thomas," *Forum* 2 [2, 1986] 15) observes that this use of a traditional saying to interpret a parable is unique in the *Gospel of Thomas* and therefore argues that it not be considered the product of the author but of an earlier stage of the tradition. He also argues that the saying "has no vestige of a distinctive language or style attributable to the author of this gospel" and that "the secondary collocation of 'pearl' and 'treasure' in *Gos. Thom.* 76 betrays no earmarks of the author's own redaction." Both of these observations should make one wary when considering the possibility of Thomas' derivation from the synoptic gospels.

similarities between Thomas 76.3 and the canonical versions of the Treasure in Heaven saying have led to a number of proposals concerning the relationship between these texts. For this reason, the cautious scholar should hesitate before arguing that the Thomas tradition represents a development completely independent of the traditions underlying the canonical gospels.

Cerfaux was first to propose that the Thomas saying was actually a composite text constructed from the canonical gospels, derived primarily from Matthew 6:20 and John 6:27, with "worm" taken from Mark 9:48.[17] Specifically, he understood the construction ⲉⲙⲁϥⲱϫⲛ̄ ⲉϥⲙⲏⲛ ⲉⲃⲟⲗ ("which does not perish, which abides") to be Johannine, with the bulk of the rest of the saying being taken up from Matthew. Robert Wilson, noting the Lukan parallels, suggested that the "most obvious explanation here is free quotation by an author familiar with all four Gospels..."[18] Wolfgang Schrage focused on the Lukan parallels and argued that Thomas' singular "treasure" and its characterization as "that which does not perish" are derived from Luke.[19] Klyne Snodgrass went beyond Schrage to argue that Thomas' ⲧϩⲛⲟ ⲉϩⲟⲩⲛ ("approach") is taken from Luke's ἐγγίζει, Thomas' ⲉⲟⲩⲱⲙ ("to eat") comes from Matthew's ἀφανίζει, and Thomas' ⲧⲁⲕⲟ ("destroy") comes from Luke's διαφθείρει.[20] Most scholars who have addressed this saying have assumed that Thomas' ϥⲛ̄ⲧ ("worm") comes from βρῶσις, whether it was derived from Matthew or not.[21] In short, with a little perseverance, one can identify a gospel source or sources for every word in Thomas 76.3.

However, such a deconstruction of Thomas' text raises certain questions. For example, *why* would the composer of Thomas 76.3 go to such trouble picking out individual words here and there from all four canonical gospels? Do any of the individual words or phrases have especial meaning in the *Gospel of Thomas*? Indeed, outside of the general concept of seeking, not one aspect of the saying has any identifiably Thomasine relevance, and a redactional rationale is

---

[17] L. Cerfaux & G. Garitte, "Les Paraboles du Royaume," 312-313.

[18] R. McL. Wilson, *Studies in the Gospel of Thomas* (London: Mowbray, 1960) 92.

[19] W. Schrage, *Das Verhältnis des Thomas-Evangeliums zur synoptischen Tradition und zu den koptischen Evangelienübersetzungen* (Berlin: A. Töpelmann, 1964) 159.

[20] K. R. Snodgrass, "The Gospel of Thomas: A Secondary Gospel," *SecCent* 7 (1989-90, 1) 36.

[21] E. g., J. Sieber, "A Redactional Analysis of the Synoptic Gospels with Regard to the Question of the Sources of the Gospel According to Thomas" (Ph. D. diss., Claremont Graduate School, 1965) 57, 60. But cf. R. M. Grant & D. N. Freedman, *The Secret Sayings of Jesus* (Garden City, NY: Doubleday, 1960) 177.

lacking for almost every compositional maneuver one can suggest. On
the contrary, several points argue against canonical derivation. For
example, the image of the "thief" as an adversary appears to be a
popular image in the *Gospel of Thomas* (*Gos. Thom.* 21, 103;[22] cf.
also *Gos. Thom.* 35, 39), and it would seem particularly appropriate
following the Parable of the Merchant (*Gos. Thom.* 76.1-2). Yet,
"worm" is found in its place.[23] For what reason would Thomas use
Matthew's order of adversaries but Luke's verbs and verb order in the
adversary clauses? Thomas' use of Luke's ἐγγίζω would seem
unnecessary: "Where moths eat and worms destroy" would make for
a simpler, more concise saying. The second object qualifier, ЄϥΜΗΝ
ЄΒΟΛ ("which abides"), also could be considered redundant. Why the
locative ΠΜΑ if Thomas has replaced "in (the) heaven(s)"? Either this
saying was constructed in a sloppy, carefree manner, or the construction ΠΜΑ...ЄΜΑΥ simply indicates that the *metaphorical* treasure is
understood to be found in a location, as the images of moths, worms
and treasures suggest. Without any rationale for a cut and paste
theory of redaction, and in light of Ron Cameron's observations that
the composition of Thomas 76 as a whole shows no distinctive signs
of authorial redaction,[24] it seems more reasonable to assume that
Thomas 76.3 is not dependent upon the synoptic gospels for its text.

A more difficult set of questions is raised by the coincidence of
Luke 12:33 and John 6:27 each having two qualifiers, one negative
and one positive, that describe the permanence of the object of the
imperative. Luke's first qualifier, ἀνέκλειπτον ("unfailing"), is a
redactional addition to Q.[25] But John has a similar qualifier in the first
position, the relative clause τὴν ἀπολλυμένην ("which perishes").

---

[22] *Gos. Thom.* 21.5 uses the Coptic construction ΡЄϥϪΙΟΥЄ ("one who steals") for
"thief," while 21.7 and 103 use the Greek loan-word ΛΗϹΤΗϹ (λῃστής: "bandit,"
"brigand," "highwayman," "robber").

[23] See *Gos. Thom.* 9.4 for the only other use of worm.

[24] See above, n. 16.

[25] So the International Q Project. See Johnson, "Q 12:33-34 Database," Q 12:33[8]:
"Harnack argued that ἀνέκλειπτος is literary Greek, and so was added by Luke. It could
be argued that Matthew eliminated the word to smooth out the saying, but that does not
answer Harnack's argument. Ἀνέκλειπτος is also Lukan terminology. Albrecht Garsky
has noted the similarity in thought to Luke 16:9's 'unjust mammon' which 'fails'
(ἐκλίπῃ). Wrege has noted Luke's use of the related ἐκλείπω in Luke 16:9, 22:32, and
23:45, but he assumes that 16:9 and 22:32 are from Lukan *Sondergut* and not a result of
Lukan redaction. Hence, he argues that ἀνέκλειπτος is traditional here. In fact, both
verses show evidence of being Lukan redaction. Hence, it appears that ἐκλείπω is Lukan
vocabulary after all, and by extension, ἀνέκλειπτος as well. By adding ἀνέκλειπτος,
Luke has created parallelism by means of apposition in the construction βαλλάντια μὴ
παλαιούμενα, θησαυρὸν ἀνέκλειπτον ἐν τοῖς οὐρανοῖς (Sellew)."

Does John reflect knowledge of the *redacted* Lukan version of this saying, though using Johannine terminology? If one argues for this point of view, then it remains to be asked where Luke got the idea of doubling the qualifiers for the object "treasure" in the first place.[26] And what is to be said for John's βρῶσις, which is found in Matthew but not in Luke: that the author used both Luke's *and* Matthew's (or Q's) version of the saying in creating John 6:27? It seems more reasonable to suggest that John used a source for this saying of Jesus that differed from both Matthew and Luke; a version that contained both βρῶσις and two object qualifiers.[27] What, then, would this source have looked like?

There is a very simple solution to the questions raised above: both John *and* Luke used a source that itself had two qualifiers for the object of the imperative. To be more specific, while it is quite certain that Luke used Q 12:33 as the basis for the Lukan version of the saying, Luke was influenced by another tradition of this saying, the same or a similar one used as the basis for John 6:27. The only other version we know of that has two object qualifiers is Thomas 76.3. The following alignment highlights the similarities between the three texts:

| | | | |
|---|---|---|---|
| Luke | θησαυρὸν | ἀνέκλειπτον | ἐν τοῖς οὐρανοῖς |
| Thomas | ⲡ(ⲉϥ)ⲉϩⲟ | ⲉⲙⲁϥⲱ̄ⲭ̄ⲛ̄ | ⲉϥⲙⲏⲛ ⲉⲃⲟⲗ |
| John | μὴ τὴν βρῶσις | τὴν ἀπολλυμένην | τὴν μένουσαν |

A Greek translation of Thomas that retains the Coptic relative clauses would look something like the following:

| | | | |
|---|---|---|---|
| Luke | θησαυρὸν | | ἀνέκλειπτον | ἐν τοῖς οὐρανοῖς |
| Thomas | τὸν θησαυρὸν | μὴ τὸν ἀπολλύμενον, | τὸν μένοντα |
| John | μὴ τὴν βρῶσις | τὴν ἀπολλυμένην | τὴν μένουσαν [28] |

---

[26] Luke probably saw fit to create an appositive parallelism of "purses which do not wear out, a treasure unfailing" (see previous note), and by inserting the adjective ἀνέκλειπτος and reversing the order of adversary clauses created a word-play with κλέπτης (So S. Anderson in Johnson, "Q 12:33-34 Database," Q 12:33.[11] But such a redactional analysis still does not answer the question of where Luke first got the idea of doubling the qualifiers for the object "treasure."

[27] Admittedly "perishing" over against "eternal life" is a Johannine theme (e.g., John 3:16), and could conceivably indicate further redaction.

[28] Kasser and Greeven translate Thomas' ⲉⲙⲁϥⲱ̄ⲭ̄ⲛ̄ with ἀνέκλειπτον: A. Huck *Synopse der drei ersten Evangelien: 13 Auflage völlig neu bearbeitet von Heinrich Greeven* (Tübingen: J.C.B. Mohr [P. Siebeck], 1981) 38; R. Kasser, *L'Evangile selon Thomas: Présentation et commentaire théologique* (Neuchatel: Delachaux et Niestlé, 1961) 98. P. Sellew ("Reconstruction of Q 12:33-59," *SBLSP* 26 [Atlanta: Scholars Press, 1987] 618) notes the problem usually raised by such retroversions: il

If we assume, not that Thomas 76.3 is based on a combining of canonical texts, but that Luke and John are influenced by a Thomas-like version of the saying, a number of questions are answered. First, we can see where Luke first got the idea for a qualifier of "treasure" that parallels the qualifier of "purses" *and* precedes the qualifier "in the heavens" (Q). Such an apposition of two qualifiers referring to the permanence of the object "treasure" already existed in the Thomas version.

Second, we can see how Luke, using better Greek style, simplified the Thomas version of the first object qualifier when adding it to the Q version of the saying, employing a terser phraseology in this clause that intentionally paralleled the redactionally added "purse" clause.

Third, we can now see where Luke got the idea for several other modifications of the Q text. Below are the Q and Luke versions of the two adversary clauses, with a proposed original Greek text of Thomas:

| Q: | ὅπου οὔτε | σὴς | |
| | οὔτε | βρῶσις | ἀφανίζει |
| | καὶ ὅπου | κλέπται οὐ | διορύσσουσιν οὐδε κλέπτουσιν. |
| Luke: | ὅπου | κλέπτης οὐκ | ἐγγίζει |
| | οὐδε | σὴς | διαφθείρει. |
| Thomas: | ὅπου οὔτε | σὴς οὔτε | βρῶσις ἐγγίζει |
| | οὐδε | σκώληξ | διαφθείρει.[29] |

---

have... quoted Greeven's Greek retroversions as though they were the original *Thomas* readings — which they could well be in many cases, though in doing that work there seems to have been a natural tendency to be influenced in both vocabulary and word order by the familiar NT parallels." It *is* possible that Thomas' Greek *Vorlage* had ἀνέκλειπτος, in which case Luke used Thomas' word and John changed it, using the more Johannine ἀπόλλυμι. However, this ignores the Coptic construction of *Gos. Thom.* 76.3. Looking to a semitic *Vorlage* does not help here, though in regard to the adversary clauses, see n. 30.

[29] Originally, I argued for a Greek *Vorlage* of Thomas best represented by a more literal translation of the Coptic: ὅπου οὐ σὴς ἐγγίζει βιβρώσκειν... However, as T. Baarda rightly pointed out in response to this paper at the Annual Meeting of the AAR/SBL (Philadelphia, November 21, 1995), that would mean that John changed Thomas' infinitive βιβρώσκειν to the rare substantive that Matthew also used, βρῶσις, but with an altogether different meaning. From a transmission-history point of view, this suggestion is admittedly very unlikely. Baarda's objection should point us instead to the problem of Coptic translation; in particular, translating βρῶσις in the context of this saying. The Sahidic version of Matt 6:19-20 employs a nifty use of homeonymous synonyms for moth: ϫⲟⲟⲗⲉⲥ—ϩⲟⲟⲗⲉ. I would argue that the translator of Thomas tried to keep the essence of the Greek root, and in so doing altered the position and

So, for example, Luke retained Q's "thieves," changing it to the singular, but used Thomas' ἐγγίζει (ⲦϨⲚⲞ ⲈϨⲞⲨⲚ) in the first clause in order to abbreviate Q's διορρύσσουσιν οὐδὲ κλέπτουσιν.[30] This assisted Luke's creation of a tight, metrical pair of clauses. It also created the possible, though not quite as likely, image of a κλέπτης that approaches someone who is carrying a "treasure" in a purse (the role of a λῃστής). The change to the singular subject "thief" to go with the third singular ἐγγίζει would have been consistent with the previous change from the plural to the singular "treasure (unfailing)," itself a change perhaps prompted by the adoption and adaptation of Thomas' singular "treasure which does not perish." Further, we can now see that Thomas' agreement with Luke's order of verbs is actually due to Luke's use of Thomas' verb in the first clause when reversing the order of Q clauses in order to create the ἀνέκλειπτον—κλέπτης word-play that more closely connects the adversary clauses with the "purse" and "treasure" clauses.

Fourth, we finally see what John's source for this saying looked like. Consequently, we can describe the process of Johannine modification of this source with greater confidence. In focusing only on the imperative of the saying, John split the qualifiers of the object of the imperative into two separate clauses, creating negative and positive imperatives (with implied verb in the second clause).[31] John achieved this simply by moving the negative μή in front of the object of the

---

function of the word from a second subject, the ambiguous substantive "eating thing," to an infinitive, "to eat," complementing ἐγγίζω.

[30] Based on a possible Aramaic paronomasia underlying the Greek text (קְרֵב for ἐγγίζω ("approach") and רְקַב ("rot") for διαφθείρω ("destroy" or "spoil")), Gundry argues that Luke's adversary clauses are original to Q. R. Gundry, *Matthew: A Commentary on his Literary and Theological Art* (Grand Rapids: Eerdmans, 1982) 112. However, this observation would apply to a Semitic *Vorlage* behind the Coptic *Gos. Thom.* 76:3 as well (ⲦϨⲚⲞ ⲈϨⲞⲨⲚ and ⲦⲀⲔⲞ). Davies' and Allison's speculation that assonance in a Semitic *Vorlage* could have extended to "moth" and "worm" can only support the priority of the Thomas version. W. D. Davies & D. C. Allison, *A Critical and Exegetical Commentary on the Gospel According to Saint Matthew. Vol. 1: Introduction and Commentary on Matthew I-VII* (ICC; Edinburgh: T. & T. Clark, 1988) 631. Furthermore, while numerous observers have noted the parallelism of the adversary clauses in Matthew, Luke, and Q, Thomas provides the best instance of Semitic synonymous parallelism in the pairing of "moth" and "worm" (Cf. Job 25:6; Is 14:11; 51:8 [עָשׁ is paired with סָס, רִמָּה with תּוֹלֵעָה]. In each case in the Hebrew Bible, synonyms of either "worm" or "moth" are paired, but cf. the LXX of Job 25:6 [σαπρία and σκώληξ] and Is 14:11 [σῆψις and σκώληξ], where רִמָּה has been rendered with cognates of σής [best translated "decay"]).

[31] Hence, the incidental agreement with Matthew (or Q) in using antithetical parallelism.

imperative, adding the negative conjunction αλλά and duplicating the object of the imperative in the new second clause. John's object βρῶσις would have come from Thomas' second subject in the first adversary clause.[32] John found the relative expression "which abides" already in the tradition and attached the Johannine "into eternal life" to the end of the traditional saying.[33]

As I have argued, apart from βρῶσις being used as the object of the imperative, John jettisoned the adversary clauses in order to focus subsequent interpretation on the terms used in the admonition proper. However, another element of Thomas' adversary clauses may have suggested the use of this saying at the beginning of John's Bread of Life Discourse, which contrasts the perishable manna in the wilderness with the abiding "true bread from heaven." According to Exodus 16:19-24, the problem with manna is that it doesn't last for more than a night. More specifically, *worm*-infestation is cited as the cause of its putrefaction.[34]

Finally, such a solution requires only that one of the five gospel versions of the saying be reliant on more than one source; even then, Luke is only reliant upon two sources. Otherwise, the best solutions would need to argue either that *both* Thomas and John rely on a minimum of two sources each for their versions of this saying, or that the form, content and provenance of the source for John's version is similar to Thomas but remains unknown.

## THOMAS, LUKE, AND JOHN

The relationship between Luke and Thomas in regard to the Treasure in Heaven saying is in some ways easier to understand than the relationship between Thomas and John. Simply put, the author of Luke was a collector and adapter of sources. While Luke's primary source was Q, aspects of the Thomas version were integrated in the process of redacting Q. The Lukan focus in this operation appears to have been less a concern for correcting the interpretation of the Thomas version and more a concern for focusing the interpretation of the Q version on specific, concrete Lukan concerns regarding wealth

---

[32] This change from subject to object only coincidentally corresponds to the change of the meaning of βρῶσις from "that which eats" to "that which is eaten."

[33] See above, n. 13. Cf. the use of μένω in John 6:52-58 (esp. 6:56), where John returns to identifying βρῶσις as Jesus' flesh, forming an inclusio to Jesus' entire discourse of 6:25-59. There, John returns to using μένω with the preposition ἐν in the more familiar immanential sense.

[34] Compare Thomas' second adversary clause "nor worms that destroy."

and almsgiving. In other words, at least in this case, the author of Luke does not appear to have had a particular bone to pick with the tradition represented by Thomas 76.3.[35]

The case is different with John, which has used only the Thomas version of this saying, but in so doing has greatly modified and then reinterpreted it. I would argue, furthermore, that the author of John knew how the interpretive potential of the saying was actualized in the Thomas communities that transmitted the saying, and so altered the form and content of the saying in order to steer its interpretation in another direction.[36]

When viewed from this anti-Thomasine perspective, the specific changes that John made to the saying become informative. For example, the imperative "seek" is replaced by the imperative "work for," which is then defined in 6:29 as "*believing* into him whom (God) has sent"; that is, believing into the Christ. Jesus is understood as the *means* of salvation and the *focus* of the admonition, not just the *transmitter* of the saying. Hence, a verb that was likely understood in the sense of a search for enlightenment is replaced by another imperative which is interpreted in a manner quite foreign, or even odious, to Thomas Christians. Yet, ζητέω is not eliminated by John. Rather, in connecting John 6:27ff. to the previous Feeding of the 5000, John has

---

[35] It is even possible (though speculative) that Luke's *inspiration* for the admonition "sell your possessions and give alms" came, not from Mark 10:21 or Tobit 4, but from the parable attached to *Gos. Thom.* 76.3, where the merchant sells all of his cargo in order to buy the so-called "pearl of great price."

Other examples of Lukan use of the Thomas tradition suggest that this is not an isolated case in Luke. For example, Patterson's analysis of *Gos. Thom.* 31 strongly suggests that Luke has used the pair of Thomas sayings in this logion in the construction of Luke 4:23-24, though reversing their order and substituting Thomas' physician proverb with another. S. J. Patterson, *The Gospel of Thomas and Jesus* (Sonoma: Polebridge, 1993) 31-32. Note that Luke has Jesus himself stating that this is a common proverb and, hence, not an original saying of Jesus. Mark 6:4-5 is probably an expansion and narrativization of this two-proverb cluster: E. Wendling, *Die Entstehung des Markus-Evangeliums* (Tübingen: J.C.B. Mohr [P. Siebeck], 1908) 54; R. Bultmann, *Die Geschichte der synoptischen Tradition* (Göttingen: Vandenhoeck & Ruprecht, 1957) 30-31. G. Riley has demonstrated Luke's addition of *Gos. Thom.* 47 to the Patches and Wineskins sayings of Mark 2:21-22, and Luke's use of *Gos. Thom.* 72's "divider" saying in creating Luke 12:13-14. Riley argues that these two sayings have "passed through [Thomas Christianity] before being used by Luke." Luke then "conflates the two readings and produces the canonical text." G. J. Riley, "Thomas Christianity and the Canonical Gospels," forthcoming in *HTR*. This kind of conflation of traditions is similar to what Luke has done with Q and Thomas in the creation of Luke 12:33.

[36] For foundational work on the existence of Thomasine (as opposed to, e.g., Matthean, Pauline, or Johannine) communities, see esp. G. Riley, *Resurrection Reconsidered* (Minneapolis: Fortress, 1995) 69-179; idem, "Thomas Tradition and the *Acts of Thomas*," *SBLSP* 30, ed. E. Lovering (Atlanta: Scholars Press, 1991) 533-542.

Jesus saying in 6:26: "You seek me, not because you saw signs, but because you ate your fill of the loaves." The relocation of ζητέω at this point in particular lends to a contrast between "seeking" and "working for" (that is, "seeking" vs. "believing") that is surely intentional.[37]

In the same way, the object "treasure," which in Thomas 76.3 is left undefined, but which may best be understood as wisdom or gnosis, is changed to "food," which is then defined in 6:32 as the "true bread from heaven" and in 6:53-58 as Jesus' flesh. Then, after attaching the typically Johannine phrase "into eternal life" to the end of what is left of the traditional saying in 6:27, John also adds the clause "which the Son of Humanity will give to you." This final clause makes certain that Jesus is the focus of the admonition.

It appears, then, that we not only have a rationale for Johannine redaction of the Thomas saying based on the narrative context of the saying in John (the Bread of Life Discourse), but a second reason as well — the reworking of a Thomas saying to stress a Johannine, *anti-Thomasine* soteriology based on "faith" over against "enlightenment."[38]

I would argue that this kind of intentional reformulation in the Gospel of John of a dominical saying popular in Thomasine communities is not an isolated phenomenon. Rather, I would argue that it is but one example of the author of John's recasting of sayings of Jesus which embody theological concepts that are central for Thomasine groups. Another example will serve to support this point. John uses a saying indicative of Thomasine soteriology:

| *John 8:51-52* | *Gos. Thom. 1* |
|---|---|
| (Jesus answered,…) | |
| "Truly, truly, I tell you, | |
| whoever observes my word | |
| will not see death forever." | |
| | |
| The Jews said to him, | |
| "…and you say | And he said, |
| 'Whoever observes | "Whoever attains the interpretation of |
| my word | these words |
| will not taste death forever.'" | will not taste death" |

---

[37] John 6:26-27 also sets up the contrast of manna and "true bread" of John 6:31-34, 48-50.

[38] Riley, *Resurrection*, 119-123, uses this terminology, I think correctly, to express the different soteriological foundations for the two communities in question.

When comparing the Gospels of John and Thomas, Raymond Brown assumed that sayings parallels were due to John's influence on the text of Thomas.[39] He observed one difficulty in this particular parallel, that "GTh has its parallel in the Jewish rephrasing of Jesus' own statement"; but he did not follow up on the ramifications of his observation.[40] If there was a choice of using John 8:51 or 8:52, it does not make sense for Thomas to have used the version of Jesus' opponents as Jesus' own.[41] Rather, if John wished to mock or attack another group's soteriology, placing the saying most indicative of their views on the lips of Jesus' opponents would be a simple, yet effective, rhetorical maneuver. Hence, if there is influence in one direction or another, it is most likely to be from Thomas to John. It is therefore quite possible that John took the saying of Jesus perhaps most representative of Thomasine soteriology, altered it in ways more conducive to Johannine soteriology, and duplicated it, keeping intact Thomas' distinctive "not taste death" expression (cf. *Gos. Thom.* 18, 19, 85) in one version and placing it on the lips of Jesus' opponents, while using the expression "not see death" in the other version and placing it on the lips of Jesus.[42] In other words, rather than Thomas having "gnosticized" one of John's versions of this saying, it was John who turned the Thomas version into a misquotation of Jesus and, by duplication and alteration, directed the *hermeneia* of the saying towards Jesus as the means to salvation. So, when the phrase "whoever discovers the interpretation" (ⲡⲉⲧⲁϩⲉ ⲉⲑⲉⲣⲙⲏⲛⲉⲓⲁ) is changed to "whoever observes" or "keeps" (ἐάν τις τηρήσῃ), the

---

[39] R. E. Brown, "The Gospel of Thomas and St. John's Gospel," *NTS* 9 (1962) 159.

[40] Ibid.

[41] For this reason alone, it is wrong to assume Thomas' dependency on John 8:52 at the beginning of one's analysis. B. Chilton, at first glance, appears to do this in his earlier article "'Not to Taste Death': A Jewish, Christian and Gnostic Usage," *StudBib* 2 (1978) 31. Fortunately, after reviewing the various theories of Schrage (*Das Verhältnis*, 28-29), as repeated by J.-E. Ménard (*L'Evangile selon Thomas* [NHS 5; Leiden: E. J. Brill, 1975] 77), Chilton decides against making any definitive source-critical claims ("Not to Taste Death," 31; 35, n. 15). However, cf., e.g., O. Hofius, "Das koptische Thomasevangelium und die Oxyrhynchus-Papyri Nr. 1, 654 und 655," *EvT* 20 (1960) 26, who states with no uncertainty, "Das Logion ist ohne Zweifel eine gnostische Umdeutung von Joh 8,52 ... "

[42] If, as Chilton claims, the expression "not taste death" carried with it an implied reference to ancient or legendary figures like Elijah and Enoch in a Jewish context ("Not to Taste Death," 29-30), then one would have no need of recourse to John 8:52 to explain the background of *Gos. Thom.* 1 if the *Gospel of Thomas* is intentionally moving beyond traditional Jewish thought in using gnostic categories (cf. *Gos. Thom.* 85). At the same time, John's placement of the expression "not taste death" on the lips of "the Jews" would serve as a subtle, but rather snide attack on the Thomas tradition.

search for enlightenment becomes an ethic of faithful piety. When "these words" (ⲛⲉⲉⲓϣⲁϫⲉ) is changed to "my word" (8:51 – τὸν ἐμὸν λόγον; 8:52 – τὸν λόγον μου), emphasis is diverted away from meditation on the *meaning* of Jesus' *sayings* and towards Jesus *himself* as Sophia-Logos whose word itself gives life if obeyed. The Johannine qualifier "forever" (εἰς τὸν αἰῶνα) is also added to each version of the saying in John.[43] Not surprisingly, the larger pericope of John 8:31-59 is concerned with the identity of Jesus, and the opening statement of Jesus in 8:31, "If you *abide in my word*, you are truly my disciples," reflects John's immanential christology.[44]

## CONCLUSION

The notions that dialogue and debate took place between Johannine and Thomasine communities and that the author of John intentionally attacked Thomasine hermeneutics are not new.[45] This study has argued, however, that the author of John has gone so far in this debate as to alter the individual sayings transmitted by the Thomas communities in an effort to combat their enlightenment soteriology and correlative lack of emphasis on the figure of Jesus as the means to salvation.

The use of the Thomas sayings tradition by Luke suggests that it had attained some degree of authoritative status in parts of Western Syria outside of specifically Thomasine communities late in the first or early in the second century CE. At the same time, John's use and alteration of the Thomas tradition indicates that a developing enlight-

---

[43] See, e.g., John 4:14; 8:35; 10:28; 11:26; 13:8 (12x in all; see also above, n. 12). Unless one assumes that Thomas uses John, there is no need to rely on theories of 1) Thomas' dependence on a Western text of John that omits the phrase, 2) Thomas' use of an *Urtext* of John that does not contain the phrase, or 3) influence from Mark 9:1—so Schrage, *Das Verhältnis*, 28-29. Indeed, when dealing with variant readings common to "Western" texts and the *Gospel of Thomas*, one should always ask if textual influence might go the other way, or if the readings reflect an early, common oral milieu.

[44] *Gos. Thom.* 111 is an indication that both expressions, "tasting death" and "seeing death," may have been known to both Thomas and John. But *Gos. Thom.* 111:1-2 understands "not seeing death" to mean that the enlightened will never die. *Gos. Thom.* 111.3 indicates why that is the case: they have found themselves. Both perspectives would be antithetical to Johannine Christianity, even with its realized eschatology. That Thomas uses both expressions with the same meaning supports Bultmann's claim that a change in meaning between John 8:51 and 8:52 is "oversubtle" (R. Bultmann, *The Gospel of John* [trans. G. R. Beasley-Murray; Philadelphia: Westminster, 1971] 325, n. 2; cited from Chilton, "'Not to Taste Death,'" 34, n. 13). Rather, as I have argued, the significance of the difference is found in the historical debate between Thomasine and Johannine communities.

[45] So Riley, *Resurrection*, 69-156.

enment-oriented form of Jesus religion had already begun to blossom by the time of John's writing. It also indicates the lengths to which some late first/early second century writers would go to counteract the perceived errors and misunderstandings of rival communities in the service of community teaching or evangelism/recruitment, and the liberties they could take with authoritative sayings traditions in this effort.

## ADDENDUM: *Reconstruction of Q 12:33*

| *Q12:33* (S. Johnson) | *Q12:33* (International Q Project) |
|---|---|
| 0ſ | 0ſ |
| 1ſ | 1ſ |
| | ⟦(μὴ θησαυρίζετε ⟦(ὑμῖν)⟧ θησαυρο( ) |
| | ἐπὶ τῆς γῆς, ὅπου σὴς ⟦καὶ βρῶσις⟧ |
| | ⟦ἀφανίζει⟧ καὶ ⟦ὅπου⟧ κλέπτ( ) διορύσσ( ) |
| [( )]² | καὶ κλεπτ( )·)²⟧ |
| (θησαυρίζετε)³ | (θησαυρίζετε)³ |
| ( )⁴ | ⟦(δέ)⁴⟧ |
| ( )⁵ | ⟦(ὑμῖν)⁵⟧ |
| []⁶ | []⁶ |
| θησαυρο( )⁷ | θησαυρο( )⁷ |
| []⁸ | ⟦[ ]⁸⟧ |
| ἐν []⁹ | ἐν [ ]⁹ |
| οὐραν[οῖς]¹⁰, | οὐραν[οῖς]¹⁰, |
| ὅπου | ὅπου |
| ¹¹ſοὔ(τε)¹² σὴς (οὔτε βρῶσις)¹² | ¹¹ſοὔ⟦(τε)¹²⟧ σὴς ⟦(οὔτε βρῶσις)¹²⟧ |
| (ἀφανίζει)¹³ʲ¹¹ | ⟦(ἀφανίζει)¹³⟧ʲ¹¹ |
| (καὶ ὅπου)¹⁴ | ⟦(καὶ ὅπου)¹⁴⟧ |
| ¹¹ſκλέπτ⟦(αι)⟧¹⁵ | ¹¹ſκλέπτ( )¹⁵ |
| οὐ (διορύσσ⟦(ουσιν)⟧)¹⁵)¹⁶ | οὐ ⟦(διορύσσ( )¹⁵)¹⁶⟧ |
| ⟦(οὐδὲ κλέπτ⟦(ουσιν)⟧)¹⁵)⟧¹⁷ʲ¹¹. | ⟦(οὐδὲ κλέπτ( )¹⁵)¹⁷⟧ʲ¹¹ |
| ʲ¹→Q 12:34 | ʲ¹→Q 12:34 |
| ι0 | ι0 |

*IQP Formatting*

| | |
|---|---|
| text | Minimal Q |
| (text) | Matthew at an A or B grade of certainty |
| [text] | Luke at an A or B grade of certainty |
| ⟦(text)⟧ | Matthew at a C grade of certainty |
| ⟦[text]⟧ | Luke at a C grade of certainty |
| ( ) | In Matthew at a D grade of certainty. |
| [ ] | In Luke at a D grade of certainty. |
| [( )] | Undecided. But both the IQP and I argue Luke ≠ Q at 12:33² at an A or B grade of certainty. |
| () | Not in Matt at a D or higher grade of certainty. |
| [] | Not in Luke at a D or higher grade of certainty. |

# THE *GOSPEL OF THOMAS*:
## PROSPECTS FOR FUTURE RESEARCH

*Philip Sellew*
University of Minnesota

### I. WHERE WE ARE NOW: LOOKING AWAY FROM *THOMAS*

Scholarship on the *Gospel of Thomas* has to this day focused its efforts mostly outside the text. This fact has come about for a variety of reasons. First, the text itself seems nearly opaque in compositional structure or design. Second, *Thomas* quickly became a means to help us see other early Christian literature in new ways: quite an interesting moment in the history of exegesis, when an apocryphal gospel emerged as the "canon" or rod by which to measure and interpret biblical and other texts! Third, the particular combination of ideas and themes in statements attributed to Jesus in *Thomas* has provoked discussion apart from its own use of those materials. And fourth, the rediscovery of *Thomas* helped to open the current discussion of the historical Jesus. After some preliminary remarks, let me treat each of these four paths that lead scholarship willy-nilly away from the text of *Thomas* before I sketch out some ideas about how we might proceed with the task of interpreting *Thomas* itself.

When a new document or written source is discovered, there are preliminary exercises that must be completed before we can place that new text in its proper context. As is well known, the process of making the Nag Hammadi codices available to the broader world of scholarship was long and contentious. But the initial tasks of transcription, translation, and a bit of preliminary codicological analysis were accomplished within the first twelve or fifteen years of Coptic *Thomas*'s discovery, with some improvements coming down into the 1980s.[1] A second stage in evaluating a literary find is then an attempt

---

[1] Editio princeps (facsimile): P. Labib, *Coptic Gnostic Papyri in the Coptic Museum at Old Cairo*, vol. 1 (Cairo: Government Press, 1956). First critical text and translation: A. Guillaumont, H.-C. Puech, G. Quispel, W. C. Till, and T. 'Abd al-Masih, *The Gospel according to Thomas* (Leiden: E. J. Brill; New York: Harper, 1959). Improved facsimile, with codicological analysis: *The Facsimile Edition of the Nag Hammadi Codices: Codex II*, ed. J. M. Robinson (Leiden: E. J. Brill, 1974); *Introduction* (1984). Improved critical text: *Nag Hammadi Codex II,2–7 together with XII,2, Brit. Lib. Or. 4926 (1) and P. Oxy 1, 654, 655*, vol. 1, ed. B. Layton (NHS 20; Leiden: E. J. Brill, 1989).

to position the new discovery on the spectrum of known or newly hinted literary types and ideological frameworks (what we in biblical studies often prefer to call "theology"). The basic lines for accomplishing this second task were well laid out in the 1960s and early 1970s with the famous debates about *Thomas*'s relationship with the New Testament gospels.[2] A third stage should then be a thoroughgoing study of the treatise itself: its structures, compositional design, symbolic system, plot, thematics, devices of characterization, and other literary effects. Though there have been sporadic advances in *Thomas* scholarship in treating one or another isolated aspect of this sort of inquiry,[3] for the most part we have failed to address *Thomas* in its own terms. As I will point out more fully below, we know more about the lost gospel Q *in a literary way* than we do about the extant *Gospel of Thomas*!

## A. Compositional Design

First, there is the difficulty of discerning a compositional design or structure in the *Gospel of Thomas*. While other gospels use a wealth of narrative devices to present and develop Jesus' character and fate, *Thomas* relies mostly on a dialogical or conversational format. Jesus makes statements, which are often presented without interruption; but these seem not to be self-directed, since they occasionally provoke questions from an audience. Jesus answers these questions, or at times seems to ignore them, or redirect them by further statements and new questions. The overall shape of the material is not obvious. This lack of direction has led critics working with our conventional tools of form criticism and *Traditionsgeschichte* to suggest that the *Gospel of Thomas* is virtually a sub-literary product. Several scholars have isolated smaller groupings of sayings, to be sure, which are said to be arranged in places either by theme and catchword or by formal type,

---

[2] The best critical surveys and extensive listings of earlier work are F. T. Fallon and R. Cameron, "The Gospel of Thomas: A Forschungsbericht and Analysis," *ANRW* 2/25.6, ed. W. Haase and H. Temporini (Berlin/New York: W. de Gruyter, 1988) 4195-4251, and G. J. Riley, "The *Gospel of Thomas* in Recent Scholarship," *Currents in Research: Biblical Studies* 2 (Sheffield: Sheffield Academic Press, 1994) 227-252.

[3] M. Lelyveld, *Les logia de la vie dans l'Évangile selon Thomas* (NHS 34; Leiden: E. J. Brill, 1987) is one example. I should also mention some of the presentations made since 1993 in the Thomas Christianity consultation of the SBL, at the invitation of Greg Riley and Jon Asgeirsson, including those prepared by the research team led by Risto Uro of Helsinki. Two scholars are now writing literary studies of Thomas: Richard Valantasis for Routledge and myself for the Polebridge series *The Scholars Bible*.

especially parables;[4] nonetheless the lack of any discernible larger narrative plan has stymied efforts to locate and explain *Thomas'* literary genre or intention.

The most successful suggestion about *Thomas'*s literary type made to date is still James M. Robinson's proposal of thirty years ago that it fits somewhere on the spectrum of proverbial wisdom, the sayings of the wise. Thus in Christian discourse, *Thomas* is a gospel of words, not deeds.[5] But such a comparison with biblical and other Near Eastern wisdom books, or with compendia of proverbs like the florilegia or *Apothegmata Patrum*, draws attention mostly to the distinctive pattern of loosely organized statements characteristic of these collections, though there is also their implicit hermeneutic of reading, engaged by the process of presenting discrete statements that often lack elaboration or explanation. In the long run, however, *Thomas* comes off rather poorly, or at least ends up at the far end of the spectrum, when Robinson's comparison with the Sayings Gospel Q is driven home.

It is ironic but characteristic that consideration of *Thomas'* compositional and generic nature has borne greater fruit elsewhere, namely in our understanding of the Q source. Especially since Helmut Koester took up Robinson's proposal, the comparison and contrast with *Thomas* has allowed scholars to recognize aspects of the Q material that were previously unseen.[6] When laid alongside *Thomas*, Q is found to have organization, relatively coherent themes, sophisticated rhetorical devices, possibly even plot. The Q Gospel has in

---

[4] See e.g. H. Koester, "Three Thomas Parables," in *The New Testament and Gnosis: Essays in Honour of R. McL. Wilson*, ed. A. H. B. Logan and A. J. M. Wedderburn (Edinburgh: T. & T. Clark, 1983) 195-203; "Introduction [to the *Gospel of Thomas*]," in Layton, *Nag Hammadi Codex II,2–7*, 38-49; *Ancient Christian Gospels: Their History and Development* (Philadelphia: Trinity Press International) 75-108; R. Cameron, "Parable and Interpretation in the Gospel of Thomas," *Forum* 2,2 (1986) 3-34.

[5] J. M. Robinson, "ΛΟΓΟΙ ΣΟΦΩΝ: Zur Gattung der Spruchquelle," *Zeit und Geschichte: Danksgabe an Rudolf Bultmann*, ed. E. Dinkler (Tübingen: J. C. B. Mohr [Siebeck], 1964) 77-96; revised English translation as "LOGOI SOPHON: On the Gattung of Q," in idem and Koester, *Trajectories through Early Christianity* (Philadelphia: Fortress, 1971) 71-113.

[6] H. Koester, "One Jesus and Four Primitive Gospels," *HTR* 61 (1968) 203-247 = *Trajectories*, 158-204; idem, "Apocryphal and Canonical Gospels," *HTR* 73 (1980) 105-130; *Introduction to the New Testament*, vol. 2: *History and Literature of Early Christianity* (Philadelphia: Fortress; Berlin/New York: W. de Gruyter, 1982) 147-154; "Q and Its Relatives," *Gospel Origins and Christian Beginnings: In Honor of James M. Robinson*, ed. J. E. Goehring et al. (Forum Fascicles, 2; Sonoma: Polebridge, 1990) 49-63; *Ancient Christian Gospels*, 128-171. There is a recent overview by B. H. McLean, "On the Gospel of Thomas and Q," in Piper, *The Gospel behind the Gospels*, 321-345 (see next note).

effect emerged from the twilight of historical and theological obscurity thanks in large part to the midwifery of *Thomas*. Surprisingly, we
know more about a gospel that is no longer extant in its independent
form than we do about this text that still survives in four ancient
manuscript copies, though to be sure three of them are mere fragments. Some still deny the probity of the Q hypothesis, of course,
usually because they also deny the priority of Mark as the chief
narrative source for Matthew and Luke; yet we no longer hear Q
described as a mere catachetical supplement to the authentic Pauline
gospel of the *theologia crucis* displayed in the canonical gospels.
*Thomas* is not so fortunate.

## B. Relation to Other Gospels

Second, this deployment of *Thomas* as a handy measuring rod for Q
scholarship draws our attention to an overall trend provoked by the
rediscovery of *Thomas*, toward reconsidering the development of
Christian gospel literature at large. This has meant, initially, the
question of how *Thomas* itself might fit into the picture. Several
logical possibilities were conceivable: a very early text, that is, a first-
generation *Thomas*, as a source for some or all other gospels, much
like we imagine being the case with Mark or Q; or a second-
generation *Thomas*, much like Matthew or Luke, an outgrowth or
revision of one or more gospels, including possibly Q itself or more
likely some of Q's sources; or *Thomas*, whether of an early or late
generation, as an autonomous representative of a stream of tradition
also found in other texts; or, finally, a late *Thomas*, a derivative
product compiled from other gospels, much like the *Protevangelium
Jacobi* in relationship to Matthew and Luke.[7] Each of these models
has had its prolific and vociferous champions, but as the debate
continues, once again our attention shifts inevitably away from the
*Gospel of Thomas* in and of itself, and on toward issues of how one
properly evaluates apocryphal literature, for example, or how one
situates a given document on one's map of Christian beginnings.
Much of this looking beyond *Thomas* has been quite fruitful. Ideological and compositional comparisons with the Gospel of John have
been particularly apt in work by Koester and his student Gregory

---

[7] These options are well explained in Fallon and Cameron, "The Gospel of Thomas"
and Riley, "The *Gospel of Thomas* in Recent Scholarship." See now too the collection
edited by R. A. Piper, *The Gospel behind the Gospels: Current Studies on Q* (NovTSup
75; Leiden: E. J. Brill, 1995).

Riley.[8] Again, however, in my judgment we have learned more about John's gospel than about *Thomas* as a result of these and similar investigations.

## C. The Doctrine of Thomas

A third factor directing our attention away from *Thomas* into other topics has been the nature of the statements ascribed to Jesus in this text. These offer such a dazzling range of religious or at times philosophical images and concepts that intense scrutiny of *Thomas* from a history-of-ideas or history-of-religions approach has been important. Debate has raged about whether to characterize *Thomas*'s ideology best as gnostic, mystic, encratite, or sapiential. All of these proposals can fit at least some of the evidence. But once again, the driving force of these investigations of ideas has been directed outside the text itself. We ask how *Thomas* illuminates the emergence of a gnosticized wisdom Christology, for example, or whether it better fits what we know about Syrian or Palestinian or Egyptian Christianity, or compare its mixture of materials with the ideologies present in other gospel texts.

Here too comparison with the Q source becomes pertinent. Koester's observation that *Thomas* lacks an apocalyptic viewpoint, whether in its overall tone or in individual statements ascribed to Jesus, has been of fundamental importance. When blended with Robinson's proposal of a sapiential genre for both *Thomas* and Q, this insight drew attention to the contrast with Q's curious intermingling of both wisdom and apocalyptic form and content. Koester, joined and furthered by John Kloppenborg, extended this observation into the hypothesis that the different types of Q material represented different moments in the development of the Q gospel.[9] But the

---

[8] Koester, "Dialog und Spruchüberlieferung in den gnostischen Texten von Nag Hammadi," *EvTh* 34 (1979) 532-556; "Gnostic Writings as Witnesses for the Development of the Sayings Tradition," *The Rediscovery of Gnosticism*, vol. 1: *The School of Valentinus*, ed. B. Layton (SHR 16; Leiden: E. J. Brill, 1980) 238-261; *Introduction to the New Testament*, 2. 178-193; "Gnostic Sayings and Controversy Traditions in John 8:12-59," *Nag Hammadi, Gnosticism, and Early Christianity*, ed. C. W. Hedrick and R. Hodgson Jr. (Peabody, MA: Hendrickson, 1986) 97-110; *Ancient Christian Gospels*, 173-187; Riley, *Resurrection Reconsidered: Thomas and John in Controversy* (Minneapolis: Fortress, 1995). For a different view cf. R. E. Brown, "The Gospel of Thomas and St. John's Gospel," *NTS* 9 (1962) 155-177. I should also mention the valuable suggestions of April De Conick in her work to place Thomas within the mystical traditions of late antiquity.

[9] Koester, "One Jesus" and "Q and Its Relatives"; *Ancient Christian Gospels*, 134-135, 149-166; J. S. Kloppenborg, "Wisdom Christology in Q," *Laval théologique et philosophique* 34 (1978) 129-148; "Tradition and Redaction in the Synoptic Sayings

impetus provided to Q research by this insight has rarely returned to explicate *Thomas* itself.[10]

## D.  Thomas and the Historical Jesus

Fourth, the discovery of *Thomas* in its Coptic form revolutionized our approach to the historical Jesus question. The portrait of Jesus offered here was essentially of a speaker of heavenly mysteries. There is apparently some overlap with the mysterious Jesus so prominent in the gospels of Mark and John, texts which themselves were compared in enlightening fashion nearly a century ago by William Wrede. Once again it was Robinson and Koester that noticed and drove home the connection with *Thomas*.[11] But in terms of overall content, apart from the personality of the central character Jesus, *Thomas* reminded scholars once again of Q, with its apparent paucity of miracle stories, its inattention to the Pauline kerygma of cross and resurrection, and especially in its focus on the teaching of Jesus. With Koester's insight about the fundamentally sapiential nature of the words ascribed to Jesus in *Thomas*, the question was reopened as to whether the consensus view of Jesus as (among other things) a preacher of apocalypse could be challenged by *Thomas*'s (and Q's) different portrait. Some Jesus scholars, notably J. Dominic Crossan and the Jesus Seminar, including Stephen Patterson, took up the case that *Thomas* provides in this aspect, at least, a truer picture of Jesus than the gospels of the New Testament canon.[12] Others, like Robinson,

---

Source," *CBQ* 46 (1984) 34-62; *The Formation of Q: Trajectories in Ancient Wisdom Collections* (Philadelphia: Fortress, 1986). Robinson spells out the terms of the discussion in his articles "On Bridging the Gulf from Q to the Gospel of Thomas (or Vice Versa)," in Hedrick and Hodgson, eds., *Nag Hammadi, Gnosticism, and Early Christianity* 127-175, and "The Q Trajectory: Between John and Matthew via Jesus," in *The Future of Early Christianity: Essays in Honor of Helmut Koester*, ed. B. A. Pearson (Minneapolis: Fortress, 1991) 173-194; see also C. M. Tuckett, "Q and Thomas: Evidence of a Primitive 'Wisdom Gospel'?" *ETL* 67 (1991) 346-360; McLean, "On the Gospel of Thomas and Q," 333-342.

[10] An exception is a stimulating article by William Arnal posing the question whether distinct sorts of sayings material in Thomas ("sapiential" and "gnostic") may reveal its compositional history. See "The Rhetoric of Marginality: Apocalypticism, Gnosticism, and Sayings Gospels," *HTR* 88 (1995) 471-494.

[11] W. Wrede, *Das Messiasgeheimnis in den Evangelien* (Göttingen: Vandenhoeck & Ruprecht, 1901); Robinson, "Kerygma and History in the New Testament," *The Bible in Modern Scholarship*, ed. J. P. Hyatt (Nashville: Abingdon, 1965) 114-150 = *Trajectories*, 20-70; *The Problem of History in Mark and Other Marcan Studies* (Philadelphia: Fortress, 1982) 11-53; Koester, "Gnostic Writings as Witnesses" and "Gnostic Sayings and Controversy Traditions," *Ancient Christian Gospels*, 107-124.

[12] J. D. Crossan, *In Parables: The Challenge of the Historical Jesus* (New York: Harper, 1973; repr. Sonoma: Polebridge, 1992); *In Fragments: The Aphorisms of Jesus*

Burton Mack, Leif Vaage, F. Gerald Downing, and Crossan too, with influence from Paul Hoffmann, Gerd Theissen, and other contributors, drew from the newly understood Q gospel a portrait of Jesus as sage or cynic.[13]

But this flurry of excitement about the implications of *Thomas*'s presentation of Jesus and his message, especially in light of its strong contrasts with the canonical gospels, has begged some central questions, indeed has flown right past them. Leaving some less important considerations aside, let me address what I see as the crucial problem. How do we justify our claim to stake out any particular reconstruction of the historical Jesus on any of these gospel texts? The problem is indeed especially acute for *Thomas*. Those scholars who rely on *Thomas* for key information about Jesus and his activities must remove and abstract the statements ascribed to Jesus from the very text in which those attractive statements are embedded. So, for example, some confirmation of Theissen's proposals about Jesus and his first followers as itinerants is claimed to lie in the famously laconic statement *Gos. Thom.* 42: "Become passers-by."[14] Not enough justification for this interpretation is offered or can be offered from *Thomas* itself, despite the composite statement *Gos. Thom.* 14.

Those trying to trace the history of the transmission of the Jesus traditions reflected in *Thomas* naturally employ form criticism; and these scholars have shown the relatively "early" character of much of the material ("early" meant in more of a phenomenological than a

---

(San Francisco: Harper & Row, 1983); *The Historical Jesus: The Life of a Mediterranean Jewish Peasant* (San Francisco: HarperCollins, 1991); R. W. Funk, R. Hoover, and the Jesus Seminar, *The Five Gospels: The Search for the Authentic Words of Jesus* (New York/London: Macmillan, 1993). For discussion see esp. S. J. Patterson, *The Gospel of Thomas and Jesus* (Sonoma: Polebridge, 1993) 217-241.

[13] P. Hoffmann, *Studien zur Theologie der Logienquelle* (Münster: Aschendorff, 1972); Gerd Theissen, *Soziologie der Jesubewegung* (Munich: Kaiser, 1977), ET as *The Sociology of Early Palestinian Christianity* (Philadelphia: Fortress, 1978); *Studien zur Soziologie des Urchristentums*, 2nd ed. (WUNT 19; Tübingen: Mohr [Siebeck]), 1983), ET as *Social Reality and the Early Christians* (Minneapolis: Fortress, 1992); Robinson, "The Jesus of Q as Liberation Theologian," in Piper, *The Gospel behind the Gospels*, 259-274; Crossan, *In Aphorisms*; B. L. Mack, *A Myth of Innocence: Mark and Christian Origins* (Philadelphia: Fortress, 1988); "The Kingdom That Didn't Come: A Social History of the Q Tradents," *SBLSP* (1988) 606-635; *The Lost Gospel: Q and Christian Origins* (San Francisco: HarperCollins, 1993); F. G. Downing, *Christ and the Cynics: Jesus and Other Radical Preachers in First-Century Tradition* (Sheffield: JSOT, 1988); L. Vaage, "Q[1] and the Historical Jesus: Some Peculiar Sayings," *Forum* 5,2 (1989) 159-176; idem, *Galilean Upstarts: Jesus' First Followers According to Q* (Philadelphia: Trinity Press International, 1994).

[14] Patterson, *Gospel of Thomas and Jesus*, 128-133.

strictly chronological sense). Historians of the tradition have focused their efforts on parables and aphorisms and chreiai that either offer close parallels to the New Testament Jesus or else remind us strongly of that sort of material. Thus the dubious category of "synoptic" and "synoptic-like" sayings has been evaluated with a claim of generally positive results. Especially when removed from their present literary contexts, many of the words ascribed to Jesus in *Thomas* do have qualities of antiquity and authenticity vis-à-vis the New Testament gospels. But using the New Testament portrait of Jesus as a criterion of authenticity for *Thomas* material seems to me quite suspect as a method. If anything, our ever-growing awareness of the ideological programs of all the gospel writers should give us pause. When Jesus makes a statement within the discourse world of the *Gospel of Thomas* that reminds us, especially in isolation, of something else the character Jesus mentions within another text's narrative world, this suggests to me a situation of intertextuality (whether of oral or written texts) rather than data providing coordinates for some sort of surveyor's triangulation back to the historical speaker Jesus.

Admittedly, in the case of *Thomas*, which is after all a gospel that strikes so many critics as a haphazard text, a virtually random stringing together of isolated statements, lacking both context and sequence, there seems to be ample room for abstracting any given statement from its literary location. For example, still today we read, in what is the best book published on gospel traditions in the 1990s, that *Thomas* is "just stringing sayings together," with "seemingly no rhyme or reason for the odd sequence in which the sayings occur.... The writer of the *Gospel of Thomas* is, in fact, not an author who deliberately composed his book according to a general master plan.... He shows no desire to express his own understanding of these sayings through the manner of composition.... Each saying has meaning in itself."[15] Yet our ease in extracting a statement from its textual life into the never-never land of scholarly reconstruction is in and of itself no defense of the procedure. We have begun to learn to tread cautiously when removing the words of Jesus contextualized in Matthew, Mark, Luke, or John, and perhaps now Q too, from their narrative settings, as though they were so many colorful pebbles with which to build a mosaic portrait of the authentic Jesus. We have no more license to treat *Thomas* as a quarry to be mined for Jesus talk, consciously or heedlessly oblivious to literary and compositional

---

[15] Koester, *Ancient Christian Gospels*, 80, 81-82.

realities, than we should have in the case of other Christian texts, be they narrative gospels in their basic orientation or sayings gospels.

## II. WHERE WE GO FROM HERE: LET *THOMAS* BE *THOMAS*

What should our primary goal be as readers and interpreters of the *Gospel of Thomas*? Which form of the gospel text should we privilege, if any? I suggest that we should now seek literary questions and literary answers about the *Gospel of Thomas*. Our difficulties in finding any obvious meaning at the compositional level suggest to me that we should try a different tack. The text obviously must have meant something, both to its author, since I claim there was an author, and to the many readers that we might imagine using the surviving Egyptian manuscripts. Perhaps we can learn something by presupposing the direct opposite of the starkly negative scholarly consensus that I have summarized: perhaps the arrangement or sequence of statements and groups of statements *does* indeed convey meaning, though not necessarily the sort of meaning that we see even in other sayings gospels or in wisdom books. To explore this possibility requires adopting a more literary sensibility, a focusing of attention on reading the text in its own terms, searching out its hermeneutical soteriology. The task is difficult, and the meanings provided by stark juxtapositions are not always obvious. Perhaps that obscurity is already part of the point.

### A. Original Text of Thomas

A key question still before us is whether there ever existed an "original" text of *Thomas*, or for that matter even a "final" text. I would deny that we have access to either a beginning or an endpoint in any meaningful sense. We have learned from the study of other, better-attested texts that also remained outside the canon of Christian scripture, that writings like *Thomas* have little protection against interpolation, rearrangement, revision, and rewriting. Even texts that eventually became canonical, as we know, were not yet in fixed form until the third century; well-known examples of an experience of interpolations, continuations, and re-editions include Luke-Acts, the Pauline corpus, and the Gospel of Mark.[16] There are some good

---

[16] On the textual tradition of the gospels in general see *Gospel Traditions in the Second Century: Origins, Recensions, Text, and Transmission*, ed. W. L. Petersen (Notre Dame: University of Notre Dame Press, 1989), esp. the contributions by Birdsall, Koester, and Epp; on Mark in particular, see Koester, *Ancient Christian Gospels*, 273-289; P. Sellew, "*Secret Mark* and the History of Canonical Mark," *The Future of Early Christianity*, ed. B. A. Pearson (Minneapolis: Fortress, 1991) 242-257. For aspects of the

parallels in classical literature: the text of Homer prior to the canon
formation of the Alexandrian scholars in the mid-second century BCE
is quite variable in terms of specific wording and the placement or
even inclusion of particular lines or episodes.[17] The Attic tragedians
had their plays altered for stage productions by both actors and
producers.[18] Closer to our literature both generically and temporally
are the Greek romances or novels, which in some cases may never
have achieved a so-called "final form."[19]

   A related issue has to do with which specific form of the *Gospel of
Thomas* deserves our primary attention. Here I would argue that we
should address our main work to the Coptic version of the text. Of
course the three Greek fragments represent a chronologically earlier
moment in the life of the gospel, yet this very fact distracts us again
into questions of the history of the text rather than its meaning. A
largely unmentioned reason that many scholars privilege the Greek
excerpts of *Thomas* over its full version in Coptic is the factor of
relative dating and value; if we are to use *Thomas* to reconstruct
Jesus, or first- and second-century Christian literary and theological

---

text of Paul see e.g. J. J. Clabeaux, *A Lost Edition of the Letters of Paul: A Reassessment
of the Text of the Pauline Corpus Attested by Marcion* (CBQMS 21; Washington, DC:
Catholic Biblical Association of America, 1989); Sellew, "*Laodiceans* and the Philippians
Fragments Hypothesis," *HTR* 87 (1994) 17-28. A useful overview of the general state of
NT textual criticism is provided in *The Text of the New Testament in Contemporary
Research: Essays on the Status Quaestionis*, ed. B. D. Ehrman and M. W. Holmes
(Grand Rapids: Eerdmans, 1995).

   [17] See e.g., S. West, *The Ptolemaic Papyri of Homer* (Cologne: Westdeutscher Verlag,
1967); "The Transmission of the Text," in A. Heubeck, S. West, and J. B. Hainsworth, *A
Commentary on Homer's Odyssey* (Oxford: Clarendon, 1988) 33-48.

   [18] D. L. Page, *Actors' Interpolations in Greek Tragedy* (Oxford: Clarendon, 1934); M.
D. Reeve, "Interpolations in Greek Tragedy," *GRBS* 13 (1972) 247-265; 451-474; 14
(1973) 145-171.

   [19] B. E. Perry, *The Ancient Romances: A Literary-Historical Account of Their Origins*
(Berkeley: University of California Press, 1967); T. Hägg, "Die Ephesiaka des Xenophon
Ephesios: Original oder Epitome?," *Classica et Medievalia* 27 (1966) 118-161; *The
Novel in Antiquity* (Berkeley: University of California Press, 1983); E. L. Bowie, "The
Greek Novel," in *Cambridge History of Classical Literature*, vol. 1, ed. P. E. Easterling
and B. Knox (Cambridge: University Press, 1985) 683-699; R. I. Pervo, *Profit with
Delight: The Literary Genre of the Acts of the Apostles* (Philadelphia: Fortress, 1987);
*Der antike Roman: Untersuchungen zur literarischen Kommunikation und Gattungs-
geschichte*, ed. H. Kuch (Berlin: Akademie-Verlag, 1989); B. P. Reardon, *The Form of
Greek Romance* (Princeton: Princeton University Press, 1991); R. Kussl, *Papyrusfrag-
mente griechischer Romane* (Tübingen: G. Narr, 1991); S. A. Stephens, "Who Read
Ancient Novels?" and Bowie, "The Readership of Greek Novels in the Ancient World,"
*The Search for the Ancient Novel*, ed. J. Tatum (Baltimore: Johns Hopkins University
Press, 1994); C. M. Thomas, "Word and Deed: The Acts of Peter and Orality,"
*Apocrypha* 3 (1992) 125-164; "The Acts of Peter, the Ancient Novel, and Early Christian
History" (Ph.D. diss., Harvard University, 1995).

developments, after all, we would want to underline the antiquity of the document, not its fourth-century appearance in Upper Egypt in a jar stuffed with other, even more outré writings. But for literary purposes, the Coptic text of *Thomas* is what we have to work with.

## B. Methods of Approach

My next topic poses the question of what sorts of techniques we could profitably use to make some headway in understanding *Thomas* as it exists. I will first discuss the notion of viewing the gospel as part of a horizontal, intertextual conversation rather than as the result of a vertical, genetic process. After a brief discussion of the topics of reception history or readership and other literary concerns, I will move to Part III of the paper, a sample of a literary probing of a major theme within the gospel—the identity of Jesus.

The SBL seminar on Christian Apocrypha has led the way in recent years in coming to terms with fluid texts like the *Acts of Paul* or *Acts of Peter* which survive in various languages and recensions.[20] The interrelationships of the apostolic acts, including the work ascribed to Luke, whether these connections be literary, social-historical, or theological, seem best approached in many cases using the techniques of intertextual analysis: how do the various stories and narratives converse with each other?

When these sorts of questions are asked of the gospel tradition, however, our resistance is stronger and our reaction much more guarded. An "intertextual" analysis of the New Testament gospels would seem to call into question important scholarly constructs on which much of our work is based: the priority of Mark, the existence and use of the Q Gospel, the independence of John, and so on. Either Matthew used Mark as a source, we might argue, or it did not; how does a model of conversation between texts work when those gospels have been defined as existing in a genetic relationship?

The postulated independence of John from the synoptic gospels is a good example of this difficulty. Several recent authors have returned to the view prominent early in the century that John either

---

[20] See contributions by members of the Seminar on Intertextuality and Christian Apocrypha published in recent years in the *SBL Seminar Papers*, among which I would mention especially D. R. MacDonald, *"The Acts of Paul* and *The Acts of Peter:* Which Came First?" *SBLSP* (1992) 214-224; R. F. Stoops, "Peter, Paul, and Priority in the Apocryphal Acts," ibid., 225-233; R. Valantasis, "Narrative Strategies and Synoptic Quandaries: A Response to Dennis MacDonald's Reading," ibid., 234-239; F. S. Jones, "Principal Orientations in the Relations between the Apocryphal Acts," *SBLSP* (1993) 485-505; cf. also F. Bovon, "The Synoptic Gospels and the Noncanonical Acts of the Apostles," *HTR* 81 (1988) 19-36.

knew and used Mark directly or as mediated through Luke. Mack, for example, points out the use of Mark's plot, characterizations, and distinctive terms in John's narrative.[21] Some scholars, myself included, have emphasized the presence of signature Marcan stylistic devices in parallel scenes in John, as for example in the episode of Peter's triple denial during Caiaphas' interrogation of Jesus.[22] Thomas Brodie sees an even more thorough permeation of John's story with Marcan and other Synoptic narrative themes that are constantly set over against each other.[23] The model of the Synoptic Problem has in fact confused our perceptions of the relations between John and other gospels, and by analogy quite possibly our view of how *Thomas* fits, too. John's knowledge or use of Mark is not as obvious as the literary dependencies among Matthew, Mark, and Luke. John represents an "autonomous" gospel tradition, to borrow the term proposed by Theissen and Patterson to describe the connection of *Thomas* to the New Testament gospels.[24] John knows Mark's story somehow, but accomplishes his aims in a more independent manner than did Matthew or Luke, nonetheless revealing his knowledge of the earlier gospel in many subtle ways—data that seem not so subtle once they are noticed.

If we accept the likelihood of John's knowledge either of Mark or, perhaps, a revision of Mark as represented by Luke, then the presuppositions that led to many of the reconstructions of first-generation Christianity since World War II are called into question. The presumed literary independence of John from the Synoptics is what requires us to postulate shared sources outside of Mark (or Luke) and thus prior to either one of them. For example, if John knows Mark, then the *need* to postulate an oral cycle of miracles (à la Achtemeier's

---

[21] Mack, *A Myth of Innocence*, 225 n. 12.

[22] Sellew, "Tracking the Tradition: On the Current State of Tradition History," *Forum* 9 (1993) 217-35, with further literature there, among which I would mention especially F. Matera, "The Incomprehension of the Disciples and Peter's Confession," *Bib* 70 (1989) 153-172.

[23] T. L. Brodie, *The Quest for the Origins of John's Gospel: A Source-Oriented Approach* (New York: Oxford University Press, 1993). See also D. M. Smith, *John among the Gospels: The Relationship in Twentieth-Century Research* (Minneapolis: Fortress, 1992), and the important essays in *John and the Synoptics*, ed. A. Denaux (BETL 101; Leuven: Peeters, 1992). Earlier advocates of John's knowledge of Mark or all three Synoptic Gospels are discussed by Smith on pp. 13-43.

[24] Patterson, *Gospel of Thomas and Jesus*, 17-110, with summary statement on pp. 109-110.

"miracle catenae"[25]) disappears. If John knows Mark, then the apparent independent attestation of "facts" about Jesus and his circle disappears, including such foundational data as Jesus calling disciples or Jesus performing public miracles. Most significantly, if we accept the conclusion that John knows Mark's story, the evidence for there needing to have been a pre-Marcan Passion Narrative disappears.

How do we apply these lessons toward improving our understanding of *Thomas*? For one thing, we see that some hypotheses may remain compelling even when they seem a bit messier than alternative explanations. The need to postulate a shared source should not be confused with the *advantages* of proposing such hypotheses, whether they be logically necessary or not. The Q hypothesis strikes few of us as logically required, but rather as an attractive or even compelling explanation for the data we see in and among the three synoptic gospels. Perhaps the hypothesis of an independent Johannine narrative tradition no longer bears the weight of its relative "messiness" over against the more elegant solution of intertextual knowledge. Therefore the question is open whether we have framed the issue correctly when we ask about the nature of *Thomas*'s relationship with the New Testament gospels and Q. I think we have been too distracted by the related problem of the historical Jesus to see this matter clearly. What is often at stake in our discussions is not merely or even mainly the history of *Thomas*, but rather a decision as to which texts are to be acknowledged as the most authentic sources for Jesus and whatever Christian theology is built on claims that depend on making his words visible. Perhaps *Thomas* is conversing with other gospels.[26]

## III. THE CONSTRUCTION OF JESUS IN THE *GOSPEL OF THOMAS*

I now want to sketch out one possible application of literary methods of interpretation to *Thomas*, since in my judgment we have reached an impasse in how we pose and answer most of those other sorts of questions. Both historical and ideological approaches tend to fragment the text, to separate and dissolve it into bits useful for whatever questions are deemed most relevant. It is no doubt useful and important to break *Thomas* down into its constitutive parts to analyze its

---

[25] P. J. Achtemeier, "Toward the Isolation of Pre-Markan Miracle Catenae," *JBL* 89 (1970) 265-291; idem, "The Origin and Function of the Pre-Marcan Miracle Catenae," *JBL* 91 (1972) 198-221.

[26] For a discussion of this and similar issues see R. Uro, "'Secondary Orality' in the Gospel of Thomas? Logion 14 as a Test Case," *Forum* 9 (1993) 305-329.

form-critical profile and its use of philosophical or religious concepts. But this atomizing of the text, this dismemberment, leaves us knowing more about the parts than the whole. I am more interested in how language is used within and across the document as it stands than in tracing the background and import of the terms outside of the text. Knowing what these terms and symbols mean elsewhere is useful, but all too often takes us too far away from the document itself.

As mentioned above, *Thomas* relies on a pattern of monologue and dialogue, creating a need for the reader to enter the world of the text to make any sense of its claims. Quite possibly the very fact of a bare bones structure made the gospel useful and appealing for particular ancient readers, for example, those seeking spiritual gnosis or enlightenment. I have suggested elsewhere that *Thomas* could be understood as something of a spiritual guide.[27] The gospel's famous absence of narrative clues is perhaps not in reality a vacuum, or a failure to conform to a literary type, but instead a deliberate silence. What clues do exist are often baffling or apparently contradictory.

A basic question facing any reader of this gospel is: Who is Jesus? The main personage of the *Gospel of Thomas* is Jesus the speaker. What are we told or shown about this Jesus in this text? We are in fact *told* very little beyond the interesting fact that he is "the one who lives" (ⲓ̄ⲥ ⲉⲧⲟⲛ̄ⳅ). We are mostly *shown* Jesus speaking: but why is he speaking? Apparently this display of the conversation is itself somehow important to the document and its meaning. A quest of Jesus and his meaning indeed lies at the heart of its message, an identity that is slowly constructed by the reader through pondering the arrangement of his statements. The reader must consider and search out the meaning of his words to attain life. This is the plan of salvation offered by the gospel, what I would term its hermeneutical soteriology.

The prologue announces that "secret words of the living Jesus" will soon follow, or his "hidden words" (ⲛ̄ϣⲁϫⲉ ⲉⲑⲏⲡ). From whom are these sayings and their import kept hidden or obscure? The text contains clues suggesting that the meaning of Jesus' words is especially mysterious to his interlocutors within the gospel itself. Clustered near the end of the gospel are questions from the disciples that deepen our impression that even then they remain in the dark.

---

[27] Sellew, "Death, the Body and the World in the Coptic Gospel of Thomas," *Proceedings of the XII International Patristics Conference, Oxford, 1995*, ed. E. A. Livingstone (*Studia Patristica* 31; Leuven: Peeters, 1996) 530-34.

Perhaps we too are still left wondering. Understanding and explanation first require an adequate description of what we see.

The gospel opens with a scene of one man speaking, Jesus, the one who lives, and one man recording his words, Didymos Judas Thomas. No other people are mentioned directly at first, though we quickly sense that the speaker's words are addressed to more than one individual. Here and there various other listeners begin to be labeled, and occasionally are even named. But other narrative clues or stage directions are missing—we know not where or when these monologues and conversations are taking place, except that they occur sometime in the undetermined narrative past. We are not told how or when these other individuals come to hear the speaker, or when or how they may at times disappear. After a bit these listeners begin to speak too—mostly by posing questions to the first named speaker.

As mentioned, these questions elicit various responses from him. Here and there we are told a questioner's name. The listeners and questioners are nearly all males, from what we can tell, though someone named Mary successfully poses a question a few pages into the text (at *Gos. Thom.* 21), as does a person called Salome, rather further along (*Gos. Thom.* 61). An unnamed third woman shouts out a blessing from the crowd in *Gos. Thom.* 79, a blessing that Jesus does not accept. The participation of Mary, the first named female questioner, is debated at the close of the text. Possibly our own acceptance and the meaning of our participation as eavesdropping readers are also in question, both at the end of the text and (retrospectively) throughout.

Going back to the opening of the gospel: After a statement by an unnamed male individual, we find the first statement that is introduced with the famous phrase "Jesus said" (ⲡⲉϫⲉ ⲓ̅ⲥ̅). Jesus' statement addresses no one in particular—it is in the mode of third-person, or better, "delocutive" speech (as opposed to the give-and-take of "interlocutive" speech). Why? Perhaps a generalized or indefinite audience is in view. Perhaps those challenged by the summons to find interpretation and avoid death are meant: "Let the one who seeks not stop seeking until that person finds ..." (*Gos. Thom.* 2). Who makes up that audience?

Without any narrative interruption or explanation, but in simple juxtaposition, the very next statement, also introduced by the formula ⲡⲉϫⲉ ⲓ̅ⲥ̅, employs the interlocutive mode. This implies that Jesus does have an audience, or envisions conversation partners beyond the scribe mentioned in the prologue. Here we see a series of conditional declarations, all addressed to an indeterminate plural "you" (*Gos.*

*Thom.* 3) — "Jesus said, If they say to you (ΝΗΤΝ̄), that is, those who lead you (ΝΕΤϹⲰΚ ϨΗΤ' ΤΗΥΤΝ̄), 'See, the kingdom of heaven is in the sky ...' Rather, the kingdom is inside of you, and it is outside of you," and so on.

The text opens as monologue: the figure named "Jesus who lives" makes several observations or pronouncements, numbered as *Gos. Thom.* 2–5 in the conventional classification, before any other labeled voices are heard. Then a group labeled "his disciples" suddenly poses a question, "Do you want us to fast? ..." (*Gos. Thom.* 6). The text reads, "His disciples questioned him and said to him..." Who these "disciples" might be, or where they might have come from, are matters left undescribed; we must presume that they have been listening all along, that *they* have been the "you" of Jesus' previous statements. But the topic of fasting and prayer will make us wonder by the end of the text whether they have been listening very well to Jesus or not.

Scholars debate whether the statement conventionally labeled *Gos. Thom.* 1 is meant as a pronouncement of Jesus: ⲀⲨⲰ ⲠⲈⲬⲀϤ ⲬⲈ ⲠⲈⲦⲀϨⲈ ...: "And he said, "Whoever *finds* the meaning of these sayings will not taste death." Who actually does begin the speaking in this gospel *of Thomas?* I suspect that it is not Jesus but the apostle. I suspect that the first statement to be tagged with the "Jesus said" formula, the so-called statement 2, is actually also Jesus' first utterance in the text. This would mean that Jesus is shown reacting to what had just been said by the unidentified "he" of statement 1: Jesus says, or, more likely, replies, "Let one who seeks not stop seeking until that person *finds* ...."[28] The initial challenge to find the interpretation of the sayings is not tagged with a speaker's name, precisely because that speaker is not Jesus who lives, but his scribe Didymos Judas Thomas. The speaker of the challenge is unnamed so as to keep the speech of Jesus in the foreground. Though other people have things to say, Jesus is the speaker *par excellence* of this text. The Jesus "who lives" comes to life, as it were, by his and our giving voice to his words.

The construction of Jesus as one who lives in speaking continues throughout the text. In *Gos. Thom.* 4 Jesus reverts to delocutive speech: "The man old in days will not hesitate ..." In *Gos. Thom.* 5 he

---

[28] The shift in verbs of finding in the Coptic (ϨⲈ in # 1 to ϬⲒⲚⲈ in # 2) need not rule out this "reply" interpretation. Unfortunately the verb translated as "find" is missing in the Greek of # 1 (Pap. Oxy. 654.4), though forms of the verb εὑρίσκειν are typically restored for both statements by editors.

then abruptly switches to second-person singular address, "Recognize what is in your sight (ⲘⲠⲈⲔⳅⲞ), and that which is hidden from you will become plain to you." Then comes a characteristic Jesus proverb: "There is nothing hidden which will not become manifest." Whatever this proverb may mean in other early Christian writings, here its only apparent reference is to the hidden quality ascribed to Jesus' words themselves. Recognize what is before you (namely, Jesus, the living one, the speaker) and what is hidden, his words, and their meaning, will become clear. Jesus lives by speaking his words; his auditors must find their meaning and thus also ... live?

When Jesus' opening monologue is broken, his audience apparently does not recognize what is right before their eyes. (This failure is something Jesus himself will complain about as late as *Gos. Thom.* 91–92.) Instead of finding meaning manifest in the hidden words, and perhaps thus finding life, they query Jesus about proper pious practice. "His disciples questioned him and said to him, 'Do you want us to fast? How shall we pray ...'" and so on. When Jesus has confronted them as individuals "Recognize that which is before *thee*," they scramble for the safety of the group: Tell *us*, Jesus, what *we* should do! Jesus accepts their group identity and addresses the group, "Don't tell lies, and don't do that which you hate." Then he repeats his proverb in two slightly new wordings, as though hoping they would now get the point: "Nothing hidden will not become manifest, and nothing covered will remain without being uncovered."

Jesus then embarks on a series of hidden or obscure words, *meshalim* or enigmas: the lion becoming human (*Gos. Thom.* 7), the wise fisherman (statement 8), and the fate of the seed (statement 9). The meaning of the juxtapositions is of interest here. We may wonder whether Jesus is meant to be the unnamed speaker of the fisher similitude, for example, or whether instead the lion-become-human is speaking. None of these obscurities provokes any response from Jesus' interlocutors, who at this point appear to be more like puzzled onlookers than real partners in conversation. Jesus tries to involve them by getting personal: "I have cast fire upon the world, and look! — I am guarding it until it blazes!" Maybe his disciples do "look," since they definitely keep their mouths shut.[29]

Finally, after comments about the "passing away" of the heavens, and the utter separation of life and death, Jesus poses them a direct question in *Gos. Thom.* 11: "In the days when you ate what is dead,

---

[29] The incomprehension of Jesus' disciples in *Thomas* is one of the features that connects this gospel thematically with Mark's; see n. 11 above.

you made it what is alive; when you come to dwell in the light, what
will you do? ... When you become two, what will you do?" This
insistent question demands a response, but it is not forthcoming. The
disciples do not discuss these central themes of the text: eating, what
is dead and what is alive, dwelling in the light, or becoming a single
one. Instead they worry about who is to lead them after Jesus'
departure — they know *that's* coming: "We know that you will depart
from us" (*Gos. Thom.* 12).

A key passage in my reading of the text is that called *Gos. Thom.*
13. Here Jesus provokes further conversation by urging his disciples
to characterize him, to give him some quality, to put him in some
classification: "Tell me whom I am like!" Two attempts by leading
disciples to characterize Jesus in conventional terms are met with
silence. First Simon Peter likens Jesus to an angel, in fact, significantly, a righteous angel or messenger, and then Matthew compares
him to a wise philosopher. But finally Thomas begins to hit the mark
by making no comparison at all, by claiming an inability of speech, a
quality beyond words; yet he gives away his true view of Jesus by his
first word, "Master, my mouth is totally incapable of saying whom
you are like!" The word usually translated "master" (ⲡⲥⲁϩ) of
course also means "teacher," and perhaps it is this role that Jesus
immediately denies himself: "I am not *your* teacher!" But he uses the
singular form, (ⲁⲛⲟⲕ ⲡⲉⲕⲥⲁϩ ⲁⲛ), he is not *Thomas's* teacher or
master. Thomas has already learned something, or, in the words of the
text, he has drunk and become intoxicated from Jesus' own bubbling
spring.

Thomas is praised for this particular intoxication. But what interests me here is still the conversation itself and its way of flowing or
bubbling along. When Thomas, as one of Jesus' disciples, or students,
opens his mouth to claim, ironically, that his mouth will not work
right in attempting to compare Jesus, but calls him "Teacher"
anyway, this for some reason strikes something positive in Jesus.
Jesus takes Thomas aside and speaks to him out of our hearing. Jesus
tells Thomas three mysterious words, and then Thomas rejoins his
friends. This all seems reminiscent of the opening of the text, as
though we were now in flashback to the prologue's statement that
"*These* are the secret words that Jesus spoke and Thomas wrote
down." But of course we now have more than three: perhaps the scene
of the private words is meant to be paradigmatic.

Upon Thomas's return from this privileged conversation we find
the only dialogue in the text that does not involve Jesus as a participant: "What did Jesus say to you, what did he say?" But Thomas

refuses to repeat anything that Jesus had told him, threatening magical violence if his companions try to force him to speak. Thomas prefers silence here too. He writes or keeps notes, he doesn't like to speak.

Juxtaposed next is *Gos. Thom.* 14, where we are shown Jesus again as the speaker, who now provides direct answers to the questions first posed to him by his disciples back in *Gos. Thom.* 6: "If you fast" (using the plural: ⲈⲦⲈⲦⲚϢⲀⲚⲚⲎⲤⲦⲈⲨⲈ) "you will give rise to sin for yourselves; and if you pray, you will be condemned, and if you give alms, you will harm your spirits." The works of the mouth, like prayer, and indeed speech itself, are dangerous: "For what goes into your mouth will not defile you, it is what comes out from your mouth—that is what will defile you!" Food and drink are key symbols here and elsewhere in the text. Their "orality" may be important. Perhaps these prohibitions correspond to the three dangerous words that Thomas had refused to repeat.

I must bring this brief sketch to a close with mention of only one or two other sections of the text that help illumine my point about the importance of speech in characterizing Jesus in this gospel. Much of what follows *Gos. Thom.* 14 shows Jesus speaking without interruption—no interruption from the narrator or from any of the other characters. But here or there the disciples again pose a question, and Jesus responds again in riddles: statement 18, about the end and the beginning, and statement 20, about the kingdom being like a mustard seed. Parables continue in statement 21, when suddenly Mary, apparently a non-disciple, asks Jesus to characterize them for a change. Up to this point one has imagined that Jesus is speaking only to his disciples, yet here is an indication that others (besides us readers) are listening in on that conversation. But as we know, Mary may yet turn out to be one of the group. In statement 43 the disciples challenge Jesus' authority, or even his identity as the living one who speaks: "Who are you that you should say these things to us?" Jesus agrees that they cannot understand his speech, nor his identity: "You do not realize who I am from what I am saying to you."

At the end of the document, a sort of ring composition emerges more clearly, when themes addressed very early in the text recur. Some unnamed group again speaks in statement 104, this time to propose prayer and fasting. If the unnamed speakers are his disciples, they have listened poorly and learned little since they first posed this topic in statement 6 and Jesus disposed of it both there and in statement 14. Now Jesus begins to quote himself even more explicitly, as in statement 111. Soon the disciples pose another topic that was earlier disposed of by Jesus back in statement 3, the when- and whereabouts of the kingdom: "His disciples said to him, "When will the kingdom come?" "It will not come by waiting for it. ... Rather, the kingdom of the father is spread out on the earth, and people do not see it" (*Gos. Thom.* 113). That kingdom is "spread out on the earth" by Jesus' words, and his disciples do not comprehend it.

We seem to be back at the entry point of the text. The disciples have listened in vain; we too seem often to have read and listened but not understood. Perhaps to symbolize this failure of understanding, Simon Peter speaks his second solo part in the gospel: "Let Mary leave us, for women are not worthy of life" (*Gos. Thom.* 114). As we all know, Jesus rejects Peter's demand and promises to make Mary into "a living spirit resembling you males." We the readers are left to hope that, along with Mary, we too will heed Jesus' voice and so first be led to understand, and then to speak Jesus' words of life.

What effect or impact does the Jesus portrayed in this fashion in the *Gospel of Thomas* have on its readers? Which ancient readers found *Thomas* compelling?—whether we mean those readers implied by the text, in the first instance, or those we can postulate based on the provenience of the manuscripts as well as hints found in other texts? What aspects of life are most illuminated by this sort of presentation of Jesus? How does *Thomas* use its central character Jesus to engage our attention, then try to redirect our interests, and finally perhaps change us in some way? These are the sorts of questions that I submit to our consideration as present and future interpreters of *Thomas*. I propose this approach because this is what seems to be demanded by the gospel text, both in its overall design and in its elementary structures. I hope that the sort of work I envision here will ultimately dovetail with more conventional form-critical and historical approaches to teach us something about both the author of the text and its readership.

# L'INTERPRÉTATION DE L'*ÉVANGILE SELON THOMAS*, ENTRE TRADITION ET RÉDACTION

*Jean-Marie Sevrin*
Louvain-la-Neuve

Dès la première génération d'études sur l'EvTh, on a vu, à côté du débat sur ses sources, se dessiner des tentatives d'en retracer la doctrine—la théologie—c'est-à-dire de l'interpréter comme un tout. Les plus significatives et les plus citées de ces tentatives furent sans doute celles de B. Gärtner et d'E. Hänchen.[1] Si depuis lors la recherche s'est poursuivie, souvent dans des commentaires suivis du texte,[2] et s'est parfois égarée dans des interprétations spirituelles sans rapport avec une démarche critique,[3] il semble que les pas essentiels aient été faits dans les débuts et qu'une interprétation d'ensemble satisfaisante soit encore à attendre. Mais dans le même temps, l'idée qu'une lecture cohérente de l'ensemble de l'EvTh soit possible, a régressé. La tendance marquée à considérer l'EvTh comme une collection de paroles, analogue à ce qu'a pu être l'hypothétique *Quelle* et apparentée à elle,[4] n'oriente pas vers la considération de l'EvTh comme un ensemble, mais vers l'interprétation isolée de chaque logion, rapporté à la tradition dans laquelle il s'origine (démarche de Formgeschichte) plutôt qu'au texte dans lequel il s'inscrit. Si l'EvTh est, en réalité comme en apparence, une collection et non un texte, le prendre au sérieux dans sa globalité consisterait principalement à faire la monographie de chacun des dits qui le

---

[1] B. Gärtner, *The Theology of the Gospel of Thomas* (London: Collins, 1961); E. Hänchen, *Die Botschaft des Thomas-Evangeliums* (Theologische Bibliothek Töpelmann 6; Berlin: Töplemann, 1961).

[2] Principalement J.E. Ménard, *L'Évangile selon Thomas* (NHS 5; Leiden: E. J. Brill, 1975). Parmi les études thématiques ou sectorielles, M. Lelyveld, *Les logia de la vie dans l'Évangile selon Thomas: à la recherche d'une tradition et d'une rédaction* (NHS 34; Leiden: E. J. Brill, 1987).

[3] Entre autres P. De Suarez, *L'Évangile selon Thomas: traduction, présentation et commentaires* (Marsanne: Metanoia, 1974); J. Y. Leloup, *L'Évangile selon Thomas* (Spiritualités vivantes 61; Paris: Albin Michel, 1986).

[4] À partir de J. M. Robinson, "LOGOI SOPHÔN: on the Gattung of Q," J. M. Robinson et H. Koester, *Trajectories through Early Christianity* (Philadelphia: Fortress, 1971) 74-85.

composent. Il est significatif que l'on puisse lire dans la conclusion du status quaestionis de F. Fallon - R. Cameron dans *Aufstieg und Niedergang der römischen Welt*: «But what has been generally overlooked is a careful assessment of the entire document in its own right, including a compositional analysis of the histories of its individual sayings».[5] Mon propos serait d'examiner dans quelle mesure et par quelles procédures il est possible de considérer encore l'EvTh comme un texte formant un tout, portant sens en tant que tout, et si la considération de l'ensemble, de certaines de ses caractéristiques constantes, peut légitimement éclairer l'exégèse des parties qui le composent, c'est-à-dire des dits individuels.

## 1. TRADITION, RÉDACTION, INTERPRÉTATION

La question des sources de l'EvTh ne connaîtra sans doute jamais, dans l'état actuel de notre documentation, de solution définitive et qui fasse le consensus. Sans doute la considération de type *Formgeschichte*, dont le Prof. H. Koester est sans contexte la figure la plus influente,[6] tend-elle de par sa nature même à proposer une origine para-synoptique aux paroles conservées dans l'Évangile selon Thomas. Le rapport mis avec la *Quelle*, qui fut basé d'abord sur la mise en évidence d'un genre littéraire de paroles de sagesses, dont l'EvTh serait une illustration, va dans ce sens et a aujourd'hui de nombreux partisans.[7] D'autre part, la dépendance à l'égard des synoptiques, si elle est difficile, voire impossible à établir pour l'ensemble du texte, n'en reste pas moins une hypothèse tenable et effectivement soutenue; les observations de C. Tuckett sur la présence de traits rédactionnels de Mc, Mt ou Lc dans l'EvTh ne manquent pas de pertinence et ne peuvent être prises à la légère,[8] même si savoir ce qui est rédactionnel dans chacun des synoptiques ne peut jamais être qu'une position théorique et non une évidence absolue; toutefois ces observations montrent bien la faiblesse d'une théorie qui exclurait de façon radicale toute dépendance à l'égard des synoptiques, et illustre

---

[5] F. Fallon et R. Cameron, "The Gospel of Thomas: A Forschungsbericht and Analysis," *ANRW* II.25.6, ed. H. Temporini and W. Hasse (Berlin and New York: de Gruyter, 1988) 4237.

[6] H. Koester, *Ancient Christian Gospels* (London: SCM; Philadelphia: Trinity Press International, 1990); idem., "Gnomai diaphorai: The Origin and Nature of Diversification in Early Christianity," HTR 58 (1965) 279-317 (= *Trajectories*, 114-157).

[7] J. S. Kloppenborg, *The Formation of Q: Trajectories in Ancient Wisdom Collections* (Philadelphia: Fortress, 1987).

[8] C. Tuckett, "Q and Thomas. Evidence of a Primitive 'Wisdom Gospel'? A Response to H. Koester," *ETL* 67 (1991) 346-360.

que l'hypothèse de cette dépendance ne saurait, en l'état actuel, être exclue. La question se réduit-elle à un dilemme? La composition de l'EvTh, considérée du point de vue de l'origine de ses matériaux est évidemment complexe; même si les synoptiques figurent parmi ses sources, il y en a évidemment d'autres (ne fût-ce que pour les dits non synoptiques) et qui peuvent être de diverse nature, incluant, peut-être pour une large part, la tradition orale. Le problème est qu'en fait de textes nous ne possédons guère que les synoptiques et, pour le reste, des traces qui nécessitent interprétation. Quoi qu'il en soit, il y a plus de vraisemblance à penser que les sources de Thomas sont complexes et sa rédaction unifiée, plutôt que l'inverse.

Ce n'est pas là une question que j'ambitionne de trancher, puisque mon intérêt se situe moins du côté de l'histoire du christianisme primitif, que de l'exégèse de l'EvTh lui-même, considéré comme un texte qu'il s'agit de comprendre. Je n'évoque la question de ses sources que parce que la manière dont on l'envisage conditionne la façon dont on traite cet évangile dans son ensemble.

Si l'on privilégie l'étude des traditions sous-jacentes, l'histoire de chaque dit, l'histoire en vient facilement à primer sur le texte, et l'exégèse de celui-ci, comme telle, perd de son intérêt: l'unité littéraire du texte s'estompe, et il ne lui demeure au mieux qu'une sorte d'unité doctrinale, résultante des tendances plus ou moins constantes manifestées par les dits individuels qui le composent.

En revanche, lorsque l'on privilégie partout où c'est possible la dépendance à l'égard des synoptiques, la part de la rédaction thomasienne s'accroît nécessairement puisque les écarts entre les synoptiques et l'EvTh doivent être expliqués par la rédaction de celui-ci, et sont même l'indice privilégié de sa doctrine propre. En d'autres termes, alors que l'hypothèse de la dépendance tend à réduire la part de la tradition en cherchant l'explication des écarts dans la rédaction, l'hypothèse de l'indépendance tend à réduire voire à supprimer la part de la rédaction en expliquant les écarts par la tradition. Il y a une convenance mutuelle entre la conception de Thomas comme une simple collection et une approche de *Formgeschichte* d'une part, et d'autre part entre la conception de Thomas comme un texte et un usage privilégié de la référence aux synoptiques comme source.

## 2. LE GENRE LITTÉRAIRE DE L'ÉVANGILE SELON THOMAS

On le voit, à côté de l'examen systématique des analogies et différences entre l'EvTh et les synoptiques (ou les autres sources de paroles de Jésus dont il subsisterait des vestiges), la question du genre littéraire est cruciale. Si cette question peut être éclairée par la prise en compte de genres littéraires attestés ou théoriquement reconstruits, telle la collection de paroles de sagesse, elle ne peut cependant être tranchée qu'à partir du texte lui-même. Sa suscription, qui a valeur de titre, est à cet égard à considérer soigneusement. Le titre d'évangile lui-même n'est évidemment pas significatif: il est obvie qu'il a été ajouté secondairement, dans une collection de manuscrits où cette appellation ne coïncide plus avec un genre littéraire, même considéré à des stades divers de son développement.[9] Quoi de commun entre la forme littéraire de l'*Évangile de vérité*, l'*Évangile de Thomas*, l'*Évangile de Philippe* et l'*Évangile des Égyptiens* (où d'ailleurs le caractère secondaire du titre d'évangile est également évident)? Le véritable titre est bien la suscription et le log.1: «Voici les paroles cachées (ἀπόκρυφοι) que Jésus le vivant a dites, et qu'a écrites Didyme Jude Thomas; celui qui trouvera l'interprétation de ces paroles ne goûtera pas la mort». Cette suscription-titre figure dans P. Oxy. 654,1-5; ce qui en subsiste ne permet pas de déceler de variantes significatives, à l'exception du nom de grec Δίδυμος, et appartient donc à la forme la plus ancienne du texte qui nous soit accessible. J.M. Robinson s'est d'ailleurs appuyé sur la désignation du texte comme des λόγοι pour caractériser EvTh comme une collection de paroles de sagesse.[10] Mais d'autre part on ne peut négliger le fait que cet incipit s'apparente de près aux, voire appartient au même genre que les incipit de plusieurs dialogues gnostiques chrétiens de révélation, qui peuvent être caractérisés comme des «évangiles gnostiques», sans en porter tous le titre. Parmi ceux-ci on peut certainement retenir la version longue de l'ApocrJn, l'ApocrJac, LivThom et EvMar.[11] Dans tous ces cas, la matière de l'écrit est décrite comme un enseignement (ou plus précisément des paroles: LivTh, EvMar, probablement ApocrJn, et la narration de ApocrJac), caractérisé comme caché ou secret, confié à un médiateur (Thomas, Marie, Jean, Pierre et Jacques), fonctionnant de façon ésotérique – c'est-à-dire réservé à des initiés; en outre dans LivTh et ApocrJac, il est fait explicitement mention de la mise par écrit (mention du livre, et rôle de Matthias dans LivTh). Il ne suffit donc point de dire, dès l'état le plus ancien

---

[9] Je me permets de renvoyer à mon article "Remarques sur le genre littéraire de l'Évangile selon Thomas (II, 2)," *Les textes de Nag Hammadi et le problème de leur classification*, ed. L. Painchaud et A. Pasquier (BCNH Études 3; Québec: Presses de l'Université Laval et Louvain: Peeters, 1995) 263-278, esp. 264-265.

[10] J. M. Robinson, "LOGOI SOPHÔN," 79-80.

[11] J. M. Sevrin, "Remarques sur le genre littéraire," 268-271.

connu, que l'EvTh se présente lui-même comme une collection de paroles. D'abord parce que la réduction à la parole ou aux enseignements est caractéristique de l'incipit analogue d'autres écrits, qui désigne chaque fois un genre littéraire clairement gnostique; ensuite parce que ce qui est clairement visé par ces auto-définitions d'écrits, c'est le caractère ésotérique de l'ouvrage, le secret, le rôle du médiateur qui en est dépositaire, la restriction virtuelle des lecteurs. Cela est particulièrement net dans l'EvTh: dites par le vivant à un intermédiaire qui les écrit, les paroles permettent au lecteur de ne pas goûter la mort, lorsqu'elles passent du statut de secrètes (telles qu'elles sont *dites* et *écrites*) au statut de dévoilées par l'interprétation. Ce sont des paroles qui ont un dedans et un dehors: un extérieur de forme, un intérieur de sens, à quoi doivent correspondre un auditoire extérieur qui n'en saisit que la forme ou le sens apparent, et un auditoire initié qui en perçoit le sens vrai. La figure de ceci est bien connue, p.ex., dans l'ApocrJac.[12] Apocryphe signifie ésotérique-gardé à l'intérieur.

Le seul passage de l'EvTh qui prête quelque peu à une analyse narrative pourrait bien illustrer ceci. Il s'agit du log.13.[13] À la question de Jésus: comparez-moi et dites-moi à qui je ressemble (dont on notera qu'elle appelle la métaphore et non la titulature qui fixe l'identité), Simon-Pierre et Matthieu répondent, Thomas, non: «Maître, ma bouche n'acceptera absolument pas de dire à qui tu ressembles». La réponse de Jésus caractérise Thomas comme un disciple ayant acquis sa pleine autonomie: «Je ne suis pas ton maître puisque tu as bu et t'es enivré à la source bouillonnante que j'ai fait jaillir». Manifestement Thomas n'est pas discrédité—seul est récusé le titre de maître donné à Jésus. Dès lors, Jésus prend Thomas à l'écart de ses compagnons («il le prit, se retira») et lui dit trois paroles. Lorsqu'il revient vers ses compagnons et est interrogé par eux sur les paroles de Jésus, Thomas refuse de répondre, même partiellement: «Si je vous dis l'une des paroles qu'il m'a dites,[14] vous prendrez des pierres, vous me les jetterez et un feu sortira des pierres et vous brûlera». Les paroles dites par Jésus à Thomas instaurent une distance infranchissable entre les autres disciples et lui. Parmi ces autres disciples, Pierre et Matthieu, qui ont formulé une doctrine sur Jésus, alors que Thomas se refusait à rien exprimer. Thomas apparaît

---

[12] ApocrJac II.1.1-29.

[13] Ev. Th 13, 34.30-35.14.

[14] Formulation identique à celle de la suscription: «des paroles que Jésus le Vivant a dites...» (32.10-11)

ici comme celui qui se tait doublement: en n'énonçant pas l'indicible à propos de Jésus, et en ne communicant pas aux autres disciples les paroles que Jésus a dites. Unique séquence narrative de l'EvTh qui ne soit pas racontée par Jésus mais appartienne à la texture du texte lui-même, ce passage décrit significativement celui qui est censé dans l'incipit avoir écrit les paroles (cachées) que Jésus a dites. Il semblerait bien que celui qui *écrit* soit ici celui qui ne *dit* pas. En d'autres termes, que les paroles demeurent non dites dans l'écriture. Par là, l'EvTh est situé quant à sa forme: il voile ce qu'il communique; et quant à son usage: il ne dit rien aux chrétiens ordinaires, représentés par les disciples, mais aux initiés seuls—c'est-à-dire à ceux qui trouveront le sens caché, l'*hermeneia* des paroles.

### 3. COMMENT THOMAS NE DIT PAS

On peut se demander dès lors comment fonctionne ce jeu du non-dire dans l'écriture. Est-ce pure fiction, artificielle, pour introduire une collection qui n'aurait rien d'ésotérique *en soi*? Est-ce le souvenir que chacun de ces dits appartient à une tradition ésotérique pré ou protognostique? Ou cela signifie-t-il que le recueil est en réalité écrit avec une certaine cohérence pour correspondre à ce qu'annonce son incipit et que confirme son unique morceau narratif non placé dans la bouche de Jésus?

Si l'on s'arrête à cette dernière possibilité, qui n'a rien d'improbable et mérite d'être posée en hypothèse, il vient aussitôt à l'idée est que la structure de l'EvTh elle-même fait partie du voile, et que la désarticulation littéraire du texte n'est qu'une apparence. Plus précisément: dans sa forme actuelle, la seule que nous puissions considérer comme un fait, la collection de dits serait artificielle. Il apparaît que la division par la clausule «Jésus dit» est floue, parce qu'elle paraît parfois manquer ou qu'elle introduit une fois au moins une parole à l'intérieur de laquelle s'emboîte un autre «Jésus dit»;[15] qu'elle sépare des paroles qui peuvent s'organiser en unités de sens[16] et que, d'autre fois, elle manque entre des paroles où le lien n'apparaît pas clairement;[17] qu'elle ne permet pas des césures nettes lorsque les paroles de Jésus sont mélangées à des questions des disciples dans le

---

[15] Ev Th log. 111 (51.6-10)

[16] p. ex. Ev Th 18 et 19; 32 et 33 (et même 34); 68 et 69; 80 et 81.

[17] Ne fût-ce qu'entre Ev Th log. 26 et 30; 100 et 101 où les éditeurs ont dû suppléer l'absence de la clausule pour séparer des dits distincts; mais on pourrait le faire davantage (voir p. ex. Ev Th log. 14; 21; 39).

dialogue;[18] bref qu'il s'agit d'une structure simpliste plus ou moins plaquée sur le texte, et qui constitue d'ailleurs une difficulté à son édition (il y avait quelque sagesse dans la division en versets proposée par R. Kasser,[19] mais qui n'a pas été suivie: au moins ne risquait-elle pas de durcir des divisions qui ne sauraient servir dans tous les cas de principe d'interprétation).

D'autre part la difficulté constamment rencontrée de proposer une structure cohérente de l'ensemble de l'EvTh s'évanouit dès lors que l'absence d'une telle structure relève de la volonté d'occulter le sens; et les articulations par mots crochets conviennent parfaitement à un arrangement du texte qui se voudrait au moins partiellement aléatoire.

### 4. PROPOSITIONS POUR UNE RECHERCHE DU SENS DANS L'EVTH, CONSIDÉRÉ COMME UN ENSEMBLE

Trois voies ont été essentiellement suivies. La première, la plus commune, est de procéder par comparaison avec les synoptiques pour évaluer les écarts, qui seraient le bien propre de l'EvTh, et d'en tenter une synthèse. La seconde de partir de préférence des paroles au contenu gnostique obvie; la troisième enfin, corollaire de l'une et de l'autre, d'éclairer l'EvTh à partir de parallèles divers récoltés dans la documentation disponible sur le gnosticisme (postuler et vérifier un sens gnostique de l'EvTh).

4.1. Il me semble qu'en bonne méthode, et si l'on se place dans l'hypothèse que l'EvTh, pris dans son ensemble, offre un sens à interpréter, mais qu'il dissimule ce sens, il convient de partir de tout le texte, sans privilégier aucune de ses composantes, en se gardant des précompréhensions du texte qui ne viendraient pas de lui—qu'elles soient tirées des évangiles canoniques, de théories sur les premières traditions chrétiennes, ou de l'horizon, au demeurant divers, des courants, textes ou écoles gnostiques. L'horizon sur lequel *pourrait* se découper le texte n'est pas son premier interprète; l'analyse de Religionsgeschichte doit suivre la critique littéraire, et non la précéder.

4.2. La critique littéraire doit autant que faire se peut porter d'abord sur l'ensemble du texte, sur son organisation et sur ce qu'il dit lui-

---

[18] Faut-il opérer une césure entre Ev Th log. 23 et 24; 42 et 43; 74 et 75; 90 et 92? Si oui, pourquoi pas entre log. 61a et 61b?

[19] R. Kasser, *L'Évangile selon Thomas. Présentation et commentaire théologique* (Bibliothèque théologique; Neuchâtel: Delachaux et Niestlé, 1961).

même de son fonctionnement et de son interprétation. C'est ce que
l'on fait lorsqu'on présente l'EvTh comme une collection de paroles, qu'on observe la façon dont les dits isolés sont enchaînés, ou
parfois regroupés en ensembles. Hors cela (qui est, comme je l'ai
suggéré), sujet à discussion, l'EvTh offre peu de prise à l'analyse
narrative, ou à l'analyse rhétorique, du moins du point de vue de
l'ensemble du texte. Je crois avoir montré plus haut cependant que
l'incipit, le log.1 et le log.13 fournissent des indications sur le
fonctionnement du texte, soit parce qu'ils s'expriment directement
sur lui (l'incipit) soit parce qu'ils mettent en scène son auteur, au
sens de celui qui est censé avoir écrit (incipit, log.13). La caracté-
risation des différents personnages qui interviennent dans les em-
bryons de dialogue trouverait ici sa place. Quelle est la fonction
exacte des disciples comme interlocuteurs? Il est remarquable, par
exemple, que malgré le caractère didactique de beaucoup de questions, les disciples sont souvent pris à contre-pied par les réponses
de Jésus[20] et sont, dans leurs questions, tenants de pratiques re-
ligieuses que récuse Jésus;[21] comme s'il y avait le plus souvent un
hiatus entre les questions et les réponses, entre Jésus et les disciples; ce qui correspond à l'image que fournissait le log.13 et à leur
contraste avec le personnage de Thomas.

4.3. L'essentiel de l'interprétation passe cependant par
l'interprétation des dits individuels. Mais comment les interpréter?
Il faudrait se libérer du carcan de la clausule «Jésus dit» pour
considérer quelles sont les unités à interpréter. Une unité minimale
est une phrase, un groupe de phrases liées, un récit. Il arrive qu'un
«dit» corresponde à une unité minimale, ou soit composé de plusieurs;[22] il peut aussi arriver que la formule sépare des éléments
qui pourraient être regroupés en unités. On partira donc des unités
élémentaires pour voir ensuite dans quelle mesure elles sont as-
semblées en des ensembles plus vastes. Les critères littéraires
doivent évidemment primer sur les critères de sens ou ceux tirés
d'une considération des sources. Par exemple, ce n'est pas parce
que «la pierre rejetée des bâtisseurs» du log.66 fait suite à la
parabole des vignerons homicides (log.65) en Mt 21,42; Mc 12,10
et Lc 20,17, qu'elle doit être associée à cette parabole du point de
vue de l'interprétation: ce n'est qu'une fois la parabole interprétée
en elle-même que 'l'on pourra décider si le log.66 fait corps avec
le log.65—ce qui n'est d'ailleurs pas le cas.

---

[20] P. ex. Ev Th log. 18; 24; 43; 52; 91; 114.

[21] P. ex. Ev Th log. 6; 53; 104.

[22] Voir ci-dessus, note 17.

4.4. Dans l'interprétation des dits individuels ou des unités ainsi dégagées, on ne peut évidemment faire l'économie d'une classique analyse formelle: examen des structures de composition, jeux de parallélisme, chiasmes, inclusions etc. Dans nombre de cas il existe des parallèles dans des textes conservés: les évangiles synoptiques, bien sûr, mais aussi dans une moindre mesure dans d'autres textes. L'analyse comparative est un bon catalyseur d'interprétation. Si cette analyse peut être menée en regardant vers l'arrière, dans une démarche de *Traditionsgeschichte* (l'EvTh dépend-il des synoptiques ou d'autres traditions?), il est aussi possible de faire ici abstraction des dépendances et de se livrer à une exégèse que j'appellerais différentielle, c'est-à-dire à une analyse qui ne se borne pas à inventorier les similitudes et les divergences pour inscrire ou non les textes dans une histoire commune, mais qui cherche à reconstruire, par contraste, le fonctionnement propre à chaque texte: ce qu'il dit, comment il le dit. Considérer chaque texte examiné non dans ses composantes ou son histoire, mais dans son fonctionnement de texte. Je prendrai rapidement deux exemples.

• Le log.100 (// Mt 22,15-22, Mc 12,13-14, Lc 20, 20-26). La question polémique des synoptiques est, dans l'EvTh, une constatation des disciples: les gens de César exigent de nous les tributs; la pièce du tribut, portant l'effigie de César et réclamée par Jésus dans la logique de son argumentation est, chez Thomas, une pièce d'or montrée par les disciples dans le même temps qu'ils parlent à Jésus. Il est clair que l'EvTh ne s'inscrit pas dans une polémique sur le tribut. On attend déjà que l'or en tant que tel soit renvoyé à César. Le dit de Jésus lui-même est plus développé dans l'EvTh. Là où les synoptiques portent: «rendez ce qui est de César à César, et ce qui est de Dieu à Dieu», l'EvTh est plus développé: «Ce qui est à César donnez-le à César, ce qui est à Dieu donnez-le à Dieu, ce qui est à moi donnez-le moi». D'une part il s'agit de donner, non de rendre; d'autre part Jésus lui-même vient s'ajouter à l'opposition Dieu-César, ce qui fait qu'au lieu d'une opposition nous avons une gradation culminant en Jésus, Dieu étant en situation intermédiaire. Si d'autre part l'on se souvient que l'EvTh évite le mot Dieu ou lui confère ordinairement un sens péjoratif, on pourra même conclure que là où les synoptiques jouent sur l'opposition Dieu/César, l'EvTh joue sur l'opposition César-Dieu/Jésus. Et comme il s'agit de savoir ce que l'on fait de l'or, on comprendra qu'il faut donner ou laisser la richesse à ce qui est de son ordre, ce qui relève de César, et probablement ce qui relève de

Dieu entendu comme le créateur: ce qui nous conduit à un sens de type gnostique. La forme du dit reste analogue à celle des synoptiques, non le sens.

* La parabole des vignerons homicides (log.65//Mt 21,33-41; Mc 12,1-9; Lc 20,9-16) constitue aussi un bon exemple d'un sens très différent dans une forme semblable.23 Je n'entrerai pas dans le détail mais me bornerai à constater que l'EvTh y met en relief la mort: le premier serviteur est frappé «et peu s'en fallut qu'ils ne le fissent mourir», et la mort du fils est la fin de l'histoire. D'autre part le maître est dit crh[stov]" ou crh[sthv]", bon ou usurier. La seconde lecture est plus probable en ce qu'elle fait écho au crh'ma de la parabole du log.63 et s'accorde avec le fait que l'homme «donne sa vigne aux ouvriers afin qu'ils y travaillent et qu'il reçoive (ou prenne) son fruit de leurs mains». L'homme de richesse, ou l'homme qui ne travaille point son champ, est privé des fruits et «goûte la mort» dans la personne de son héritier. La mort est au rendez-vous final, comme dans la parabole du log.63. Ici encore, cela paraît la même histoire que dans les synoptiques, mais le sens est radicalement différent.

4.5. Les deux exemples précédents (que je n'ai pas argumentés mais esquissés à gros traits) montre que l'exégèse différentielle, dans le cas des paraboles en tout cas, gagne beaucoup à un examen du récit en tant que récit, aux rapports entre ses personnages, à la position de l'intrigue, à son nœud et à son dénouement. J'ajouterais comme exemple supplémentaire de ceci l'importance de la séquence des événements dans deux paraboles où elle diffère des synoptiques.

Au log.57 (// Mt 13,24-30), la parabole de l'ivraie nous montre dans l'évangile de Mt des serviteurs qui annoncent au maître que de l'ivraie pousse dans son champ; le maître leur ordonne d'attendre la moisson pour faire le tri. Dans l'EvTh, les ivraies n'apparaissent qu'au moment de la moisson et sont alors arrachées et brûlées; et comme les ivraies ne deviennent apparentes ou révélées qu'à la fin, l'intervention des serviteurs qui les ont découvertes est nécessairement omise.

De même au log.109 (//Mt 13,44), le trésor caché. En Mt, l'homme (1) trouve le trésor (2) vend tout ce qu'il a (3) achète le

---

[23] J'ai formulé cette interprétation avec plus de détail dans "Un groupement de trois paraboles contre les richesses dans l'Évangile selon Thomas (Ev Th log. 63, 64, 65)," *Les paraboles évangélique: Perspectives nouvelles* (Lectio divina 135; Paris: Cerf, 1989) 425-439.

champ. Dans l'EvTh (1) un homme a un trésor dans son champ, sans le savoir (2) il meurt (3) l'héritier ignore aussi le trésor et il vend le champ (4) l'acheteur laboure le champ et (5) trouve le trésor. Ce qui est au début dans les synoptiques est à la fin dans l'EvTh. Les synoptiques parlent de vendre ce qu'on a pour acheter le trésor découvert; l'EvTh parle du rapport entre l'ignorance (du trésor) et la mort, ou la perte et, inversement, entre le labeur (en l'occurrence le labour) et la trouvaille.

Sur un même thème, deux séquences narratives ordonnées différemment, produisent un sens différent. Aucune de ces deux paraboles ne dit la même chose, ne parle de la même chose que les deux paraboles synoptiques.

4.6. L'analyse différentielle du fonctionnement des dits de l'EvTh fait apparaître des constantes, tant dans les procédés rédactionnels que dans les modes d'écriture. Ainsi, dispersées seules ou par petits groupes dans l'ensemble du texte, les paraboles se répondent. La *bonne* terre produit vers le ciel en fruit *bon* (log.9), la terre *travaillé* produit une *grande* branche (log.20). Après qu'il ait *peiné*, le berger trouve la *grande* brebis et l'aime plus que toutes les autres, qu'il a quittées (log.107) comme le pêcheur intelligent choisit sans *peine* le *grand* poisson (log.8); l'homme qui a du *bien* (χρῆμα, log.63) meurt comme l'héritier de l'*usurier* (χρηστής, log.5), qui voulait prendre les *fruits* des *travailleurs* de la vigne. Les correspondances, coïncidant avec les écarts d'interprétation par rapport aux synoptiques, dessinent entre elles un réseau, et ce réseau indique un sens. Lequel sens consonne avec la doctrine exprimée par l'incipit et le log.1, que continue le log.2: celui qui *trouvera* l'interprétation (le sens caché) de ces paroles ne goûtera pas de la *mort*.[24] Ce sont là les indices manifestes d'une cohérence d'écriture et de doctrine qui, incluant l'incipit du texte, doit bien appartenir à son actuelle rédaction, et encourage à le considérer comme un tout organique.

4.7. Il n'est légitime d'interpréter l'EvTh à partir d'éclairages extérieurs et de le situer dans une trajectoire historique qu'après avoir mené à bien, ou du moins suffisamment conduit, une telle interprétation du texte à partir de lui-même, sans quoi l'on y projettera fatalement ce qu'on s'attend à y trouver, et l'on s'enfermera

---

[24] Synthèse de l'analyse différentielle des paraboles de l'Ev Th: J.-M. Sevrin, "La rédaction des paraboles dans l'Évangile selon Thomas," *Actes du IVe Congrès copte (Louvain-la-Neuve, 5-10 septembre 1988)*, ed. M. Rassart-Debergh et J. Ries (PIOL 41; Louvain-la-Neuve: Université catholique de Louvain, Institut orientaliste, 1992) 343-354.

dans un cercle heméneutique. Ainsi le sens gnostique de l'EvTh,
même s'il est déjà suggéré par l'étroite parenté de son incipit avec
le cadre de plusieurs dialogues gnostiques chrétiens de révélation,
ne peut être posé au départ, et pas davantage exclu par hypothèse.
C'est seulement lorsque l'interprétation intra-textuelle (appuyée au
besoin sur une exégèse différentielle) a dégagé un fonctionnement
et une doctrine, qu'il est possible de dire pourquoi, comment et
dans quelle mesure cette doctrine peut être qualifiée de gnostique.

## 5. CONCLUSIONS PROVISOIRES

Recherchant s'il est possible d'interpréter l'EvTh comme un texte
cohérent, j'ai fait quelques observations sur le caractère ésotérique
qu'il revendique, et sur ce qu'implique ce caractère ésotérique. J'ai
ensuite avancé quelques règles de méthode propres à aider le cher-
cheur moderne, qui n'est ni un ascète paléochrétien, ni un gnostique
initié interprétant le texte à partir de son expérience de vie, à forcer
l'apparence pour en extraire le sens caché. Ces règles visent à
restreindre autant que possible ou à contrôler la part de la subjectivité
dans la lecture, mais elles ne sauraient exorciser complètement les
risques de la lecture, sans lesquelles aucune interprétation n'est
possible.

Les quelques exemples évoqués pour illustrer ces propositions
méthodologiques sont bien sûr trop partiels et trop sommairement dits
pour constituer des preuves. Ils n'en suggèrent pas moins qu'il reste
possible d'interpréter l'EvTh comme une relecture interprétative et
ésotérique d'évangiles reçus, tels que sont les synoptiques ou des
textes analogues. C'est là un modèle d'interprétation.

Sans nul doute, ce modèle est simplificateur. L'exégèse différentielle sur laquelle il repose en partie ne peut s'appuyer avec rigueur
que sur des textes actuellement connus, beaucoup moins sûrement sur
des textes hypothétiques ou hypothétiquement reconstruits. Elle est
légitime, en ce qu'elle ne présuppose que des analogies, non des
relations de dépendance; mais elle est simplificatrice parce qu'elle
ignore la complexité possible de la genèse de l'EvTh et de ses sources.

Enfin ce modèle est un modèle théorique. Mais à quoi l'exégèse
d'un texte peut-elle prétendre d'autre? Comme modèle théorique,
comme théorie de ce texte particulier, il ne peut revendiquer d'être
vrai, sous peine de sombrer dans un scientisme naïf. Il ne peut
revendiquer que d'être valide, c'est-à-dire de rendre compte du texte
et de tous ses éléments, avec la plus grande simplicité possible, de
façon cohérente et en offrant le maximum de sens. La validité d'un tel
modèle se mesurera aussi à sa capacité de conduire à des observations

nouvelles dans le texte et à les intégrer, en d'autres mots, à sa capacité d'enrichir et d'approfondir la lecture du texte.

Construire un tel modèle—interpréter l'EvTh comme un texte—reste pour une bonne part, cinquante ans après la découverte des textes de Nag Hammadi, une tâche à accomplir.

## ENGLISH SUMMARY

1. Despite the increasing success of the critical approach that considers the Gospel of Thomas as independent of the synoptics, the discussion over its sources cannot be considered concluded. There are good arguments in favor of an—at least partial—dependency on the Synoptic tradition, especially given the presence of redactional traces of Mark, Matthew and Luke in certain traditional sayings of Thomas' Gospel. The answer given to the question of the sources conditions the interpretation of the text itself. The thesis of independence tends to diminish the significance of the redactional process by appealing to the tradition for explaining the differences between the Synoptics. Meanwhile, the hypothesis of dependency tends to amplify the redactional process by attributing the differences to the redaction. There is a mutual fitness between the critical approach and the conception of Thomas' Gospel as a simple collection, on the one hand, and the privileged use of a reference to the Synoptics as the main source and the conception of Thomas' Gospel as a text, in the full sense of the term, on the other.

2. At first sight, it is difficult to consider the *Gos. Thom.* as a simple collection of sayings. Up to this day, it has been impossible to propose a satisfying organization of the text. However, the incipit of the text (which is the real title) and log. 1 are related to the frame (title or narrative structure) of several Christian gnostic revelation dialogues. More than signifying a mere collection of sayings—a banality in this kind of title—they underscore the hidden or secret (*apocryphoi*) character of these words.
This hiddenness can be understood in two complementary senses: On the one hand, the apparent sense underlies a secret meaning; on the other, because of their secret meaning, these words are reserved for the insider; their real sense is hidden from simple believers. The function of Thomas in log. 13—which is the unique narrative passage of any size outside the sayings of Jesus—corroborates this interpretation. The Gospel of Thomas obscures

the real meaning of what it says. The disorganized character of a collection of sayings contribute to that effect.

3. The interpretation of the meaning (*hermeneia*) is the task entrusted to the reader by the *incipit* of the text. That consists in discovering the sense hidden in the apparent sayings. How could it be discovered? The answer given by the text itself is a moral one: searching and continuing to search. But what are the means for that research? We could propose a methodology:

• Not to presuppose a background for the text that too quickly determines its meaning (neither Gnosis, which nevertheless is probable, nor the synoptic tradition, nor any other). The *Religionsgeschichtliche* approach must follow literary criticism, rather than precede it.

• Make the critical analysis on the whole text, using at a most the few possibilities allowed by the literary analysis of the narrative itself (e.g. the characters of Jesus, Thomas, and the disciples).

# JOHN AND THOMAS IN CONFLICT?

*Ismo Dunderberg*
University of Helsinki

## 1. INTRODUCTION

The relationship of the Gospel of John and the *Gospel of Thomas*, not unlike that of the Synoptics and the *Gospel of Thomas*, has called forth different solutions.[1] A few scholars hold that the *Gospel of Thomas* has been influenced by the Gospel of John either directly,[2] or, as Raymond E. Brown has asserted, through a Gnostic intermediary.[3] Less specifically, Miroslav Marcovich has maintained "that the *GTh* was inspired by John."[4] On the other hand, affinities between the Gospel of John and the *Gospel of Thomas* have been explained in terms of early, pre-Johannine traditions. These traditions have been identified with a Jewish Christian Gospel tradition by Gilles Quispel,[5] whereas Helmut Koester traces them back to early, possibly gnosticizing traditions of Jesus' sayings,[6] and Stevan Davies has suggested

---

[1] For a closer view of the state of the question, see my "Thomas' I-Sayings and the Gospel of John," *Thomas at the Crossroads*, ed. R. Uro (forthcoming).

[2] J. Sell, "Johannine Traditions in Logion 61 of The Gospel of Thomas," *Perspectives in Religous Studies* 7 (1980) 24-37.

[3] R. E. Brown, "The Gospel of Thomas and St John's Gospel," *NTS* 9 (1962-1963) 155-177, esp. 176.

[4] M. Marcovich, "Textual Criticism on the *Gospel of Thomas*," *JTS* 20 (1969) 53-74, esp. 74.

[5] G. Quispel, "Qumran, John and Jewish Christianity," *John and the Dead Sea Scrolls*, 2nd. ed., ed. J. Charlesworth (New York: Crossroad, 1991) 137-155, esp. 144-146.

[6] Cf. H. Koester, "Dialog und Sprachüberlieferung in den gnostischen Texten von Nag Hammadi," *EvTh* 39 (1979) 532-556; id., "Gnostic Writings as Witnesses for the Development of the Sayings Tradition," *The Rediscovery of Gnosticism*, 2 vols., ed. B. Layton (Studies in the History of Religions 41, Leiden: E. J. Brill, 1980) 1.238-261; id., *Introduction to the New Testament* (Philadelpia: Fortress; Berlin and New York: de Gruyter, 1982) 2.178-180; id., "Gnostic Sayings and Controversy Traditions in John 8:12-59," *Nag Hammadi, Gnosticism, and Early Christianity*, ed. C. W. Hedrick and R. Hodgson (Peabody, MA: Hendrickson, 1986) 97-110; id., *Ancient Christian Gospels: Their History and Development* (London: SCM; Philadelphia: Trinity Press International, 1990) 256-263.

that the *Gospel of Thomas* originated in the same community "that, in a later decade, produced the Gospel of John."[7]

More recent studies are inclined to the view that the Johannine writings react against ideas visible in the *Gospel of Thomas*. Koester already points to this direction by maintaining that the parallels to John 8:12-36 derived from the *Gospel of Thomas* "reveal a typical gnostic understanding of salvation" which is "refuted by the author of the Gospel [of John]."[8] In a detailed study devoted to *Gos. Thom.* 17, Takashi Onuki concludes that the author of 1 John reacts against this saying which was circulated by the author's opponents.[9] The notion of a conflict between Johannine and Thomas Christians has been developed further in two recent monographs on the *Gospel of Thomas* by April D. De Conick and Gregory J. Riley. According to De Conick, the *Gospel of Thomas* displays a mystical soteriological scheme which consists of seeking, ascension, and the *visio dei*; it is this scheme against which the Gospel of John argues.[10] Riley holds that the Gospel of John and the *Gospel of Thomas* bear witness to a reciprocal controversy between Johannine and Thomas Christianities. According to Riley, the Gospel of John and the *Gospel of Thomas* "are much closer to each other in spirit than either is to the Synoptics."[11] However, Riley argues that the groups behind these texts were engaged in a controversy about the importance of faith, the deity of Christ, and especially about physical resurrection, on which Johannine Christianity insisted but which Thomas Christianity denied.[12] In

---

[7] S. L. Davies,"The Christology and Protology of the Gospel of Thomas," *JBL* 111 (1992) 663-682, esp. p. 682; cf. ibid., *The Gospel of Thomas and Christian Wisdom* (New York: Seabury 1983) 116.

[8] Koester, *Ancient Christian Gospels* 263. The "gnostic understanding of salvation" is defined by Koester in terms of divine origins of the believer, and attested by *Gos. Thom.* 19, 24, 38, 43 and 49 (ibid. 260-263).

[9] T. Onuki, "Traditionsgeschichte von Thomasevangelium 17 und ihre christologische Relevanz," *Anfänge der Christologie*, ed. C. Breytenbach and H. Paulsen (Festschrift F. Hahn; Göttingen: Vandenhoeck & Ruprecht, 1991) 399-415.

[10] A. D. De Conick, *Seek to see Him: Ascent and Vision Mysticism in the Gospel of Thomas* (VCSup 33; Leiden: E. J. Brill, 1996) 72-73. The idea of the *visio dei* in the *Gospel of Thomas* has been developed already by A. D. De Conick & J. Fossum, "Stripped Before God: A New Interpretation of Logion 37 in the Gospel of Thomas," *VC* 45 (1991) 123-150, esp. pp. 135-139. As to *Gos. Thom.* 37, it is nevertheless uncertain whether this saying speaks of 'seeing God.' Riley has aptly suggested the reading ⲧⲟⲧ[ⲉ ⲧⲉⲧ]ⲛ̅[ⲛ]ⲏⲩ, "then you will come", instead of ⲧⲟⲧⲉ [ⲧⲉⲧ]ⲛ̅ⲁⲛⲁⲩ, "then you will see"; cf. G. J. Riley, "A Note on the Text of *Gospel of Thomas* 37," *HTR* 88 (1995) 179-181.

[11] G. J. Riley, *Resurrection Reconsidered: Thomas and John in Controversy* (Minneapolis: Fortress 1995) 3.

[12] Riley, *Resurrection* 5; cf. id., "The Gospel of Thomas in Recent Scholarship," *Currents in Research: Biblical Studies* 2 (1994) 227-252, esp. 240.

Riley's opinion, the *Gospel of Thomas* reflects a debate with the Johannine community before the Gospel of John was written, whereas the author of the Gospel of John addressed not only the Johannine community, but also Thomas Christians.[13]

The adherents of the controversy theories do not usually maintain that the Gospel of John would react against the *Gospel of Thomas* as it now stands. They affirm more cautiously that the extant *Gospel of Thomas* attests to some ideas of Thomas Christianity which are attacked by the Johannine writers. Riley takes one step further, but even this has been done with great caution:

> The elements present and positions countered in the pericope [of the Doubting Thomas] cohere well with those in the *Gospel of Thomas*, and lead to the conclusion that the *Gospel of Thomas* itself was already *at some stage of completion*, either written or oral, and that its contents were known to the author of John, probably through verbal contact with members of this rival community.[14]

There are a number of different theories concerning the relationship between the *Gospel of Thomas* and the Gospel of John, but there is surprisingly little interaction between these theories. In some cases, some critical remarks are made but they remain superficial and insufficient. For example, Davies criticizes Brown—with good reason—for having taken the late dating of the *Gospel of Thomas* for granted, and comments on different scenarios Brown provides with regard to the relationship of the *Gospel of Thomas* and the Gospel of John, but never discusses Brown's analyses of distinct sayings. Riley's critique of Brown is even shorter. He asserts simply that Brown's theory of the Gnostic intermediary (which is to explain the lack of verbatim quotations of John in the *Gospel of Thomas*) is a "desperate solution."[15] Instead of a more detailed demonstration of this judgment, Riley affirms:

> "Dependency" of Thomas on John not only is not demonstrable, it is indeed nothing more than a presupposition of some early *Thomas* scholarship to which Brown and others subscribed, which obscured the actual relationship of the texts.[16]

---

[13] Riley, *Resurrection* 178.

[14] Riley, *Resurrection* 178 (emphasis added).

[15] Riley, *Resurrection* 2.

[16] Riley, *Resurrection* 3.

More surprisingly, there is hardly any interaction between those models which are based on an early dating of the *Gospel of Thomas*. Neither De Conick nor Riley take any detailed position on Koester's theory of gnosticizing sayings traditions, or on Davies' theory that the *Gospel of Thomas* had its origins in the same community as the Gospel of John.[17] One expression of the lack of a detailed discussion between different solutions is certainly that totally opposite views continue to be defended with similar lists of parallels between the Gospel of John and the *Gospel of Thomas*.[18]

On the other hand, De Conick's and Riley's studies mark an important shift in scholarship on the *Gospel of Thomas*. Neither of them concentrates on the 'traditional' question to what extent the *Gospel of Thomas* can be used as a source for the quest of the historical Jesus. Instead, they raise another issue of equal or even greater importance: what form of early Christianity gave rise to the *Gospel of Thomas*, and how was the community behind this text related to other early Christian groups? Both De Conick and Riley also locate the *Gospel of Thomas* in a wider context of either hermetic and Jewish mystic traditions (De Conick), or of contemporary Graeco-Roman thought (Riley). Moreover, Riley makes an important effort to draw a trajectory of Thomas Christianity from the *Gospel of Thomas* through the *Book of Thomas* to the *Acts of Thomas*.

Hence both of these studies provide a new impetus for subsequent research of the *Gospel of Thomas*. In view of their wide approach, the theory about rivalry between Johannine and Thomas communities is only one part of more comprehensive and compelling pictures of the *Gospel of Thomas*. Nevertheless, this part is of crucial importance for locating the *Gospel of Thomas* within early Christianity. In this article I will focus on the question whether there is sufficient basis to posit an actual controversy between Johannine and Thomas Christians. My point of departure is that the extant differences between the

---

[17] To be sure, Riley presents both views in his *Forschungsbericht* (Riley, "The Gospel of Thomas in Recent Scholarship" 239f.).

[18] The most recent demonstration of this is the way James H. Charlesworth and Craig E. Evans deal with the John-Thomas relationship. They give a list of parallels (John 1:9//*Gos. Thom.* 24; John 1:14//*Gos. Thom.* 28; John 4:13-15//*Gos. Thom.* 13; John 7:32-36//*Gos. Thom.* 38; John 8:12; 9:5//*Gos. Thom.* 77) which is used—without any closer qualification of these parallels—in favor of the conclusion: "...the presence of M, L, and Johannine elements in *Thomas* indicate that the latter, at least in its extant Coptic form, has been influenced by the New Testament Gospels" (J. H. Charlesworth & C. E. Evans, "Jesus in the Agrapha and Apocryphal Gospels," *Studying the Historical Jesus: Evaluations of the State of Current Research*, ed. B. Chilton & C. E. Evans [NTTS 19; Leiden: E. J. Brill] 479-533, esp. 498f.).

Johannine literature and the *Gospel of Thomas* in themselves are not sufficient to prove this hypothesis. To draw detailed conclusions of the "real-life situation" of the communities behind these documents, there should be more specific signs of interaction between them. Whether such signs are available, will be examined in the following in light of Onuki's, Riley's, and De Conick's respective arguments.

## 2. *GOSPEL OF THOMAS* 17

Onuki devotes his article to the tradition history of *Gos. Thom.* 17. He takes 1 John 1:1-3 as a negative affirmation of an early existence of this saying, yet he does not develop any theory about Thomas Christianity against which the author of 1 John would argue. Those who are supposed to have used this saying are identified with the author's docetic opponents (cf. 1 John 4:2; 5:6) whose Christology is characterized as "gnosticizing" by Onuki.[19]

*Gos. Thom.* 17 is a *Wanderlogion*; a similar saying occurs not only in 1 Cor 2:9 but is also widely attested in extracanonical literature. The specific linkage to the prologue of 1 John is provided by the clause "and what no hand has touched" in *Gos. Thom.* 17. This clause is missing in most parallels to *Gos. Thom.* 17,[20] but its positive counterpart occurs in 1 John 1:1 ("which we have... touched with our hands"). Since 1 John 1:1 also affirms 'hearing' and 'seeing' of Jesus, *Gos. Thom.* 17 has even been called "the exact reverse of 1 John 1:1."[21]

The tradition history of *Gos. Thom.* 17 is closely related to that of 1 Cor 2:9.[22] This verse is introduced by Paul as a scriptural quotation (ἀλλὰ καθὼς γέγραπται), and it refers at least to two OT passages (Is 64:3; 65:16), yet it cannot be explained as a mere combination of them. The different closure might be due to the Pauline adaptation of Is 64:3, but other differences indicate that Paul made use of a traditional saying. The beginning of 1 Cor 2:9 differs significantly from Is 64:3 (LXX),[23] and ἀνθρώπου is not attested in Is 65:16 (LXX).

---

[19] Onuki, "Traditionsgeschichte" 413f.

[20] The clause appears also in the Manichaean Turfanfragment Nr. 789, but this text is most likely influenced by *Gos. Thom.* 17 (Onuki, "Traditionsgeschichte" 407).

[21] R. M. Grant & D. N. Freedman, *The Secret Sayings of Jesus* (London - Glasgow: Collins Fontana Books, 1960) 13.

[22] As to the tradition history of 1 Cor 2:9, cf. K. Berger, "Zur Diskussion über die Herkunft von I Kor II.9," *NTS* 24 (1978) 270-283; Onuki, "Traditionsgeschichte" 400-408.

[23] "What no eye has seen nor ear heard," 1 Cor 2:9//"we have not heard nor did our eyes see God," Is 64:3 (LXX).

More importantly, a similar form of the saying can be found not only in writings that are or can be dependent on 1 Cor 2:9,[24] but also in texts which most likely are independent of Paul's letters.[25]

Given the multiple attestation of this saying, it is impossible to say with certainty whether *Gos. Thom.* 17 was originally based on 1 Cor 2:9 or on some other variant of the saying; the lack of the Pauline conclusion of 1 Cor 2:9 ("what God has prepared for those who love him") in *Gos. Thom.* 17 speaks rather in favor of the latter possibility. On the other hand, that the clause "what no hand has touched" of *Gos. Thom.* 17 is missing in the other versions of the saying can point to a later development of the saying. In any case, this clause adds conveniently to the non-concrete nature of what Jesus promises to give to his followers.

Several difficulties are involved in the further interpretation of *Gos. Thom.* 17. To begin with, the temporal aspect of the saying differs from 1 Cor 2:9. Paul connects the saying with something that has been hidden thus far but has now been made manifest (ἡμῖν δὲ ἀπεκάλυψεν ὁ θεός, 1 Cor 2:10). This distinction between past and present is missing in *Gos. Thom.* 17. The opening sentence provides the saying with a future meaning (ϯⲚⲀϯ ⲚⲎⲦⲚ̄, "I shall give you..."). Since the time which the future form of ϯ refers to is not defined, it remains unclear whether the promise is expected to be fulfilled in a near future or whether it waits for an eschatological fulfillment. In the former case the saying could be taken as a reference to subsequent teachings by Jesus, whereas in the latter case it would rather depict the final share of believers in the divine realm.

Another problem is associated with the future tense used in *Gos. Thom.* 17. Like 1 Cor 2:9 and most other versions of the saying, *Gos. Thom.* 17 appears to distinguish divine reality from normal human experience. But on account of the future tense at the outset of the saying, it is not clear whether *Gos. Thom.* 17 intends to affirm that the things which Jesus will give have not *yet* been perceptible to the senses but are to be revealed to them later, or whether it speaks of a divine reality that the senses will not be able to discern at all. Moreover, the meaning of *Gos. Thom.* 17 is opaque not only because of the future tense, but also on account of the verb ϯ. Paul obviously

---

[24] 1 Clem 34:8; 2 Clem 11:7; *Acts of Thomas* 36; *Acts of Peter* 39; Hippolytus, *Ref.* 5.24.1; 26.16; 27.2; 6.24.4; Clement of Alexandria, *Exc. Theod.* 10.5; *Dial. Sav.* 57 (140.2-4).

[25] A similar beginning of the saying can be found, e.g., in Ps.-Philo, *Ant. Bibl.* 26:13 and in the Syriac *Apocalypse of Daniel* 6.4-5; cf. Berger, "Diskussion" 272-273; Onuki, "Traditionsgeschichte" 402.

associated this saying with *revelation* of hidden things (ἀπεκάλυψεν, 1 Cor 2:10). In *Gos. Thom.* 17 this association is not clear, for the verb ϯ ('to give') does not primarily bear the meaning of 'revelation' or 'teaching.'[26] The following relative clauses supply the verb with grammatical objects, but they do not clarify the meaning of the verb itself.

As to the grammatical structure of *Gos. Thom.* 17 and its indistinct use of ϯ, a close parallel is provided by *Gos. Thom.* 88: "The angels and the prophets will come to you and give to you those things you (already) have (ϲⲉⲛⲁϯ ⲛⲏⲧⲛ̄ ⲛ̄ⲛⲉⲧⲉⲩⲛ̄ⲧⲏⲧⲛ̄ⲥⲉ)." In this saying the future tense and the precise meaning of ϯ are as difficult to explain as they were in *Gos. Thom.* 17. In any case, *Gos. Thom.* 88 can be contrasted with *Gos. Thom.* 17, for according to it the addressees already are in possession of what the angels and the prophets will give them, whereas Jesus promises to give to his followers in *Gos. Thom.* 17 something new which has not been thought of before.

A further interpretation of this contrast is dependent on the identification of 'the angels and the prophets' mentioned in *Gos. Thom.* 88. Ménard suggests that this expression originally referred to early Christian preachers,[27] but his proof-text, *Did.* 11:3-6, speaks of 'apostles' instead of 'angels.' As an alternative it might be proposed that 'the angels and the prophets' refer to the OT writings. In *Gos. Thom.* 52 'prophets' seem to designate the books of the OT, for their number ('twenty-four') is tantamount to a reckoning of the OT writings attested by 4 Ezra 14:45.[28] The tradition that the *law* was given at Sinai through angels, on the other hand, is widely attested both by Jewish and Christian authors.[29] Hence *Gos. Thom.* 88 may give expression to a similar, distanced view of the OT as does *Gos. Thom.* 52. In consequence, the superiority of what Jesus will give (*Gos. Thom.* 17), in comparison to what the angels and prophets will give (*Gos. Thom.* 88), could be understood primarily in terms of two

---

[26] Cf. W. E. Crum, *A Coptic Dictionary* (Oxford: Clarendon 1939, repr 1993) s.v.

[27] J.-É. Ménard, *L'Évangile selon Thomas* (NHS 5, Leiden: E. J. Brill, 1975) 189.

[28] This reckoning appears also in the talmudic traditions; cf., e.g., B. Gärtner, *Ett nytt evangelium? Thomasevangeliets hemliga Jesusord* (Stockholm: Diakonistyrelse 1960) 139; A. Marjanen, "Thomas and Jewish Religious Practices," *Thomas at the Crossroads*, ed. R. Uro (forthcoming).

[29] As parallels to this view in Gal 3:19, H. Räisänen, *Paul and the Law* (Philadelphia: Fortress 1986) 133 n. 29; 140 n. 61, mentions the following texts: Deut 33:2 LXX; Josephus, *Ant.* 15.136; Jub 1:29; T. Dan. 6:2; Philo, *Somn.* 1.141ff.; Acts 7:38, 53; Heb 2:2; *Apoc. Mos.* 1; PesiqR 21, and Epiphanius, *Panarion* 28.1.3 (as an opinion of Cerinthus).

exclusive revelation traditions, and 'giving' as referring to Jesus' subsequent teachings.

Be that as it may, the main difficulty with Onuki's view that the author of 1 John knew a saying similar to *Gos. Thom.* 17 is the underlying theory about the origins of the prologue of 1 John. According to Onuki, 1 John 1:1-3 betrays no less than three subsequent phases of composition: The original form of the prologue consisted only of 1 John 1:1a, 3; yet the author responsible for this form added later 1 John 1:1b-e (ὃ ἀκηκόαμεν... ἐψηλάφησαν), and even later made another addition, 1 John 1:1-2 (περὶ τοῦ λόγου τῆς ζωῆς κτλ.).[30] According to Onuki, it is above all the earlier addition that indicates the author's knowledge of a tradition similar to *Gos. Thom.* 17; by reversing this tradition to its opposite the author sought to rebut the claims made by the opponents.

Onuki's argumentation raises several questions. It is not entirely plausible that the same author composed the prologue of 1 John and then felt it necessary to expand it twice without integrating these additions more smoothly into the earlier composition, i.e., without rewriting the whole prologue. It is not clear, either, that 1 John 1:1 in fact opposes what has been said in *Gos. Thom.* 17; to assert the tactility of Jesus does not necessarily exclude the idea that he reveals to his disciples things that have thus far been hidden. Moreover, the notion that Jesus was touched by his followers does not have to be explained in light of *Gos. Thom.* 17 at all. This feature is connected with the more general emphasis the Johannine epistles lay on the incarnation of Jesus. In fact, the extant *Gospel of Thomas* accords well with this doctrine to which the Johannine epistles measure great importance as they distinguish the right belief (and insiders!) from that of 'deceivers' and 'antichrists' (1 John 4:2; 2 John 7; cf. *Gos. Thom.* 28). To point out the tactility of Jesus is also in line with a more common tendency visible in different early Christian texts (e.g., Ign. *Smyrn.* 3:2; *Gos. Truth* 30.26-32).[31] The wide attestation of this notion turns the view that the author of 1 John would in specific react against a saying like *Gos. Thom.* 17 to a remote possibility.

---

[30] Onuki, "Traditionsgeschichte" 410f.

[31] To be sure, unlike these passages, which speak of touching the risen Jesus, 1 John 1:1 does not indicate whether this motif is to be associated with the earthly or the risen Jesus.

Finally, it is at least an interesting coincidence that the quotation of
1 John 1:1 in the *Muratorian Canon* brings this text essentially closer
to *Gos. Thom.* 17 than it originally was.[32]

| 1 Cor 2:9 | Gos. Thom 17 | 1 Jn 1:1 | Muratorian II. 29-31 |
|---|---|---|---|
| ἀλλ' καθὼς | ΠΕΧΕ ΙC ΧΕ | | |
| γέγραπται· | ΤΝΑΤ ΝΗΤΝ | | |
| | | ὁ ἀκηκόαμεν, | Quae |
| ἃ | ΜΠΕΤΕ | ὃ ἑωράκαμεν τοῖς | vidimus |
| ὀφθαλμὸς | ΜΠΕΒΑΛ | ὀφθαλμοῖς ἡμῶν, | oculis nostris |
| οὐκ εἶδεν | ΝΑΥ ΕΡΟϤ | ὁ ἐθεασάμεθα | |
| καὶ | ΑΥⲰ ΠΕΤΕ | | et auribus |
| οὓς οὐκ | ΜΠΕ ΜΑΑΧΕ | | audivimus |
| ἤκουσεν | COΤΜΕϤ | | |
| | ΑΥⲰ ΠΕΤΕ | καὶ | et |
| | ΜΠΕϬΙΧ | αἱ χεῖρες | manus |
| | | ἡμῶν | nostrae |
| | ϬΜϬⲰΜϤ | ἐψηλάφησαν | palpaverunt |
| καὶ ἐπὶ | ΑΥⲰ ΜΠΕϤΕΙ | | |
| καρδίαν | ΕϨΡΑΪ ϨΙ ϤΗΤ | | |
| ἀνθρώπου | ῬῬⲰΜΕ | | |
| οὐκ ἀνέβη ... | | | |

The following similarities are shared by the *Muratorian canon* and
*Gos. Thom.* 17 against the more original text of 1 John 1:1:

1. The *Muratorian Canon* reverses the order of seeing and hearing of
   1 John 1:1.
2. In addition to 1 John 1:1, the *Muratorian Canon* mentions 'ears'.
3. The reference to hearing is introduced by the *Muratorian canon*
   with 'et', which is equivalent to the use of ΑΥⲰ in *Gos. Thom.* 17.
4. The *Muratorian Canon* omits another reference to the seeing in 1
   John 1:1 (ἐθεασάμεθα).

[32] The edition of the *Muratorian Canon* followed here is *Das Muratorische Fragment
und die Monarchianischen Prologe zu den Evangelien*, 2nd. ed., ed. H. Lietzmann (KlT
1, Berlin: de Gruyter, 1933). The *Muratorian Canon* is usually dated about 200 CE and
located in Rome; for a short overview of these questions, see B. M. Metzger, *The Canon
of the New Testament: Its Origin, Development, and Significance* (Oxford: Clarendon,
1987) 193f.

This list is not to suggest that the text of *Gos. Thom.* 17 would be dependent on the *Muratorian Canon* or *vice versa*. Most differences between 1 John 1:1 and the *Muratorian Canon* can be explained as a result of loose quoting;[33] in addition, the reversed order of seeing and hearing appears already in 1 John 1:3. In fact, some differences between 1 John 1:1 and the *Muratorian Canon* are similar to those between 1 Cor 2:9 and its OT parallels.[34] Even the possibility that 1 Cor 2:9 would have indirectly influenced the wording of the *Muratorian Canon* cannot be ruled out; in this case the 'negative form' of the saying could have exerted some influence on its 'positive' counterpart. Basically, a similar, but reversed process could be suggested in the case of *Gos. Thom.* 17. The clause "what no hand has touched" did not occur in other negative versions of the saying, nor did its positive parallel in 1 John 1:1 lend any reliable evidence for the view that there was a traditional saying which would have included this clause. Yet these remarks leave the possibility open that this clause in *Gos. Thom.* 17 could at some stage of development have been inspired by or juxtaposed with 1 John 1:1.

This suggestion remains, of course, very tentative. It is by no means unexpected that 'touching with hands' is added to a saying which have already mentioned other senses and sense organs (eyes–seeing; ears–hearing). In consequence, similarities between 1 John 1:1 and *Gos. Thom.* 17 can also be entirely coincidental. In any case, the above comparison of the *Muratorian Canon* and 1 John 1:1 admits of one conclusion about the value of verbatim quotations or their lack with regard to the question of literary dependency: since the *Muratorian Canon*, even though it *intends* to quote 1 John 1:1 verbatim, fails to do so, the *lack of verbatim quotations* alone hardly suffices to prove independence of one early Christian text from another.

## 3. THE JOHANNINE FIGURE OF THOMAS

In Riley's view, the notion of a conflict between Johannine and Thomas Christians is closely related to the literary portrayal of Thomas in the Gospel of John.[35] In the NT only the Gospel of John displays any closer interest in Thomas (John 11:16; 14:5; 20:24-29;

---

[33] Cf. Th. Zahn, *Geschichte der Neutestamentlichen Kanons*, 2 vols. (Erlangen: Deichert; Leipzig: Böhme, 1890) 2.51.

[34] Hearing and seeing, asserted by Is 64:3, occur in a reversed order 1 Cor 2:9; in addition, 1 Cor 2:9 adds to Is 64:3 'ear' as the means of hearing.

[35] Cf. Riley, *Resurrection* 78-126.

21:2),[36] and its portrayal of him is not very favorable; he is even called ἄπιστος by Jesus in John 20:27. Given the high estimation Thomas assumes in the Thomas literature,[37] his negative portrayal in the Gospel of John could be seen as polemic against the main authority of Thomas Christianity. Nevertheless, to establish such a link between two early Christian groups is not without difficulties. The following remarks focus on the presentation of Thomas in the Gospel of John both with regard to the terminology applied to him and to his literary figure.

## a. Terminology

The apposition ὁ λεγόμενος Δίδυμος is attached three times to the name of Thomas in the Gospel of John (John 11:16; 20:24; 21:2). This apposition functions as a translation, for both the Aramaic noun תאומא and the Greek noun δίδυμος mean "twin". Moreover, the repeated use of this epithet in the Gospel of John suggests that it was already fixed with Thomas as the Gospel was written. However, attempts to establish a linkage between the Johannine figure of Thomas and the Thomas literature on this basis suffer from the fact that the Gospel of John betrays no acquaintance with two other characteristics of the Thomas literature. It does not identify Thomas with Judas (cf., e.g., *Gos. Thom.* incipit; *Thom. Cont.* 138.2; *Acts of Thomas* 1),[38] nor does it betray (or combat) the tradition that Thomas was regarded as *Jesus'* twin brother (*Thom. Cont.* 138.7-8; *Acts of Thomas* 11, 31, 39). The Johannine Thomas is neither associated with Jesus' brothers whom the author of the Gospel of John apparently opposes (John 7:5).[39] That ὁ λεγόμενος, attached to 'Didymos', would have been used pejoratively, in the meaning of 'so-called',[40] is unlikely, for in John 4:25 the same expression is applied to the Christ. In fact, a passive voice is sustained also in the Thomas literature with regard to Thomas (ⲁⲩⲭⲟⲟⲥ ⲭⲉ ⲛ̄ⲧⲟⲕ ⲡⲁⲥⲟⲉⲓϣ, "it has been said that you are my twin," *Thom. Cont.* 138.8-9; trans. Turner).

---

[36] The Synoptics mention Thomas only in the list of disciples (Mark 3:18//Matt 10:3//Luke 6:15).

[37] In the following, this term includes the *Gospel of Thomas*, the *Book of Thomas*, and the *Acts of Thomas*.

[38] As is well known, this identification occurs in the early Syriac translations of John 14:22. Yet this tradition cannot be taken as a more original reading of John 14:22; it rather reflects a later textual development of the Gospel of John.

[39] Unbelief is maintained both with regard to Jesus' brothers and to Thomas; the crucial difference is that this is all that has been said of Jesus' brothers, whereas Thomas, encouraged by Jesus to overcome his unbelief, finally confesses his belief (John 20:28).

[40] Cf. Paul Morisette's suggestion, reported by Riley, *Resurrection* 114 n. 46.

Nevertheless, it can be pondered whether the Gospel of John refers
to the Judas Thomas tradition more implicitly. The increasingly
popular notion has it that, because of its meaning 'twin,' 'Thomas' is
only a nickname, and that this nickname was originally connected
with the name Judas.[41] This Judas, on the other hand, could be
identified with Judas, Jesus' brother.[42] Hence the fixed expression ὁ
λεγόμενος Δίδυμος in the Gospel of John might—even without the
author's knowledge[43]—refer to an early Judas Thomas tradition. It
has also been argued that the expression 'one of the Twelve' (εἷς ἐκ
τῶν δώδεκα), attached to Thomas in John 20:24, links him with Judas
the Betrayer, for in John 6:70 he is singled out by Jesus as one of the
Twelve (οὐκ ἐγὼ ὑμᾶς τοὺς δώδεκα ἐξελεξάμην... καὶ ἐξ ὑμῶν εἷς
κτλ.).[44]

As to this terminological derivation, the first difficulty lies in the
Thomas literature itself. Among two different versions of the *Gospel
of Thomas*, 'Didymos' occurs together with 'Judas Thomas' only in
the Coptic *incipit* of the *Gospel of Thomas*; it is not attested by the
Greek version, which most likely reads ['Ἰούδα ὁ] καὶ Θωμᾶ (P. Oxy
654.2-3).[45] The possibility that 'Didymos' is a later addition to an
earlier textual tradition of the *Gospel of Thomas* would conform with
the textual development of the NT text, for manuscript D adds

---

[41] Cf. H.Koester, "GNOMAI DIAPHOROI: The Origin and Nature of Diversification in
the History of Early Christianity," in J. M. Robinson and H. Koester, *Trajectories
through Early Christianity* (Philadelphia: Fortress, 1971) 114-157, esp. 134; id.,
*Introduction* 2.152; id., "Introduction [to the Gospel of Thomas]," *Nag Hammadi Codex
II,2-7*, 2 vols., ed. B. Layton (NHS 20-21, Leiden: E. J. Brill, 1989) 1.38-49, esp. 39; see
also Davies, *Wisdom* 18f.; S. J. Patterson, "Gospel of Thomas: Introduction," in: J. S.
Kloppenborg, Marvin W. Meyer, S. J. Patterson, and M. Steinhauser, *Q–Thomas Reader*
(Sonoma: Polebridge, 1990) 77-123, esp. 90f.; Riley, *Resurrection* 110.

[42] Koester, "GNOMAI DIAPHOROI" 134; id., "Introduction" 39; Riley, *Resurrection*
111f. A slightly different view is provided by Patterson, "Introduction" 91: "... in Syria,
the figure of Judas, the brother of Jesus came to be identified with the apostle Thomas,
perhaps since both were known in some circles as 'the Twin.'"

[43] Cf. Riley, *Resurrection* 114: "It is enticing to speculate that John knew that the
Thomas community, at least, was calling Thomas the 'twin,' but because of their
esotericism, did not yet know why."

[44] Riley, *Resurrection* 110: "Thus 'Judas the One Who Betrays' and 'Judas the One
Who Denies' are both and uniquely designated in John by the same expression, 'one of
the twelve,' the second use here recalling the first" (for a similar linkage, see E.
Ruckstuhl, "Θωμᾶς," *EWNT* 1.407-409, esp. 408). It remains unclear whether this is to
suggest that the author nonetheless was aware of the Judas–Thomas identification (cf.
above n. 42) or whether it only applies to the Syriac textual tradition of John 14:22,
mentioned immediately before this quotation.

[45] I follow the reading provided by H. Attridge, "The Greek Fragments [of the Gospel
According to Thomas]," *Nag Hammadi Codex II,2-7* 1.95-128, 113.

'Didymos' to the name of Thomas in Luke 6:15 (τὸν ἐπικαλούμενον Δίδυμον), and in John 14:6 (ὁ λεγόμενος Δίδυμος). Moreover, even the name 'Judas Thomas' is not firmly rooted in the Thomas literature. The only saying which in the *Gospel of Thomas* portrays Thomas as a narrative figure employs the name 'Thomas' (*Gos. Thom.* 13), and the same notion applies to the narrative figure of Thomas in the *Book of Thomas* (*Thom. Cont.* 138.4.19.21.37; 139.12.22.25; 140.6.37; 141.2.19; 142.3.19; 145.17) with one exception (*Thom. Cont.* 142.8).[46]

Second, the tradition that Thomas was regarded as the twin brother of Jesus is not consistently held by the Thomas literature.[47] This tradition comes to expression in the *Book of Thomas* and in the *Acts of Thomas*, but is not spelled out in the *Gospel of Thomas*.[48] The suggestion that the three secret words in *Gos. Thom.* 13 include this identification[49] remains as conjectural as any other attempt to disclose the contents of these words. In addition, even the *Acts of Thomas* which does indeed portray 'Judas Thomas' as Jesus' twin, and makes extensive use of this identification, distinguishes him from 'Judas, Jesus' brother' (*Acts of Thomas* 1). Third, אמת is attested as a proper name at least by one Semitic inscription (CIS I.46.3);[50] hence 'Thomas' cannot be regarded only as a nickname.[51] Fourth, the

---

[46] In the *Acts of Thomas*, the double name "Judas Thomas" appears more frequently; cf., e.g., *Acts of Thomas* 1f., 11, 70, 73f., 128f., 170.

[47] Cf. B. Chilton, "The Gospel According to Thomas as a Source of Jesus' Teaching," *Gospel Perspectives: The Jesus Tradition outside the Gospels*, ed. D. Wendham (Sheffield: JSOT 1985) 155-175, esp. 156. Yet by maintaining that Judas Thomas is identified as Jesus' twin only in the *Acts of Thomas*, Chilton ignores the attestation of this view in *Thom. Cont.*

[48] That *Gos. Thom.* also attests to this identification has been suggested, e.g., by J. D. Turner, "A New Link in the Syrian Judas Thomas Tradition," *Essays on the Nag Hammadi Texts in Honour of Alexander Böhlig*, ed. M. Krause (NHS 3; Leiden: E. J. Brill, 1972) 109-119, esp. 117.

[49] This suggestion has been made by Riley, *Resurrection* 113, on the basis of the three epithets used of Thomas by Jesus in *Thom. Cont.* 138.7-8 (ⲡⲁⲥⲟⲉⲓϣ, ⲡⲁϣⲃⲣ ⲙ̄ⲙⲉ. ⲡⲁⲥⲟⲛ). To be sure, Riley is careful not to claim too much certainty for his suggestion: "Confidence is impossible in such a case" (ibid. n. 41).

[50] Cf. M. Lidzbarski, *Handbuch der Nordsemitischen Epigraphik nebst ausgewählten Inschriften*, 2 vols. (Hildesheim: Georg Olms, 1962) 1.383. The inscription is Phoenician; the same name most likely occurs also in another Phoenician inscription (CIS I.66.1: [ם]אמת).

[51] W. Bauer & K. Aland & B. Aland, *Griechisch-deutsches Wörterbuch zu den Schriften des Neuen Testaments und der frühchristlichen Literatur*, 6th ed. (Berlin and New York: de Gruyter, 1988), s.v. Θωμᾶς. Yet the assertion of this entry that "Thomas" has been attested as a *Greek* proper name is based only on the reference to the Greek

Gospel of John offers no specific linkage between Judas the Betrayer and the Doubting Thomas. The phrase εἶς ἐκ τῶν δώδεκα is used of Thomas but it is not used of Judas. As for him, the exact wording is ἐξ ὑμῶν εἶς (John 6:70). Moreover, the phrase εἶς ἐκ τῶν δώδεκα itself does not bear any connotative sense in John. It appears to be interchangeable with a more common idiom εἶς ἐκ τῶν μαθητῶν αὐτοῦ which can be used as a definition of different disciples, Judas included (John 12:6; cf. 6:8; 13:23).[52]

### b. Characterization of Thomas

Although terminological connections between John and the Judas Thomas tradition remain vague, the negative characterization of Thomas in the Gospel of John cannot be denied. The crucial problem is whether this feature justifies us to leap from the story to the real-life situation of the communities behind the texts. This leap is usually difficult to take, and it is especially difficult with regard to the characters of the Johannine story, for in fact most of them are portrayed negatively—no doubt in order to create a foil for Jesus, the main character of the story.[53] Hence much is dependent on the question of how negative the portrayal of Thomas is in comparison to other characters of the Gospel.

Riley is without doubt right in insisting that "As a character in John, Thomas is cast as one who is wrong, ignorant and unbeliev-ing."[54] But on the other hand, in the Johannine story Peter can also be wrong (John 13:37-38), Philip is ignorant of Jesus' true identity (John 14:8-9), and despite her full-blown confession Martha can be rebuked by Jesus as if she has not believed in the first place (John 11:27,40). Even the sarcastic question, addressed by Jesus to Thomas after his confession (John 20:29), appears to be a conventional feature,

---

*Incipit* of *Gos. Thom.* Otherwise Thomas appears as a Greek proper name only in papyri that are considerably later than the NT. The earliest of them, as far as I have been able to check thus far, dates from 381 CE (P. Rain. Cent. 001,87.2).

[52] Cf. R. Schnackenburg, *Das Johannesevangelium,* 4 vols. (HTKNT 4; Freiburg–Basel–Wien: Herder 1975) 3.392. Riley's question: "Why did John use this expression here? Anyone at all familiar with the tradition knew that Thomas was one of the Twelve" (*Resurrection* 109) could be applied equally well to John 6:8, where Andrew is designated as εἶς ἐκ τῶν μαθητῶν αὐτοῦ—regardless of the fact that he has been defined as Jesus' disciple already in John 1:40.

[53] To be sure, the Beloved Disciple appears to be a dominantly positive figure in John; but even he is included in the narrator's comment of the disciples' misunderstanding in John 13:28.

[54] Riley, *Resurrection* 79.

whenever the Johannine Jesus encounters his disciples' confession of faith or understanding (cf. John 1:50; 16:31-32).[55]

In fact, Thomas seems to be associated with rather than dissociated from the general Johannine portrait of Jesus' followers. In a few occasions Thomas appears as a representative of all the disciples; he can speak on their behalf (John 11:16; John 14:5), as do Peter (John 6:68-69), Philip (John 14:8), and Judas 'not the Iscariot' (John 14:22) elsewhere. As a character Thomas can also embody a more general attitude of Jesus' disciples. His exhortation in John 11:16 ("Let us also go, that we may die with him") is addressed to all the disciples, and in effect it repeats the concern expressed a little earlier by all the disciples that Jesus will be in danger in Judea (John 11:8).[56] In John 14 Thomas is one of the interlocutors, characterized by his misunderstanding of Jesus. Yet this does not distract him from the other disciples, for within the Johannine Last Supper scene, misunderstandings are ascribed to all the disciples (cf. John 13:28-29; 16:16-20). Thomas's question—unlike that of Philip (John 14:8-9)—is not even rebuked by Jesus. In light of its narrative context, Jesus' answer to this question, complaining that the recipients have not yet known the Father (John 14:7), is not addressed to Thomas in specific (nor to Thomas Christians),[57] but to all the disciples.

### c. Doubting Thomas

The Johannine portrait of Thomas attains its most negative features within the Doubting Thomas pericope (John 20:24-29). Here Thomas is singled out as the disciple who was not present when Jesus appeared to his disciples, and as the one who demands additional proof for the resurrection of Jesus. Yet even this passage adds to those in which the figure of Thomas is associated with the general characterization of all disciples of Jesus. This view is suggested by the strong parallelism of the Doubting Thomas pericope to the preceding appearance story (John 20:19-23). Both passages are introduced by an eyewitness testimony addressed to those who have not yet seen the

---

[55] Even in John 6:66-71 (unlike in Matt 16:17) Jesus does not praise Peter's confession, made on behalf of all the disciples, but encounters it by referring to the betrayer among them.

[56] It is not clear whether Thomas is "shown to be wrong" in John 11 (Riley, *Resurrection* 78f.), for the Johannine author connects the Raising of Lazarus with the death of Jesus (John 11:47-53), and hints elsewhere to the possibility that the followers of Jesus are in danger of being killed by Jews (John 12:9-11; 16:1-4). Later Riley seems to interpret John 11:16 slightly differently: Thomas' remark does not refer to Jesus' death, but to that of Lazarus (ibid., 118).

[57] This interpretation is suggested by Riley, *Resurrection* 123.

risen Lord (ἑώρακα τὸν κύριον, 20:18; ἑωράκαμεν τὸν κύριον, 20:25); what convinces the addressees, however, is in both cases their personal encounter with the risen Jesus.[58] The repeated sequence consisting of the eyewitness testimony and its verification underscores the reliability of these testimonies for the intended audience of the Gospel. Hence not only the Doubting Thomas pericope but the Johannine resurrection narrative as a whole prepares for the blessing of those who believe without seeing (John 20:29).[59] This closure also betrays the author's perspective to the Doubting Thomas pericope; the focus of this passage is not so much on Thomas, but on those 'later generations' who have to believe without seeing.[60]

Riley's interpretation of John 20:24-29 is closely related to the notion that the *Gospel of Thomas* as well as the later Thomas literature renounce the body and the idea of physical resurrection. That a trajectory through the Thomas literature can be drawn on this basis is well demonstrated by Riley's study. In addition, as Riley points out, different applications of the Temple saying in John 2:19-21 and in the *Gos. Thom.* 71 may reflect distinct views regarding the bodily resurrection of Jesus.[61] This interpretation would admit of the conclusion that the Johannine and Thomas Christians had adopted different views concerning the future resurrection of believers.[62]

In light of this overall view, it would be tempting to maintain that in John 20:24-29 Thomas "doubts the possibility of bodily resurrection."[63] However, the Doubting Thomas pericope itself allows for an

---

[58] At least no reaction of disciples is mentioned after Mary's eyewitness testimony (John 20:18); cf. Riley, *Resurrection* 125: "All of the disciples had to see to believe, in all of the canonical Gospels."

[59] Cf. also Riley, *Resurrection* 125.

[60] Cf. Schnackenburg, *Johannesevangelium* 3.391.

[61] Riley, *Resurrection* 146-156. Yet given the fragmentary text of *Gos. Thom.* 71, the exact interpretation of the saying remains uncertain. In specific, it is not fully clear what the "house" refers to in the saying.

[62] Yet the view that the Thomas Christians denied the future resurrection in body can be sustained consequently only by declaring the sentence καὶ θεθαμμένον ὃ ο[ὑκ ἐγερθήσεται] (*Gos. Thom.* 5, P.Oxy 654.31) to be a secondary addition. That this sentence appears to be secondary to the Synoptic attestation of the same saying (Mark 4:22//Matt 10:26//Luke 8:17; 12:2) and is missing in the Coptic *Gospel of Thomas* does not prove yet that it would be added to the original *Gospel of Thomas* (thus Riley, *Resurrection* 165f.). The otherwise anti-eschatological tendency of the *Gospel of Thomas* could have motivated the omission of this sentence at some later stage of transmission as well.

[63] Riley, *Resurrection* 119; cf. ibid. 104f.: "Thomas... will not believe in the physical nature of the resurrection, and must touch the body of Jesus." The last feature, at least, does not occur in John: Thomas is invited by Jesus to touch him, but the seeing proves to be sufficient even here.

alternative reading as well. Taking the text as it stands,[64] Thomas doubts the claim that the other disciples have seen the Lord (ἑωράκαμεν τὸν κύριον, John 20:25), and is presented as the disciple who demands more concrete proof instead of a mere vision. Hence it is possible to consider Thomas to be a "realist more than doubter"[65] also in this story. It belongs to the narrator's irony that the proofs demanded by Thomas were just given to the other disciples by Jesus. Although the other disciples—and the audience of the Gospel—are aware of them, according to the narrative they have not yet been transmitted to Thomas.

The proofs demanded by Thomas might lead to the conclusion that the Johannine author makes Thomas require evidence for the physical resurrection of Jesus. Yet Riley's survey of different Graeco-Roman views concerning post-mortem existence demonstrates that the dead could be considered as having scars and, occasionally, even as being palpable.[66] These features lend some support to the possibility that what is at stake in the Doubting Thomas pericope is the *identification* of the risen Jesus rather than his physical resurrection.[67] In any case, Riley's observations make us more sensitive to the fact that the most concrete elements of the Lucan resurrection story are missing in the Gospel of John. The explicit contrast between "spirit that has no flesh and bones" and the risen Jesus (Luke 24:39; cf. Ign. *Smyrn.* 3:2) does not occur in the Gospel of John, nor does its author maintain that Jesus ate after his resurrection (like in Luke 24:41-42; cf. Ign. *Smyrn.* 3:3).

In any case, it is striking that the Johannine author not only includes Thomas in the group of believers, but also grants him a full-blown confession of Jesus. Moreover, Thomas' confession ("My lord

---

[64] According to Riley, the demand of physical proofs indicates that "John *meant* the disciples to say, 'We have seen the Lord in the same physical body he had before his death'" (Riley, *Resurrection* 115; italics added).

[65] R. Alan Culpepper, *Anatomy of the Fourth Gospel: A Study in Literary Design*, 2nd. ed. (Philadelphia: Fortress, 1987) 124.

[66] For στίγματα and the possible palpability of the dead, cf. Riley, *Resurrection* 50-58; of crucial importance is Riley's comparison between Homer and Virgil: as to the latter, "the 'life' in the underworld has by his time become far more substantial, and the dead had become correspondingly more tangible" (ibid. 55).

[67] The identification of the Risen Jesus is a crucial theme in the Johannine resurrection narratives: in John 20:11-18 Mary does not recognize the Risen Jesus immediately (20:14), and John 21:4 asserts that the disciples did not recognize Jesus in the first place. The theme naturally occurs also in other Gospels (cf. Luke 24:13-32). As to this issue, a similar interpretation is proposed by A. De Conick, "'Blessed are those who have not seen' (Jn 20:29): Johannine Dramatization of an Early Christian Discourse," included in the present volume.

and my God", John 20:28) is unique even to the Gospel of John, for it provides an impressive inclusion to and confirmation of the Prologue of the Gospel (cf. John 1:1,18). It is beyond any doubt that this confession is presented as paradigmatic to the audience of the Gospel. If Johannine and Thomas Christians were in conflict, such a portrayal of Thomas would not have been without problems. It might have been understood as a friendly gesture by Thomas Christians, but it also could have appeared as a hazardous concession in the eyes of the Johannine audience of the Gospel. However that may be, Thomas' confession is repeated twice in the *Acts of Thomas* (10; 166), which shows that the Johannine Doubting Thomas pericope could easily be adapted also by those who thought highly of Thomas. Hence at least the reception history of John 20:24-29 does not confirm the idea that Thomas in this pericope was regarded as a "false hero."[68]

### 3. SEEKING AND FINDING IN JOHN

De Conick deals with the relationship of the *Gospel of Thomas* to John only very briefly in her recent monograph.[69] In this study emphasis is laid on the Johannine sayings of seeking and finding (John 7:33-34; 8:21; 13:33). These sayings together with John 13:36 are taken as critique against mystic ascension soteriology attested by the *Gospel of Thomas*.[70] According to De Conick, the Johannine soteriological model is not that a believer ascends, but that Jesus ascends and then returns to take his followers to himself (John 14:3). The Johannine figure of Thomas is involved in De Conick's argumentation only insofar as she points out the fact that in John 14:5 Thomas is made to confess that he does not know the way.[71]

De Conick's comparison between the Gospel of John and the *Gospel of Thomas* is helpful in pointing out differences in their soteriologies. In support of her view, one could easily add the emphasis the Gospel of John lays on the claim that nobody (John 1:18) or the Son

---

[68] The category of a "false hero" was linked with the Doubting Thomas pericope by De Conick in her article mentioned in the preceding note.

[69] This is due to a separate study devoted to this issue (above n. 66), announced by De Conick, *Seek to See Him*, 72 n. 25.

[70] De Conick, *Seek to See Him*, 72-3. De Conick's view of ascension mysticism in the *Gospel of Thomas* is based on her detailed study on *Gospel of Thomas* 50. This study consists of comprehensive tradition-historical analysis of the saying, demonstrating that its closest parallels are connected with either post-mortem or mystic ascension of the believer (ibid., 64 ff.). Yet, strictly speaking, the ascension terminology itself ("to go/come above") does not occur in the *Gospel of Thomas*.

[71] Ibid.

only (John 5:19) has seen the Father. In addition, Jesus' rebuke of Philip, who asks him to show the Father to the disciples, appears to reflect the same conviction: "Who has seen me has seen the Father" (John 14:9).

The difficulty, again, is in demonstrating that these differences bear witness to an actual conflict between Johannine and Thomas Christians. To begin with, the Johannine sayings of seeking and finding do not react against the seeking of Jesus. Instead, they express the seeking through declarative sentences and thus take it for granted. Admittedly the sayings of seeking and finding can be used polemically in the Gospel of John, but only insofar as they are directed against the Jews. As for them, these sayings affirm that they will not see Jesus any longer (John 7:33-34; 8:21). Yet no similar condemnation is attached to the believers who seek Jesus (John 13:33). In contrast, their failure to find Jesus will be only temporary (cf. John 16:16). The distinction between the world which is no longer able to see Jesus and the believers who are to see him is explicitly drawn in John 14:18-19.[72] Finally, John 13:36 cannot be associated with any kind of conlict between Johannine and Thomasine soteriologies, for Peter's inability to follow Jesus is resolved already within the 'narrated time' of the Gospel of John. The subsequent promise has it that Peter will follow Jesus later, and this promise finds its fulfilment already in the closing scene of the Gospel (John 21:19).

## 4. CONCLUSION

The main concern of this paper has been the use of the Johannine writings as the negative attestation of Thomas Christianity. In my opinion, the controversy theories have managed to highlight substantial differences between the Gospel of John and the *Gospel of Thomas*. Yet the hypothesis that the Gospel of John reacts directly against another early Christian group that traced its origins back to the disciple (Judas) Thomas remains questionable. This is, of course, partly due to the nature of our sources. Even if there were in fact a conflict between these groups, their stories of Jesus—or their manner of treating his sayings—possibly did not provide the best forum to deal with such a conflict. However, traits of polemics *could* have been more visible. For example, neither the Gospel of John nor the *Gospel of Thomas* leave any doubts concerning their hostile attitude against

---

[72] Given the fact that in the Johannine resurrection narratives Jesus only appears to his followers, John 14:18-9 can, of course, be taken as a reference to these stories.

the Jews. In addition, the *Gospel of Thomas* is able to contrast its
views with the opinions of "those who lead you" (ΝΕΤϹШΚ ϨΗΤ
ΤΗΥΤΝ; *Gos. Thom.* 3). Moreover, the *Gospel of Philip* demonstrates that also the genre of saying collection allows the author(s) to
express polemics against other Christian groups very explicitly. In
this Gospel other Christian views are frequently opposed by using the
phrase "some said/those who say... are in error (or: deceive)" (*Gos.
Phil.* 55.23-24; 56.15-17; 67.35-37; 73.1-3). Whatever be the
relationship of the Gospel of John and the *Gospel of Thomas*, such
unmistakable features of controversy do not mark it.

Due to the limited scope of this paper, many crucial issues have
been left unnoticed. For example, Davies' notion that coincidences
between Johannine christology and that of the *Gospel of Thomas* can
be explained in terms of similar adaptations of Jewish Wisdom myth
deserves more attention than it has gained thus far. In light of the
above analysis of *Gos. Thom.* 17, it also seems that more traditional
questions, such as the textual criticism of the *Gospel of Thomas*, or
even the possibility of direct or indirect influence of the Johannine
literature on the *Gospel of Thomas* are not yet entirely outdated
issues. The mere fact that the *Gospel of Thomas* has been circulated
in various recensions[73] leaves us with several points of possible
interaction between it and the Johannine writings. The existence of
different recensions speaks in favor of the view that saying collections
like the *Gospel of Thomas* could easily have been modified by adding
and omitting individual sayings.[74] This warns us against making
generalizations concerning the relationship of the *Gospel of Thomas*
to the Johannine writings; their relationship may vary from one saying
to another.[75]

---

[73] This is not only attested by the extant fragments found in Oxyrynchos in the beginning of this century (for example, as is well known, in P. Oxy 1.23-30 the sayings 33 and
77b of the Coptic *Gospel of Thomas* occur together), but also by the excerpts from the
Naassene version of the *Gospel of Thomas*, attested by Hippolytus' *Refutatio*, that betray
a significant degree of variance.

[74] Cf. Riley, "The Gospel of Thomas in Recent Scholarship" 236; J. M. Robinson, "Die
Bedeutung der gnostischen Nag-Hammadi Texte für die neutestamentliche Wissenschaft," *Religious Propaganda and Missionary Competition in the New Testament
World: Essays Honoring Dieter Georgi*, ed. L. Bormann, K. Del Tredici, A. Standhartinger (Leiden: E. J. Brill, 1994) 23-41, esp. 30-31.

[75] A similar view concerning the relationship of the *Gospel of Thomas* to the canonical
Gospels has, of course, been already asserted by many scholars; cf. Riley, "The Gospel of
Thomas in Recent Scholarship" 236.

# "BLESSED ARE THOSE WHO HAVE NOT SEEN" (JN 20:29): JOHANNINE DRAMATIZATION OF AN EARLY CHRISTIAN DISCOURSE

*April D. De Conick*
University of Michigan

The relationship of the Gospel of John to early Jewish mysticism has been the focus of several previous studies beginning with W. Baldensperger who recognized the polemical nature of 3:3 and 3:13 and suggested that this polemic was aimed at Jewish mystics.[1] H. Odeberg has followed suit, also arguing that the polemic contained within these verses was directed against Jewish visionaries who sought salvation through an ascent to heaven and visual encounter with God.[2] P.

---

[1] W. Baldensperger, *Der Prolog des vierten Evangeliums* (Tübingen: J. C. B. Mohr, 1898). On the connections between John and early Jewish mysticism, see H. Odeberg, *The Fourth Gospel Interpreted in its Relationship to Contemporaneous Religious Currents in Palestine and the Hellenistic-Oriental World* (Uppsala: Almqvist & Wiksell, 1929; Amsterdam: Bruner, 1929, repr. 1968, 1974); G. Quispel, "Nathanael und der Menschensohn (Joh 1:51)," *ZNW* 47 (1956) 281-283; idem. "Het Johannesevangelie en de Gnosis," *NedTTs* 11 (1956/57) 173ff.; idem, "L'Évangile de Jean et la Gnose," L'Évangile de Jean, ed. M. E. Boismard (RechBib 3; Bruges: Desclée de Brouwer, 1958) 197-208; N. A. Dahl, "The Johannine Church and History," *Current Issues in New Testament Interpretation: Essays in Honor of Otto A. Piper*, ed. W. Klassen and G. Synder (New York, Evanston, and London: Harper & Row, 1962) 124-142; P. Borgen, *Bread From Heaven: An Exegetical Study of the Concept of Manna in the Gospel of John and the Writings of Philo* (NovTSup 10; Leiden: E. J. Brill, 1965); idem, *Philo, John and Paul: New Perspectives on Judaism and Early Christianity* (BJS 131; Atlanta: Scholars Press, 1987) 103-120, 171-184; W. A. Meeks, *The Prophet-King: Moses Traditions and the Johannine Christology* (NovTSup 14; Leiden: E. J. Brill, 1967); A. F. Segal, *Two Powers in Heaven: Early Rabbinic Reports About Christianity and Gnosticism* (SJLA 25; Leiden: E. J. Brill, 1978) 213-214; C. Rowland, "John 1.51, Jewish Apocalyptic and Targumic Tradition," *NTS* 30 (1984) 498-507. J. Dunn, "Let John be John: A Gospel for Its Time," *Das Evangelium und die Evangelium, Vorträge vom Tübinger Symposium 1982*, ed. P. Stuhlmacher (WUNT 28; Tübingen: J.C.B. Mohr [P. Siebeck], 1983) 322-325, provides a brief summary of some of these ideas.

[2] Odeberg, *The Fourth Gospel*, 72-98; cf. R. Bultmann, *The Gospel of John: A Commentary*, ed. R. W. N. Hoare and J. K. Riches, trans. by G.R. Beasley-Murray (Philadelphia: Westminster, 1971), 150 n. 1; Borgen, *Philo, John and Paul*, 103-120, 171-184; W. A. Meeks, "The Man from Heaven in Johannine Sectarianism," *JBL* 91 (1972) 52; F. Moloney, *The Johannine Son of Man* (Rome: Las, 1976) 54. On ascent, see: W. Bousset, "Die Himmelsreise der Seele," *ARW* 4 (1901) 136-169, 229-273; G. Widengren, *The Ascension of the Apostle and the Heavenly Book* (UUÅ 7; Uppsala: Lundequistka Bokhandeln, 1950); C. Colpe, "Die 'Himmelsreise der Seele' ausserhalb und innerhalb der Gnosis," *Le Origini dello Gnosticismo, Colloquio di Messina 13-18*

Borgen believes that the polemic serves a more specific purpose: to discourage adepts in the Johannine community who maintained that they were visionaries like Moses.[3]

Discussions of 1:18 have served to advance this investigation. C. Rowland argues that the claim in this verse that only Jesus can make God known must be recontextualized alongside the claims made by Jewish mystics that they revealed the divine secrets. So the Fourth Gospel contains several rebuttals against those mystics who claimed that they knew God apart from the revelation of God in Jesus (1:18; 3:13; 5:37; 6:46).[4] Rowland's discussion seems to have been influenced by earlier works such as those by G. Quispel and A. Segal who previously argued that 6:46 is a polemic against ascension and theophany themes.[5]

The work of these scholars has made it clear that the Johannine author was in dispute with mystical pre-mortem ascent theology, especially in verses 1:18, 3:3, 3:13, 5:37, and 6:46. To these passages, I would add the series of verses in John where Jesus proclaims that he will not be able to be followed into heaven (at least not before the Eschaton). No less than four times, Jesus repeats to different audiences that "you will seek me...(but) where I am going, you cannot come" (7:33-34; 8:21; 13:33; 13:36).

---

*Aprile 1966,* ed. U. Bianchi (SHR 12; Leiden: E. J. Brill, 1967) 429-447; A. Segal, "Heavenly Ascent in Hellenistic Judaism, Early Christianity, and their Environment," *ANRW* 2.23.2 (Berlin/New York: de Gruyter, 1980) 1333-1394; U. Mann, "Geisthöhe und Seelentiefe: Die vertikale Achse der numinosen Bereiche," *Eranos* 50 (1981) 1-50; M. Smith, "Ascent to the Heavens and the Beginning of Christianity," *Eranos* 50 (1981) 403-429; I. P. Culianu, "L''Ascension de l'âme' dans les mystères et hors des mystères," *La Soteriologia dei culti orientali nell'Impero romano,* ed. U. Bianchi and M. J. Vermaseren (Leiden: E. J. Brill, 1982) 276-302; idem, *Psychanodia I: A Survey of the Evidence Concerning the Ascension of the Soul and Its Relevance* (Leiden: E. J. Brill, 1983); idem, *Expériences de l'Extase* (Paris: Payot, 1984); M. Dean-Otting, *Heavenly Journeys: A Study of the Motif in Hellenistic Jewish Literature* (Frankfurt am Main: P. Lang, 1984); J. D. Tabor, *Things Unutterable: Paul's Ascent to Paradise in its Greco-Roman, Judaic, and Early Christian Contexts* (Studies in Judaism; Lanham, MD: University Press of America, 1986); M. Himmelfarb, *Ascent to Heaven In Jewish and Christian Apocalypses* (New York: Oxford University Press, 1993).

[3] Borgen, *Philo, John and Paul,* 103. There certainly were those who maintained that Moses was divinized. See Quispel's comments on Ezekiel the Tragedian in "Judaism, Judaic Christianity, and Gnosis," *The New Testament and Gnosis: Essays in Honour of Robert McLachlan Wilson,* ed. A.H.B. Logan and A.J.M. Wedderburn (Edinburgh: T. & T. Clark, 1983) 48-52.

[4] Rowland, "John 1:51," 499-500.

[5] G. Quispel, "Gnosticism and the New Testament," *Gnostic Studies, vol. 1* (Nederlands Historisch-Archaeologisch Instituut te Istanbul 34; Istanbul: Nederlands Historisch-Archaeologisch Instituut in het Nabije Oosten, 1974) 211. Segal, *Two Powers,* 213-214.

Indisputably, the Johannine author was discoursing against the notion of ecstatic pre-eschatological ascent and visionary experience. It is to this idea that John is reacting when he makes the statements that no one has ascended into heaven except Jesus nor has anyone ever seen the Father except the Son. But is it possible to further identify the factions of this discourse from this textualized Johannine environment?

Developing upon the methodological model of R. Wuthnow who has advanced our understanding of the process of articulation of actual discourse as textual ideology,[6] I suggest that in addition to uncovering the ideology of the general religious environment to which John may be responding, we can also determine what I call the "religio-social horizon," the specific religious community with which John is in dispute, and the "discursive field," the particular point of dispute between the two communities.

It must be recognized, however, that the religio-social horizon represented in the Johannine text may only resemble partially the actual community which is in dialogue with John. The actual discourse will be masked due to the theoretical representation of the conflict. The articulation of the discursive field will be done on a symbolic level so that the actual features of the religio-social horizon are incorporated at the textual level as symbolic acts and events. The real opposition between the factions is dramatized. Such dramatizations provide a contrast to the religio-social horizon and evoke a space for creative reflection on the part of the author. The result of the discourse between the two communities is the textualization of critical ideology which will have thematized particular features of the horizontal horizon.

In order to assist in recovering the discourse from its textual environment, three major passages will be analyzed: 14:3-7, 14:20-23, and 20:24-29. This analysis will identify more precisely the discursive field as understood by the Johannine author and reveal the nature of the religio-social horizon. It must be remembered, however, that this horizon will only be reflective of Johannine space and thus will only bear a relative relationship to the actual discourse itself. Common to all these passages is the portrayal of (Judas) Thomas as the Fool who does not have the correct understanding of the way to heaven or of the manner of encountering God since he insists on visions.

---

[6] R. Wuthnow, *Communities of Discourse* (Cambridge, MA: Harvard University Press, 1989) esp. 1-22.

The dialogue in the first of these passages, John 14:3-7, centers around the crucial term "the way (ἡ ὁδός):"

> "And when I go and prepare a place for you, I will come again and will take you to myself, that where I am you may be also. And you know the way (τὴν ὁδόν) where I am going." Thomas said to him, "Lord, we do not know where you are going; how can we know the way (τὴν ὁδόν)?" Jesus said to him, "I am the way (ἡ ὁδος), and the truth, and the life; no one comes to the Father, but by me. If you had known me, you would have known my Father also; henceforth you know him and have seen him."

According to R. Bultmann, "the way" is a reference to the mythology that, when the soul separates from the body, it journeys to the sacred realm often guided by a superior being.[7] In other words, it is the route to heaven and divinity.

A vivid instance of this in Christian literature is seen in the Syrian *Odes of Solomon* 39.9-13, where the Lord's footsteps to heaven create a path for his own to follow and, in this manner, "the Way has been appointed for those who cross over after him, and for those who adhere to the path of his faith; and who adore his name" (39.13). In *Ode* 11, the hymnist tells us that "I ran in the Way in his peace, in the Way of truth" (11.3). This verse functions as the beginning of a song about the hymnist's ascent to Paradise (11.16), his vision of the Lord (11.13), and his transformation into a light-being (11.11). The Lord caused the mystic odist to "ascend from the regions below" (22.1) and this is the Lord's "Way" which is "incorruptible" (22.11).

This use of the concept "the way" as the heavenly route is already present in Judaism as evidenced in Philo. In *De Migratione Abrahami* 168-175, Philo explains that Exodus 24:1, "Come up to thy Lord, thou and Aaron and Nadab and Abihu and seventy of the Senate of Israel," means that the soul must "come up" to "behold the Existent

---

[7] R. Bultmann, *John*, 603ff. where he refers to Hippolytus, *Ref.* 5.10.2, 5.16.1, 5.26.23; *Exc. Theod.* 38, 74; Irenaeus, *Haer.* 1.13.6; 1.21.5; Epiphnius, *Panarion*, 36.3.2-5; Origen, *c. Celsus* 6.31; *Acts Thom.* 148, 167; *Odes Sol.* 39.9ff. [cp. 7.3, 13f.; 11.3; 22.7, 11; 24.13; 33.7ff, 41.11]; *Mand. Lit.* 38, 77, 97f., 101, 132f., 134f.; *Joh.-B.* 198.20f., 199.3f., 239.14; Ginza 95.15, 247.16ff., 271.26f., 395.3ff., 429.17ff., 439.14ff., 487.8ff., 523.23ff., 550.1ff; *C.H.* 1.26, 1.29, 4.11, 7.2, 9.10, 10.21. He states that the parabolic usage of the way in the Old Testament (e.g. Ps 143:10; Isa 63:14) is of little relevance here, 604 n. 5. Furthermore, he notes that "the way" belongs together with "the door" in 10:7 which mythologically represents the entrance into life or the world of light, 377-378 n. 7, 604 n. 5. Cf. idem, "Die Bedeutung der neuerschlossenen mandäischen und manichäischen Quellen für das Verständnis des Johannesevangeliums," *ZNW* 24 (1925) 100-146, esp. 135. Odeberg, *Fourth Gospel*, 319-327, convincingly argues that the expression "door" in John 10:9 refers to the door or gate of heaven being opened and is the same spiritual reality as described in John 1:51.

One" (169). Furthermore, Aaron (= combining understanding and speech), Nadab (= voluntarily honoring the Deity), and Abihu (= having need of God), are "the powers that form the bodyguard of the mind" (170). These "bodyguards" are necessary because "the soul has reason to fear ascending in its own strength to the sight of Him that IS, ignorant as it is of *the way* (δι' ἑαυτὴν ἀγνοούσῃ τὴν ὁδὸν)" (170).⁸ So Moses, Philo's paradigm mystic, in Exodus 33:15 "prays that he may have God Himself, to guide him to the way that leads to Him (πρὸς τὴν πρὸς αὐτὸν ἄγουσαν ὁδόν)" (171).⁹ Philo warns unprepared mystics, however, that it is better to forego mystic ascent and roam through mortal life, then to ascend without "Divine direction" and become shipwrecked along the way (171).

The study of J. Pascher indicates that Philo interprets the "royal way (βασιλικὴ ὁδός)" of Numbers 20:17 as the way to the knowledge and vision of God.¹⁰ Philo describes the "royal way" as the road of "wisdom" by which the "souls can make their escape to the Uncreated. For we may well believe that he who walks unimpeded along the King's way (ὁδοῦ τῆς βασιλικῆς) will never flag or faint, till he comes into the presence of the King" (*Quod deus* 159-161). Philo explains that the "royal way" is the eternal and indestructible way described in Genesis 6:12 which leads to the recognition and knowledge of God; those who are endowed with "vision," that is Israel, are able to journey along this road although they will be tempted to swerve off course by the earthly senses (ibid., 142-144; cf. 162; *Gig.* 64; *Mig.* 146).

Philo's employment of ὁδός in the technical sense as the road to heavenly ascent and vision is similar to the manner in which Hermeticism uses ὁδος. In *Corpus Hermeticum* 4.11, Hermes tells Tat that "if your vision of it [god's image] is sharp and you understand it with the eyes of your heart, believe me, child, you shall discover *the way* (τὴν ὁδόν) that leads above or, rather, the image itself will show you the way (ὁδηγήσει)." He continues by informing Tat that vision has a special drawing power, taking hold of the mystic and drawing him up to God like a "magnet stone draws iron" (cf. C.H. 1.26-27). In the *Excerpts* of Stobaeus 6.18, Hermes explains that the one who has

⁸ Philo, *Migr.* 170 (trans. F. H. Colson and G. H. Whitaker), emphasis mine.
⁹ Philo, *Migr.* 171.
¹⁰ J. Pascher, *Η ΒΑΣΙΛΙΚΗ ΟΔΟΣ Der Königsweg zu Wiedergeburt und Vergöttung bei Philon von Alexandreia, Studien zur Geschichte und Kultur des Altertums 17, 3-4* (Paderborn: F. Schoningh, 1931). Cf. E. Goodenough, *By Light, Light* (New Haven: Yale University Press, 1935), who understands the "Way" to be the Mystic Road to God: 14, 136, 145, 214, 219, 244, 280, 316, 355-356.

seen God is blessed but this visionary experience is not possible while one is in the body. One "must train his soul in this life, in order that, when it has entered the other world, where it is permitted to see God, it may not miss the way (ὁδοῦ) <which leads to Him>."

Since the goal of the ascent and vision is to become divinized like Hermes, *the way* of Hermes is "*the way* of immortality (ⲉⲑⲓⲏ ⲛ̄ⲧⲙ̄ⲛ̄ⲧⲁⲧⲙⲟⲩ)," the ascent to the ninth heavenly sphere (*Disc.* 8-9 63.10-14; cf. *C.H.* 10.7; 13.3).[11] So the Hermetics speak of the experience of becoming God (*C.H.* 13.3,10,14) by casting off materiality, ascending to heaven, and being absorbed into God (*C.H.* 1.24-26; 10.13; *Disc.* 8-9 57.28-58.22; cf. *C.H.* 11.20; 12.1; *Ascl.* 6.22). Thus, they explain: "If you ask about god, you ask also about the beautiful. Only one *way* (ὁδός) travels from here to the beautiful - reverence combined with knowledge" (*C.H.* 6.5; cf. 11.22).[12]

A passage from the *Excerpts* of Stobaeus 2B.3-8 contains a synthesis of this theology. Tat is taught about "the only *way* that leads to Reality (ἡ πρὸς ἀλήθειαν ὁδός)" (2B.5).[13] This way is a "holy and divine way (ὁδός)" which is difficult to travel while the soul "is in the body" (2B.5).[14] The soul must feud against the vices and strive toward the Good (2B.6-7). Once the soul has won this contest, it is able to "mount upward" and begin the "journey to the world above" (2B.8). The soul yearns for the Good and must learn to know the Father so that the soul is freed and will not fail "to know whither it must wing its upward flight" (2B.3-4).

Connected to this is the discussion in *Corpus Hermeticum* 13 where Tat inquires about the way to be "born again" (13.3). Hermes explains that he is incapable of relating anything about this except to share a specific visionary experience when he left his human body and assumed "an immortal body (ἀθάνατον σῶμα)" (13.3).[15] He goes on to describe a vision of his spiritual Self. He tells Tat that the Self must be cleansed of the twelve vices under the influence of the ten powers of God. Hermes, of course, is referring to the way of ascent

---

[11] For an excellent summary of the Hermetic immortalization process, see J.-P. Mahé, "La voie d'immortalité à la lumière des Hermetica de Nag Hammadi et de découvertes plus récentes," *VC* 45 (1991) 347-375.

[12] A. D. Nock and A.-J. Festugière, *Corpus Hermeticum, Tome I, Traités I-XII* (Paris: Les Belles Lettres, 1945) 75.

[13] A.-J. Festugière, *Corpus Hermeticum, Tome III, Fragments extraits de Stobée I-XXII* (Paris: Les Belles Lettres, 1954) 14.

[14] Ibid., 14.

[15] A. D. Nock and A.-J. Festugière, *Corpus Hermeticum, Tome II, Traités XIII-XVIII. Asclepius* (Paris: Les Belles Lettres, 1945) 201.

through the planetary spheres, the removal of particular vices at each sphere, and the final absorption into the divine (cf. *C.H.* 1.24-26). Once this has happened, the new spiritual birth is possible and with it, divinity (13.10). Thus the road of ascent and vision is the way of rebirth.[16]

It is significant that all these texts, whether describing pre- or post-mortem ascent, agree that ὁδός means the path that the soul will journey when it goes to heaven. It is quite certain that the Johannine author employs the terminology "the way" in this technical sense. Thus Thomas' reply makes sense: "Lord, we do not know where you are going; how can we know the way?" (14:5). It appears that Thomas' answer reflects the popular association of ὁδός with proleptic heavenly ascents.

At the same time, the disciple Thomas is portrayed by the Johannine author as the fool in this discourse because of this ignorant statement.[17] Clearly, in this passage, the Johannine author attributes to Thomas the confession that he *and* others with him are ignorant of the true way or route to heaven.

It is probable that here we see evidence of the textualization of discourse from the point of view of the Johannine community. The author, by deliberately characterizing Thomas as a fool in this passage, condemns the hero of Thomasine Christianity. Moreover, his articulation of the discourse points to a particular feature of the dispute: the journey or ascent to heaven. John tells us that such ascent is not necessary, that Jesus himself is the only "way" into heaven. This is stated in contradistinction to the Thomasine belief which, from Thomas' answer in 14.5, appears to have encouraged proleptic heavenly ascents.

The next pericope which requires attention is John 14:20-23 where a certain Judas who is distinguished from Judas Iscariot (Ἰούδας οὐχ ὁ Ἰσχαριώτης)[18] is given the dunce cap:

---

[16] C.H. Dodd, *The Interpretation of the Fourth Gospel* (Cambridge: Cambridge University Press, 1953) 44-53, discusses C.H. 13 and notes "expressions which recall the language of the Fourth Gospel and the First Epistle of John" including the notion of rebirth. He argues that there lie "real similarities in thought" behind these verbal parallels (49). He provides a useful chart which compares passages from *C.H.* 13 and John (50-51).

[17] Contra. J. Charlesworth, *The Beloved Disciple: Whose Witness Validates the Gospel of John?* (Valley Forge, PA: Trinity Press International, 1995) 261-264.

[18] The gloss, "not Iscariot," was probably added to this passage by the Johannine redactor since Judas Iscariot had left the scene earlier.

"In that day you will know that I am in my Father, and you in me, and I in you. He who has my commandments and keeps them, he it is who loves me; and he who loves me will be loved by my Father, and I will love him and manifest (ἐμφανίσω) myself to him." Judas (not Iscariot) (᾿Ιούδας οὐχ ὁ ᾿Ισχαριώτης) said to him, "Lord, how is it that you will manifest (ἐμφανίζειν) yourself to us, and not to the world?" Jesus answered him, "If a man loves me, he will keep my word, and my Father will love him, and we will come to him and make our home with him."

Judas is concerned about the method by which the followers of Jesus will be able to have a vision of Jesus when he is not in the "world" anymore. Judas has interpreted the phrase "manifest myself to him (ἐμφανίσω αὐτῷ ἐμαυτόν)" to refer to a theophany since he demands to know how the followers of Jesus will be able to behold the manifestation while others in the world will not see it.

The word ἐμφανίζειν is used only in the New Testament in John 14:21-22 in this sense, but it is a word which is associated with the theophany in Exodus 33:13,18 which is quoted by Philo in *Legum Allegoriae* 3.101. He states that Moses represents the "mind more perfect and more thoroughly cleansed, which has undergone initiation into the great mysteries" and which lifts its eyes "above and beyond creation" and "obtains a clear vision (ἔμφασιν) of the uncreated One" (*Leg. Al.* 3.100). Thus Moses says in Exodus 33:13: "Manifest Thyself to me (᾿Εμφάνισόν μοι σαυτὸν), let me see Thee that I may know Thee (γνωστὸς ἴδω σε)" (*Leg. Al.* 3.101). Philo exegetes this passage, stating that Moses meant that he did not want God to "be manifested (ἐμφανισθείης)" to him "by means of heaven or earth or water or air or any created thing at all" (*Leg. Al.* 3.101). He believed that one can only receive "the clear vision (ἔμφασιν) of God directly from the First Cause Himself" (*Leg. Al.* 3.102). Thus Philo employs the term ἐμφανίζειν to describe the vision of God himself.

According to the Johannine author, it is actually a misunderstanding that Judas expects Jesus' manifestation to be a theophany. When Jesus speaks of manifesting himself in the future to his followers, according to John, he intends to do this through a manifestation of divine love, not through a mystical visionary encounter such as that which Judas is anticipating.

The identity of this "Judas" is arguably linked with the Syrian Thomas tradition where the apostle Thomas has the unique appellation "Judas Thomas."[19] Careful analysis of the use of this name in

---

[19] H.-Ch. Puech, "The Gospel of Thomas," *New Testament Apocrypha*, 2 vols., ed. E. Hennecke and W. Schneemelcher; Eng. trans. R. McL. Wilson (Philadelphia: Westminster, 1963) 1.278-307; followed by H. Koester, "GNOMAI DIAPHOROI: The Origin and

various Syrian texts suggests that, in addition to Judas Iscariot, there was a disciple of Jesus whose actual name was "Judas." In order to differentiate him from Judas Iscariot, the nickname "Thomas" or "Twin"[20] was appended to Judas probably at an early date. Thus, "Judas Thomas" is preserved in the Syrian traditions. Eventually the name "Judas" fell out of favor because it was so closely linked to the man who betrayed Jesus (how often do we hear of anyone naming their child "Judas" even today?). As the name "Judas" became unfavorable, "Judas" was dropped in some traditions and the disciple was addressed by his nickname "Thomas" or "Twin."[21]

That John was aware of the fact that "Thomas" was only a title meaning "Twin" and not the actual name is evidenced in John's phrase "ὁ λεγόμενος Δίδυμος" which is added to the name Thomas in 11:16, 20:24, and 21:2 (cf. 14:5D).[22] Moreover, the presence of the disciple's actual name "Judas" in 14:22 probably suggests that the Johannine author or redactor was familiar with the very early tradition that there was an apostle named Judas. It is plausible that John

---

Nature of Diversification in the History of Early Christianity," in J. M. Robinson and H. Koester, *Trajectories through Early Christianity* (Philadelphia: Fortress, 1971) 127-128. For further discussions, see A. F. J. Klijn, *The Acts of Thomas: Introduction - Text - Commentary* (NovTSup 5; Leiden: E. J. Brill, 1962) 158; A. F. J. Klijn, "John XIV 22 and the Name Judas Thomas," *Studies in John Presented to Professor Dr. J. N. Sevenster on the occasion of his Seventieth Birthday* (NovTSup 24; Leiden: E. J. Brill, 1970) 92; J. D. Turner, *The Book of Thomas the Contender from Codex II of the Cairo Gnostic Library from Nag Hammadi (CG II.7): The Coptic Text with Translation. Introduction, and Commentary* (SBLDS 23; Missoula: Scholars, 1975) 8-9.

[20] δίδυμος (twin) is a Greek rendition of the Aramaic תאמא (twin) which has been transliterated into Greek letters as θωμᾶς). See Klijn, "Judas Thomas," 89-9l; and Turner, *The Book of Thomas*, 114. H. Koester suggests that this Judas is to be identified with Judas the brother of James in Jude 1 and was probably a brother of Jesus according to primitive traditions, "GNOMAI DIAPHOROI," 134-135. Cf. Judas is a brother of Jesus in Mark 6:3, Matthew 13:55; Luke 6:16 and Acts 1:13 know of a Ἰούδαν Ἰακώβου. This latter tradition is likely a later confusion.

[21] Cf. Klijn, "Judas Thomas," 88-96. The author of Luke 6:15-16 and Acts 1:13b shows how confusing the traditions surrounding the name "Judas Thomas" were by the late first century. He has recorded both a "Thomas" and a "Judas son of James" in his list of the disciples, thereby seemingly representing this singular disciple twice in his lists. The gospels of Matthew and Mark, however, only record this disciple once under the name "Thomas" and present the twelfth disciple as "Thaddaeus" (Mt 10:3; Mk 3:18). The tradition that Judas was the son of James rather than the brother of James and Jesus is likely to also be a later confusion. On the tendency to soften the stress on the sibling relationship between Judas Thomas and Jesus, see Koester, "GNOMAI DIAPHOROI," 134-135. Refer as well to J. Dart's treatment of the name Judas in his article, "Jesus and His Brothers," *Jesus in History and Myth*, ed. R. Joseph Hoffman and G. A. Larue (Buffalo, NY: Prometheus Books, 1986) 181-190.

[22] Klijn, *The Acts of Thomas*, 158; idem, "Judas Thomas," 89; cf. C. K. Barrett, *The Gospel according to St. John* (London: SPCK, 1978 [1955]) 327.

14:22 represents a very early layer of tradition belonging to the Johannine community about the disciple "Judas Thomas." It is highly significant that the Johannine author has assigned the same role to Judas in 14:22 as he does to Thomas in 14:5 and, as we will see, in 20:25: that of a fool who misunderstands salvation as ascent and vision mysticism.[23]

Thus it would seem that, in the Gospel of John, there are preserved two of the stages in the development of the name "Thomas:" the earliest stage where this disciple was known by his actual name "Judas," and the later stage where the disciple was beginning to be known by his epithet "Twin" or "Thomas." This signals that the Johannine author was familiar with early Syrian Thomasine traditions and had some type of contact with the Thomasine community.[24]

In this story we see remnants of the discourse between these two communities. The discursive field, as articulated by the Johannine author, focuses on the question of visionary experience. Fragments of this discourse recovered from its textual environment tell us that the Thomasine tradition expected theophany experiences whereas the Johannine Christians did not. In textualizing the discursive field, the Johannine author has painted the hero of Thomasine Christianity as an ignoramus, a fool who repeatedly misunderstands salvation.[25]

The third passage which merits analysis is John 20:24-29 which reads:

> Now Thomas, one of the twelve, called the Twin, was not with them when Jesus came. So the other disciples told him, "We have seen the Lord." But he said to them, "Unless I see in his hands the print of the nails, and place my finger in the mark of the nails, and place my hand in his side, I will not believe." Eight days later, his disciples were again in the house, and Thomas was with them. The doors were shut, but Jesus came and stood among them, and said, "Peace be with you." Then he said to Thomas, "Put your finger here, and see my hands; and put out your hand, and place it in my side; do not be faithless, but believing." Thomas answered, "My Lord and my God!" Jesus said to him, "Have you believed because you have seen me? Blessed are those who have not seen and yet believe."

---

[23] Of interest as well is the foolish statement made by Thomas in 11:16. Thomas does not seem to understand that life is imparted through belief in Jesus as God's Glory on earth and that Jesus' journey to Lazarus' tomb was intended to witness to this (11:15).

[24] R. Schnackenburg, *The Gospel According to St. John*, 3 vols. (New York: Crossroad, 1968) 1.152, concludes that "the Johannine tradition, originating in Palestine, was subjected to Syrian influences before it reached Asia Minor (Ephesus), where it was fixed and edited."

[25] Contra: Charlesworth, *Beloved Disciple*, esp. 267.

This story must be read as the third and climactic story about Jesus' appearances after his death and is best understood within this larger context. The main issue in all three of these episodes is one of *identity*, not Jesus' corporeality as some have suggested.[26]

The sequence of stories begins in 20:14-18, where Mary Magdalene encounters Jesus outside his tomb. The text is very clear that the point of the story is one of Jesus' identity: "She turned around and saw Jesus standing, but she did not know that it was Jesus (καὶ οὐκ ᾔδει ὅτι 'Ιησοῦς ἐστιν)" (20:14). Jesus even talks to her and she still does not recognize him. In fact, the reader can only be humored by the subsequent narrative when it says that Mary even confided in him, considering him to be the gardener who had stolen Jesus' body. She pleads with him to take her to the missing body. It is not until he addresses her by name that she finally recognizes the man as Jesus. This point of recognition is driven home at the end of this pericope when Mary meets with the other disciples and announces: "I have seen the Lord" (20:18).

This resurrection story, as presented by John, bears the hallmark structure of traditional folktale. According to the Russian Formalist, V. Propp, any individual folktale is a combination of a concrete set of elements or "functions" which are gathered into spheres of action. According to Propp, the characters or actors are defined by the spheres of action in which they participate. These are classified as seven actants and include such figures as the hero and the false hero. Each of the spheres of action consists of clusters of functions which are attributed to the actors. Thus a tale is characterized by an inventory of thirty-one functions and their sequential order.[27]

This model was later revised and condensed by A. Greimas.[28] He specifically reduces the number of Propp's functions to twenty concrete elements by coupling several of them because of their binary character. Moreover, he emphasizes the transformational nature of the folktale, particularly in regard to the sequential order. Thus he defines narrative as "a discursive manifestation, unfolding, by means of the consecution of its functions, an implicit transformational model."[29]

---

[26] Most recently, G. Riley, *Resurrection Reconsidered: Thomas and John in Controversy* (Minneapolis: Fortress, 1995).

[27] V. Propp, *Morphologie du Conte* (Paris: Seuil, 1928, reprint 1965 and 1970). I am indebted to Ellen Johns for this and the following reference.

[28] A. Greimas, *Sémantique Structurale: Recherche de Méthode* (Paris: Larousse, 1966); see now, *Structural Semantics: An Attempt at a Method*, trans. D. McDowell, R. Schleifer, and A. Velie (Lincoln, NE: University of Nebraska Press, 1983).

[29] Ibid., 225.

In both of these models, we find at the finale of the sequences of functions, and thus at the conclusion of the narrative, a cluster of elements which are particularly significant for the present analysis of John 20. Greimas articulates them in the following manner:

16. unrecognized arrival of the hero
17. difficult trial versus success
18. recognition of the hero
19. exposure of the false hero versus revelation of the hero[30]

In the episode where Mary encounters Jesus, we discover the actant, the hero, playing out his proper function at this point in the narrative: his incognito arrival. Function 17, the victory, has been ingeniously hinged by the author on element 18, the recognition of the hero. Jesus, by overcoming his death, is successful in his trial. This victory is revealed through Mary's exclamations, "Rabboni!" (20:16) and "I have seen the Lord!" (20:18). Thus, Mary, by recognizing Jesus, acknowledges his victory over death.

This cluster of functions is duplicated, and therefore emphasized and reinforced in the second episode when Jesus appears to the disciples who are in hiding. He shows them his hands and his side. Through this visionary experience, the disciples are able to recognize Jesus. The text reiterates the theme of vision: "The disciples were glad when they *saw* the Lord" (19:20). Here again the emphasis is on identification, through vision, of the hero Jesus who has arrived incognito. This identification is a celebration of Jesus' victory.

A common *topos* in ancient Greek literature is the identification of a character through the exposure of his wounds and the touching of his body. Nowhere is this more evident than in the *Odyssey* when the disguised hero, Odysseus, arrives at his home.[31] Eurykleia is asked to wash Odysseus' feet after his long journey (19.357-360). Odysseus withdraws into the shadows in order to keep his identity secret (19.388-389). But alas, as she takes his feet into her hands, she notices a scar which a boar had inflicted on him years ago (19.392-394). Thus lines 467-475 read:

> The old woman, holding him in the palms of her hands, recognized this scar as she handled it. She let his foot go, so that his leg, which was in the basin,

---

[30] Ibid., 225.

[31] My thanks to Dennis MacDonald who reminded me of this story in his response to my presentation of this paper at the 1995 SBL Annual Meeting in Philadelphia.

fell free, and the bronze echoed...Pain and joy seized her at once, and both eyes filled with tears, and the springing voice was held within her. She took the beard of Odysseus in her hands and spoke to him: "Then, dear child, you are really Odysseus. I did not know you before; not until I had touched my lord all over."[32]

The special connection between identifying the hero and touching him is brought out here and goes a long way to explain John 20:17 where Mary touches Jesus and exclaims, "Rabboni," as she recognizes him.

This generic *topos* spilled over into literature about the dead so that quite often the dead are found displaying their wounds to the living.[33] For instance, when the murdered Clytemnestra appears in the famous scene in *Eumenides*, she cries out, "Do you see these wounds (ὁρᾶτε πληγάς τάσδε)?!" (103) as a way to identify herself and her violent death, and to elicit pity for her dreadful fate.[34] There are several scenes in Virgil's *Aeneid* which speak to this end, scenes in which Aeneas is able to identify several of the dead by their death wounds. For example, the Trojan hero stops by the side of the woman Dido. He sees "her wound still fresh," "recognizing her dim form in the darkness." In that instant he wept and spoke softly to her, "So the news they brought me was true, unhappy Dido? They told me you were dead and had ended your life with the sword" (6.450-458).[35] Following this, he sees Deiphobus standing there, "his whole body mutilated and his face cruelly torn. The face and both hands were in shreds. The ears had been ripped from the head. He was noseless and hideous" (6.450-458)![36] Perhaps the most vivid example is Aeneas' vision of the dead Hector found in 2.272-273, 277-279:

In a dream, behold, before my eyes most sorrowful Hector seemed to be present and be weeping copiously, as of old dragged by [Achilles'] chariot,

---

[32] Eng. trans. by R. Lattimore, *The Odyssey of Homer* (New York: Harper & Row, 1965, 1967) 294.

[33] Cf. the warriors in Homer, *Iliad* 11.41; Clytaemnestra in Aeschylus, *Eumenides* 103; Eurydice in Ovid, *Metamorphose* 10.48-49; Sychaeus in Virgil, *Aeneid* 1.355; Eriphyle in *Aeneid* 6.445-446; Dido in *Aeneid* 6.450; Deiphobus in *Aeneid* 6.494-497; Plato, *Gorgias* 524-525; Tibullus 1.10.37; 2.6.38-40; Propertius 4.7.7; Statius, *Silvae* 2.1.154-156; Silius Italicus 12.547-550; Apuleius, *Metamorphoses* 8.8. For a discussion of these texts, see J. N. Bremmer, *The Early Greek Concept of the Soul* (Princeton: Princeton Universiry Press, 1983) 70-84; Riley, *Resurrection*, 50-51. The dead are often depicted on vases with their wounds. Refer to J. Chamay, "Des défunts portant bandages," *Bulletin Antieke Beschaving* 52-53 (1977-1978) 247-251.

[34] A. J. Podlecki, *Aeschylus. Eumenides* (Warminster: Aris & Phillips, 1989) 68-69.

[35] D. West, *Virgil. The Aeneid* (New York: Penguin, 1990) 146.

[36] Ibid., 148.

> black with gory dust, and pierced in his swollen feet with thongs...wearing a squalid beard and hair clotted with blood, and those many wounds he received around the walls of his fatherland.[37]

Thus the ancient readers of the Gospel of John would have understood the display of the death marks in the second pericope to be his badge of identification. So the story emphasizes that Jesus showed them his hands and side. This display revealed his true identity and celebrated his victory over death. Thus the story builds on the premise that the disciples identified Jesus by seeing him.

Finally, in the crucial third episode, the climax of the narrative, we find Thomas "the Twin," the one who is reported to have missed the resurrection appearance of Jesus to his disciples (20:24), singled out. The reader expects Thomas to receive the third vision in a row and identify Jesus on this basis, following the pattern set up in the two previous encounters. The reader may even be waiting for Thomas to finally be absolved from his past misunderstandings since he has been chosen for his own special vision of Jesus.

Thus the narrative functions of the first two episodes are triplicated here. They are amplified to the extreme. Thomas does not believe the reports of the others that they have seen the Lord (20:25). He must see for himself Jesus and the death wounds.

Therefore, Thomas' statement in 20:25, "Unless I see in his hands the print of the nails, and place my finger in the mark of the nails, and place my hand in his side, I will not believe," is a rhetorical intensification of the storyline begun in 20:20 when Jesus showed his death wounds to the other disciples in order to reveal his identity to them. Like Eurykleia in the *Odyssey* who did not recognize Odysseus until she had touched his scar, Thomas must handle the death wounds before he recognizes Jesus and is able to proclaim his identity.

So the story may surprise the reader when Jesus appears to Thomas and rebukes him, "Do not be faithless, but believing" (20:27), because Thomas confesses his belief that Jesus is God on the basis of his vision of Jesus (20:28). The effect of this rebuke has a dyadic function in the narrative. First, the Johannine author has written Thomas into the role of the actant, the false hero, and has forwarded the movement of the narrative so that we find function 19 being articulated: the false hero is exposed through the revelation of the hero's identity. By identifying the specific actor, Thomas, with the

---

[37] Ibid., 148.

actant, the false hero, the Johannine author is driving home his point that the hero of the Thomasine Christians is really no hero at all.[38]

Second, the Johannine author has created space for his own message, for his critique of the visionary experience and his praise of the faith experience. The exposure of the false hero erupts in the climactic saying in verse 29 where Thomas is admonished by Jesus that visions of him are not necessary for belief: "Have you believed because you have seen me? (῞Οτι ἑώρακάς με πεπίστευκας) Blessed are those who have not seen and yet believe (μακάριοι οἱ μὴ ἰδόντες καὶ πιστεύσαντες)" (20:29). Clearly, a conflict is set up here between the false hero, Thomas, who insists that a *visio Dei* is necessary, and John's hero, Jesus, who rebuts this in favor of faith.

The Johannine story, therefore, should not be confused with the Lukan post-resurrection narratives. It was not meant to be understood as Luke 24:37-43: as a demonstration of the corporeality of Jesus' resurrection. It should be noted that ancient readers were familiar with the notion that the dead soul could interact with the living. It could be touched, and even made love to.[39] So for the dead Jesus to appear and be touched was not *necessarily* a demonstration of his corporeality. Even Luke has to *inform* his readers that Jesus' appearance was not an appearance of his spirit *as they supposed*, but of "flesh and bones": "See my hands and my feet, that it is I myself; handle me, and see; for a spirit has not flesh and bones as you see that I have" (Luke 24:36). How different from John's statement in 20:25, where Luke's definitive qualification, "for a spirit has not flesh and bones as you see that I have," does not appear!

The Johannine scholar, J. Ashton, in his balanced monograph on the Gospel of John, warns us about plunging into a morass when interpreting this story, of reading beyond the intent of the author as does the statement of B. Lindars: "According to the Jewish idea of bodily resurrection presupposed by John, Jesus is touchable, and perfectly able to invite Thomas to handle him."[40] Ashton reminds us to keep the *author's* point of the story foremost in mind: "If John invented this story, as there is every reason to believe, it was not,

---

[38] Contra: Charlesworth, *Beloved Disciple*, 226-233, 274-285.

[39] For a summary of the ancient texts, see Riley, *Resurrection*, 51-58. In this discussion, he makes obvious the dispute among the ancient Greeks over the palpability of the soul.

[40] B. Lindars, *Behind the Fourth Gospel* (London: S.P.C.K., 1971) 607.

surely, to stimulate his readers to reflect upon the tangibility of risen bodies, but to impress upon them the need for faith."[41]

Based on this reading of the gospel, I therefore disagree with G. Riley's suggestion that John 20:24-29 represents a dispute between the Johannine community and the Thomasine Christians over the issue of bodily resurrection.[42] Aside from the fact that the intent of John 20:24-29 is not to confirm a fleshly resurrection but to criticize visionary experience in favor of faith, it must be noted that nowhere does the *Gospel of Thomas* mention resurrection as a *spiritual* raising.

In Logion 51, it is said that the "rest of the dead" has already happened, but the nature of this resurrection is not discussed. It is clear that many early Christians including Paul held that the resurrection had already started with Jesus' own resurrection. Some of these Christians, especially those who espoused an encratite lifestyle like the Thomasites, interpreted Luke 20:34-36 as evidence for the fact that their life *on earth now* was part of this new era, the age of the resurrection. They believed that they had to imitate the angels in the way that they conducted their lives (Clement of Alexandria, *Strom.* 3.12.87).[43] But nothing is delineated regarding the nature of this resurrection.

Thus I maintain that this story is not about bodily resurrection and must be distinguished from Luke 24:36. Rather the impetus of this story for the Johannine writer is encapsulated in the climatic saying attributed to Jesus which blesses those who have faith in Jesus even though they have not had a visionary encounter (20:29). Behind this articulation we can reconstruct the discursive field. For Johannine Christians faith in Jesus was the basis of their salvation, whereas for the Thomasine Christians, the mystical visionary encounter was paramount. The discourse between these communities on this subject is preserved here from the perspective of the Johannine community which presents its "correct" version of soteriology that developed as a result of the discourse.

Clearly, in each of these three scenarios, Thomas is the actant, the false hero, a fool who misunderstands the path of salvation. In the

---

[41] J. Ashton, *Understanding the Fourth Gospel* (Oxford: Clarendon, 1991) 514.

[42] Riley, *Resurrection*, 107-126.

[43] On this, see U. Bianchi, "The Religio-Historical Relevance of Lk 20:34-36," *Studies in Gnosticism and Hellenistic Religions. Presented to Gilles Quispel on the Occasion of his 65th Birthday*, ed. R. van den Broek and M. J. Vermaseren (EPRO 91; Leiden: E. J. Brill, 1981) 31-37.

words of C. Barrett: "Thomas...appears in John as a loyal but dull disciple, whose misapprehensions serve to bring out the truth."[44] According to John, Thomas' misunderstanding is that he believes that in order to achieve life, one must seek the "way" to Jesus, the route of ascent into heaven, and a *visio Dei*.

The methodology of articulation when applied to the Gospel of John has borne results. It has revealed a discourse between the Thomasine and Johannine Christians.[45] The discursive field has emerged as a dispute over soteriology, specifically over the validity of proleptic visionary flights to heaven. The assumption of this methodology is that the Johannine author is not painting an arbitrary picture of the apostle Thomas, the hero of Syrian Christianity, when he portrays him as a false hero whose mystical soteriology is corrected by Jesus. Thus he created his discursive field by dramatizing actual features of the religio-social horizon and incorporating them at the textual level. The articulation certainly mirrors Johannine space and perspective, reflecting only partially the historical discourse itself.

These conclusions become more than provocative because they can be substantiated by the *Gospel of Thomas* itself, which promotes a visionary scheme of salvation. There is evidence that the Thomasine Christians were mystics seeking visions of God for the purpose of immortalization.[46] Such a scheme defines Jesus' role as the esteemed model mystic and mystagogue. Each individual becomes responsible for saving himself. It may be against this consequence of the *Gospel of Thomas'* soteriology that John reacts so harshly.

In any event, John disparages this system and, in response, articulates his own system which centers around the transforming essence of the faith experience. This experience is more than cognitive belief. It is experiential. In Jesus' absence, the Paraclete or Spirit has descended to earth. Now the divinity of Jesus is encountered through the Spirit, particularly in the two sacraments, Baptism and the Lord's

---

[44] Barrett, *The Gospel According to St. John*, 382.

[45] The implications for dating the Thomas tradition and perhaps even the Gospel of Thomas are paramount. Since the Johannine tradition is connected with Palestine and later, Asia Minor (see n. 29), it is quite possible that the author was familiar with the Syrian Gospel of Thomas. If John is writing in response to the Gospel of Thomas itself rather than traditions associated with it, this would suggest a first century date for the composition of the Gospel of Thomas probably around 70-80 CE. This lends support to S. Patterson's recent and convincing arguments for a 70-80 CE date for Thomas; refer to his discussion in *The Gospel of Thomas and Jesus* (Sonoma: Polebridge, 1993) 113-120.

[46] On this see A. D. De Conick, *Seek to See Him: Ascent and Vision Mysticism in the Gospel of Thomas* (VCSup 33; Leiden: E. J. Brill, 1996).

Supper. But how John develops this ideology is a subject for another essay.[47]

I leave this essay, however, with a few comments on a passage from the *Acts of John* 90:

> He took us three [John, James, and Peter] likewise up the mountain, saying "Come with me." And again we went; and we saw him at a distance praying. Then I, since he loved me, went quietly up to him, as if he could not see me, and stood looking at his hinder parts; and I saw him not dressed in clothes at all but stripped of those <that> we (usually) saw (upon him), and not like a man at all. (And I saw that) his feet were whiter than snow, so that the ground there was lit up by his feet; and that his head stretched up to heaven, so that I was afraid and cried out; and he, turning about, appeared as a small man and caught hold of my beard and pulled it and said to me, "John, do not be faithless, but believing, and not inquisitive."

This was written in Syria shortly after the Gospel of John[48] and preserves a story in which John, *not* Thomas, is rebuked by Jesus: "John, do not be faithless, but believing." And what provoked this rebuke? That John went up a mountain (which is a metaphor for ascent), and was afraid of the vision he had of Jesus as the Glory![49]

It is plausible that this represents the theoretical construction of continued discourse between the mystic Christians of Syria who applauded Thomas and those who continued to follow John. Here they remind the Johannine Christians that visions of God are essential to the Christian faith experience. So they remember and portray not a Doubting Thomas, but a Doubting John.

---

[47] I will take up this subject in a paper to be delivered at the 1996 Annual SBL Convention in the Early Jewish and Christian Mysticism Consultation: "'He who sees me sees him who sent me' (Jn 12:45): The Johannine Theologian and Early Christian Mysticism." See also my forthcoming *Faith Mysticism in the Gospel of John: The Johannine Community as a Community of Discourse*, to be published by Sheffield in the Supplements to *JSNT*.

[48] R. Cameron, *The Other Gospels* (Philadelphia: Westminster, 1982) 88-89; cf. H. Koester, *Introduction to the New Testament, Vol. 2: History and Literature of Early Christianity* (Philadelphia: Fortress, 1982) 196-198.

[49] See J. Fossum, "Partes posteriores dei: The 'Transfiguration' of Jesus in the Acts of John," in his forthcoming book, *The Image of the Invisible God: Essays on the Influence of Jewish Mysticism on Early Christianity* (NTOA 20; Göttingen: Vandenhoeck & Ruprecht, 1995) 95-108.

PART FIVE

ISSUES OF SOCIAL LOCATION, COMPOSITION,
AND REWRITING

# VALENTINIAN GNOSTICISM:
# TOWARD THE ANATOMY OF A SCHOOL

*Christoph Markschies*
University of Jena

For Martin Hengel as a small greeting for Dec. 14, 1996

When one opens Bentley Layton's book, *The Gnostic Scriptures*, one finds that the section on "Valentinian Gnosticism" is entitled, "The School of Valentinus."[1] Layton writes, "Thus the Valentinian movement had the character of a philosophical school, or network of schools, rather than a distinct religious sect."[2] I can only agree emphatically with Layton in accepting this widely held judgment which goes back in its essentials to the heresiologists of the early church and has long been a point of agreement in the notoriously splintered scholarship on Gnosticism.[3] It is all the more surprising that research has been done on "the Greek school" and the Nag Hammadi writings,[4] on the Christological "school" differences between "Valentinisme Italien et Valentinisme oriental"[5] and, of course, on various aspects of the prosopography and doxography of individual members of the school and its alleged head, but (to my

---

[1] The same title appears in Volume One of the essays contributed to the 1978 conference on Gnosticism at Yale: *The Rediscovery of Gnosticism. Proceedings of the International Conference on Gnosticism at Yale, New Haven, Connecticut, March 28-31, 1978, Vol. I, The School of Valentinus*, ed. B. Layton (SHR 41/1; Leiden: E. J. Brill, 1980). I am grateful to Michael Waldstein for assistance with the translation.

[2] B. Layton, *The Gnostic Scriptures: A New Translation with Annotations and Introductions* (Garden City, NY and London: Doubleday, 1987) 267.

[3] See, for example, A. Hilgenfeld, *Die Ketzergeschichte des Urchristentums, urkundlich dargestellt* (Darmstadt: Olms, 1963; = Leipzig: Fues, 1884) 290: "Valentinus stands at the origin of a school with many branches in which his teaching was again and again transformed and developed."

[4] A. Böhlig, "Die griechische Schule und die Bibliothek von Nag Hammadi," *Zum Hellenismus in den Schriften von Nag Hammadi*, ed. A. Böhlig and F. Wisse (GOF.H VI,2; Wiesbaden: Harrassowitz, 1978) 9-53 = idem, *Gnosis und Synkretismus, Gesammelte Aufsätze zur spätantiken Religionsgeschichte*, 2 vols. (WUNT 47; Tübingen: J. C. B. Mohr [P. Siebeck], 1989) 1.251-286.

[5] J.-D. Kaestli, "Valentinisme Italien et Valentinisme oriental: Leurs divergences à propos de la nature du corps de Jésus," *The Rediscovery of Gnosticism, Vol. I*, ed. B. Layton, 391-403; R. P. C. Casey, "Two Notes on Valentinian Theology," *HTR* 23 (1930) 275-298, here 291-298.

knowledge) not on the theme "Valentinian Gnosticism as a school in Antiquity." The point applies even to the essays written for the 1978 Gnosticism conference at Yale, collected and edited by Layton under this very title, *The School of Valentinus*.[6]

But do the Valentinians really have the character of a philosophical school? John Whittaker, certainly an expert on this matter, has answered the question in the negative, at least with respect to the contents of philosophical teaching. "We have only indications of a watered down Biblical Platonism, and any second-century intellectual could be made to look like some sort of Platonist."[7] And Barbara Aland points out again and again that there may be "certain analogies between Gnosticism and contemporary philosophy in the Second and Third Century," but she goes on to stress,

> Gnosticism differs fundamentally from philosophy. When elements of philosophical form are adopted in Gnostic texts, they are adopted as a mere addition, without true insight into the consequences of such a step—which is the case in the *Apophasis*—or the philosophical system is consciously used but broken at a decisive place and thus transformed into its opposite—which is the case in Valentinianism. Gnosticism is thus neither "corrupted" nor incipient philosophy, but a religion of revelation and redemption.[8]

For this reason we raise the following question. Is this character of a philosophical school one of the "certain analogies" alluded to by Barbara Aland? Or are we dealing with a conscious (or even unconscious) misinterpretation by which the church fathers disguise the true character of the enterprise? Did the Valentinians understand themselves as a philosophical school? In order to find an answer to these questions which have been largely ignored in the scholarly literature, Part One of my paper clarifies what really constituted a philosophical school in the early Roman imperial period. It shows what concepts were used to refer to the philosophical school and what happened there. It is only then, in Part Two, that the extant reports about the Valentinians as a school can be analyzed in terms of the questions raised above. In Part Three, finally, I will draw the conclusions which emerge from the comparison of the first two parts. Of course, such an analysis of details will not answer the larger question of the relation

---

[6] Layton, ed., *The Rediscovery of Gnosticism, Vol. 1, The School of Valentinus*.

[7] In the discussion of the paper by Christopher Stead at Yale: *The Rediscovery of Gnosticism*, ed. B. Layton, 1.96.

[8] B. Aland, "Gnosis und Philosophie," *Proceedings of the International Colloquium on Gnosticism, Stockholm, August 20-25, 1973*, ed. G. Widengren (VHAAH.FF 17; Stockholm: Almqvist & Wiksell, 1977) 34-73.

between "philosophy" and "Gnosticism." Rather, it proposes a few mosaic stones for a future reconsideration of this theme. At the same time I understand the reflections below as an attempt to meet at least a small part of the obligations I incurred when in the preface of my monograph on Valentinus I rashly announced a sequel to my investigations.[9]

Let me begin with remarks on the phenomenon of "philosophical schools" and philosophical professional life in the first two centuries after Christ.

## 1. SOME OBSERVATIONS ON PHILOSOPHICAL SCHOOLS IN THE EARLY IMPERIAL PERIOD

Since we have many reports about student-teacher relations, indeed about philosophical schools from all periods of antiquity,[10] I shall concentrate in what follows on *Rome*, for the capital was a "Valentinian metropolis" (at least Valentinus and Ptolemy lived and taught there for some time) and many philosophical teachers of the most diverging orientations were active in it. In this, as in other respects, Rome was the "epitome of the entire inhabited world" (ἐπιτομὴ τῆς οἰκουμένης).[11] In his Heidelberg Habilitation in Classical History, Johannes Hahn has been able to show from inscriptions and other literary reports that (and how) the influx and presence of Greek philosophers increased especially in the second century under the graecophile emperors Hadrian and Marcus Aure-

---

[9] Christoph Markschies, *Valentinus Gnosticus? Untersuchungen zur valentinianischen Gnosis mit einem Kommentar zu den Fragmenten Valentins* (WUNT I.65; Tübingen: J. C. B. Mohr [P. Siebeck], 1992) VII. The terrain surrounding this planned monograph includes also the discussion of the value of Irenaeus' reports on the Gnostics in my *RAC* article "Kerinth" (to appear in 1997). We need a thorough new treatment of the question on what Gnostic presuppositions the Valentinian system could be built.

[10] See H. von Arnim, *Leben und Werke des Dion von Prusa* (Berlin: Weidmann, 1898) esp. the introductory chapter "Sophistik, Rhetorik und Philosophie in ihrem Kampfe um die Jugendbildung"; J. M. Dillon, "Les écoles philosophiques aux deux premiers siècles de l'Empire," *ANRW* II.36.1 (Berlin & New York: de Gruyter, 1987) 5-77; L. Friedländer, G. Wissowa, *Darstellungen aus der Sittengeschichte Roms in der Zeit von Augustus bis zum Ausgang der Antonine III*, 9th ed. (Leipzig: S. Hirzel, 1920) 243-297; G. Fowden, "The Platonist Philosopher and his Circle in Late Antiquity," *Philosophia* 7 (1977) 359-383; R. Goulet, "Les vies de philosophes dans l'Antiquité tardive et leur portée mystérique," in F. Bovon, ed., *Les Actes Apocryphes des Apôtres: Christianisme et monde païen* (Publications de la faculté de théologie de l'université de Genève 4; Geneva: Labor et fides, 1981) 161-208.

[11] A statement by the Sophist Polemon: Athenaeus, *Deipnosophistae* 1.36.3 [Kaibel]; Galen, *hum. prol.* (XVIII/1, 347.16 Kühn); cf. H. Fuchs, *Der geistige Widerstand gegen Rom in der Antike* (Berlin: Walter de Gruyter, 1938) 27, note 1.

lius. He counts attestations of about fifty persons.[12] Among them (apart from "visiting lectures" by philosophers residing elsewhere) there are "domestic philosophers," who belong to a *familia* residing in Rome, "parlor philosophers," that is, "popular philosophers" and philosophers in the strict sense of the discipline "philosophy" ("professional philosophers")—there is, by the way, at least one woman philosopher.[13] Hahn has also shown in the monograph just mentioned that contemporaries of the Roman imperial period had a relatively fixed image of the philosopher's "profession," to speak anachronistically; they also had definite expectations about these different types of philosophical teaching. We still do not have, as far as I know, a thorough treatment of the life of philosophical schools and their members,[14] to which we now briefly turn.

Since Aristotle and Theophrastus the word μαθητής has been used in Greek literature above all (but not, of course, exclusively) to refer to personal students of the philosophers or to members of the same school or philosophical orientation.[15] (Unlike German and its term "Schüler," English has no equivalent of μαθητής that can be used across the same broad range of meanings. The translation below adopts various expressions, such as "disciple," "student," and "member of the school of...") Many other Greek terms were used— for example, ἀκουστής, ἀκροατής, γνωριμός, οἱ ἀμφί τινα or οἱ περί τινα—both as self-designations and as designations by outsiders. These concepts are not sufficient to draw clear boundaries between the phenomena of religious "disciple" and "student" or "member of a philosophical school." The various terms for members of philosophical schools mentioned above are not limited to the four

---

[12] J. Hahn, *Der Philosoph und die Gesellschaft: Selbstverständnis, öffentliches Auftreten und populäre Erwartungen in der hohen Kaiserzeit* (HABES 7; Stuttgart: Steiner, 1987) 150, cf. also the texts cited 149, notes 7-12. On the basis of paleographic observations of his teacher Alföldy, Hahn dates the inscription *CIL* VI.9785 = H. Dessau, *ILS* II/2, 7778 826 "Second Century, perhaps beginning of the Third" (171, note 28).

[13] *CIL* VI.33898 = H. Dessau, *ILS* II/2, 7783 (p. 827): *Euphrosyne pia, docta novem musis, philosopha v(ixit) a(nnos) XX.* For the concept of "parlor philosopher," see Hahn, *Der Philosoph und die Gesellschaft,* 97; the other terms are my own; cf. also F. Millar, *The Emperor in the Roman World (31 BC–AD 337),* 2nd ed. (London: Duckworth, 1992) 494-498; 501-503.

[14] See, however, R. Valantasis, *Spiritual Guides of the Third Century. A Semiotic Study of the Guide-Disciple Relationship in Christianity, Neoplatonism, Hermetism, and Gnosticism* (Minneapolis: Fortress, 1991).

[15] Aristotle, *metaph.* A 5 (986 b 22)/Theophrastus, *physic. opin.* Frg. 4 (479.17f Diels). I am making use here of the conclusions reached in the article "Jünger" by Roland Kany, where all the relevant texts are presented; the author has kindly put at my disposal the manuscript to appear in *RAC.*

"professional philosophical schools" of Antiquity, namely, Plato's Academy, Aristotle's Lyceum, Epicurus' Kepos and Zeno's Stoa. A group of students belonged also to the public image of the popular philosophers and Sophists of the imperial period. The semantic field of "student" appears with corresponding frequency. For example, according to the extant fragments, Musonius, who taught at the end of the First Century in Rome, always appeared in conversation with his students and listeners. Also the term σχολή is not applied exclusively to the great "professional" philosophical schools, although it often appears, of course, in these contexts—in Diogenes Laertius, for example, who probably wrote toward the end of the third century. Already the poet Alexis (frg. 158 Kock = 163 Kassel/Austin. Olympiodorus, line 3) asks, ταῦτ' οὐ σχολὴ Πλάτωνος; According to Diogenes, Speusippus transferred leadership of the Academy to Xenocrates shortly before his suicide, καὶ τὴν σχολὴν διαδέξασθαι. Of course, the Academy can also be named after its present scholiarch, ἡ Ξενοκράτους σχολή.[16] The concept σχολή is used also for the student-teacher relation in popular philosophy, by Epictetus, for example.[17]

Such a survey of the terminology of "school" and "student" or "member of a philosophical school" shows that the phenomenon of forming a "school" is to be expected not only among "professional" philosophers and after the model of the early Platonic Academy. We should thus turn our interest also to the two other groups, that is, domestic and popular or parlor-philosophy, for it is not clear from the outset that the Valentinian school is best compared to "professional" philosophical schools—quite on the contrary, the legitimacy of this comparison is often strongly contested. We now ask: What was the daily life of a school and what were its subject-matters?

Just as there is no terminological difference between popular and "professional" philosophical schools in the description of teacher-student relations, so also the daily life of the school (viewed formally) differed in relatively few respects. The schools in *Rome* illustrate this point. The life of the popular philosophical circles around the Stoics

---

[16] III.28 (SCBO I.133.15); IV.3 (165.2f)—identical formulations, for example, in IV.16 (173.15) and 21 (175.15); IV.16 (173.11f). Cf., for example, about Arcesilaus and the Academy in IV.32, Κράτητος δὲ ἐκλιπόντος κατέσχε τὴν σχολήν (SCBO I, 181.3f Long). Diogenes does not use the term διδασκαλεῖον; cf. also W. v. Kienle, "Die Berichte über die Sukzessionen der Philosophen in der hellenistischen und spätantiken Literatur" (Ph.D. dissertation, Berlin 1961).

[17] Diss. II.8.15 (BiTeu 139.12 Schenkl) or IV.5.37 (409.15), cf. also P. Zarella, "La concezione del 'discepolo' in Epitteto," *Aevum* 40 (1966) 211-229.

Musonius Rufus,[18] Epictetus and around the "professional" philosopher and Platonist Calvenus Taurus[19] can be drawn rather clearly from lecture notes and reports of students. Calvenus was head of the Academy in the middle of the second century. Epictetus taught philosophy in Rome before his expulsion in 89 CE and his teacher Musonius taught there for some time as well. The list of three names (Musonius, Epictetus and Calvenus) can be supplemented (for example, by Seneca, Annaeus Cornutus and Favorinus)—and the list is certainly not complete. The difference between the two categories of philosophical teaching lay above all in the degree of professionalism and in the relatively little weight given to formal-logical elaboration among popular philosophers. In "professional" philosophical instruction, above all, there is a sort of fixed fundamental pattern of scholarly activity which applies—*mutatis mutandis*—also to popular philosophical diatribe. The teacher offered "regular lectures" fixed in their program ahead of time, but occasionally improvised; "students took notes, made speeches and engaged in discussions."[20] Iamblichus accordingly knows of "conversations, discussions with each other, notes and written documents" in the school of Pythagoras (διδασκαλεῖον)[21] and Gellius reports that central texts were interpreted in the Platonic Academy, at times—according to our taste—rather freely and loosely. The students joined in memorizing the most important passages of these central texts, they engaged in guided discussions of their form and content, and also took time for questions

---

[18] O. Hense, ed., *C. Musonii Rufi Reliquiae* (Leipzig: Teubner, 1905 = 1990) XIV-XXVI; A. C. v. Geytenbeek, *Musonius Rufus and the Greek Diatribe* (Assen: Van Gorcum, 1963) as well as R. Laurenti, "Musonio, maestro di Epitteto," *ANRW* II.36.3 (1989) 2105-2146.

[19] H. Dörrie, "L. Kalbenos Tauros, Das Persönlichkeitsbild eines platonischen Philosophen um die Mitte des 2. Jahrh. n. Chr.," *Kairos* 15 (1973) 24-35, in idem, *Platonica minora* (Studia et testimonia antiqua VIII; München: W. Fink, 1976) 310-323; U. Neymeyr, *Die christlichen Lehrer im zweiten Jahrhundert. Ihre Lehrtätigkeit, ihr Selbstverständnis und ihre Geschichte* (Supplements to VC 4; Leiden: E. J. Brill, 1989) 218-220; 224-226 on Calvenus Taurus.

[20] H. Cancik, "Gnostiker in Rom. Zur Religionsgeschichte der Stadt Rom im 2.Jahrhundert nach Christus," J. Taubes, ed., *Gnosis und Politik: Religionstheorie und politische Theologie vol. 2* (München: W. Fink, 1984) 163-184, here 177. On the written character of the διαλέξεις see the controversy between H. Hobein and W. Kroll in their article, "Maximus" *Paulys Real-Encyclopädie der classischen Altertumswissenschaft (PW)*, XIV/2, 2559.

[21] *VP* 104 (110 v. Albrecht) διαλέξεις καὶ τὰς πρὸς ἀλλήλους ὁμιλίας καὶ τοὺς ὑπομνηματισμούς τε καὶ ὑποσημειώσεις καὶ αὐτὰ ἤδη τὰ συγγράμματα καὶ ἐκδόσεις πάσας; cf. also W. Bousset, *Jüdisch-Christlicher Schulbetrieb in Alexandria und Rom. Literarische Untersuchungen zu Philo und Clemens von Alexandria, Justin und Irenäus* (FRLANT 23; Göttingen: Vandenhoeck & Ruprecht, 1915 = 1975) 4f.

not directly related to the matter at hand.[22] Questions about what life one ought to lead played an important role—we would fall below the level of Hadot's work on "Philosophy as a Way of Life"[23] if we did not see these questions as an indication that many of these popular and "professional" philosophical circles and schools had the character of a "community of learning" and "of life." There were differences in the selection of the circle of listeners. Some philosophers, says Dio Chrysostom, the student of Musonius, "utterly refuse to mix with the common people, (...) while others strain their voices in so-called lecture halls, gathering before themselves listeners who are familiar and used to them."[24] The most likely audience comprised wealthy young men. In addition, we are often told that people who were traveling through Rome attended lectures. It is a noteworthy feature of the overall picture, "how frequently we are told that outsiders attended lectures or joined the circle of a particular philosopher's students, either as accidental visitors and relatives or as people seeking counsel."[25] (By the way, in the third work of his *Moralia*, *De recta ratione audiendi*, Plutarch offers a number of norms for appropriate behavior when attending a lecture). Only in the case of a few teachers should one imagine "a separate piece of land with a colonnade, a covered lecture hall or a little odeon in the open."[26] Most philosophers probably taught in public places, in the *forum* or in the baths and, of course, in rented dwellings. Maximus of Tyre could have delivered his roughly half-hour διαλέξεις in places like the *Athenaeum* founded by Hadrian, which had rooms for events of Greek language and culture.[27] Its exact location in Rome remains unfortunately unclear. A few years ago Konrad Gaiser assembled the extant visual representations of such school situations, some of them from Rome.[28]

---

[22] Aulus Gellius, *noct.* XVII.20.1-9 (SCBO 528.28-530.8 Marshall).

[23] P. Hadot, *Philosophy as a Way of Life: Spiritual Exercises from Socrates to Foucault* (Oxford: Blackwell, 1995) = *Exercices spirituels et philosophie antique*, 2nd ed. (Paris: Études augustiniennes, 1987).

[24] Dio Chrysostom, *Or.* 32.8, οἱ μὲν γὰρ αὐτῶν ὅλως εἰς πλῆθος οὐκ ἴασον οὐδὲ θέλουσι διακινδυνεύειν, ἀπεγνωκότες ἴσως τὸ βελτίους ἂν ποιῆσαι τοὺς πολλούς· οἱ δ' ἐν τοῖς καλουμένοις ἀκροατηρίοις φωνασκοῦσιν, ἐνσπόνδους λαβόντες ἀκροατὰς καὶ χειροήθεις ἑαυτοῖς (BiTeu 342.22-343.1 Budé).

[25] J. Hahn, *Der Philosoph und die Gesellschaft*, 70.

[26] H. Cancik, "Gnostiker in Rom," 177.

[27] This is the appealing hypothesis of J. Hahn, *Der Philosoph und die Gesellschaft*, 94 note 36 on Max. Tyr. I.10 (... ἀλλ' ὁμιλεῖν ἀξιόχρεως θεάτροις Ἑλλενικοῖς...).

[28] K. Gaiser, *Das Philosophenmosaik in Neapel. Eine Darstellung der platonischen Akademie* (AHAW.PH 2/1980; Heidelberg: C. Winter, 1980) esp. 8-23.

We should now take a closer look at the contents of philosophical teaching. First a few remarks on *domestic philosophers*, whose life Lucian caricatures with his usual sarcasm in *De mercede conductis* and of which we have some inscriptions and literary evidence from Rome.[29] Their activity was, of course, determined especially by the interest of the respective *pater familias*; generalizations are therefore ruled out of court.

We are somewhat better informed about the *popular* or *parlor-philosophers*, for, in addition to the fragments of Musonius and the diatribes of his pupil Epictetus, forty-one lectures of such a philosophizing rhetorician have been preserved. Maximus of Tyre flourished in Rome probably in the second half of the second century (at the same time as Valentinus, Justin and Ptolemy, among others). Michael B. Trapp published a new critical edition of these διαλέξεις in 1994.[30] Delivery of Maximus' extant Greek lectures probably took half an hour or less. These texts are addressed to educated Romans living in the city who knew some philosophical and literary texts but who were interested, at the same time, in an entertaining presentation of the subject.[31] In addition to the "great" philosophical themes (What is philosophy? What is god? What is the origin of evil? How ought one to live?), Maximus also addresses various "lesser" problems (for example, how to face suffering injustice, *Or*. XII), immediate questions of life (for example, freedom from anxieties, *Or*. XXVIII) and problems of Platonic doxography. Persius, a student of the Roman Stoic Annaeus Cornutus, reflects these themes already a century before Maximus in the satire:

> Learn, you miserable ones, and investigate the nature of things. What are we? For what purpose were we born? In what order are we placed? ... What is the proper measure of gain and what may one pray for? What is the use-

---

[29] Lucian, *merc. cond.* 1-42 (SCBO II, 212-236 Macleod); J. Hahn, *Der Philosoph und die Gesellschaft*, 151-153. § 17 introduces the title διδάσκαλος (221.25).

[30] M. B. Trapp, ed., *Maximus Tyrius: Dissertationes* (Stuttgart/Leipzig: Teubner, 1994); on Maximus cf. also H. Hobein/W. Kroll, "Maximus (37) von Tyrus," *PW* XIV/2 (1930) 2555-2562; J. Puigalli, *Études sur la Dialexeis de Maxime de Tyre, conférencier platonicien du IIième siècle* (Lille, 1983) und M. Szarmach, *Maximos von Tyros. Eine literarische Monographie* (Torun: Uniwersytet Mikolaja Kopernika, 1985).

[31] H. Hobein/W. Kroll, "Maximus," *PW* XIV/2, 2558 and 1561f; cf. also H. Mutschmann, "Das erste Auftreten des Maximus von Tyros in Rom," *Sokrates* 5 (1917) 185-197; here 188-192; and on the "philosophical program," see J. Hahn, *Der Philosoph und die Gesellschaft*, 54-60.

fulness of money? ... What has a god called you to? What is your place in the workings of the world, in human society?[32]

We must finally mention the *"professional" philosophers* and their schools. Let me begin with some remarks on terminology. A petition addressed to Hadrian in 121 CE by the widowed wife of Trajan (who was controversial because of her role in her husband's death) mentions the applicable technical terms, in this case for the Epicureans. In the school (here, *secta Epicuri*; αἵρεσις) there is a *successio* (διαδοχή). The school chooses its head (*diadochus*/διάδοχος) in accord with certain rules.[33] Of course, the founder and first teacher, to whom and to whose δόγματα others give their προκλίσις, is the authority constitutive of such αἱρέσεις κατὰ φιλοσοφίαν.[34] But precisely the Platonic Academy, which is in many respects the model for later Antiquity, shows how a remarkable discontinuity in teachings arose despite personal continuity in its history. An entire world obviously separates the Athenian heads of the Academy Carneades ( 129/128 BCE) and Calvenus Taurus (ἀκμή 145 CE). One cause of this divergence may have been the open, dialogical conception of philosophical teaching represented by the school's founder, Plato—we cannot pursue the issue here. At any rate, the continuity between the dogmatizing Older Academy, the aporetic Middle Academy and the probabilistic New Academy consisted mainly in the unbroken succession of its scholiarchs. Since the Platonic Academy financed itself through bequests and endowments, it was interested in its continuous existence already in the economic sense, independent from

---

[32] *Sat.* III.66-72 (cf. R. L. Wilken, "Kollegien, Philosophenschulen und Theologie," in W. A. Meeks, ed., *Zur Soziologie des Urchristentums. Ausgewählte Beiträge zum frühchristlichen Gemeinschaftsleben in seiner gesellschaftlichen Umwelt* (TBü 62, München: Kaiser, 1979) 165-193, here 171.

*Discite, o miseri, et causas cognoscite rerum:*

*Quid sumus, et quidnam victuri gignimur; ordo*

*Quis datus, aut metae quam mollis flexus et unde;*

*Quis modus argento, quid fas optare, quid asper*

*Utile nummus habet; patriae carisque propinquis*

*Quantum elargiri deceat, quem te deus esse*

*Iussit, et humana qua parte locatus es in re.*

[33] H. Dessau, ILS II/2, 7784 (p. 827f); cf. J. Ferguson, "Epicureanism under the Roman Empire," *ANRW* II.36.4 (1990) 2257-2327; here 2285; R. Hanslik, "Pompeia Plotina," *PW* XXI/2, 2293-2298, here 2296.

[34] On the role of the Platonic Academy as model, see H. J. Krämer, "Die ältere Akademie," in: H. Flashar, ed., *Ältere Akademie. Aristoteles - Peripatos* (Basel/Stuttgart: Schwabe, 1983) 1-174, here 4-7; for the concept see H. Schlier, "αἱρέομαι κτλ," *ThWNT* 1 (1933) 179-184; 179f (with attestations).

disparate contents of its teaching. One should not, of course, exaggerate here. No head of the school (προστάτης or ἄρχων) wanted to establish conscious *discontinuity* as the principle of tradition, for example in the controversy about the question whether the world really came to be or not (*Tim.* 28 b 7). Everyone, of course, attempted to establish a relation between the new and the old, to justify new teachings by statements of previous teachers.[35] On the other hand, a normative process of tradition of the sort intended by the Christian church in the form of the *regula fidei* lay largely outside the field of vision. A further reason for this phenomenon was probably the fundamental importance of the individual personality of the teacher. He spoke "immediately in his own name and communicated to his students the fruits of his own thinking and his wisdom."[36] As a result boundaries are occasionally blurred between a philosophical school in the strict sense (that is, in a continuous institutionalized succession of teaching) and the individual persons "who teach in their own name in the city in which they have settled."[37] For there was also a consensus that—as Maximus of Tyre says—one needs such a teacher to become knowledgeable in philosophical questions (*Orat.* I.9).

At the beginning we spoke of "the character of a philosophical school" which Valentinian Gnosticism possesses according to Bentley Layton and many other scholars. Our remarks about philosophical schools in Rome's early imperial period give rise to three questions for the further development of this investigation. What terms did the Valentinians use to refer to themselves and what terms were used to refer to them? Did they themselves understand themselves as a "school" or did only their opponents, the heresiologists, see them in this manner? And with what type of philosophical school should the "Valentinian School" really be compared with respect to its themes and forms of organization? Before one can answer these questions,

---

[35] Numenius, who proposed an interpretation of Plato which was undoubtedly new, original and largely rejected by his contemporaries, rejected innovations explicitly and vehemently (frg. 24 [62.5-65.79 des Places]). The καινοτομηθέν is παρανόμημα and ἀσέβημα (ibid. [63.30f]); on this issue see also M. Frede, "Numenius," *ANRW* II.36.2 (1987) 1034-1075, here 1041-1046; J. Dillon, "Self-Definition in Later Platonism," in B. F. Meyer and E. P. Sanders, eds., *Jewish and Christian Self-Definition, Vol. 3* (London: SCM Press, 1982) 60-75.

[36] See H. I. Marrou, *Geschichte der Erziehung im klassischen Altertum* (München: Deutscher Taschenbuch Verlag, 1977) 393f; Marrou insists on "the personal character of education in Antiquity." Ibid. 394.

[37] H. I. Marrou, *Geschichte der Erziehung im klassischen Altertum*, 391. As an example Marrou mentions Epictetus; on this point see now also U. Neymeyr, *Die christlichen Lehrer*, 220-224.

the ancient reports about the phenomenon "Valentinian Gnosticism" must once more be investigated thoroughly in view of the questions we raised.

## 2. THE VALENTINIANS AS A SCHOOL

We begin this section—like the first—with detailed remarks on the terms used for membership in a philosophical school. We first recall a trivial observation which is, however, of great importance for our questions. The concept "school" is applied to the Valentinians, as far as I can see, for the first time in Irenaeus, that is, as a designation applied by an outsider. Irenaeus says in his work against the Gnostic heresy, in Anne McGuire's translation, "Valentinus, the first (of these), adapted the principles (or beginnings)[38] of the so-called γνωστική αἵρεσις to the distinctive style of his own school (διδασκαλεῖον)."[39]

It need not detain us here that the bishop of Lyon adds to this thesis a compilation which is highly problematic from the point of view of literary criticism. One cannot simply use this compilation without any further ado for the historical Valentinus as Quispel unfortunately did again in a recent contribution (and A. H. B. Logan in his wake); Quispel refuses to engage recent research and comes to correspondingly problematic results in his new quest for the "original doctrine of Valentinus the Gnostic."[40] One point at least should be made clear. The clear trinitarian organization of *Haer.* I.11.1 shows that this section is designed by Irenaeus as a "heretical counterpart" to the church's *regula fidei*. The church believes in *one* god; the heresiarch allegedly introduces a dyad consisting of "Αρρητον and Σιγή. The church teaches the one Jesus Christ, the son of god; Valentinus, according to Irenaeus, teaches yet a ἕτερον υἱόν. The church and the heresiarch differ

---

[38] I here correct my own translation in *Valentinus Gnosticus*, 409; how the Latin translation (*antiquas doctrinas*) came about is explained by the editors, SC 263.229f.

[39] *Haer.* I.11.1 Ὁ μὲν γὰρ πρῶτος ἀπὸ τῆς λεγομένης Γνωστικῆς αἱρέσεως τὰς ἀρχὰς εἰς ἴδιον χαρακτῆρα διδασκαλείου μεθαρμόσας, Οὐαλεντῖνος, οὕτως ὡρίσατο· Irénée de Lyon. *Contre les hérésies. Livre I*, ed. A. Rousseau and L. Doutreleau, (SC 264; Paris: Cerf, 1979) 167.1197-1199; A. M. McGuire, "Valentinus and the 'Gnostike Hairesis': An Investigation of Valentinus' Position in the History of Gnosticism," (Ph.D. dissertation, Yale 1983) 11; see her entire discussion 9-16.

[40] Paper for the 12th International Conference on Patristic Studies, Aug. 22, 1995, "The Original Doctrine of Valentinus the Gnostic," (VC 50 [1996] 327-352). Quispel here simply repeats claims made in his essay, "The Original Doctrine of Valentine" *VC* 1 (1947) 43-73); cf. in contrast C. Markschies, *Valentinus Gnosticus*, 364-379 and idem, "Alte und neue Texte und Forschungen zu Valentin und den Anfängen der 'valentinianischen' Gnosis - Von J. E. Grabe und F. C. Baur bis B. Aland," *Gnosis und Manichäismus. Forschungen und Studien zu Texten von Valentin und Mani sowie zu den Bibliotheken von Nag Hammadi und Medinet Madi*, ed. A. Böhlig and C. Markschies (BZNW 72; Berlin/New York: de Gruyter, 1994) 39-111; here 77f.

also in their teaching about the πνεῦμα—one can neither add to nor subtract from the church's faith,[41] while Valentinus modifies the character of the teaching.

The term "school" applied to the Valentinians stands thus—one would hardly expect otherwise—in the context of heresiological conceptions and it must always be investigated in their light. This brief note suffices for our purposes at present. We investigate now first the terms by which the fathers of the church refer to the Valentinians, in approximately chronological order (2.1). Then we examine the terms the "Valentinians" used for themselves (2.2), gather information about the life of the school (2.3) and search for indications of the character of belonging to a school in the prosopographic reports about the Valentinians (2.4). At the end the reports about the two Valentinian schools will be analyzed (2.5). Space here does not permit consideration of most doxographic questions or of the stemma of the early church's heresiologists (together with the question of the *syntagmata* composed by Justin and Hippolytus).

## 2.1. The Terminology of the Church Fathers
### 2.1.1. Irenaeus of Lyon
As we already saw, Irenaeus introduces Valentinus in *Haer.* 1.11.1 not only as the reformer of a classical Gnostic myth, but also connects him with a school, a διδασκαλεῖον, a *Ualentini scola*.[42] The degree to which we are dealing here with something at the heart of Irenaeus' heresiological conception[43] becomes clear a little later in the same work where he ascribes to Marcion the development or elaboration of a school (διδασκαλεῖον), probably—to judge from the context—the elaboration of Cerdon's school. At any rate the two are linked in a

---

[41] *Haer.* I.10.2 Μιᾶς γὰρ καὶ τῆς αὐτῆς πίστεως οὔσης, οὔτε ὁ <τὸ> πολὺ περὶ αὐτῆς δυνάμενος εἰπεῖν ἐπλεόνασεν οὔτε ὁ τὸ ὀλίγον ἠλαττόνησεν (161.1148-1150).

[42] Thus the late Latin translation; cf. C. Markschies, *Ambrosius von Mailand und die Trinitätstheologie. Kirchen- und theologiegeschichtliche Studien zu Antiarianismus und Neunizänismus bei Ambrosius und im lateinischen Westen (364-381)* (BHTh 90, Tübingen: J. C. B. Mohr [P. Siebeck], 1995) 13-19; in *Haer.* I.30.15 (384.279). The editors propose as the Greek original (SC 263, 211) ἡ Οὐαλεντίνου σχολή; as a parallel one can note *Haer.* II.19.8 (196.154) *scola eorum qui sunt a Ualentino*, as well as *Haer.* I praef. 2 = Epiphanius, *Haer.* 31.9.8 (23.44f = 400.5f).

[43] Bibliography (selection): P. Perkins, "Irenaeus and the Gnostics," *VC* 30 (1976) 193-200; R. A. Greer, "The Dog and the Mushrooms. Irenaeus' View of the Valentinians Assessed," *The Rediscovery of Gnosticism* 1:146-175; N. Brox, *Offenbarung, Gnosis und gnostischer Mythos bei Irenäus von Lyon. Zur Charakteristik der Systeme* (SPS 1; Salzburg/München: A. Pustet, 1966) 116-133; A. Le Boulluec, *La notion d'hérésie dans la littérature grecque IIe-IIIe siècles, Tome I De Justin à Irénée* (Paris: Études augustiniennes, 1985) 113-188.

διαδοχή.[44] Quite analogously, the διαδοχή of Menander gives rise to two distinct schools, that of Saturninus in Syria and that of Basilides in Egypt.[45] The analogy with the two Valentinian schools separated geographically and doxographically is striking; we will have to return to this observation. Moreover, in his description of the development of Tatian's thought and life, Irenaeus uses terms that are quite analogous to those he uses for Valentinus, "a form proper to his school (διδασκαλεῖον)."[46] Irenaeus constructs an unbroken διαδοχή of heretics which competes with the διαδοχή of the church's orthodox bishops. The heretical διαδοχή, however, establishes in short periods of time ever new "specific forms of school." And, as Irenaeus himself says, new falsehoods are adopted in the course of this process.[47] The form of the church and its teaching remains, by contrast, ever the same. Among the apostles there was not yet any heretical διδασκαλεῖον.[48] Thus the concept of school (διδασκαλεῖον), which fits the Valentinians apparently so well, stands in the service of Irenaeus' anti-heretical polemics. Since Justin does not use the term διδασκαλεῖον in his extant writings, it probably goes back to the bishop of Lyon. Whether or to what extent it also describes historical reality is a separate question.

In addition to the concept "school of Valentinus" Irenaeus uses the term Οὐαλεντίνου μαθηταί in one passage and the more neutral formulation *qui sunt a Ualentino*, in Greek οἱ ἀπὸ Οὐαλεντίνου.[49] It is noteworthy that the bishop of Lyon evidently does not know a term familiar to us, namely, οἱ Οὐαλεντινιανοί or *ualentiniani*. Justin, by contrast, uses it once and, as far as I can see, for the first time in the *Dialogue*, οἱ Οὐαλεντινιανοί, and explains that the name is taken ἀπὸ τοῦ ἀρχηγέτου τῆς γνώμης—this conceptual framework

---

[44] *Haer.* 27.2 διαδεξάμενος δὲ αὐτὸν Μαρκίων ὁ Ποντικὸς ηὔξησε τὸ διδασκαλεῖον, *succedens autem ei Marcion Ponticus adampliauit doctrinam* (351.8-10 and 350.9f).

[45] *Haer.* I.24.1 (320.3f) *distantes doctrinas ostenderunt, alter quidem in Syria, alter uero in Alexandria.*

[46] *Haer.* I.28.2 ἴδιον χαρακτῆρα διδασκαλείου συνεστήσατο· *proprium characterem doctrinae constituit* (357.13f or 356.21f); cf. also 24.7 *in suum characterem doctrinae transtulerunt* (332.6f).

[47] *Haer.* II.31.1 *ea quae sunt extra ueritatem transferentes ad characterem suae doctrinae* (SC 294, 326.27-29). Whether *doctrina* translates διδασκαλία or διδασκαλεῖον is difficult to decide. On the basis of the parallel with *Haer.* I.11.1, I tentatively incline toward the latter possibility.

[48] *Haer.* III.4.2 (SC 211, 50.44); cf. the commentary of the editors in SC 210, 242-244.

[49] For example, in *Haer.* IV *praef.* 2 (SC 100, 384.17 Rousseau).

belongs, of course, in the context of terms for philosophical schools.[50] I do not, however, believe that one can conclude from this that between 155 and 160 (the consensus for dating the *Dialogue* which goes back to Harnack)[51] there existed in Rome a group with the self-designation "Valentinians." For one thing, before Justin introduces the various groups, he himself points out that there are people who falsely call themselves Χριστιανοί. Thus the people whom he calls "Valentinians" probably called themselves simply "Christians." In addition, nothing in Irenaeus' anti-Valentinian writings points to a self-designation which corresponds to Justin's presumably artificial concept. We will, however, have to examine whether the two expressions Οὐαλεντίνου μαθηταί and οἱ ἀπὸ Οὐαλεντίνου could have been self-designations of the group.

### 2.1.2. Clement of Alexandria

A situation in many respects similar can be observed in Clement of Alexandria. In the large majority of cases (nine times) he uses οἱ δὲ ἀπὸ Οὐαλεντίνου[52] or (once) οἱ (...) ἀμφὶ τὸν Οὐαλεντῖνον.[53] In

---

[50] *Dial.* 35.6 (131 Goodspeed); for the philosophical significance, cf. Julian, *Or.* IX [VI] 6, 188b (CUFr 154 Rochefort, τὸν ἀρχηγέτην τῆς φιλοσοφίας) or Philodemus, *Sto. Herc.* Pap. Hercul. 339.12.

[51] Cf. the evidence laid out by O. Skarsaune, "Justin der Märtyrer," *Theologische Realenzyklopädie*, ed. G. Krause and G. Müller (Berlin/New York: de Gruyter, 1988 = 1993) XVII: 471-478; here note 472; on the passage itself, see A. Le Boulluec, *La notion d'hérésie dans la littérature grecque IIᵉ-IIIᵉ siècles, Tome I De Justin à Irénée*, 62.

[52] *Strom.* II.10.2. Clemens Alexandrinus ed. Stählin/Früchtel/Treu (GCS 15; Leipzig: Hinrichs, 1906) II.118.13f., likewise III.29.3 (209.26f); VII.108.1 (III.76.21) and stereotypically in *Exc. Theod.* 2.1 (III.105.14f); 6.1 (107.18f); 16 (112.5); 23.1 (114.16); 25.1 (115.10) and 28.1 (116.19).

[53] *Strom.* III.1.1 (195.3). This passage, by the way, plays a central role in Quispel's attempt to reconstruct Valentinus' "original doctrine" (see above, 411 with note 40; here, 334f.), because he relies on the exact Greek (that is, Classical Greek) meaning of the preposition. Since ἀμφί is allegedly always understood in the inclusive sense, Valentinus together with his disciples had a positive view of marriage and was, therefore, not a "Catholic" but a "Gnostic." I need not comment on Quispel's curious prejudices regarding "the Catholic position" but I do want to say something about the philological side of his argument (cf. J. Humbert, *Syntaxe grecque*, 2nd ed. [Paris: Klincksieck, 1954] § 72). That Quispel's claim, as it stands, cannot be applied to the post-Classical Greek of Clement is something the Alexandrian shows already in *Eclog.* 1.1. In this passage οἱ ἀμφὶ τὸν Σεδράχ, Μισάκ, Ἀβδεναγώ (p. 137.2) applies, of course, to exactly these *three* young men (and not to a fourth or fifth anonymous person in addition to them). I abstain from further confirmation of the point in the other thirteen passages in which Clement combines οἱ with ἀμφί. Quispel does not mention and discuss a single one of them! Besides, between grammar and historical reconstruction there is still a gulf, as *Strom.* III.16.3-4 shows. In this passage Clement writes that Plato attributed a certain view to Orpheus. He goes on to speak of a quite similar view held by the Orphics (οἱ ἀμφὶ Ὀρφέα [203.10]). Now, should we go on and attribute this view also to the historical Orpheus?

four passages of his (?) *excerpta ex Theodoto* (see below p. 433) one encounters the expression οἱ Οὐαλεντινιανοί.[54] One cannot, however, consider this expression part of the original text identified by literary criticism, but it always appears in the redactional additions by the author Clement. It is remarkable how rarely Clement speaks about a "school of Valentinus"—only twice. In one passage the Alexandrian links Iulius Cassianus with the school, ὁ δ' ἐκ Οὐαλεντίνου ἐξε-φοίτησε σχολῆς.[55] Also Heracleon, whom we usually count as a member of the "Italic school" of the Valentinians, is described in this "school" terminology, but without any geographical differentiation, ὁ τῆς Οὐαλεντίνου σχολῆς δοκιμώτατος.[56] On the other hand, Clement does not use Irenaeus' term διδασκαλεῖον. This reserve in describing the Valentinians as a school is doubtless to be explained by the fact that Clement did not develop the same heresiological aversion to the phenomenon "school" as Irenaeus. In Alexandria people evidently did not (yet) sense a contrast between the church's majority position and its transformation "into a form proper to a certain school."[57]

### 2.1.3. Tertullian

The concept "Valentinians," which is lacking in Irenaeus and still rare in Clement, is first consistently used, it would appear, in Tertullian, who uses it almost thirty times.[58] Also this author shows that the term was probably not a self-designation, "We know why *we* call them Valentinians."[59] The term "Valentinians" corresponds in the first place to the normal Roman practice of identifying "any adherents of a

---

[54] *Exc. Theod.* 17.1 (GCS Clem. Al. III.112.9); 21.1 (113.19); 24.1 (115.3) and 37.1 (115.3).

[55] *Strom.* III.92.1 (238.22).

[56] *Strom.* IV.71.1 (280.10f).

[57] Cf. on this point also G. May, "Platon und die Auseinandersetzung mit den Häresien bei Klemens von Alexandrien," *Platonismus und Christentum. Festschrift für H. Dörrie*, ed. H.-D. Blume and F. Mann (JAC Ergb. 10; Münster: Aschendorff, 1983) 123-132.

[58] Cf., for example, *Traité de la prescription contre les heretiques*, ed. R. F. Refoulé (SC 46; Paris: Cerf, 1957) 29.1 (209.3); 33.7 (214.14); 42.8 (222.18); *Contre les Valentiniens*, ed. J.-C. Fredouille (SC 280; Paris: Cerf, 1980) 1.1 (78.1); 1.3 (80.24); 4.1 (86.2); 4.3 (86.17f); 7.3 (92.12); 39.2 (154.15); *De anima*, ed. J. H. Waszink (Amsterdam: J. M. Meulenhoff, 1947) 18.4 (807.29f); *Scorpiace, Q. S. F. Tertulliani Opera*, ed. A. Reifferscheid and G. Wissowa (CSEL 20; Vindobonae: Tempsky, 1890) 1.5 (1069.8).

[59] "*Nouimus, inquam, optime originem quoque ipsorum et scimus, cur valentinianos appellemus, licet non esse uideantur.*" *Tertullien. Contre les Valentiniens*, ed. J.-C. Fredouille (SC 280; Paris: Cerf, 1980) 4.1 (86.1-3).

party" in the plural by analogy to the adjectives ending in -*ianus*. The most famous example is the expression Christiani/Χριστιανοί (Acts 11:26). According to a broad consensus of New Testament scholarship, Χριστιανοί was not originally a self-designation, but a designation by outsiders which was rather hesitantly accepted by Christians.[60] The North African theologian offers a kind of reason for this concept, *Ualentiniani, qui per Ualentinum*,[61] which one could translate into Greek with the phrase used by Irenaeus and Clement, οἱ ἀπὸ Οὐαλεντίνου, "people who come from Valentinus." The claim expressed in the same text, namely, that the Valentinians fell away from the teaching of their founder, is a more than typical anti-heretical commonplace, as I have attempted to show in detail elsewhere.[62] Also Tertullian uses Irenaeus' model of the Valentinians as a *schola*. In fact, he uses this term in an even clearer analogy with the philosophical schools of Plato and Epicurus.[63] "Students" or "disciples" arose from the school of Ptolemy[64] as others arose from the school of the Carthaginian rhetorician Phosphorus.[65] The famous lines about the split of the *doctrina Ualentini* into two schools will be discussed below (section 2.5). At any rate, Tertullian differs from the authors discussed so far in speaking of the church as the *schola Christi*.[66] He supplies us with a further interpretive term when he speaks of a *collegium* at the beginning of his writing on the Valentinians (he

---

[60] See E. Peterson, "Christianus," *Miscellanea Giovanni. Mercati* I (Studi e testi 121, Rome: Città del Vaticano, 1946) 355-372 = idem, *Frühkirche, Judentum und Gnosis. Studien und Untersuchungen* (Darmstadt: Wissenschaftliche Buchgesellschaft, 1982 = 1959) 64-87. A recent discussion of the term Χριστιανοί can be found in R. Riesner, *Die Frühzeit des Apostels Paulus. Studien zur Chronologie, Missionsstrategie und Theologie* (WUNT 71; Tübingen: J. C. B. Mohr [P. Siebeck], 1994) 98-101.

[61] *Val.* 4.3. (Fredouille, 86.18).

[62] Markschies, *Valentinus Gnosticus*, esp. 303-311; cf. also *praescr.* 42.8f (222.17-21).

[63] *Apol.* 46, *Clavis patrum latinorum*, ed. E. Dekkers (CCSL, Turnhout: Brepols, 1954) 1. 161.52; *Marc.* 1.25.3, ed. E. Kroymann (Vindobonae: Tempsky, 1906) 468.14; *res.* 1.4 (921.13 Borleffs).

[64] *Val.* 33.1 (148.5-8) *Extiterunt enim de schola ipsius* (sc. Ptolemaei, C. M.) *discipuli super magistrum, qui duplex coniugium bytho suo adfingerent: cogitationem et voluntatem.*

[65] *Val.* 8.3 (96.15-17). See F. J. Dölger, "Der Rhetor Phosphorus von Karthago und seine Stilübung über den braven Mann," *Antike und Christentum* 5 (1936) 272-274; R. Braun, "Notes de lecture sur une édition récente de l'Adversus Valentinianos de Tertullian," *REAug* 28, (1982) 189-200, here 193-195; G. Schöllgen, *Ecclesia sordida? Zur Frage der sozialen Schichtung frühchristlicher Gemeinden am Beispiel Karthagos zur Zeit Tertullians* (JAC Ergb. 12; Münster: Aschendorff, 1984) 144f.

[66] *Scorp.* 9.1 (1084.14) and 12.1 (1092.5f).

otherwise avoids this term for Christians).[67] Adolf Harnack accordingly spoke about "Gnostic societies."[68] The term is probably meant in the extended sense, for we have no indications that Valentinian schools organized themselves as *collegia* in the juridical sense. Purely private societies for the pursuit of intellectual goals were unknown to Roman law and it would have been difficult to organize as a cultic or professional society. There is no evidence that the four great philosophical schools were organized as cultic societies.[69] Tertullian's remark about "*collegium*" yields little for the comparison between "Valentinian school" and philosophical schools.

### 2.1.4. Hippolytus and Epiphanius

It is surprising that in *Hippolytus'* extant writings "the Valentinians" play no role, at least terminologically. He mentions Valentinus καὶ αὐτοῦ σχόλη and even uses a combination of Irenaeus' two expressions, οἱ ἀπὸ τῆς Οὐαλεντίνου σχολῆς,[70] but the school remains essentially a pale list of names, "Secundus and Ptolemy and Heracleon" together with the "disciple" Mark.[71] Hippolytus does not speak of "Valentinians." The expression was apparently not yet widely current at the beginning of the Third Century.

We conclude our survey of the early church's heresiologists with Epiphanius. He uses the expression οἱ Οὐαλεντινιανοί one single time,[72] otherwise always the curious short form Οὐαλεντῖνοι.[73] Like Irenaeus he knows (in addition to Οὐαλεντῖνον) also ἡ γὰρ Οὐαλεν-

---

[67] *Val.* 1.1 *Valentiniani, frequentissimum plane collegium inter haereticos* (SC 280, 78.1 Fredouille; cf. his commentary in SC 281, 168).

[68] A. Harnack, *Der Brief des Ptolemäus an die Flora* (SBPAW.PH; 1902) 507-545; here 535; repr., idem, *Kleine Schriften zur Alten Kirche, Berliner Akademieschriften 1890-1907 mit einem Vorwort v. J.Dummer, Opuscula IX/1* (Leipzig: Zentralantiquariat der Deutschen Demokratischen Republik, 1980) 591-629, here 619.

[69] J. P. Lynch, *Aristotle's School. A Study of a Greek Educational Institution* (Berkeley: University of California Press, 1972) 108-127.

[70] *Haer.* VI.42.2 (GCS Hippolyt III.173.20 Wendland) and VI.55.1 (189.4); cf. also X.13.1 ὁ δὲ Οὐαλεντῖνος καὶ οἱ ἀπὸ τῆς τούτου σχολῆς (273.25).

[71] *Keph.* for *Haer.* V.28 (134.12) and VI.29.1 (155.19f) as well as VI.39.1 (170.11).

[72] *Anc.* 63.6 (76.12).

[73] *Anc.* 13.3, Epiphanius, *Ancoratus und Panarion*, ed. K. Holl (GCS 25; Leipzig: Hinrichs, 1915) I.21.20; *Haer. praef.* 4.3 (158.7); *praef.* 5.4 (160.7); 31.1.1 (382.11.17); 31.32.9 (435.9); 42.12.3 *Ref.* 26 (II.174.19 Holl/Dummer) and 56.2.1 (340.10). Following him, the author of the *Anac.* for Epiphanius, *Haer.* II.31.1 (236.23). A similar case is the confusion between Valentinus and Valentinianus in Hegemonius, *Acta Archelai* 42 (38), ed. C. F. Beeson (GCS 16; Leipzig: Hinrichs, 1906) 32f: "*Marcionem et Ualentinianum ac Basilidem.*"

418 CHRISTOPH MARKSCHIES

τίνου σχολή[74] and τὴν αὐτοῦ διδασκαλίαν.[75] Irenaeus' old expression οἱ ἀπὸ Οὐαλεντίνου is attested only in a quoted passage.[76]

## 2.1.5. Nag Hammadi Writings

In the Nag Hammadi writings there is one (and only one) possible attestation for the self-understanding of the Valentinians as a "school," namely in the writing commonly entitled *Testimony of Truth* (NHC IX,3), which is critical of the Valentinians (thus again from an opponent's perspective). In a badly damaged passage an unknown person, probably one of the better known Valentinian teachers,[77] is accused of "completing the course of Valentinus" by speaking about the ὀγδοάς. The text continues, "His disciples (μαθητής) resemble [the disc]iples of Valentinus."[78]

> In an extensive and most stimulating review of my book on Valentinus, Hans-Martin Schenke proposed a new reconstruction of the text which seems to me possible, but by no means compelling. For he starts with the premise that one cannot complete the course of another: "Does not everyone complete only his or her own course?" Hence he reconstructs in the lacuna "in place of the object marker ... the introductory particle for the post-positive nominal subject which explicates the preceding pronominal subject" and translates, "Valentinus completed his (own) course." This would suggest, as Schenke quite correctly concludes, that the heresiarch died a martyr's death.[79] The reconstruction suggested by Schenke—the New Testament scholar from Berlin does not mention this point—sounds like a modified Scripture quotation based on 2 Tim 4:7 τὸν δρόμον τετέλεκα. The Valentinus of Nag Hammadi would thus be viewed as parallel to the Paul of the pastoral epistles. I am not sure that one can really complete only one's own course. For example, according to Tertullian Ptolemy proceeds further along the course of Valentinus.[80] The passage thus remains problematic.

---

[74] *Haer.* 35.23 Epiphanius. *Panarion*, ed. K. Holl, J. Dummer (GCS 31; Berlin: Akademie-Verlag, 1980) 2.41.17.

[75] *Haer.* 31.1.6 (383.19f); 31.36.7 (438.20).

[76] Epiph., *Haer.* 32.5.2 (444.20), cf. R. A. Lipsius, *Zur Quellenkritik des Epiphanios* (Vienna: Braumüller, 1865) 156-164.

[77] B. A. Pearson, ed., *Nag Hammadi Codices IX and X* (NHS 15; Leiden: E. J. Brill, 1981) 172 *ad locum* joins K. Koschorke, *Die Polemik der Gnostiker gegen das kirchliche Christentum* (NHS 12; Leiden: E. J. Brill, 1978) 153, of Ptolemy, Heracleon or Axionicus.

[78] ⲀϤⲬⲰⲔ ⲈⲂ[ⲞⲖ] ⲘⲠⲠⲰⲦ [ⲘⲠⲞⲨⲀⲖ]ⲈⲚⲦⲒⲚⲞⲤ ⲚⲦⲞϤ ϨⲰⲰϤ [ⲘⲈⲚ] ⲈϤϢⲀⲬⲈ ⲈⲐⲞⲢ·ⲖⲞⲀⲤ ⲚⲈ[ϤⲘⲀⲐ]ⲎⲦⲎⲤ ⲖⲈ ⲞⲨⲦⲚ̄ⲦⲰⲚ [ⲈⲘⲘⲀ]ⲐⲎⲦⲎⲤ ⲘⲠⲞⲨⲀⲖⲈⲚⲦⲒⲚ[ⲞⲤ·] (56.1-5 [NHS 15, 172 Pearson]; cf. Markschies, *Valentinus Gnosticus*, 378f).

[79] ⲀϤⲬⲰⲔ ⲈⲂ[ⲞⲖ] ⲘⲠⲠⲰⲦ [Ⲛ̄ϬⲒ (Ⲡ)ⲞⲨⲀ][Ⲗ]ⲈⲚⲦⲒⲚⲞⲤ...; cf. H.-M. Schenke, "Rev. Markschies," *JAC* 38 (1995) 173-177, and B. A. Pearson in his commentary (NHS 15; Leiden: 1981) 133.

[80] *Val.* 4.3 (SC 280, 86.11-15); text quoted below, note 108.

The passage just quoted is interesting despite all of its textual uncertainty because it shows that the phrase, "disciple of Valentinus" or "member of the school of Valentinus" is not only an external identification of a Gnostic group considered heretical by the church fathers, but also a phrase by which one Gnostic orientation draws its boundaries over against another.

### 2.1.6. The Terminology of the Church Fathers—Summary

Our survey of the attestations of the use of the term "school" and related expressions for Valentinians has produced in immediate terms a relatively meager result. Apart from the fact *that* this group appears to be a school, one finds out almost nothing concrete about it. Above all, the importance of the category "school" for the heresiological conceptual grid of Irenaeus, for example, raises doubts whether "the people who stem from Valentinus" really constitute a "school" or whether we are not rather dealing with an anti-heretical topos. A first indication lies in the fact that besides the many texts from the majority church there is also one clearly Gnostic text from Nag Hammadi that speaks of "disciples of Valentinus" or "members of the school of Valentinus." In order to address the questions that have been raised, we must now investigate possible self-designations of the Valentinians.

### 2.2. The Self-Designations of the "Valentinians"

In the preface of his work against heresies the bishop of Lyon reports that he came upon writings of people, ὡς αὐτοὶ λέγουσιν Οὐαλεντίνου μαθητῶν.[81] Since he does not return to this expression in what follows, it can hardly be his own polemically motivated invention. But who are these "members of the school of Valentinus?" A first glance already suggests that one could use the reference to Ptolemy—or more exactly, to οἱ περὶ Πτολεμαῖον—as part of the answer and suppose that Irenaeus calls the teaching of "the people around Ptolemy" an ἀπάνθισμα ... τῆς Οὐαλεντίνου σχολῆς.[82] If the views of those *qui sunt circa Ptolemaeum* (thus the Latin translation of οἱ περὶ Πτολεμαῖον) are a blossom of the school of Valentinus, one may suppose that it was these people who called themselves "members of the school of Valentinus." I am inclined to suppose further that the bishop of Lyon does not speak directly about Ptolemy,

---

[81] *Haer.* I *praef.* 2 (22.35).

[82] *Haer.* I *praef.* 2 (23.44f); Latin, *uelut flosculum Valentini scolae* (22.44f).

because in the 180s[83] he was only dealing with the circle around him and his students, not with Ptolemy himself. These data are most easily explained by the hypothesis that Ptolemy had already died or moved away from Rome. Gerd Lüdemann has shown that in Irenaeus the formulation οἱ περί ... does not imply even philologically that Ptolemy was part of the group of "Ptolemeans" in the sense of still being alive when Irenaeus wrote, that is, in the eighties.[84] It is consistent with this hypothesis that the unknown author of the "Anacephalaiosis" to Epiphanius' *Panarion* (end of the fourth century) speaks also about "Ptolemaeans" and identifies them with "disciples" or "members of the school of Valentinus"[85] We are immediately faced with the next question, Why does Irenaeus not, as it were, "concede" to these "Valentinians" their self-designation Οὐαλεντίνου μαθηταί in the further course of his work? As we saw above, he always uses the more neutral οἱ ἀπὸ Οὐαλεντίνου. Also this fact could be explained by chronological and substantive reservations of the bishop. Valentinus left Rome perhaps already in 155, at the latest in 161. When Irenaeus visited Rome for the first time, probably in 177/178, about twenty years had passed since the Egyptian Valentinus lived in Rome.[86] There were probably no longer any direct, personal students of Valentinus among the "Valentinians" of the circle around Ptolemy in Rome. Perhaps people in the majority community still remembered the differences between Valentinus, who after all was never expelled from the community, and persons whom they saw as "heretics" but who called themselves "members of the school of Valentinus." Irenaeus calls them οἱ περὶ Πτολεμαῖον, a circle around Ptolemy, and refers to this group, a "school of Ptolemy," also in another passage.[87]

As an aside, these observations about a school of Ptolemy would provide an excellent explanation for the striking plural forms in Sagnard's so-called "Grande notice" (*Haer.* I.1.1-8.5) and also in the report on Johannine exegesis *Haer.* I.8.5, λέγουσιν, καλοῦσιν, παρ'

---

[83] On the date of composition of this work see my summary, C. Markschies, *Arbeitsbuch Kirchengeschichte* (UTB; Tübingen: J. C. B. Mohr [P. Siebeck], 1995) 126f, with notes 214-216.

[84] "Zur Geschichte des ältesten Christentums in Rom," *ZNW* 70 (1979) 86-114; 97f with notes 31-33.

[85] *Anac.* for Epiphanius, *Haer.* II.33, Πτολεμαῖοι, μαθηταὶ ὄντες καὶ αὐτοὶ Οὐαλεντίνου, οἷς συνάπτεται ἡ Φλώρα (GCS Epiph. I.237.9).

[86] For the dates see the arguments and quotes in Markschies, *Valentinus Gnosticus*, 293-336.

[87] *Haer.* I.12.1, οἱ δὲ περὶ τὸν Πτολεμαῖον (181.1).

αὐτοῖς, αὐτῶν, etc. all of them forms found already in *Haer.* I.1.1. If these texts went back to Ptolemy himself, as has often been supposed, all of this would have to be formulated in the singular. In addition, the well known note preserved only in Latin at the end of the passage *Haer.* I.8.5, *Ptolemaios quidem ita*, does not correspond—contrary to Adelin Rousseau's explicit assurances—"parfaitment" to the preceding αὐταῖς λέξεσι λεγοντες οὕτως (beginning of *Haer.* I.8.5). In one case there is the singular (*Ptolemaeus*), in the other the plural (*qui sunt circa Ptolemaeum*).[88] *Ptolemaios quidem ita* may thus be a redactional gloss. At any rate, Irenaeus is dealing with the writings of a group, probably precisely that *school of Ptolemy*.

Differences between a "school of Valentinus" and a "school of Ptolemy" have been noted already a long time ago, after the Gnosticism conference at Yale 1978, by Gerd Lüdemann and Ekkehard Mühlenberg.[89] Their observations have unfortunately not been noticed at all. One can sharpen their observations as follows. Irenaeus is dealing with a school of Ptolemy which understands itself as a school of Valentinus—and the bishop distinguishes these two school contexts. It does not seem at all surprising to me that the Roman Gnostics appealed to Valentinus, who was never anathematized during his life in Rome. Of course, little or nothing is thereby said about the question whether they rightly or wrongly appeal to Valentinus with respect to the content of their teaching. We have thus reached the problem of a Valentinian διαδοχή or *successio*. The few remaining references to the school show that being a "member of the school" is here to be understood in the precise sense of being member of a *philosophical* school.

## 2.3. Valentinian Gnosticism as a "Philosophical School"
### 2.3.1. The Succession(s) in the School of Valentinus
Further important information for our question of the character of Valentinian Gnosticism as a school is offered by a passage from the *Stromata* ("quilts") of Clement of Alexandria. He reports that "followers of heresies" (in this case the Valentinians) claim "that Valentinus heard Theodas who was, in turn, a disciple of Paul.[90] One

---

[88] Cf. A. Rousseau, SC 263, 218 on *Haer.* I.8.5 (136.189) and 8.5 (129.909f). See the brief discussion of the problem in Markschies, *Valentinus Gnosticus*, 365, note 119.

[89] G. Lüdemann, "Zur Geschichte des ältesten Christentums in Rom," *ZNW* 70 (1979) 86-114, here 105 with note 51f.

[90] *Strom.* VII.105.5 οἱ τὰς αἱρέσεις μετιόντες (75.16-18) and 106.4, ὡσαύτως δὲ καὶ Οὐαλεντῖνον Θεοδᾶ δακηκοέναι φέρουσιν· γνώριμος δ' οὗτος γεγόνει Παύλου (75.16-18); on this passage see Markschies, *Valentinus Gnosticus*, 298-302 and W. A.

could thus consider whether establishing a "school of Valentinus" was accompanied also among those around Ptolemy by the construction of a διαδοχή. Clement reports the διαδοχή Paul-Theodas-Valentinus-(Valentinians); Irenaeus the διαδοχή Valentinus-Ptolemy-Valentinians. Perhaps the Roman school also had a combined list of succession such as Paul-Theodas-Valentinus-Ptolemy (which remains, of course, pure conjecture). Interestingly, the bishop of Lyon denies the διαδοχή to a person whom we usually classify as "Valentinian," namely, the Roman presbyter Florinus. Not even οἱ ἔξω τῆς ἐκκλησίας αἱρητικοί—Irenaeus claims—propounded δόγματα of the sort held by his addressee Florinus. The overall thrust of the letter (CPG I, 1308)[91] suggests that Irenaeus denies Florinus not only the conformity of his doctrines with those of the church—Florinus claimed such conformity as Ptolemy evidently had done before him (see below)—but also his διαδοχή. Since Irenaeus alludes to persons outside the Church, Valentinus or Ptolemy could be the persons in question, but unfortunately the segment of the letter preserved for us by Irenaeus does not say anything on this point.[92]

The information in Clement shows, at any rate, that some part of the "school of Valentinus" passed on a διαδοχή or *successio* of its leaders, following the general custom of antiquity, and this observation deserves being noted quite independently from the question whether this succession is historically reliable.

### 2.3.2. *Evidence for the Life of the School*

Evidence for the concrete activities of "members of the school of Valentinus" is harder to come by. It is highly questionable, for example, whether one can accept Irenaeus' accusation that the Valentinian teachers engaged in sharp financial practices. It is highly unlikely that the Valentinian myth was artificially lengthened and made more mysterious just to get more money out of the audience by

---

Löhr, "Basilides und seine Schule. Eine Studie zur Theologie- und Kirchengeschichte des zweiten Jahrhunderts" (WUNT 83; Tübingen: J. C. B. Mohr [P. Siebeck], 1996) 19-23.

[91] M. Geerard, ed., *Clavis Patrum Graecorum. Vol. 1* (Turnhout, Belgium: Brepols, 1974).

[92] Eusebius, *H. E.* 5.20.4 ταῦτα τὰ δόγματα, Φλωρῖνε, ἵνα πεφεισμένως εἴπω, οὐκ ἔστιν ὑγιοῦς γνώμης· ταῦτα τὰ δόγματα ἀσύμφωνά ἐστιν τῇ ἐκκλησίᾳ ... ταῦτα τὰ δόγματα οὐδὲ οἱ ἔξω τῆς ἐκκλησίας αἱρετικοὶ ἐτόλμησεν ἀποφήνασθαί ποτε· (482.15-19 Schwartz). For the claim of belonging to the church see also the letter to Victor of Rome preserved in Syriac (CPG I, 1311) and H. Langerbeck, "Zur Auseinandersetzung von Theologie und Gemeindeglauben in der römischen Gemeinde in den Jahren 135-165," in idem, *Aufsätze zur Gnosis, aus dem Nachlaß hg. v. H. Dörries* (AAWG.PH 69; Göttingen: Vandenhoeck & Ruprecht, 1967) 38-62.

longer lectures on these matters—as the bishop of Lyon claims.[93] On the other hand, analysis of and commentary on important texts of the school's supposed founder—as in the schools of the philosophers—is well attested by the transmission of the Valentinus hymn θέρος (fragment 8). For Hippolytus transmits it together with a sort of commentary[94] which superimposes "normal Valentinian theology" on the cosmology of the text, a cosmology which is in my judgment quite different. The probable origin of this commentary in an interpretation of the school is still indicated by its grammar, more specifically by the shift from singular (Valentinus) to the plural (of the members of the school, κατ' αὐτούς).[95] Such commentaries were evidently produced not only orally. We know from Tertullian that a Valentinian Gnostic by the name of Alexander (see below p. 431) quoted psalms by Valentinus in his writings.[96] In this context I want to turn briefly to the texts in Nag Hammadi Codex XI which are usually entitled "A Valentinian Exposition" (NHC XI,2).

The beginning of this writing looks to me more like a revelatory discourse than a scholarly commentary (I am following the reconstruction of the text by John Turner), "[I will speak] my μυστήριον [to those who are] mine and [to those who will be mine]."[97] Stretching matters a little one could compare this text in its form with the more strongly religious texts of some Neo-Platonists, but at this point the differences in the content of teaching between the Valentinians who composed this text and the philosophical schools of the early imperial period manifest themselves also in formal terms. If one applies Barbara Aland's point on the fundamental difference between

---

[93] Irenaeus, *Haer.* I.4.3 (69.410-416) = Epiphanius, *Haer.* 31.17.4 (411.8-12).

[94] Hymn: VI.37.7 (GCS Hipp. III.167.17-23 Wendland; PTS 25, 253.31-38 Marcovich; text and translation also in Markschies, *Valentinus Gnosticus*, 218-259; commentary, *Haer.* VI.37.8 (167.24-168.4/254.39-44; on this topic see C. Markschies, "Platons König oder Vater Jesu Christi? Drei Beispiele für die Rezeption eines griechischen Gottesepithetons bei den Christen in den ersten Jahrhunderten und deren Vorgeschichte," *Königsherrschaft Gottes und himmlischer Kult im Judentum, im Urchristentum und in der hellenistischen Welt,* ed. M. Hengel and A. M. Schwemer (WUNT 1.R 55; Tübingen: J. C. B. Mohr [P. Siebeck], 1991) 385-439, here 429-438. Objections have recently been made against my interpretation of this Valentinus fragment. I have discussed them in my survey of the literature, "Alte und neue Texte und Forschungen" (n. 40 above), 90-96.

[95] VI.37.8 (167.24/254.39).

[96] Carne 17.1 (903.1-4 Kroymann).

[97] NHC XI,2.16-18: [†ΝΑ]ϪⲈ ⲠⲀⲘⲨⲤ[ⲦⲎⲢⲒⲞⲚ ⲀⲚⲈⲈⲒ ⲈⲦ]ϢⲞⲞⲠ ⲚⲎⲈⲒ M̄Ⲛ̄ [ⲚⲈⲦⲚⲀϢⲰⲠⲈ Ⲛ]ⲎⲈⲒ (NHS 28, 106 Turner). H. Strutwolf, *Gnosis als System. Zur Rezeption der valentinianischen Gnosis bei Origenes* (FKDG 56; Göttingen: Vandenhoeck & Ruprecht, 1993) 40, n. 61, calls the text an "esoteric revelatory writing."

philosophy and religions of revelation (quoted above p. 402) to this late Valentinian text, one will have to say that despite its contacts with techniques of philosophical schools it belongs more on the side of religions of revelation—to judge from the extant beginning. The same applies probably to a further Valentinian writing. The remarkable parallel between the beginning of the exposition from Nag Hammadi and the beginning of the so-called "Valentinian Doctrinal Letter" in Epiphanius has, as far as I know, been overlooked. "Indestructible Mind greets the Indestructible Ones: unknown and unutterable trans-celestial mysteries (μυστήρια) do I announce to you."[98] Now, the questions we raise about the genre "philosophical school commentary" do not imply that elements of such literature do not appear at all in the Coptic writing from Nag Hammadi (I want to forego a more detailed analysis of the "Doctrinal Letter" in this context). Quite the opposite. The passages in NHC XI,2 which follow after the introduction in the style of a revelation discourse do not really return to this genre. With some justification one can classify the continuation rather as an "expository commentary" on the central *topoi* of Valentinian teaching (god, creation, redemption) and assign it to a school context after all. The text even deals with diverging opinions in the school with a certain polemical note (NHC XI 27.30-38) and thus attests a discussion about specific points of doctrine within the school. A commentary belonging to a school setting was quite superficially stylized into a religious tractate. Now, despite this comparatively narrow textual basis, I suspect that such observations are pertinent to the history of Valentinianism as a whole. At some point in time, elements of a religion of revelation were superimposed on the activities of the Valentinians that were originally more similar to those of a philosophical school. Corresponding interpretations would, of course, have to be presented also for the other Nag Hammadi writings classified as Valentinian—we cannot do so here. It should be pointed out that evidently there were still groups which did not accept this development toward a religion of revelation. Mark J. Edwards has recently interpreted the *Letter to Rheginus* as a document of the enduring and critical reception of Platonic philosophy in the Valentinian school of later centuries.[99] At any rate, already in this

---

[98] Epiphanius, *Haer.* 31.5.1f νοῦς ἀκατάργητος τοῖς ἀκαταργήτοις χαίρειν. Ἀνονομάστων ἐγὼ καὶ ἀρρήτων καὶ ὑπερουρανίων μνείαν ποιοῦμαι μυστηρίων πρὸς ὑμᾶς ... (390.6-8 Holl); on the doctrinal letter see the brief introductory remarks in Markschies, *Valentinus Gnosticus*, 45, n. 217 and 312, nn. 131-136.

[99] M. J. Edwards, "The Epistle to Rheginus: Valentinianism in the Fourth Century," *NovT* 37 (1995) 76-91.

preliminary stage of such analyses there cannot be any doubt that there was a "Valentinian" program of lectures and discussions.

Unfortunately we know nothing about the corresponding audience. The one Roman noblewoman Flora, the addressee of Ptolemy's letter, is not sufficient evidence for conclusions on this matter, not even if we identify her with Justin's converted noblewoman who wants to be divorced from her husband.[100] The same point applies to location. On the basis of epigraphic sources, Peter Lampe located an alleged group of noble Valentinians among the *honoratiori* on the Roman *Caelius*, but he has rightly been criticized for his weak arguments.[101]

If, then, the application of the model "philosophical school" to the Valentinians and the construction of a διαδοχή implies, at least in part, heresiological categorization and evaluation, the question arises all the more urgently whether we possess any independent further reports that show and present the Valentinians as a "school." Can one perhaps use the ancient reports about Valentinus' so-called "disciples," Ptolemy, Heracleon, Theodotus and the rest, as reports independent from the reports gathered so far to reconstruct a "school of Valentinus?"

### 2.4. Valentinians as "Disciples" of Valentinus

The question of "disciples" among the Valentinians can be truly answered only by proportionately extensive doxographic investigations on Valentinian Gnosticism as attested in the church fathers and Nag Hammadi. I promised such a monograph in my Valentinus book and I cannot, of course, fulfill this promise in the present limited framework, for one would first have to present detailed *Literarkritik* of the various sources, in order to see their historical sequence and

---

[100] *2Apol.* 2.1-10 (79f). For the discussion on the identity of this anonymous person with Ptolemy's Flora see G. Lüdemann, "Zur Geschichte des ältesten Christentums in Rom," 100-102. Lüdemann assembles arguments for the hypothesis first proposed by Harnack that the teacher of the noble-woman, Ptolemy and the Roman Gnostic of the same name are identical. This identification is the basis for calling the anonymous woman "Flora." Of course, it would be strange if Justin branded the "Valentinians" as heretics (see above, note 51), and at the same time wrote, without any commentary, in support of the Valentinian Ptolemy. At the very least one would have to assume a change in Justin's views between the *Apology* and the *Dialogue*.

[101] P. Lampe, *Die stadtrömischen Christen in den ersten beiden Jahrhunderten. Untersuchungen zur Sozialgeschichte*, 2nd ed. (WUNT 2.R. 18; Tübingen: J. C. B. Mohr [P. Siebeck], 1989) 257-264; against this position, see C. Scholten, "Gibt es Quellen zur Sozialgeschichte der Valentinianer Roms?," *ZNW* 79 (1988) 244-261 and G. Schöllgen, "Probleme der frühchristlichen Sozialgeschichte," *JAC* 32 (1989) 23-40. However, Lampe (ibid. 50, note 121a) rightly warns against a misunderstanding of Tertullian, *Val.* 7.3 (92.11-13) as an indication of addresses of Valentinians.

grouping. Two (in my judgment not unproblematic) contributions on this topic have recently been submitted; in any case, they will stimulate the discussion and make it more fruitful.[102] Let me note that no progress is made when one follows Quispel's recent contribution in simply attributing the lowest common denominator of all Valentinian sources to Valentinus as his "original doctrine" and simply dismisses all doubts that have arisen in recent years with the trumpet blast that such an approach "brings confusion."[103] Imagine as a test-case that we were to attribute the lowest common denominator of the three Synoptic Gospels without much further ado to the historical Jesus. I am inclined to suppose that *this* approach would rather "bring" considerable "confusion." An independent value for the interpretation of texts is something which such general considerations do not, at any rate, have.

In the present context, of course, I cannot anticipate these necessary labors. Instead, I will develop the brief prosopographic remarks I made in my Valentinus book—at least for Ptolemy. What Hans Leisegang summarized briefly already many years ago calls in many respects for a new analysis.[104] One must first focus upon those who assert links between Valentinus and his so-called "disciples" or "members of his school," and upon the degree of proximity such assertions really imply. Such an investigation leads partly to rather surprising results. We turn first to Ptolemy. The famous split of the Valentinians into two schools will occupy us at the end.

### 2.4.1. Ptolemy as a "Valentinian?"

Was Ptolemy a Valentinian at all or did only the people around him call themselves "members of the school of Valentinus" after his death or departure from Rome, thereby turning their teacher into a posthumous "Valentinian?" Nowhere do we find the claim that Ptolemy was *personally* a disciple of Valentinus. At the most, one can argue for such a relation on the basis of the circumstances of his life and his temporary sojourn in Rome. And the exact dating of this sojourn depends essentially upon the (to say the least) not unproblematic

---

[102] J. Holzhausen, *Der 'Mythos vom Menschen' im hellenistischen Ägypten. Eine Studie zum "Poimandres"(= CH I), zu Valentin und dem gnostischen Mythos* (Theoph. 33, Bodenheim: Athenäum Hain Hanstein, 1994); H. Strutwolf, *Gnosis als System. Zur Rezeption der valentinianischen Gnosis bei Origenes* (FKDG 56; Göttingen: Vandenhoeck & Ruprecht, 1993).

[103] In his contribution mentioned above, p. 411, note 40; he simply repeats here what he had said already in 1947 in "The Original Doctrine of Valentine," *VC* 1 (1947) 46f.

[104] H. Leisegang, "Valentinus; Valentinianer," *PW*, 2d ed., VII A (Waldsee [Württemberg]: Alfred Druckenmüller, 1948) 2261-2273, here 2269-2273.

identification of the Christian teacher and martyr Ptolemy in Justin with the Gnostic teacher in Irenaeus and Epiphanius (see above p. 419). If we accept this identification despite all misgivings, then Ptolemy and Valentinus did indeed both live in Rome at the beginning of the 250s[105]—but what does that prove? Personal discipleship was indeed not the decisive nor even the only criterion of belonging to a school. Even after Plato's death, as we saw, there existed ἡ Πλάτωνος σχολή. Did Ptolemy, then, belong to the "school of Valentinus?"

For an answer one can turn first to the corresponding classification asserted by the church fathers. Of course, Irenaeus and Hippolytus give him a place among the "Valentinians." Οὐαλεντῖνος ... καὶ Ἡρακλέων καὶ Πτολεμαῖος καὶ πᾶσα ἡ τούτων σχολή.[106] Among Valentinus' *sectatores* Irenaeus first simply mentions Ptolemy and Heracleon without further information. "*Sectator*" is probably a translation of ἀκόλουθος, an expression which can also be used in the contexts of philosophical schools.[107] And Tertullian says only that Ptolemy continued further along Valentinus' course and modified the teaching of his—here quite literally—predecessor.[108] In Epiphanius the information is apparently more extensive. He brings Ptolemy into a διαδοχή with Secundus, whom he had previously introduced as Valentinus' διάδοχος. Ptolemy's relation to Valentinus as his "disciple" is thus in the view of the later bishop of Salamis a mediated and interrupted one. Secundus was allegedly a "Valentinian," but developed his thought beyond Valentinus and departed from his teaching at many points. Epiphanius accordingly knows "Secundians," people who adhere to the "heresy of Secundus."[109] And Irenaeus' ἐπιφανὴς διδάσκαλος, that is, the "recognized" (but anonymous) Valentinian teacher, turns in Epiphanius into Ἐπιφάνης, Isidor's disciple and Carpocrates' son (!).[110] Ptolemy follows—at

---

[105] For all dates see Markschies, *Valentinus Gnosticus*, 393, notes 32-34.

[106] Hippolytus, *Haer.* VI.29.1 (155.18-20).

[107] Irenaeus, *Haer.* II.4.1 (SC 294, 46.21); cf. also G. Kittel, "ἀκολουθέω κτλ," *ThWNT* 1, 210-216, here 210f.

[108] *Val.* 4.3 *Eam postmodum Ptolemaeus intrauit, nominibus et numeris aeonum distinctis in personales substantias, sed extra deum determinatas, quas Valentinus in ipsa summa diuinitatis ut sensus et affectus, motus incluserat* (SC 280, 86.11-15); for an interpretation of this sentence, see W. A. Löhr, "La doctrine de Dieu dans la Lettre à Flora de Ptolémée," *RHPR* 75 (1995) 177-191, here 178f; and Markschies, *Valentinus Gnosticus*, 303-311.

[109] *Haer.* 32.1.1-1.5 (438.25-439.11) and 3.1 (442.1f).

[110] Compare Irenaeus, *Haer.* I.11.3 *clarus ... magister* (172.44 or 173.1) with Epiphanius, *Haer.* 32.3.2 (19). We need not enter into the question whether this teacher

least according to Epiphanius—after Secundus and Epiphanes or their schools, thus twice mediated after Valentinus, τοὺς περὶ Σεκοῦνδον καὶ τὸν ὀνομασθέντα ̓Επιφάνην ... Πτολεμαῖος διαδέχεται (*Haer.* 33.1.1 p. 448.2f). These apparently more precise reports are probably a mere misunderstanding by the author, who likes drawing connections but is not very careful. One can, at any rate, interpret the sequence Valentinus-Secundus-Epiphanes-Ptolemy as a mistaken combination based on the text of Irenaeus, who discusses, in sequence, Valentinus (11.1), Secundus (11.2), the other anonymous teacher (11.3) and finally those of Ptolemy's school (12.1). Already the connection between Secundus and Basilides' son Isidor in Epiphanius looks extremely strange. Besides, one must not ignore a tendency characteristic of the author of the *Panarion*, namely, the artificial "invention," as it were, of new heresies (such as the Merinthians whom he deduces from the Cerinthians). Is his διαδοχή worthless? We already pointed out the differentiations between the "school of Valentinus" and the "school of Ptolemy" reported by Irenaeus. At any rate, Epiphanius had no additional information about a direct relation between Valentinus and Ptolemy. Whether Ptolemy was indeed a disciple of Valentinus, or understood himself as such, can thus no longer be determined reliably in the designations imposed by the church fathers.

The only thing that remains for examining the question of Ptolemy's membership in a "school of Valentinus" is a glance at the one and only indubitably authentic work of the Gnostic Ptolemy. In its didactic-schematic composition, his letter to Flora (CPG I, 1135) is reminiscent of the manner in which a philosophical problem was discussed in ancient schools, as Jaap Mansfeld pointed out recently.[111] When the author speaks of the ἀποστολικὴ παράδοσις, a tradition ἣν ἐκ διαδοχῆς καὶ ἡμεῖς παρειλήφαμεν and introduces as the decisive standard ἡ τοῦ σωτῆρος ἡμῶν διδασκαλία, one can observe a convergence of Pauline tradition (cf. 1 Cor 15:1-3) and the terminology of philosophical schools (keyword διαδοχή).[112] This convergence, of course, also gives greater plausibility to claims that Ptolemy

---

is to be identified with a known Valentinian. Harnack proposed Heracleon; *Zur Quellenkritik der Geschichte des Gnosticismus* (Leipzig: Bidder, 1873) 62f.

[111] J. Mansfeld, *Heresiography in Context: Hippolytus' Elenchos as a Source for Greek Philosophy* (PhAnt 56; Leiden: E. J. Brill, 1992) 279f; on this set of issues cf. also the forthcoming *TRE* article, "Ptolemäus, Gnostiker" by W. A. Löhr. I thank the author for having made this article available to me.

[112] Epiphanius, *Haer.* 33.7.9 (457.14-16); cf. N. Brox, *Offenbarung, Gnosis und gnostischer Mythos*, 130f.

and his school stood in chains of succession of the form Paul-Theodas-Valentinus-Ptolemy cited above (p. 421). Some further details allow comparison with works of philosophical schools of that period. Already some time ago Eduard Norden pointed out the high stylistic level of the letter.[113] The various allusions to the Bible and Platonic *topoi* such as πατήρ, δημιουργὸς καὶ ποιητής and νομοθέτης presuppose a certain level of education in the addressee, ἀδελφή μου Φλώρα. The text is a kind of "introductory lecture" on the problem of the law which begins with a review of previous and unsatisfactory γνώματα. In what follows Ptolemy develops his own anti-Marcionite solution as a διαίρεσις. In an excellent and thorough article Winrich A. Löhr has recently discussed this argumentation (also from the point of view of its contents) as a text-book example of Christian Platonism and pointed out decisive philological and conceptual misunderstandings in Quispel's edition/commentary of 1949 (2nd ed. 1966).[114]

We cannot enter here into a more extensive discussion of the doxographic side of the problem whether Ptolemy was a Valentinian. What follows must suffice at present. If one follows Löhr's approach, one is compelled to explain considerable tensions between the Letter and the so-called "Grande Notice" in Irenaeus, that is, differences between Ptolemy's authentic teaching and the teaching of "the people around Ptolemy," who call themselves "disciples" of Valentinus or "members of the school of Valentinus." These differences, in my judgment, shatter the conventional model of exoteric teaching (in the letter to Flora) and esoteric teaching (in Irenaeus' extensive report). Löhr himself considers several hypotheses to explain these tensions. At any rate, on the basis of these tensions one can perhaps further elucidate Irenaeus' differentiation between the school of Ptolemy and Ptolemy. Perhaps one can also note closer relations between Valentinus' teaching as expressed in the fragments and the teaching of Ptolemy in the *Letter to Flora*. We need a separate study on this topic. It has become clear in any case that Ptolemy's membership among the Valentinians, which was still a matter of course for the church fathers, should at least be discussed anew. We turn only briefly to other Valentinians.

---

[113] E. Norden, *Die antike Kunstprosa vom VI. Jahrhundert v. Chr. bis in die Zeit der Renaissance*, Vol. 2, 9th ed. (Stuttgart: B. G. Teubner, 1983 = 3rd ed., Leipzig/Berlin: Teubner, 1915) 920-922.

[114] Cf. note 107.

## 2.4.2. Other "Valentinians," Especially Heracleon

The various anti-heretical works of the ancient church fathers contain references to *nine* other Valentinian teachers: Alexander, Florinus,[115] Heracleon and Theotimus on the one hand; and on the other Axionicus,[116] Colarbasos, Marcus and Theodotus. In almost all cases, unfortunately, one can say little or nothing about the foundation on which this classification rested. Clear exceptions, of course, are Heracleon and Theodotus, some of whose writings have been preserved. There seem to have been no direct and personal disciples of Valentinus among these "Valentinians." According to the title of the *Excerpta*, Theodotus belongs "in the time of Valentinus," but this statement raises considerable problems (see below, p. 433); and, anyway, one cannot deduce direct discipleship from it.[117]

Also *Heracleon*, whom we now discuss in a little more detail, is not as closely linked to Valentinus as one is generally ready to assume. His dates and place can only be approximately determined. Origen is the first and only one who reports, with a certain reservation, that Heracleon was considered a personal disciple of Valentinus.[118] Since he is counted as a member of the "Italic school" in Hippolytus, he may perhaps have taught in Rome. On the other hand, the members of his school (οἱ ἀπ' αὐτοῦ and οἱ ἀπὸ τῆς γνώμης αὐτοῦ) at the time of Origen are in Alexandria.[119] That the Valentinian Heracleon is an excellent witness for the character of Valentinian Gnosticism as a philosophical school hardly requires lengthy argumentation. It is evident already in the simple fact that (perhaps around 170 CE) he wrote the first "scholarly" commentary on the Gospel of John. When one compares what is preserved of the commentary with the demands made by exegetical method in Antiquity one can only come to a positive judgment about the work (as Origen himself puts

---

[115] A. Jülicher, "Florinus," *PW* VI/2 (1909) 2760 and A. von Harnack, *Geschichte der altchristlichen Litteratur I/2* (1894 = 1958) 593f.

[116] About this Valentinian from Antioch we know not much more than Tertullian tells us (*Val.* 4.3: *Solus ad hodiernum Antiochiae Axionicus memoriam Valentini integra custodia regularum eius consolatur* [86.19f Fredouille]).

[117] *Exc. Theod.* title, κατὰ τοὺς Οὐαλεντίνου χρόνους (52 Sagnard/40 Casey).

[118] *Comm. in Joh.* II.14.100 (GCS Origenes IV.70.3f Preuschen) = frg. 1 (63.24f Völker), Βιαίως δὲ οἶμαι καὶ χωρὶς μαρτυρίου τὸν Οὐαλεντίνου λεγόμενον εἶναι γνώριμον Ἡρακλέωνα διηγούμενον...

[119] Hippolytus, *Haer.* VI.35.6 (165.5f/249.28f) and Orig., *Comm. in Joh.* XX.20.170 (352.34 Preuschen = frg. 44 Brooke); cf. C. Bammel, "Herakleon," *TRE* XV (1986 = 1993) 54-57; Markschies, *Valentinus Gnosticus*, 393f and E. Pagels, *The Johannine Gospel in Gnostic Exegesis: Heracleon's Commentary on John* (SBL MS 17; Nashville: Abingdon Press, 1973; Atlanta: Scholars Press, 1989).

it, despite all his criticism, οὐκ ἀπιθάνως δή φησιν ... *Comm. in Joh.* VI.23.126 [p. 134.8]). The commentary evidently proceeded verse by verse; what is preserved are mainly explanations of things (ἱστορικόν) which partly enter into great philological detail and thus presuppose the explanation of words (γλωσσηματικόν) and grammatical-rhetorical exegesis (τεχνικόν), although the corresponding passages are hardly ever transmitted by Origen. For example, δι' οὗ in John 1:3 is distinguished from the prepositional phrase ἀφ' οὗ and ὑφ' οὗ.[120] In a very critical remark about the quality of Heracleon's interpretations Origen did not designate the work of his predecessor with the technical terms σημείωσεις, σχόλια, τόμοι or ζητήματα, but as ὑπομνήματα. It remains uncertain whether this was the original title of the work. For a scholarly commentary one would not use this—admittedly rather vague—expression. It places this member of the school of Valentinus side by side with the various authors of ancient *memorabilia*, such as Plutarch (but also Hegesippus).[121] One should, however, consider that the majority of ancient commentaries also had comparatively non-specific titles. The Valentinian commentary may thus perhaps have been analogously entitled, ʿΗρακλέωνος εἰς τὸν ʾΙωάννου Εὐαγγέλιον.

The magician Marcus claimed, according to Irenaeus, that he "improved" upon his teacher. It remains unclear, however, who this (Valentinian) teacher was.[122] Tertullian reports about Alexander that he supports his Christological views with logical proofs, *syllogismis, quos argumentationibus torquet*, and that he wove "psalms of Valentinus," that is, his hymns, into his proofs.[123] All in all one can say that the character of Valentinian Gnosticism as a philosophical

---

[120] Origen, *Comm. in Joh.* II.14.102 (70.25-27) = Herakleon, Fragment 1. For the terms and steps of philological method in Antiquity I gratefully rely on B. Neuschäfer, *Origenes als Philologe* (*Schweizerische Beiträge zur Altertumswissenschaft* 18/1-2, Basel: Friedrich Reinhardt Verlag, 1987) 138-246.

[121] Origen, *Comm. in Joh.* VI.92 (125.19) and Diogenes Laertius IV.4 (SCBO I.165.17); cf. J.-M. Poffet, *La Méthode exégetique d'Héracléon et d'Origène, commentateurs de Jn 4: Jésus, la Samaritaine et les Samaritains* (Paradosis 28, Fribourg: Éditions Universitaires, 1985) 3f n. 5. For the concept ὑπομνήματα cf. N. Hyldahl, "Hegesipps Hypomnemata," *StTh* 14 (1960) 70-113; Th. Zahn, *Geschichte des neutestamentlichen Kanons I/2* (Erlangen/Leipzig: A. Deichert, 1889) 471-476.

[122] *Haer.* I.13.1 ʾΆλλος δέ τις <τῶν παρ' αὐτοῖς, τοῦ διδασκάλου> διορθωτὴς εἶναι <καυχώμενος>, Μάρκος <δὲ> αὐτῷ ὄνομα ... (189, 1-3 in the reconstruction by A. Rousseau). In his commentary Rousseau suggests identifying the unknown teacher with Valentinus (SC 263, 240). He proceeds, however, to show that an analysis of the doctrine ascribed to him shows that the "système de Marc le Magicien" is only "le simple écho de celui de Ptolémée" (ibid.).

[123] *Carn.* 17.1 (CChr.SL 2, 903.1-3 Kroymann).

school is still rather well expressed in the extant literary works and in reports about them.

Finally, the famous split of Valentinian Gnosticism into an eastern and a western school still remains to be discussed.

## 2.5. The Two Valentinian Schools

That the language of two schools must be some sort of Valentinian self-designation is shown, at least for the Third Century, by *Hippolytus*: καὶ καλεῖται ἡ μὲν ἀνατολική τις διδασκαλία κατ' αὐτούς, ἡ δὲ Ἰταλική.[124] I see no reason for doubting the correctness of this statement. The self-designation of the Valentinians as "members of the school of Valentinus" is attested clearly before Hippolytus, namely—as we saw—in Irenaeus. "Teaching," διδασκαλία, stands here as *pars pro toto* for the school, διδασκαλεῖον. And since some people perceived two different variants—variants of a unified teaching—one will hardly be able to deny the fact of a "Valentinian" identity, of a "Valentinian consciousness." It was thus not "inappropriate ... for them to think of themselves as Valentinians."[125] The analogous models of schools with primarily geographic epithets need not be taken as evidence against the historicity of the terms. Clement, like other contemporaries, distinguished within philosophy "three schools, named according to the area which was their home," the Italic, the Ionic and the Eleatic.[126] One will not exclude the possibility that the expressions "Italic" and "eastern school" were formed by analogy to these categorizations.

On the instructive map "Followers of Valentinus and their Enemies" of his *Gnostic Scriptures* (p. 268f) Bentley Layton introduces the two Valentinian schools in two neatly arranged little boxes: "'Italic' School (Rome, second cent.): Heracleon, Ptolemy, Secundus, Alexander, Flora, Florinus, Theotimus" and "'Eastern' School (mostly Alexandria; second cent.): Axinonicus of Antioch, Kolorbasos (?), Mark,[127] Theodotus; (third cent.): Ambrose, Candidus."[128]

---

[124] *Haer.* VI.35.5 (165.4f).

[125] This is the view of F. Wisse, "The Nag Hammadi Library and the Heresiologists," *VC* 25 (1971) 205-223, here 218.

[126] *Strom.* I.62.1 Φιλοσοφίας τοίνυν ... τρεῖς γεγόνασι διαδοχαὶ ἐπώνυμοι τῶν τόπων περὶ οὓς διέτριψαν (39.14-17); on the matter itself, see, for example, H. Diels, *Doxographi Graeci*, 4th ed. (Berlin: de Gruyter, 1965 = 1879) 244f.

[127] A. von Harnack also considers the hypothesis that Marcus flourished in Gaul; *Geschichte der altchristlichen Litteratur II/1* (Leipzig: J. C. Hinrichs, 1958 = 1896) 295f.

[128] The map is based on K. Koschorke, "Patristische Materialien zur Spätgeschichte der valentinianischen Gnosis," M. Krause, ed., *Gnosis and Gnosticism. Papers read at*

The conventional picture that especially the Roman school was the productive and flourishing school is thereby corrected already in graphic terms. Valentinianism survived above all in Egypt, Valentinus' native country. Regarding the split itself, a chronological order of investigation is once again appropriate.

### 2.5.1. The Two Schools according to Clement

Clement of Alexandria, if I am not mistaken, tends to be cited as the first to attest a difference between two Valentinian schools. As we have seen (section 2.1.1), Irenaeus knows two geographically and doxographically different non-Valentinian schools, which originated from the διαδοχή of Menander (the school of Saturninus in Syria and of Basilides in Egypt),[129] but in his excerpts he mixes various Valentinian systems together without any reference to two Valentinian schools. In the Eighties of the second century, was there as yet no differentiation into an Italic and an eastern school? It seems to me that here we have a clear need for further clarification and material for a thorough analysis of sources in Irenaeus.

The apparently first attestation for the split is the title of CPG 1.1139 (*Excerpta ex Theodoto*). The following excursus will show that the attestation is highly questionable.

### Excursus: The Title of the Excerpta ex Theodoto

This title is attested simply (that is, without *subscriptio*) in the one and only authentic manuscript of the work, the Florentine Laur. V.3 (apart from this manuscript there is only a late Parisian copy) from the eleventh century.[130] It reads (fol. 358ʳ), ἐκ τῶν Θεοδότου καὶ τῆς 'Ανατολικῆς καλουμένης διδασκαλίας κατὰ τοὺς Οὐαλεντίνου χρόνους ἐπιτομαί, that is, "excerpts from the works of Theodotus and the so-called eastern teaching (or school), at the time of Valentinus." Do the title and the work really go back to Clement of Alexandria? We can deal here only briefly with this highly complicated matter, for considerable doubts about the ascription of the work and its title to Clement have never become silent. The basis on which such an ascription could be made is quite narrow. In contrast to the *Stromateis*, whose second to fifth book in the same manuscript bear the author's name in

---

the 8th International Conference on Patristic Studies (Oxford, September 3rd-8th 1979) (NHS 12; Leiden 1981) 120-139.

[129] *Haer.* I.24.1 (320.3f) *distantes doctrinas ostenderunt, alter quidem in Syria, alter uero in Alexandria.*

[130] Cf. the description by O. Stählin in GCS *Clemens Alexandrinus I* (Leipzig: Hinrichs, 1905) XL-XLIII and the remarks by R. P. Casey, *The Excerpta ex Theodoto of Clement of Alexandria* (StD 1, London: Christophers, 1934) 3-5. According to Stählin (GCS Clem. Al. II, 137 apparatus) and Casey (p. 3) the title of the work which immediately follows in the manuscript, namely, ἐκ τῶν προφητικῶν ἐκλογαί on fol. 377 verso is designed like a *subscriptio* of the preceding Excerpta.

the genitive, Κλήμεντος, and in the *subscriptio* the title of the book, ὁ πρῶτος (δεύτερος κτλ) στρωματεύς, the excerpts lack an explicit mention of their author (the beginning of Book I is lost; the Codex Laurentinianus fails to mention the author's name for Books VI, VII and VIII). The manuscript title points to the literary genre ἐπιτομή, but the work corresponds to this title only in a most general sense. Of course, such "excerpts" from other works among pagans and Christians of Antiquity are in themselves nothing unusual,[131] but in this case already the epitomator's customary preface on method is missing. The work simply begins with a quote and with the indication of a quote, φησί. The author (or epitomator?), by contrast, begins to speak after seven lines of quote somewhat abruptly in the first person plural (φαμέν or ἡμεῖς ... δέ) and offers the opposite opinion. In purely statistical terms, of eighty-six chapters one fourth (eighteen entirely and six partly) contain the author's majority-church and anti-Valentinian reflections. The work is thus a fragmentary counter-commentary rather than an ἐπιτομή— but, in contrast to the anonymous commentary on Plato's *Theaetetus* by a Middle-Platonist (Pap. Berol. 9782),[132] it is a *critical* refutation. The contamination of perhaps four different Valentinian sources may best fit the genre "ἐπιτομή,"[133] but the *Excerpta* are not a particularly characteristic specimen of the genre. Harnack formulated the point more definitely, "The title is completely arbitrary." By the same token statements implicit in the title and guesses about the author become problematic. Is the work a series of private excerpts by Clement for further books of the *Stromateis* which friends published after his death as fragments, giving the work its title as well (Ruben, von Arnim and von Harnack),[134] or a later excerpt from the lost eighth book of this work (Zahn),[135] or similarly late excerpts from the *Hypotyposes* (Nautin)?[136] Whether Clement was truly the author of the present text should be examined once again, despite Hans von Arnim's work. If one considers, in addition, the history and the character of the Florentine manuscript mentioned above, it becomes further unlikely that Clement himself gave the work its title. There is some possibility that the Florentine codex was copied from a manuscript of the learned bishop Arethas of Caesarea. At the end of the Ninth Century, this student of Photius acquired and glossed manuscripts of pagan and Christian authors on a large scale.[137] Perhaps he

---

[131] I. Opelt, "Epitome," *RAC* V (1962) 944-973. The author does not count our text among "theological *epitomai*" (963f). Harnack (*Geschichte der altchristlichen Litteratur I/1*, 181) even writes, "They are thus excerpts from excerpts."

[132] Hg. H. Diels/W. Schubart, Anonymer Kommentar zu Platons Theaetet (Papyrus 9782) (Berliner Klassikertexte, Heft 2, Berlin: Weidmann, 1905).

[133] I. Opelt, "Epitome," *RAC* V, 961f.

[134] P. Ruben, *Clementis Alexandrini Excerpta ex Theodoto* (Leipzig: Teubner, 1892); H. von Arnim, *De Octavo Clementis Stromateorum Libro* (Rostock: Typis Academicis Adleranis, 1894); A. von Harnack, *Geschichte der altchristlichen Litteratur II/2*, 17.

[135] Th. Zahn, *Supplementum Clementinum* (FGNK 3; Erlangen: Deichert, 1884) 93-103; 119-121.

[136] P. Nautin, "La fin des Stromates et les Hypotyposes de Clément d'Alexandrie," *VC* 30 (1976) 268-302.

(or some other knowledgeable scholar) simply added this superscript to the anti-Valentinian work.

One must thus warn against all too certain conclusions from controversial materials like the title of the *Excerpta*!

### 2.5.2. The Two Schools According to Tertullian

Tertullian and his work against the Valentinians is chronologically the next in line. The North-African makes it even clearer that one should understand the two schools by analogy to philosophical schools, for he joins the two expressions, *duae scholae, duae cathedrae*.[138] In his instructive commentary on this work, Jean-Claude Fredouille has shown that Tertullian applies the terms *schola* and *cathedra* to heretics only in this one place. He uses them elsewhere for the corresponding pagan educational institutions or for the various biblical doctrinal authorities (*cathedra Moysi, apostolorum* etc.). What is meant in our context is not, of course, the prominent throne of the Jewish synagogue or that of the apse of a Christian Church,[139] but a teaching chair and a philosophical school. Of course, the expression "teaching chair" (καθέδρα, also θρόνος) is not to be understood in the sense in which it is used on the base of a statue from Eleusis, Νικαγόρας ... ἐπὶ τῆς καθέδρας σοφιστής, that is, as a fixed teaching chair institutionalized by the state as in the example, ὁ Ἀθήνῃσι τῶν σοφιστῶν θρόνος, that is, one of the four teaching positions set up for the philosophical schools by Marcus Aurelius and funded with 60,000 sesterces.[140] Here there were indeed *duae cathedrae*, the chair for Greek rhetoric in the city of Rome and the Athe-

---

[137] A. Jülicher, "Aretas 9," *PW* (Stuttgart: J. B. Metzler, 1895) II/1:675-677; A. von Harnack, *Die Überlieferung der griechischen Apologeten des zweiten Jahrhunderts in der alten Kirche und im Mittelalter* (TU 1/1; Berlin: Akademie Verlag, 1991 = Leipzig: J. C. Hinrichs, 1882) 36-46; H. G. Beck, *Kirche und theologische Literatur im byzantinischen Reich* (Handbuch der Altertumswissenschaft XII 2/1, München: Beck, 1959) 591-594; O. Stählin, *Untersuchungen über die Scholien zu Clemens Alexandrinus* (Beilage zum Jahresbericht des Nürnberger Gymnasiums, Nürnberg, 1897).

[138] *Val.* 11.2 (SC 280, 104.9-12 Fredouille) *munus enim his datur unum: procurare concinnationem aeonum, et ab eius officii societate duae scholae protinus, duae cathedrae, inauguratio quaedam diuidendae doctrinae valentini*; cf. the commentary on the passage in SC 281, 258f.

[139] B.-J. Diebner, ʹΕΠΙ ΤΗΣ ΜΟΥΣΕΩΣ ΚΑΘΕΔΡΑΣ ʹΕΚΑΘΙΣΑΝ (Mt 23:2): Zur literarischen und monumentalen Überlieferung der sogn. 'Mosekathedra'," O. Feld and U. Peschlow, eds., *Studien zur spätantiken und byzantinischen Kunst II* (Bonn: R. Habelt, 1986) 147-155.

[140] W. Dittenberger, SIG 845 Z. 2f; Philostrat, *Vitae soph.* II.27.618 and 33.628; for Nikagoras (I.) cf. W. Stegemann, "Nikagoras 8," *PW* XVII/1 (1936) 216-218 and for the teaching chairs, H.-I. Marrou, *Geschichte der Erziehung im klassischen Altertum*, 554.

nian chair for the same purpose (with a much lower salary). The exact meaning of the passage in Tertullian now becomes clear. A sharp irony characterizes the use of the expressions. As if the issue were the highest educational goods, rhetoric and philosophy, the Valentinians "play university," to speak anachronistically, and establish two *scholae* with their chairs. Such polemics have a real meaning especially when the "members of the school of Valentinus" distinguished themselves as two schools.

While on the basis of Tertullian and Hippolytus one can make a somewhat plausible case that the Valentinians divided themselves into two schools, the reason given for this division looks rather strange. Can it really be that a comparatively minor difference about the nature of the redeemer's body brings about the split of a school (or let us say more cautiously, a self-differentiation of distinct schools)? This is what Hippolytus at least has us believe, but it seems to me this is not the last word on the matter. For, the separation of "schools" can also have had quite trivial biographic reasons, a possibility suggested by the geographical epithets of both Valentinian schools. It is not surprising that in the passage of time distinct circles of teachers and students differentiated themselves doxographically as well. It is also not surprising that the heresiologists of the early church attempted to derive meaning from such dissociation and to gain from it materials for the propaganda against the Valentinians.

Before confronting in a third and final section the results of this analysis of Valentinian Gnosticism as a "school" with our observations on philosophical schools in Rome there is one thing that must be stressed. Of course, the category "school" does not provide a comprehensive approach to the quite disparate and colorful reality of "Valentinian Gnosticism" (and even less does it allow a comprehensive sociological description of this phenomenon). But it illustrates at least a large number of prosopographical and doxographical reports we possess of this enterprise.

## 3. Conclusion

### Philosophical Schools and the School of Valentinus

First of all, it has become clear at different points how little we know, at least at this point, about the "school of Valentinus." We are at best "on the way toward an anatomy of this school." Nevertheless, it has become clear that this category "school" is not merely an interpretive device of the heresiologists, but part of the self-understanding of (at least) Ptolemy and the group around him, as shown by Irenaeus, the *Letter to Flora*, and other texts of the church fathers. People from the group around Ptolemy called themselves "members of the school of Valentinus" and at the beginning of the third century (at the latest) the Valentinians themselves distinguished themselves as two schools. In addition to these terminological indications of the character of Valentinian Gnosticism as a "school," a number of technical and doctrinal analogies with philosophical schools can be demonstrated with comparatively great certainty. Also the "school of Valentinus" is constituted by a teacher-student relation; it knows a διαδοχή or *successio* of teachers. In view of this personal continuity the doctrinal differences are less weighty. Such phenomena of simultaneous continuity and discontinuity were, as we saw, familiar to Antiquity.[141] The Valentinian school, like its probable pagan paradigms, works with lectures, commentaries and discussions. Important texts of the teachers are interpreted, problems are approached by the method of division (διαίρεσις) and solutions are proposed. How similar the themes were in the different forms of instruction is shown by the famous and well-known series of questions which Clement of Alexandria excerpts from Theodotus.[142] And the community of learning seems to have implied on occasion also a community of life. At any rate, the address of Flora as "sister" is an expression of the same sibling relation which is customary in the Christian community. One should investigate also the extant reports about "sacraments" and cultic actions in Valentinian Gnosticism from this point of view. As we said already at the beginning, it is with good justification that Layton attributes to the movement the "character of a philosophical school." Non-polemical contemporary observers probably saw at least the group's claim in this manner.

One important point of comparison has not yet been developed in this sketch. Should we compare Valentinus, Ptolemy and their students with domestic philosophers, parlor-philosophers (that is, popular philosophers) or professional philosophers? In this conclusion I do not want to return to complaints about the difficulties of giving a truly certain answer here, but I want to be courageous and venture a hypothesis. Could it not be that in Valentinus and the Ptolemy of the letter to Flora we are dealing with quite well educated theologians who attempted to measure up to the qualitative level and sometimes to the style of professional philosophers? We are usually quite sensitive

---

[141] Cf. also the texts cited in Markschies, *Valentinus Gnosticus*, 395f., note 48.

[142] *Exc. Theod.* 78.2 (202 Sagnard; 88.677-679 Casey); on the interpretation, see Markschies, *Valentinus Gnosticus*, 391, note 22 with further literature.

in perceiving the differences between Valentinian Gnosticism and the various philosophical schools and we stress how, for example, Middle-Platonic theologoumena are read and interpreted against their meaning—and this is quite accurate. In his essay mentioned above, however, Winrich Löhr has shown how thoroughly the demi-urge/creator of Ptolemy's letter corresponds to the second god of Numenius. There is probably no one who would want to deny the character of a professional philosopher to the latter, though he was highly idiosyncratic. And at what level Valentinus' level of education is to be pegged has already been discussed many times. My own research is not needed for this judgment. Thus much speaks for supposing that both attempted to orient themselves in their own teaching by the teaching style and qualitative level of professional philosophers—this is quite independent of the question how one judges the success of this intention.[143] And could it not be, further, that the mythologoumena of "members of the school of Valentinus," that is, of the people around Ptolemy, Heracleon, etc., were stories told more on the level of parlor philosophy and no longer arose from independent engagement with professional philosophical literature?[144] The colorful myth may well have had its own philosophical quality, its charm and effect,[145] but it does not, of course, belong to the same level as discourses about the law proceeding by διαίρεσις and poetic essays in cosmology expressed in the form of a hymn. And whether the Valentinian writings from Nag Hammadi are a popular philo-sophical variant of Valentinianism or rather a documentation of its development away from its philosophical origins needs to be investi-gated in its own right. If all of this is correct, one must say that the highly gifted teachers Valentinus and Ptolemy simply did not have the right students, that is—at least in the sense of professional philoso-phy—not sufficiently educated students. And no one, unfortunately, is entirely immune from this misery.

---

[143] In no case would I go as far as considering Ptolemy "one of the most important theologians of the Second and Third Centuries, indeed of the Early Church as a whole" (Löhr at the end of the *TRE* article cited above, note 110).

[144] On the basis of other texts H. W. Attridge reaches a similar conclusion in "What Gnostics Knew," paper for the Conference on Theology, Scientific Knowledge and Society in Antiquity, Center of Theological Inquiry, Princeton, November 16, 1993. I am grateful to Prof. Attridge for making this text available to me.

[145] On the theme "myth and philosophy" (with further bibliography) see C. Mark-schies, "Die Krise einer philosophischen Bibel-Theologie in der Alten Kirche, oder: Valentin und die valentinianische Gnosis zwischen philosophischer Bibelinterpretation und mythologischer Häresie," *Gnosis und Manichäismus*, ed. A. Böhlig and C. Markschies (BZNW 72; Berlin: de Gruyter, 1994) 1-37, here 30-36.

# THE "KINGLESS GENERATION" AND THE POLEMICAL REWRITING OF CERTAIN NAG HAMMADI TEXTS

*Louis Painchaud* and *Timothy Janz*
Université Laval[1]

## SUMMARY

The occurrences of the adjective *ἀβασίλευτος and of the expression *ἡ ἀβασίλευτος γενεά in the Nag Hammadi texts appear often to have polemical connotations and to involve literary problems. This paper seeks to demonstrate that this motif is interpolated in most of these texts; that these interpolations are linked to a revision or to a rewriting of these texts in the context of a controversy between different doctrinal circles; and that they are probably the hallmark of a circle which used rewriting as a means of adapting texts to their specific needs.

*

There is every reason to believe that rewriting was a widespread phenomenon in the production and reception of the texts of the Nag Hammadi collection, as it was in the case of Christian apocrypha such as, for example, the apocryphal acts of the apostles. This is shown by the transformation of the theological treatise entitled *Eugnostos the Blessed* (henceforth *Eugnostos*) into a dialogue between the risen Saviour and his disciples, the *Sophia of Jesus Christ* (henceforth *Soph. Jes. Chr.*)[2] (two copies each of the original and of the rewritten version have come down to us), as well as by the

---

[1] Louis Painchaud is Professor at the Collège de Sainte-Foy and Associate Professor at the Université Laval (Québec). Timothy Janz is lecturer at the Université Laval and student at the Université de Paris IV. This paper was produced thanks in part to a research grant from the Social Sciences and Humanities Research Council of Canada and the Fonds pour la Formation de Chercheurs et l'Aide à la Recherche du Québec.

[2] See M. Krause, "Das literarische Verhältnis des Eugnostosbriefes zur Sophia Jesu Christi," *Mullus, Festschrift Theodor Klauser* (JAC 1; Münster/Westfalen: Aschendorffsche Verlagsbuchhandlung, 1964) 215-223; C. Barry, "Un exemple de réécriture à Nag Hammadi, la Sagesse de Jésus Christ," *Les textes de Nag Hammadi et le problème de leur classification. Actes du colloque tenu à Québec du 21 au 25 septembre 1993*, ed. L. Painchaud and A. Pasquier (BCNH, section "Études" 3; Québec: Presses de l'Univeristé Laval; Leuven-Paris: Peeters, 1995) 151-168.

extant versions of the *Apocryphon of John*.[3] It can also be demonstrated by a comparison between the letter quoted by Epiphanius in
his description of the Valentinians, and the treatise *Eugnostos the
Blessed*, which seems to have been the source of this letter.[4]

It seems unlikely that this phenomenon was restricted to those texts
of which two or more versions have come down to us; rather, we must
assume that an unspecified number of those of which we possess only
one version were also the object of revisions or of more or less radical
rewritings. This seems the more likely in light of the many literary
problems raised by the ancient Gnostic texts; in fact, few of them
have not seen their redactional homogeneity called into question.[5]
However, for those texts which are attested by only one witness,
internal evidence is our only resource for attempting to discover the
transformations they may have undergone and for reconstructing their
trajectory and the reception they may have encountered in the different circles where they were read.

In this paper, we propose to explore the phenomenon of rewriting
as a means used in antiquity for the reception and the production of

---

[3] See M. Krause and P. Labib, *Die drei Versionen des Apokryphon des Johannes im
Koptischen Museum zu Alt-Kairo* (Abhandlungen des Deutschen Archäologischen
Instituts Kairo, Koptische Reihe 1; Wiesbaden: Harassowitz, 1962) 37; A. Kragerud,
"Apocryphon Johannis: En Formanalyse," *Norsk Teologisk Tidsskrift* 66 (1965) 15-38;
B. A. Pearson, "Apocryphon Johannis Revisited," *Apocryphon Severini (Mélanges
Giversen)*, ed. P. Bilde, K. Nielsen, J. P. Sørensen (Aarhus: Aarhus University Press,
1993) 155-165; and especially S. Giversen, *Apocryphon Johannis* (Acta Theologica
Danica 5; Copenhagen: Munksgaard, 1963) 276-282.

[4] The text of this letter is quoted by Epiphanius, *Haer.* 31.5.1-8; see M. Tardieu,
*Écrits gnostiques. Codex de Berlin* (Sources gnostiques et manichéennes 1; Paris: Cerf,
1984) 60. Also worth mentioning are some cases of different recensions, if not actual
rewritings, of the same text: for example, the Greek fragments of the Gospel of Thomas
display several marked differences with the Coptic version of the same text in Nag
Hammadi Codex II (see M. Marcovich, "Textual Criticism on the Gospel of Thomas,"
*JTS* 20 [1969] 53-74). Also very different are the two recensions of *Eugnostos* in Nag
Hammadi Codices III and V (see D. M. Parrott, *Nag Hammadi Codices III,3-4 and V,1*
[NHS 27; Leiden: E. J. Brill, 1991] 16-18); the differences between the two versions of
the Untitled Writing, one from Nag Hammadi and the other from the London fragments,
are less marked (see C. Oeyen, "Fragmente einer subachmimischen Version der
gnostischen Schrift ohne Titel," in *Essays on the Nag Hammadi Texts in Honor of Pahor
Labib*, ed. M. Krause [NHS 6; Leiden: E. J. Brill, 1975] 125-144; *Nag Hammadi Codex
II,2-7*, 2 vols., ed. B, Layton [NHS 21; Leiden: E. J. Brill, 1989] 2:96-99; W.-P. Funk,
"Les fragments Brit. Lib. Or. 4926 (1)," in L. Painchaud *L'Écrit sans titre. Traité sur
l'origine du monde* [BCNH, section "Textes" 21; Québec: Presses de l'Université Laval;
Leuven-Paris: Peeters, 1995] 529-570).

[5] See L. Painchaud, "La classification des textes de Nag Hammadi et le phénomène
des réécritures," *Les textes de Nag Hammadi et le problème de leur classification*, ed. L.
Painchaud and A. Pasquier (BCNH, section "Études" 3; Québec: Presses de l'Université
Laval; Leuven-Paris: Peeters, 1995) 51-86.

texts, beginning our observations with the occurrence of the adjective *ἀβασίλευτος or of the expression *ἡ ἀβασίλευτος γενεά in certain Nag Hammadi texts. As we progress through the *Tripartite Tractate* (*Tri. Trac.*), the "Untitled Writing" *On the Origin of the World* (*Orig. World*), *Eugnostos the Blessed*, the *Sophia of Jesus Christ*, the *Apocalypse of Adam* (*Apoc. Adam* ) and the *Hypostasis of the Archons* (*Hyp. Arch*), we shall attempt to demonstrate: 1) that there was a controversy between different doctrinal circles linked with the use of this term; 2) that redactional interventions in certain Nag Hammadi texts are linked to this controversy; and 3) that this expression was probably the hallmark of a specific circle which used rewriting as a means of receiving certain texts. Inasmuch as this phenomenon bears witness to the conditional reception of texts by a group or groups foreign to their original milieu, it will perhaps shed some light on the particularly obscure question of the mutual relationships which were shared by different or rival Gnostic groups.

## I. THE ADJECTIVE ἀβασίλευτος IN DIRECT AND INDIRECT SOURCES

### A. Corpus

The use of the Greek adjective ἀβασίλευτος in the context which interests us here is directly attested only in Hippolytus' description of the Naassenes[6] and in the anonymous writing of the Bruce Codex.[7] As for the other Coptic sources, they must be interpreted carefully, since Coptic did not possess an exact equivalent of this Greek adjective; however, the retroversion can be considered almost certain in cases where the word seems to be used in the same way as in Hippolytus. In the Nag Hammadi texts, we find two occurrences of the Coptic adjective ⲁⲧⲣ̅ⲣⲟ which belong to this category: one in *Tri. Trac.* (100.7-9: *Οὐδεὶς ἄναρχος, οὐδεὶς ἀβασίλευτος); and one in *Orig. World* (125.1-2: * Ἐποίησε ... καὶ ἄλλους πολλοὺς ἀβασιλεύτους). As for the expression "kingless generation," it is to be found in two other passages, one in *Hyp. Arch* (97.4-5: * Τὸ δοθὲν αὐτῷ ὑπὸ τῆς ἀβασιλεύτου γενεάς) and one in *Apoc. Adam* (82.19-21: * Ἡ δὲ ἀβασίλευτος γενεὰ εἶπεν ...).[8]

---

[6] Hippolytus, *Ref.* V.8.2.30, uses the adjective once and the expression ἡ ἀβασίλευτος γενεά once.

[7] C. Schmidt and V. MacDermot, *The Books of Jeu and the Untitled Text in the Bruce Codex* (NHS 13; Leiden: E. J. Brill, 1978.

[8] Here are the Coptic texts of these passages: Tri. Trac. 100.7-9: ⲁⲩⲱ ⲙ̅ⲛ̅ⲗⲁⲩⲉ ⲉϥⲟⲉⲓ ⲛ̅ⲁⲧⲟⲩⲉϩ ⲥⲁϩⲛⲉ ⲁⲩⲱ ⲙ̅ⲛ̅ⲗⲁⲩⲉ ⲉϥⲟⲉⲓ ⲛ̅ⲁⲧⲧⲣ̅ⲣⲟ (Thomassen and

Moreover, we also find in *Orig. World* a reference to a "kingless race" (< * τὸ δὲ τέταρτον γένος ἀβασίλευτόν ἐστιν),[9] as well as one to an abstraction which might be translated "kinglessness" (p. 127.14: ⲙⲚⲧⲁⲧⲢⲢⲟ, perhaps < *ἀβασιλεία, although this word does not seem to be attested elsewhere in Greek).

The most difficult passages to interpret are the appearances of this motif in *Eugnostos*, which Codices III and V preserve in two different recensions (*Eugnostos* V and *Eugnostos* III), and in *Soph. Jes. Chr.*, which is a rewriting of *Eugnostos* and is also extant in two versions, one in Codex III, and one in Berlin Codex 8502 (*Soph. Jes. Chr.* III and *Soph. Jes. Chr.* BG). There are three passages in this group which are of interest here: the first two are common to *Eugnostos* and *Soph. Jes. Chr.*, while the last appears only in the conclusion of *Soph. Jes. Chr.* In only one of these passages do all the witnesses agree, namely *Eugnostos* III 85.15-16 = *Eugnostos* V 13.15-16 = *Soph. Jes. Chr.* BG 108.12-14 (*Soph. Jes. Chr.* III has a lacuna here), which speaks of a kingless aeon, (probably < *ἀβασίλευτος αἰών).[10] In the other passage, which is common to *Eugnostos* and *Soph. Jes. Chr.* (*Eugnostos* III 75.16-23; *Eugnostos* V 5.3-9; *Soph. Jes. Chr.* III 99.17-100.2; *Soph. Jes. Chr.* BG 92.4-13), and which seems to contain two references to our concept, the witnesses disagree; a retroversion will allow us to clearly identify the disagreements, which tend to be exaggerated by the different Coptic translations:[11]

---

Painchaud). *Orig. World* 125.1-2: ⲁϥⲧⲁⲙⲓⲟ (...) ⲁⲩⲱ ⲖⲚⲕⲟⲟⲩⲉ ⲉⲛⲁϣⲱⲟⲩ ⲉⲅⲟ ⲚⲁⲧⲢⲢⲟ (Painchaud). *Hyp. Arch* 97.4-5: Ⲛⲧⲁⲩⲧⲁⲁϥ ⲛⲁϥ ⲉⲃⲟⲗ ⲍⲚ ⲧⲧⲉⲛⲉⲁ ⲧⲉⲧⲘⲙⲚⲧⲉⲥ Ⲣⲣⲟ (Barc). *Apoc. Adam* 82.19-21: †ⲧⲉⲛⲉⲁ ⲇⲉ ⲚⲛⲁⲧⲢ Ⲣⲣⲟ ⲉⲍⲣⲁⲓ ... ⲉⲭⲱⲥ ⲭⲱ Ⲙⲙⲟⲥ ⲭⲉ (...) (Morard).

[9] *Orig. World* 125.2-3: ⲡⲙⲁⲍϥⲧⲟⲟⲩ ⲇⲉ Ⲛⲅⲉⲛⲟⲥ ⲟⲩⲁⲧⲢⲢⲟ ⲡⲉ (Painchaud).

[10] *Eugnostos* III 85.15-16 ⲡⲉⲧⲉⲙⲁⲍⲧⲉ Ⲛⲛⲁⲓ... ⲡⲁⲓⲱⲛ ⲡⲉⲧⲉ ⲙⲚⲙⲚⲧⲢⲢⲟ ⲍⲓⲭⲱϥ (Parrott); *Eugnostos* V 13.15-16 ⲡⲓⲏ ⲇⲉ ⲉⲧⲁⲙⲁⲍⲧⲉ Ⲛⲛⲁⲓ... ⲡⲉ ⲡⲓⲉⲱⲛ [Ⲛⲛ]ⲁⲧⲢⲢⲢⲟ ⲉⲍⲣⲁⲓ... ⲉⲭⲱϥ (Pasquier); *Soph. Jes. Chr.* BG 108.12-14 ⲡⲉⲧⲁⲙⲁⲍⲧⲉ Ⲛⲛⲁⲓ... ⲡⲓⲁⲓⲱⲛ ⲡⲉ ⲉⲧⲉ ⲙⲚ ⲙⲚⲧⲢⲢⲟ ⲍⲓⲭⲱϥ (Barry). Probable retroversion: ὁ δὲ τούτους περιέχων (or: τούτων κρατῶν) ἐστὶν ὁ ἀβασίλευτος αἰών.

[11] We shall simply give here the Coptic texts from Codex III: *Eugnostos* III 75.16-23: ⲉϣⲁⲩⲙⲟⲩⲧⲉ ⲉⲣⲟⲟⲩ ⲭⲉ ⲧⲧⲉⲛⲉⲁ ⲉⲧⲉ ⲙⲚⲙⲚⲧⲢⲢⲟ ⲍⲓⲭⲱⲥ Ⲛⲍⲣⲁⲓ... ⲍⲚⲙⲙⲚⲧⲢⲢⲁⲓ... ⲉⲧⲕⲏ ⲉⲍⲣⲁⲓ... ⲡⲓⲙⲉⲉⲩⲉ ⲇⲉ ⲧⲏⲣϥ Ⲙⲡⲓⲙⲁ ⲉⲧⲉ ⲙⲚⲙⲚⲧⲢⲢⲟ ⲍⲓⲭⲱϥ ϣⲁⲩⲭⲟⲟⲥ ⲉⲣⲟⲟⲩ ⲭⲉ Ⲛϣⲏⲣⲉ Ⲛⲡⲁⲅⲉⲛⲛⲏⲧⲟⲥ Ⲛⲉⲓⲱⲧ (Parrott). Note that the text of *Eugnostos* V is very fragmentary here and that the retroversion is therefore based on reconstructions; we have followed those of A. Pasquier (forthcoming in the BCNH collection). *Soph. Jes. Chr.* III 99.17-100.2: ⲉϣⲁⲩⲙⲟⲩⲧⲉ ⲉⲡⲉⲩⲅⲉⲛⲟⲥ ⲭⲉ ⲧⲧⲉⲛⲉⲁ ⲉⲧⲉ ⲙⲚⲙⲚⲧⲢⲢⲟ ⲍⲓⲭⲱⲥ (ⲉⲃⲟⲗ ⲍⲘ ⲡⲉⲛⲧⲁⲧⲉⲧⲚⲟⲩⲱⲛⲍ Ⲛⲍⲏⲧϥ ⲍⲱⲧ·ⲧⲏⲟⲩⲧⲚ ⲉⲃⲟⲗ ⲍⲚⲛⲓⲣⲱⲙⲉ ⲉⲧⲙⲙⲁⲩ ⲡⲙⲏⲛϣⲉ ⲇⲉ ⲧⲏⲣϥ ⲉⲧⲙⲙⲁⲩ ⲉⲧⲉ ⲙⲚⲙⲚⲧⲢⲢⲟ ⲍⲓⲭⲱⲟⲩ ϣⲁⲩⲙⲟⲩⲧⲉ ⲉⲣⲟⲟⲩ ⲭⲉ ⲛϣⲏⲣⲉ Ⲙⲡⲁⲅⲉⲛⲛ]ⲏⲧⲟⲥ Ⲛⲉⲓⲱⲧ (Barry).

| Eugnostos III 75.16-23 | Eugnostos V 5.3-9 | Soph. Jes. Chr. III 99.17-100.2 | Soph. Jes. Chr. BG 92.4-13 |
|---|---|---|---|
| οἳ καλοῦνται | οἳ καλοῦνται | ὦν καλεῖται τὸ γένος | οὖ καλεῖται τὸ γένος |
| γενεά ἐφ᾽ ἧς οὔκ ἐστι βασιλεία ἐκ τῶν οὐσῶν βασιλειῶν. | γενεά ἐφ᾽ ἧς οὔκ ἐστι βασιλεία ἐκ τῶν οὐσῶν βασιλειῶν. | γενεά ἐφ᾽ ἧς οὔκ ἐστι βασιλεία, | γενεά ἐφ᾽ ἧς οὔκ ἐστι βασιλεία, |
| | | ἐν ᾧ δὲ ἐφανερώθητε ὑμεῖς ἐκ τούτων τῶν ἀνθρώπων. | ἐν ᾧ δὲ ἐφανερώθητε ὑμεῖς. Ἐκ δὲ τούτων τῶν ἀνθρώπων |
| Πᾶν δὲ τὸ πλῆθος τοῦ τόπου τοῦ ἀβασιλεύτου καλεῖται υἱοὶ τοῦ ἀγεννήτου πατρός | Πᾶν δὲ τὸ πλῆθος τούτων τῶν ἀβασιλεύτων καλεῖται υἱοὶ τοῦ ἀγεννήτου καὶ αὐτοφυοῦς | Πᾶν δὲ τὸ πλῆθος τοῦτο τὸ ἀβασίλευτον καλοῦνται υἱοὶ τοῦ ἀγεννήτου πατρός | τοῦ τόπου τοῦ ἀβασιλεύτου καλοῦνται ἀγέννητος |

The first occurrence in this passage does not seem to involve the adjective ἀβασίλευτος itself, but rather a paraphrase, which nevertheless parallels the expression used by Hippolytus, namely "the kingless generation." In addition, *Soph. Jes. Chr.* mentions a kingless "race," which parallels the vocabulary of *Orig. World*. At the end of the passage, we read of a "kingless place" (*Eugnostos* III et *Soph. Jes. Chr.* BG), or of a "kingless multitude" (*Soph. Jes. Chr.* III), or, finally, of the "multitude of these kingless ones" (*Eugnostos* V). It is difficult to distinguish here between scribal errors and deliberate changes. At any rate, all the themes which are to be found here in the context of kinglessness are repeated elsewhere in our corpus: we will come back later to the "multitude;" as for the "place," it reappears in the Berlin Codex version of the end of *Soph. Jes. Chr.* (*Soph. Jes. Chr.* BG p. 124; *Soph. Jes. Chr.* III p. 118), associated now not only with kinglessness, but also with the themes of "wealth" and of "rest." In this passage, the risen Christ says that the revelation he has just given to his disciples aims to transmit to all a portion of the goodness of the Great Invisible Spirit, as well as of "the kingless wealth of his resting place," according to *Soph. Jes. Chr.* BG (according to *Soph. Jes. Chr.* III, the "wealth of the kingless repose").[12]

## B. An Unusual Use

The uses of the adjective ἀβασίλευτος which we have surveyed here differ not only as to the realities which are thus qualified, but also as to the function of the motif in each of the texts. Whatever the meaning of this diversity, these texts attest to a specialized use of the motif which goes beyond the literal and figurative uses of the term ἀβασίλευτος in Greek literature which have been presented by F. T. Fallon,[13] in that it is here used exclusively to characterize realities belonging to the upper world or to an historical group which itself belongs to the upper world. Only one of our texts seems to use the word in a straightforward, non-specialized way, namely *Tri. Trac.*, a survey of Valentinian theology. It is found there in a passage which describes the hierarchical relationships which govern the world of the archons (100.3-14):[14]

> Each one of the archons with his race and his perquisites to which his lot has claim, just as they appeared, each was on guard, since they have been en-
> trusted with the organization (οἰκονομία). And none lacks a command
> (ⲚⲀⲦⲞⲨⲈϨⲤⲀϨⲚⲈ), and none is kingless (ⲚⲀⲦⲦⲢⲢⲞ < *ἀβασίλευτος):
> from [the e]nds of the heavens to the ends of the [earth] and to the inhabited
> regions of the [earth] and to the regions beneath the earth, there [are] kings
> and lords and those whom they command... (transl. Attridge and Mueller,
> modified).

The meaning of this passage is clear: among the archons, there are kings and lords and those whom they command; but those who command and those who obey are not two distinct groups: on the contrary, all of them are at the same time subject to those over them

---

[12] To this corpus from Nag Hammadi must be added, for the sake of completeness, two further occurrences, in the extant Coptic literature, either of ἀβασίλευτος or of a Coptic equivalent. The first is in a Gnostic text, an anonymous treatise of the Bruce Codex, 249.22 Schmidt (see C. Schmidt and V. MacDermot, *The Books of Jeu and the Untitled Text in the Bruce Codex*), where ἀβασίλευτος, appearing in its Greek form, is an attribute of a heavenly aeon also called Jerusalem, Incorruptibility, New Land, etc. As for the Coptic equivalent (ⲀⲦⲢⲢⲞ), we find it in a speech by Shenoute which seems to attack adversaries who claimed to be "kingless:" Ⲏ ⲈⲨⲚⲀϪⲞⲞⲤ ϨⲈⲚⲚⲈⲒ ⲚⲚⲒⲢⲰⲘⲈ ⲈⲦϪⲎⲔ ⲈⲂⲞⲖ ⲚⲔⲢⲞϤ ⲚⲒⲘ ϨⲒⲔⲀⲔⲒⲀ ⲚⲒⲘ ϪⲈ ⲚⲈϨⲈⲚⲀⲦⲢⲢⲞ ⲚⲈ Leipoldt 88, 20 (*Sinuthii Archimandritae Vita et Opera Omnia III*, ed. J. Leipoldt (CSCO 42, Scriptores coptici, 2; Louvain: Secrétariat du Corpus SCO, 1955).

[13] F. Fallon, "The Gnostics: the Undominated Race" *NovT* 21 (1979) 271-288.

[14] Ibid., 168-169.

and commanders of those under them. The phrase "no one is without command and no one is kingless" expresses this idea in a negative way.[15]

Thus, the Valentinian author uses the adjective ἀβασίλευτος simply to express the idea of lack of submission or of domination: to be ἀβασίλευτος means, for him, not to be submitted to a superior power or authority. This is an unremarkable metaphorical use of the adjective ἀβασίλευτος, which reminds us of the opinion of Artemidorus of Ephesus, who, in the second century, writes in a treatise on the interpretation of dreams that no nation lacks a god (ἄθεος) or a king (ἀβασίλευτος).[16] Here, the Valentinian author takes up this metaphorical use of the term and uses it negatively to describe the relationships among the archons.

It is important that this occurrence of ἀβασίλευτος is the only one which is found in a Valentinian text, for reasons which we shall see presently. It is also worth noting that this passage was not mentioned by the two scholars who have thus far studied the use of the adjective in these texts, Francis T. Fallon and Roland Bergmeier,[17] although it corresponds well to the metaphorical meaning of the word which Fallon identified in Greek literature and proposed to translate "undominated."[18] The importance of the Valentinian context of this occurrence is due to the fact that, by denying the possibility of the archontic powers being ἀβασίλευτος,[19] the *Tri. Trac.* implicitly

---

[15] A little earlier in the text, the same idea is expressed (99.23-100.2): "He (the Logos) gave to each one the appropriate rank, and it was ordered that each one be a ruler over a place and an activity. He yields to the place of the one more exalted than himself, in order to command the other places in an activity which is in the allotted activity which falls to him to have control over because of his mode of being. As a result, there are commanders and subordinates in positions of domination and subjection among the angels and archangels, while the activities are of various types and are different" (transl. Attridge and Mueller). Although this passage involves some syntactic problems, the general meaning seems to be that in order to satisfy the desire for power which is present both in the powers of the right and in those of the left, the Logos permitted both to exercise authority in order to prevent conflicts between them and the power which is superior to them.

[16] Οὐδὲν γὰρ ἔθνος ἀνθρώπων ἄθεον ὥσπερ οὐδὲ ἀβασίλευτον (R. A. Pack, *Artemidori Daldiani Onirocriticon Libri V* [Bibliotheca Scriptorum Graecorum et Romanorum Teubneriana; Leipzig: Teubner, 1963] 17.1.8). On the use of the adjective ἀβασίλευτος in Greek literature, see Fallon's article referred to in note 13.

[17] While Fallon (see note 13) is especially interested in the function of this motif as an expression of Gnostic disenchantment with the world, Bergmeier ("'Königlosigkeit' als nachvalentinianisches Heilsprädikat," *NovT* 24 [1982] 316-339) tries to demonstrate that the use of this motif presupposes a post-valentinian doctrinal context.

[18] See F. T. Fallon, art. cit., 276.

[19] With the exception of the demiurge or archon of the oikonomia (τὸν τῆς οἰκονομίας ... ἄρχοντα, *Excerpts from Theodotus* 33.3), "to whom no one gives orders,

reserves this qualification for those beings which escape their domin-
ion, namely the pleromatic world itself, which is beyond the archontic
spheres. In so doing, it opens the way for the specialized use of the
term which we find in the other texts.

## C. Eschatological, Non-Polemical Use

Among the non-Valentinian texts which attest the use of the term
ἀβασίλευτος, we may distinguish two categories: those which place
the things thus designated within the realm of history and use the
motif in a clearly polemical way, and those which place it outside of
history. Within this last group, we may note particularly the group
comprising *Eugnostos* and *Soph. Jes. Chr.*, where a "kingless
generation," a "kingless place," and a "kingless aeon" are part of a
description of the pleromatic spheres. Now, contrary to the archontic
realm mentioned by *Tri. Trac.*, the pleromatic realm and its description have direct implications for eschatology. Thus we shall not be
surprised to encounter this motif again in an eschatological context in
the conclusion of *Soph. Jes. Chr.*, where it occurs among the reasons
given for the Savior's revelation of the main contents of the treatise:

> (...) in order that all might take from his goodness and from the wealth over
> which no kingdom rules, (that) of their resting place (*Soph. Jes. Chr.* BG
> 125.6-10 = *Soph. Jes. Chr.* III 118.12-15).

The motif of kinglessness appears again in an eschatological context
in the conclusion to *Hyp. Arch*, where the angel Eleleth announces to
Norea:

> "When the Tr[ue] Man [rev]eals, within a modelled form, [the Spirit of]
> Truth which the Father has sent, then he will teach them about [every]thing
> and he will anoint them with the unction of life eternal, which was given
> him by the kingless generation (...)" (96.33-97.4).

Leaving aside the interpretation of these rather difficult passages, let
us simply note here that the insertion of the kinglessness motif into the
pleromatic world—and as a consequence into an eschatological
framework—profoundly changes its function. However, it is in
another text, Hippolytus' description of the Naassenes, that the
implications of this change become clear, especially for the role which

---

since he is the lord of them all" (100.19-21) and who holds the title of "king" (ⲢⲢⲞ <
*βασιλεύς, *Tri. Trac.* 100.29), among others.

the notion of kinglessness is to play in the identity of the group which uses it.

Here is the first passage where we find the expression ἡ ἀβασίλευτος γενεά[20] in Hippolytus:

> They say, "He who affirms that everything is made up of a single element errs; he who affirms that everything is made up of three elements tells the truth and will explain the universe. For one of them, as he says, is the blessed nature of the blessed man of above, Adamas; another one is the mortal nature of below; and the third one is the kingless generation (ἡ ἀβασίλευτος γενεά) which is born of above, of the place, as he says, where are Miriam who is sought after, Iothor (Jethro) the great sage, Sepphora the seer, and Moses, who has no birth in Egypt, since his children were born in Midian.

These "Naassenes," then, according to Hippolytus' source, use a tripartite system including 1) the blessed nature of the Man of Above, Adamas; 2) an intermediate nature, born of above, the kingless generation (ἡ ἀβασίλευτος γενεά), and 3) a mortal nature here below. This "kingless generation" included major Old Testament figures such as Miriam "who is sought after," Jethro "the great Sage," and Moses "who has no birth in Egypt." Although the text does not say so explicitly, it seems very likely that the author quoted by Hippolytus identified himself and the group he belonged to with this "kingless generation," whether in its historical reality or in an eschatological perspective, since another passage which Hippolytus seems to have borrowed from the same source affirms that kinglessness was linked to the attainment of eschatological salvation by the perfect Gnostics, with whom the author must have identified both himself and his readers:[21]

---

[20] Hippolytus, *Ref.* V.8.1: λέγουσι δέ· ὁ λέγων τὰ πάντα ἐξ ἑνὸς συνεστάναι πλανᾶται, ὁ λέγων ἐκ τριῶν ἀληθεύει καὶ περὶ τῶν ὅλων τὴν ἀπόδειξιν δώσει. μία γάρ ἐστι, φησίν, ἡ μακαρία φύσις τοῦ μακαρίου ἀνθρώπου τοῦ ἄνω, τοῦ Ἀδάμαντος· μία δὲ ἡ θνητὴ κάτω· μία δὲ ἡ ἀβασίλευτος γενεὰ ἡ ἄνω γενομένη, ὅπου, φησίν, ἐστὶ Μαριὰμ ἡ ζητουμένη καὶ Ἰοθὼρ ὁ μέγας σοφὸς καὶ Σεπφώρα ἡ βλέπουσα καὶ Μωσῆς, οὗ γένεσις οὐκ ἔστιν ἐν Αἰγύπτῳ· γεγόνασι γὰρ αὐτῷ παῖδες ἐν Μαδιάμ (P. Wendland, *Hippolytus Werke*, vol. 3: *Refutatio omnium haeresium* [GCS 26; Leipzig: Teubner, 1916]).

[21] Hippolytus, *Ref.* V.8.28: οὐδεὶς τούτων τῶν μυστηρίων ἀκροάτης γέγονεν εἰ μὴ μόνοι οἱ γνωστικοὶ τέλειοι. αὕτη, φησίν, ἐστὶν ἡ καλὴ καὶ ἀγαθή, ἣν λέγει Μωϋσῆς· "εἰσάξω ὑμᾶς εἰς γῆν καλὴν καὶ ἀγαθήν, εἰς γῆν ῥέουσαν γάλα καὶ μέλι." τοῦτο, φησίν, ἐστὶ τὸ μέλι καὶ τὸ γάλα, οὗ γευσαμένους τοὺς τελείους ἀβασιλεύτους γενέσθαι καὶ μετασχεῖν τοῦ πληρώματος (Wendland).

> ... no one has heard these mysteries except the *perfect Gnostics*. This, says he, is the beautiful and good land of which Moses says, "I shall lead you into a beautiful and good land, a land flowing with milk and honey." It is by tasting this milk and this honey, says he, that *the perfect Gnostics become kingless* and partake of the pleroma.

We may conclude from what we have seen thus far that in the "Naassene" source quoted by Hippolytus toward the end of the third century,[22] the motif of the "kingless generation" appears, so to speak, at the junction between the theme of history and that of eschatology, at the heart of the identity discourse of the circle which produced it. We may also conclude from this indirect witness that the kingless generation has its place within a tripartite system in which it occupies the intermediate position, and that this theme does not seem to have a polemical function. However, it is possible that the polemical connotation which this theme will acquire in another context is already latent here, since the "mysterious race of the Perfect Ones," which we can identify with the perfect Gnostics of the preceding passage and who seek the eschatological state of kinglessness, is implicitly opposed to other races. Nevertheless, this opposition seems to be aimed at preceding generations and not at contemporaries:

> For, says he, all things were made through him and nothing was made without him; and what was made by him is life [Jn 1:3-4]. This life, he adds, is the mysterious race of Perfect Humans, which was unknown to previous generations.[23]

## D. Polemical and Historical Use

In the *Apocalypse of Adam*, on the contrary, the polemical tone surrounding the motif of kinglessness is clear. Here, the "kingless generation" (82.19-21) is opposed to thirteen kingdoms to whom the treatise attributes erroneous opinions concerning the nature and the origin of the Saviour. However, as F. Morard has shown convincingly,[24] while the text attributes to the twelve first kingdoms de-

---

[22] We assume the authenticity of the Elenchos, in spite of Pierre Nautin's arguments in *Hippolyte et Josipe. Contribution à l'histoire de la littérature chrétienne du troisième siècle* (Paris: Cerf, 1947).

[23] Hippolytus, *Ref.* V.8.28: πάντα γάρ, φησί, δι' αὐτὸν ἐγένετο καὶ χωρὶς αὐτοῦ ἐγένετο οὐδὲ ἕν. ὃ δὲ γέγονεν ἐν αὐτῷ ζωή ἐστιν. αὕτη, φησίν, ἐστὶν ἡ ζωὴ ἡ ἄρρητος γενεὰ τῶν τελείων ἀνθρώπων, ἣ ταῖς προτέραις γενεαῖς οὐκ ἐγνώσθη.

[24] F. Morard, *L'Apocalypse d'Adam* (BCNH, section "Textes" 15; Québec: Presses de l'Université Laval, 1985) 112.

scended from Ham and Japheth opinions which combine Jewish and Biblical traditions, as well as pagan, Greek and oriental ones, the thirteenth kingdom distinguishes itself from these in that its opinions seem rather to evoke Christianity. Thus it is in opposition to these thirteen kingdoms, and perhaps particularly to the thirteenth,[25] that the treatise mentions the kingless generation (ϯⲅⲉⲛⲉⲁ ⲛ̄ⲛⲁⲧⲣ̄ⲣⲟ ⲉⲍⲣⲁⲓ̈ ... ⲉⲭⲱⲥ < *ἡ ἀβασίλευτος γενεά 82.19-20) which alone possesses true knowledge (ⲟⲩⲅⲛⲱⲥⲓⲥ ⲛ̄[ⲧ]ⲉ ⲧⲙⲉ < *γνῶσις τῆς ἀληθείας).

> But the generation without a king over it (ϯⲅⲉⲛⲉⲁ ⲛ̄ⲛⲁⲧⲣ̄ⲣⲟ ⲉⲍⲣⲁⲓ̈ ... ⲉⲭⲱⲥ) says, "He caused knowledge of the undefiled one of truth to come to be [in] him." <It> said, "[Out of] a foreign air, [from a] great aeon, [the great] illuminator came forth. [And he made] the generation of those men whom he had chosen for himself shine, so that they could shine upon the whole aeon. Then the seed, those who will receive his name upon the water and (that) of them all, will fight against the power. And a cloud of darkness will come upon them. Then the peoples will cry out with a great voice, saying, 'Blessed is the soul of those men because they have known God with a knowledge of the truth! They shall live forever, because they have not been corrupted by their desire, along with the angels, nor have they accomplished the works of the powers, but they have stood in his presence in a knowledge of God like light that has come forth from fire and blood. But we have done every deed of the powers senselessly. We have boasted in the transgression of [all] our works. We have [cried] against [the God] of [truth] because all his works [ ... ] is eternal. These are against our spirits. For now we have known that our souls will die the death'" (82.19-84.3, transl. G. MacRae, modified)

Here the expression "kingless generation" designates neither heavenly entities, nor an eschatological status which is sought after, but a given historical group which claims, like the "Naassenes" of Hippolytus, to be in sole possession of true knowledge and uses this expression to affirm its superiority over a group or groups holding differing opinions.

In *Orig. World*, it is a "kingless race" rather than a "generation" whose superiority over other groups is asserted (124.33-125.7):[26]

> Then the Saviour created [ ... ] of them all, and the spirits (ⲙ̄ⲡⲛ̄ⲁ <*τὰ πνεύματα) of these [ ... e]lect, being blessed (< μακάριοι) and varying in

---

[25] It is to be expected that the adversary be mentioned last, after a series of heretical opinions and immediately preceding a statement of the true doctrine. Besides this, according to *Apoc. Adam* 73.25-27, there are twelve kingdoms, while the litany adds a thirteenth. It is possible that this thirteenth kingdom was added especially for the purposes of the author of *Apoc. Adam* or of a final redactor.

[26] See L. Painchaud, *L'Écrit sans titre*.

election (< ἐκλογή), and many other beings, which are kingless and are superior to everyone that was before them. Consequently, four races (< γένος) exist. There are three that belong to the kings of the eighth heaven. But the fourth race (< γένος) is kingless (ογατῆρο < *ἀβασίλευτος) and perfect (< τέλος), being the highest of all.

This passage tells us that, for the author of this document, there is a superior γένος, which escapes the domination of the kings of the Ogdoad, that is, of the archons, and is said to be numerous and kingless (ἀβασίλευτον). This is a fourth γένος, as opposed to three other γένη which are no doubt the Pneumatics, the Psychics and the Hylics (or, to use the terminology of *Orig. World*, the Earthly Ones [< χοϊκοί) who are in submission to the archons.[27]

## II. LITERARY PROBLEMS ASSOCIATED WITH THE OCCURRENCES OF THE ADJECTIVE *ΑΒΑΣΙΛΕΥΤΟΣ* IN THE NAG HAMMADI TEXTS

Almost all the treatises where the adjective ἀβασίλευτος appears present numerous literary problems which could be the result of more or less far-reaching textual rearrangements, if not of an actual rewriting such as is clearly attested in the case of *Eugnostos* and *Soph. Jes. Chr.* The only exception seems to be *Tri. Trac.*, which in any case occupies an exceptional position in our corpus. Furthermore, these problems seem to be particularly concentrated in contexts where we meet the adjective ἀβασίλευτος. We shall leave aside for now the *Apoc. Adam* and *Hyp. Arch*, which involve especially difficult literary problems,[28] in order to concentrate on *Orig. World*, *Eugnostos*, and *Soph. Jes. Chr.*

---

[27] On this passage, Fallon writes as follows: "By introducing a fourth category above and beyond that of the pneumatics, who would normally be considered the gnostics, the author is moving in the direction of Manichaeism, which also distinguished two grades within its gnostic community: the "elect" as the more perfect and then the catechumens or hearers." ("The Undominated Race," 285). But the *Orig. World* does not introduce two distinct categories among Gnostics: it opposes a fourth category to all others and thus reduces the pneumatics to the same status as the psychics and even the hylics. It is true that a fourth race is mentioned in the *Kephalaia*, but there it has a negative connotation and means a foreign group within the Church of Mani (1 *Kephalaia* 354.7; 360.12, and 362. 4).

[28] Most commentators of *Apoc. Adam*, with the exception of F. Morard (see note 24), distinguish at least two sources; in general, the litany of the thirteen kingdoms, including the "kingless generation" which is annexed to it, is at the centre of one of them (thus R. Kasser, "Bibliothèque gnostique V, Apocalypse d'Adam," *RTP*, 3° série, 17 [1967] 316-333; and C. W. Hedrick, *The Apocalypse of Adam, A Literary and Source Analysis* [SBLDS 46; Chico, CA: Scholars Press, 1980, followed by J. D. Turner, "Sethian Gnosticism, A Literary History," *Nag Hammadi, Gnosticism and Early Christianity*, ed. Ch. W. Hedrick and R. Hodgson (Peabody, MA: Hendrickson, 1986] 55-86). Douglas M.

## A. The Untitled Writing

In *Orig. World*, the affirmation of the superiority of the fourth, kingless race contradicts the tripartite anthropology of the treatise, which is resumed in the following sentence (122.6-9):

> There are three men—and his descendants unto the consummation of the world—the Pneumatic of this world (ⲡⲚⲉⲨⲘⲀⲦⲒⲔⲞⲤ ⲘⲠⲀⲒⲰⲚ < * ὁ τοῦ αἰῶνος πνευματικός), the Psychic and the Earthly.

This passage echoes precisely the anthropogonical summary of the treatise (117.27-118.2), which is itself a polemical paraphrase of 1 Cor 15:45-47:[29]

> Now the first Adam, Adam of Light, is pneumatic, and appeared on the first day. The second Adam is psychic. He appeared on the [six]th day, which is called Aphrodite. The third Adam is earthly, that is, the Man of the Law who appeared on the eighth day, [after the r]epose of poverty, which is called the Day of the Sun.

Regardless of the question of the attribution of these passages to the earliest or to later redactional layers of the treatise,[30] the addition of a

---

Parrott's article ("The Thirteen Kingdoms of the Apocalypse of Adam: Origin, Meaning and Significance," *NovT* 31 [1989] 67-87) is especially interesting here, because, while he assumes, like his predecessors, that the litany of the 13 kingdoms forms a separate document, Parrott distinguishes the "kingless generation" as an element foreign to the original form of that document. As for the *Hypostasis of the Archons*, it has been the object of widely divergent redactional hypotheses, from the simple one proposed by A. Böhlig and P. Labib, in their edition of the Untitled Writing (A. Böhlig and P. Labib, *Die koptisch-gnostische Schrift ohne Titel aus Codex II von Nag Hammadi*, [Deutsche Akademie der Wissenschaften zu Berlin Institut für Orientforschung 58; Berlin: Akademie Verlag, 1963) 27), which distinguishes only two sources, to that of R. Kasser ("Formation de 'l'Hypostase des archontes'," *Bulletin de la Société d'Archéologie Copte* 21 [1975] 83-103) which distinguished twelve redactional layers, not to mention B. Barc's hypothesis (*L'Hypostase des archontes* [BCNH, section "Textes" 15; Québec: Presses de l'Université Laval, 1980), which distinguished between two sources which would have been first combined and then successively revised by two different revisors.

[29] See L. Painchaud, "Le sommaire anthropogonique de l'Écrit sans titre (127.17-118.2) à la lumière de 1 Co 15, 45-47," *VC* 44 (1990) 382-393.

[30] According to L. Painchaud's redactional hypothesis, these passages belong to the first revision of the original text, which would probably have taken place in a Valentinian circle or one close to Valentinianism; see "The Writing without Title of Nag Hammadi Codex II: A Redactional Hypothesis," *SecCent* 8 (1991) 217-234; and *L'Écrit sans titre*, (BCNH, section "Textes" 21; Quebec: Presses de l'Université Laval; Louvain-Paris: Peeters, 1995) 106-121. E. Thomassen has criticized the association of this revision with a Valentinian milieu ("Notes pour la délimitation d'un corpus valentinien à Nag Hammadi," in *Les textes de Nag Hammadi et le problème de leur classification. Actes du colloque tenu à Québec, du 19 au 23 septembre 1993*, ed. L. Painchaud and A.

fourth race is clearly incoherent within this tripartite anthropology. What is more, besides being incompatible with the overall doctrine of the treatise, this statement about a γένος ἀβασίλευτον is also incompatible with its immediate context. The sentence which immediately precedes this statement, though its precise meaning is unclear because of its lacunae, contains a series of technical terms used in Valentinian soteriology and ecclesiology: "spirits" (< τὰ πνεύματα); "the elect" (ⲉⲧ- or ⲉⲩ|ⲥⲟⲧⲡ < *ἐκλεκτός), being "blessed" (< μακάριοι) and "different" or "excellent" (ⲉⲩⲱ̄ⲃⲉⲓⲟⲉⲓⲧ) as a result of their "election" (< ἐκλογή).[31] Coming immediately after this series of terms usually used by Valentinians to describe the Pneumatics, a statement which implies the superiority of a fourth γένος over these same Pneumatics and puts them on the same level with Psychics and "Choics," makes no sense unless it is an interpolation aimed at correcting the text on this point.

Incidentally, this hypothesis, which seems to us best to explain the text of 124.33-125.7, also has the advantage of offering a framework within which the unexpected expression "the Pneumatic of this world" in 122.8 might be explained.[32] The words τοῦ αἰῶνος could have been interpolated in this anthropological summary in order to express the idea that the Pneumatics really are submitted to the kings of the Ogdoad, that is, to the archons. Thus both of these interpolations are indications of a polemical reception of *Orig. World* in a circle whose members claimed to be ἀβασίλευτοι and superior to a group of Pneumatics which they disdainfully called "of this world."

In *Orig. World*, the theme of kinglessness reappears once more in 127.14, in a passage (127.7-17) which literary criticism again invites us to interpret as an interpolation and where the polemical tone is clear:[33]

---

Pasquier [BCNH, section "Études" 3; Quebec: Presses de l'Université Laval; Louvain-Paris: Peeters, 1995], 243-259).

[31] See e. g. the *Excerpts from Theodotus* 58.1 (Sagnard 176-177) and the *Tri. Trac.* 122.12-136.24 (Thomassen and Painchaud 222-255); cf. F. Sagnard, *La gnose valentinienne et le témoignage de saint Irénée* (Paris: Vrin, 1949) index, s.v.

[32] This surprising expression has simply been rendered as "the spirit-endowed of the aeon" (or the equivalent) in modern translations of this passage; only H.-G. Bethge and B. Layton differ in proposing "the spirit-endowed of eternity," apparently taking ⲙ̄ⲡⲧⲁⲓⲱⲛ to be a poor translation of αἰῶνος ("On the Origin of the World," in *Nag Hammadi Codex II,2-7*, vol. II, ed. B. Layton [NHS 21; Leiden: E. J. Brill, 1989] 79). While not impossible, this solution assumes a rather unlikely degree of ignorance either of Greek or of Coptic on the part of the translator; more fundamentally, appeals to a hypothetical misunderstood *Vorlage* do not produce a translation of the Coptic text and must be used with caution.

[33] See Louis Painchaud, *L'Écrit sans titre*, commentary ad loc.

And the glory of the unbegotten will appear, and it will fill all the aeons, as soon as the prophecy and the account of those that are king become known and are fulfilled by those who are called perfect. And those who are not perfect in the Unbegotten Father will receive their glories in their aeons and in the immortal kingdoms, but they will never enter into kinglessness (TMNTATP͞PO).

We thus have considerable evidence that *Orig. World* underwent a coherent revision or rewriting in a circle whose members called themselves ἀβασίλευτοι. This rewriting seems to have been principally aimed at asserting the superiority of these ἀβασίλευτοι over pneumatics who expressed their own identity in terms of categories in current use within Valentinianism.

## B. Eugnostos and the Sophia of Jesus Christ

The case of *Eugnostos* and of *Soph. Jes. Chr.* is entirely different: here we are clearly dealing with an original document and a rewritten form of that same document;[34] but, contrary to what we have observed in *Orig. World*, it is not at all clear at first sight that the appearance of the theme of kinglessness is connected to this phenomenon. On the contrary, this theme appears both in *Eugnostos*, a sort of primer on the heavenly realm which presents itself as a letter, and in *Soph. Jes. Chr.*, a dialogue between the risen Christ and his disciples which inserts the contents of *Eugnostos* into a narrative framework and transforms it into a series of answers given by the Lord to the questions of the Apostles.

Moreover, the theme of kinglessness seems to fit better into the framework of *Eugnostos* and *Soph. Jes. Chr.* than into that of *Orig. World*, for here it is paralleled by the theme of kingship, which often occurs in the context of the introduction of a new entity and of its aeons (e. g. the Immortal Man in *Eugnostos* III 77.10-16 parr; the Son of Man in *Eugnostos* V 8.18-27). At the end of the treatise, we find this summary:

All the immortals, whom I have just described, all have authority from the power of Immortal Man and Sophia, his consort, (...). Since the imperishabilities had the authority, each provided great kingdoms in all the immortal

---

[34] In fact, the reverse hypothesis was common in the earliest investigations of these texts, most notably in J. Doresse, "Trois livres gnostiques inédits," *VC* 2 (1948) 137-160; but ever since Martin Krause's definitive article ("Das literarische Verhältnis," 1964), the consensus has been that *Eugnostos* is the *Vorlage* of *Soph. Jes. Chr.*, not the reverse.

heavens and their firmaments, thrones (and) temples, corresponding to their
own majesty (*Eugnostos* III 88.3-17; the three other texts are similar).

The exception to this behavior is the supreme entity, whose realm
precedes the aeons (cf. *Eugnostos* III 76.9-10) and does not appear to
be linked to the notion of kingship in any way, since kingship is
introduced only with the appearance of an inferior entity:

> Through Immortal Man appeared the first designation, namely, divinity and
> kingdom (*Eugnostos* III 77.9-10; the parallels are similar).

One should expect, then, that kinglessness be an exclusive feature of
the realm of the supreme entity; but, on the contrary, kinglessness is
said elsewhere to be common to the aeons of the Immortal Man, of the
Son of Man, and of the Son of the Son of Man (we quote *Eugnostos*
V 13.8-20):

> [The fir]st aeon is that of I[mmor]tal Man. The second is t[hat of the Son of]
> Man, who is call[ed] "Firstborn." The third is that of the Son of the Son of
> Man, who is called "Saviour." Now that which embraces (ЄⲘⲀ2ⲦЄ Ñ-)
> these is the king[les]s (< *ἀβασίλευτος) aeon of the eternal and in[finite]
> [Go]d (...).[35]

The only way to reconcile these two passages would appear to be to
consider kingdom and kinglessness as two different ways of expressing the same idea, i.e. the fact that there is no domination within these
aeons. Understood in this way, this passage would appear to fit very
well into the theology of the treatise. Upon closer examination,
however, there is something surprising about this series of three aeons
enumerated from top to bottom and then followed by a fourth which
embraces the others, since in the rest of *Eugnostos* and *Soph. Jes.
Chr.*, we find only three aeons (e. g. in *Eugnostos* III 86.10-15 parr).
On the other hand, there is something odd in this replacement of the
pair "divinity/kingdom" by the pair "eternal God/kinglessness." This
shift could well be the result of a revision of *Eugnostos* aiming to
bring its contents closer to the language of a group where kinglessness
appeared as a central theologoumenon. The situation in this passage
could thus be analogous to that which we noted in the *Untitled
Writing*, where a fourth race which seemed out of place seems to have
been added to the three which were expected, the difference being that

---

[35] We follow the text established by A. Pasquier, forthcoming in the BCNH series. The
two other witnesses for this passage (*Soph. Jes. Chr.* III has a lacuna here) omit the
second aeon due to a *saut du même au même*, cf. M. Tardieu, *Écrits gnostiques*, 384.

in *Eugnostos* and *Soph. Jes. Chr.*, we are speaking of aeons instead of races—but this is only natural, since *Eugnostos* (and its parallels in *Soph. Jes. Chr.*) is entirely concerned with heavenly things.[36]

The other reference to kinglessness which is to be found both in *Eugnostos* and in a parallel passage in *Soph. Jes. Chr.* is in a description of the unknowable Forefather and of his "confronter" (ἀντωπός), which would appear to be his intelligible counterpart. Having mentioned the existence of the latter, *Eugnostos* III continues as follows (*Eugnostos* III 75.12-76.7; cf. *Eugnostos* V 4.29-5.16):

> After him, he revealed a multitude of self-begotten confronters (ἀντωποί), equal in age, equal in power, glorious and without number, which are called "the generation over which no kingdom rules among the kingdoms that exist." And the whole multitude of the kingless (< *ἀβασίλευτος) place (*Eugnostos* V: the multitude of these kingless ones) is called "the sons of the Unbegotten Father" (*Eugnostos* V: "the sons of Unbegotten and of He Who Brings Himself Forth).

Nothing in the vocabulary of this passage would seem to brand it as an interpolation, as was the case in the preceding one; note, however, that the intrusion of a "multitude" in the middle of a description of the supreme entity is perhaps slightly surprising, especially since the description of the Forefather continues immediately afterwards: "Now he is unknowable (...)." Perhaps more significant is the fact that here the redactor of *Soph. Jes. Chr.* seems to be very concerned with this motif since he or she introduced certain modifications into the text of *Eugnostos*; we quote *Soph. Jes. Chr.* III 99.13-100.1 (main differences between *Soph. Jes. Chr.* III and *Eugnostos* italicized):

> After him, he revealed a multitude of confronters (ἀντωποί), who are all self-begotten, equal in age, equal in power, glorious and without number, *whose race* (γένος) *is called* "the generation over which no kingdom rules," *in which you yourselves appeared from those men.* And that whole kingless (< *ἀβασίλευτος) multitude is called "the sons of the Unbegotten Father."

Clearly the redactor of *Soph. Jes. Chr.* is emphasizing the identity (or at least the affinity) between the heavenly "kingless generation" on the

---

[36] This difference in content between *Eugnostos–Soph. Jes. Chr.* and *Orig. World* may not be coincidental: it seems likely that the two original texts come from one and the same circle and that they were designed by their author(s) to be complementary. See L. Painchaud, "The Literary Contacts between the Writing without Title On the Origin of the World (CG II,5 and XIII,2) and Eugnostos the Blessed (CG III,3 and V,1)," *JBL* 114 (1995) 81-101. Thus it is not surprising to find that they also seem to have shared a common trajectory.

one hand, and, on the other, the Apostles to whom these words are addressed in *Soph. Jes. Chr.*, and with whom he no doubt identifies himself and his group. Moreover, he must have had a reason for adding the term "race" (γένος) to the term "generation" (γενεά), which was probably already there. Perhaps the expression ἀβασί-λευτον γένος (cf. *Orig. World*) was more familiar to him than the one the original author had used; or perhaps this was a way for him to emphasize the link between the heavenly group and his earthly one, since γένος would appear to be a more appropriate description for a social group than γενεά.[37]

There is another clue to the interest of the redactor of *Soph. Jes. Chr.* in the theme of kinglessness: besides modifying *Eugnostos'* statements concerning the "kingless generation," he introduced it into the conclusion which he added at the end of the text. The precise meaning of this passage is obscure: it speaks of the "kingless wealth of the resting place" (according to *Soph. Jes. Chr.* BG 125.8-9), or of the "wealth of the kingless rest" (according to *Soph. Jes. Chr.* III 118.14-15). However this is to be interpreted, the mere presence of this rare and evocative adjective in the ending of *Soph. Jes. Chr.* is in itself sufficient to suggest the hypothesis that its appearance in *Eugnostos* (and in the parallel passages of *Soph. Jes. Chr.*) is due to interpolation. For if this word is the hallmark of a certain circle, as we are led to believe by what we have seen so far, then *Eugnostos* and its rewritten version must either both have been produced within that same circle—but this would seem unlikely—or, alternatively, that same circle must have first added certain interpolations to *Eugnos-tos*,[38] and then transformed it completely into *Soph. Jes. Chr.* at a

---

[37] In *Orig. World* and in *Eugnostos/Soph. Jes. Chr.*, the theme of kinglessness is more or less closely associated with that of numerousness. Thus in *Orig. World* (125.2), the γένος ἀβασίλευτος is numerous (ⲉⲛⲁϣⲱⲟⲩ); in the passages common to Eug and Soph. Jes. Chr., it is a "multitude without number" (ⲟⲩⲙⲏⲏϣⲉ (...) ⲉⲙⲛ̄ⲧⲟⲩ ⲏⲡⲉ <* πλῆθος ἀναρίθμητον in Eug III 75.13-16); while this same notion of πλῆθος is found once again in the conclusion of Soph. Jes. Chr. (BG 125.16). In *Apoc. Adam*, this theme is not directly associated with the use of ἀβασίλευτος; however, the "others," the descendants of Ham and of Japheth who leave their own and enter into another land where they live together with those who came out of the great eternal Gnosis, and who are no doubt to be identified with the kingless generation, are said to number 400,000 (*Apoc. Adam* 73.13-24; on the use of this symbolic number see the commentary by Françoise Morard, *L'Apocalypse d'Adam*, 90). This insistence could have something to do with the historical situation in which these texts were written or revised.

[38] It could be that the initial greeting is also one of these "Sethian" additions: it is the only epistolary element in the text, and as such, it breaks the otherwise remarkable symmetry in literary form and content between *Eugnostos* and *Orig. World*; further, the name Eugnostus, which would be secondary in this hypothesis, is also associated with another major "Sethian" document, the *Holy Book of the Great Invisible Spirit*. This of

later date. In that case, the *Eugnostos–Soph. Jes. Chr.* group would be the result of two consecutive and coherent rewritings of a single original text, the first one minor, the second one more thorough, both tending in the same direction and both being comparable to what we have observed in the case of *Orig. World*, in terms of form and especially in terms of content.

## III. THE IDENTITY OF THE CIRCLES INVOLVED

Thus the motif of kinglessness seems to be associated with circles whose members identified themselves as ἀβασίλευτοι and used rewriting as a means of adapting foreign texts to their needs. As for those texts which we have not been able to examine in detail here, especially the *Apoc. Adam* and *Hyp. Arch.*, as we have noted, they also involve literary problems which could point to a secondary insertion of this motif; however, they could also be original products of the circle or circles whose work we believe may have produced the revisions of *Orig. World* and of the *Eugnostos–Soph. Jes. Chr.* complex. Do we have any indications as to the identity of this or these circles and of their opponents or those people they were facing?

### A. *"Gnostic" Circles*

The expression ἡ ἀβασίλευτος γενεά is found in one or more than one of the sources used by Hippolytus in his description of the so-called Naassenes who, according to the haeresiologist, called themselves "Gnostics," and it is strongly related to the idea of the possession of the perfect or true knowledge. On the other hand, it is also found in two texts which have been considered "Sethian" ever since the work of Hans-Martin Schenke, or, in Layton's categories, "Gnostic," namely *Hyp. Arch.* and the *Apoc. Adam*, as well as in a third text which belongs marginally to this tendency, the anonymous treatise of the Bruce Codex.[39] In one of these texts, the *Apoc. Adam*,

---

course calls into question Paulinus Bellet's reasoning concerning the name Eugnostos and the adjective "blessed" which is attached to it; see "The Colophon of the Gospel of the Egyptians: Concessus and Macarius of Nag Hammadi," in *Nag Hammadi and Gnosis. Papers read at the First International Congress of Coptology* (Cairo, December 1976) , ed. R. McL. Wilson (NHS 14; Leiden: E. J. Brill, 1978) 54-55.

[39] H.-M. Schenke, "Das sethianische System nach Nag-Hammadi-Handschriften" *Studia Coptica*, ed. P. Nagel (Berliner Byzantinische Arbeiten 45; Berlin: Akademie Verlag, 1974, 165-173; id., "The Phenomenon and Significance of Gnostic Sethianism" in *The Rediscovery of Gnosticism, Vol. 2, Sethian Gnosticism*, ed. B. Layton (SHR, NumenSup 41;) Leiden: E. J. Brill, 1981) 588-616. See also J. D. Turner, "Sethian Gnosticism, A Literary History;" and idem, "Typologies of the Sethian Gnostic Treatises from Nag Hammadi" in *Les textes de Nag Hammadi et le problème de leur classifica-*

the motif is strongly related to the possession of the perfect or true knowledge, as it is in the Naassene source(s). Finally, ἀβασίλευτος is also found in the ending of *Soph. Jes. Chr.*, which C. Barry has recently shown to be influenced by "Sethianism."[40]

As for the revision of *Orig. World* which involves the motif of kinglessness, L. Painchaud has suggested that it may be related to the insertion in this same treatise of a passage borrowed from a written source, which seems to have formed the core around which another Nag Hammadi treatise was constructed, namely *Thunder* in Codex VI.[41] Now the function of this insertion in *Orig. World* seems to be precisely to allow the redactor to introduce into the treatise's proto-gonic narrative allusions to a "lordly man" and to a "lordly genera-tion" (113.34-35), which no doubt refer to Seth, who was the first to invoke the *Name of the Lord* (Gn 4:25, LXX), and to his descen-dants.[42] Thus the function of the insertion of this source in the final redaction of *Orig. World* would have been to provide the γένος ἀβασίλευτον with a prototype to be the counterpart of the Spiritual Adam who is both the ancestor (122.5-9 ⲁⲇⲁⲙ ⲘⲚ Ⲧⲉⲹⲅⲉⲛⲉⲁ) and the prototype of the "Pneumatics" of the preceding redaction. On this basis it would appear likely that the circle responsible for the final redaction of *Orig. World* saw itself as the descendants of Seth, and gave Seth an important position in its soteriological system.

According to the available evidence, then, the Gnostic use of kinglessness as an eschatological motif is first attested in the Gnostic circle which is behind the Naassene source(s), quoted by Hippolytus before the end of the first quarter of the third century. Since this source necessarily predates Hippolytus' work, the emergence of this specialized use of the motif may be placed with some confidence toward the end of the second century. The fact that Irenaeus does not

---

*tion*, 169-219. B. Layton considers them as "classic Gnostic scriptures" together with the Apocryphon of John and the Holy Book of the Great Invisible Spirit; see *The Gnostic Scriptures* (Garden City, NY: Doubleday, 1987) Part One.

[40] See "Un exemple de réécriture à Nag Hammadi, la Sagesse de Jésus Christ;" and J. D. Turner, "Typologies of the Sethian Gnostic Treatises."

[41] On this matter, see L. Painchaud, *L'Écrit sans titre (NH II,5)* (BCNH 21; Quebec: Presses de l'Université Laval; Louvain-Paris: Peeters, 1996) 115, and P.-H. Poirier, *Le Tonnerre, intellect parfait (NH VI,2)* (BCNH 22; Quebec: Presses de l'Université Laval; Louvain-Paris: Peeters, 1996).

[42] This is George W. MacRae's interpretation of the passage ("Seth in Gnostic texts and Traditions," *SBLSP 1977* [Missoula: Scholars Press, 1977] 19); however, Birger A. Pearson interprets it as an allusion to Cain ("The Figure of Seth in Gnostic Literarure," in *The Rediscovery of Gnosticism, Vol. II, Sethian Gnosticism*, ed. B. Layton, 481). On the use of ὁ κυριακὸς ἄνθρωπος, see L. Painchaud, *L'Écrit sans titre*, Commentary ad loc.

mention it may indicate that it is later than 180. On the other hand, a specialized use of the term ἀβασίλευτος as a means of self-designation by a group (*Soph. Jes. Chr.*) charactarized by the possession of knowledge (*Apoc. Adam*) or by its superiority to other Pneumatics (*Orig. World*) emerges in the secondary and interpolated passages to be found in several Christian gnostic texts. The fact that this usage is found in a rewritten text like *Soph. Jes. Chr.*, as well as in passages which seem to be interpolated in *Orig. World* and in *Eugnostos*, is an indication both of its lateness and of its importance for the Christian gnostic circles responsible for these rewritings.

We may thus formulate the hypothesis that there were, in the third century, a circle or circles which described themselves using the adjective ἀβασίλευτος and the expression ἡ ἀβασίλευτος γενεά/τὸ ἀβασίλευτον γένος that belonged to the literary tradition known as "Sethianism," and whose literary activity consisted in part of rewritings (*Soph. Jes. Chr.*) or substantial revisions (*Eugnostos, Orig. World, Apoc. Adam?*) of earlier treatises.[43]

## B. A Valentinian Target

As we have already mentioned, the appearance of the kinglessness motif seems to be linked to a polemical context, at least in *Apoc. Adam* and *Orig. World*. An analysis of these contexts could perhaps allow us to identify the target(s) of this polemic. In the case of *Orig. World*, the "kingless race" seems to be defined in opposition to "Pneumatics" who could well represent a Valentinian target. In *Apoc. Adam*, as we suggested earlier, the function of the litany of the thirteen kingdoms could well be to oppose the true opinion of the "kingless generation" to that of the thirteenth kingdom, which seems to be aimed at a Christian doctrine, as we have seen. Further examination would be necessary to determine whether it might be a Valentinian one.

Whatever the precise identity of the targets of these attacks may have been, it would seem that this motif and the rewritings and revisions associated with it demonstrate that, in the third century, there was a polemic going on between different Christian Gnostic circles. Moreover, this hypothesis and this date are compatible with the conclusions reached by Roland Bergmeier, who has claimed that

---

[43] Although the term ἀβασίλευτος and its Coptic equivalents are absent from this text, there is clearly a link which would be worth investigating between the secondary literary activity of "sethian" circles and the obviously secondary title of the *Second Treatise of the Great Seth*.

the use of the adjective ἀβασίλευτος in these sources presupposes a Valentinian background.[44]

## CONCLUSION

To summarize, the problems we have explored here show the importance of rewriting as a means used to receive and appropriate these texts in the circles through which they passed. This is true for *Orig. World*, whose revision is highly polemical. It is also true, probably in two stages, for *Eugnostos*, a treatise which was probably first revised and only later rewritten as a dialogue between Jesus and his disciples. Our analysis of this phenomenon leads us to question the commonly held opinion that the Nag Hammadi texts are free from polemics aimed at groups other than what was to become orthodox Christianity.[45]

In conclusion, we raise the question of a possible link between these ἀβασίλευτοι who seem to be behind the rewriting of certain Nag Hammadi texts and those who were the target of Shenoute's invectives in the region of Pneuit at the beginning of the fifth century. In a speech directed against "the idolaters" (Ⲛⲣⲉϥϣⲙϣⲉ ⲉⲓⲆⲰⲖⲟⲚ) of this region, Shenoute expresses his opposition to adversaries who claimed to be "kingless" (ⲁⲧⲣⲣ̅ⲟ).[46] While the precise identity of this group remains enigmatic,[47] it could be that this text is a witness to the survival, well into the fifth century, not only of a polemical use of the word ἀβασίλευτος, but also of the the religious trends and of the theological discourse which accompany it in the older sources and, probably, of the socio-religious group whose identity was connected with it.[48]

---

[44] Note that Roland Bergmeier (above, n. 17) reached this same conclusion without using the literary approach we offer here and without being aware of the occurrence of ἀβασίλευτος in *Tri. Trac.* Criticism of his work by M. A. Williams, *The Immovable Race* (NHS 29; Leiden: E. J. Brill, 1985) 174, n. 16, and Kurt Rudolph, *Die Gnosis*[3] (Göttingen, Vandenhoeck und Ruprecht, 1990) 417, n. 102a, seems to be concerned rather with his method than with his conclusions, which are supported by our analysis.

[45] See F. Wisse, "The Nag Hammadi Library and the Heresiologists," *VC* 25 (1971) 221.

[46] 88.20 Leipoldt: *Sinuthii Archimandritae vita et opera omnia III* (CSCO 42, Scriptores Coptici, 2; Louvain: Secrétariat du Corpus SCO, 1955).

[47] *Pace* Paulinus Bellet, who identified them as Gnostics, art. cit. 64-65.

[48] As for the idea that the members of this group were the last owners of the Nag Hammadi Codices and were thus those responsible for their burying due to a flight to the South (thus P. Bellet, art. cit., 65), this is pure speculation.

# THE ACTS OF PETER AND THE TWELVE APOSTLES: A RECONSIDERATION OF THE SOURCE QUESTION

*Andrea Lorenzo Molinari*
Marquette University

The *Acts of Peter and the Twelve Apostles*, discovered along with 46 other tracts at Nag Hammadi, Egypt in 1945, is still very much in its infancy of scholarly analysis. While with some early Christian texts scholarly history is measured in centuries, the study of *ActsPet-12Apost.* must be measured in decades. Until now the scholarly approach has been primarily that of introductions to the text; half of the available literature serves this purpose. Most of these introductions and several of the other studies have focused upon dividing and describing the text in light of its most obvious problem, the problem of peculiar voice shifts.[1] In the following pages I shall begin to address these peculiar voice shifts by discussing the various positions that have been proposed as solutions to this problem. I shall present these theories according to the individual scholar with a general regard for the chronological order in which they were proposed. After reviewing these theories, I shall present my own theory as to how the divisions in the text and corresponding source questions should be treated.

## A. MARTIN KRAUSE

In 1972, Martin Krause argued that the title reflects the composite nature of the text. He argued that the text actually contains two separate "acts": first, an act of Peter and second, an act of the apostolic group.[2] Krause divided the text into three originally independent parts: a contextual framework section (1.3-1.29), a first narrative (1.29-7.23) and a second narrative (8.13-12.19).[3] Observing

---

[1] Simply put, the narrative voice of the text begins in the first person plural, then shifts to the first person singular. After a peculiar shift to the third person, the text successively shifts back to the first person plural, then to the first person singular, finally ending in the third person.

[2] M. Krause, "Die Petrusakten in Codex VI von Nag Hammadi," in idem, ed., *Essays in Honour of Alexander Böhlig* (NHS 3; Leiden: E. J. Brill, 1972) 38.

[3] Ibid., 49-51.

that there are inconsistencies in the text, he notes the changes in the voice of narration. According to Krause, the first person plural "we" is used in the framework section, the first person singular "I" is used in the first narrative and the voice of narration changes from the first person plural to the third person singular in the second narrative section.[4]

## B. HANS-MARTIN SCHENKE

In 1973, Hans-Martin Schenke proposed, then rejected, an explanation of the text's peculiar voice shifts as a choir-sermon with Peter as soloist. Instead, he found the text to be half sermon, half narrative, the original framework being that of a sermon.[5] Later, in 1989, Schenke contended, apparently building from the work of Krause, that *ActsPet12Apost.* came into existence through the combination of three different texts. The first text was a "legendary narrative" of a fantastic voyage involving Peter and the other apostles. They are brought "out of time and space" to an imaginary island which signifies the world. This island is symbolically named according to its situation.[6] Schenke viewed the phrase, "So that in this way, the city of everyone who endures the burden of his yoke of faith will be inhabited, and he will be included in the kingdom of heaven" (7.15-19), as the original ending of this story.

Schenke's second text was not added to the first, but was inserted into it. This second text was the description of a vision (presumably by Peter) of a pearl-merchant named Lithargoel who appears in a strange city offering a mysterious pearl to rich and poor alike. Schenke argued that this was a transparent allegory of Jesus' preaching of salvation and its reception in the world. For Schenke this second text originally had no relationship with the first.[7]

---

[4] Ibid., 49.

[5] Schenke views this sermon as having been altered at the end to a narrative. This sermon was originally only Peter's, although the other apostles were dealt with in the text. See Schenke, "Die Taten des Petrus und der zwölf Apostel," *TLZ* 98 (1973) 15.

[6] Schenke sees the key aspects of this story as being: a) the imparting of the name "since the island city still endures although it ought properly to be swallowed up by the sea"; b) the statements concerning the power and significance of endurance; and c) a sermon-like application of the name; Schenke, "The Acts of Peter and the Twelve Apostles," *New Testament Apocrypha*, vol. 2, ed. W. Schneemelcher (Louisville: Westminster/Knox, 1992) 417.

[7] Schenke reasons that there is a "breakdown in the internal logic of the imagery." Since there are no black dogs, wolves, lions or bulls on the sea, the original location of Lithargoel's city "must be conceived as lying in the midst of a desert." For Schenke, Peter's intervention in his own vision makes the whole description less clear; "the only

Schenke's third text demonstrates its original character by a collection of motifs typical of canonical Easter stories. Imagining this text as an Easter or Pentecost story, Schenke believes its original setting to be before the gates of Jerusalem, where Peter and the disciples meet the risen Jesus.

As for the possible motivation for three so supposedly different texts to be united, he proposes that:

> what is common to all three, and could arouse the temptation to form such a hybrid, was *probably* that in all of them a city stood mysteriously at the centre, and *possibly* also that all three, although in different ways, may have been Peter texts. The second and third must also have been bound together through the name Lithargoel, which the central figure in each case bears. Each text was marked by characteristic clusters of motifs, specific to the genre or peculiar to that text, and here it is not difficult to recognize where they really belong, even when they have been displaced in the weaving-together of the texts.[8]

## C. DOUGLAS M. PARROTT

In 1979, Douglas M. Parrott offered an analysis of the source question that differed slightly from that of Krause. Although, it was not his intention to offer a detailed source analysis, Parrott did make some points that furthered the discussion. He began by noting that Krause's analysis is weakened by its reliance upon divisions that are suggested by a secondary and inaccurate title.[9] Instead, Parrott argues that the text is comprised of four originally independent accounts: 1) the story of a pearl merchant who is rejected by the rich but accepted by the poor, 2) a story about a city called Habitation, 3) a story about a journey which required the abandonment of food and possessions for successful completion rather than the expected reverse, and 4) an

---

logical sequence—and so it may have originally have been related—is that the poor themselves ask the pearl-merchant his name and that of his city, and also about the way to that city." Schenke is also disturbed by what he terms "the inconceivable clothing of Lithargoel." He suggests that the reference to "a napkin" (σουδάριον, 2.14) is actually a reference to "grave clothes" used to help people recognize the crucified Jesus. This reference migrated into this section from the third text, ibid., 418.

[8] Schenke, *New Testament Apocrypha*, 417.

[9] Parrott states that the title must be secondary because of the contradiction between the explicit statement of the text ("we comprised eleven disciples") and the title's reference to twelve. Parrott concludes, "The title, then, was probably provided by someone who had not read the tractate carefully or who followed the common practice of the second and third centuries of using the number twelve to refer to the apostles as a group." See D. Parrott, "The Acts of Peter and the Twelve Apostles (VI,1:1.1-12.22)," in *Nag Hammadi Codices V,2-5 and VI*, ed. idem (NHS 11; Leiden: E. J. Brill, 1979) 189.

account of Christ's commission of his disciples so that they may undertake a mission of preaching and healing among poor and sick Christians. Parrott believes that the first three of these four "probably began as parables or allegories, somewhat resembling those found in the *Shepherd of Hermas*."[10]

## D. STEPHEN J. PATTERSON

Until the work of Stephen J. Patterson in 1991, the ideas of Krause, Schenke and Parrott went virtually unchallenged. Patterson's work may well mark a new era in scholarly consideration of this text.[11] In his analysis of the various literary and source theories, Patterson reviewed and critiqued the work of Krause, Schenke and Parrott in the most comprehensive treatment of the source question to date.

Patterson begins his treatment of literary and source theories by referring to a study by Vernon K. Robbins which helps explain some of the "we passages" in *ActsPet12Apost.* with reference to similar "we passages" in the canonical Acts of the Apostles.[12] By comparing a variety of ancient sea voyage accounts, including those in Homer's *Odyssey*, Virgil's *Aeneid*, and Aeschylus' *Seven Against Thebes*, Robbins demonstrates that it was a common literary convention for ancient narrators to shift from either a first person singular or third person singular to a first person plural when narrating a sea voyage. Robbins also offers another possible explanation for this convention in terms of social relationships:

> Since first person narration emerged naturally in relation to sea voyage lit-
> erature, there could be no complete reversal of the trend. The dynamic of

---

[10] D. Parrott, "The Acts of Peter and the Twelve Apostles (VI,1)," *The Nag Hammadi Library in English,* ed. J. M. Robinson (San Francisco: Harper, 1988) 287-288. Parrott argues that an editor related these accounts to one another by the common presence of Peter and the other disciples, by the name Lithargoel, which links the pearl merchant (Parrott's second section) with the one who gives directions about the way to the city (third section) and Christ (section four) who commissions the disciples.

[11] S. J. Patterson, "Sources, Redaction and Tendenz in The Acts of Peter and the Twelve Apostles (NH VI,1)," *VC* 45 (1991) 1-17.

[12] V. K. Robbins, "By Land and By Sea: The We-Passages and Ancient Sea Voyages," *Perspectives on Luke-Acts,* ed. C. H. Talbert (Perspectives in Religious Studies 5; Edinburgh: T. & T. Clark, 1978) 215-42. While this study by Robbins presents an original solution to the "we passages" in Acts, the discussion of the source or sources behind these texts is an old one; for a summary of past discussion see, J. Dupont, *The Sources of the Acts,* trans. K. Pond (New York: Herder and Herder, 1964) 75-112; also Stanley E. Porter, "The 'We' Passages," *The Book of Acts in its First Century Setting,* vol. 2, ed. B. W. Winter (Grand Rapids: Eerdmans, 1994) 545-74. Both include extensive bibliographies.

voyaging on the sea brings with it the experience of working with others to achieve a safe voyage and of sharing with others the fear and desperation when a storm threatens to end the voyage in shipwreck. The social setting that emerges through a voyage on the sea gave rise to the sea voyage genre recounted with the personal plural dynamic: "We thought we were lost, we did what we could, and we made it through."[13]

In his study, Robbins also briefly addresses *ActsPet12Apost.* and implies that this ancient literary convention may explain the use of the first person plural in the sea voyage sections of *ActsPet12Apost.* Patterson agrees with this suggestion. He notes that the shift from the first person plural to the first person singular voice of Peter at 1.29-30 occurs at the moment in the text that the sea journey comes to an end. Also, at 7.23-8.20 the shift from first person singular to first person plural occurs at the point in the story when Peter and the disciples journey to Lithargoel's city, although this is not specifically presented as a sea journey.[14]

At this juncture, Patterson makes what I believe to be one of his best points. He notes that Robbins's study is only helpful in the above-mentioned cases but does not serve to explain all the narrative shifts in *ActsPet12Apost.* He states: "in contrast to the we-passages in Acts, the narrative shifts in the *ActsPet12Apost.* often involve not simply a shift in voice (third person to first, or singular to plural), but an actual shift in the narrative perspective of the text." He further clarifies his point by distinguishing between shifts in voice and shifts in identity of the narrator (Peter vs. a narrator). Thus, he concludes that while Robbins's study is helpful in explaining the existence of the we passages in the canonical Acts and even the two shifts in *ActsPet12Apost.*, something more is required to explain the other shifts present in this text.

---

[13] V. Robbins, "By Land and By Sea," 223. It should also be noted that Porter has argued against Robbins' conclusions. He cited a 1) mix of literatures, 2) range of centuries and 3) variety of genres as key weaknesses in Robbins' theory, Porter, op. cit. n. 12, 554. However, I am not entirely convinced by Porter's arguments. While I hesitate to describe the use of the first person plural in such set terms as "literary convention," I would agree with Robbins and C. K. Barrett in suggesting a sociological motivation for this tendency. See C. K. Barrett, "Paul Shipwrecked," *Scripture: Meaning and Method*, ed. B. P. Thompson (Festschrift A. T. Hanson; Hull: Hull University Press, 1987) 53-54.

[14] Patterson, 6. It seems important to point out that Patterson does not include 7.23-8.20 as I have written but rather 9.17-26. I have made this change because Patterson describes 9.17-26 as "the point where Peter and the disciples undertake the journey to Lithargoel's city." These line quotations are incorrect. Therefore, I have assumed an error and replaced 9.17-26 with 7.23-8.20, which properly fits Patterson's point.

Patterson proceeds to briefly examine and critique the theories of Krause, Schenke and Parrott. Of the three, Patterson seems most amenable to the theory of Schenke, which he describes as "a more fruitful attempt to deal with this problem"[15] He viewes Schenke's idea of multiple levels of composition, with one level inserted into another and separate material attached at the end of the text, as possibly offering the basis for a solution to the problem.

Before offering his solution, Patterson makes four methodological observations which he believes must be seen as lessons learned from the previous attempts to solve the problem. The first is related to the lesson taught to us by the work of Robbins. Patterson notes that Robbins's study has shown us that not every shift in narrative voice in this text need signal a different source or redactional layering. Some shifts can be attributed to ancient literary convention.

Second, Patterson points out that, although some shifts can be attributed to literary convention, there are other aporias in the text that must be explained. Therefore, any compositional theory must take these aporias into account.

Patterson's third observation built upon this idea of aporias. He states that "the aporias alone will not always provide one with the neat divisions in the text one would hope for in trying to clarify where one voice stops and another begins."[16] The aporias signal a shift in the textual sources but do not necessarily mark where the shift has taken place. Thus, Patterson urges the interpreter to pay attention not only to aporias and places where new voices emerge but also to the episodic structure of the text as a whole and the places where these elements coincide.

Patterson's fourth observation is that any theory which attempts to explain the compositional history of this text must have the necessary complexity to deal with the various voice shifts which can be found in the text. He argues that there are at least three different voices in the text: 1) the "I, Peter" voice, 2) the first person plural voice of the disciples, and 3) the anonymous third person voice. Thus, he concludes that at least three sources are required.

Therefore, Patterson proposes a "Three-Source Hypothesis." The first is called the "I, Peter Source," consisting of 1.1-3.11 and 5.5-8.9. Originally, this source consisted of the encounter of Peter with

---

[15] Ibid., 8.

[16] Ibid., 9. Patterson argues that only once in *ActsPet12Apost.* can a narrative aporia be said to mark a textual seam. Patterson points to the shift between first and third person which occurs at 9.29-30.

the angel Lithargoel in a symbolic city, Habitation. A discussion occurs about a heavenly city called Nine Gates and Lithargoel gives ascetical instructions on how to safely arrive at this city. The cities and the ascetical instructions would have been the point of this story. Patterson compares this source with such heavenly journey texts as *The Enthronement of the Archangel Michael* and *The Book of the Enthronement of the Archangel Gabriel*.

The second source is the "Third Person Source" because it is characterized by this voice. Primarily, Patterson sees two episodes stemming from this proposed source: 1) the story of the pearl merchant (3.11-5.5), which he thinks was "inserted" into the "I, Peter" text, and 2) the more obvious commissioning scene (9.30-12.29).[17] Patterson assigns these sections to the same source because of their common third person voice and their common concern for the poor. Patterson envisions the original version of the story as featuring Jesus himself as the pearl merchant. Thus, Jesus' emphatic instructions to shun the rich in 11.26-12.8 would have been a calculated repayment for their rejection of the pearl merchant in 3.14-31.

The third source is called the "We Source." Patterson strongly argues that what he calls "the resurrection appearance" in 8.10-9.29 was part of this source.[18] Although Patterson was unsure whether 1.1-29 should be included in this source, he suggests that if the above-mentioned "resurrection appearance" scene of the "We Source" originally came out of an Easter text, then it may have included a commissioning and sending-out scene of which 1.1-29 may be a remnant.[19]

---

[17] While Patterson sees the commissioning scene as obviously from another source, he recognizes that the story of the pearl merchant is far less easy to identify as such. By way of explaining this point, Patterson notes that the shift to third person at 3.11 is presented as Peter's third person remembrance of the event. However, Patterson reminds his reader that at 5.1 a "source using a non-Petrine third person voice" has been inserted. Patterson argues that this "insertion" has already occurred back at 3.11. The three points he puts forward in favor of this thesis are as follows: 1) this story of the pearl merchant does not need to include Peter as he only appears at the end as a "tutor" for the poor; 2) 3.11-5.5 is tangential to the main Petrine narrative as one could pass from 3.11 to 5.5 and not miss the intervening section; and 3) the presence of "a redactional seam" in 5.4-5. This seam is indicated by Peter telling the poor about the hardships of the way to Lithargoel's city and then turning around and asking Lithargoel about these same hardships, ibid., 11-12.

[18] Patterson recognizes the tenuous location of the "We Source" seam at 8.10. Part of the problem is that the "I, Peter" source is using its plural voice at this point and until 8.21, where Peter is specifically mentioned it is hard to tell where a new source is being inserted.

[19] Patterson points out a number of changes and additions which were made to these three sources by the hand of a redactor: 1) a lengthy description of Lithargoel's appearance (2.14-29); 2) the cry "Pearls, Pearls" in 2.32; 3) the third person voice in 5.5-

## E. A DIFFERENT PROPOSAL

In light of Patterson's detailed study of the various types, I suggest that there are possibly five different varieties of voice shifts in *ActsPet12Apost.* I would stress that at this point these are not sources, but rather merely types of voice shifts present in the text. It is my contention (in agreement with Patterson) that these voice shifts are only one factor to be considered when examining the question of sources in *ActsPet12Apost.*; as I hope to demonstrate, aporias, shifts in vocabulary, and thematic discrepancies are of equal significance. I shall ultimately argue that there are three main sections in *ActsPet12Apost.* The first two are originally separate sources that have undergone redaction by the author, and the third is the author's own material appended to the two previous sections. These three sources are: 1) *The Story of the Pearl Merchant* (1.1-9.1); 2) *A Resurrection Appearance* (9.1-9.29); and 3) *The Author/Redactor's Position and Theology* (9.30-12.19). I begin begin this analysis by delineating the five types of voice shifts present in *ActsPet12Apost.* and then proceed to examine the specific parameters of these sections.

The five voice shift types are as follows: 1) *I, Peter*—first person narration from Peter's perspective; found in 1.30-3.11 and 6.9-7.22; 2) Robbins' *"We of journeys"*—first person plural narration often found in travel literature of the Greco-Roman period; found in 1.1-29 and 7.23-8.20; 3) *We - apostolic voice*—first person plural narration which could be considered the voice of one in the apostolic group due to its proximity to lines which refer to Peter in the third person; found only in 9.15-29; 4) *The Narrator*—third person narration which refers to Peter as a character in the story and not as the storyteller; found in 5.1-14; 8.21-9.15 and 9.30-12.19; and 5) *Problematic Sections*—passages in the third person, yet difficult to classify under "The Narrator" because they could be understood as being connected with the "I, Peter" texts (i.e., third person narration by a first person narrator); found in 3.11-5.1 and 5.14-6.8.

### Voice Shift Types

| | | | |
|---|---|---|---|
| 1) | I, Peter | a. 1.30-3.11; | b. 6.9-7.22 |
| 2) | We of Journeys | a. 1.1-29; | b. 7.23-8.20 |

---

7, which Patterson attributes to a redactor's attempt to smooth out the problem of voice; and 4) the difficulty created between 8.13 and 9.19, where the physician is first identified as Lithargoel in disguise and then identified as Jesus. Patterson describes these lines as the section where the redactor attempted to splice together the "I, Peter" source and the "resurrection appearance" of the "We Source."

| 3) | We - Apostolic Voice | a. 9.15-29 | | |
|---|---|---|---|---|
| 4) | The Narrator | a. 5.1-14; | b. 8.21-9.15; | c. 9.30-12.19 |
| 5) | Problematic Sections | a. 3.11-5.1; | b. 5.14-6.8 | |

## 1. A Unity from 1.1 to 8.20?

There may be more unity in *ActsPet12Apost*. than one might first suppose, given the variety of these shifts in voice shifts. For example, in shift types 1) and 2) there is a consistent first person narrative voice (singular and plural). To these sections might be added 3.11-5.1, which was classed above as part of shift type (5). This text follows directly upon an "I, Peter" section (1.30-3.11) and could be easily seen as Peter narrating events as they unfolded around him. Therefore, it would not be incorrect (in terms of literary technique) for these lines to be written in the third person and yet occur within the larger context of a first person narrative.[20] The second "Problematic Sections" text (5.14-6.8) might for the same reason also be added to the texts associated with the first person. However, its relationship with 5.1-14, a text classed under "The Narrator" shift type (third person), must be explained.

### a. First Person Narration: Greek, Roman, and Early Christian Texts

To understand 5.1-14, a text which breaks up an otherwise continuous first person narrative flow spanning 1.1 to 8.20, a brief examination of other occurrences of first person narration in Greek, Roman, and early Christian literature would be helpful. According to Robert Scholes and Robert Kellogg, the development of first person narration and all eye-witness narrative forms reached their first significant development in Roman times. Scholes and Kellogg do not claim that first person narration did not previously exist; rather:

> ... narrative forms designed to exploit first person presentation in one way or another had not been developed before; so that a Xenophon, writing of his own experiences in Asia Minor in the *Anabasis*, automatically wrote of himself in the third person, just as Caesar later did in *De Bello Gallico*...Such men chose this mode of narration not out of pride or humility, but because

---

[20] Patterson seems to agree with this evaluation: "At 3.11 there is a shift from the first to third person, but the third person narrative is placed ostensibly on the lips of Peter, who tells the story of Lithargoel now as an observer of events, not as a participant in them. Narratively this poses no problem," ibid., 9.

they associated the third person with formal narratives of the epic and historical kind, with which they associated their own works.[21]

According to Scholes and Kellogg the first person is less formal and
more intimate:

> In early literature the first person is generally associated with such loose and
> personal forms as the epistle and the memoir, the forms of the amateur
> rather than the professional author. We find occasionally a sense of self-
> awareness in the authors of works which are essentially neither first person
> in form nor autobiographical in spirit, as when Hesiod opens the Theogony
> with a reminiscence of the time when a delegation of Muses visited Hesiod
> (referring to himself in the third person) and persuaded him to enlighten the
> world with the true histories of the deathless gods; but we find almost no
> first person narrative in early Greek literature, with the important exception
> of the story of his travels told by Odysseus to the Phaeacians, which is em-
> bedded in the larger narrative structure of Homer. This portion of the Odys-
> sey is of great interest. It is the most magical, fabulous, and romantic thing
> in Homer. It is a traveler's tale, a road or journey narrative, and it is told in
> the first person. The traveler's tale is a persistent oral form in all cultures. It
> is, in a sense, the amateur's answer to the professional rhapsodist, skald, or
> jongleur. Its form is the simple linear form of voyage by land or sea, and in
> it fiction, which in its highest sense involves ordering and shaping for an es-
> thetic end, is reduced to its most humble form—the lie. Traveler's tales in
> all countries are notoriously untrustworthy, and untrustworthy in proportion
> to the distance of the travels from familiar territory, just as ancient maps
> become less reliable toward their edges. The prose writers of the Roman
> Empire developed the first person journey narrative as an art form and also
> established the pattern of the inward journey, the autobiography, in its two
> usual forms—the apology and the confession.[22]

To illustrate their point, Scholes and Kellogg referred to several
examples. Among these were Petronius Arbiter, *Satyricon* (ca. 64);
Lucius Apulieus, *Metamorphoses* (ca. 150); and Lucian of Samosata,
*A True Story* (ca. 180). Each of these pieces of literature is written
almost exclusively in the first person, as a personal account of the
main character's adventures while traveling.

In the NT, the "we source" texts in Acts 16:10-17; 20:5-15; 21:1-
18 and 27:1-28:16, mentioned above, are the most famous examples
of first person narration. Furthermore, the book of Revelation, like
other apocalypses,[23] also includes extensive first person narration.[24]

---

[21] R. Scholes and R. Kellogg, *The Nature of Narrative* (New York: Oxford University
Press, 1966) 72. The third chapter of this book, "The Classical Heritage of Modern
Narrative," is especially helpful in its overview of Greco-Roman literary development.

[22] Ibid., 72-73.

[23] For example, the Coptic *Apocalypse of Paul* and *Apocalypse of Peter* (both from
Nag Hammadi) and the Greek *Apocalypse of Paul*. In other non-canonical early Christian

The first person is also present in the various epistles of the NT, whether authentic or pseudepigraphical,[25] a typical aspect of a personal letter. There are also brief occurrences of the first person in both Luke 1:1-4 and John 21:24-25.

While these examples are helpful, the closest parallel I have found to the oddly placed voice shifts in *ActsPet12Apost.* 5.1-14 also occurs in the Nag Hammadi literature.[26] In the *Apocryphon of James* (NHC I,1) the reader is, much as in the text surrounding *ActsPet12Apost.* 5.1-14, confronted with a confusing voice shift from first to third person, back to first again. *Ap.Jas.* begins with a pseudepigraphical letter in which "James" claims to be sending a book containing material revealed to Peter and himself (1.8-12):

> Since you asked that I send you a secret book which was revealed to me and Peter by the Lord, I could not turn you away or gainsay you; but [I have written] it in the Hebrew alphabet and sent it to you, and you alone. But since you are a minister of the salvation of the saints, endeavor earnestly and take care not to rehearse this text to many—this that the Savior did not wish to tell to all of us, his twelve disciples. But blessed will they be who will be saved through the faith of this discourse.
>
> I also sent you, ten months ago, another secret book which the Savior had revealed to me. Under the circumstances, however, regard that one as revealed to me, James; but this one [untranslatable fragments] the twelve disciples [were] all sitting together and recalling what the Savior had said to each one of *them*, whether in secret or openly, and [putting it] in books— [But I] was writing that which was in [my book]—lo, the Savior appeared, [after] departing from [us while we] gazed after him. And five hundred and fifty days since he had risen from the dead, we said to him, "Have you departed and removed yourself from us?"
>
> But Jesus said, "No, but I shall go to the place from whence I came. If you wish to come with me, come!"
>
> *They* all answered and said, "If you bid us, we come."

---

texts, somewhat related to apocalyptic literature, there are such examples of first person narration as: *Shepherd of Hermas* and *Ascension of Isaiah* 7.1-11.35.

[24] David E. Aune has described the function of the first person in apocalypses: "the autobiographical style of apocalypses requires emphasis since this feature is an important aspect of the legitimization of the revelatory experience, and the first-person style in oral performance enables the audience to experience the vividness and vitality of the original revelatory experience," ("The Apocalypse of John and the Problem of Genre," *Semeia* 36 [1986] 87).

[25] See R. F. Collins, *Letters That Paul Did Not Write* (Good News Studies 28; Wilmington, DE: Michael Glazier, 1988) 69-86, and also W. G. Doty, *Letters in Primitive Christianity* (Philadelphia: Fortress, 1973) for a detailed description of ancient letter writing technique as well as the practice of pseudepigraphy.

[26] By "oddly placed" I refer to the peculiar and unexpected switch to third person narration in the middle of an otherwise first person text.

> He said, "Verily I say unto you, no one will ever enter the kingdom of heaven at my bidding, but (only) because you yourselves are full. Leave James and Peter to me that I may fill them." And having called these two, he drew them aside and bade the rest occupy themselves with that which they were about (1.8-2.39).

In this letter James refers to the twelve disciples as "us" (first person plural; 1.24-25), reinforcing his "identity" as one of Jesus' inner circle. However, this identity begins to break down in 2.12 when the twelve are referred to as "them" (third person plural). This peculiar shift is followed by a return to the first person as the plural is once again used to refer to the group of disciples. This shift is short-lived, as in 2.26 the disciples are referred to in the third person plural. In 2.36-37, the identity of the narrator is compromised, revealing itself not to be James. James is referred to as separate from the narrator as he and Peter are referred to as "these two" and "them." Interestingly enough, from this point on in the text the voice of narration remains constant, referring to James as "I" and Peter and James as "we" and "us" while referring to the rest of the twelve as "they."[27]

The *Epistula Apostulorum* provides us with yet another shift in voice which can be compared to that found in *ActsPet12Apost.* 5.1-14. Julian V. Hills has noted a peculiar occurrence in this document. The Epistula, as a whole reported from the point of view of the disciples, contains a list of miracles in chapter 5. This list begins: "Then there was a marriage in Cana of Galilee. And he was invited with his mother and his brothers. And he made water into wine..." Hills notes the connection of this Cana wedding to its canonical

---

[27] Also from the Nag Hammadi literature there is the *1 Apocalypse of James* which contains both first person narration and an abrupt shift from the first to the third person. *1 Ap.Jas.*, cast in the form of a dialogue within a narrative framework, has narration which begins with the first person singular "me" in reference to James (24.11; see also 25.12; 27.18). However, the text then switches over almost completely to the third person, using "James said" to introduce James' questions to the Lord, leaving the reader to ask the reason for this sudden shift in narrative technique. William R. Schoedel claims, "Although most of the report is in the third person, there are three places where the author speaks of himself in the first person. This may indicate the artificiality of the narrative framework," ("The First Apocalypse of James, V,3:24.10-44.10," *Nag Hammadi Codices V,2-5 and VI with Papyrus Berolinensis 8502,1 and 4*, ed. D. M. Parrott [NHS 11; Leiden: E. J. Brill, 1979] 5). Another example of first person narration and abrupt voice shifts from within the Nag Hammadi corpus is *Hypostasis of the Archons. Hyp.Arch.* begins as a "learned treatise in which a teacher addresses a topic ostensibly suggested by the dedicatee of the work." This introduction is written in the first person singular (86.22.26). The work then proceeds to switch to the third person, only to resume the first person in what Bentley Layton has called "an angelic revelation dialogue" from 93.13 until the end of the text. See B. Layton, *The Gnostic Scriptures* (Garden City, NY: Doubleday, 1987) 65.

counterpart in John 2:1 and observes the difference in terminology from "disciples" in John to "brothers" in the *Epistula*:

> In relating the presence of "his brothers," however, either the author is drawing on material independent of John, or he is making a conscious change; or, finally, a later hand has been at work. It has long been noted that Jesus' brothers, perhaps understood by John to be the disciples, appear in John 2:12, and it was even affirmed by Bultmann that John's source at 2:2, and therefore possibly the Epistula's source, read "and his brothers."[28]

Hills noted the peculiarity that in three separate places the Epistula expressly calls the disciples "brothers."[29] If the Epistula saw "disciples" and "brothers" as related, even interchangeable, terms, then the question arises, "Why doesn't this section of the text use "we" or "us" (in place of "brothers") as are found in eight other places within this same list of miracles?" Thus, there is a subtle (and short-lived) switch in from the first to third person narration.[30]

Several conclusions that can be drawn from these examples of first person narration. First, the first person tends to be associated with travel/adventure literature (e.g., Lucian, *A True Story* and Lucius Apulieus, *Metamorphoses*). Second, it also is associated with revelatory literature (e.g., Revelation, *Ascension of Isaiah* and *Apocryphon of James*). Third, it tends to represent a less formal (as compared to Homer's *Iliad*), more amateurish literary effort, (being influenced by the form of the traveler's tale). Fourth, in some of these works there are peculiar and sometimes sudden shifts in the voice of narration (from first to third). It seems that *ActsPet12Apost.* has connections with each of these aspects.

### b. First Person as a Literary Device

Now that I have briefly discussed the uses of first person narration in Greek, Roman, and early Christian literature, it seems possible to examine more closely the voice change that occurs in 5.1-14. Up until

---

[28] J. Hills, *Tradition and Composition in the Epistula Apostolorum* (HDR 24; Minneapolis: Fortress, 1990) 48. For the reference to Bultmann; see R. Bultmann, *The Gospel of John: A Commentary* (Philadelphia: Westminster, 1971) 114 and n. 6.

[29] These three are: 10.2 (part of a retelling of Jesus' appearance to three women outside the tomb, "go to your brothers and say, "Come, our Master has risen from the dead.""); 19.5 ("Truly I say unto you, you will be my brothers and companions"); and 32.4 ("Truly I say unto you, you are my brothers, companions in the kingdom of heaven").

[30] Hills suggested that this section may represent a later addition to the text. However, in verbal discussions with me he admitted that this occurrence is difficult to explain and may represent an authorial mistake or "slip."

this point in the text the voice of narration has been consistently first person, both plural and singular. However, at 5.1-14, especially at 5.2-7, the voice switches to third person for no obvious reason.

As far as I can determine there are three possible explanations for the change in voice at 5.1-14: 1) a change in sources; 2) a deliberate literary choice on the part of the author[31] and 3) a mistake or "slip" on the part of the author (i.e., sloppy pseudonymity). I reject the first of these explanations because I see nothing other than this change in voice that would suggest a change in source. It seems that the material included in 5.1-14, is in agreement with previously given information. That is, when the merchant offers the pearl to the poor he clearly indicates that he does not actually have the pearl on his person. Rather, he expressly invites the poor to come to his city "so that I may not only show it before your (very) eyes, but give it to you for nothing" (4.10-15; 30-34). We assume that Peter, as a member of the assembled crowd, was also extended this invitation. Therefore, it seems that the question Peter asks of the merchant in 5.7-14 as to the way to the merchant's city is a logical progression or response to the merchant's appeal to the people present in Habitation. One must go to the merchant's city to receive the pearl. Thus, if anything is ever to be made of this invitation, it is necessary to know the way to this city.[32]

---

[31] This understanding of voice changes in literature is explained by the comments of French literary theorist Gérard Genette in *Narrative Discourse: An Essay in Method*, trans. J. E. Lewin (Ithaca, NY: Cornell University Press, 1980) 246. (Note, however, that Genette admits the possibility of a deliberate literary choice on the part of the author but only for modern literature). Genette wrote concerning unexpected shifts in voice: "An even more glaring violation is the shift in grammatical person to designate the same character: for instance, in *Autre étude de femme*, Bianchon moves all of a sudden from "I" to "he," as if he were unexpectedly abandoning the role of narrator; for instance, in *Jean Santeuil*, the hero moves inversely from "he" to "I." In the field of the classical novel, and still in Proust, such effects obviously result from a sort of narrative pathology, explicable by last-minute reshufflings and states of textual incompleteness. But we know that the contemporary novel has passed that limit, as it has so many others, and does not hesitate to establish between narrator and character(s) a variable or floating relationship, a pronominal vertigo in tune with a freer logic and a more complex conception of "personality." The most advanced forms of this emancipation are perhaps not the most perceptible ones, because the classical attributes of "character"—proper name, physical and moral "nature"—have disappeared and along with them the signs that direct grammatical (pronominal) traffic."

[32] In 5.7-14, it is interesting to note that Peter does not mention the pearl. His interest in the merchant's city is not basely associated with a desire for gain. (Frankly, this would be rather embarrassing for the community, their role-model scurrying off like some crazed bargain shopper in search of a complementary gift). Rather, his thought is to pursue the commission given him in 1.10-11. However, he still needs to know the way to the city. Thus, two different motivations are given for attaining "Nine Gates": a spiritual one (evangelism) and a simpler, more common motivation (lifting the poor out of their beggarly state).

As for the second possible explanation, a deliberate literary choice on the part of the author, I must admit that I am at a loss to see how this switch in voice could serve the progression of the story. Any possible explanation of 5.1-14 in light of this suggestion is further complicated by the reappearance of the first person in 6.9-8.20. The immediate reappearance of the first person in 6.9-27 seems to assume a dialogue between the merchant and Peter that has been narrated in the first person. In short, there is no special indication of a deliberate return to the first person. It is as if the voice change of 5.1-14 never happened. Obviously, an inability to supply a literary motive for the voice change in 5.1-14 does not eliminate its possibility. However, any theory which attempts to adopt this explanation must explain the immediate return to the first person in 6.9, a task which will not be easy.

I propose that the third explanation, a mistake or "slip" (i.e., sloppy pseudonymity) on the part of the author, makes the most sense of this perplexing voice shift in 5.1-14. To understand this suggestion, it is important to consider the literary role of first person narration. Let us consider that, despite the above examples, the typical voice in which the majority of ancient narratives are written is third person. Virgil's *Aeneid*, Thucydides' *Peloponnesian War*, Genesis, the canonical gospels and many Nag Hammadi documents may be used as examples. However, the writer of this text made a conscious decision to write in the first person—a voice typically reserved for personal testimony. This literary decision creates the narrative illusion of a personal account of actual events occurring in the life of the narrator (in this case, Peter). In short, this technique has the effect of historicizing the story by personalizing it. Clearly this is a deliberate literary device.

Recognition of the first person as a literary device may be an important step to understanding the intrusion of the third person in 5.1-14. If the author was not Peter, then he/she had not experienced these events first hand. Thus, writing in the first person may have been more demanding[33] in that it required (and still does require) the writer to "get inside" the character and "see" the unfolding events through the character's eyes. I would juxtapose this to third person narration, which allows the author to visualize the characters' actions and

---

[33] Consider some of the difficult textual transitions caused by using first person narration, such as description of actions unfolding before the eyes of the main character and description or narration given by a character other than the main character.

statements as unfolding before his or her imagination as actors on a
stage.

I believe the work of literary theorist Ellen Peel sheds some interesting light on the phenomenon of sudden shifts in voice. Peel describes such sharp shifts between first person narration by the
protagonist and third person narration about the protagonist as
"alternating narration." While she acknowledges the presence of this
literary technique in works with male protagonists, Peel suggested
that alternating narration in modern literature is part of a feminist
aesthetic:

> I considered the tendency toward alternating narration in contemporary
> novels about women to be merely interesting until I began to wonder what
> the technique signified in these writings. The answer seems to lie in the fe-
> male protagonists' uneasy view of themselves as both subject and object,
> both self and other. First person point of view presents the protagonist as
> subject (at least of narration); third person narration presents her as object
> (at least of narration); and sharp alternation between the two vividly presents
> her unease.[34]

Peel connects this narrative unease between the protagonist's view of
herself as both subject and object with the actual situation of women
in a patriarchal society:

> The answer lies in the feminist analysis of women's role as subject and ob-
> ject. A woman may consider herself a subject but face strong pressure from a
> society that urges her to see herself as object, as other. Simone de Beauvoir
> says that woman "is defined and differentiated with reference to man and not
> he with reference to her; she is the incidental, the inessential as opposed to
> the essential. He is the Subject, he is the Absolute—she is the Other."
> Probably the issue of self and other, like the related issue of subject and ob-
> ject, has concerned every human being. But, for the reasons articulated by
> Beauvoir, the issue has particular urgency for women in a sexist society.... I
> contend that alternating narration is a particularly effective technique for
> expressing a feminist awareness of women's condition.[35]

Peel's literary-theoretical study in effect develops the second of my
proposed explanations for sudden voice shifts or "alternating narration," i.e., a deliberate literary choice on the part of the author.

---

[34] E. Peel, "Subject, Object, and the Alternation of First and Third Person Narration in
Novels by Alther, Atwood, and Drabble: Toward a Theory of Feminist Aesthetics,"
*Critique* 98 (1989) 108.

[35] Ibid., 118-19. De Beauvoir's insightful comments are from her work, *The Second
Sex*, trans. H. M. Parshley (New York: Vintage-Random House, 1974).

However, her discussion of subject and object has something to add to my third suggestion that 5.1-14 represents a mistake or "slip" (i.e., sloppy pseudonymity) on the part of the author. Peel's principle suggests that alternating narration can be deliberately used by an author to reflect a character's unease with themselves (i.e., tension between the character's view of their self as subject and external pressure to view their self as an object). Is it not possible to argue that an *author* might experience this same unease in relation to one of his/her own characters? In our case the author is using Peter as the subject ("I, Peter"), yet is not Peter. Therefore, from the author's perspective, Peter is really not subject (self), but object (other). It is precisely this tension between the subject of the author and the subject of the character that makes writing a story in first person narration difficult and susceptible to a "slip" into the author's natural view of the character, as object (i.e., third person).[36] Thus, I conclude that the third person in 5.1-14 may represent the writer "slipping" into a more natural third person voice—natural, that is, for a person who is not describing personally witnessed events.[37] This "slip" was either unnoticed or simply disregarded by the author due to the complications inherent in using first person narration.

*c. Difficulties Posed by 5.1-6*

A second area of concern when dealing with voice shifts and 5.1-14 is the difficulties posed by 5.1-6. The problems of 5.1-6 are twofold: 1) the change in voice, an explanatory theory for this has been

---

[36] In discussing this concept with my wife, a social worker, I was inadvertently given a modern example of just such a circumstance. It seems my wife is required to write reports detailing the specific steps she has taken in aiding her various clients. These reports, as formal documents, are supposed to be written in the third person in which the social worker is supposed to refer to him- or herself "this social worker." However, my wife stated that upon rereading her reports and the reports of many other social workers she noticed that virtually every report fluctuated between the third and first person. When asked to explain this phenomenon my wife noted that the third person did not seem natural and, try as she might, over the course of a long report she and other social workers could not help but revert back to the first person, which seemed more natural. I recognize that this does not conclusively prove the validity of my argument. However, it should prove that such unintentional "slips" in voice do happen in real life circumstances.

[37] Patterson argues that "somewhere between 3.7 and 5.3 there has been a shift from the first person voice of Peter to the third person voice of an anonymous narrator." However, Patterson is unsure as to where this transition has actually taken place. He attributes this discrepancy to a redactor: "It is as though a redactor was able to accomplish a smooth transition from one source to another, but once he/she was well into the second source the identity of the voice in the original narrative was soon forgotten as the scribe dutifully copied exactly what was on the page before him/her. By 5.3 the redactor has simply forgotten that it is Peter who is telling the story," Patterson, 9-10. Patterson attributes the words "Peter" in 5.3 and the Coptic prefix "he" in 5.7 to error.

proposed above, and 2) a peculiar narrative order, which presents Peter answering the poor's questions about "the hardships of the way" only to turn around in 5.7-10 and ask Lithargoel about these same hardships.[38]

This second problem could lead an interpreter to posit a literary seam indicating a change in sources. However, the problem may not be so much a narrative problem as a problem with the translation of the Coptic text. Most of the first few letters in the sentence beginning in 5.1 and translated in NHS 11 as "The men asked Peter about the hardships"[39] are gone. Therefore, the ΝΙ] / ΡⲰ[Ⲙⲉ, "the men," is only a theoretical reconstruction of how the text might have read. Certainly, the translator's assumption that the original text included ΡⲰⲘⲉ is well within the realm of possibility. In fact, I agree that the text did in fact read ΡⲰⲘⲉ. However, I disagree with the translator's assumption that at the end of 5.1 the original text included a plural article. I suggest that the original text used the Coptic singular article and originally read "The man asked Peter..." This slight change is quite significant in determining who is asking Peter about the hardships. Based upon the tendencies manifested in *ActsPet12Apost.* to this point in the text, I suggest that it is not the poor who are asking this question, but rather "the man who sells this pearl" (i.e., the pearl merchant). I have come to this conclusion based upon the following three considerations.

First, the translators assume that the text is referring to the poor and the beggars, and thus postulate a plural prefix for ΡⲰⲘⲉ. However, the Coptic text never refers to these groups as "the men." Rather, they are systematically referred to as the "poor of the city" (3.32; 4.16) or simply "the poor" (4.6; 4.28; 4.35). The beggars are referred to as such (4.29; 4.35).[40] In fact, the logic of referring to any group within the city of Habitation as "the men" (i.e., in generic terms) is bad in that it defeats the strict dichotomy the author has set

---

[38] Patterson notes this narrative problem, calling it a "jolting aporia." This leads Patterson to suggest that there has been a shift in sources, yet he finds it difficult to locate this seam with much specificity, ibid., 3, 9-10.

[39] The translation in *The Nag Hammadi Library in English* mirrors this wording. Schenke's translation in *New Testament Apocrypha* (vol. 2) is slightly different: "The people asked Peter about the hardships," (*New Testament Apocrypha*, 421).

[40] In the Coptic there are two terms translated in the English as "beggar." In 4.18, 20 ⲚϬⲀΤⲘⲚΤΝⲀⲉ is used by the poor to describe themselves and their condition, while in 4.29, 35 the term ΡⲉϥΤⲰⲂϨ seems to be used to describe a distinct group among the poor.

up between the rich, who reject the pearl merchant, and the poor, who rejoice because of his promise.[41]

The second reason I believe the text to have originally referred to "the man who sells this pearl" is that to this point in the text it has been typical for the author to refer to the pearl merchant by using the word ⲣⲱⲙⲉ. Granted, ⲣⲱⲙⲉ may have different prefixes as is called for by its respective situations in the text, but the pattern is undeniable (see 2.10; 2.17; 2.33; 3.31; 4.2 and even 5.7).

The third reason has to do with narrative flow. (I have saved this reason until now as I recognize that "narrative flow" can be a very subjective thing. What sounds good or makes sequential logic for one reader may be perceived differently by another.) In the text leading up to 5.1-14, Peter meets and converses with the pearl merchant (2.17-3.11). This conversation is interrupted by the intrusions of Habitation's two factions, the rich and the poor. While the rich disdain the merchant and do not acknowledge him (3.25-27), the poor converse with him (4.3-34). Meanwhile, Peter apparently remains close so as to narrate the action and conversation. At 4.35-5.1, the conversation between the poor and the merchant is resolved in a positive manner ("the poor and the beggars rejoiced"). Thus, the poor as a group recede from view and, logically, the merchant resumes his conversation with Peter. This understanding of the text would make the merchant's question to Peter similar in kind to Jesus' question in Mark 8:27, "Who do men say that I am?" In other words, a question asked to reveal the answerer's partial knowledge so as to complete that knowledge by further revelation (see Mark 8:31, 34-38).

The author, then, originally intended to present the reader with a solidly first person narrative from 1.1 to 8.20. It is here that the pattern of first person narration begins to break down permanently (excepting the "We–Apostolic voice" passage in 9.15-29) and it is here that our most intriguing shifts occur.

## 2. A Problematic Section (8.21-35)— The Case of the Missing Text

In addition to the obvious voice shift at this juncture there is a more subtle indicator of a possible transition in the underlying sources. It seems that a key to understanding this transition lies in a careful reading of the Coptic in 8.21. When these lines are more closely examined a rather peculiar usage of the verb (ⲟⲩⲱϣⲃ̄, "to re-

---

[41] This theory of a singular subject ("the man") is allowed by the remaining fragment of the verb "to ask." The alpha of its prefix could easily be third person singular, allowing the prefix+verb to read "he asked": ⲁ[ϥϣ]ⲓⲛⲉ ⲛ̄ϭⲓ ⲡ[ⲓ]/ⲣⲱⲙⲉ ⲛ̄ⲥⲁ....

spond") is discovered. This verb is not uncommon to
*ActsPet12Apost.*, appearing 13 times over its 12 pages.[42] What is
peculiar to this instance is that in every other occurrence it refers to a
"response" by a character to a statement, request or question posed by
another character. It is only at 8.20-21 that it is used to initiate
dialogue. Thus, based upon previous usage, it would appear that there
is some text missing, though, it is virtually impossible to guess how
much preceded 8.21. Furthermore, it is difficult to determine this
missing section's relationship to the surrounding texts. The possibility
of text, originally preceding these lines, but now missing, coupled
with an obvious voice shift leads me to separate it somewhat from the
Petrine narration spanning 1.1 to 8.20.

Yet the issue is far from decided by this point. On the other hand
there are several significant thematic aspects which link it with the
previous text, such as 1) the use of the term "stranger" (8.24 to
3.7.10); 2) the reference to Lithargoel (8.25 to 5.16); and 3) the
reference to medical topics (8.34 to 8.15-19). Suffice it to say here
that I consider this text to be related to the rest of the pearl merchant
story in 1.1-8.20.

### 3. An Inserted Resurrection Appearance (9.1-29)

At 9.1, there appears to be yet another indication of a textual break.
Following the rather plastic "He hurried and came (back) quickly" in
8.35-9.1, there is a rather abruptly introduced section to which I shall
refer, following Schenke and Patterson's lead,[43] as a resurrection
appearance. In this section, I include 9.1 to 9.29, which contains my
third voice shift type, "We - Apostolic Voice." My reasons for
regarding this as stemming from an originally separate source are
fourfold.

The first reason is related to the voice shift present within this
section, "We - Apostolic Voice." As Patterson has noted, "the
narrative shifts in *ActsPet12Apost.* often involve not simply a shift in
voice (third person to first, or singular to plural), but an actual shift in
the narrative perspective of the text." Patterson notes that in this text

---

[42] 3.1; 4.10-11, 29-30; 5.3, 15; 7.6; 8.20-21; 9.4-5, 8, 13; 10.13, 22; 11.14. Patterson
also noted this peculiarity, describing this usage as an "aporia;" Patterson, 4.

[43] Patterson describes this resurrection appearance as being in 8.10-9.29 and links it
with his proposed third source—"We Source;" Patterson, 12. Schenke's view is similar.
He calls the text "an Easter and Pentecost story;" Schenke, *New Testament Apocrypha*,
418.

the voice is one of the apostolic group, not Peter.[44] Thus, this narrative perspective is unique to this section of *ActsPet12Apost.*, a fact which sets it apart from the rest of the document.

The second reason has to do with the problematic relationships between Lithargoel, the physician and Jesus. In 8.11-20, Lithargoel is introduced for the first time as a physician. The narrator (presumably Peter—still in the "We of Journeys") declares that the group did not recognize him. Thus, the reader expects a recognition scene where the physician is revealed as Lithargoel and, presumably, Lithargoel's relationship with physicians is explained. Instead, Lithargoel is referred to as "the Savior" in 9.5, a term that is otherwise foreign to *ActsPet12Apost.* Thus, Lithargoel is never "recognized" as the physician and subsequently drops out of the narrative.[45]

Third, there is a natural break in the text as it now stands. Lithargoel, now a physician, leaves and promises to return. I regard the cursory mention of Lithargoel's departure and return as secondary. It just doesn't seem to make a great deal of narrative sense. Why take the trouble to narrate a departure of a key character and then not do anything with the other characters in the meantime?

The fourth reason is a minor point. In 9.20 the "we" is referred to as eleven "disciples." The word μαθητής appears only twice in *ActsPet12Apost.* (9.20; 12.13), and it is only in 9.20 that a numerical designation is associated with the term "disciples." Elsewhere those with Peter are called brothers (3.6); strangers (3.7; 8.25); friends (6.28; 7.21) and possibly even apostles (1.5) and yet none of these terms has any kind of numerical designation as in 9.20.

## 4. The Author/Redactor's Own Material

The final section to be examined is 9.30-12.19. As noted above, this is one of those sections which I have classed under "The Narrator." These lines are the defining section of *ActsPet12Apost.* and representative of the author's own hand. The section begins with a reference to the unguent box and pouch that were mentioned in 8.16-19. However, it seems clear from what follows that this is merely the author's attempt to link his/her work with the previous material, since the

---

[44] Patterson, 6-7. Patterson groups this first person plural voice in 9.15-29 with his third source, the "We Source."

[45] The significance of this point should not be overlooked—this is nothing less than the absorption of the characteristics of Lithargoel into Jesus. Lithargoel was to be revealed as a heavenly physician but now it is Jesus who is depicted as the physician. As Schenke states, "the central figure now wears one disguise too many," Schenke, *New Testament Apocrypha*, 418.

reference in 9.30-31 to the unguent box and pouch is not expanded upon. Instead, it is not until 10.31-32, when the text presents Jesus as once again giving the pouch to Peter and the others, that the subject of healing is seriously broached. It is only in the following text that it becomes clear that the author's own views on healing are slightly different from the previous material. While the author is obliged by his/her usage of the previous material to mention the unguent box and pouch, it seems clear in 11.14-26 (especially lines 19-23) that the author envisions bodily healing as being able to be brought about "without medicine of the world"—thus making Lithargoel's tools of the healing trade practically obsolete.[46]

In summary, I suggest that in *ActsPet12Apost.* we have two main bodies of source material which have been brought together and expanded by an author/redactor. It is important at this point to stress that I do not believe that the first and second sources have remained inviolate from the author/redactor's hand. On the contrary, I believe that the author/redactor has added material and thereby altered these sources. For now it is sufficient to paint with broad strokes as follows:

1) *The Story of the Pearl Merchant* (1.1-9.1, except for redactional additions): a first-person narrative; parable-like or allegorical in nature; involved a mysterious pearl merchant, two symbolic cities and a mystical journey to one of these cities so as to attain "the pearl" which was most likely spiritual healing of the soul (i.e., heaven, oneness with God); there was probably a return from the heavenly city so as to pass on the knowledge of how to make the journey and any other "knowledge" that might have been revealed at "Nine Gates."

2) *A Resurrection Appearance* (9.1-9.29): told from the perspective of one of the followers of Jesus, not Peter (first person yet employing third person within this overall structure); possibly docetic or gnostic in tone;[47] its reference to the "eleven disciples" associates it with a post-crucifixion period and with the traditions like those recorded in the canonical gospels.

---

[46] Presumably this envisioned healing would be like many of the miracles of Jesus as reported by the canonical gospels where no aides were used (e.g., Mark 1:29-31; 40-2 but not John 9:1-7).

[47] This would seem to be evidenced by the instance when Jesus loosens his garment and is recognized by his disciples. One expects there to be reference made to identifying scars or wounds. However, the garment is shown in the text to be the body into which Jesus had changed, almost as if it were a costume. Thus, it seems to be not the flesh which the disciples recognize but what lies underneath, presumably the spirit?

3) *The Author/Redactor's Position and Theology* (9.30-12.19): third person narration; didactic or hortatory in tone; attempts to echo themes from the pearl merchant source; it shifts the emphasis of first source from a heavenly hereafter to an earthly or pastoral focus.

# INTERPRETATION OF THE PROLOGUE TO JOHN'S GOSPEL IN SOME GNOSTIC AND PATRISTIC WRITINGS: A COMMON TRADITION

*Anne Pasquier*
Université Laval, Québec

In his Commentary on John's Gospel, Origen writes: "But if there are letters of God, as there are, which the saints read and say they have read what is written in the tablets of heaven, those letters are the thoughts about the Son of God which are broken up into alpha and the letters that follow to omega, that heavenly matters might be read through them."[1] The Greek term here translated by "thoughts" about the Son, *ennoiai*, is central for Origen's interpretation of Christ. The other word used more often by him in the same context is *epinoiai* which means "titles," "expressions," or "concepts." The *epinoiai*, just as the *ennoiai*, have a subjective and an objective side: they are thoughts about the Son and may correspond to the spiritual growth of the saints. But these thoughts or names also "have a corresponding objective reality. From a Christological point of view the *epinoiai* are the objective perfections of Christ which display a hierarchy within themselves."[2] They are like letters, which are divided from alpha to

---

[1] *Comm. in Joh.* I.221, transl. by R. E. Heine, *The Fathers of the Church. A New Translation*, vol. 80, 1989, 77. Also Origène. *Commentaire sur Saint Jean. Tome I, Livres I-V*, ed. and trans. C. Blanc (*SC* 120; Paris: Cerf, 1966) 168-169.

[2] A. Grillmeier, *Christ in Christian Tradition, Vol. I: From the Apostolic Age to Chalcedon (451)*, 2nd ed. (Oxford: Mowbrays, 1975) 141. Also: F. Bertrand, *Mystique de Jésus chez Origène* (Paris, Aubier, 1951); H. Crouzel, "Le contenu spirituel des dénominations du Christ selon le Livre I du Commentaire sur Jean d'Origène," *Origeniana Secunda: Second colloque international des études origéniennes (Bari, 20-23 septembre 1977)*, ed. H. Crouzel and A. Quacquarelli (Quaderni di Vetera Christianorum 15; Rome: Ed. dell' Ateneo and Desclée de Brouwer, 1980) 131-150; Id., *Origène et la connaissance mystique* (Paris-Bruges: Desclée de Brouwe, 1961) 389ff; A. Orbe, *En los albores de la exegesis johannea. Estudios valentinianos*, vol. II (Analecta Gregoriana 65; Rome: Libreria Editrice dell' Università Gregoriana, 1955); idem, *Hacia la primera teologia de la procesion del Verbo. Estudios valentinianos*, vol. I (Analecta Gregoriana 99-100; Rome, Libreria Editrice dell' Università Gregoriana, 1958); idem, *La uncion del verbo: Estudios valentinianos*, vol. III (Analecta Gregoriana 113; Rome: Libreria Editirice dell' Università Gregoriana, 1961). R. Van den Broek, "Jewish and Platonic Speculations in Early Alexandrian Theology: Eugnostus, Philo, Valentinus, and Origen," *The Roots of Egyptian Christianity*, ed. B. A. Pearson and J. E. Goehring (Studies in

omega and which describe aspects of the function of the Son whereby he reveals himself.[3] These designations of Christ do not dissolve his unity: "the same one is beginning and end, but he is not the same insofar as the aspects (*epinoiai*) are concerned." (*Comm. in Joh.* I.222 [trans. R. E. Heine, ANF IV.77])

Whereas God the Father is absolute simplicity, the Son is multiple in respect of his very constitution. So Christology is explained on the basis of a Platonic hierarchy of being. But at the same time, those names or concepts applied to the Son, which display a hierarchy among themselves, derive from Scripture. Such an attempt to build a Christology on titles found in Scripture is typical of Valentinian Gnostics. Moreover, Origen distinguishes between *epinoiai* which belong to the Son himself in his relation to God and *epinoiai* which he possesses in his relation to human beings. Now the first ones—the fundamental ones—are taken from the prologue to John's Gospel: the Son is Beginning (*arche*), Word (*logos*), Life (*zoe*) and Truth (*aletheia*).[4] It is easy to perceive the connection with the Valentinian exegesis of the same prologue: Origen and the Valentinians partake of the same tradition, the latter having very probably exerted an influence upon the former in a positive and a negative way.[5] So it is possible to make a comparison between them that could help us to perceive more exactly the philosophical background of the Gnostic interpretation of the prologue to John's Gospel. Despite the theological differences between Origen and them, it could also retrospectively

---

Antiquity & Christianity; Philadelphia, Fortress, 1986) 201-203 draws some interesting parallels between Origen's doctrine and Gnostic speculations on the pleroma; also J. Collantes, *La Teologia Gnostica en el primer comentario al Evangelio de San Juan* (Diss. theol. Pontificia Universitas Gregoriana; Madrid, 1953). E. H. Pagels, *The Johannine Gospel in Gnostic Exegesis: Heracleon's Commentary on John* (Nashville: Abingdon Press, 1973).

[3] This is the reason why R. Lorenz (*Arius Iudaizans? Untersuchungen zur dogmengeschichtlichen Einordnung des Arius* [Göttingen: Vandenhoeck & Ruprecht, 1979] 83) translated *epinoiai* by "structures of knowledge."

[4] *Comm. in Joh.* I.1.123.

[5] Cf. A. Le Boulluec, "La place de la polémique antignostique dans le *Peri Archôn* d'Origène," *Origeniana* (Quaderni di Vetera Christianorum 12; Bari: Istituto di Letteratura christiana antiqua, Università Bari, 1975) 47-61; idem, "Y a-t-il des traces de la polémique antignostique d'Irénée dans le Peri Archôn d'Origène?" *Gnosis and Gnosticism*, ed. M. Krause (NHS 8; Leiden, E. J. Brill, 1977) 138-147; Id., *La notion d'hérésie dans la littérature grecque, II-IIIe siècle* vol. II: *Clément d'Alexandrie et Origène* (Paris: Études augustiniennes, 1985) 514-18 (against Heracleon). Also: A. B. Scott, "Opposition and Concession: Origen's Relationship to Valentinianism," *Origeniana Quinta*, ed. R. J. Daly (Bibliotheca Ephemeridum theologicarum Lovaniensium 105; Leuven: Leuven University Press, 1992) 79-84; J. Rius-Camps, "Origenes frente al desafio de los Gnosticos," *Origeniana Quinta*, 57-78.

help us to clarify some aspects of their Christology, in so far as Origen is much more explicit on that matter. For the Gnostic interpretation is known above all from indirect sources, principally from the accounts of Irenaeus (*Adv. haer.* I.8.5).[6] Here I present some first reflections on that topic that could lead to a deeper study.

## THE BEGINNING OR PRINCIPLE

According to Irenaeus' account (*Adv. haer.* I.8.5), Valentinians teach that "John, the disciple of the Lord, wishing to set forth the origin of all things, so as to explain how the Father produced the whole, lays down a certain principle, that, namely, which was first-begotten by God, which Being he has termed both the only-begotten Son and God, in whom the Father, after a seminal manner (*spermatikôs*), brought forth all things. By him the Word was produced, and in him the whole substance of the Aeons, to which the Word himself afterwards imparted form."[7]

This passage may be compared with Origen's doctrine on the *epinoiai* which is found especially in *On First Principles* and in the *Commentary on John*. The first title and the most important one is "principle" or "beginning", *arche*. And this *arche* is Sophia, for the Son "is the beginning insofar as he is wisdom, as we have learned in Proverbs. Therefore it has been written, 'God created me the beginning of his ways for his works.'" (*Comm. in Joh.* I.31.222 [trans. R. E. Heine, ANF IV.77).[8] Abiding in the uninterrupted vision of the Father's profundity, Wisdom contains the types and principles (*logoi*) of all things which she has formed within herself beforehand. She contains in herself the *initia*, that is to say, not only the ideal Platonic forms in the general sense (*genus* and *species*), but also the individual germs or seeds (*logoi spermatikoi*) of all beings (*Princ.* I.4.5).[9]

---

[6] Also, Clement of Alexandria, *Ex. Theod.* 6.1-4.

[7] *The Ante-Nicene Fathers. Translations of The Writings of the Fathers down to A. D. 325*, vol. 1, ed. A. Roberts and J. Donaldson, rev. A. C. Coxe. (New York: Scribners, 1969) 328-329.

[8] For the whole interpretation of Jn 1:1: *Comm. in Joh.* I.90-292. Also: *Princ.* I.2.1-3.

[9] Also, *Princ.* I.2.2-3: see H. Crouzel and M. Simonetti, eds. and trans., *Origène. Traité des Principes* (SC 253; Paris: Cerf, 1978) 31 and 36, n. 13; also W.R. Schoedel, "Jewish Wisdom and the Formation of the Christian Ascetic," *Aspects of Wisdom in Judaism and Early Christianity*, ed. R. L. Wilken (Notre Dame and London: University of Notre Dame Press, 1975) 174-194; H. Jaeger, "The Patristic Conception of Wisdom in the Light of Biblical and Rabbinical Research," *StudPat* IV (TU 79; Berlin: Akademie-Verlag, 1961) 90-106. One should add that even if he is the beginning of all things, the Son is himself without beginning.

Origen develops more explicitly what heresiologists merely summarize about Valentinian exegesis, that is to say, the idea that all the creative power of the coming creation is included in the Son as beginning and as *Nous* (intelligence; see *Ex. Theod.* 6.3: the only-begotten Son is *Nous*). Just as the Plotinian *Nous*, Wisdom is a multiplicity in her very nature, being a mediator between the One and the multiplicity of creatures. She is a cosmos, an eternal archetypal world who embraces Plato's world of intelligibles. Thus is she presented in terms of exemplary causality.

In order to express the theme of the Son as being the instrument of God in the creation of all things, Origen makes use of Col 1:16-18 and Ps 104:24,[10] in addition to Jn 1:3:[11] "And in Him were all things created that are in heaven and earth, visible and invisible, whether they be thrones, or dominions, or principalities, or powers; all things were created by Him, and in Him, and He is before all, and He is the head."[12]

This means first that the Only-begotten Son precedes the constitution of all things. As in Christian Gnostic thought, the Son not only precedes the constitution of the *pleroma*; he *is* the *pleroma*: he contains all the beings that are prefigured in him as the beginning and end of all things. He is, as Origen puts it, the only one who is by nature a Son and is therefore termed Only-begotten. Thus, the multiplicity of the archetypal world in God's Wisdom is to some extent expressed through the other *epinoiai* or titles of Christ found in Scripture: Logos, Life, and so on, that are part of himself.

However, Origen lays great stress on the fact that the Father and his image, Wisdom, are "one in the agreement of their minds, in the concord of their utterance and in the identity of their will." Wisdom is the "spotless mirror of his activity" (Wis 7:26). Origen objects to the Gnostics' view that the existence of the visible cosmos depends upon the double subordinate agency of the Savior and of an inferior Wisdom with the help of the Demiurge (a Wisdom whose initial act is

---

[10] "In wisdom hast Thou made them all" (*Princ.* I.3.10 [ANF IV.250]).

[11] "All things were made by Him, and without Him was nothing made."

[12] See also: "He (Paul) therefore manifestly declares that in Christ and through Christ were all things made and created, whether things visible, which are corporeal, or things invisible, which I regard as none other than incorporeal and spiritual powers. But of those things which he had termed generally corporeal or incorporeal, he seems to me, in the words that follow, to enumerate the various kinds, viz., thrones, dominions, principalities, powers, influences." (*Princ.* I.7.1, [ANF IV.262])

committed without Theletos, without the Father's assent, that is to say, without the Son.[13]

## LOGOS AND LIFE

According to the Valentinian teaching, "by him (the beginning or principle) the Word was produced, and in him the whole substance (*ousia*) of the Aeons, to which the Word himself afterwards imparted form" (Irenaeus, *Adv. haer.* I.1.18, 7-9). Origen too distinguishes between *arche* (beginning) and *Logos* (Word): "But insofar as he is Word, he is not the beginning, for 'in the beginning was the Word'" (*Comm. in Joh.* II.19.133, 3-5), that is to say, in Wisdom was the Logos. "His aspects, therefore, have a beginning, and something that is second beyond the beginning, and third, and so on to the end."[14] One of the functions of the Logos is to communicate to spiritual beings (the *logikoi*) the things which have been contemplated in Wisdom: "Now, in the same way in which we have understood that Wisdom was the beginning of the ways of God, and is said to be created, forming beforehand and containing within herself the species and beginnings of all creatures, must we understand her to be the Word of God, because of her disclosing to all other beings, i.e., to universal creation, the nature of the mysteries and secrets which are contained within the divine wisdom; and on this account she is called the Word, because she is, as it were, the interpreter of the secrets of the mind."[15] Thus, the Son "unites the Model and the Demiurge of the *Timaeus*."[16] The Logos looks in two directions, towards the mind as well as towards those who need salvation and formation; he implants *form* upon chaotic matter in accordance with the archetypes residing in Wisdom, inasmuch as he is the rational principle behind creation.

---

[13] *C. Cels.* 8.12 and *Princ.* I.2.12: see A. Orbe, *Estudios Valentinianos*, I.388f., 449f.; II.35-46; III.211-2. See Irenaeus, *Adv. haer.* I.2.2: *theletos* is one of the names of the Savior and is called Wisdom's husband.

[14] *Comm. in Joh.* I.222-223 [transl. R. E. Heine], 77-78 (see also I.111-115). According to Gnostic exegesis (*Adv. haer.* I.8.5), these designations of Christ do not dissolve the unity of God: "Having first of all distinguished these three—God, the Beginning, and the Word—he (John) again unites them, that he may exhibit the production of each of them, that is of the Son and of the Word, and may at the same time show their union with one another, and with the Father."

[15] *Princ.* I.2.3, [ANF IV.246; *Comm. in Joh.* I.111: "It is wisdom which is understood, on the one hand, taken in relation to the structure of the contemplation and thoughts of all things, but it is the Word which is received, taken in relation to the communication of the things which have been contemplated to spiritual beings" (trans. R. E. Heine, 57).

[16] J. A. Lyons, *The Cosmic Christ in Origen and Teilhard de Chardin. A Comparative Study* (Oxford: Oxford University Press, 1982) 94.

For the Gnostics, formation and disclosure of the secrets of the mind are also two functions of the Logos. In their interpretation, it is a question of spiritual formation only, while for Origen, the Logos, as a cosmic aspect of the Son, has penetrated the whole creation, including the non-rational creation. Of course, Origen too is chiefly concerned with the Son's presence in rational creatures. Initially, the Son is united with them in a pre-mundane existence, where they form the preexistent church.[17]

According to the Gnostic interpretation of John, the Logos plays two roles: "But 'what was made in Him,' says John, 'is life.' Here again he indicated conjunction; for all things, he said, were made *by* Him, but *in* Him was life. This, then, which is in Him, is more closely connected with Him than those things which were simply made by Him, for it exists along with Him, and is developed by Him." (*Adv. haer.* I.8.5). The saying "All things were made *by* him" was commented upon previously as follows: "for the Word was the author of form and beginning to all the Aeons that came into existence *after Him*" (*Adv. haer.* I.1.18, 23-25). This activity is distinguished from the development of life *in* him. This shows very likely the distinction that exists between the Logos as the Savior who is Life intrinsically and those who are not yet saved. For the Aeons first exist in the Father's thought (that is, in the Son as mind or beginning) as intellectual substance. Being in the Father's thought means being in a potential state; it means that the spiritual germ is not yet developed or that human beings or some humans are not yet conscious of that. But any spiritual germ or seed comes from the Father who sows it in the Logos. By means of the Logos, this seed enables the birth of spiritual humans. Such an interpretation seems to distinguish the *ousia*, the spiritual substance, from the imposition of the qualities whereby this original substance becomes differentiated into individual beings:[18] "In Stoicism this is the process of individuation within shared being; the different activity produces a distinct, if essentially related individual."[19] As an immanent seminal principle, the Logos is the instrumen-

---

[17] Idem, 136: see Origen's *Comm. in Cant.* 2. 8.

[18] See Origen's *Comm. in Joh.* II.137: according to Heracleon, "For he (the Logos) furnished their first form at their origin, bringing the things sown by another into form and illumination and their own individuality, and bringing them forth" (trans. adapted from R. E. Heine, 131).

[19] J. R. Lyman, *Christology and Cosmology. Models of Divine Activity in Origen, Eusebius, and Athanasius* (Oxford Theological Monographs; Oxford: Clarendon Press, 1993) 72, who refers to A. J. Voelke, *L'Idée de volonté dans le stoicisme*, (Paris: Presses universitaires de France, 1973) 13-18.

tal cause of a spiritual understanding, which will afterwards impart form to the Aeons by the development of the spiritual germ. In fact, the pleroma here is an initial pleroma:

> "Le Plérôme en tant que plénitude n'existe en effet qu'à la fin et non au début du récit, puisque le Plérôme initial est complété par des êtres spirituels, les semences, qui sont formés dans la création. Il apparaît alors que la constitution du Plérôme ne peut être considérée sans référence à la création. Le monde et son histoire sont indispensables pour communiquer la gnose aux spirituels."[20]

The Savior, who is at the same time "Son, and Aletheia, and Zoe, and the Word made flesh" will be "the fruit of the entire Pleroma" (*Adv. haer.* I.8.5) only at the end.

Origen sometimes agrees with Valentinians on the fact that "he alone who participates in this Word, insofar as he is such, is 'rational.' Consequently, we could also say that the saint alone is 'rational,' that is to say 'spiritual'" (*Comm. on Joh.* II.114).[21] But this immanent all-pervading presence of the Logos is offered up to all humans, not only to some in particular. Origen opposes, in his *Commentary on John*, II.130-131, the reading "what was in him was life": "Life was not in the Word, but life was made, if indeed 'life is the light of men.'"[22] And "This life indeed comes into existence *after the Word*, being inseparable from him after it has come into existence." (II.129). He thus argues against Heracleon: "But when Heracleon came to the passage, 'What was made in him was life,' he took 'in him' in a very forced manner to mean 'in spiritual men,' as though he thought the Word and spiritual humans were the same, although he did not say this explicitly" (*Comm. on Joh.* II.137, trans. R. E. Heine, 131).[23]

In Origen and in Gnostic interpretation, one can discern the Stoic doctrine of the *logos spermatikos*, in addition to some Platonic

---

[20] J. Fantino, *La théologie d'Irénée. Lecture des Écritures en réponse à l'exégèse gnostique: Une approche trinitaire* (Paris: Cerf, 1994) 193.

[21] ANF IV.125-128. See also II.132: "Some copies, however, have, and perhaps not without credibility, 'What was made in him is life.' Now if life is equivalent to the light of men,....Consequently only the one who is alive,....is a son of light". (*Comm. in Joh.* I.221, trans. R. E. Heine, 129).

[22] Origen's comment is as follows: anything which has "come to be" is not in itself life. But the possession of life did not come upon the Logos from without, but he is life. Unlike creatures, the Logos is life intrinsically; see G. L. Prestige, *God in Patristic Thought* (London: SPCK, 1959) 137.

[23] See E. H. Pagels, *The Johannine Gospel in Gnostic Exegesis: Heracleon's Commentary on John* (Nashville: Abingdon Press, 1973) 48 and 98-113.

ingredients. According to the Stoic doctrine, the *logos* is represented in the act of "sowing" *gnosis* . Either the human receives what the Logos sows but is not part of it, or a portion of the Logos is present in the human, something deposited by the Logos, which, before being deposited, is part of it, a seed or a particle of the divine Logos.[24] Thus the being of the pneumatics is either a mere participation in the substance of the Logos, or else an actual derivative of that substance.

Origen, for his part, does not seem to assume the presence of a portion of the Logos in the human even if the latter partakes of the former[25]. Only the Son emanates from the Father, whereas rational creatures are not of his being (*ousia*). Jerome, however, charges him with holding the consubstantiality of rational creatures and God (*Epist. ad Avitum* 14). On the other hand, the Gnostic exegesis amounts to the doctrine of the saved Savior. The Logos "individualizes" himself in a multitude of beings that he will in turn gradually gather together as his own members. However, such a doctrine does *not necessarily* mean a theory of automatic salvation for those of a spiritual nature: the spiritual germ, which is sown in the soul, is not something perfect but has to be disciplined or educated along with the soul. Thus, it is not able to assure its own salvation automatically. According to Irenaeus, Valentinians rank human souls into various categories "say that some are by nature good, and others by nature evil. The good are those who become capable of receiving the [spiritual] seed." In other words, there exist two classes of humans, the *hylics* and the *psychics* and a third element, namely:

> la nature spirituelle n'est qu'une virtualité du psychique. Il n'y a pas, du moins ici-bas, de pneumatiques purs; il n'y a que des psychiques qui reçoivent, par grâce, comme dit Tertullien (*Val.* 29.2.3), une semence spirituelle et la font fructifier avec plus ou moins de bonheur.[26]

---

[24] See S. R. C. Lilla, *Clement of Alexandria. A Study in Christian Platonism and Gnosticism* (Oxford Theological Monographs; Oxford: Oxford University Press, 1971) 199-212 (cited by A. Grillmeier, *Christ in Christian Tradition,* 1.135: Lilla has stressed the development of the inner different stages of existence of the Logos and has pointed to the contacts between some Church Fathers (specially Clement of Alexandria) and Jewish-Alexandrian philosophy, Middle Platonism and Neo-Platonism: first of all the Logos is the mind of God which contains his thoughts; then, in a second stage, he represents the immanent law of the universe or a kind of world-soul.

[25] D. L. Balas, "The Idea of Participation in the Structure of Origen's thought. Christian Transposition of a Theme of the Platonic Tradition," *Origeniana* (1975) 257-275. Also H. Crouzel, *Théologie de l'image de Dieu chez Origène* (Paris: Aubier, 1956).

[26] J.-P. Mahé, "Le Témoignage véritable et quelques écrits valentiniens de Nag Hammadi," *Les textes de Nag Hammadi et le problème de leur classification (Actes du Colloque tenu à Québec du 15 au 19 septembre 1993),* ed. L. Painchaud and A. Pasquier (BCNH, section "Études" 3; Québec: Presses de l'Université Laval; Louvain; Paris:

## THE MAN OF THE CHURCH

Philo, Clement of Alexandria, and Origen all state that the Logos, the true Son of Mind, is the image of God, and that the image of the Logos is the true human, the human mind.[27] They all associate the Logos with the word of God in the Old Testament accounts of the creation when "God spoke and it was done." The Valentinians do likewise. However, according to them, the human in question is the Church united with the Son. Or, in other words, the Logos has become human and revealed himself through the church, his body: "When, again, he (John) adds, 'And the life was the light of men,' while thus mentioning Anthropos, he indicated also Ecclesia by that one expression, in order that, by using only one name, he might disclose their fellowship with one another, in virtue of their conjunction. For Anthropos and Ecclesia spring from Logos and Zoe. Moreover, he styled life (Zoe) the light of men, because they are enlightened by her, that is formed and made manifest.....Since, therefore, Zoe manifested and begat both Anthropos and Ecclesia, she is termed their light" (*Adv. haer.* I.8.5).

A similar idea can be found in Origen, even if he doesn't seem to assume the term human as an *epinoia:* the end or consummation that is the perfection and completion of things may, according to him, be confirmed by Paul (*Eph.* 4:13): "Until we all come in the unity of the faith to a perfect man, to the measure of the stature of the fullness of Christ." (*Princ.* I.6.2 [trans. Roberts and Donaldson, ANF IV.261]). And the church here below is the form of that kingdom which is to come, because it has the similitude of unity.[28] Such a doctrine could also be found in Augustine's *City of God* (XV.17-18), where life means also resurrection: Seth means

> "'resurrection,' and the name of his son Enos means 'man.'....Thus, Enos was a 'son' of 'resurrection,'... 'Resurrection' is the father of those generations which are mentioned apart from the others... 'Abel' means 'sorrow' and the name of Seth, his brother, means 'resurrection.' Thus, these two are

---

Peeters, 1995) 240-241. See also M. Desjardins, *Sin in Valentinianism* (SBLDS; Atlanta: Scholars Press, 1990) 120-126, where on can find a discussion of: E. H. Pagels, "Conflicting Versions of Valentinian Eschatology: Irenaeus' Treatise vs. the Excerpts from Theodotus," *HTR* 67 (1974) 35-53 and *The Johannine Gospel in Gnostic Exegesis,* 94-97.

[27] See Prestige, *God in Patristic Thought,* 112-128.

[28] However, see *Comm. in Joh.* I.107-108: owing to the fact that "'the Word became flesh'...he is not only the first-born of all creation, but also Adam, [which] means 'man,'" because we are able to receive him only in this manner at first.

> prophetic symbols of the death of Christ and of His resurrection from the dead. And it is from faith in the Resurrection that the city of God is born ...,"

That is to say, Enos was "destined to be a symbol of man, in the sense of a community of men." This human is the church that has a share in the City which is above, the prefiguration of the church above.[29]

As A. Orbe has written, the pleroma is the "pattern" according to whose image and similitude the economy of salvation must take its course through the sensible world.[30] The general depiction of God as a mind may have brought about the transformation of the Platonic Ideas into the thoughts of God, assuming an analogy between the human and the divine mind. The divine thoughts are just like the ideas of human beings, that is, universal concepts, or individual reasons.[31] It is this for which Irenaeus reproaches the Valentinian Gnostics in *Adv. haer.* II.11 ff. In the mind of the divine Son, who is at the same time *logos endiathetos* and *logos prophorikos* or *nous* and *logos*, there arises and is manifested a specific thought: the man of the church, the archetypal form of the church below. According to the Valentinians, the prologue to John's Gospel depicts a spiritual genesis, the model for the material one, and it is seen as a spiritual interpretation of the Old Testament accounts of the creation: the male and female beings represent the spiritual generation, where Adam as mind begot Seth, the Logos called "life" or "resurrection", because he is himself the father of a spiritual seed, from which springs a living generation: Enos, the man of the church.

## CONCLUSION

In the Christology of Origen, built on titles found in Scripture, the Son reveals facets of his divine nature through his various names. Origen ordered them so as to correspond to the hierarchy of being and the spiritual growth of the Christians. Even if he is a committed opponent of theirs, it seems to me that Origen's doctrine reflects some

---

[29] *Saint Augustine. The City of God,* Books VIII-XVI, trans. G. G. Walsh and G. Monahan, *The Fathers of the Church, A New Translation* (New York: Fathers of the Church, Inc., 1952) 455-457. See also in Origen: "He is the invisible image of the invisible God, in the same manner as we say, according to the sacred history, that the image of Adam is his son Seth. The words are, "And Adam begat Seth in his own likeness, and after his own image." Now this image contains the unity of nature and substance belonging to Father and Son" (*Princ.* I.2.6, trans., 248).

[30] *La uncion del Verbo. Estudios Valentinianos* III, 211-212.

[31] See A. Rich, "The Platonic Ideas as the Thoughts of God," *Mnemosyne* 4.7 (1954) 127.

of the presuppositions and language of the Valentinians. Of course, both have been influenced by Jewish speculations about the names of God and by Jewish-Alexandrian and Platonic philosophy. The main idea is participation in the Father through the Son: God "is altogether one and simple. Our Savior, however, because of the many things...becomes many things..." (*Comm. in Joh.* I.119 [trans. R. E. Heine, ANF IV.58]). From the point of view of the spiritual growth of Christians, this kind of Christology resembles the Platonic process of transformation, where one has to go up through and grasp different levels in order to attain the summit, that is the Son as mind: being the only one who contemplates and perfectly knows God the Father, he is thus the perfect image of the Father's will. But from another point of view, this Christology brings to light the mediation of the Son between God and the visible world: this is a kind of precosmic Passion or an "extension" of the Son for salvation.

However, the question remains whether the different names or forms of the Son in the Gnostic doctrine are just "*epinoiai*" or some kind of distinct "hypostases." The comparison between Irenaeus' two accounts, that is, *Adv. haer.* I.8.5 and *Adv. haer.* I.1ff., leads me to think that there exists perhaps a difference between these two passages about this question. I summarize this hypothesis as follows:

In *Adv. haer.* I.8.5, it is written:

> Since, therefore, he (John) treats of the first origin of things, he rightly proceeds in his teaching from the beginning, that is, from God and the Word. And he expresses himself thus: 'In the beginning was the Word, and the Word was with God, and the Word was God; the same was in the beginning with God.' Having first of all distinguished these three—God, the beginning, and the Word—he again unites them, that he may exhibit the production of each of them, that is, of the Son and of the Word, and may at the same time show their union with one another, and with the Father.

Furthermore, in *Adv. haer.* I.8.5, the Aeons are described as a spiritual seed (the Father brings forth all things in the Son, after a seminal manner: *spermatikôs* ), which will only later be made actual in the Logos. The expression "*ousia*" of the Aeons, used by Irenaeus to designate what is manifested in the mind and in the Logos, perhaps means that the Aeons, in the initial pleroma, exist in the Father's thought only (that is, in the Son as mind and Logos): as intellectual substance, as *logikoi* . But the Logos is also "the author of form and beginning to all the Aeons that *came into existence after Him.*" They will manifest themselves as the images of the ideal form contained in the mind of God, that is, the form of archetypal humanity. So it seems to me that in Irenaeus I.8.5 there is no real distinction between the different forms of the Son: beginning, Logos, Savior, human; we find an emanative hierarchy mediating between the first principle and the world in which the distinctions between one level and the next seem more notional than real.[32]

On the other hand, the passage in *Adv. haer.* I.1ff., lays stress upon the distinctions between mind, Logos and human (even if it is a temporary distinction).[33] For example, the *Propator* is only known to the only-begotten Son or mind, and not to the other Aeons, including the Logos. Further, the Aeons included in the Logos and in the man of the church are nominally and numerically distinguished, that is to say, divided into a decad and a duodecad. In other words, there is an "hypostatizing" of the preexistent church. So I wonder if one could perhaps perceive between these two accounts the same distinction that was made by Tertullian in *Val.* 4.1: while on the one hand Valentinus (or some of the first Valentinians) considered the Aeons to be thoughts or emotions included in the Godhead, that is (according to the same Tertullian in *De anima* 18), to be the ideas in the mind of God, according to which the Logos forms afterwards their images, on the other hand, in Ptolemaeus those Aeons are numerically and nominally distinguished, because Ptolemaeus regarded them as individual substances.[34]

---

[32] The author of the *Tripartate Tractate* is vague about such a distinction between the different notions of the Son, just as the *Gospel of Truth*, which speaks of the pleroma that is in the thought and the intellect of the Father, and from which proceeds the Logos who will be manifested as Savior.

[33] And between the first principle and the mediating levels of divinity.

[34] In the Greek version of Epiphanius, there is nothing that corresponds to the words "Such are the views of Ptolemaeus," which are the conclusion in the Latin translation of Irenaeus *Adv. Haer.* I.8.5. One should add that, in this account, the Savior, revealing the pleroma, is at the same time Son, Aletheia, Zoe and Logos, and not man and church as in other accounts: this perhaps means that the Aeons are not yet manifested but are still thoughts in the mind of God.

PART SIX

BIBLIOGRAPHY

# BIBLIOGRAPHY

Achtemeier, Paul J. "The Origin and Function of the Pre-Marcan Miracle Catenae." *JBL* 91 (1972) 198-221.

——. "Toward the Isolation of Pre-Markan Miracle Catenae." *JBL* 89 (1970) 265-291.

Aland, Barbara. "Die Paraphrase als Form gnostischer Verkundigung." In Robert McL. Wilson, ed. *Nag Hammadi and Gnosis*. Leiden: E. J. Brill, 1978, 75-90.

——. "Gnosis und Philosophie." In Geo Widengren, ed. *Proceedings of the International Colloquium on Gnosticism, Stockholm, August 20-25, 1973*. VHAAH.FF 17. Stockholm: Almqvist & Wiksell, 1977, 34-73.

Albright, William F. *New Horizons in Biblical Research*. London: Oxford University Press, 1966.

Argall, Randal. *1 Enoch and Sirach: A Comparative Literary Analysis of the Themes of Revelation, Creation and Judgment*. SBLEJL. Atlanta: Scholars Press, 1995.

Armstrong, Arthur H. "Gnosis and Greek Philosophy." In Barbara Aland, ed. *Gnosis. Festschrift für Hans Jonas*. Göttingen: Vandenhoeck & Ruprecht, 1978, 67-124.

Arnim, Hans von. *Leben und Werke des Dion von Prusa*. Berlin: Weidmann, 1898.

Ashton, John. *Understanding the Fourth Gospel*. Oxford: Clarendon, 1991.

Attridge, Harold W. "The Gospel of Truth as an Exoteric Text." In Charles W. Hedrick and Robert Hodgson, Jr., eds. *Nag Hammadi, Gnosticism, and Early Christianity*. Peabody, MA: Hendrickson, 1986, 239-255.

——. "The Greek Fragments [of the Gospel According to Thomas]." In Bentley Layton, ed. *Nag Hammadi Codex II, 2-7 Together with XIII, 2\*, Brit. Lib. Or. 4926(1), and P. Oxy. I, 654, 655*. NHS 20-21. Leiden: E. J. Brill, 1989, 95-128.

——. "The Original Language of the Acts of Thomas." In John Collins, Harold W. Attridge, and Thomas Tobin, eds. *Of Scribes and Scholars*. Lanham, MD: University Press of America, 1990, 241-250.

——. "What Gnostics Knew." Paper presented at Conference on Theology, Scientific Knowledge and Society in Antiquity, Center of Theological Inquiry, Princeton, New Jersey, 1993.

Attridge, Harold W. and George W. MacRae. "Gospel of Truth." In James M. Robinson, ed. *The Nag Hammadi Library in English*. San Francisco: Harper & Row, 1988, 38-51.

Aune, David E. "The Apocalypse of John and the Problem of Genre." In Adela Yarbro Collins, ed. *Semeia 36: Early Christian Apocalypticism: Genre and Social Setting*. Decatur: Scholars Press, 1986, 65-96.

——. "The Phenomenon of Early Christian 'Anti-Sacramentalism'." In David E. Aune, ed. *Studies in New Testament and Early Christian Literature: Essays in Honor of Allen P. Wikgren*. Leiden: E. J. Brill, 1972, 194-214.

Balas, David L. "The Idea of Participation in the Structure of Origen's Thought. Christian Transposition of a Theme of the Platonic Tradition." In Henri Crouzel, Gennaro Lomiento, and Josep Rius-Camps, eds. *Origeniana*. Bari: Istituto di Letteratura christiana antiqua, Università Bari, 1975, 1975, 257-75.

Baldensperger, Wilhelm. *Der Prolog des vierten Evangeliums*. Freiburg: J. C. B. Mohr, 1898.

Bammel, Caroline. "Herakleon." *TRE* 15 (1986) 54-57.

Barc, Bernard. *L'Hypostase des archontes*. BCNH, section "Textes" 15. Québec: Les Presses de l'Université Laval, 1980.

——. "Les Noms de la Triade dans l'Évangile selon Philippe." In Julien Ries, Yvonne Janssens, and Jean-Marie Sevrin, eds. *Gnosticisme et Monde Hellénistique*. Louvain-la-neuve: Université catholique de Louvain, Institut orientaliste, 1982, 361-376.

Barrett, Charles K. *The Gospel According to St. John*. 2nd ed. London: SPCK, 1978.

——. "Paul Shipwrecked." In Barry P. Thompson, ed. *Scripture: Meaning and Method: Essays Presented to Anthony Tyrrell Hanson for his Seventieth Birthday*. Hull: Hull University Press, 1987, 51-64.

Barry, Catherine. "Un exemple de réécriture à Nag Hammadi: La Sagesse de Jésus Christ (BG,3; NH III,4)." In Louis Painchaud and Anne Pasquier, eds. *Les textes de Nag Hammadi et le problème de leur classification: Actes du colloque tenu à Québec du 15 au 19 septembre 1993*. BCNH, Section "Études" 3. Québec: Les Presses de l'Université Laval; Louvain/Paris: Éditions Peeters, 1995, 151-168.

Bauer, Walter, Kurt Aland, and Barbara Aland. *Griechisch-deutsches Wörterbuch zu den Schriften des Neuen Testaments und der frühchristlichen Literatur*. 6th ed. Berlin/New York: de Gruyter, 1988.

Beauvoir, Simone de. *The Second Sex*. Trans. by H. M. Parshley. New York: Vintage-Random House, 1974.

Beck, Hans Georg. *Kirche und theologische Literatur im byzantinischen Reich*. HABES 12.2.1. München: Beck, 1959.

Bellet, Paulinus. "The Colophon of the Gospel of the Egyptians: Concessus and Macarius of Nag Hammadi." In Robert McL. Wilson, ed. *Nag Hammadi and Gnosis. Papers Read at the First International Congress of Coptology (Cairo, December 1976)*. NHS 14. Leiden: E. J. Brill, 1978, .

Berger, Klaus. "Zur Diskussion über die Herkunft von I Kor II.9." *NTS* 24 (1978) 270-283.

Bergmeier, Roland. "'Königslosigkeit' als nachvalentinianisches Heilsprädikat." *NovT* 24 (1982) 316-339.

Bertrand, Frederic. *Mystique de Jésus chez Origène*. Paris: Aubier, 1951.

Betz, Otto. "Das Problem der Gnosis seit der Entdeckung der Texte von Nag Hammadi." *Jesus, der Herr der Kirche*. Tübingen: J. C. B. Mohr (P. Siebeck), 1990, 361-385.

Bianchi, Ugo. "Le gnosticisme et les origines du christianisme." In Julien Ries, Yvonne Janssens, and Jean-Marie Sevrin, eds. *Gnosticisme et Monde Hellénistique*. Louvain-la-Neuve: Institut Orientaliste, 1982, 211-228.

——. "The Religio-Historical Relevance of Lk 20:34-36." In Roelof van den Broek and Maarten J. Vermaseren, eds. *Studies in Gnosticism and Hellenistic Religions: Presented to Gilles Quispel on the Occasion of his 65th Birthday*. EPRO 91. Leiden: E. J. Brill, 1981, 31-37.

——. "Some Reflections on the Greek Origins of Gnostic Ontology and the Christian Origin of the Gnostic Saviour." In Alastair H. B. Logan and Alexander J. M. Wedderburn, eds. *The New Testament and Gnosis: Essays in Honour of Robert McLachlan Wilson*. Edinburgh: T. & T. Clark, 1983, 38-45.

Bikai, P. M. "Update on the Scrolls." *ACOR Newsletter* 7 (1995) 11.

Blackstone, Warren J. "A Short Note on the Apocryphon of John." *VC* 19 (1965) 163.

Blume, Horst-Dieter and Friedhelm Mann, eds. *Platonismus und Christentum. Festschrift für Heinrich Dörrie*. JAC Ergbd. 10. Münster Westfalen: Aschendorff, 1983.

Böhlig, Alexander. "Die Adamsapokalypse aus Codex V von Nag Hammadi als Zeugnis Jüdisch-Iranischer Gnosis." *Oriens Christianus* 48 (1964) 44-49.

——. "Die Bedeutung der Funde von Medinet Madi und Nag Hammadi für die Erforschung des Gnostizismus." In Alexander Böhlig and Christoph Markschies, eds. *Gnosis und Manichäismus: Forschungen und Studien zu Texten von Valentin und Mani sowie zu den Bibliotheken von Nag Hammadi und Medinet Madi*. Berlin/New York: de Gruyter, 1994, 113-242.

——. "Die griechische Schule und die Bibliothek von Nag Hammadi." In Alexander Böhlig, ed. *Gnosis und Synkretismus: Gesammelte Aufsätze zur spätantiken Religionsgeschichte, Vol. 1.* WUNT 47. Tübingen: J. C. B. Mohr (P. Siebeck), 1989, 251-286.

——. "Die griechische Schule und die Bibliothek von Nag Hammadi." In Alexander Böhlig and Frederik Wisse, eds. *Zum Hellenismus in den Schriften von Nag Hammadi.* Wiesbaden: Harrassowitz, 1978, 9-53.

——. *Gnosis und Synkretismus: Gesammelte Aufsätze zur spätantiken Religionsgeschichte.* 2 vols. WUNT 47. Tübingen: J. C. B. Mohr, 1989.

Böhlig, Alexander and Pahor Labib. *Die koptisch-gnostische Schift ohne Titel aus Codex II von Nag Hammadi.* Deutsche Akademie der Wissenschaften zu Berlin Institut für Orientforschung 58. Berlin: Akademie Verlag, 1963.

——. *Koptisch-gnostische Apokalypsen aus Codex V von Nag Hammadi im Koptischen Museum zu Alt-Kairo.* Sonderband of the Wissenschaftliche Zeitschrift der Martin-Luther-Universität. Halle-Wittenberg: Martin-Luther Universität, 1963.

Böhlig, Alexander and Frederik Wisse. *Nag Hammadi Codices III,2 and IV,2: The Gospel of the Egyptians (The Holy Book of the Great Invisible Spirit).* NHS 4. Leiden: E. J. Brill, 1975.

——. *Zum Hellenismus in den Schriften von Nag Hammadi.* GOF.H 6.2. Wiesbaden: Harrassowitz, 1978.

Borchert, Gerald Leo. "An Analysis of the Literary Arrangement and Theological Views in the Gnostic Gospel of Philip." Th.D. Dissertation, Princeton Theological Seminary, 1967.

Borgen, Peder. *Bread From Heaven: An Exegetical Study of the Concept of Manna in the Gospel of John and the Writings of Philo.* NovTSup 10. Leiden: E. J. Brill, 1965.

——. *Philo, John and Paul: New Perspectives on Judaism and Early Christianity.* BJS 131. Atlanta: Scholars Press, 1987.

Bourdieu, Pierre. *Outline of a Theory of Practice.* Trans. by Richard Nice. 16 vols. Cambridge Studies in Social Anthropology 8. Cambridge: Cambridge University Press, 1977.

Bousset, Wilhelm. "Die Himmelsreise der Seele." *ARW* 4 (1901) 136-169, 229-273.

——. "Gnosis." *PW* VII.2 (1912) 1502-1534.

——. *Jüdisch-Christlicher Schulbetrieb in Alexandria und Rom. Literarische Untersuchungen zu Philo und Clemens von Alexandria, Justin und Irenäus.* FRLANT 23. Göttingen: Vandenhoeck & Ruprecht, 1915; repr. 1975.

Bovon, François. "The Synoptic Gospels and the Noncanonical Acts of the Apostles." *HTR* 81 (1988) 19-36.

Bowie, Ewen L. "The Greek Novel." In Patricia E. Easterling and Bernard Knox, eds. *Cambridge History of Classical Literature, Vol. 1.* Cambridge: University Press, 1985, 683-699.

——. "The Readership of Greek Novels in the Ancient World." In James Tatum, ed. *The Search for the Ancient Novel.* Baltimore: Johns Hopkins University Press, 1994, 435-459.

Boyce, Mary and Frantz Grenet. *A History of Zoroastrianism, Vol. 3: Zoroastrianism under Macedonian and Roman Rule.* Leiden: E. J. Brill, 1991.

Braun, René. "Notes de lecture sur une édition récente de l'Adversus Valentinianos de Tertullian." *REAug* 28 (1982) 189-200.

Bremmer, Jan N. *The Early Greek Concept of the Soul.* Princeton: Princeton University Press, 1983.

Briggs, Charles L. *Competence in Performance. The Creativity of Tradition in Mexicano Verbal Art.* Philadelphia: University of Pennsylvania Press, 1988.

Brodie, Thomas L. *The Quest for the Origins of John's Gospel: A Source-Oriented Approach.* New York: Oxford University Press, 1993.

Broek, Roelof van den. "Autogenes and Adamas: The Mythological Structure of the Apocryphon of John." In Martin Krause, ed. *Gnosis and Gnosticism: Papers Read at the Eighth Inter-*

national Conference on Patristic Studies (Oxford, September 3rd-8th 1979). NHS 17. Leiden: E. J. Brill, 1981, 16-25.

——. "The Creation of Adam's Psychic Body in the Apocryphon of John." In Roelof van den Broek and Maarten J. Vermaseren, eds. *Studies in Gnosticism and Hellenistic Religions Presented to Gilles Quispel on the Occasion of his 65th Birthday.* EPRO 91. Leiden: E. J. Brill, 1981, 38-57.

——. "Eugnostos and Aristides on the Ineffable God." In Roelof van den Broek, Tjitze Baarda, and Jaap Mansfeld, eds. *Knowledge of God in the Graeco-Roman World.* EPRO 112. Leiden: E. J. Brill, 1988, 202-218.

——. "Jewish and Platonic Speculations in Early Alexandrian Theology: Eugnostos, Philo, Valentinus, and Origen." In Birger A. Pearson and James Goehring, eds. *The Roots of Egyptian Christianity.* SAC. Philadelphia: Fortress, 1986, 190-203.

——. "The Theology of the Teachings of Silvanus." *VC* 40 (1986) 1-23.

Brown, Peter. *The Body and Society.* New York: Columbia University Press, 1988.

Brown, Raymond E. *The Gospel According to John (I-XII).* AB 29. Garden City, NY: Doubleday, 1982.

——. "The Gospel of Thomas and St. John's Gospel." *NTS* 9 (1962) 155-177.

Brox, Norbert. *Offenbarung, Gnosis und gnostischer Mythos bei Irenäus von Lyon. Zur Charakteristik der Systeme.* SPS 1. Salzburg/München: A. Pustet, 1966.

Buckley, Jorunn Jacobsen. "Conceptual Models and Polemical Issues in the Gospel of Philip." *ANRW* II.25.5 (1988) 4167-4194.

——. *Female Fault and Fulfilment in Gnosticism.* Chapel Hill: University of North Carolina Press, 1986.

Bultmann, Rudolf. "Die Bedeutung der neuerschlossenen mandäischen und manichäischen Quellen für das Verständnis des Johannesevangeliums." *ZNW* 24 (1925) 100-146.

——. *Die Geschichte der synoptischen Tradition.* Göttingen: Vandenhoeck & Ruprecht, 1957.

——. *The Gospel of John: A Commentary.* Trans. by George R. Beasley-Murray. Edited by Rupert W. N. Hoare and John K. Riches. Oxford: Blackwell; Philadelphia: Westminster, 1971.

Cameron, Alan. *The Greek Anthology from Meleager to Planudes.* Oxford: Clarendon, 1993.

Cameron, Ron. *The Other Gospels: Non-Canonical Gospel Texts.* Philadelphia: Westminster, 1982.

——. "Parable and Interpretation in the Gospel of Thomas." *Forum* 2 (1986) 3-34.

Cameron, Ron and Arthur J. Dewey, eds. *The Cologne Mani Codex: "Concerning the Origin of His Body."* SBLTT 15. Chico: Scholars Press, 1979.

Cancik, Hubert. "Gnostiker in Rom. Zur Religionsgeschichte der Stadt Rom im 2. Jahrhundert nach Christus, Vol. 2." In Jacob Taubes, ed. *Gnosis und Politik: Religionstheorie und politische Theologie.* München: W. Fink, 1984, 163-184.

Carroll, Scott T. "The *Apocalypse of Adam* and Pre-Christian Gnosticism." *VC* 44 (1990) 263-279.

Casey, Robert P. *The Excerpta ex Theodoto of Clement of Alexandria.* SD 1. London: Christophers, 1934.

——. "Two Notes on Valentinian Theology." *HTR* 23 (1930) 275-298.

Cerfaux, Lucien and Gerard Garitte. "Les Paraboles du Royaume dans l'Evangile de Thomas." *Le Muséon* 70 (1957) 307-327.

Chadwick, Henry. *The Sentences of Sextus: A Contribution to the History of Early Christian Ethics.* Cambridge: Cambridge University Press, 1959.

Chamay, Jacques. "Des défunts portant bandages." *Bulletin Antiede Beschaving* 52-53 (1977-78) 247-251.

Charlesworth, James H. *The Beloved Disciple: Whose Witness Validates the Gospel of John?* Valley Forge: Trinity Press International, 1995.

——. "A Critical Comparison of the Dualism in 1QS 3:13-4:26 and the 'Dualism' contained in the Gospel of John." *NTS* 15 (1968-69) 389-418.

——. "A Critical Comparison of the Dualism in 1QS 3:13-4:26 and the 'Dualism' contained in the Gospel of John." In James H. Charlesworth, ed. *John and the Dead Sea Scrolls.* New York: Crossroad, 1991, 76-106.

——, ed. *The Old Testament Pseudepigrapha: Apocalyptic Literature and Testaments.* Vol. 1. Garden City, NY: Doubleday, 1983.

Charlesworth, James H. and Craig E. Evans. "Jesus in the Agrapha and Apocryphal Gospels." In Bruce Chilton and Craig E. Evans, eds. *Studying the Historical Jesus: Evaluations of the State of Current Research.* NTTS 19. Leiden: E. J. Brill, 1994, 479-533.

Chilton, Bruce. "The Gospel According to Thomas as a Source of Jesus' Teaching." In David Wendham, ed. *Gospel Perspectives, Vol. 5: The Jesus Tradition outside the Gospels.* Sheffield: JSOT, 1985, 155-175.

——. "'Not to Taste Death': A Jewish, Christian and Gnostic Usage." *StudBib* 2 (1978) 29-36.

Clabeaux, John J. *A Lost Edition of the Letters of Paul: A Reassessment of the Text of the Pauline Corpus Attested by Marcion.* CBQMS 21. Washington, DC: Catholic Biblical Association of America, 1989.

Collantes, Justus. "La Teologia Gnostica en el primer comentario al Evangelio de San Juan." Th.D. Dissertation, Pontificia Universitas Gregoriana, 1953.

Collins, Raymond F. *Letters That Paul Did Not Write: The Epistle to the Hebrews and the Pauline Pseudepigrapha.* GNS 28. Wilmington: Michael Glazier, 1988.

Colpe, Carsten. "Die 'Himmelsreise der Seele' ausserhalb und innerhalb der Gnosis." In Ugo Bianchi, ed. *Le Origini dello Gnosticismo, Colloquio di Messina 13-18 Aprile 1966.* SHR 12. Leiden: E. J. Brill, 1967, 429-447.

Couliano, Ioan P. "The Angels of the Nations and the Origins of Gnostic Dualism." In Roelof Van Den Broek and Maarten J. Vermaseren, eds. *Studies in Gnosticism and Hellenistic Religions presented to Gilles Quispel on the Occasion of his 65th Birthday.* EPRO 91. Leiden: E. J. Brill, 1981, 78-91.

——. *Expériences de l'Extase: extase, ascension, et récit visionnaire de l'hellenisme au Moyen Age.* Paris: Payot, 1984.

——. "L'Ascension de l'âme' dans les mystères et hors des mystères." In Ugo Bianchi and Maarten J. Vermaseren, eds. *La Soteriologia dei culti orientali nell'Impero romano.* Leiden: E. J. Brill, 1982, 276-302.

——. *Psychanodia I: A Survey of the Evidence Concerning the Ascension of the Soul and Its Relevance.* Leiden: E. J. Brill, 1983.

——. *The Tree of Gnosis.* San Francisco: HarperSanFrancisco, 1990.

Cramer, Peter. *Baptism and Change in the Early Middle Ages.* Cambridge: Cambridge University Press, 1993.

Crossan, John Dominic. *The Historical Jesus: The Life of a Mediterranean Jewish Peasant.* San Francisco: HarperCollins, 1991.

——. *In Fragments. The Aphorisms of Jesus.* San Francisco: Harper & Row, 1983.

——. *In Parables: The Challenge of the Historical Jesus.* New York: Harper & Row, 1973; repr. Sonoma: Polebridge, 1992.

Crouzel, Henri. "Le contenu spirituel des dénominations du Christ selon le Livre I du Commentaire sur Jean d'Origène." In Henri Crouzel and Antonio Quacquarelli, eds. *Origeniana Secunda.* Quaderni di Vetera Christianorum 15. Rome: Edizioni dell' Ateneo and Desclée de Brouwer, 1980, 131-150.

——. *Théologie de l'image de Dieu chez Origène.* Paris: Aubier, 1956.

Crouzel, Henri and Antonio Quacquarelli, eds. *Origeniana Secunda: Second colloque international des études origéniennes (Bari, 20-23 septembre 1977).* Quaderni di Vetera Christianorum 15. Rome: Edizioni dell' Ateneo and Desclée de Brouwer, 1980.

Crum, Walter Ewing. *A Coptic Dictionary.* Cairo: Institut Français d'archéologie orientale: 1939, 1964; Oxford: Clarendon, 1972.

Culpepper, Alan. *Anatomy of the Fourth Gospel: A Study in Literary Design.* 2nd ed. Philadelphia: Fortress, 1987.

Dahl, Nils A. "The Arrogant Archon and the Lewd Sophia: Jewish Traditions in Gnostic Revolt." In Bentley Layton, ed. *The Rediscovery of Gnosticism, Vol. 2: Sethian Gnosticism.* SHR 41. Leiden: E. J. Brill, 1981, 689-712.

——. "The Johannine Church and History." In William Klassen and Graydon F. Synder, eds. *Current Issues in New Testament Interpretation.* New York/Evanston/London: Harper & Row, 1962, 124-142.

Dart, John. "Jesus and His Brothers." In R. Joseph Hoffman and Gerald A. Larue, eds. *Jesus in History and Myth.* Buffalo, NY: Prometheus Books, 1986, 181-190.

Dauer, Anton. "Zur Herkunft der Tomas-Perikope Joh 20, 24-29." In Helmut Merklein and J. Lange, eds. *Biblische Randbemerkungen: Schülerfestschrift für Rudolf Schnackenburg zum 60. Geburtstag.* Augsburg: Echter-Verlag, 1974, 56-76.

Davies, Stevan. "The Christology and Protology of the Gospel of Thomas." *JBL* 111 (1992) 663-682.

——. *The Gospel of Thomas and Christian Wisdom.* New York: Seabury, 1983.

Davies, W. D. and Dale C. Allison. *A Critical and Exegetical Commentary on the Gospel according to Saint Matthew, Vol. 1: Introduction and Commentary on Matthew I-VII.* ICC. Edinburgh: T. & T. Clark, 1988.

De Conick, April. *Faith Mysticism in the Gospel of John: The Johannine Commuinty as a Community of Discourse,* forthcoming.

——. "'He who sees me sees him who sent me' (Jn 12:45): The Johannine Theologian and Early Christian Mysticism." Paper presented at Annual Meeting, SBL, Early Jewish and Christian Mysticism Consultation, New Orleans, LA, 1996.

——. "'Seek to See Him': The Influence of Early Jewish Hermeticism on the Gospel of Thomas." Ph.D. Diss., University of Michigan, 1994.

——. *Seek to See Him: Ascent and Vision Mysticism in the Gospel of Thomas.* VCSup 33. Leiden: E. J. Brill, 1996.

De Conick, April D. and Jarl Fossum. "Stripped Before God: A New Interpretation of Logion 37 in the Gospel of Thomas." *VC* 45 (1991) 123-150.

De Suarez, P. *L'Évangile selon Thomas: traduction, présentation et commentaires.* Marsanne: Metanoia, 1974.

De Villard, U. Monneret. *Le leggende orientali sui magi evangelici.* Studi e testi 163. Città del Vaticano: Biblioteca Apostolica Vaticana, 1952.

Dean-Otting, Mary. *Heavenly Journeys: A Study of the Motif in Hellenistic Jewish Literature.* Frankfurt: P. Lang, 1984.

Denaux, Adelbert, ed. *John and the Synoptics.* BETL 101. Leuven: Éditions Peeters, 1992.

Desjardins, Michel. "Baptism in Valentinianism." Paper presented at Annual Meeting, SBL, Boston, 1987.

——. *Sin in Valentinianism.* SBLDS. Atlanta: Scholars Press, 1990.

Dibelius, Martin. *James: A Commentary on the Epistle of James.* Trans. by Michael A. Williams. Hermeneia. Philadelphia: Fortress, 1976.

Diebner, Bernd Jorg. "'ΕΠΙ ΤΗΣ ΜΟΥΣΕΩΣ ΚΑΘΕΔΡΑΣ ΈΚΑΘΙΣΑΝ (Mt 23:2): Zur literarischen und monumentalen Überlieferung der sogenannten 'Mosekathedra'." In Otto

Feld and Urs Peschlow, eds. *Studien zur spätantiken und byzantinischen Kunst, Vol. 2.* Bonn: R. Habelt, 1986, 147-155.

Diels, Hermann, ed. *Doxographi Graeci.* 4th ed. Berlin: de Gruyter, 1965; first published 1879.

Dillon, John, ed. *Alcinous: The Handbook of Platonism.* Clarendon Later Ancient Philosophers. Oxford: Clarendon, 1993.

———. "Les écoles philosophiques aux deux premiers siècles de l'Empire." *ANRW* II.36.1 (1987) 5-77.

———. *The Middle Platonists: 80 B.C. to 220 A.D.* London: Duckworth, 1977.

———. "Self-Definition in Later Platonism." In Ben F. Meyer and E. P. Sanders, eds. *Jewish and Christian Self-Definition, Vol. 3.* London, 1982, 60-75.

Dodd, C. H. *The Interpretation of the Fourth Gospel.* Cambridge: Cambridge University Press, 1953.

Dölger, Franz J. "Der Rhetor Phosphorus von Karthago und seine Stilübung über den braven Mann." *Antike und Christentum* 5 (1936) 272-274.

Doresse, Jean. "A Gnostic Library from Upper Egypt." *Archaeology* 3 (1950) 69-73.

———. "Le roman d'une grande découverte." *Les Nouvelles Littéraires,* July 25, 1957, 1, col. 4-6; 5, col. 4-6.

———. "Les gnostiques d'Egypte." *La Table Ronde* 107 (1956) 85-96.

———. *Les livres secrets des gnostiques d'Egypte, Vol. 1: Introduction aux écrits gnostiques coptes découverts à Khénoboskion.* Paris: Librairie Plon, 1958.

———. *Les livres secrets des gnostiques d'Egypte, Vol. 2: L'Evangile selon Thomas ou les paroles secrètes de Jésus.* Paris: Librairie Plon, 1959.

———. *The Secret Books of the Egyptian Gnostics: An Introduction to the Gnostic Coptic Manuscripts Discovered at Chenoboskion.* Trans. by P. Mairet. New York: Viking; London: Hollis & Carter, 1960.

———. "Sur les traces des papyrus gnostiques: Recherches à Chénoboskion." *Académie royale de Belgique: Bulletin de la Classe des Lettres et des Sciences morales et politiques, 5ème Série* 36 (1950) 432-439.

———. "Trois livres gnostiques inédits." *VC* 2 (1948) 137-160.

———. "Une bibliothèque gnostique copte." *La Nouvvelle Clio* 2 (1949) 59-70.

———. "Une extraordinaire découverte archéologique en Haute-Egypte: Quarante-neuf livres secrètes relèvent la religion gnostique." *La Tribune de Genève* February 1-2, 1958 13.

———. "Une importante découverte: Un papyrus gnostique copte du IVème siècle." *Chronique d'Egypte* 23 (1948) 260.

Dörrie, Heinrich. "L. Kalbenos Tauros, Das Persönlichkeitsbild eines platonischen Philosophen um die Mitte des 2. Jahrhundert nach Christus." *Platonica minora.* Studia et testimonia antiqua 8. München: W. Fink, 1976, 310-323.

———. "L. Kalbenos Tauros, Das Persönlichkeitsbild eines platonischen Philosophen um die Mitte des 2. Jahrhundert nach Christus." *Kairos* 15 (1973) 24-35.

Doty, William G. *Letters in Primitive Christianity.* Philadelphia: Fortress, 1973.

Downey, Glanville. *A History of Antioch in Syria: From Seleucus to the Arab Conquest.* Princeton: Princeton University Press, 1961.

Downing, Francis Gerald. *Christ and the Cynics: Jesus and Other Radical Preachers in First-Century Tradition.* Sheffield: JSOT, 1988.

Drijvers, Han J. W. "Facts and Problems in Early Syriac-Speaking Christianity." *SecCent* 2 (1982) 157-175.

Dubois, Jean-Daniel. "Contribution à l'interprétation de la Paraphrase de Sem (NH VII.1)." In Jean-Marc Rosentiehl, ed. *Deuxième Journée d'Études Coptes.* Louvain: Éditions Peeters, 1986, 150-160.

Duchesne-Guillemin, Jacques. "Gnosticisme et Dualisme." In Julien Ries, Yvonne Janssens, and Jean-Marie Sevrin, eds. *Gnosticisme et Monde Hellénistique*. Louvain-la-Neuve: Institut Orientaliste, 1982, 89-101.

——. "On the Origin of Gnosticism." In Jacques Duchesne-Guillemin and Didier Marcotte, eds. *A Green Leaf: Papers in Honour of Professor Jes P. Asmussen*. Leiden: E. J. Brill, 1988, 349-363.

Dulière, Walter. "Les Chérubins du troisième Temple à Antioche." *ZRGG* 13 (1961) 201-219.

Dunn, James. "Let John be John: A Gospel for Its Time." In Peter Stuhlmacher, ed. *Das Evangelium und die Evangelien: Vorträge vom Tübinger Symposium 1982*. WUNT 28. Tübingen: J. C. B. Mohr, 1983, 322-325.

Dupont, Jacques. *The Sources of the Acts*. Trans. by Kathleen Pond. New York: Herder & Herder, 1964.

Dupont-Sommer, André. *The Essene Writings from Qumran*. Cleveland: World Publishing Co., 1962.

Edwards, M. J. "*The Epistle to Rheginus*: Valentinianism in the Fourth Century." *NovT* 37 (1995) 76-91.

Ehrman, Bart D. and Michael W. Holmes, eds. *The Text of the New Testament in Contemporary Research: Essays on the Status Quaestionis*. Grand Rapids: Eerdmans, 1995.

Emmel, Stephen L. "Shenoute's Literary Corpus." Ph.D. Dissertation, Yale University, 1993.

Evans, Craig A. "On the Prologue of John and the *Trimorphic Protennoia*." *NTS* 27 (1981) 395-401.

Fallon, Francis T. "The Gnostics: The Undominated Race." *NovT* 21 (1979) 271-288.

Fallon, Francis T. and Ron Cameron. "The Gospel of Thomas: A Forschungsbericht and Analysis." *ANRW* II.25.6 (1988) 4195-4251.

Fantino, Jacques. *Le théologie d'Irénée. Lecture des Écritures en réponse à l'exégèse gnostique: Une approache trinitaire*. Paris: Cerf, 1994.

Ferguson, John. "Epicureanism under the Roman Empire." *ANRW* II.36.4 (1990) 2257-2327.

Festugière, André-Jean. *Corpus Hermeticum, Tome III, Fragments extraits de Stobée I-XXII*. Paris: Belles Lettres, 1954.

Filoramo, Giovanni. "Sulle Origini dello Gnosticismo." *Rivista di Storia e Letteratura Religiosa* 39 (1993) 493-510.

Fokkema, Douwe Wessel and Elrud Kunne-Ibsch. *Theories of Literature in the Twentieth Century*. London: C. Hurst & Co., 1977.

Fossum, Jarl. *The Image of the Invisible God: Essays on the Influence of Jewish Mysticism on Early Christianity*, forthcoming.

——. *The Name of God and the Angel of the Lord: Samaritan and Jewish concepts of Intermediation and the Origin of Gnosticism*. WUNT 36. Tübingen: J. C. B. Mohr (P. Siebeck), 1985.

Fowden, Garth. "The Platonist Philosopher and His Circle in Late Antiquity." *Philosophia* 7 (1977) 359-383.

Fradier, Georges. "Découverte d'une religion." *UNESCO Features*, August 1, 1949, 11-13.

Frankfurter, David. "The Magic of Writing and the Writing of Magic: The Power of the Word in Egyptian and Greek Traditions." *Helios* 21 (1994) 189-221.

Frede, Michael. "Numenius." *ANRW* II.36.2 (1987) 1034-1075.

Friedländer, Ludwig and Georg Wissowa. *Darstellungen aus der Sittengeschichte roms in der Zeit von Augustus bis zum Ausgang der Antonine III*. 9th ed. Leipzig: S. Hirzel, 1920.

Fuchs, Harald. *Der geistige Widerstand gegen Rom in der antiken Welt*. Berlin: de Gruyter, 1938.

Funk, Robert W., Roy Hoover, and the Jesus Seminar. *The Five Gospels: The Search for the Authentic Words of Jesus*. New York/London: Macmillan, 1993.

Funk, Wolf-Peter. "Ein doppelt überliefertes Stück spätägyptischer Weisheit." *Zeitschrift für Ägyptische Sprache und Altertumskunde* 103 (1976) 8-21.

———. "Gedanken zu zwei faijumishen Fragmenten." In Jean-Marc Rosenstiehl, ed. *Christianisme d'Egypte: Hommages à René-Georges Coquin.* Cahiers de la Bibliothèque 19. Louvain/Paris: Éditions Peeters, 1995, 93-100.

———. "Les fragments Brit. Lib. Or. 4926 (1)." In Louis Painchaud, ed. *L'Écrit sans titre. Traité sur l'origine du monde.* BCNH, Section "Textes" 21. Québec: Les Presses de l'Université Laval; Louvain/Paris: Éditions Peeters, 1995, 529-570.

———. "The Linguistic Aspect of Classifying the Nag Hammadi Codices." In Louis Painchaud and Anne Pasquier, eds. *Les textes de Nag Hammadi et le problème de leur classification: Actes du colloque tenu à Québec du 15 au 19 septembre 1993.* BCNH, Section "Études" 3. Québec: Les Presses de l'Université Laval; Louvain/Paris: Éditions Peeters, 1995, 107-147.

———. "Toward a Linguistic Classification of the 'Sahidic' Nag Hammadi Texts." In David W. Johnson, ed. *Acts of the Fifth International Congress of Coptic Studies: Washington, 12-15 August 1992, Vol. 2, Papers from the Sections.* Rome: Centro Italiano Microfiches, 1993, 163-177.

Gaffron, Hans-Georg. "Studien zum koptischen Philippusevangelium unter besonderer Berücksichtigung der Sakramente." Th.D. Dissertation, Friedrich-Wilhelms-Universität, Bonn, 1969.

Gaiser, Konrad. *Das Philosophenmosaik in Neapel. Eine Darstellung der platonischen Akademie.* AHAW.PH 2. Heidelberg: C. Winter, 1980.

Gamble, Harry Y. *Books and Readers in the Early Church. A History of Early Christian Texts.* New Haven and London: Yale University Press, 1995.

Gärtner, Bertil. *Ett nytt evangelium? Thomasevangeliets hemliga Jesusord.* Stockholm: Diakonistyrelse, 1960.

———. *The Theology of the Gospel of Thomas.* London: Collins, 1961.

Genette, Gérard. *Narrative Discourse: An Essay in Method.* Trans. by Jane E. Lewin. Ithaca: Cornell University Press, 1980.

Geytenbeek, Anton C. van. *Musonius Rufus and Greek Diatribe.* Assen: Van Gorcum, 1973.

Giversen, Søren. *Apocryphon Johannis: The Coptic Text of the Apocryphon Johannis in the Nag Hammadi Codex II with Translation, Introduction and Commentary.* ATDan 5. Copenhagen: Munksgaard, 1963.

———. *Filips Evangeliet: Indledning, studier oversaettelse og noter.* Copenhagen: G. E. C. Gads Forlag, 1966.

Goehring, James A. "A Classical Influence in the Gnostic Sophia Myth." *VC* 35 (1981) 16-23.

Good, Deirdre J. *Reconstructing the Tradition of Sophia in Gnostic Literature.* Atlanta: Scholars Press, 1987.

Goodenough, Erwin R. *By Light, Light.* New Haven: Yale University Press, 1935.

Goody, Jack and Ian Watt. "The Consequences of Literacy." *Comparative Studies in Society and History* 5 (1963) 304-345.

Goulder, Michael. "Colossians and Barbelo." *NTS* 41 (1995) 601-19.

Goulet, Richard. "Les vies de philosophes dans l'Antiquité tardive et leur portée mystérique." In François Bovon, ed. *Les Actes Apocryphes des Apôtres: Christianisme et monde païen.* Publications de la faculté de théologie de l'Université de Genève 4. Geneva/Paris: Labor et fides, 1981, 161-208.

Graham, William A. *Beyond the Written Word. Oral Aspects of Scripture in the History of Religion.* Cambridge: Cambridge University Press, 1987.

Grant, Robert M. "The Mystery of Marriage in *The Gospel of Philip.*" *VC* 15 (1961) 129-140.

——. "Two Gnostic Gospels." *JBL* 79 (1960) 1-11.

Grant, Robert M. and Freedman, David N. *The Secret Sayings of Jesus*. London and Glasgow: Collins Fontana Books; Garden City, NY: Doubleday, 1960.

Greer, Rowan A. "The Dog and the Mushrooms: Irenaeus's View of the Valentinians Assessed." In Bentley Layton, ed. *The Rediscovery of Gnosticism, Vol. 1: The School of Valentinus*. SHR 41. Leiden: E. J. Brill, 1980, 146-175.

Greimas, Algirdas. *Sémantique Structurale: Recherche de Méthode*. Paris: Larousse, 1966.

——. *Structural Semantics: An Attempt at a Method*. Trans. by Danielle McDowell, Ronald Schleifer, and Alan Velie. Lincoln: University of Nebraska Press, 1983.

Grillmeier, Alois. *Christ in Christian Tradition, Vol. 1: From the Apostolic Age to Chalcedon (451)*. Oxford: Mowbrays, 1975.

Gruenwald, Ithamar. "Aspects of the Jewish-Gnostic Controversy." In Bentley Layton, ed. *The Rediscovery of Gnosticism, Vol. 2: Sethian Gnosticism*. SHR 41. Leiden: E. J. Brill, 1981, 713-723.

Guillaumont, André, ed. *Gospel according to Thomas: Coptic Text Established and Translated*. Leiden: E. J. Brill, 1959.

Gundry, Robert H. *Matthew: A Commentary on his Literary and Theological Art*. Grand Rapids: Eerdmans, 1982.

Hadot, Pierre. "Être, Vie, Pensée chez Plotin et avant Plotin." *Les sources de Plotin*. Entretiens sur l'antiquité classique 3. Geneva: Fondation Hardt, 1966, 107-141.

——. *Exercices spirituels et philosophie antique*. 2nd ed. Paris: Études augustiniennes, 1987.

——. *Philosophy as a Way of Life: Spiritual Exercises from Socrates to Foucault*. Oxford/New York: Blackwell, 1995.

——. *Porphyre et Victorinus*. 2 vols. Paris: Études augustiniennes, 1968.

Hägg, Tomas. "Die Ephesiaka des Xenophon Ephesios: Original oder Epitome?" *Classica et Medievalia* 27 (1966) 118-161.

——. *The Novel in Antiquity*. Berkeley: University of California Press, 1983.

Hahn, Johannes. *Der Philosoph und die Gesellschaft: Selbstverständnis, öffentliches Auftreten und populäre Erwartungen in der hohen Kaiserzeit*. HABES 7. Stuttgart: F. Steiner, 1989.

Hänchen, Ernst. *Die Botschaft des Thomas-Evangeliums*. Theologische Bibliothek Töpelmann 6. Berlin: Töpelmann, 1961.

Hanslik, Rudolf. "Pompeia Plotina." *PW* XXI/2 2293-2298.

Harnack, Adolf von. *Der Brief des Ptolemäus an die Flora*. SBPAW.PH. Bonn, 1902.

——. *Die Überlieferung der griechischen Apologeten des zweiten Jahrhunderts in der alten Kirche und im Mittelalter*. TU 1.1. Leipzig: Hinrichs, 1882.

——. *Geschichte der altchristlichen Litteratur, Vol. 1*. 2d. ed. TU 12. Leipzig: Hinrichs, 1894; 1958.

——. *Kleine Schriften zur Alten Kirche, Berliner Akademieschriften 1890-1907 mit einem Vorwort v. J. Dummer, Opuscula 9.1*. Leipzig: Zentralantiquariat der Deutschen Demokratischen Republik, 1980.

Harris, William V. *Ancient Literacy*. Cambridge: Harvard University Press, 1989.

Hartin, Patrick J. *James and the Q Sayings of Jesus*. JSNTSup 47. Sheffield: JSOT Press, 1991.

Hauschild, Wolf-Dieter. *Gottes Geist und der Mensch. Studien zur Frühchristlichen Peumatologie*. BEvT 63. München: Chr. Kaiser Verlag, 1972.

Havelar, Henrietta W. "The Coptic Apocalypse of Peter (NHC VII, 3). Text Edition with Translation, Commentary and Interpretative Essays." Ph.D. Dissertation, University of Groningen, 1993.

Hays, Richard. *Echoes of Scripture in the Letters of Paul*. New Haven: Yale University Press, 1989.

Hedrick, Charles W. "Adam, Apocalypse of." In David N. Freedman et al., eds. *ABD, Vol. 1.* New York: Doubleday, 1992, 11.

———. *The Apocalypse of Adam: A Literary and Source Analysis.* SBLDS 46. Chico: Scholars Press, 1980.

———. "Gnosticism." In Watson E. Mills et al., eds. *Mercer Dictionary of the Bible.* Macon, GA: Mercer University Press, 1990, 335.

———. "Introduction." In Charles W. Hedrick and Robert Hodgson, Jr., eds. *Nag Hammadi, Gnosticism, and Early Christianity.* Peabody, MA: Hendrickson Publishers, 1986, 1-11.

———. "Thomas and the Synoptics: Aiming at a Consensus." *SecCent* 7 (1989-90) 39-56.

Hellholm, David. "The Mighty Minorities of Gnostic Christians." In David Hellholm et al., eds. *Mighty Minorities: Minorites in Early Christianity—Positions and Strategies.* Oslo: Scandinavian University Press, 1995, 41-66.

Hendrickson, George L. "Ancient Reading." *Classical Quarterly* 25 (1929) 182-196.

Hennecke, Edgar and Wilhelm Schneemelcher, eds. *New Testament Apocrypha, Vol. 1: Gospels and Related Writings.* Louisville: Westminster/John Knox, 1992.

Henrichs, Albert. "Mani and the Babylonian Baptists: A Historical Confrontation." *Harvard Studies in Classical Philology* 77 (1973) 23-59.

Herrmann, Wilhelm. *Systematic Theology (Dogmatik).* Trans. by Nathaniel Micklem and Kenneth A. Saunders. London: G. Allen & Unwin, Ltd.; New York: Macmillan, 1927.

Hilgenfeld, Adolf. *Die Ketzergeschichte des Urchristentums, urkundlich dargetstellt.* Leipzig: Fues, 1884; Darmstadt: Olms, 1963.

Hills, Julian V. *Tradition and Composition in the Epistula Apostulorum.* HDR 24. Minneapolis: Fortress, 1990.

Himmelfarb, Martha. *Ascent to Heaven in Jewish and Christian Apocalypses.* Oxford: Oxford University Press, 1993.

Hobein, Hermann and Wilhelm Kroll. "Maximus (37) von Tyrus." *PW* XIV/2 (1930) 2555-2562.

Hoffman, Paul. *Studien zur Theologie der Logienquelle.* Münster: Aschendorff, 1972.

Hofius, Otfried. "Das koptische Thomasevangelium und die Oxyrhynchus-Papyri Nr. 1,654 und 655." *EvT* 20 (1960).

Holzhausen, Jens. *Der 'Mythos vom Menschen' im hellenistischen Ägypten. Eine Studie zum "Poimandes" (=CH I), zu Valentin und dem gnostischen Mythos.* Theophaneia 33. Bodenheim: Athenaum Hain Hanstein, 1994.

Hopfe, Lewis M. and Gary Lease. "The Caesarea Mithraeum." *BA* 38 (1975) 1-10.

Horsley, G. H. R. "Names, Double." In David N. Freedman et al., eds. *ABD, Vol. 4.* New York: Doubleday, 1992, 1011-1017.

———. *New Documents Illustrating Early Christianity.* North Ryde N. S. W. (Australia): The Ancient History Documentary Research Centre, Macquarie University, 1981.

Huck, Albert. *Synopse der drei ersten Evangelien: 13 Auflage völlig neu bearbeitet von Heinrich Greeven.* Tübingen: J. C. B. Mohr (P. Siebeck), 1981.

Hunzinger, C.-H. "Aussersynoptisches Traditionsgut im Thomas-Evangelium." *TLZ* 85 (1960) 843-846.

———. "Unbekannte Gleichnisse Jesu aus dem Thomas-Evangelium." In Walther Eltester, ed. *Judentum, Urchristentum, Kirche: Festschrift für Joachim Jeremias.* BZNW 26. Berlin: Töpelmann, 1960, 209-220.

Hyldahl, Niels. "Hegesipps Hypomnemata." *StTh* 14 (1960) 70-113.

Idel, Moshe. "Rabbinism versus Kabbalism: On G. Scholem's Phenomenology of Judaism." *Modern Judaism* 11 (1991) 281-296.

Isenberg, Wesley W. "The Coptic Gospel According to Philip." Ph.D. Dissertation, University of Chicago, 1968.

——. "Introduction, Tractate 3: The Gospel according to Philip." In Bentley Layton, ed. *Nag Hammadi Codex II,2-7 Together with XIII,2,\* Brit. Lib. Or. 4926(1), and P. Oxy. 1, 654, 655.* NHS 20. Leiden: E. J. Brill, 1989, 129-217.

Jaeger, H. "The Patristic Conception of Wisdom in Light of Biblical and Rabbinical Research." *Studia Patristica IV.* TU 79. Berlin: Akademie-Verlag, 1961, 90-106.

Jaffee, Martin S. "How Much 'Orality' in Oral Torah? New Perspectives on the Composition and Transmission of Early Rabbinic Tradition." *Shofar* 10 (1992) 53-72.

Janssens, Yvonne. "L'Apocryphon de Jean." *Le Muséon* 84 (1971) 43-64, 403-432.

——. *La prôtennoia trimorphe (NH XIII,1).* BCNH 4. Québec: Laval University Press, 1978.

——. "Le Codex XIII de Nag Hammadi." *Le Muséon* 7 (1974) 341-413.

——. "The Trimorphic Protennoia and the Fourth Gospel." In Alastair H. B. Logan and Alexander J. M. Wedderburn, eds. *The New Testament and Gnosis: Essays in Honour of Robert McLachlan Wilson.* Edinburgh: T. & T. Clark, 1983, 229-243.

——. "Une source gnostique du Prologue." In Marinus de Jonge, ed. *L'Evangile de Jean: sources, redaction, théologie.* BETL 44. Gembloux: Duculot, 1977, 355-358.

Jauss, Hans Robert. *Literaturgeschichte als Provokation.* Frankfurt: Suhrkamp, 1970.

Johnson, Mark. *The Body in the Mind. The Bodily Basis of Meaning, Imagination, and Reason.* Chicago and London: The University of Chicago Press, 1987.

Johnson, Steven R. "Q 12:33-34." In James M. Robinson et al., eds. *Documenta Q.* Louvain: Éditions Peeters, forthcoming.

Jomier, Jacques. *Bible et Coran.* Paris: du Cerf, 1959.

Jonas, Hans. "Evangelium Veritatis and the Valentinian Speculation." In Frank L. Cross, ed. *Studia Patristica 6.* Berlin: Akademie-Verlag, 1962, 96-111.

——. *The Gnostic Religion.* Boston: Beacon, 1963.

——. "Response to G. Quispel's 'Gnosticism and the New Testament'." In J. Philip Hyatt, ed. *The Bible in Modern Scholarship.* Nashville: Abingdon, 1965, 279-93.

Jones, F. Stanley. "Principal Orientations in the Relations between the Apocryphal Acts." *SBLSP* 32 (1993) 485-505.

Jülicher, Adolf. "Aretas 9." *PW* II/1 (1895) 675-677.

——. "Florinus." *PW* VI/2 (1909) 2760.

Junod, Eric and Jean-Daniel Kaestli. *Acta Johannis.* CChr, Series Apocryphorum. Turnhout: Brepols, 1983.

Kaestli, Jean-Daniel. "Valentinisme Italien et Valentinisme oriental: Leurs divergences a propos de la nature du corps de Jesus." In Bentley Layton, ed. *The Rediscovery of Gnosticism, Vol. 1: The School of Valentinus.* SHR 41. Leiden: E. J. Brill, 1980, 391-403.

Kapera, Zdzislaw J. "An Anonymously Received Pre-Publication of the 4Q MMT." *The Qumran Chronicle* 2 (1990).

Kasser, Rodolphe. "Bibliothèque gnostique V, Apocalypse d'Adam." *RTP, ser. 3,* 17 (1967) 316-333.

——. "Bibliothèque gnostique VIII: L'Évangile selon Philippe." *RTP, ser. 3,* 20 (1970) 12-35, 82-106.

——. "Formation de 'l'Hypostase des archontes'." *Bulletin de la Société d'Archéologie Copte* 21 (1975) 83-103.

——. "L'Évangile selon Philippe." *RTP, ser. 3,* 20 (1970) 12-106.

——. *L'Evangile selon Thomas: Présentation et commentaire théologique.* Neuchâtel: Delachaux et Niestlé, 1961.

Kelber, Werner H. "Modalities of Communication, Cognition, and Physiology or Perception: Orality, Rhetoric, and Scribality." *Orality and Textuality in Early Christian Literature.* Semeia 65 (1995) 193-216.

——. *The Oral and the Written Gospel: The Hermeneutics of Speaking and Writing in the Synoptic Gospel Tradition, Mark, Paul, and Q.* Philadelphia: Fortress, 1983.

Khosroyev, Alexandr L. "Bemerkungen über die vermutlichen Besitzer der Nag-Hammadi-Texte." In Cäcilia Fluck et al., eds. *Divitiae Aegypti: Koptologische und verwandte Studien zu Ehren von Martin Krause.* Wiesbaden: Dr. Ludwig Reichert Verlag, 1995, 200-205.

Khosroyev, Alexandr L. *Die Bibliothek von Nag Hammadi: Einige Probleme des Christentums in Ägypten während der ersten Jahrhunderte.* Arbeiten zum spätantiken und koptischen Ägypten 7. Altenberge: Oros Verlag, 1995.

King, Karen L. "The Quiescent Eye of the Revelation: Nag Hammadi Codex XI.3, 'Allogenes,' A Critical Edition." Ph.D. Dissertation, Brown University, 1984.

——. "Sophia and Christ in the *Apocryphon of John.*" In Karen L. King, ed. *Images of the Feminine in Gnosticism.* SAC. Philadelphia: Fortress, 1988, 158-176.

Kittel, Gerhard. "δοκέω, δόξα, δοξάζω, κτλ." In Gerhard Kittel, ed. *TDNT, Vol. 2.* Grand Rapids: Eerdmans, 1964, 232-255.

Klijn, A. F. J. *The Acts of Thomas: Introduction, Text, Commentary.* NovTSup 5. Leiden: E. J. Brill, 1962.

——. "John XIV 22 and the Name Judas Thomas." *Studies in John Presented to Professor Dr. J. N. Sevenster on the Occasion of his Seventieth Birthday.* NovTSup 24. Leiden: E. J. Brill, 1970, .

Kloppenborg, John S. *The Formation of Q: Trajectories in Ancient Wisdom Collections.* Philadelphia: Fortress, 1986.

——. *Q Parallels: Synopsis, Critical Notes and Concordance.* Sonoma: Polebridge, 1988.

——. "Tradition and Redaction in the Synoptic Sayings Source." *CBQ* 46 (1984) 34-62.

——. "Wisdom Christology in Q." *LTP* 34 (1978) 129-148.

Koester, Helmut. *Ancient Christian Gospels: Their History and Development.* Philadelphia: Trinity Press International, 1990.

——. "Apocryphal and Canonical Gospels." *HTR* 73 (1980) 105-130.

——. "Dialog und Spruchüberlieferung in den gnostischen Texten von Nag Hammadi." *EvT* 34 (1979) 532-556.

——. "GNOMAI DIAPHOROI: The Origin and Nature of Diversification in the History of Early Christianity." In Helmut Koester and James M. Robinson. *Trajectories Through Early Christianity.* Philadelphia: Fortress, 1971, 114-157.

——. "Gnostic Sayings and Controversy Traditions in John 8:12-59." In Charles W. Hedrick and Robert Hodgson, Jr., eds. *Nag Hammadi, Gnosticism, and Early Christianity.* Peabody, MA: Hendrickson, 1986, 97-110.

——. "Gnostic Writings as Witnesses for the Development of the Sayings Tradition." In Bentley Layton, ed. *The Rediscovery of Gnosticism, Vol. 1: The School of Valentinus.* SHR 41. Leiden: E. J. Brill, 1980, 238-261.

——. "The History-of-Religions School, Gnosis, and Gospel of John." *StTh* 40 (1986) 115-136.

——. *Introduction to the New Testament: History and Literature of Early Christianity.* 2 vols. Philadelphia: Fortress; Berlin/New York: de Gruyter, 1982.

——. "Introduction [to the Gospel of Thomas]." In Bentley Layton, ed. *Nag Hammadi Codex II,2-7 together with XII,2, Brit. Lib. Or. 4926 (1) and P. Oxy 1, 654, 655.* NHS 20. Leiden: E. J. Brill, 1989, 38-49.

——. "One Jesus and Four Primitive Gospels." *HTR* 61 (1968) 203-247.

——. "Q and Its Relatives." In James E. Goehring, Charles W. Hedrick, and Jack T. Sanders, eds. *Gospel Origins and Christian Beginnings: In Honor of James M. Robinson.* Forum Fascicles 1. Sonoma: Polebridge, 1990, 49-63.

——. "Three Thomas Parables." In Alastair H. B. Logan and Alexander J. M. Wedderburn, eds. *The New Testament and Gnosis: Essays in Honour of R. McL. Wilson.* Edinburgh: T. & T. Clark, 1983, 195-203.

Koester, Helmut and James M. Robinson. *Trajectories through Early Christianity.* Philadelphia: Fortress, 1971.

Koschorke, Klaus. "Die 'Namen' im Philippusevangelium. Beobachtungen zur Auseinandersetzung zwischen gnostischen und kirchlichen Christentum." *ZNW* 64 (1973) 307-322.

——. *Die Polemik der Gnostiker gegen das kirchliche Christentum.* NHS 12. Leiden: E. J. Brill, 1978.

——. "Patristische Materialien zur Spätgeschichte der valentinianischen Gnosis." In Martin Krause, ed. *Gnosis and Gnosticism. Papers read at the 8th International Conference on Patristic Studies (Oxford, September 3rd-8th 1979).* NHS 12. Leiden: E. J. Brill, 1981, 120-139.

Kotansky, Roy. "Incantations and Prayers for Salvation on Inscribed Greek Amulets." In Christopher A. Faraone and Dirk Obbink, eds. *Magika Hiera. Ancient Greek Magic and Religion.* New York and Oxford: Oxford University Press, 1991, 107-137.

Kragerud, Alv. "*Apocryphon Johannis*: En Formanalyse." *NorTT* 66 (1965) 15-38.

Krämer, Hans Joachim. *Der Ursprung der Geistmetaphysik: Untersuchungen zur Geschichte des Platonismus zwischen Platon und Plotin.* Amsterdam: B. R. Grüner, 1967.

——. "Die ältere Akademie." In Hellmut Flashar, ed. *Ältere Akademie: Aristoteles - Peripatos.* Basel/Stuttgart, 1983, 1-174.

Krause, Martin. "Das literarische Verhältnis des Eugnostosbriefes zur Sophia Jesu Christi." *Mullus: Festschrift Theodor Klauser.* JAC Ergbd. 1. Münster Westfalen: Aschendorff, 1964, 215-223.

——. "Die Petrusakten in Codex VI von Nag Hammadi." In Martin Krause, ed. *Essays in Honor of Alexander Bohlig.* NHS 3. Leiden: E. J. Brill, 1972, .

Krause, Martin and Pahor Labib. *Die drei Versionen des Apokryphon des Johannes im Koptischen Museum zu Alt-Kairo.* Abhandlungen des Deutschen Archäologischen Instituts Kairo, Koptische Reihe 1. Wiesbaden: Harrassowitz, 1962.

Kuch, Heinrich, ed. *Der antike Roman: Untersuchungen zur literarischen Kommunikation und Gattungsgeschichte.* Berlin: Akademie-Verlag, 1989.

Kuhn, Karl G. "Die in Palästina gefundenen hebräischen Texte und das Neue Testament." *ZTK* 47 (1950) 192-211.

Kümmel, Werner Georg. "Das Gleichnis von den bösen Weingärtnern (Mark 12:1-5)." *Aux Sources de la tradition chrétienne: Mélanges offerts à M. Maurice Goguel à l'occasion de son soixante-dixième anniversaire.* Neuchâtel: Delachaux et Niestlé, 1950, 120-131.

Kuntzmann, Raymond. *Le symbolisme des jumeaux au Proche-Orient ancient.* Religions 12. Paris: Beauchesne, 1983.

Kussl, Rolf. *Papyrusfragmente griechischer Romane.* Tübingen: G. Narr, 1991.

Labib, Pahor. *Coptic Gnostic Papyri in the Coptic Museum of Old Cairo, Vol. 1.* Cairo: Government Press, 1956.

——. "Les papyrus gnostiques coptes du Musée Copte du Vieux Caire." *La Revue du Caire* 195-196 (1956) 275-278.

Lampe, Peter. *Die stadtrömischen Christen in den erster beiden Jahrhunderten. Untersuchungen zur Sozialgeschichte.* 2nd ed. WUNT 2.R 18. Tübingen: J. C. B. Mohr (P. Siebeck), 1989.

Langerbeck, Hermann. "Zur auseinandersetzung von Theologie und Gemeindeglauben in der römischen Gemeinde in den Jahren 135-165." In Hermann Langerbeck, ed. *Aufsätze zur Gnosis, aus dem Nachlass hg. v. Heinrich Dörries.* AAWG.PH 69. Göttingen: Vandenhoeck & Ruprecht, 1967, 38-62.

LaSor, William S. *The Dead Sea Scrolls and the New Testament*. Grand Rapids: Eerdmans, 1972.

Laurenti, Renato. "Musonio, maestro di Epitteto." *ANRW* II.36.3 (1989) 2105-2146.

Layton, Bentley. *The Gnostic Scriptures: A New Translation with Annotations and Introductions*. Garden City, NY and London: Doubleday, 1987.

——. *The Gnostic Treatise on Resurrection from Nag Hammadi*. HDR 12. Missoula: Scholars Press, 1979.

——, ed. *Nag Hammadi Codex II, 2-7 Together with XIII, 2\*, Brit. Lib. Or. 4926(1), and P. Oxy. I, 654, 655*. 2 vols. NHS 20-21. Leiden: E. J. Brill, 1989.

——. "Prolegomena to the Study of Ancient Gnosticism." In L. Michael White and O. Larry Yarbrough, eds. *The Social World of the First Christians: Essays in Honor of Wayne A. Meeks*. Minneapolis: Augsburg Fortress, 1995, 334-350.

——. "The Recovery of Gnosticism: The Philologist's Task in the Investigation of Nag Hammadi." *SecCent* 1 (1981) 85-99.

——, ed. *The Rediscovery of Gnosticism: Proceedings of the International Conference on Gnosticism at Yale, New Haven, Connecticut, March 28-31, 1978. Vol. 1: The School of Valentinus; Vol. 2: Sethian Gnosticism*. SHR 41. Leiden: E. J. Brill, 1980-81.

——. "The Riddle of the Thunder (NHC VI,2): The Function of Paradox in a Gnostic Text from Nag Hammadi." In Charles W. Hedrick and Robert Hodgson, Jr., eds. *Nag Hammadi, Gnosticism, and Early Christianity*. Peabody, MA: Hendrickson Publishers, 1986, 37-54.

Le Boulluec, Alain. *La Notion d'heresie dans la littérature grecque, IIe-IIIe siècles*. Paris: Études augustiniennes, 1985.

——. "La place de la polémique antignostique dans le *Peri Archôn* d'Origène." In Henri Crouzel, Gennaro Lomiento, and Josep Rius-Camps, eds. *Origeniana*. Quaderni di Vetera Christianorum 15. Bari: Istituto di Letteratura christiana antiqua, Università Bari, 1975, 1975, 47-61.

——. "Y a-t-il des traces de la polémique antignostique d'Irénée dans le *Peri Archôn* d'Origène?" In Martin Krause, ed. *Gnosis and Gnosticism*. NHS 8. Leiden: E. J. Brill, 1977, 138-147.

Leipoldt, Johannes. "Ein neues Evangelium? Das koptische Thomasevangelium übersetzt und besprochen." *TLZ* 83 (1958) 481-496.

——, ed. *Sinuthii Archimandritae Vita et Opera Omnia, Vol. 3*. CSCO 42; Scriptores coptici 2. Louvain: Secrétariat du Corpus SCO; L. Durbecq, 1955.

Leisegang, Hans. "Art. Valentinus 1) Valentinianer." *PW* VII.A. 2d ed. (1948) 2261-2273.

Leloup, J. Y. *L'Évangile selon Thomas*. Spiritualités vivantes 61. Paris: Albin Michel, 1986.

Lelyveld, Margarethe. *Les logia de la vie dans l'Évangile selon Thomas: À la recherche d'une tradition et d'une rédaction*. NHS 34. Leiden: E. J. Brill, 1987.

Lichtheim, Miriam, ed. *Ancient Egyptian Literature: A Book of Readings*. 3 vols. Berkeley: University of California Press, 1980.

——. *Late Egyptian Wisdom Literature in the International Context: A Study of Demotic Instructions*. OBO 52. Freiburg: Universitätsverlag; Göttingen: Vandenhoeck & Ruprecht, 1983.

Lidzbarski, Mark. *Handbuch der nordsemitischen Epigraphik nebst ausgewählten Inschriften*. 2 vols. Weimar: Felber, 1898; Hildesheim: Olms, 1962.

Liechtenhan, Rudolf. "Die pseudepigraphe Litteratur der Gnostiker." *ZNW* 3 (1902) 222-237.

Lietzmann, Hans. *Das Muratorische Fragment und die Monarchianischen Prologe zu den Evangelien*. 2nd ed. Kleine Texte 1. Berlin: de Gruyter, 1933.

Lilla, Salvatore R. C. *Clement of Alexandria. A Study in Christian Platonism and Gnosticism*. Oxfrod Theological Monographs. Oxford: Oxford University Press, 1971.

514 BIBLIOGRAPHY

Lindars, Barnabas. *Behind the Fourth Gospel*. Studies in Creative Criticism 3. London: SPCK, 1971.

Logan, Alastair H. B. "John and the Gnostics: The Significance of the Apocryphon of John for the Debate about the Origins of the Johannine Literature." *JSNT* 43 (1991) 41-69.

Löhr, Winrich A. *Basilides und seine Schule. Eine Studie zur Theologie- und Kirchengeschichte des zweiten Jahrhunderts*. WUNT 83. Tübingen: J. C. B. Mohr (P. Siebeck), 1996.

——. "Basilides und seine Schule. Eine Studie zur Theologie- und Kirchengeschichte des zweiten Jahrhunderts." Habilitation, Bonn, 1993.

——. "La doctrine de Dieu dans la Lettre à Flora de Ptolémée." *RHPR* 75 (1995) 177-191.

Lord, Albert B. "Homer as Oral Poet." *Harvard Studies in Classical Philology* 72 (1967) 1-46.

Lorenz, Rudolf. *Arius Judaizans? Untersuchungen zur dogmengeschichtlichen Einordnung des Arius*. Göttingen: Vandenhoeck & Ruprecht, 1979.

Lüdemann, Gerd. *Heretics: The Other Side of Early Christianity*. London: SCM Press; Minneapolis: Fortress, 1996.

——. *Ketzer: Die andere Seite des frühen Christentums*. Stuttgart: Radius, 1995.

——. "Zur Geschichte des ältesten Christentums in Rom." *ZNW* 70 (1979) 86-114.

Luttikhuizen, Gerard P. "Early Christian Judaism and Christian Gnosis, and their Relation to Emerging Mainstream Christianity." *Neot. Journal of the New Testament Society of South Africa. Critical Scholarship and the New Testament: A Dialogue with Willem S. Vorster* 28 (1994) 219-34.

——. "A Gnostic Reading of the Acts of John." In Jan N. Bremmer, ed. *The Apocryphal Acts of John*. Studies in the Apocryphal Acts 1. Kampen: Kok-Pharos, 1995, 119-52.

——. "Intertextual References in Readers' Responses to the Apocryphon of John." In Sipke Draaisma, ed. *Intertextuality in Biblical Writings: Essays in Honour of Bas van Iersel*. Kampen: J. H. Kok, 1989, 117-26.

——. "The Jewish Factor in the Development of the Gnostic Myth of Origins." In Tjitze Baarda et al., eds. *Text and Testimony: Essays on New Testament and Aprocryphal Literature in Honour of A. F. J. Klijn*. Kampen: J. H. Kok, 1988, 152-161.

——. "Johannine Vocabulary and the Thought Structure of Gnostic Mythological Texts." In Holger Preißler and Hubert M. Seiwert, eds. *Gnosisforschung und Religionsgeschichte. Festschrift für Kurt Rudolph zum 65. Geburtstag*. Marburg: Diagonal-Verlag, 1994, 175-81.

Lyman, J. Rebecca. *Christology and Cosmology. Models of Divine Activity in Origen, Eusebius, and Athanasius*. Oxford Theological Monographs. Oxford: Clarendon Press, 1993.

Lynch, John P. *Aristotle's School: A Study of a Greek Educational Institution*. Berkeley: University of California Press, 1972.

Lyons, James A. *The Cosmic Christ in Origen and Teilhard de Chardin. A Comparative Study*. Oxford: Oxford University Press, 1982.

Maccoby, Hyam. *Paul and Hellenism*. London: SCM Press; Philadelphia: Trinity Press International, 1991.

MacDonald, Dennis R. "*The Acts of Paul* and *The Acts of Peter*: Which Came First?" *SBLSP* 31 (1992) 214-224.

Mack, Burton L. *A Myth of Innocence: Mark and Christian Origins*. San Francisco: HarperCollins, 1988.

MacRae, George W. "The Apocalypse of Adam." In Douglas M. Parrott, ed. *Nag Hammadi Codices V,2-5 and VI with Papyrus Berolinensis 8502,1 and 4*. NHS 11. Leiden: E. J. Brill, 1979, 151-195.

———. "The Ego-Proclamation in Gnostic Sources." In Daniel J. Harrington and Stanley B. Marrow, eds. *Studies in the New Testament and Gnosticism*. Wilmington: Michael Glazier, 1987, 203-217.

———. "Introduction to the Apocalypse of Adam." In James H. Charlesworth, ed. *The Old Testament Pseudepigrapha, Vol. 1: Apocalyptic Literature and Testaments*. Garden City, NY: Doubleday, 1983, 707-711.

———. "The Jewish Background of the Gnostic Sophia Myth." *NovT* 12 (1970) 86-101.

———. "Nag Hammadi and the New Testament." In Barbara Aland, ed. *Gnosis: Festschrift for Hans Jonas*. Göttingen: Vandenhoeck & Ruprecht, 1978, 144-157.

———. "Seth in Gnostic Texts and Traditions." *SBLSP 1977*. Missoula: Scholars Press, 1977, 17-24.

Magne, Jean. *From Christianity to Gnosis and from Gnosis to Christianity*. Atlanta: Scholars Press, 1993.

Mahé, Jean-Pierre. "La voie d'immortalité à la lumière des *Hermetica* de Nag Hammadi et de découvertes plus récentes." *VC* 45 (1991) 347-375.

———. "Le Témoignage véritable et quelques écrits valentiniens de Nag Hammadi." In Louis Painchaud and Anne Pasquier, eds. *Les textes de Nag Hammadi et le problème de leur classification*. Québec: Les Presses de l'Université Laval; Louvain/Paris: Éditions Peeters, 1995, 233-42.

Majercik, Ruth. "The Existence-Life-Intellect Triad in Gnosticism and Neoplatonism." *Classical Quarterly* 42 (1992) 475-488.

Mann, Ulrich. "Geisthöhe und Seelentiefe: Die vertikale Achse der numinosen Bereiche." *Eranos* 50 (1981) 1-50.

Mansfeld, Jaap. "Compatible Alternatives: Middle Platonist Theology and the Xenophanes Reception." In Roelof van den Broek, Tjitze Baarda, and Jaap Mansfeld, eds. *Knowledge of God in the Graeco-Roman World*. EPRO 112. Leiden: E. J. Brill, 1988, 92-117.

———. *Heresiography in Context: Hippolytus' Elenchos as a Source for Greek Philosophy*. Philosophia Antiqua 56. Leiden: E. J. Brill, 1992.

Marcovich, Miroslav. "Textual Criticism on the *Gospel of Thomas*." *JTS* 20 (1969) 53-74.

Marjanen, Antti. "Thomas and Jewish Religious Practices." In Risto Uro, ed. *Thomas at the Crossroads*, forthcoming.

Markschies, Christoph. "Alte und neue Texte und Forschungen zu Valentin und den Anfängen der 'valentinianischen' Gnosis--von J. E. Grabe und F. C. Baur bis B. Aland." In Alexander Böhlig and Christoph Markschies, eds. *Gnosis und Manichäismus. Forschungen und Studien zu Texten von Valentin und Mani sowie zu den Bibliotheken von Nag Hammadi und Medinet Madi*. BZNW 72. Berlin/New York: de Gruyter, 1994, 39-111.

———. *Ambrosius von Mailand und die Trinitätstheologie. Kirchen- und theologiegeschichtliche Studien zu Antiarianismus und Neunizänismus bei Ambrosius und im lateinischen Westen (364-381)*. BHT 90. Tübingen: J. C. B. Mohr (P. Siebeck), 1995.

———. *Arbeitsbuch Kirchengeschichte*. UTB. Tübingen: J. C. B. Mohr (P. Siebeck), 1995.

———. "Die Krise einer philosophischen Bibel-Theologie in der Alten Kirche, oder: Valentin und die valentinianische Gnosis zwischen philosophischer Bibelinterpretation und mythologischer Häresie." In Alexander Böhlig and Christoph Markschies, eds. *Gnosis und Manichäismus*. BZNW 72. Berlin: de Gruyter, 1994, 1-37.

———. "Platons König oder Vater Jesu Christi? Drei Beispiele für die Rezeption eines griechischen Gottesepithetons bei den Christen in den ersten jahrhunderten und deren Vorgeschichte." In Martin Hengel and Anna Maria Schwemer, eds. *Königsherrschaft Gottes und himmlischer Kult im Judentum, im Urchristentum und in der hellenistischen Welt*. WUNT 55. Tübingen: J. C. B. Mohr (P. Siebeck), 1991, 385-439.

——. *Valentinus Gnosticus? Untersuchungen zur valentinianischen Gnosis mit einem Kommentar zu den Fragmenten Valentins.* WUNT I/65. Tübingen: J. C. B. Mohr (P. Siebeck), 1992.

Marrou, Henri I. *Geschichte der Erziehung im klassischen Altertum.* München: Deutscher Taschenbuch Verlag, 1977.

——. "La technique de l'edition a l'epoque patristique." *VC* 3 (1949) 208-224.

Matera, Frank. "The Incomprehension of the Disciples and Peter's Confession." *Bib* 70 (1989) 153-172.

May, Georg. "Platon und die Auseinandersetzung mit den Häresien bei Klemens von Alexandrien." In Horst-Dieter Blume and Friedhelm Mann, eds. *Platonismus und Christentum. Festschrift für Heinrich Dörrie.* JAC Ergbd. 10. Münster Westfalen: Aschendorff, 1983, 123-132.

McGuire, Anne. "Conversion and Gnosis in the Gospel of Truth." *NovT* 28 (1986) 338-355.

——. "Valentinus and the Gnostike Hairesis: Irenaeus, *Haer.* I.11 and the Evidence of Nag Hammadi." In Elizabeth A. Livingstone, ed. *Studia Patristica: Proceedings of the IXth International Conference on Patristic Studies at Oxford University.* Kalamazoo: Cistercian Press, 1985, 247-252.

——. "Valentinus and the 'Gnostike Hairesis': An Investigation of Valentinus's Position in the History of Gnosticism." Ph.D. Dissertation, Yale University, 1983.

McLean, Bradley H. "On the Gospel of Thomas and Q." In Ronald A. Piper, ed. *The Gospel behind the Gospels: Current Studies on Q.* Leiden: E. J. Brill, 1995, 321-345.

Meeks, Wayne A. "The Man from Heaven in Johannine Sectarianism." *JBL* 91 (1972) 44-72.

——. *The Prophet-King: Moses Traditions and the Johannine Christology.* NovTSup 14. Leiden: E. J. Brill, 1967.

Ménard, Jacques E., ed. *L'Evangile de Vérité.* Leiden: E. J. Brill, 1972.

——. *L'Évangile selon Philippe.* Montréal: Université de Montréal; Paris: P. Lethielleux, 1964.

——. *L'Évangile selon Philippe: Introduction, texte, traduction, commentaire.* Paris: Letouzy & Ané, 1967.

——. *L'Évangile selon Thomas.* NHS 5. Leiden: E. J. Brill, 1975.

Metzger, Bruce M. *The Canon of the New Testament: Its Origin, Development, and Significance.* Oxford: Clarendon, 1987.

Meyer, Marvin and Richard Smith. *Ancient Christian Magic. Coptic Texts of Ritual Power.* San Francisco: HarperSanFrancisco, 1994.

Meyer, Marvin W. and James M. Robinson, eds. *The Nag Hammadi Library in English.* Leiden: E. J. Brill; San Francisco: Harper & Row, 1977.

Millar, Fergus. *The Emperor in the Roman World (31 BC-AD 337).* 2nd ed. London: Duckworth, 1992.

Mimouni, Simon. "1. Thomas (apôtre)." *Dictionnaire de spiritualité, Vol. 15.* Paris: Beauchesne, 1991, 708-718.

Mina, Togo. "Le papyrus gnostique du Musée Copte." *VC* 2 (1948) 129-136.

Morard, Françoise. *L'Apocalypse d'Adam (NH V,5).* BCNH, Section "Textes" 15. Québec: Les Presses de l'Université Laval, 1985.

——. "L'Apocalypse d'Adam du Codex V de Nag Hammadi et sa polémique anti-baptismale." *RevScRel* 51 (1977) 214-233.

Moreland, Milton C. and James M. Robinson. "The International Q Project Work Sessions 23-27 May, 22-26 August, 17-18 November 1994." *JBL* 114 (1995) 475-485.

Mutschmann, Hermann. "Das erste Auftreten des Maximus von Tyros in Rom." *Sokrates* 5 (1917) 185-197.

Nautin, Pierre. "La fin des Stromates et les Hypotyposes de Clément d'Alexandrie." *VC* 30 (1976) 268-302.

Neuschäfer, Bernhard. "Origenes als Philologe." *Schweizerische Beiträge zur Altertumswissenschaft* 18 (1987) 138-246.

Neymeyr, Ulrich. *Die christlichen Lehrer im zweiten Jahrhundert: Ihre Lehrtätigkeit, Ihr Selbstverständnis und ihre Geschichte.* VCSup 4. Leiden: E. J. Brill, 1989.

Nickelsburg, George. "Apocalyptic and Myth in I Enoch 6-11." *JBL* 96 (1977) 383-405.

Nock, Arthur Darby. "Gnosticism." *HTR* 57 (1964) 255-79.

Nock, Arthur Darby and André-Jean Festugière. *Corpus Hermeticum, Tome I, Traites I-XII.* Paris: Belles Lettres, 1945.

———. *Corpus Hermeticum, Tome II, Traités XIII-XVIII: Asclepius.* Paris: Belles Lettres, 1945.

Norden, Eduard. *Die antike Kunstprosa vom VI. Jahrhundert v. Chr. bis in die Zeit der Renaissance, Vol. 2.* Leipzig/Berlin: Teubner, 1915; Stuttgart: Teubner, 1983.

O'Callaghan, José. *Nomina sacra in papyris Graecis saeculi III neotestamentariis.* AnBib 46. Rome: Pontifical Biblical Institute, 1970.

Odeberg, Hugo. *The Fourth Gospel Interpreted in its Relationship to Contemporaneous Religious Currents in Palestine and the Hellenistic-Oriental World.* Uppsala: Almqvist & Wiksell, 1929; Amsterdam: B. R. Gruner, 1929, 1968, 1974.

Oeyen, Christian. "Fragmente einer subachmimischen Version der gnostischen *Schrift ohne Titel.*" In Martin Krause, ed. *Essays on the Nag Hammadi Texts in Honour of Pahor Labib.* NHS 6. Leiden: E. J. Brill, 1975, 125-144.

Ong, Walter J. *Orality and Literacy. The Technologizing of the Word.* New York/London: Routledge, 1982; repr. 1993.

Onuki, Takashi. *Gnosis und Stoa. Eine Untersuchung zum Apokryphon des Johannes.* NTOA 9. Göttingen: Vandenhoeck & Ruprecht, 1989.

———. "Traditionsgeschichte von Thomasevangelium 17 und ihre christologische Relevanz." In Cilliers Breytenbach and Henning Paulsen, eds. *Anfänge der Christologie.* Göttingen: Vandenhoeck & Ruprecht, 1991, 399-415.

Opelt, Ilona. "Epitome." *RAC* 5 (1962) 944-973.

Orbe, Antonio. *La Uncion del Verbo. Estudios Valentinianos, Vol. 3.* Analecta Gregoriana 113. Rome: Libreria Editrice dell' Università Gregoriana, 1961.

Orlandi, Tito. *Evangelium Veritatis.* Testi del Vicino Oriente antico 8.2. Brescia: Paideia Editrice, 1992.

Paap, Anton H. *Nomina Sacra in the Greek Papyri of the First Five Centuries A. D.: The Sources and Some Deductions.* Papyrologica Lugduno-Batavia 8. Leiden: E. J. Brill, 1959.

Page, Denys L. *Actors' Interpolations in Greek Tragedy.* Oxford: Clarendon, 1934.

Pagels, Elaine H. "Adam and Eve, Christ and the Church: A Survey of Second Century Controversies Concerning Marriage." In Alastair H. B. Logan and Alexander J. M. Wedderburn, eds. *The New Testament and Gnosis: Essays in Honour of Robert McLachlan Wilson.* Edinburgh: T. & T. Clark, 1983, 146-175.

———. "Conflicting Versions of Valentinian Eschatology: Irenaeus' Treatise vs. the Excerpts from Theodotus." *HTR* 67 (1974) 35-53.

———. *The Gnostic Paul: Gnostic Exegesis of the Pauline Letters.* Philadelphia: Fortress, 1975.

———. *The Johannine Gospel in Gnostic Exegesis: Heracleon's Commentary on John.* SBLMS 17. Nashville: Abingdon, 1973.

———. "The 'Mystery of Marriage' in the *Gospel of Philip* Revisited." In Birger A. Pearson et al., eds. *The Future of Early Christianity.* Minneapolis: Fortress, 1991, 442-454.

———. "A Valentinian Interpretation of Heracleon's Understanding of Baptism and Eucharist and Its Critique of 'Orthodox' Sacramental Theology and Practice." *HTR* 65 (1972) 153-169.

Painchaud, Louis, ed. *L'Écrit sans titre: Traité sue l'origine du monde (NH II,5 et XIII,2 et Brit. Lib. Or. 4926[1]*. BCNH, section "Textes" 21. Québec: Les Presses de l'Université Laval; Louvain/Paris: Éditions Peeters, 1995.

——. "La classification des textes de Nag Hammadi et le phénomène des réécritures." In Louis Painchaud and Anne Pasquier, eds. *Les textes de Nag Hammadi et le problème de leur classification: Actes du colloque tenu à Québec du 15 au 19 septembre 1993*. BCNH, Section "Études" 3. Québec: Les Presses de l'Université Laval; Louvain/Paris: Éditions Peeters, 1995, 51-86.

——. "Le Christ vainqueur de la mort (EvPhil NH II 68,17b-29a): une exégèse valentinienne de Mt 27,46." *NovT* 38 (1996) 1-11.

——. "Le sommaire anthropogonique de l'Écrit sans titre (127.17-118.2) à la lumière de 1 Co 15,45-47." *VC* 44 (1990) 382-393.

——. "The Literary Contacts between the Writing without Title On the Origin of the World (CG II,5 and XIII,2 and Eugnostos the Blessed (CG III,3 and V,1)." *JBL* 114 (1995) 81-101.

——. "The Writing without Title of Nag Hammadi Codex II: A Redactional Hypothesis." *SecCent* 8 (1991) 217-234.

Painchaud, Louis and Anne Pasquier. *Les textes de Nag Hammadi et le problème de leur classification: Actes du colloque tenu à Québec du 15 au 19 septembre 1993*. BCNH, Section "Études" 3. Québec: Les Presses de l'Université Laval; Louvain/Paris: Éditions Peeters, 1995.

Parrott, Douglas M. "The Acts of Peter and the Twelve Apostles (VI,1)." In James M. Robinson, ed. *The Nag Hammadi Library in English*. San Francisco: Harper & Row, 1988, 287-289.

——. "The Acts of Peter and the Twelve Apostles (VI,1:1.1-12.22)." In Douglas M. Parrott, ed. *Nag Hammadi Codices V,2-5 and VI*. NHS 11. Leiden: E. J. Brill, 1979, 197-202.

——. "Eugnostos and the Sophia of Jesus Christ." In David N. Freedman et al., eds. *ABD, Vol. 2*. New York: Doubleday, 1992, 668-669.

——. "Eugnostos the Blessed (III,3 and V,1) and The Sophia of Jesus Christ (III,4 and BG 8502,3)." In James M. Robinson, ed. *The Nag Hammadi Library in English*. San Francisco: Harper & Row, 1988, 220-243.

——. "Gnosticism and Egyptian Religion." *NovT* 29 (1987) 73-93.

——. "Introduction to the Apocalypse of Adam (V,5)." In James M. Robinson, ed. *The Nag Hammadi Library in English*. San Francisco: Harper & Row, 1988, 278.

——. *Nag Hammadi Codices III,3-4 and V,1 with Papyrus Berolinensis 8502,3 and Oxyrhynchus papyrus 1081: Eugnostos and the Sophia of Jesus Christ*. NHS 27. Leiden: E. J. Brill, 1991.

——. "The Thirteen Kingdoms of the Apocalypse of Adam: Origin, Meaning, and Significance." *NovT* 31 (1989) 67-87.

Parry, Milman. "Language and Characterization in Homer." *Harvard Studies in Classical Philology* 76 (1972) 1-22.

Pascher, Josef. *HE BASILIKE HODOS: Der Königsweg zu Wiedergeburt und Vergöttung bei Philon von Alexandreia*. Studien zur Geschichte und Kultur des Altertums 17, vols. 3-4. Paderborn: F. Schöningh, 1931; New York: Johnson Reprint, 1968.

Pasquier, Anne. "Prouneikos: A Colorful Expression to Designate Wisdom." In Karen L. King, ed. *Images of the Feminine in Gnosticism*. SAC. Philadelphia: Fortress, 1988, 47-66.

Patterson, Stephen J. *The Gospel of Thomas and Jesus*. Sonoma: Polebridge, 1993.

——. "The Gospel of Thomas and the Synoptic Tradition: A Forschungsbericht and Critique." *Forum* 8 (1992) 45-97.

——. "Gospel of Thomas: Introduction." In John S. Kloppenborg, Marvin W. Meyer, Stephen J. Patterson, and Michael G. Steinhauser, eds. *Q-Thomas Reader*. Sonoma: Polebridge, 1990, 77-123.

——. "Sources, Redaction and Tendenz in The Acts of Peter and the Twelve Apostles (NH VI,1)." *VC* 45 (1991) 1-17.

Pearson, Birger A. "*Apocryphon Johannis* Revisited." In Per Bilde, Helge Kjaer Nielsen, and Jörgen Podemann Sørensen, eds. *Apocryphon Severini presented to Søren Giversen.* Aarhus: Aarhus University Press, 1993, 155-165.

——. "Biblical Exegesis in Gnostic Literature." In Michael E. Stone, ed. *Armenian and Biblical Studies.* Jerusalem: St. James, 1977, 70-80.

——. "The Figure of Seth in Gnostic Literature." In Birger A. Pearson, ed. *Gnosticism, Judaism, and Egyptian Christianity.* SAC 5. Minneapolis: Fortress, 1990, 52-83.

——. "From Jewish Apocalypticism to Gnosis." Paper presented at Fiftieth Anniversary of the Nag Hammadi Discovery: Copenhagen International Conference on the Nag Hammadi Texts in the History of Religions, Danish Academy of Sciences and Letters, 1995.

——. "Gnosticism as Platonism." In Birger A. Pearson, ed. *Gnosticism, Judaism, and Egyptian Christianity.* SAC 5. Minneapolis: Fortress, 1990, 52-83.

——. "Jewish Elements in Gnosticism and the Development of Gnostic Self-Definition." In E. P. Sanders, ed. *Jewish and Christian Self-Definition, Vol. 1.* Philadelphia: Fortress, 1981, 151-160.

——. "Jewish Elements in Gnosticism and the Development of Gnostic Self-Definition." In Birger A. Pearson, ed. *Gnosticism, Judaism, and Egyptian Christianity.* SAC 5. Minneapolis: Fortress, 1990, 124-35.

——. "Jewish Sources in Gnostic Literature." In Michael E. Stone, ed. *Jewish Writings of the Second Temple Period. Apocrypha, Pseudepigrapha, Qumran Sectarian Writings, Philo, Josephus.* Assen: Von Gorcum; Philadelphia: Fortress, 1984, 443-481.

——. *Nag Hammadi Codex VII.* NHMS 30. Leiden: E. J. Brill, 1996.

——. "Nag Hammadi Codices." In David N. Freedman et al., eds. *ABD, Vol. 4.* New York: Doubleday, 1992, 984-993.

——. "Philo and Gnosticism." *ANRW* II.21.1 (1984) 295-342.

——. "Philo, Gnosis and the New Testament." In Alastair H. B. Logan and Alexander J. M. Wedderburn, eds. *The New Testament and Gnosis: Essays in Honour of Robert McLachlan Wilson.* Edinburgh: T. & T. Clark, 1983, 73-89.

——. "The Problem of Jewish Gnostic Literature." In Charles W. Hedrick and Robert Hodgson, Jr., eds. *Nag Hammadi, Gnosticism and Early Christianity.* Peabody, MA: Hendrickson, 1986, 15-35.

——. "Theurgic Tendencies in Gnosticism and Iamblichus's Conception of Theurgy." In Richard T. Wallis and Jay Bregman, eds. *Neoplatonism and Gnosticism.* Studies in Neoplatonism: Ancient and Modern 6. Albany: SUNY Press, 1992, 253-275.

——. "Use, Authority, and Exegesis of Mikra in Gnostic Literature." In Martin J. Mulder, ed. *Mikra: Text, Translation and Interpretation of the Hebrew Bible in Ancient Judaism and Early Christianity.* CRINT, Section 2: The Literature of the Jewish People in the Period of the Second Temple and the Talmud, 1. Assen/Maastiricht: Van Gorcum; Philadelphia: Fortress, 1988, 635-52.

Peel, Ellen. "Subject, Object, and the Alternation of First and Third Person Narration in Novels by Alther, Atwood, and Drabble: Toward a Theory of Feminist Aesthetics." *Critique: Studies in Contemporary Fiction* 98 (1989) 107-122.

Perkins, Pheme. *The Gnostic Dialogue. The Early Church and the Crisis of Gnosticism.* Studies in Contemporary Biblical and Theological Problems. New York: Paulist, 1980.

——. "Irenaeus and the Gnostics." *VC* 30 (1976) 193-200.

Perry, Ben E. *The Ancient Romances: A Literary-Historical Account of Their Origins.* Berkeley: University of California Press, 1967.

Pervo, Richard I. *Profit with Delight: The LIterary Genre of the Acts of the Apostles.* Philadelphia: Fortress, 1987.

Petersen, Norman R. "The Literary Problematic of the Apocryphon of John." Ph.D. Dissertation, Harvard University, 1967.

Petersen, William L., ed. *Gospel Traditions in the Second Century: Origins, Recensions, Text, and Transmission.* Notre Dame: University of Notre Dame Press, 1989.

Peterson, Erik. "Christianus." In Erik Peterson, ed. *Miscellanea Giovanni Mercati, Vol. 1: Letteratura cristiana antica.* Studi e Testi 121. Rome: Città del Vaticano, 1946, 355-372.

——. *Frühkirche, Judentum und Gnosis. Studien und Untersuchungen.* Freiburg: Herder & Herder, 1959; Darmstadt: Wissenschaftliche Buchgesellschaft, 1982.

Pétrement, Simone. "Les quatres 'illuminateurs' sur les sens et l'origine d'un thème gnostique." *REAug* 27 (1981) 1-23.

——. *A Separate God: The Christian Origins of Gnosticism.* Trans. by Carol Harrison. San Francisco: HarperSanFrancisco, 1990.

Piper, Ronald A., ed. *The Gospel behind the Gospels: Current Studies on Q.* Leiden: E. J. Brill, 1995.

Plisch, Uwe-Karten. "Die Auslegung der Erkenntnis (NHC XI,1) herausgegeben, übersetzt und erklärt." Th.D. Dissertation, Berlin, 1994.

Podlecki, Anthony J. *Aeschylus. Eumenides.* Warminster: Aris & Phillips, 1989.

Poffet, Jean-Michel. *La Méthode exégetique d'Héracléon et d'Origène, commentateurs de Jn 4: Jésus, la Samaritaine et les Samaritains.* Paradosis 28. Fribourg: Éditions universitaires, 1985.

Poirier, Paul-Hubert. *L'Hymne de la Perle des Actes de Thomas.* Homo religiosus 8. Louvain-la-Neuve: Centre d'histoire des religions, 1981.

——. "L'Hymne de la Perle des Actes de Thomas: Étude de la tradition manuscrite." *Symposium syriacum 1976.* Orientalia christiana analecta 205. Rome: Pontificium Insitutum Orientalium Studiorum, 1978, 19-29.

——. *Le Tonnerre, intellect parfait (NH VI,2).* BCNH, section "Textes" 22. Québec: Les Presses de l'Université Laval; Louvain/Paris: Éditions Peeters, 1996.

Porter, Stanley E. "The 'We' Passages." In Bruce W. Winter, ed. *The Book of Acts in its First Century Setting, Vol. 2.* Grand Rapids: Eerdmans, 1994, 545-574.

Prestige, George L. *God in Patristic Thought.* London: SPCK, 1959.

Pritchard, James B., ed. *The Ancient Near East: An Anthology of Texts and Pictures.* Princeton: Princeton University Press, 1958.

Propp, Vladimir. *Morphologie du Conte.* Paris: Seuil, 1928; repr. 1965 and 1970.

Puech, Henri-Charles. "Découverte d'une bibliothèque gnostique en Haute-Egypte." *Encyclopédie Française, Vol. 19: Philosophie, Religion.* Paris: Societé Nouvelle de l'Encyclopédie Française, 1957, 42.4-42.13.

——. *En quête de la Gnose. II. Sur l'Évangile selon Thomas. Esquisse d'une interprétation systématique.* Bibliothèque des sciences humaines. Paris: Gallimard, 1978.

——. "Gnostic Gospels and Related Documents." In Edgar Hennecke and Wilhelm Schneemelcher, eds. *New Testament Apocrypha, Vol. 1: Gospels and Related Writings.* London: SCM Press Ltd., 1963, 286-287.

——. "Les nouveaux écrits gnostiques découverts en Haute-Egypte (premier inventaire et essai d'identification)." *Coptic Studies in Honor of Walter Ewing Crum.* Bulletin of the Byzantine Institute 2. Boston: Byzantine Institute of America, 1950, 91-154.

——. "Nouveaux écrits gnostiques découverts à Nag Hammadi." *RHR* 134 (1948) 244-248.

Puech, Henri-Charles and Jean Doresse. "Nouveaux écrits gnostiques découverts en Egypte." *Académie des Inscriptions et Belles-Lettres: Comptes Rendus des Séances de l'Année* (1948) 87-89.

Puigalli, J. *Études sur la Dialexeis de Maxime de Tyre, conférencier platonicien du IIième siècle*. Lille, 1983.

Quispel, Gilles. "Ezekiel 1:26 in Jewish Mysticism and Gnosis." *VC* 34 (1980) 1-13.

——. *Gnosis: de derde component van de Europese cultuurtraditie*. Utrecht: HES Uigevers, 1988.

——. "Gnosticism and the New Testament." *VC* 19 (1965) 65-85.

——. "Gnosticism and the New Testament." In J. Philip Hyatt, ed. *The Bible in Modern Scholarship*. Nashville: Abingdon, 1965, 252-271.

——. "Gnosticism and the New Testament." *Gnostic Studies, Vol. 1*. Nederlands Historisch-Archaeologisch Instituut te Istanbul 34. Istanbul: Nederlands Historisch-Archaeologisch Instituut in het Nabije Oosten, 1974, 197-212.

——. "Het Johannesevangelie en de Gnosis." *NedTTs* 11 (1956/57) 173-203.

——. "Judaism, Judaic Christianity, and Gnosis." In Alastair H. B. Logan and Alexander J. M. Wedderburn, eds. *The New Testament and Gnosis: Essays in Honour of Robert McLachlan Wilson*. Edinburgh: T. & T. Clark, 1983, 48-52.

——. "L'Évangile de Jean et la Gnose." In Marie Émile Boismard, ed. *L'Évangile de Jean: Études et problèmes*. RechBib 3. Bruges: Desclée de Brouwer, 1958, 197-208.

——. "Nathanael und der Menschensohn (Joh 1:51)." *ZNW* 47 (1956) 281-283.

——. "The Original Doctrine of Valentine." *VC* 1 (1947) 43-73.

——. "The Original Doctrine of Valentinus the Gnostic." *VC* 50 (1996) 327-352.

——. "Qumran, John and Jewish Christianity." In James Charlesworth, ed. *John and the Dead Sea Scrolls*. New York: Crossroad, 1991, 137-155.

Räisänen, Heikki. *Paul and the Law*. Philadelphia: Fortress, 1986.

Reardon, Bryan P. *The Form of Greek Romance*. Princeton: Princeton University Press, 1991.

Reeve, Michael D. "Interpolations in Greek Tragedy." *GRBS* 13 (1972) 451-474; 14 (1973) 145-171.

Rich, Audrey N. M. "The Platonic Ideas as the Thoughts of God." *Mnemosyne* 4.7 (1954) 123-133.

Riesner, Rainer. *Die Frühzeit des Apostels Paulus. Studien zur Chronologie, Missionsstrategie und Theologie*. WUNT 71. Tübingen: J. C. B. Mohr (P. Siebeck), 1994.

Riley, Gregory J. "*The Gospel of Thomas* in Recent Scholarship." *Currents in Research: Biblical Studies, Vol. 2*. Sheffield: Sheffield Academic Press, 1994, 227-252.

——. "A Note on the Text of *Gospel of Thomas* 37." *HTR* 88 (1995) 179-181.

——. *Resurrection Reconsidered: Thomas and John in Controversy*. Minneapolis: Fortress, 1995.

——. "Thomas Christianity and the Canonical Gospels." *HTR*, forthcoming.

——. "Thomas Tradition and the Acts of Thomas." *SBLSP* 30 (1991) 533-542.

Rius-Camps, Josep. "Origenes frente al desafio de los Gnosticos." In Robert J. Daly, ed. *Origeniana Quinta*. BETL 105. Leuven: Leuven University Press, 1992, 57-78.

Robbins, Vernon K. "By Land and By Sea: The We-Passages and Ancient Sea Voyages." In Charles H. Talbert, ed. *Perspectives on Luke-Acts*. Perspectives in Religious Studies 5. Edinburgh: T. & T. Clark, 1978, 215-242.

Roberge, Michel. "Anthropogonie et anthropologie dans la *Paraphrase de Sem* (NH VII,1)." *Le Muséon* 99 (1986) 229-248.

——. "Introduction to The Paraphrase of Shem (VII,1)." In James M. Robinson, ed. *Nag Hammadi Library in English*. San Francisco: Harper & Row, 1988, 339-341.

——. "La crucifixion du Sauveur dans la Paraphrase de Sem (NH VII,1)." In Marguerite Rassart-Debergh and Julien Ries, eds. *Actes du IVe Congrès copte: Louvain-la-Neuve, 5-10 septembre 1988.* Louvain-la-Neuve: Université catholique de Louvain, 1992, 381-387.

Robinson, Gesine M. "Trimorphic Protennoia." In David N. Freedman et al., eds. *ABD, Vol. 6.* New York: Doubleday, 1992, 663-64.

——. "The Trimorphic Protennoia and the Prologue of the Fourth Gospel." In James E. Goehring et al., eds. *Gnosticism and the Early Christian World.* Sonoma: Polebridge, 1990, 37-50.

Robinson, James M. "The Coptic Gnostic Library." *NovT* 12 (1970) 81-85.

——. "Die Bedeutung der gnostischen Nag-Hammadi Texte für die neutestamentliche Wissenschaft." In Lukas Bormann, Kelly Del Tredici, and Angela Standhartinger, eds. *Religious Propaganda and Missionary Competition in the New Testament World: Essays Honoring Dieter Georgi.* NovTSup 74. Leiden/New York: E. J. Brill, 1994, 23-41.

——. "The Discovering and Marketing of Coptic Manuscripts: The Nag Hammadi Codices and the Bodmer Papyri." *Sundries in Honour of Torgny Säve-Söderbergh.* Acta Universitatis Upsaliensis. Uppsala Studies in Ancient Mediterranean and Near Eastern Civilizations 13. Uppsala/Stockholm: Almqvist & Wiksell, 1984, 97-114.

——. "The Discovering and Marketing of Coptic Manuscripts: The Nag Hammadi Codices and the Bodmer Papyri." In Birger A. Pearson and James A. Goehring, eds. *The Roots of Egyptian Christianity.* SAC. Philadelphia: Fortress, 1986, 1-25.

——. "The Discovery of the Nag Hammadi Codices." *BA* 42 (1979) 206-224.

——. "Ethics in Publishing Manuscript Discoveries: Panel Discussion." In Michael O. Wise et al., eds. *Methods of Investigation of the Dead Sea Scrolls and the Khirbet Qumran Site: Present Realities and Future Prospects.* Annals of the New York Academy of Sciences 722. New York: New York Academy of Sciences, 1994, 468-471.

——. *The Facsimile Edition of the Nag Hammadi codices: Introduction.* Leiden: E. J. Brill, 1984.

——. "From the Cliff to Cairo: The Story of the Discoverers and the Middlemen of the Nag Hammadi Codices." In Bernard Barc, ed. *Colloque international sur les textes de Nag Hammadi (Québec, 22-25 août 1978).* BCNH, Section "Études" 1. Québec: Les Presses de l'Université Laval, 1981, 21-58.

——. "Handling Future Manuscript Discoveries." *BA* 54 (1991) 235-240.

——. "Introduction." In Marvin W. Meyer and James M. Robinson, eds. *The Nag Hammadi Library in English.* Leiden: E. J. Brill, 1977, 1-25.

——. "Jesus as Sophos and Sophia: Wisdom Tradition and the Gospels." In Robert L. Wilken, ed. *Aspects of Wisdom in Judaism and Early Christianity.* Notre Dame: University of Notre Dame Press, 1975, 1-16.

——. "The Jesus of Q as Liberation Theologian." In Ronald A. Piper, ed. *The Gospel Behind the Gospels: Current Studies on Q.* Leiden: E. J. Brill, 1995, 259-274.

——. "Jesus: From Easter to Valentinus (Or to the Apostles' Creed)." *JBL* 101 (1982) 5-37.

——. "The Jung Codex: The Rise and Fall of a Monopoly." *RelSRev* (1977) 17-30.

——. "Kerygma and History in the New Testament." In J. Philip Hyatt, ed. *The Bible in Modern Scholarship.* Nashville: Abingdon, 1965, 114-150.

——. "ΛΟΓΟΙ ΣΟΦΩΝ: Zur Gattung der Spruchquelle." In Erich Dinkler, ed. *Zeit und Geschichte: Danksgabe an Rudolf Bultmann.* Tübingen: J. C. B. Mohr (P. Siebeck), 1964, 77-96.

——. "Manuscript Discoveries of the Future." *Zeitschrift für Papyrologie und Epigraphik* 92 (1992) 281-296.

——. *Manuscript Discoveries of the Future.* Occasional Papers, The Institute for Antiquity and Christianity 23. Claremont: Institute for Antiquity and Christianity, 1991.

——. *Nag Hammadi: The First Fifty Years.* Occasional Papers, The Institute for Antiquity and Christianity 34. Claremont: The Institute for Antiquity and Christianity, 1995.

——. "On Bridging the Gulf from Q to the Gospel of Thomas (or Vice Versa)." In Charles W. Hedrick and Robert Hodgson, Jr., eds. *Nag Hammadi, Gnosticism, and Early Christianity.* Peabody, MA: Hendrickson, 1986, 127-175.

——. *The Problem of History in Mark and Other Marcan Studies.* Philadelphia: Fortress, 1982.

——. "The Q Trajectory: Between John and Matthew via Jesus." In Birger A. Pearson, ed. *The Future of Early Christianity: Essays in Honor of Helmut Koester.* Minneapolis: Fortress, 1991, 173-194.

——. "Sethians and Johannine Thought: The Trimorphic Protennoia and the Prologue of the Gospel of John." In Bentley Layton, ed. *The Rediscovery of Gnosticism, Vol. 2: Sethian Gnosticism.* SHR 41. Leiden: E. J. Brill, 1981, 643-662.

——. "The Three Steles of Seth and the Gnostics of Plotinus." In Geo Widengren, ed. *Proceedings of the International Colloquium on Gnosticism, Stockholm August 20-25, 1973.* VHAAH.FF 17. Stockholm: Almqvist & Wiksell, 1977, 133-142.

Robinson, James M. et al., eds. *Documenta Q: Reconstructions of Q through Two Centuries of Gospel Research Excerpted, Sorted, and Evaluated. Q 11:2b-4.* Louvain: Éditions Peeters, 1996.

Robinson, James M. and Marvin W. Meyer, eds. *The Nag Hammadi Library in English.* Translated by members of the Coptic Gnostic Library Project for the Institute for Antiquity and Christianity. New York: Harper & Row, 1977.

Robinson, James M. (General) and Richard Smith (Managing), eds. *The Nag Hammadi Library in English.* 3rd rev. ed. Leiden: E. J. Brill; San Francisco: Harper & Row, 1988.

Rose, Peter W. *Sons of the Gods, Children of Earth: Ideology and Literary Form in Ancient Greece.* Ithaca and London: Cornell University Press, 1992.

Rowland, Christopher C. "John 1:51, Jewish Apocalyptic and Targumic Tradition." *NTS* 30 (1984) 498-507.

Ruckstuhl, Eugen. "Θωμα." In Horst Balz and Gerhard Schneider, eds. *Exegetisches Wörterbuch zum Neuen Testament, Vol. 1.* Stuttgart: Kohlhammer, 1978, 407-409.

Rudolph, Kurt. "Coptica-Mandaica: Zu einiger Ubereinstimmungen zwischen koptisch-gnostischen und mandäischen Texten." In Martin Krause, ed. *Essays on the Nag Hammadi Texts in Honour of Pahor Labib.* Leiden: E. J. Brill, 1975, 191-216.

——. "Gnosis and Gnostizismus, ein Forschungsbericht." *TRu* 34 (1969) 121-175, 181-231, 358-361.

——. "Gnosis and Gnostizismus, ein Forschungsbericht." *TRu* 36 (1971) 1-61, 89-124.

——. *Gnosis: The Nature and History of Gnosticism.* Trans. by R. McL. Wilson. Edinburgh: T. & T. Clark, 1977; San Francisco: Harper & Row, 1983.

Runia, David T. "Themes in Philonic Theology with Special Reference to the *De mutatione nominum.*" In Roelof van den Broek, Tjitze Baarda, and Jaap Mansfeld, eds. *Knowledge of God in the Graeco-Roman World.* EPRO 112. Leiden: E. J. Brill, 1988, 67-91.

——. "Was Philo a Middle Platonist? A Difficult Question Revisited." *Studia Philonica Annual* 5 (1993) 112-140.

Sagnard, François. *La Gnose Valentinienne et le témoignage de Saint Irénée.* Paris: Vrin, 1947.

Sayre, Kenneth M. *Plato's Late Ontology: A Riddle Resolved.* Princeton: Princeton University Press, 1983.

Schenke, Hans-Martin. "The Acts of Peter and the Twelve Apostles." In Edgar Hennecke and Wilhelm Schneemelcher, eds. *New Testament Apocrypha, Vol. 2: Writings Related to the Apostles, Apocalypses and Related Subjects.* Cambridge: J. Clarke; Louisville: Westminster/John Knox, 1992, 412-425.

524 BIBLIOGRAPHY

——. "Das Evangelium nach Philippus." In Wilhelm Schneemelcher, ed. *Neutestamentliche Apokryphen in deutscher Übersetzung, Bd 1: Evangelien.* Tübingen: J. C. B. Mohr (P. Siebeck), 1987, 148-173.

——. "Das Evangelium nach Philippus: Ein Evangelium der Valentinianer aus dem Funde von Nag-Hammadi." In Johannes Leipoldt and Hans-Martin Schenke, eds. *Koptisch-gnostische Schriften aus den Papyrus-Codices von Nag-Hammadi.* TF 20. Hamburg/Bergstedt: Herbert Reich, 1960, 31-65.

——. "Das Evangelium nach Philippus: Ein Evangelium der Valentinianer aus dem Funde von Nag-Hammadi." *TLZ* 84 (1959) 1-26.

——. "Das sethianische System nach Nag-Hammadi-Handschriften." In Peter Nagel, ed. *Studia Coptica, Vol. 45.* Berliner Byzantinistische Arbeiten 45. Berlin: Akademie Verlag, 1974, 165-172.

——. *Das Thomas-Buch (Nag-Hammadi-Codex II,7).* Berlin: Akademie-Verlag, 1989.

——. *Der Gott "Mensch" in der Gnosis: Ein Religionsgeschichtlicher Beitrag zur Diskussion über die Paulinische Kirche als Leib Christi.* Göttingen: Vandenhoeck & Ruprecht, 1962.

——. "Die Rolle der Gnosis in Bultmanns Kommentar zum Johannesevangelium aus heutiger Sicht, Protokoll der Tagung 'Alter Marburger'." *Hofgeismar* 2.5 (1991) 49-83.

——. "'Die Taten des Petrus und der zwölf Apostel:' Die erste Schrift aus Nag-Hammadi-Codex VI: Eingeleitet und übersetzt vom Berliner Arbeitskreis für koptisch-gnostische Schriften." *TLZ* 98 (1973) 13-19.

——. "Gnosis: Zum Forschungsstand unter besonderer Berücksichtigung der religions–geschichtlichen Problematik." *VF* 32 (1987) 2-22.

——. "Introduction to the Gospel of Philip." In Edgar Hennecke and Wilhelm Schneemelcher, eds. *New Testament Apocrypha, Vol. 1: Gospels and Related Writings.* Cambridge: Cambridge University Press, 1991, 179-208.

——. "Nag Hammadi Studien I: Das Literarische Problem des Apocryphon Johannis." *ZRGG* 14 (1962) 57-63.

——. "The Phenomenon and Significance of Gnostic Sethianism." In Bentley Layton, ed. *The Rediscovery of Gnosticism, Vol. 2: Sethian Gnosticism.* SHR 41. Leiden: E. J. Brill, 1981, 588-616.

——. "The Problem of Gnosis." *SecCent* 3 (1983) 73-87.

——. "The Relevance of Nag Hammadi Research to New Testament Scholarship." Paper presented at Annual Meeting, SBL, Chicago, 1994.

——. "The Role of Gnosis in Bultmann's Commentary on the Gospel of John Reconsidered in the Light of Nag Hammadi Research." Paper presented at The Nag Hammadi Codices: Fifty Years of Scholarship (1945-1995), Harvard Divinity School, 1995.

——. "Vom Ursprung der Welt, Eine Titellose Gnostische Abhandlung aus dem Funde von Nag-Hammadi." *TLZ* 84 (1959) 243-256.

——. "Zur Exegese der Philippus-Evangeliums." In Søren Giversen, Martin Krause, and Peter Nagel, eds. *Coptology: Past, Present, and Future, Studies in Honour of Rodolphe Kasser.* Orientalia Lovaniensia Analecta 61. Leuven: Édition Peeters, 1994, 123-137.

——. "Zur Faksimile-Ausgabe der Nag-Hammadi-Schriften Nag-Hammadi-Codex VI." *OLZ* 69 (1974) 229-243.

Schlier, Heinrich. "αἱρέομαι κτλ." In Gerhard Kittel and Gerhard Friedrich, eds. *TWNT, Vol. 1.* Stuttgart: Kohlhammer, 1933, 179-184.

Schmidt, Carl. "Ein vorirenäisches gnostisches Originalwerk im koptischer Sprache." *Sitzungsberichte der preussischen Akademie der Wissenschaften zu Berlin.* Berlin: Verlag der Akademie der Wissenschaften, 1896, 839-847.

——. "Irenäus und seine Quelle in adv. haer. I,29." In Adolf von Harnack et al., eds. *Philotesia: Paul Kleinert zum LXX Geburtstag.* Berlin: Trowitzsch & Sohn, 1907, 317-336.

Schmidt, Carl and Violet MacDermot. *The Books of Jeu and the Untitled Text in the Bruce Codex*. NHS 13. Leiden: E. J. Brill, 1978.

Schmithals, Walter. *Die Gnosis in Korinth*. FRLANT 66. Göttingen: Vandenhoeck & Ruprecht, 1965.

——. *Neues Testament und Gnosis*. Darmstadt: Wissenschaftliche Buchgesellschaft, 1984.

Schnackenburg, Rudolf. *Das Johannesevangelium*. HTKNT 4. Freiburg/Basel/Wien: Herder & Herder, 1975.

——. *The Gospel According to St. John, Vol. 1*. London: Burns & Oates; New York: Herder & Herder, 1968.

Schneemelcher, Wilhelm, ed. *Neutestamentliche Apokryphen in deutscher Übersetzung. Bd. 1: Evangelien; Bd. 2: Apostolisches, Apokalypsen und Verwandtes*. Tübingen: J. C. B. Mohr (P. Siebeck), 1987, 1989.

Schoedel, William R. "The First Apocalypse of James, V,3:24.10-44.10." In Douglas M. Parrott, ed. *Nag Hammadi Codices V,2-5 and VI with Papyrus Berolinensis 8502,1 and 4*. NHS 11. Leiden: E. J. Brill, 1979, .

——. "Jewish Wisdom and the Formation of the Christian Ascetic." In Robert L. Wilken, ed. *Aspects of Wisdom in Judaism and Early Christianity*. Notre Dame/London: University of Notre Dame Press, 1975, 169-199.

Schoenborn, Ulrich. *Diverbium Salutis: Literarische Struktur und theologische Intention des gnostischen Dialogs am Beispiel der koptischen 'Apokalypse des Petrus'*. SUNT 19. Göttingen: Vandenhoeck & Ruprecht, 1995.

Scholem, Gershom. *Major Trends in Jewish Mysticism*. 3rd ed. New York: Schocken, 1974.

——. *On the Kabbalah and Its Symbolism*. New York: Schocken, 1969.

Scholer, David M. *Nag Hammadi Bibliography 1948-1969*. NHS 1. Leiden: E. J. Brill, 1971.

Scholes, Robert and Robert Kellogg. *The Nature of Narrative*. New York: Oxford University Press, 1966.

Schöllgen, Georg. *Ecclesia sordida? Zur Frage der sozialen Schichtung frühchristlicher Gemeinden am Beispiel Karthagos zur Zeit Tertullians*. JAC Ergbd. 12. Münster: Aschendorff, 1984.

——. "Probleme der frühchristlichen Sozialgeschichte." *JAC* 32 (1989) 23-40.

Scholten, Clemens. "Die Nag-Hammadi-Texte als Buchbesitz der Pachomianer." *JAC* 31 (1988) 144-172.

——. "Gibt es Quellen zur Sozialgeschichte der Valentinianer Roms?" *ZNW* 79 (1988) 244-261.

Schrage, Wolfgang. *Das Verhältnis des Thomas-Evangeliums zur synoptischen Tradition und zu den koptischen Evangelienübersetzungen*. Berlin: Töpelmann, 1964.

Schüssler Fiorenza, Elisabeth. *In Memory of Her: A Feminist Theological Reconstruction of Christian Origins*. New York: Crossroad, 1984.

Scott, Alan B. "Opposition and Concession: Origen's Relationship to Valentinianism." In Robert J. Daly, ed. *Origeniana Quinta*. BETL 105. Leuven: Leuven University Press, 1992, 79-84.

Segal, Alan F. "Heavenly Ascent in Hellenistic Judaism, Early Christianity, and their Environment." *ANRW* II.23.2 (1980) 1333-1394.

——. *The Other Judaisms of Late Antiquity*. Atlanta: Scholars Press, 1987.

——. *Two Powers in Heaven: Early Rabbinic Reports about Christianity and Gnosticism*. SJLA 25. Leiden: E. J. Brill, 1978.

Segelberg, Eric. "The Coptic-Gnostic Gospel According to Philip and its Sacramental System." *Numen* 7 (1960) 189-200.

Sell, Jesse. "Johannine Traditions in Logion 61 of the Gospel of Thomas." *Perspectives in Religious Studies* 7 (1980) 24-37.

Sellew, Philip. "Death, the Body and the World in the Coptic Gospel of Thomas." In Elizabeth A. Livingstone, ed. *Proceedings of the XII International Patristics Conference, Oxford, 1995*. Studia Patristica 31. Leuven: Éditions Peeters, 1996, 530-534.

——. "Laodiceans and the Philippians Fragments Hypothesis." *HTR* 87 (1994) 17-28.

——. "Reconstruction of Q 12:33-59." *SBLSP* 26 (1987) 617-668.

——. "Secret Mark and the History of Canonical Mark." In Birger A. Pearson, ed. *The Future of Early Christianity: Essays in Honor of Helmut Koester*. Minneapolis: Fortress, 1991, 242-257.

Sevrin, Jean-Marie. "À propos de la 'Paraphrase de Sem'." *Le Muséon* 88 (1975) 69-96.

——. *L'Exegese de l'ame: NH II, 6. Texte établi et presenté*. BCNH 9, Section "Textes" 9. Québec: Les Presses de l'Université Laval; Louvain: Éditions Peeters, 1983.

——. "La rédaction des paraboles dans l'Évangile selon Thomas." In Marguerite Rassart-Debergh and Julien Ries, eds. *Actes du IVe Congrès copte (Louvain-la-Neuve, 5-10 septembre 1988)*. Publications de l'Institut orientaliste de Louvain 41. Louvain-la-Neuve: Université catholique de Louvain, 1992, 343-354.

——. *Le dossier baptismal séthien: Études sur la sacramentaire gnostique*. BCNH, Section "Études" 2. Québec: Les Presses de l'Université Laval, 1986.

——. "Les Noces Spirituelles dans l'Évangile selon Philippe." *Le Muséon* 87 (1974) 143-193.

——. "Les rites et la gnose, d'après quelques textes gnostiques coptes." In Julien Ries, Yvonne Janssens, and Jean-Marie Sevrin, eds. *Gnosticisme et Monde Hellénistique*. Louvain-la-Neuve: Institut Orientaliste, 1982, 440-450.

——. "A propos de la 'Paraphrase de Sem'." *NovT* 12 (1970) 130-140.

——. "Un groupement de trois paraboles contre les richesses dans l'Évangile selon Thomas (Ev Th log. 63, 64, 65)." In Jean Delorme, ed. *Les paraboles évangélique: Perspectives nouvelles (XIIe congrès de l'ACFEB, Lyon [1987])*. Lectio divina 135. Paris: Cerf, 1989, 425-439.

Shanks, Hershel. "Correction: Photographs of Unpublished Dead Sea Scrolls at Ancient Biblical Manuscript Center." *BAR* 16 (1990) 67.

——. "How to Break a Scholarly Monopoly: The Case of the Gospel of Thomas." *BAR* 16 (1990) 55.

——. "New Hope for the Unpublished Dead Sea Scrolls." *BAR* 15 (1989) 55-56, 74.

Shellrude, G. M. "The Apocalypse of Adam: Evidence for a Christian Provenience." In Martin Krause, ed. *Gnosis and Gnosticism*. Leiden: E. J. Brill, 1981, 82-91.

Sieber, John. "The Barbelo Aeon as Sophia." In Bentley Layton, ed. *The Rediscovery of Gnosticism, Vol. 2: Sethian Gnosticism*. SHR 41. Leiden: E. J. Brill, 1981, 788-795.

——. "A Redactional Analysis of the Synoptic Gospels with Regard to the Question of the Sources of the Gospel According to Thomas." Ph.D. Dissertation, Claremont Graduate School, 1965.

Simonetti, Manlio. "Alcune riflessioni sul rapporto tra gnosticismo e cristianesimo." *Vetera Christanorum* 28 (1991) 337-374.

Skarsaune, Oskar. "Justin der Märtyrer." *TRE* 17 (1988) 471-478.

Smith, D. Moody. *John Among the Gospels: The Relationship in Twentieth-Century Research*. Minneapolis: Fortress, 1992.

Smith, Morton. "Ascent to the Heavens and the Beginning of Christianity." *Eranos* 50 (1981) 403-429.

Snodgrass, Klyne R. "The Gospel of Thomas: A Secondary Gospel." *SecCent* 7 (1989-90).

Stählin, Otto. *Untersuchungen über die Scholien zu Clemens Alexandrinus*. Nürnberg: Beilage zum Jahresbericht des Nürnberger Gymnasiums, 1897.

Stambaugh, John and David Balch, eds. *The Social World of the First Christians*. London: SPCK, 1986.

Standaert, Benoit. "'L'Évangile de Verité': Critique et Lecture." *NTS* 22 (1976) 243-275.

Stark, Rodney. "Antioch as the Social Situation for Matthew's Gospel." In John Stambaugh and David Balch, eds. *The Social World of the First Christians*. London: SPCK, 1986, 189-210.

Stegemann, Willy. "Nikagoras 8." *PW* XVII/1 (1936) 216-218.

Stendahl, Krister. "The Apostle Paul and the Introspective Conscience of the West." In Krister Stendahl, ed. *Paul Among Jews and Gentiles*. Philadelphia: Fortress, 1976, 78-96.

Stephens, Susan A. "Who Read Ancient Novels?" In James Tatum, ed. *The Search for the Ancient Novel*. Baltimore: Johns Hopkins University Press, 1994, 405-418.

Stone, Michael E. and John Strugnell. *The Books of Elijah, Parts 1-2*. SBLTT 18. Missoula: Scholars Press, 1979.

Stoops, Robert F. "Peter, Paul, and Priority in the Apocryphal Acts." *SBLSP* 31 (1992) 225-233.

Stroumsa, Gedaliahu G. "Aher: A Gnostic." In Bentley Layton, ed. *The Rediscovery of Gnosticism, Vol. 2: Sethian Gnosticism*. SHR 41. Leiden: E. J. Brill, 1981, 808-818.

——. *Another Seed: Studies in Gnostic Mythology*. NHS 24. Leiden: E. J. Brill, 1984.

——. "Form(s) of God: Some Notes on Metatron and Christ." *HTR* 76 (1983) 269-288.

——. "Polymorphie divine et transformations d'un mythologème: l'*Apocryphon de Jean* et ses sources." *VC* 35 (1981) 412-434.

Strutwolf, Holger. *Gnosis als System. Zur Rezeption der valentinianischen Gnosis bei Origenes*. FKDG 56. Göttingen: Vandenhoeck & Ruprecht, 1993.

Sumney, Jerry L. "The Letter of Eugnostos and the Origins of Gnosticism." *NovT* 31 (1989) 172-181.

Szarmach, Marian. *Maximos von Tyros. Eine literarische Monographie*. Torun: Uniwersytet Mikolaja Kopernika, 1985.

Tabor, John D. *Things Unutterable: Paul's Ascent to Paradise in its Greco-Roman, Judaic, and Early Christian Contexts*. Studies in Judaism. Lanham, Md.: University Press of America, 1986.

Tardieu, Michel. *Écrits Gnostiques: Codex de Berlin*. Sources gnostiques et manichéennes 1. Paris: Cerf, 1984.

Theissen, Gerd. *Social Reality and the Early Christians*. Minneapolis: Fortress, 1992.

——. *The Sociology of Early Palestinian Christianity*. Philadelphia: Fortress, 1978.

——. *Soziologie der Jesubewegung*. München: Kaiser, 1977.

——. *Studien zur Soziologie des Urchristentums*. WUNT 19. Tübingen: J. C. B. Mohr (P. Siebeck), 1983.

Thomas, Christine M. "The Acts of Peter, the Ancient Novel, and Early Christian History." Ph.D. Dissertation, Harvard University, 1995.

——. "Word and Deed: The Acts of Peter and Orality." *Apocrypha* 3 (1992) 125-164.

Thomas, Rosalind. *Literacy and Orality in Ancient Greece*. Cambridge: Cambridge University Press, 1992.

Thomassen, Einar. "Gnostic Semiotics: The Valentinian Notion of the Name." *Temenos* 29 (1993) 141-156.

——. "Notes pour la délimitation d'un corpus valentinien à Nag Hammadi." In Louis Painchaud and Anne Pasquier, eds. *Les textes de Nag Hammadi et le problème de leur classification. Actes du colloque tenu à Québec, du 15 au 19 septembre 1993*. BCNH, section "Études" 3. Québec: Les Presses de l'Université Laval; Louvain/Paris: Éditions Peeters, 1995, 243-259.

——. "The Philosophical Dimension of Gnosticism: The Valentinian System." In Roald Skarsten et al., eds. *Understanding and History in Arts and Sciences*. Acta Humaniora Universitatis Bergensis 1. Oslo: Solum Forlag, 1991, 69-79.

——. "The Valentinianism of the *Valentinian Exposition* (NHC XI,2)." *Le Muséon* 102 (1989) 225-236.

Thomassen, Einar and Louis Painchaud. *Le Traité Tripartite*. BCNH, Section "Textes" 19. Québec: Les Presses de l'Université Montreal, 1989.

Till, Walter C. *Das Evangelium nach Philippos*. Berlin: de Gruyter, 1963.

——. "The Gnostic Apocryphon of John." *JEH* 3 (1952) 14-22.

——. *Koptische Grammatik (Saïdischer Dialekt)*. 2nd ed. Leipzig: VEB Verlag Enzyklopädie, 1961.

Tov, Emanuel. *The Dead Sea Scrolls on Microfiche: A Comprehensive Facsimile Edition of the Texts from the Judean Desert*. Leiden: E. J. Brill; IDC Microform Publishers, 1993.

Trakatellis, Demetrios. *The Transcendent God of Eugnostos*. Trans. by Charles Sarelis. Brookline, MA: Holy Cross Orthodox Press, 1991.

Trapp, Michael B., ed. *Maximus Tyrius: Dissertationes*. Stuttgart/Leiqzig: Teubner, 1994.

Traube, Ludwig. *Nomina Sacra: Versuch einer Geschichte der christlichen Kürzung*. Darmstadt: Wissenschaftliche Buchgesellschaft, 1967.

Tripp, David H. "The Original Sequence of Irenaeus 'Adversus Haereses' I: A Suggestion." *SecCent* 8 (1991) 157-162.

——. "The 'Sacramental System' of the Gospel of Philip." In E. A. Livingstone, ed. *Studia Patristica*. Oxford: Pergamon Press, 1982, 251-267.

Tröger, Karl Wolfgang. "The Attitude of the Gnostic Religion towards Judaism as Viewed in a Variety of Perspectives." In Bernard Barc, ed. *Colloque international sur les textes de Nag Hammadi*. Québec: Les Presses de l'Université Laval, 1981, 86-98.

——. "Christianity and Gnosticism." *Theology Digest* 34 (1987) 219-225.

Tuckett, Christopher M. *Nag Hammadi and the Gospel Tradition*. Edinburgh: T. & T. Clark, 1986.

——. "Q and Thomas: Evidence of a Primitive 'Wisdom Gospel'?" *ETL* 67 (1991) 346-360.

Turner, John D. *The Book of Thomas the Contender from Codex II of the Cairo Gnostic Library from Nag Hammadi (CG II,7): The Coptic Text with Translation, Introduction and Commentary*. SBLDS 23. Missoula: Scholars Press, 1975.

——. "Gnosticism and Platonism: The Platonizing Sethian Texts from Nag Hammadi in their Relation to Later Platonic Literature." In Richard T. Wallis and Jay Bregman, eds. *Neoplatonism and Gnosticism*. Studies in Neoplatonism: Ancient and Modern 6. Albany: SUNY Press, 1992, 425-459.

——. "A New Link in the Syrian Judas Thomas Tradition." In Martin Krause, ed. *Essays on the Nag Hammadi Texts in Honour of Alexander Böhlig*. NHS 3. Leiden: E. J. Brill, 1972, 109-119.

——. "Notes to Text and Translation: NHC XI,3: *Allogenes*." In Charles W. Hedrick, ed. *Nag Hammadi Codices XI, XII, XIII*. NHS 28. Leiden: E. J. Brill, 1990, 243-267.

——. "Ritual in Gnosticism." *SBLSP* 33 (1994) 136-181.

——. "Sethian Gnosticism: A Literary History." In Charles W. Hedrick and Robert Hodgson, Jr., eds. *Nag Hammadi, Gnosticism, and Early Christianity*. Peabody, MA: Hendrickson, 1986, 55-86.

——. "Trimorphic Protennoia: Introduction and Translation." In Charles W. Hedrick, ed. *Nag Hammadi Codices XI, XII, XIII*. NHS 28. Leiden: E. J. Brill, 1990, 511-522.

——. "Typologies of the Sethian Gnostic Treatises from Nag Hammadi." In Louis Painchaud and Anne Pasquier, eds. *Les textes de Nag Hammadi et le problème de leur classification: Actes du colloque tenu à Québec du 15 au 19 septembre 1993*. Québec: Les Presses de l'Université Laval; Louvain/Paris: Éditions Peeters, 1995, 169-219.

——. "The Virgin that Became Male: The Feminine Principle in Platonic and Gnostic Metaphysics." Unpublished manuscript, 1995.

Turner, Martha Lee. *The Gospel according to Philip: The Sources and Coherence of an Early Christian Collection.* NHMS 38. Leiden: E. J. Brill, 1996.

——. "The Sources and Organization of the Gospel According to Philip." Ph.D. Dissertation, University of Notre Dame, 1994.

Vaage, Leif. *Galilean Upstarts: Jesus' First Followers According to Q.* Philadelphia: Trinity Press International, 1994.

——. "Q and the Historical Jesus: Some Peculiar Sayings." *Forum* 5 (1989) 159-176.

Valantasis, Richard. "Narrative Strategies and Synoptic Quandaries: A Response to Dennis MacDonald's Reading." *SBLSP* 31 (1992) 234-239.

——. *Spiritual Guides of the Third Century: A Semiotic Study of the Guide-Disciple Relationship in Christianity, Neoplatonism, Hermetism and Gnosticism.* Minneapolis: Fortress, 1991.

van Unnik, Wilhelm C. "Die 'geöffneten Himmel' in der Offenbarungsvision des Apocryphon Johannis." In Walther Eltester and F. H. Kettler, eds. *Apophoreta: Festschrift für Ernst Hänchen zu seinem seibzigsten Geburtstag am 10. Dezember 1964.* BZNW 30. Berlin: Alfred Töpelmann, 1964, 269-280.

——. "Die Gotteslehre bei Aristides und in Gnostischen Schriften." *TZ* 17 (1961) 168-174.

——. "A Formula Describing Prophecy." *NTS* 9 (1963) 86-94.

Veilleux, Armand. "Monasticism and Gnosis in Egypt." In Birger A. Pearson and James E. Goehring, eds. *The Roots of Egyptian Christianity.* SAC 1. Philadelphia: Fortress, 1986, 271-306.

Voelke, André-Jean. *L'Idée de volonté dans le stoicisme.* Paris: Presses universitaires de France, 1973.

Völker, Walther, ed. *Quellen zur Geschichte der christlichen Gnosis.* SAQ n.s. 5. Tübingen: J. C. B. Mohr (P. Siebeck), 1932.

Wacholder, Ben Z. and Martin G. Abegg. *A Preliminary Edition of the Unpublished Dead Sea Scrolls: The Hebrew and Aramaic Texts from Cave 4.* Fascicle 1. Washington, D.C.: Biblical Archaeology Society, 1991.

Waldstein, Michael. "On the Relation Between the Two Parts of the *Apocryphon of John.*" In Walter Beltz, ed. *Der Gottesspruch in der koptischen Literatur. Hans-Martin Schenke zum 65. Geburtstag.* Hallesche Beiträge zur Orientwissenschaft 15. Halle: Druckerie der Martin-Luther-Universität Halle Wittenberg, 1995, 99-112.

——. "The Providence Monologue in the *Apocryphon of John* and the Johannine Prologue." *JECS* 3 (1995) 369-402.

Waldstein, Michael and Frederik Wisse. *The Apocryphon of John: Synopsis of Nag Hammadi Codices II,1; III,1; and IV,1 with BG 8502,2.* NHMS 33. Leiden: E. J. Brill, 1995.

Walter, Nikolaus. "Paulus und die urchristliche Jesustradition." *NTS* 31 (1975) 498-522.

Weiss, Konrad. "χρηστός." In Gerhard Kittel and Gerhard Friedrich, eds. *TDNT, Vol. 9.* Grand Rapids: Eerdmans, 1974, 483-492.

Welburn, Andrew J. *The Beginnings of Christianity: Essene Mystery, Gnostic Revelation and the Christian Vision.* Edinburgh: Floris Books, 1991.

——. "Iranian Prophetology and the Birth of the Messiah: The Apocalypse of Adam." *ANRW* II.25.4 (1988) 4752-4794.

——. "The Identity of the Archons in the *Apocryphon Johannis.*" *VC* 32 (1978) 241-254.

Wendling, Emil. *Die Entstehung des Markus-Evangeliums.* Tübingen: J. C. B. Mohr (P. Siebeck), 1908.

Werner, Andreas. "Das Apokryphon des Johannes in seinen vier Versionen synoptisch betrachtet und unter besonderer Berücksichtigung anderer Nag-Hammadi Schriften in Auswahl erläutert." Th.D. Dissertation, Humboldt Universität Berlin, 1977.

West, Stephanie. *The Ptolemaic Papyri of Homer*. Cologne: Westdeutscher Verlag, 1967.

——. "The Transmission of the Text." In Alfred Heubeck, Stephanie West, and John B. Hainsworth, eds. *A Commentary on Homer's Odyssey*. Oxford: Clarendon, 1988, 33-48.

Wey, Heinrich. *Die Funktionen der bösen Geister bei den griechischen Apologeten des zweiten Jahrhunderts nach Christus*. Wintermur: Keller, 1957.

Whittaker, John. "Self-Generating Principles in Second-Century Gnostic Systems." In Bentley Layton, ed. *The Rediscovery of Gnosticism, Vol. 1: The School of Valentinus*. SHR 41. Leiden: E. J. Brill, 1980, 176-189.

Whittaker, John and Pierre Louis, eds. *Alcinoos, Enseignement des doctrines de Platon*. Paris: Belles Lettres, 1990.

Widengren, Geo. *The Ascension of the Apostle and the Heavenly Book*. UUÅ 7. Uppsala: Lundequistska Bokhandeln, 1950.

Wilken, Robert L. "Philosophenschulen und Theologie." In Wayne A. Meeks, ed. *Zur soziologie des Urchristentums: Ausgewählte Beiträge zum frühchristlichen Gemeinschaftsleben in seiner gesellschaftlichen Umwelt*. TBü 62. München: Kaiser, 1979, 165-193.

Williams, Michael A. "The Demonizing of the Demiurge: The Innovation of Gnostic Myth." In Michael A. Williams, Collett Cox, and Martin S. Jaffee, eds. *Innovation in Religious Traditions*. Berlin: de Gruyter, 1992, 73-107.

——. *The Immovable Race. A Gnostic Designation and the Theme of Stability in Late Antiquity*. NHS 29. Leiden: E. J. Brill, 1985.

——. "Interpreting the Nag Hammadi Library as 'Collection(s)' in the History of 'Gnosticism(s)'." In Louis Painchaud and Anne Pasquier, eds. *Les textes de Nag Hammadi et le problème de leur classification: Actes du colloque tenu à Québec du 15 au 19 septembre 1993*. BCNH, Section "Études" 3. Québec: Les Presses de l'Université Laval; Louvain/Paris: Éditions Peeters, 1995, 3-50.

——. "Psyche's Voice: Gnostic Perceptions of Body and Soul." Paper presented at Annual Meeting, SBL, Joint Session of Nag Hammadi and Gnosticism Section/Platonism and Neo-platonism Group, Kansas City, 1991.

——. "Realized Eschatology in the Gospel of Philip." *ResQ* 3 (1971) 1-17.

——. *Rethinking "Gnosticism": An Argument for Dismantling a Dubious Category*. Princeton: Princeton University Press, 1996.

——. "Stability as a Soteriological Theme in Gnosticism." In Bentley Layton, ed. *The Rediscovery of Gnosticism, Vol. 2: Sethian Gnosticism*. SHR 41. Leiden: E. J. Brill, 1981, 819-829.

——. "Variety in Gnostic Perspectives on Gender." In Karen L. King, ed. *Images of the Feminine in Gnosticism*. SAC. Philadelphia: Fortress, 1988, 2-22.

Wilson, Robert McL. *The Gospel of Philip*. London: Mowbray, 1962.

——. *Studies in the Gospel of Thomas*. London: Mowbray, 1960.

Winkler, Gabriele. "The Original Meaning of the Prebaptismal Anointing and its Implications." *Worship* 52 (1978) 24-45.

Winston, David. *Logos and Mystical Theology in Philo of Alexandria*. Cincinnati: Hebrew Union College Press, 1985.

Wire, Antoinette Clark. "Performance, Politics and Power: A Response." *Orality and Textuality in Early Christian Literature*. *Semeia* 65 (1995) 129-135.

Wisse, Frederik. "The Apocryphon of John." In David N. Freedman et al., eds. *ABD, Vol. 3*. New York: Doubleday, 1992, 899-900.

——. "The Coptic Versions of the New Testament." In Bart D. Ehrman and M. W. Holmes, eds. *The Text of the New Testament in Contemporary Research: Essays on the Status Quaestionis*. Studies and Documents 46. Grand Rapids: Eerdmans, 1995, 131-141.

——. "Gnosticism and Early Monasticism in Egypt." In Barbara Aland, ed. *Gnosis: Festschrift für Hans Jonas*. Göttingen: Vandenhoeck & Ruprecht, 1978, 431-440.

——. "The Nag Hammadi Library and the Heresiologists." *VC* 25 (1971) 205-223.

——. "The Redeemer Figure in the Paraphrase of Shem." *NovT* 12 (1970) 130-140.

——. "Shem, Paraphrase of." In David N. Freedman et al., eds. *ABD, Vol. 5*. New York: Doubleday, 1992, 1196.

Wissowa, Georg, ed. *Paulys Real-Encyclopädie der classischen Altertumswissenschaft*. Stuttgart: J. B. Metzler, 1894-1963.

Wrede, William. *Das Messiasgeheimnis in den Evangelien*. Göttingen: Vandenhoeck & Ruprecht, 1901.

Wright, William, ed. *Apocryphal Acts of the Apostles*. 2 vols. London/Edinburgh: Williams & Norgate, 1871; Amsterdam: Philo Press, 1968; Hildesheim/Zurich/New York: Olms, 1990.

Wuthnow, Robert. *Communities of Discourse*. Cambridge: Harvard University Press, 1989.

Yamauchi, Edwin M. "The Apocalypse of Adam, Mithraism, and Pre-Christian Gnosticism." In Jacques Duchesne-Guillemin, ed. *Études Mithraiques*. Leiden: E. J. Brill, 1978, 537-563.

——. "The Crucifixion and Docetic Christology." *Concordia Theological Quarterly* 46 (1982) 1-20.

——. "History-of-Religions School." In Sinclair B. Ferguson and David F. Wright, eds. *New Dictionary of Theology*. Leicester/Downers Grove, IL: InterVarsity Press, 1988, 308-309.

——. "The Magi Episode." In Jerry Vardaman and Edwin M. Yamauchi, eds. *Christos, Chronos, and Kairos*. Winona Lake, IN: Eisenbrauns, 1989, 15-39.

——. *Persia and the Bible*. Grand Rapids: Baker Book House, 1990.

——. *Pre-Christian Gnosticism*. Grand Rapids: Baker Book House, 1983.

——. "Qumran and Colossae." *Bibliotheca Sacra* 121 (1964) 141-152.

——. "Religions of the Biblical World: Persia." In Geoffrey W. Bromiley, ed. *ISBE, Vol. 4*. Grand Rapids: Eerdmans, 1988, 123-129.

——. "Review of E. Yarshater, ed., *The Cambridge History of Iran III: The Seleucid, Parthian and Sasanian Periods*." *American Historical Review* 89 (1984) 1055-56.

Zahn, Theodor. *Forschungen zur Geschichte des neutestamentlichen Kanons und der altkirchlichen Literatur, Vol. 3: Supplementum Clementinum*. Erlangen: Deichert, 1884.

——. *Geschichte des neutestamentlichen Kanons*. Erlangen: Deichert; Leipzig: Böhme, 1890.

Zandee, Jan. *The Teachings of Sylvanus (Nag Hammadi Codex VII,4): Text, Translation, Commentary*. Egyptologische Uitgaven. Leiden: Nederlands Instituut voor Het Nabije Oosten, 1991.

Zarella, P. "La concezione del 'discepolo' in Epitteto." *Aevum* 40 (1966) 211-229.

# NAG HAMMADI AND MANICHAEAN STUDIES

FORMERLY

## NAG HAMMADI STUDIES

1. Scholer, D.M. *Nag Hammadi bibliography, 1948-1969.* 1971. ISBN 90 04 02603 7

2. Ménard, J.-E. *L'évangile de vérité.* Traduction française, introduction et commentaire par J.-É. Ménard. 1972. ISBN 90 04 03408 0

3. Krause, M. (ed.). *Essays on the Nag Hammadi texts in honour of Alexander Böhlig.* 1972. ISBN 90 04 03535 4

4. Böhlig, A. & F. Wisse, (eds.). *Nag Hammadi Codices III, 2 and IV, 2. The Gospel of the Egyptians.* (The Holy Book of the Great Invisible Spirit). Edited with translation and commentary, in cooperation with P. Labib. 1975. ISBN 90 04 04226 1

5. Ménard, J.-E. *L'Évangile selon Thomas.* Traduction française, introduction, et commentaire par J.-É. Ménard. 1975. ISBN 90 04 04210 5

6. Krause, M. (ed.). *Essays on the Nag Hammadi texts in honour of Pahor Labib.* 1975. ISBN 90 04 04363 2

7. Ménard, J.-E. *Les textes de Nag Hammadi.* Colloque du centre d'Histoire des Religions, Strasbourg, 23-25 octobre 1974. 1975. ISBN 90 04 04359 4

8. Krause, M. (ed.). *Gnosis and Gnosticism.* Papers read at the Seventh International Conference on Patristic Studies. Oxford, September 8th-13th, 1975. 1977. ISBN 90 04 05242 9

9. Schmidt, C. (ed.). *Pistis Sophia.* Translation and notes by V. MacDermot. 1978. ISBN 90 04 05635 1

10. Fallon, F.T. *The enthronement of Sabaoth.* Jewish elements in Gnostic creation myths. 1978. ISBN 90 04 05683 1

11. Parrott, D.M. *Nag Hammadi Codices V, 2-5 and VI with Papyrus Berolinensis 8502, 1 and 4.* 1979. ISBN 90 04 05798 6

12. Koschorke, K. *Die Polemik der Gnostiker gegen das kirchliche Christentum.* Unter besonderer Berücksichtigung der Nag Hammadi-Traktate 'Apokalypse des Petrus' (NHC VII, 3) und 'Testimonium Veritatis' (NHC IX, 3). 1978. ISBN 90 04 05709 9

13. Schmidt, C. (ed.). *The Books of Jeu and the untitled text in the Bruce Codex.* Translation and notes by V. MacDermot. 1978. ISBN 90 04 05754 4

14. McL. Wilson, R. (ed.). *Nag Hammadi and Gnosis.* Papers read at the First International Congress of Coptology (Cairo, December 1976). 1978. ISBN 90 04 05760 9

15. Pearson, B.A. (ed.). *Nag Hammadi Codices IX and X.* 1981. ISBN 90 04 06377 3

16. Barns, J.W.B., G.M. Browne, & J.C. Shelton, (eds.). *Nag Hammadi Codices.* Greek and Coptic papyri from the cartonnage of the covers. 1981. ISBN 90 04 06277 7

17. KRAUSE, M. (ed.). *Gnosis and Gnosticism*. Papers read at the Eighth International Conference on Patristic Studies. Oxford, September 3rd-8th, 1979. 1981. ISBN 90 04 06399 4

18. HELDERMAN, J. *Die Anapausis im Evangelium Veritatis*. Eine vergleichende Untersuchung des valentinianisch-gnostischen Heilsgutes der Ruhe im Evangelium Veritatis und in anderen Schriften der Nag-Hammadi Bibliothek. 1984. ISBN 90 04 07260 8

19. FRICKEL, J. *Hellenistische Erlösung in christlicher Deutung*. Die gnostische Naassenerschrift. Quellen, kritische Studien, Strukturanalyse, Schichtenscheidung, Rekonstruktion der Anthropos-Lehrschrift. 1984. ISBN 90 04 07227 6

20-21. LAYTON, B. (ed.). *Nag Hammadi Codex II, 2-7, together with XIII, 2\* Brit. Lib. Or. 4926(1) and P. Oxy. 1, 654, 655*. I. Gospel according to Thomas, Gospel according to Philip, Hypostasis of the Archons, Indexes. II. On the origin of the world, Expository treatise on the Soul, Book of Thomas the Contender. 1989. 2 volumes. ISBN 90 04 09019 3

22. ATTRIDGE, H.W. (ed.). *Nag Hammadi Codex I* (The Jung Codex). I. Introductions, texts, translations, indices. 1985. ISBN 90 04 07677 8

23. ATTRIDGE, H.W. (ed.). *Nag Hammadi Codex I* (The Jung Codex). II. Notes. 1985. ISBN 90 04 07678 6

24. STROUMSA, G.A.G. *Another seed. Studies in Gnostic mythology*. 1984. ISBN 90 04 07419 8

25. SCOPELLO, M. *L'exégèse de l'âme*. Nag Hammadi Codex II, 6. Introduction, traduction et commentaire. 1985. ISBN 90 04 07469 4

26. EMMEL, S. (ed.). *Nag Hammadi Codex III, 5*. The Dialogue of the Savior. 1984. ISBN 90 04 07558 5

27. PARROTT, D.M. (ed.) *Nag Hammadi Codices III, 3-4 and V, 1 with Papyrus Berolinensis 8502,3 and Oxyrhynchus Papyrus 1081*. Eugnostos and the Sophia of Jesus Christ. 1991. ISBN 90 04 08366 9

28. HEDRICK, C.W. (ed.). *Nag Hammadi Codices XI, XII, XIII*. 1990. ISBN 90 04 07825 8

29. WILLIAMS, M.A. *The immovable race*. A gnostic designation and the theme of stability in Late Antiquity. 1985. ISBN 90 04 07597 6

30. PEARSON, B.A. (ed.). *Nag Hammadi Codex VII*. 1996. ISBN 90 04 10451 8

31. SIEBER, J.H. (ed.). *Nag Hammadi Codex VIII*. 1991. ISBN 90 04 09477 6

32. SCHOLER, D.M. *Nag Hammadi Bibliography*. (in preparation)

33. WISSE, F. & M. WALDSTEIN, (eds.). *The Apocryphon of John*. Synopsis of Nag Hammadi Codices II,1; III,1; and IV,1 with BG 8502,2. 1995. ISBN 90 04 10395 3

34. LELYVELD, M. *Les logia de la vie dans l'Evangile selon Thomas*. A la recherche d'une tradition et d'une rédaction. 1988. ISBN 90 04 07610 7

35. WILLIAMS, F. (Tr.). *The Panarion of Epiphanius of Salamis*. Book I (Sects 1-46). 1987. ISBN 90 04 07926 2

36. WILLIAMS, F. (Tr.). *The Panarion of Epiphanius of Salamis*. Books II and III (Sects 47-80, De Fide). 1994. ISBN 90 04 09898 4

37. GARDNER, I. *The Kephalaia of the Teacher*. The Edited Coptic Manichaean Texts in Translation with Commentary. 1995. ISBN 90 04 10248 5

38. TURNER, M.L. *The Gospel according to Philip.* The Sources and Coherence of an Early Christian Collection. 1996. ISBN 90 04 10443 7
39. VAN DEN BROEK, R. *Studies in Gnosticism and Alexandrian Christianity.* 1996. ISBN 90 04 10654 5
40. MARJANEN, A. *The Woman Jesus Loved.* Mary Magdalene in the Nag Hammadi Library and Related Documents. 1996. ISBN 90 04 10658 8
41. REEVES, J.C. *Heralds of that Good Realm.* Syro-Mesopotamian Gnosis and Jewish Traditions. 1996. ISBN 90 04 10459 3
42. RUDOLPH, K. *Gnosis & spätantike Religionsgeschichte.* Gesammelte Aufsätze. 1996. ISBN 90 04 10625 1
43. MIRECKI, P. & J. BEDUHN, (eds.). *Emerging from Darkness.* Studies in the Recovery of Manichaean Sources. 1997. ISBN 90 04 10760 6
44. TURNER, J.D. & A. McGUIRE, (eds.). *The Nag Hammadi Library after Fifty Years.* Proceedings of the 1995 Society of Biblical Literature Commemoration. 1997. ISBN 90 04 10824 6